Creative Propagation

Creative Propagation

SECOND EDITION

Peter Thompson

with line drawings by Josie Owen

> I think the true gardener is a lover of his flowers, not a critic of them. I think the true gardener is the reverent servant of Nature, not her truculent wife-beating master. I think the true gardener, the older he grows should more and more develop a humble, grateful and uncertain spirit, cocksure of nothing except the universality of beauty.
>
> Reginald Farrer, *In a Yorkshire Garden*

Timber Press
Portland ❧ Cambridge

Published in 2005 by
Timber Press, Inc.
The Haseltine Building
133 S.W. Second Avenue, Suite 450
Portland, Oregon 97204-3527, U.S.A.

Timber Press
2 Station Road
Swavesey
Cambridge CB4 5QJ, U.K.

www.timberpress.com

Printed in Hong Kong

Library of Congress Cataloging-in-Publication Data

Thompson, Peter, 1948-
    Creative propagation / Peter Thompson ; with line drawings by Josie Owen.—2nd ed.
        p.   cm.
    Includes bibliographical references and index.
    ISBN 0-88192-681-7 (flexibind)
    1. Plant propagation. I. Title.
SB119.T46 2005
631.5'3—dc22
                                                                    2004009966

A Catalogue record for this book is also available from the British Library.

This book about propagation is dedicated to the Joyce family:
my daughter, Anna; her husband, Al;
and their five children, Jenny, Paddy and Ollie, Meghan, and Dominic.

Contents

Preface

Nobody ever yet rooted a cutting or germinated a seed. Those are things that only plants can do. The propagator's job is to provide them with the conditions they need to get on with it. That was the message in the first edition of *Creative Propagation*, written some 20 years ago. Since then I have had no reason to change my conviction that the surest guide to successful propagation is to observe how plants do it naturally, and then apply what we see to what we get up to in the potting shed.

In those 20 years, gardening itself has changed. Then, the "English" garden held centre stage. Interest centred on a quorum of trees, shrubs, perennials, annuals, and other plants that had served gardeners well for many years—not just in western Europe but in other parts of the temperate world, too. Plants which only the wildly optimistic or dedicated would have dreamt of growing then have become almost commonplace now. The comfortable conservatism that condemned anything outlandish or unknown as "not for us" has largely evaporated. Garden centres set out their stalls with plants they formerly would never have dreamt of attempting to sell—and as for nurseries! The range of plants that a little delving can bring to light beggars the imagination.

Not so long ago, gardeners in the United States, New Zealand, southern Europe, Australia, South Africa, and even Japan—despite its own strong traditions of gardening—seemed eager to find ways to assimilate the contents of the "English" garden, lock, stock and barrel, into their own creations. Not so today. Now, plants that contribute texture, form and character rather than just flowers; plants that demand a second look; plants that are decidedly outlandish; and plants that excite interest and challenge the imagination have reached the boundaries of our gardens and are plunging through them like a flood.

When I read the first edition of this book, I look in vain for ways to propagate many plants that are now attracting widening interest. Tree ferns and palms are not mentioned. I search in vain for ways to propagate almost all the plants Australia contributes to our gardens; practically nothing from the Californian chaparral is there. Bulbs and annuals from South Africa make limited appearances, but I can find no guidance on the propagation of trees and shrubs from that country. Plants from New Zealand, and even from Chile, receive almost equally little attention. These omissions find a place in this edition by increasing the number of genera for which information about methods of propagation is provided from about 600 to more than 1600.

Locations of photographs

It is a pleasure to take this opportunity to thank the owners, curators and managers of the following gardens or reserves where photographs used in the second edition of *Creative Propagation* were taken:

Chapter 4. Australian Native Plant Nursery, Ventura, California

Chapter 5. Bob O'Neil's Garden, Katandra, Wandin, Victoria, Australia

Chapter 7. Little Malvern Court, Malvern, Worcestershire; Orakei Korako Reserve, Taupo, New Zealand; Kutusova, Ussuriland, Russia; Fernz Fernery, the Domain, Auckland, New Zealand; Sandra van Mast, Superba Farm, Whenuapai, New Zealand; Parque Nacional Queulat, Aisén, Chile

Chapter 8. Sir Harold Hillier Arboretum, Ampfield, Romsey, Hampshire; Strybing Arboretum, Golden Gate Park, San Francisco, California; National Botanical Institute, Kirstenbosch, Cape Town, South Africa

Chapter 15. Avon Ryan's Garden, Morningside Road, Whangarei, New Zealand

Chapter 16. Guy Bowden, Native Plant Nursery, Tutukaka, New Zealand

Chapter 17. Jim Hopkirk's Garden, Maranui, New Zealand; Gethsemane Garden, Sumner, Christchurch, New Zealand; Australian Native Plant Nursery, Ventura, California; Wayne Clarke's Garden, Parikiori Gardens, Whangarei, New Zealand

All other photographs were taken in the author's garden.

Overture to Propagation

Creative propagation, like creative accounting, might be described as the art of making much from little—sometimes very little indeed. But ideas of getting something for nothing are misconceived. Like almost everything else worthwhile, costs are levied in payments contributed by care, effort, and imagination.

Propagation is one of the most creative aspects of gardening, because it constantly provides new opportunities and challenges. It is enjoyable in itself, above all for the affection we feel toward plants we have raised and nurtured ourselves.

This book could have been burdened with the title "The Propagation of Plants in Relation to their Anatomy, Morphology, Physiology and Ecology," for that is what it is about. The title that appears on the cover was chosen because it is snappier, more appealing, and more likely to encourage you to buy the book. More to the point, the shorter, simpler title conveys the tone and contents of the book more accurately.

The tissues from which plants are put together make up their *anatomy*. The ways they are put together to form leaves, stems, roots, and other plant parts of varied shapes and compositions constitute their *morphology*. The ways they respond to their surroundings, coordinating their growth and development with the changing seasons, is referred to as their *physiology*. Their relationships with other plants, with predators, sym- bionts, and all the inhabitants of their communities are loosely lumped together in a basket labeled *ecology*.

We need not go all scientific to garden successfully. We all know green-fingered gardeners whom we envy for their success with the most obdurate seeds and unobliging cuttings, while being pretty certain they could not sniff out a pheromone from a hormone, nor be relied on to distinguish a meristem from a mericarp. Anyone feeling daunted by such a sudden and early appearance of these "ologys" should take heart now. Although this book will repeatedly link practical matters concerned with plant propagation with the anatomy, morphology, physiology, and ecology of plants, this is the last time these words appear on its pages. They disappear, but their unseen presence haunts almost every page.

The road to the great garden dump dignified by some as "the compost heap" is lined with our failures—pots of seeds that never sprung, cuttings that withered before our eyes, divisions caught out by frosts or drying winds. We may blame lack of expensive equipment for our failures and compensate by falling for gadgets on garden centre shelves, cunningly devised, so we are assured to make further failures a thing of the past. Expensive equipment has little to do with it. The corpses in our wake are more likely to be mute evidence of our lack of understanding of plants.

We turn those failures into successes when, guided by instinct, observation, and accumulating experience, we learn to provide the conditions plants need to function effectively and perform all the things they are capable of. When the right things are done at the right times, seeds germinate, cuttings produce roots, and divisions flourish using very simple methods.

Gardening skills, like any other craft, develop from an ability to observe what is happening, understand the materials we work with, and do whatever is needed to offset or avoid problems and make the most of favourable situations. They depend on recognising that plants grow in different parts of the world in different situations and under different conditions because they themselves differ from one another in their tolerances and their sensitivities. Conditions that provide a dying hell for one kind of plant are a veritable heaven for another.

Gardeners have become increasingly aware of the importance of matching plant to place in their gardens. The extension of the idea to the ways plants are propagated evidently came as a surprise to some readers of the first edition of this book. It clearly struck a cord with others and is developed as the dominant theme of this edition.

Plants names create perennial problems. Latin names, some insist, are sent to try us, and there can be no doubt they are a source of difficulty. References to familiar annuals by their Latin names may sound pretentious, but familiar names are familiar only in particular contexts. Australians who know the purple flowers in the wheat fields of Western Australia as Paterson's Curse might be confused by references to Salvation Sally in other parts of their own country, and they are probably completely perplexed when confronted by Viper's Bugloss.

The unregulated, unofficial, evocative, and attractively homely names, whether English, Spanish, Cherokee, Xhosa, Maori or whatever, work admirably within the family or within wider communities of gardeners who all speak the same language—literally or figuratively. On a broader, especially international, scale, where no consensus exists to guide decisions on which names are acceptable, and where we know little even of the extent and variety of names in common use, using anything but Latin names leads to a hotchpotch of misunderstandings.

Latin names follow a system devised to address problems of international usage, and they do so most effectively. Problems introduced by differences in nomenclature are trivial compared to those created by attempts to use any other system. So Latin names it has to be.

Plants are usually referred to by their genus throughout the book, rather than by their specific names. This is done to embrace numerous species, which for lack of space could not be covered individually. The genus is a most useful category for gardeners. It is broad enough to cover a wide range of variation and avoid hair-splitting distinctions, and narrow enough to group plants sharing significantly similar qualities. Generalisations, based on genera, provide a valuable means of communicating information about plants—not only in relation to propagation, but about other aspects of their life cycles, preferences, and responses. Like other generalisations, generic names should be applied in a reasonable and reasoning fashion—not rigidly, blindly or too literally. While it is quite sensible to think about hostas collectively, it would be supremely optimistic to hope for helpful information about growing Andean rosulate violets under a broad reference to *Viola*.

Particular groups of plants are covered in separate chapters. This involves making decisions about the characteristics used to identify ferns, annuals, herbaceous perennials, trees, climbers, shrubs, and other plant types. It is all too easy to get bogged down in endless arguments based on hair-splitting examinations of precisely what is meant by this or implied by that.

Plants widely grown as annuals may actually be perennials. The boundaries between climbers and shrubs, and shrubs and perennials, are not always clear. Differences that make one woody plant a tree and another a shrub may depend on how the plants are used, how they are pruned, or where they are grown. Most plants fit naturally and easily into a particular category, and common consent recognises them as trees, conifers, shrubs, perennials or whatever. Those that cross the boundaries and provoke the interest of nitpickers are a tiny minority. The ways plants are categorised seldom affect the ways they are propagated.

Creative Propagation has been written for gardeners with quite modest facilities; those whose glasshouses must provide for annuals, perennials, bulbs, ferns, shrubs, and anything else that attracts their owner's eye. It is written for those who have other things to do than garden all the time; for those who cannot be constantly on hand to water, open or close framelights and ventilators, or attend to other time-consuming details. It is written for those whose interest in plants takes them to parts of the plant world where mass marketing and commercial interests seldom venture.

Finally, on a matter of attitude. *Anthropomorphism* is a long word that represents a long-running source of friction, accompanied by derision and ridicule, from those who take a strictly "scientific" attitude toward the behaviour of plants and animals, directed at those who seek to understand their responses in simple, easily understood, familiar terms. In places, the scientists' dictate that the reactions of animals and plants to their surroundings and circumstances are not to be thought of in terms of human responses is transgressed. Having been a scientist and having become a gardener, I recognise the distaste of the former and the affinity of the latter for anything that smacks of attributing feelings to plants. But I am convinced anthropomorphism lies at the heart of trying to understand the world in which they live, which is so very different from our own.

My efforts to discuss these matters with my own plants have drawn no response. But I do know that when I open the door of my glasshouse on a day when the sun is shining, the plants have been fed and watered, and the atmosphere within is light and buoyant, the plants, too, emanate lightness, buoyancy, and happiness. When I open that door on a February day, after a fortnight of lowering, overcast skies, chill temperatures, and clagging humidity, I sense the feeling of oppression, the struggle for survival, and the grim resolve to hang on to better times. While that may not be a scientific response, I am sure it is a gardener's one, and that those who know it are better growers and propagators than those who do not.

PART ONE

Equipment and Facilities Used to Propagate Plants from Seeds, Cuttings and by Division

Creative Propagation is written for those who garden anywhere in the temperate world. That necessitates agreement on a number of matters in which gardeners share an interest. Seasons are used rather than months to make references equally intelligible to readers in the northern and southern hemispheres. Each season is divided into "early," "mid-" or "late" so that, in total, the year is divided into the familiar 12 divisions. However, it is still necessary to establish when, for example, spring starts and ends. This is done in accordance with Table 1.

Regions of the Temperate World

Conditions for gardening vary widely in different parts of the temperate world, and very often it is necessary to specify where a particular operation is likely, or unlikely, to be successful. Five regions have been defined for the purposes of this book. These are based primarily on the lowest temperatures likely to be experienced during their winters, which in turn correspond to some of the Hardiness Zones in the USDA system of climatological divisions.

The five regions are

- **Cold Temperate:** USDA Zone 7 and lower. Minimum temperatures down to −18°C (0°F) or below.
- **Cool Temperate:** USDA Zone 8. Minimum temperatures down to −12°C (10°F).
- **Mild Temperate:** USDA Zone 9. Minimum temperatures down to −7°C (19°F).
- **Warm Temperate:** USDA Zone 10. Minimum temperatures down to −2°C (28°F).
- **Mediterranea:** Characterised by mild, moist winters and hot, arid summers. Note that *Mediterranea* applies to a number of places in different parts of the world which share a Mediterranean climate. These are defined in the introduction to Part Two. The natural growing season, limited by rainfall, extends from autumn through winter into spring. In gardens and other situations where water is available, growth may be maintained throughout the summer, and conditions are comparable to those in warm temperate regions. Elsewhere, growing seasons are defined by the severity of winter cold. They extend from spring through summer and into autumn. In cool and cold temperate regions (especially at high latitudes, as in western Europe), short days and low light levels in mid-winter, as well as cold, affect prospects of plant survival.

Table 1. Months in relation to seasons: northern and southern hemispheres

Northern Hemisphere	Season	Southern Hemisphere
February	Early spring	August
March	Mid-spring	September
April	Late spring	October
May	Early summer	November
June	Mid-summer	December
July	Late summer	January
August	Early autumn	February
September	Mid-autumn	March
October	Late autumn	April
November	Early winter	May
December	Mid-winter	June
January	Late winter	July

Recommendations for timing operations are for guidance only. They should be interpreted in relation to local conditions. Advice to sow seeds in mid-spring might be modified to early spring in very mild situations or deferred to late spring in situations where late frosts are a hazard.

Definitions of Intensity of Frost

Frost is variously defined in the world of gardening. A frost regarded by gardeners in New Zealand's winterless north as a killer would pass almost unnoticed in most parts of Britain. An unremarkable winter night in upper New York state would be a once-in-a-lifetime event in coastal California. Terms such as *light*, *hard* or *severe* applied to freezing temperatures have completely different meanings to gardeners in different parts of the world—yet anyone who writes about gardening has to use such words. Within the context of this book, such terms are intended to convey the following impressions:

- **Light:** Down to −3°C (27°F). Winter minima at this level occur in warm temperate regions and the milder parts of Mediterranea. Many tender plants are able to survive such minima, and in a gardening context, the conditions they provide are effectively frost-free.
- **Moderate:** Down to −7°C (19°F). Mild temperate regions and many parts of Mediterranea experience at least occasional frosts at this level. Provided they are neither frequent nor persistent, they are accompanied by mild, sunny days, and conditions during the previous autumn ensure the ripening of woody shoots before the onset of winter; only markedly tender plants will be killed. In cool temperate regions where such frosts are the norm,

they limit the range of plants that can be grown but are unlikely to be damaging to established members of the garden flora.

- **Hard:** Down to −11°C (12°F). Minimum temperatures at around this level occur more or less sporadically, at least during some winters, in cool temperate regions. Only plants recognised as fully hardy can be relied on not to be killed, but semi-hardy species survive in favourable situations and in favourable (usually dry, sunny) seasons.
- **Severe:** Down to −15°C (5°F). Temperatures falling to this level are a normal occurrence in cold temperate regions. In the absence of snow, none but reliably hardy plants survive and anything dubiously hardy is killed, even when growing in sheltered situations, such as against south-facing walls.
- **Penetrating:** Down to −19°C (−2°F). In cold temperate regions where temperatures fall to this level if only for a few nights, many plants generally regarded as hardy are killed or severely cut back. Prolonged periods of exposure to such temperatures destroy all but the hardiest species. Snow cover protects buds and shoots below and just above the surface of the ground and extends the range of plants able to survive. Gardeners can obtain similar benefits by burying vulnerable woody shoots of roses, raspberries and other plants beneath the soil during the winter.
- **Extreme:** Below −19°C (−2°F).

CHAPTER 1

Natural Reproduction: The Propagator's Guide

Every garden plant looks back to a wild ancestor—sometimes several. Some are separated by lineages extending for thousands of years, and others came in from the wild only yesterday. Cultivation changes plants. No plant that produced tightly sheathed and impenetrable cobs, as cultivated maize does, would survive in the wild; the development of cultivated forms from the small, loosely wrapped heads of their wild ancestors is a long and fascinating tale. The size, diversity of shape, and range of colour of garden dahlias and roses exceed beyond imagination any variations to be found among their wild relatives. One of the world's major staples, wheat, is an intricately complex hybrid between three species from two genera. Heads of wheat, as seen today, are unrecognisably different from those of their wild forebears and a true example of genetic engineering—though whether by divine intervention or nature's happenchances, who can say?

These changes are skin deep. They are not necessarily, or even usually, accompanied by extensive changes in the ways the plants work or respond to their surroundings. The stratagems by which their wild ancestors survived persist through generations in cultivation often with little or no change, including hardiness, responses to day length through which plants control the seasons when flowers and fruits are produced, the conditions in which seeds do or do not produce

seedlings, and the ability of shoots to form roots when attempts are made to propagate them from cuttings.

Propagation is concerned with how plants work—not what they look like. Cultivated dahlias with peaches-and-cream petals on flowers as big as dinner plates may not look much like their wild ancestors, whose faded pink flowers fit easily into the palm of a hand, but both are equally sensitive to frost; both produce tubers, flowers and seeds in the same way; and as far as propagation is concerned, what works for one works equally well for the other.

Recently developed techniques of genetic engineering (transgenics) by which genes from unrelated organisms can be incorporated in a plant's genotype may fundamentally change the responses of some, and eventually many, of the plants we grow. One day we will fill our gardens with hardy kinds of petunias and cease to worry about spring frosts—but for many years to come, the best guide to the conditions most of the plants in our gardens depend on to flourish and reproduce will be the responses that enabled them to survive in the places where they grew naturally, inherited from their wild ancestors.

No plant lives forever, though some make impressive efforts to do so, and under natural conditions a species survives only when and where it can reproduce. Reproduction is a risky and uncertain process, during which the offspring must separate from their parents and succeed in establishing themselves elsewhere. Plants have two basic choices: to reproduce sexually from seed or asexually through vegetative reproduction.

Sexual Reproduction

When plants ceased to be free spirits, opting instead to live rooted to the spot, they had to find solutions to the problem of having sex without being able to move around in search of partners. Water provided a way for mobile male cells to reach nubile ovules, and for eons mosses, ferns and similar plants depended on complex life cycles to make that possible. It was, and is, an uncertain process, limited by the availability of water and more likely to result in self-fertilisation than in cross-fertilisation, but until something better turned up it made gene exchange and the benefits of sexual reproduction possible.

Pollen and seeds were the great invention of the gymnosperms, transforming the efficiency of sexual reproduction. Pollen carried from one plant to another on the wind provided opportunities for cycads and later conifers to matchmake over considerable distances. Seeds enabled their offspring to be distributed across the countryside by the wind, animals and birds. The production of brightly coloured fleshy arils, like those found on yews and podocarps, heralded the invention of succulent fruits, increasing the attractions of seeds to birds and animals.

Then, more than 100 million years ago, angiosperms refined the process by producing conspicuous, brightly coloured, often intricately constructed flowers to attract pollinators. Alliances with birds, animals, insects, snails, the wind and a dozen other agencies led to an astonishing variety of ways of ensuring pollination and seed distribution. Such improvements should have consigned mosses, ferns and other less sophisticatedly endowed plants—even conifers—to obsolescence and oblivion. Failing to get the message, they continue to coexist and compete effectively with the flowering plants.

Reproduction by seed is a sexual process as a rule, though not always. It ensures every plant in a population is an individual with its own particular genetic constitution. The differences between individuals provide the diversity that enables populations of plants to adapt to changing circumstances by selection over the generations. However, the odds against any seed growing up to produce flowers and seeds under natural conditions are not ten to one and seldom even as favourable as a thousand to one. They can be tens or hundreds of thousands, not infrequently millions to one against survival, and a population of plants survives under natural conditions only for so long as it is able to produce so many seeds that some individuals still remain after all the agents of death and decay have done their work.

A single sallow, or goat willow tree (*Salix caprea*), in a single year can produce sufficient seeds to give rise to 1300 seedlings per square metre (1100 seedlings per square yard) over an area of some 3 hectares (7.5 acres)—about 15 million seedlings in all. That same tree may enjoy 20 or 30 fruitful years during a lifetime in which it produces 200 to 300 million seeds. And the result of this enormous output? On average, just two trees, one male and one female (because this is a dioecious species), grow up to maturity, bear seed themselves and maintain the population.

Willow seeds have brief lives. Their minimal storage reserves sustain life only for a few days, and they make minimal demands on the plants that produce them. Most species provide more generously for their offspring before launching them into the world—correspondingly improving their chances of survival—so they do not need to produce so many. Nevertheless, extra provisions put greater strains on the resources of the parents. Balances must be struck between producing millions of poorly endowed seeds with almost infinitesimal chances of individual success or producing fewer, better endowed seeds with correspondingly better prospects.

The carbohydrates, oils, fats and waxes with which seeds are stuffed are energy-rich foodstuffs, expensive to produce and highly sought after by birds and mammals, insects, bacteria and fungi. Larger seeds provide greater support for seedlings but are even more desirable to predators and easier to find than smaller ones. Small or large, numerous or few, there is no clear-cut best option in the equations linking seed size and numbers with reproductive success.

An alternative strategy is to produce genetically better tuned seeds so that higher proportions establish themselves successfully and grow into mature plants. Pursuing this strategy has led to some curious results—even to second thoughts on the value of sexual reproduction itself.

Towards Vegetative Reproduction

Sex creates offspring composed of mixtures of their parents' genes in innumerable different combinations. This diversity, so we are told, ensures that when disasters strike or opportunities occur, some individuals are likely to be endowed with genotypes which enable them to adapt, cope or seize the moment. Sexual reproduction, and the genetic turmoil that goes with it, is the insurance policy which "guarantees" the long-term survival of a species.

Like all insurance policies, premiums have to be paid, and in the short term premiums represent unrewarded costs. A successfully established plant has already demonstrated its possession of an appropriate genotype for the location. That being so, the best inheritance it can confer on its progeny is its own genotype, unchanged. The most likely result of exposing its genes to the melting pot of random mixing with those of another plant is the production of numerous variations—some, possibly most, of which will be genetically ill-matched individuals with reduced chances of survival.

Botanists are fascinated by the myriad devious, elaborate and ingenious gambits plants have devised to ensure cross-pollination of their flowers. They are a truly mind-boggling anthology often so intricate in their details that it beggars belief to imagine how they could have evolved. With so much emphasis on miscegenation (interbreeding), it comes as a surprise to discover that many plants jealously guard their pollen for their own use, or even dispense with pollination and fertilisation altogether. They rely on the tried-and-tested genotypes that have enabled them to survive, rather than experiment with untried combinations of genes. They pay reduced insurance premiums, or none at all!

Gardeners favour these self-pollinated plants because they produce seed regularly and abundantly; they germinate with fewer problems, and their seedlings develop evenly and predictably; they simplify selection for desirable characteristics; and they behave very much like clones—which is not surprising, since, like clones, their members are genetically homogenous.

Most self-pollinating plants, though largely dedicated to the concept of genetic purity, leave room for the occasional accident—the occasional payment of an insurance premium—in the form of cross-pollination. The first violets of the year open to the world and to the possibilities of cross-pollination. Subsequently, the plants produce masses of cleistogamous flowers hidden amongst their leaves—that is, their buds never open and the ovules within them are pollinated exclusively with their own pollen. The anthers of a corncockle (*Agrostemma githago*) emerge as the flowers open and as their pollen matures. The developing styles thrust the receptive stigmas through the pollen, almost—but not absolutely certainly—ensuring that every ovule is fertilised before the stigmas become available to foraging bees. Just occasionally, a pollen grain brought by a visiting bee from a flower on another plant may find a waiting unfertilized ovule.

Some plants, including dandelions, some rowans (mountain ash) and crabapples, turn their backs on miscegenation, leaving no opportunities for alternatives. In a phenomenon known as *apomixis*, their ovules do not stop developing as those in other flowers do while waiting for the arrival of a pollen grain with which to engage in the duet of mutual reduction division and recombination to create a new genotype. The ovules continue to develop without reduction division or genetic scrambling to produce seedlings genetically identical to their parents. This is sexual reproduction without sex; the siblings produced by each plant, and the offspring of their offspring, are truly members of a clone.

Hitherto, gardeners have made little use of the few naturally apomictic plants available to them. The advent of transgenic techniques and the promise they offer of using the bountiful production of seeds as the sources of clones has made it a much more interesting phenomenon. Nevertheless, whether they are the result of cross-pollination, self-pollination or the virgin offspring of apomicts, all seeds are subject to the hazards and uncertainties of that unrewarding passage from seed to maturity, a passage that demands the production of thousands to ensure the survival of one or two.

Seeds are not cheap to make. They put such demands on a plant's resources that many trees—the goat willow is an example—cannot summon the energy needed to be fruitful every year. Periods of two, three, five or even more years may intervene between successive crops. Not surprisingly, faced with the uncertainties and costs of producing seedlings, plants have explored the possibilities of other methods of reproduction.

Vegetative (or Asexual) Reproduction

Branches bend down and layer themselves to form thickets. Earthbound mats of stems develop roots as they grow. Short shoots elongate to produce offsets or stolons, known to gardeners as runners. Subterranean, exploratory rhizomes or tubers are produced. These are asexual methods of reproduction, referred to by gardeners as vegetative forms of propagation.

Offspring produced in these ways are all of a kind—they are clones. Every individual possesses exactly the same genetic constitution—that of the plant that gave rise to them—and some plants reproduce vegetatively so successfully that they scarcely depend on sexual propagation at all, even in the wild. Asexual modes of reproduction come in many forms but share three things in common: The offspring continue to benefit from the support and shelter of their parents till they are big enough to set up as independent individuals. They cost a great deal more to produce than seeds, but their chances of survival are incomparably higher. They are constructed from economical, relatively unnutritious, hard-to-digest leaves and stems of limited appeal to most birds, animals or insects.

Apomictic seeds may guarantee the offspring a winning genetic combination, but they suffer from all the problems associated with seeds, while losing any prospect of benefiting from the advantages. Vegetable logic dictates that if flowers fulfill no sexual role, there is no point in producing them—better to find some other means of reproduction, and vivipary provides one answer.

A comparatively few plants, especially amongst the monocots, produce buds in places where flowers would normally be. Compressed plants with tiny leaves and vestigial roots develop before dropping from the parents onto the ground below, all ready to go. These viviparous plants have much better prospects of establishing themselves than seeds and are produced in much smaller numbers. With a few exceptions, including *Furcraea* and *Kalanchoe tubiflora* (in which they are produced on succulent branchlets), the phenomenon has little significance for gardeners.

Stolons, or runners, as some gardeners call them, are more familiar and useful but still limited only to a few plants. Runners from a single seedling of a wild strawberry may rapidly cover several square metres and eventually form a widely dispersed colony along the entire length of a hedgerow—and gardeners rely on runners when propagating cultivated strawberries. They are literally ready-made plants. Each remains attached to and nourished by its parent until it has become completely independent. There is nothing easier than cutting the connections—this happens naturally anyway—and moving the small but perfectly formed plant to another part of the garden.

Rhizomes, the name given to shoots that grow underground or along the surface, are almost equally easy, just as productive and much more widely distributed amongst the plants gardeners are interested in growing. A word of warning, though: Plants equipped with rhizomes include bracken, couch grass (twitch or quack grass), Japanese knotweed and ground elder (bishop's weed). Rhizomatous plants tend to be vigorous and invasive, the flip side of the "Easy to Propagate" coin.

Rhizomes are easy to propagate because of the way they are constructed. Although they grow underground, they are essentially stems, and like other stems, they possess leaves. Since normal leaves would be useless beneath the ground, their leaves are reduced to papery bracts or scales, but like normal leaves each has a bud (or buds) lodged in the angles where it joins the stem. Every one of these buds is capable of growing out to form a shoot, and roots develop at its base as it grows, so that almost immediately it becomes a separate plant. This serves the plant's purpose by allowing it to extend its hold on the ground almost indefinitely. It also serves the gardener's needs—not for bracken and Japanese knotweed, for which there is no need—but for lesser, more desirable plants such as bergenias, epimediums and bamboos with shorter, more manageable rhizomes. These can be cut into sections each containing a single bud, or shoot with roots, capable of transforming itself with minimum fuss or bother into an independent individual.

Layers are formed when branches from an established plant in contact with the ground form roots. In nature, a small forest of Western red cedar (*Thuja plicata*) will originate from one ancient mother plant whose branches bend to the ground and develop roots wherever they touch.

Then in ever widening circles the offspring do the same, until each appears to be a separate tree. Nurserymen follow similar methods, employing formalised, fairly elaborate methods to obtain the greatest possible number of plants. Amateurs do it in simpler, informal fashion by bending branches to the ground when opportunities arise.

Many trees and shrubs produce suckers spontaneously. These have only to be dug up and transplanted to provide a ready source of plants—some from species that are difficult to propagate in other ways. Few trees and shrubs are propagated commercially from suckers, because apart from such plants as snowberries (*Symphoricarpos* spp.) and some sumachs (*Rhus* spp.) which sucker inordinately, they are seldom numerous enough to satisfy demands. Amateur gardeners in search of one or two or even half a dozen plants have more chance of finding all they need, and for them suckers can provide a fruitful means of propagation.

Paradoxically, the method of vegetative propagation most widely used by gardeners is a relatively unusual means of natural reproduction. Gardeners long ago discovered that short lengths of shoot removed from a shrub or other plant would form roots and develop into replicas of their parents if they could be kept alive long enough to do so. That is easy enough in hot, consistently moist climates, where the humidity enables detached shoots to continue to function and the warmth encourages the rapid formation of roots. It presents no problems with many succulent plants, which reproduce naturally in this way from broken off bits and pieces. It becomes progressively more unlikely under natural conditions with unspecialised plants in drier, more taxing situations, such as those found throughout temperate regions, where plants reproduce naturally from cuttings only in unusual circumstances.

However, gardeners, bringing with them an inheritance of techniques and lore originating in the tropics, adapted methods learnt there to new situations. The progress of innovation was so slow and steady that the continually evolving craft of gardening came to be regarded as one of the most conservative—literally stuck in the mud—by those who saw only what was happening today and were unaware of the challenges and changes encountered along the way.

Latterly, gardeners have moved beyond lessons learnt directly from nature to explore possibilities provided by the innermost secret ways in which plants function. They have taken buds from the tips of stems and stripped away the leaves one by one to expose tiny assemblages of cells—the growing points, or *meristems*. They have discovered ways to keep these alive by providing them with nutrients, water and other vital substances, and how to use them to produce new plants. They have developed an industry devoted to the production of test-tube plants (tissue culture), an industry almost wholly beyond the ken of amateur gardeners. Nevertheless, tissue culture is already responsible for the propagation of vast numbers of the plants we buy, plants that started their lives growing on agar jelly in glass or plastic flasks in laboratories.

Finally, abandoning their guise as gardeners altogether, botanists donned white coats and reduced plants to their smallest functioning unit—a single cell taken from meristematic cells in the root of a carrot. They discovered that even this fragment of plant organisation could grow into a carrot plant complete with roots and shoots, leaves and flowers capable of producing seeds from which more carrots could be grown. They had entered the world of *totipotency*, the resonant, evocative name given to the power to recreate the entire plant possessed by any cell within it capable of division.

Forty years later amid a fanfare of acclaim, zoologists produced Dolly the sheep. They, too, had demonstrated that a single cell taken from an adult individual, and suitably nurtured, could produce a replica of its parent. Stem cells in Dolly and other animals; meristems in carrots and other plants.

Despite slight differences in terminology, the discovery of totipotency and the realisation that all the genetic information necessary to grow a new organism is contained in a single cell is enormously significant in both disciplines and ex-

plains an age-old gardening mystery which has grown so commonplace with familiarity that few, if any, regard it as mysterious. "Why," someone might have asked, "should a snippet of shoot grow roots after removal from the parent plant when it would never have done so, left where it was?" It could equally have been asked why sections of roots, used as cuttings, produce shoots.

Cells in different parts of a plant combine to build up the tissues of organs such as roots, shoots, leaves, and fruits in a process known as *differentiation*. Differentiation is highly organised, highly predictable and controlled by hormones. It operates so effectively that leaves normally consist only of tissues composed of the kind of cells one would expect to find in leaves, roots consist of tissues of root cells and so on, as though cells in different organs are capable of fulfilling only the functions appropriate to the organ of which they are a part. But if that were so, cells located in stems would be obliged to fulfill their destiny to develop into stem tissues. They would not be able to form roots, and propagation from cuttings would be impossible.

The discovery of *totipotency*, meaning all powerful or totally potent, explains all by demonstrating that cells arising by division from the meristems are not limited in their capabilities to particular functions. Each contains all the information needed to contribute to any part of the plant. They have no destiny; the course of their development is flexible, directed according to their situation and circumstances. Where leaves are needed they develop into leaf tissues; where flowers, flower tissues; where roots, root tissues.

When part of a plant becomes detached, the situation is recognised and responded to by the new cells produced from the meristems. Provided they continue to function, cells produced by meristems in appropriate places are programmed to replace whatever parts have been lost. This is the practical consequence of totipotency. This capacity for total renewal of an entire plant from whatever bits and pieces may be available forms the basis on which gardeners propagate plants from cuttings.

Missing parts can be renewed only when the part of the plant used as a cutting contains meristematic cells capable of dividing. Shoots, roots and buds normally contain well-organised and effective meristems, though their distribution is much more restricted amongst monocots than amongst dicots.* Mature leaves of some plants also contain effective meristematic cells capable of producing new plants, but cells in the leaves of most species lose their capacity to divide as the leaves mature and are unlikely to serve satisfactorily as cuttings. Flowers and tubers are even less likely to contain active meristematic tissues. They can be used as cuttings only in exceptional circumstances.

Monocots and *dicots* are abbreviations for the two great divisions of the flowering plants. In monocotyledons, the embryos have a single cotyledon, the veins usually run parallel to one another in the leaves, the flowers are composed of parts in threes, and the stems and roots contain very limited meristematic tissues. They include grasses, palms, lilies, and most bulbs and orchids. In dicotyledons, the embryos, with very few exceptions, contain two cotyledons, the veins usually form networks originating from the midribs or rarely to the bases of the leaves, the flowers are most frequently composed of parts in fours or fives but not in threes, and stems and roots contain extensive meristematic tissues that are capable of supporting indefinite increases in diameter and complexity. They include broad-leaved herbs, shrubs and trees.

CHAPTER 2

Seed Collection and Storage

The word *seed* conjures an image of something small, hard, dry and a shade of brown. Seeds are unchanging and appear to be inert. They are produced singly, by the dozen or in hundreds of thousands, in fruits. They are derived from the ovules within the carpels of flowers. *Fruits* in colloquial usage are juicy, succulent and sweet. For the botanist, they are any of a broad variety of organs, dry or succulent, derived from the carpels.

Botanical definitions of fruits can surprise— not to say confuse. Succulent objects such as raspberries, pineapples, plums and pears are dismissed by botanists as false fruits because their fleshy tissues are derived from parts of the flower other than the carpels. Perversely, it may seem, other obvious seeds—such as those of lettuces, celery, French marigolds, strawberries and grasses—are recognised by botanists as fruits, because each is formed from a carpel containing a single ovule. Most botanical fruits—including the capsules of poppies and orchids, pea pods and catalpa beans, the follicles of delphiniums or banksias—are dry and not succulent at all. More about the types of fruits and the ways they are defined will be found in the introduction to Part Two of this book.

These botanical niceties mean little to gardeners. As far as they are concerned, if it looks like a seed, feels like a seed and behaves like a seed, it is a seed. Throughout this book a gardener's view prevails on these matters.

Seeds are grouped into two great divisions of crucial importance to gardeners, *orthodox* and *recalcitrant,* referring to the responses of seeds to long-term storage in a dry condition at subzero temperatures. Orthodox seeds are dry and usually small, comprising the great majority of seeds. Although they appear to be inert, they are responsive to their surroundings and can deteriorate rapidly when stressed. They are able to survive intense desiccation, and given favourable conditions remain alive for decades readily, centuries probably and thousands of years possibly. Recalcitrant seeds are moist and usually large. These comprise most nuts and other analogous structures such as acorns. Their fleshy tissues remain alive only while moist. They die if they become dehydrated and are short-lived under any conditions.

Seeds provide gardeners with the means of exploring the possibilities of unusual and interesting plants beyond the generally available offerings of garden centres and mass marketing. The ease with which orthodox seeds can be stored for long periods enables them to be kept alive almost indefinitely, to be used as and when the opportunity or need arises.

Seed Production

Many garden plants produce seeds regularly and with little attention. Their seeds can be gathered without difficulty, prepared for storage and then kept alive using facilities available in almost any household. Some plants need more attention because their seeds are produced erratically, seldom or never, unless specially provided for; they are inaccessible or hard to obtain for other reasons; they are contained in succulent fruits and are awkward to prepare for storage; or they are recalcitrant and unsuitable for long-term storage.

Collecting and Cleaning Seeds in Dry Fruits

Many plants pose no problems at all when collecting their seeds. For example, campanulas, galtonias, poppies and tulips produce seed in capsules which can be left till they are ripe, and then upended straight into a paper bag. Others pose all kinds of problems, ranging from the difficulties of reaching seeds produced by some tall trees to the near impossible situation with sun cups (*Oenothera ovata*). The seed capsules of this plant from the coastal valleys of central and northern California are located directly on top of the taproot—some 20 cm (8 in.) below the surface—where they reveal nothing of their presence or their state of development.

Three principles govern successful seed collecting:

- *Collect only when seeds are ripe.* The correct time can usually be judged by the appearance of the fruits. Dry fruits change colour from green to yellowish before becoming more or less completely desiccated and turning straw-coloured or brown as they mature. As with all rules, there are exceptions, and immature (green) seeds are sometimes deliberately collected—for example, from members of the buttercup family, because they produce seedlings more readily than mature seed. Some capsules, such as the follicles of hellebores, release their seeds before they are completely dry.

- *Collect only in fine weather when the plants are as dry as possible.* This kind of smug advice arouses fury when the rain is pouring down and time is running short. Nevertheless, almost any effort to achieve it is worthwhile. Collecting seeds from soggy plants is one of gardening's more dispiriting jobs, and seeds collected when wet are vulnerable to moulds, especially when packed closely together. Seeds unavoidably collected when wet should immediately be dried—gently spread them out on sheets of kitchen towel above a radiator or in a dry, airy room, and provide low-level heat for several days rather than the hot blast of an oven.

- *Remember it is seeds that are wanted—not seeds plus bits and pieces of plants and odds and ends of soil, sand or dead leaves.* Although collections of seeds mixed with miscellaneous detritus can be cleaned up later, this is tedious and time consuming. If sown with the seeds, these bits and pieces provide sites for infection by pathogenic fungi, threatening the survival of the seeds around them.

Orthodox seeds are kept in dry, well-ventilated conditions from the time they are collected till they complete their ripening processes and lose surplus moisture. Suitable post-harvest containers include the following:

- Unglazed brown manila paper bags, provided their corners are sealed. These are permeable to water and easily hung up in a glasshouse (greenhouse) or potting shed, and they're large enough to hold the cut ends of spikes, capsules and other plant parts while the drying processes proceed, leading to the release of the seeds inside them.
- Seed trays (flats) lined with paper can be a convenient way to hold bulkier collections.
- Plastic pots lined with paper, or polystyrene cups, are convenient for small quantities, but they're likely to topple over and spill their contents unless held securely in a pot holder.

Figure 1. As a rule, seeds should be gathered when mature. Those with capsules, such as lilies, are tipped straight into paper bags or upended in suitable containers. Some plants, such as acanthus, produce ballistic seeds, which must be enclosed to prevent seeds being scattered far and wide. Others, such as agapanthus, may need a little persuasion—gentle detachment to extract the seeds. Avoid breaking up capsules with the risk of mixing seeds with fragments of plants. Seeds of some species with impermeable seed coats—such as many members of the pea family and some malvas, as shown here—may need chipping before they are sown to enable water to reach the embryo.

- Polythene (plastic) bags are to be used only for succulent fruits—never for seeds from capsules and other dry fruits.

Note that sealed containers, including stoppered bottles, plastic boxes, tins or film canisters, prevent the escape of water vapour and create the humid conditions in which moulds flourish.

Numerous plants—including geraniums, many members of the pea family, violas, acanthus, streptocarpus, impatiens, lathraea, buxus and cresses—distribute their seeds ballistically. The structures enclosing their seeds spring open suddenly when dry to hurl the seeds through the air, sometimes for several metres. For obvious reasons, these should never be put in open containers to dry out after collection; they are best stored

Causes of poor seed production or failures to breed true to type in garden plants

The problems listed here may appear discouraging, but they should more positively be regarded as cautionary. Dwelling on these problems diverts attention from the fact that a great many garden plants do produce quantities of seed of undoubted value.

Self-sterility
Some species can be fertilised only by pollen from another genetically distinct individual (not another member of the same clone) of the same species.

Dioecious species
Only female plants growing close to a male plant will produce fertile seeds. In the northern hemisphere where it is a fairly unusual condition, familiar examples include willows, hollies, mistletoes, ginkgos and red campions. In the southern hemisphere, especially within the New Zealand flora, much higher proportions of species are dioecious.

Position on inflorescence
Flowers in "junior" positions on inflorescences—for example, towards the tops of spikes, the outer florets of umbels or the tertiary branches of a cyme—are more likely to produce infertile seeds than those located higher in the hierarchy. Seeds should be collected selectively from the more advantageously placed seed capsules whenever possible.

Sterility barriers
Such barriers cause problems when plants of a kind—for example, cherries—are grown individually or in insufficient numbers to provide the diversity needed to circumvent restrictions imposed by genetic incompatibilities. Pin-eyed and thrum-eyed forms of primulas and dyonisias (heterostyly) similarly restrict opportunities for successful fertilisation.

Infertile hybrids
Some garden plants include numerous deliberate or inadvertent hybrids; like mules, they may be incapable of producing offspring.

Pollination failures
Pollination failures can be caused by something as simple as an absence of honey bees. However, many plants depend for pollination on specialised interactions with particular insects, birds, mam-

mals, reptiles and other animals. Certain species of gladioli, pelargoniums and sparaxis depend on flies with exceptionally long tongues for pollen transfer; hummingbirds, sunbirds and other nectar feeders are the main—often the exclusive—pollinators of shrubs with long, tubular flowers, especially those that produce crimson or scarlet flowers, including fuchsias, *Ribes speciosum*, correas and grevilleas. Bats pollinate some vireya rhododendrons, banksias and the pendant, shallowly cup-shaped flowers of baobabs; ground-hugging dryandras depend on honey possums in Australia; and massonias in South Africa depend on small rodents. Some species of acacia are said to be dependent on giraffes! In the absence of these pollinators, it may be necessary to hand-pollinate the flowers to obtain fertile seeds.

Breakdown of sterility barriers
In some parts of the world, including Western Australia and New Zealand, native bees act as extremely specific pollinators, each in alliance with a single species or small group of species. The honey bee is not only industrious, but promiscuous in its search for honey and nectar and a leading cause of hybridisation wherever it is present.

Species interfertility
Many genera—rhododendrons, hebes, wahlenbergias, celmisias, aquilegias and verbascums, amongst others—include numerous interfertile species. These are isolated from each other by preferences for different habitats, altitudinal ranges, and pollination mechanisms in the wild. In gardens, when grown close together, they may hybridise freely.

Wind pollination
The airborne pollen of conifers, broad-leaved trees, shrubs and grasses travels great distances and is produced in enormous quantities—a single birch catkin may release some five million pollen grains. Unless each species is grown as a group in splendid isolation, high proportions of hybrids may be produced.

Parthenocarpy
Most fruits fail to develop unless they contain some fertile seeds, but fruits may be produced in which seeds have either failed to develop at all, as in acers; in which very few seeds are viable, as in eucalyptus; or in which the embryos have aborted during development, as in some gentians and meconopsis.

in closed paper bags to prevent the ripe seeds being scattered far and wide.

Preparation for storage

When thoroughly dry—usually within three weeks following collection—seeds are ready to prepare for storage, either short or longer term.

Separate the seeds from any other plant parts harvested with them. Shake seeds free without breaking up the fruits containing them, if possible. Temptations to crush capsules or other structures to extract every last seed should be resisted. Seeds which fail to come free readily are likely to be immature or infertile. Vigorous action contaminates the sample with fragments of the capsules, bits of dried leaves and poorly developed seeds, leading to trouble later.

Linums, medicagos, hakeas, eucalyptus, callistemons and proteas, amongst others, may retain their seeds naturally. Heating the capsules releases the seeds of eucalyptus, hakeas, and callistemons, but securely enclosed fruits like those produced by linums and medicagos must be broken up to release the seeds within them. This should be done as gently as possible.

Clean the seeds before packaging and storing them. Unless this is done, it is impossible to tell how much seed there is, or even whether there are any seeds at all. Seeds of most species can be cleaned in three stages:

- *Sieving* removes hairs, grains of sand and miscellaneous bits of plant larger or smaller than the seeds. Kitchen sieves are adequate, especially if a set can be assembled with a range of mesh sizes.
- *Winnowing* removes undeveloped or infertile seeds and miscellaneous debris. Viable seeds are comparatively dense. They can be separated from most plant fragments by putting everything into a shallow cardboard box and blowing lightly across the surface, removing the rubbish while leaving the seeds behind. The technique is easily acquired but brings the operator into close contact with hairs and other small fragments of plants and should be approached with caution.
- *Hand-picking* by tipping the sample onto a sheet of white paper or light card and carefully separating the good from the bad with the point of a knife is highly effective, but it is so tedious that it soon teaches the virtues of avoiding any activity likely to increase the level of contamination of seeds with other plant parts.

Clean, dry seeds are put into paper envelopes with securely sealed corners and clearly identified by writing on them the names of the plants, the dates and places when and where they were obtained, plus other needful information. Water-soluble inks should be avoided (pencil is reliably persistent), and no faith should be placed on stick-on labels, which possess magical abilities to become unstuck-on labels when used for any purpose where their presence is vital.

Collecting and Cleaning Seeds in Fleshy Fruits

Succulent fruits are sweet, juicy and colourfully attractive to animals. Birds, animals and reptiles eat them, digest them and excrete the seeds at a distance from their parent plants, where their seedlings can grow without competing with them. That is the object of the exercise. As fleshy fruits mature and ripen, they become more or less soft as starch is converted to sugars, which attracts water osmotically, and they become highly coloured to advertise their presence and ripeness to birds, mammals, sometimes reptiles and occasionally fish, which eat the fruits and distribute the seeds within them.

The seeds in berries and other succulent fruits are usually small, though those in drupes, such as plums, podocarps and palms, are comparatively large. They tolerate desiccation and are mostly orthodox as far as storage is concerned. Before storing them, we must imitate the digestive systems of birds and animals by separating flesh from seeds. Collect the fruits when they are completely or almost completely ripe. Generally, the riper and softer the tissues the easier it is to remove them later. However, many are so enticing to birds—and daphnes provide familiar examples—that the only way gardeners can be sure of a share of the crop is to collect fruits just before they are fully ripe. The seeds they contain are mature by this time, and the final stages of ripening follow automatically after they have been picked.

Fruits soon start to lose water, shrivel, become tacky, or foul with moulds. Most remain in reasonable condition in polythene bags in a refrigerator for a week or so. They can be stored for much longer periods in a freezer, and it is often easier to remove the soft tissues after freezing, though the seeds of some species may be damaged by the experience.

Separating seeds from soft tissues

Seeds are separated from soft tissues in several ways. They can be cleaned by hand, macerated in water, or mixed with grit.

By hand

This is the quickest and most satisfactory way to deal with small to moderate quantities of fruits containing relatively large seeds. The berries, arils, drupes and fleshy pods of daphnes, yews, ginkgos, gaultherias, manzanitas, decaisneas, podocarps, rowans, poncirus, coprosmas, palms, amelanchiers, roses and many others can simply be opened up and the seeds extracted, and set out to dry in an airy room or shed on sheets of absorbent paper.

Maceration

Maceration provides an effective way to remove numerous small seeds from currants, solanums, fuchsias, ribes, coriarias, fragarias, actinidias, dianellas, clintonias, and passifloras. Extracting these by hand is messy and unrewarding, and a kitchen liquidiser (food processor) or food blender provides a better way to remove the soft tissues.

Figure 2. *Daphne mezereum* seeds are hand-cleaned and ready to be sown fresh in a grit topping above potting mix. Alternatively, the seeds could be dried in preparation for long-term storage, but they are unlikely to germinate so well afterwards.

- Wrap the blades in a layer of tape before starting in order to reduce damage to the seeds.
- Mix the fruits with at least five times their volume of water and pour the mixture into the blender. Alternatively, put them into a bowl of water and use a hand-held liquidiser.
- Run the blender/liquidiser at minimum speed in short bursts of a few seconds until the skin and tissues of the fruits have completely disintegrated.
- Stir the mixture to produce a suspension of intact seeds and fragmented fruit tissues, adding more water if necessary.

- Leave it to stand for a few minutes; fully developed seeds sink to the bottom, leaving lighter tissues and infertile seeds suspended.
- Decant the flotsam, taking care to retain the seeds.
- Repeat the sequence of adding water, providing time to settle, and pouring off until a clean sample of seeds remains.
- Swill the seeds out through a kitchen sieve and spread them over hard-surfaced absorbent paper, such as a kitchen roll (paper towel), to dry in a warm, well-ventilated room. Soft paper tissues should be avoided as residual gums on the surface of the seeds stick to them.
- When dry, the seeds are treated in exactly the same way as those from dry fruits—packaged in envelopes and stored in a cool, dry place.

Mixing with grit

Mixing seed with grit is the best way to deal with large quantities of fleshy fruits. Combine the seed with several times their volume of grit and pack into polythene bags. Put them in a sheltered, shaded place for a few weeks or several months while the fleshy tissues decompose. After the soft tissues have decomposed, sow the seeds, still mixed with grit, in nursery beds out of doors.

Since it is generally impracticable to separate seeds from grit, this method is unsuitable for seeds destined for long-term storage. However, as part of a weathering treatment (see pp. 326–327), it provides a practical means of cleaning the seeds and enhancing their prospects of germination.

tempting, but set aside after collection, they age within a week or two to a dull chocolate brown. Their shine goes, their shrunken surfaces become creased and folded and the moist, ivory flesh within the nuts becomes leathery, discoloured and yellowish. Death comes with desiccation.

Thus we discover that large, moist, recalcitrant seeds such as nuts and acorns need different treatment from those obtained from capsules and berries. They cannot be kept alive for long periods by using the simple storage conditions applicable to small, dry seeds. Indeed, even in the most favourable conditions they cannot be kept alive for longer than about a year. Unless precautions are taken to ensure that they do not become desiccated, many are very short-lived indeed.

Nuts and acorns are mixed with damp—not sodden—sand or grit, sphagnum moss, peat, shredded bark or some other moisture-retaining substance immediately after collection; then they are packed into polythene bags. These are securely sealed and stored in a cool, frost-free place. A cellar is ideal, a corner of a frost-free garage, and in mild areas anywhere outside that is sheltered and shaded. Sooner or later, depending on temperature, they will start to germinate and should be sown as soon as radicles appear.

Many recalcitrant seeds will survive short-term storage for up to a year in refrigerated stores just above freezing point (approximately 2°C, or 36°F). On a small scale, the salad compartment of a domestic refrigerator serves the same purpose but is unlikely to provide conditions in which the seeds will remain ungerminated for more than a few months.

Collecting and Cleaning Large, Moist Seeds

Almost all large, moist seeds are recalcitrant. The horse chestnut (*Aesculus*) is widely grown in parks and gardens but is a severely threatened plant in the wild, where it grows only in a few wooded valleys between Albania and Macedonia. Its lustrous, large, brown seeds, or conkers, are infinitely

Testing Viability

Before going to the trouble of storing seeds, it is worth checking that they are capable of producing seedlings. Some trees, amongst them conifers and maples, produce healthy looking but hollow seeds. A few are cut open to make sure they are not empty. If they are filled at all, it is most likely that they contain embryos and other essentials. An ivory white, healthy looking interior usually indicates a viable seed. A yellowish tinge, brown spots, and partially shriveled or leathery textures are indications of reduced vitality.

The capsules and follicles of gentians, meconopsis, delphiniums, digitalis, primulas, and hydrangeas and the heads of celmisias and many other members of the daisy family often contain mixtures of fertile and infertile seeds. These infertile seeds (chaff) are less dense than fertile seeds and can usually be eliminated by winnowing, but when they predominate it becomes difficult to summon the ruthlessness to blow away almost everything that has been collected. A short examination, preferably using a hand lens, will show whether seeds in a sample are mostly round and glossy or flat and lacklustre. If the latter, another attempt at winnowing is needed—and sometimes ruthlessness, too. Only a tiny proportion of a sample may consist of viable seeds, and reducing a seemingly abundant sample to a tiny minority of good seeds then becomes an act of faith based on conviction gardening.

As an alternative or additional test, a small sample of seeds are dropped into a cup of water to which a few drops of liquid detergent have been added; then the mixture is stirred. Fully developed seeds sink, though that does not necessarily mean they are still viable. Partially developed or empty seeds that would not be worth sowing float on the surface. Finally, a simple germination test can be set up in the way described in the box below.

Larvae of weevils, bruchid beetles and other insects infest seeds of many species in the pea family including vetches, carmichaelias and lathyrus as well as acacias, hoherias, and plagianthus, amongst others. Eggs are laid on the surface of the seeds just before they mature, and the larvae feast on the embryo and storage tissues inside them. These infestations can comprehensively ruin the prospects of seeds stored at room temperatures, and samples of seed should be examined for the telltale exit holes before they are stored.

Storing Seeds

Storage means different things, depending on what is intended: Short-term storage refers to the time between harvesting and sowing, when storage may be combined with treatments—such as after-ripening or weathering in order to enhance

---

A germination test to establish the viability of samples of seed

Sow samples of seed on a sheet of damp paper towel, kept moist in a plastic box with a tight-fitting lid. Set out pinches of seed in small clusters from as many different kinds as need to be tested in a grid pattern, identifying what is where with a plan. Put the box in a warm (18° to 25°C, or 64° to 75°F) room.

If a high proportion in a cluster (gauged by eye) germinate within a short time and produce healthy looking seedlings, all is well. If none germinate, do not assume the seeds are dead. Those that remain firm and unchanged after a fortnight are probably healthy. If most of the seeds in a cluster have gone mouldy within a fortnight, or they disintegrate when squeezed between finger and thumb, they are not viable.

Most seeds, living or dead, swell as they imbibe water after being sown; those that do not may have hard seed coats that are impermeable to water. They will imbibe after a fragment of the seed coat is removed with the point of a knife, and they will usually germinate soon after.

the prospects of germination when the seeds are sown. Long-term storage is intended to keep seeds alive for many years, perhaps to keep surpluses to sow another day, safeguard plants that are difficult to obtain commercially or seldom available, retain breeding material for future use, or conserve rare plants that might otherwise be lost from gardens or in the wild.

Short-term storage

Apart from large, moist recalcitrant seeds, those that are to be sown within a year of harvesting require minimal attention. Most can be kept in paper bags or envelopes (with the corners sealed with masking tape) in a drawer in a dry, warm room. Problems are likely only if they are not kept dry, and the humid conditions found during the winter in unheated garden or potting sheds quickly lead to serious losses, especially if the seeds go mouldy.

Long-term storage

What follows applies only to small, dry seeds with orthodox storage responses. These can be stored for very long periods indeed. Provided the seeds are dry, they are not damaged by below-freezing temperatures. The nature of the seed, not the conditions in which the plants grow naturally, determines whether or not it can be stored. Seeds of aquatic plants, provided they are small and dry, as many are, tolerate the affects of desiccation, necessary to prolong their lives in store. Seeds of tender plants, provided they are small and dry, tolerate the below-freezing temperatures needed to preserve them in store.

Successful storage conditions are defined by a simple rule: *The drier and colder the longer the storage life.* Seeds live longer in cool, dry rooms than in damp potting sheds. They live longer still in an airtight box over a desiccant. Silica gel is an effective desiccant for this purpose and amongst the safest and easiest to handle. It is not a hazard to health or to other materials, including food. Seeds in a desiccator in a refrigerator live longer than they live in a dry, warm room, and they live longer still in a freezer cabinet at temperatures around $-15\,^\circ\mathrm{C}$ ($5\,^\circ\mathrm{F}$)—long enough to satisfy almost any purpose for which seeds are stored.

Boxes containing seeds can be removed and kept at room temperature for a time if the freezer is temporarily needed for other things. Periods

---

A simple, inexpensive, long-term storage system

A plastic box with a close-fitting, airtight lid—the kind of thing used to store food—can be used to store seeds and placed in a freezer cabinet.

- Pour silica gel crystals into the box to form a layer about 1 cm (0.5 in.) deep.
- Place paper envelopes containing seeds over the silica gel.
- Replace the lid of the box and put it into a freezer, where it remains until the seeds are needed.
- Remove the box from the freezer. Leave it at room temperature for an hour or two; this avoids the possibility of water condensing on the cold surfaces of the seeds when the box is opened.
- Remove the lid of the box and take out the envelopes containing seeds from which samples are to be sown. Temporarily replace the lid.
- Sow the seeds, retaining any surplus in the envelopes.
- Put the envelopes containing surplus seeds back in the box, replace the lid and return the box to the freezer until more seeds are needed.

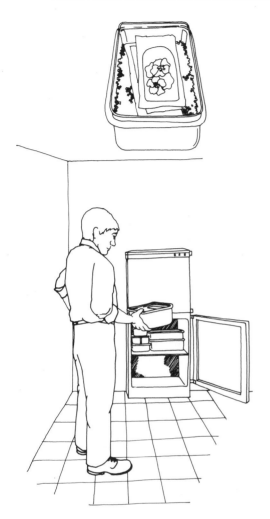

extending to several weeks have minimal effects on storage life, provided the dry atmosphere within the boxes is maintained.

Sooner or later, silica gel crystals become saturated with water, and blue indicator crystals mixed with them for the purpose will turn pink. When this happens, remove the silica gel and pour it into a shallow baking dish to be dried in an oven. A temperature of approximately 150°C (300°F), maintained for two or three hours, will drive off the excess water. The reactivated desiccant is returned to the boxes, the packets of seeds and the box lids are replaced, and the boxes are put back in the freezer.

Stored seed is treated just like good quality unstored seed—its germination responses will not have been affected. Seeds which require after-ripening should be kept at room temperatures for two to three months before being frozen to enable them to after-ripen. Similarly, there will be no weathering effects due to the low temperature while the seeds are in the cold store.

The system described is essentially the same as that used for the long-term storage of seeds in seed banks. Temperatures of −13 to −15°C (5 to 10°F) ensure prolonged viability but are not so low that they create problems for the operator. Normally short-lived seeds, such as those of delphiniums, primulas and meconopsis, will live 15 years or more. Those that are tougher and more resilient live virtually indefinitely.

Figure 3. Place seeds in unglazed paper packets above a layer of silica gel at the bottom of a plastic box with a tight-fitting lid. For long-term storage, put the boxes into a freezer at approximately −15°C (5°F). A refrigerator can be used for short-term storage—such as overwinter storage.

CHAPTER 3

Seed Science

We garden in the shadow of gardening lore—the inheritance of thousands of years of digging, weeding, sowing, harvesting and enjoying our little Edens. Like folklore—accumulated in a similar way—some is useful, much is interesting, and a certain amount is fit only for the compost heap. Gardening lore looks over our shoulders when we propagate plants from cuttings and when we sow their seeds—often helpfully, sometimes dubiously. Amongst many other things, it decrees that some seeds germinate only in the dark; others do so only when they see light. It tells us that seedlings are likely to grow best from seeds sown at the birth of a new moon, that orchid seeds must find a fungal partner before they can develop into seedlings, and that when seeds do not germinate they are probably dormant, a condition from which they must be released before they are able to produce seedlings. Like holy writ, gardening lore is a mixture of superstition, common sense and pure inspiration. This chapter looks at some of these beliefs and tries to assess to what extent they accurately reflect how seeds respond to their surroundings and how gardeners can benefit from them when sowing seeds.

What Is a Seed?

The vast majority of seeds hold a single embryo; a tiny minority, including hostas and citrus, may contain extra embryos derived from the tissues of the nucellus within the ovule. (Nucellar tissues surround the embryo sac within the unfertilised ovule.) Seeds contain storage reserves to support germination and early growth of seedlings. The protective outer wrapping, the seed coat, of a true seed is derived from tissues enclosing the ovules within the carpels. However, in a great many so-called seeds, including those of lettuces, grasses and buttercups, the seed coat is formed from the tissues of the carpel itself. In strict botanical parlance, the latter are fruits. No functional significance has been traced to this difference and from a gardener's point of view they are, and are treated as, seeds.

Functions of seeds

Seeds are packages enclosing an embryo. They provide the following:

Protection
The leathery, sometimes woody, seed coats possessed by most seeds safeguard the soft, vulnerable tissues of the embryos from abrasion, knocks and predation.

36

Regulation

The seed is a complex organism which, amongst other functions, controls uptake of water through the seed coat and its availability to the tissues of the embryo. The seed is a means of controlling the uptake of gases, allowing oxygen to diffuse into the seed to support respiration and carbon dioxide to diffuse out.

Sensors

These respond to features of the environment, including temperature and the spectral composition and intensity of light, through photoreceptive pigments and possibly crystalline structures just below the surface of the seed coat.

Nutrition

Most seeds, apart from notable exceptions such as orchids and willows, act as food stores packed with reserves in the form of starch, oils, and proteins to sustain life while the seed lies in the soil and to support seedlings till they become self-sufficient. Storage reserves may be contained within the seed leaves, or cotyledons, of the embryo itself, or in a separate storage tissue known as the endosperm. The seed coats may also act as storage reserves, with an exceptional situation found in palms, in which the "stone," or seed, is composed of hemicellulose.

Distribution in space and time

Seeds of many species are designed to be mobile. They have wings and other devices that act aerodynamically, or with a variety of attachments or lures that enable them to hitch rides, willingly or unwillingly, on animals, birds and other creatures. Seeds may germinate soon after they mature and separate from their parents; a few even germinate before they separate, or they may lie in the soil for varying periods.

Relatively short periods, measured in weeks, months, or exceptionally a year or two, are likely to be due to the need for seeds to germinate at seasons of the year favourable for the survival of their seedlings. But some seeds do not germinate for decades or even centuries, forming a reserve population in the soil known as the Soil Seed Bank. They can survive long after the parent plants have ceased to occupy the site, and they provide security in case of calamities afflicting plants above ground.

Final stages in the development of a seed

When the embryo is fully grown—sometimes before—and all the storage reserves are in place, the fertilised ovules complete their transformation into seeds. The developing embryo within the ovule is an actively metabolising part of the plant, dependent on water and nutrients received from its parent through the placenta. Seeds are independent, metabolically almost inactive individuals. The transformation from one to the other is a fundamental and critical change.

Tissues within the ovule lose water, while maintaining sufficient organisation to sustain the minimal levels of metabolic activity necessary to sustain life. Many seeds tolerate extremely low (less than 5 percent) moisture contents without harm. Surrounding tissues harden into seed coats, highly structured coverings composed of lipids and carbohydrates, usually as cellulose or lignin, and often including crystals.

Seed coats, despite their apparently inert and rather uninteresting appearance, are the critical interface between the embryo within the seed and the outside world. Their integrity is vital to the functioning of the seed, and it is crucially important to ensure they are able to complete their development and are fully mature before harvesting seeds.

Germination

Gardeners mark germination by the appearance of seedlings, but these are the visible expression of a previous event. Germination, like becoming pregnant, is a no-going-back event, one which irreversibly changes the behaviour of the tissues within the seed. It sets in motion a process that depends on the correct sequencing and coordination of a huge variety of different regulatory systems. The intensely desiccated, metabolically almost inert tissues in the seeds have to kick start the embryo, leading to the reactivation of enzyme systems and pathways of energy transfer, the mobilisation of storage reserves, and culminating in the appearance of seedlings.

Water uptake by seeds is often regarded as the start of the process of germination, but although germination cannot start without water, that is a misleading view. Water uptake by colloids within the seed is a physical process. Even dead seeds imbibe water. Imbibed seeds do not necessarily germinate; they can lie apparently inert within the soil for years.

Seeds germinate only when they are provided with all the components of their natural environment necessary for germination, in a form and sequence, which sets off the chain of events leading to the production of seedlings. That may seem a pompous combination of pedantry and imprecision when applied to sowing mustard, cress, lettuce, and many other plants which germinate so readily that we pay little attention to the conditions in which they do so. It becomes decidedly relevant when trying to unravel the responses of seeds of more obdurate species. These produce seedlings only in response to a series of events which must relate very closely to the conditions they would experience naturally. All too often we find ourselves lamentably ignorant of the nature and duration of these events.

When we sow seeds, one of the most helpful things to know is whether they are likely to produce seedlings more or less immediately, with no special treatment, or after a delay while they respond to the conditions they find themselves in, in preparation for germination later. Prospects of "immediate" or "delayed" seedling emergence crucially affect the equipment we use, the times when we sow the seeds, and how we treat them.

Immediate germination

Immediate germination can occur within 24 hours or after several weeks. The time taken is characteristic of the species—for example, at 20°C (70°F), *Salvia aethiopis* seeds produce seedlings in less than 24 hours; *Lavatera trimestris* in about 48 hours; *Delphinium* cvs. within eight days; and *Gentiana cruciata* after about 20 days. Times vary with temperature, but the gentian will always be slower than the delphinium, lavatera much faster than either, and the salvia first.

These variations are puzzling and the reasons for them obscure. Once a seed has "decided" to germinate, it would seem that the sooner it does so the better. Early risers have a competitive advantage over later entries; they are better placed to make use of transitory or intermittent rainfall, and seedlings which grow quickly are vulnerable to slugs and other predators for a shorter time.

Seeds that produce seedlings fastest are likely to come from arid areas and Mediterranea. In arid areas where falls of rain may be erratic, (for plants such as salvia) rapid germination followed by a vigorous thrusting of the radicle into lower levels of the soil, where moisture is likely to remain available for longer, are useful attributes. In Mediterranea (for plants such as lavatera), transitions from summer aridity to autumn humidity can be sharply defined by early rainfalls. This creates a starting gate effect which gives a clear advantage to those first off the mark.

Elsewhere, the advantages of rapid germination are apparently less decisive. Tardy responders such as the gentian from sub-alpine grasslands and *Delphinium elatum*—the principal progenitor of the garden hybrids—from open deciduous woodlands, can survive without having to hassle from seed to seedling.

Many seeds are wanna-be immediate germinators, prevented from being so by impediments, including hard, wax-impregnated seed coats, which prevent water reaching the embryo; impermeable seed coats, which deprive embryos of oxygen; or soluble growth inhibitors, which suppress germination until leached out. These impediments can be removed by damaging the seed coats to enable water or oxygen to reach the embryos inside them, or by leaching out the inhibitors by soaking the seeds in water. When the impediments have been removed, these seeds usually germinate spontaneously and rapidly.

Delayed germination

Delays range from a few weeks to many years. The essential difference between seeds capable of producing seedlings immediately and those which do so after a delay is the latters' need for a prior experience or treatment during which changes occur inside the seed, possibly within the embryo itself. The devices developed by seeds to control the seasons when their seedlings emerge are summarised in the box on the following pages and discussed in detail in the sections that follow.

After-ripening

The seeds of many species after-ripen, especially those growing in Mediterranea, and chart 1 illustrates typical germination responses for such species. Seeds are cleaned and dried immediately after collection. They are then stored in permeable paper envelopes in a warm, dry room for several weeks or a month or two before being sown. Seeds intended for long-term storage at subzero temperatures are treated similarly. After-ripening does not take place at subzero temperatures and the process must be completed before they are stored.

Low-temperature responses

Weathering at low temperatures, like after-ripening, usually requires periods of weeks or months to be effective. A very few seeds—for example *Lathyrus vernus*—produce seedlings following a single exposure to temperatures near freezing point. Seeds must be fully imbibed in order to respond and in gardens are sown in the normal way before starting the treatment. The most satisfactory way to weather seeds at low or high temperatures is to sow them in tune with the seasons so their responses follow natural patterns. When this is not possible, a refrigerator provides an acceptable

substitute for winter weather. Similarly, supplementary warmth, for example in a propagator, can be used to simulate summer temperatures.

Light and dark

Responses to light and dark, like those illustrated in chart 3, are widespread amongst species from Mediterranea—that is, germination depends on light only at higher temperatures. At lower temperatures, seeds germinate equally well both in light and dark. However, this principle cannot be applied to seeds in general, and responses to light are extremely complex. Lists in which species are categorised into those whose seeds "need light," those that "need darkness" and those that are "neutral" in order to germinate should be taken with more than a pinch of salt. Depending on temperature and other conditions, the same species can display all three responses.

Under natural conditions, the ability to sense light and its spectral composition enables seeds to sense their proximity to the surface: the deeper they are buried, the darker their surroundings. The absence of light conveys the message that they are so deeply buried that seedlings would be unable to reach the surface. This ability also enables seeds to sense the presence of overhanging vegetation. Changes in the spectral composition of light as it passes through leaves are detected by seeds. This enables them to avoid producing seedlings in situations where they would be overshadowed by competing vegetation.

Fluctuating temperatures and day length

Under natural conditions in most parts of the temperate world, nights are appreciably colder than days, resulting in falls in temperature of approximately 5° to 15°C (10° to 30°F) between night and day. A great many seeds produce seedlings only in response to these diurnal cycles. Constant temperatures are found naturally in situations where recently emerged seedlings would have little chance of survival, notably beneath the soil surface, beneath deep mats of existing vegetation or in deep shade, and in water. Beneath the soil surface, temperatures fluctuate only in the

Summary of devices by which seeds delay germination to control the seasons when seedlings emerge

The underlying causes of delayed germination are often complex, combining two or more of the controls outlined here. Even after immature embryos become fully developed, they may need to experience low temperatures before they germinate. Seeds may need to experience sequences of high to low soil temperatures before they germinate. Repeated exposures to high or low temperatures may be a necessary part of the processes leading to germination.

After-ripening
Freshly gathered seeds of species from Mediterranea frequently germinate reluctantly, or only, at temperatures below approximately 15 °C (60 °F). Seeds germinate more rapidly over a broader temperature range after storage for several weeks in warm, dry conditions.

Hard or impermeable seed coats
The seed coats of members of the pea family, and some species in the mint and cistus families, are heavily thickened and impermeable to water. Bacterial action, heat or mechanical damage degrade or fracture the seed coats. Water is able to reach the embryo and germination usually follows within days. This fairly haphazard strategy relies for success on spreading germination over long periods, sometimes many, many years. Gardeners cope with it by chipping the seeds.

Seed coats impervious to gases
Seed coats restrict movement of gases, including the entry of oxygen, preventing growth and germination of the embryo; the escape of carbon dioxide, leading to narcotic effects within the seed; and uptake of other gaseous components found in the soil, such as ethylene. Some promote germination and others inhibit it. The seed coats may not appear unusual and the condition cannot be spotted visually. This impediment has been identified in seeds of species in the lily family but is probably more widespread. Impervious seed coats result in persistent germination failures, despite treatments intended to enhance germination. Their presence is revealed by removing a small sliver of seed coat, close to the embryo, with a needle or the point of a sharp knife, after which the seed germinates.

Weathering at low temperatures (1° to 5°C, or 35° to 40°F)
Some seeds germinate only after exposure to cold, which must usually be maintained for weeks or months. The condition occurs in the seeds of many species from cool and cold temperate regions. Only imbibed seeds are responsive, and seeds stored dry at low temperatures are not affected. The condition is well known to gardeners, who respond to it by exposing seeds to winter conditions or by putting them in a refrigerator after sowing.

Weathering at moderate to high temperatures (15° to 25°C, or 60° to 75°F)

Seeds of many bulbs, perennials and shrubs germinate only after exposure to warm conditions. Seedlings emerge following falls in temperature to approximately 10°C (50°F). Despite being widespread, the condition is less well known than similar responses to low temperatures. It plays little part in the repertoire of most gardeners. In gardens, the effects are reproduced by exposing seeds to summer temperatures followed by cooler conditions in autumn, or by using a heated propagator after sowing before transferring to lower temperatures.

Immature embryos

The embryos within the seeds of many members of the buttercup family, notably hellebores and aconites, are immature when the seed is shed. Embryos complete their development in warm, moist soil, maturing during the autumn. Most require exposure to cold before germinating. Seeds are sown as they ripen, exposing them to summer temperatures, followed by low temperatures in early winter. Late-sown seed is placed for two months in a propagator at approximately 15°C (60°F), followed by low temperature weathering.

Specific temperature requirements

In a simple process, seeds germinate within defined temperature limits, characteristic of the species and the state of the seeds. Abrupt cutoff points define maximum and minimum temperatures above and below which few, if any, seeds produce seedlings.

In more complex processes, far more species than we are aware of respond to diurnal temperature fluctuations, similar to those occurring between night and day. Minimum effective fluctuations are approximately 5°C (10°F), with optima of approximately 7° to 10°C (15° to 20°F). Gardeners should avoid constant day/night temperatures—such as a propagator provides—when sowing seeds.

Responses to light or dark

Many seeds germinate better when exposed to light regularly or periodically. A few appear to be favoured by darkness. The responses are strongly affected by other environmental conditions, especially temperature. In the absence of contrary information, sow all seeds in situations where they receive light for part of each day. Avoid using opaque, light-excluding covers. The diffused light provided by translucent covers—for example, expanded polystyrene or bubble polythene—is ideal.

Chart 1. Seeds of a Mediterranean *Silene* sp. sown just after harvesting produced seedlings only at low temperatures and in low numbers. When sown after being stored dry at room temperatures for periods of one month or three months, the numbers of seedlings produced and the range of temperatures over which germination occurred increased progressively.

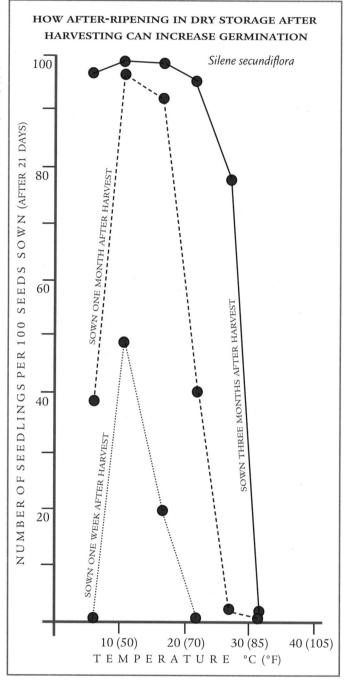

HOW AFTER-RIPENING IN DRY STORAGE AFTER HARVESTING CAN INCREASE GERMINATION

Silene secundiflora

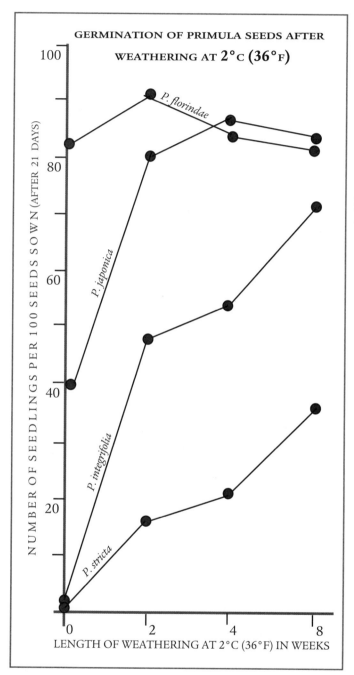

GERMINATION OF PRIMULA SEEDS AFTER
WEATHERING AT 2°C (36°F)

NUMBER OF SEEDLINGS PER 100 SEEDS SOWN (AFTER 21 DAYS)

100

80

60

40

20

P. florindae

P. japonica

P. integrifolia

P. stricta

0   2   4   8

LENGTH OF WEATHERING AT 2°C (36°F) IN WEEKS

Chart 2. Seeds of some primulas germinate better after exposure to low temperatures. *Primula florindae* did not need this treatment. With the other three species, the longer the exposure to low temperatures, the more seedlings were produced. Extending the period would probably have led to further increases of *P. integrifolia* and *P. stricta*.

Chart 3. Many seeds are reputed to produce seedlings only when exposed to light; others only in darkness. Much more usually, seeds respond to light—or dark—in particular situations. These ageratum seeds germinated to the same extent in light or dark at low temperatures, and light improved germination only at high temperatures.

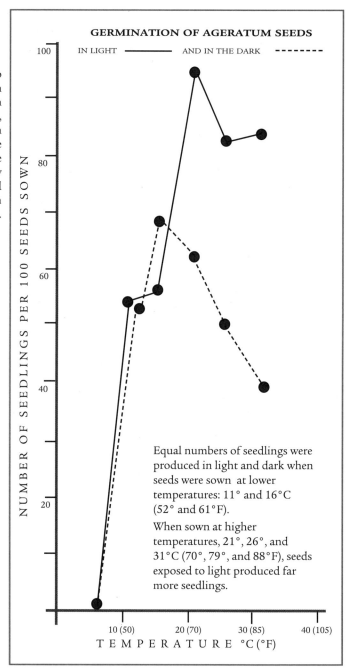

GERMINATION OF AGERATUM SEEDS

IN LIGHT ——————— AND IN THE DARK - - - - - - -

NUMBER OF SEEDLINGS PER 100 SEEDS SOWN

Equal numbers of seedlings were produced in light and dark when seeds were sown at lower temperatures: 11° and 16°C (52° and 61°F).

When sown at higher temperatures, 21°, 26°, and 31°C (70°, 79°, and 88°F), seeds exposed to light produced far more seedlings.

TEMPERATURE °C (°F)

surface layers, and this provides another means of assessing depth of burial. Seeds located beneath deep mats of existing vegetation, or in deep shade, provide another means of avoiding producing seedlings in excessively competitive conditions. In water, seeds floating on the surface or lying at the bottom of ponds are not exposed to diurnal temperature fluctuations.

Responses to light and fluctuating temperatures are frequently linked. Some of the effects are shown in chart 4, which provides an idea of how complex the responses of seeds to light and fluctuating temperatures can be.

The conventional wisdom which pigeonholes seeds into three categories—defined as those that require light in order to germinate, those that germinate only in darkness, and those capable of producing seedlings in light or dark—is a facile simplification of the true situation. It is so shot through with exceptions and ambiguities, not the least of those arising from the use in the past of some very peculiar light sources, that it is not even a useful practical guide.

As a general rule, *seeds should always be sown in such a way that light is part of their daily environment.* Covers of any kind which exclude light completely should always be avoided. There is no logical explanation why seeds should geminate in total darkness when they fail to produce seedlings under other conditions. This would literally be a leap into the dark and one most likely to expose the emerging seedlings to conditions in which they could not survive.

Reports on the ways seeds respond to light and dark are based on a partial, probably misleading, view of the dislocated fragments of an as-yet-undiscovered picture. We are now able to see that temperature has profound effects on these responses, but we remain unaware of the crucial links that would draw the fractured elements of the picture together and make sense of the composition.

The likeliest candidate as the missing factor in the equation is day length. Responses to day length are an unknown country, as far as seed germination is concerned, and few if any reports of their effects are available. We do know that the same photoreceptor systems are used by seeds to "see" light and by plants to measure day length. These systems are so sensitive it would be difficult to set up conditions in the garden that effectively consigned seeds to utter darkness.

Day lengths rule so many plant responses that it would be remarkable if they did not play any part in germination, especially as there are numerous situations in which plants would seem likely to benefit from them. For instance, if seeds of plants from Mediterranea responded to *shortening* day lengths, it would increase the likelihood of seedlings emerging under favourable conditions in the autumn and discourage the emergence of seedlings during the long, hot days of summer. Alternatively, if seeds of some species from cold temperate regions responded to *lengthening* day lengths, it would increase the likelihood of germinating under favourable conditions in the spring and discourage seedling emergence in the autumn just before the onset of winter. Nevertheless, such responses do not seem to have been identified, and thoughts about day lengths play no part in our plans when we set out to sow seeds.

Gibberellins

Treatments with several chemicals can be used to short-circuit restrictions on germination. By far, the most effective is a group of plant growth hormones known as *gibberellins*. Chart 5 shows how a mixture of two gibberellins improved the germination of several different primulas, which would normally need to be exposed to low temperatures before producing seedlings.

Treatment with gibberellins also leads to seedling production from seeds grown in darkness which normally require light, seeds in constant temperatures which normally require temperatures fluctuations, and seeds grown at constant temperatures in the dark which normally require fluctuating temperatures and light. These broad-spectrum effects on germination could make gibberellins extremely valuable aids—except for their side effects, notably excessive elongation of the seedlings' hypocotyls. Gibberellins can be useful when other, more natural, methods fail, but

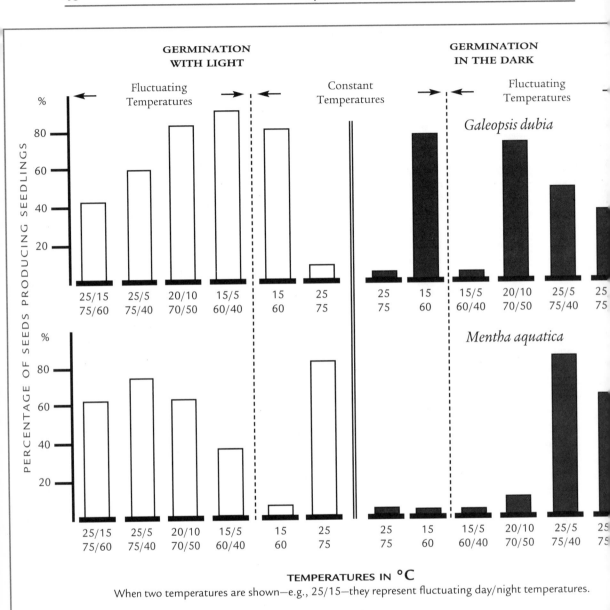

GERMINATION
WITH LIGHT

GERMINATION
IN THE DARK

Chart 4. Some of the ways light and temperature interact to control the germination of four species in the mint family. Seeds germinated in broader ranges of temperature in light than in constant darkness. They were also more likely to produce seedlings when temperatures fluctuated between day and night. Despite the unfavourable effects of darkness, especially at constant temperatures, high germination rates occurred at at least one temperature combination for every species.

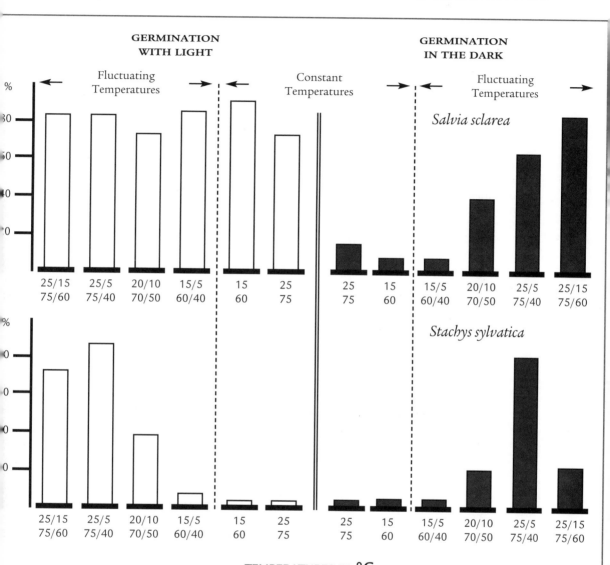

GERMINATION
WITH LIGHT

GERMINATION
IN THE DARK

Fluctuating
Temperatures

Constant
Temperatures

Fluctuating
Temperatures

Salvia sclarea

Stachys sylvatica

TEMPERATURES IN °C

When two temperatures are shown—e.g., 25/15—they represent fluctuating day/night temperatures.

Chart 5. How the seeds of several primulas, which normally would have germinated after low temperature weathering, responded to treatment with gibberellins. Similar results would have been obtained from exposure to winter weather or after a sojourn of four to eight weeks in a refrigerator.

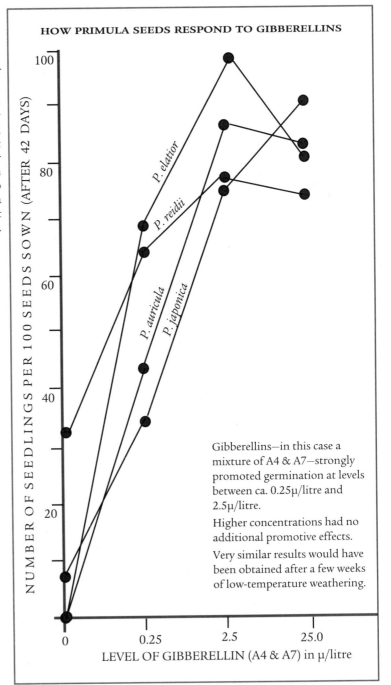

HOW PRIMULA SEEDS RESPOND TO GIBBERELLINS

NUMBER OF SEEDLINGS PER 100 SEEDS SOWN (AFTER 42 DAYS)

P. elatior

P. reidii

P. auricula

P. japonica

Gibberellins—in this case a mixture of A4 & A7—strongly promoted germination at levels between ca. 0.25μ/litre and 2.5μ/litre.

Higher concentrations had no additional promotive effects.

Very similar results would have been obtained after a few weeks of low-temperature weathering.

LEVEL OF GIBBERELLIN (A4 & A7) in μ/litre

whenever possible physical treatments similar to those operating under natural conditions are preferable.

How seeds respond to temperature

Faced with a packet of common garden seeds—the kind that come up, more or less to order, soon after they are sown—gardeners work on the broad assumption that they will produce seedlings faster in warm soil than in cold and not much more than that. This act of faith is usually vindicated in the garden. It conceals, or fails to reveal, a great deal about the precision with which seed germination is controlled by temperature. The responses of the seeds of the vegetables shown in chart 6 are characteristic of the responses of seeds in general.

Seeds display clearly defined maxima, where performance becomes extremely sensitive to temperature, and differences of only 1°C (2°F) can draw the line between success and failure. They display optimal temperature ranges, over which variations of several degrees scarcely affect the speed at which seeds produce seedlings or the numbers that do so. They display sub-optimal ranges, in which seeds take progressively longer to produce seedlings as temperatures are reduced. And they display well-defined maxima and minima, above and below which no seedlings are produced even after lengthy periods.

Under natural conditions, where soil temperatures change continuously with the seasons, responses to temperature play highly significant roles in the timing of seedling emergence, and many species control seedling emergence mainly by their responses to temperature without recourse to more complex mechanisms. For example, they prevent the germination of seeds of species from Mediterranea at high temperatures, safeguarding seedlings from exposure to summer drought. They prevent the germination of species from cold temperate regions, at moderate temperatures (less than 10°C, or 50°F), avoiding the emergence of seedlings in the autumn immediately before winter.

Traditional methods of sowing seeds pay little attention to these temperature responses, hence our lack of awareness of their existence. However, the sensitivity of lettuces and leeks still causes failures of summer sowings when soil temperatures are high.

When using supplementary heat to raise seedlings on glasshouse benches or in propagators, these responses become much more significant. It is easy to turn up the heat to a point where it exceeds the maxima even for such easy-to-grow species as leeks. When sowing seeds of less familiar plants—especially those from Mediterranea—quite moderate temperatures are sometimes high enough to cause failure. Alternatively, similarly moderate temperatures of approximately 10° to 15°C (50° to 60°F) are below the minima for germination of some warm temperate species and of freshly shed seeds of many cool and cold temperate species.

Function of germination controls

Seeds are dispersed at different times of the year, depending on the life cycles of different plants. The season when they hit the ground is not necessarily a good time to produce seedlings; it may coincide with the start of severe winter weather or intense summer droughts. Germination controls provide seedlings with a chance of survival. That is all.

It is frequently suggested the controls enable seeds to germinate at a time which provides them with the best possible chance of survival, but that is not necessarily so. The only requirement for the survival of a population is that over the years, and taking one thing with another, sufficient seedlings grow to maturity and produce seeds in their turn to replace their parents—more or less.

This may seem to be splitting hairs, but the distinction between germinating at the best possible time and one that merely enables survival is significant. If it was necessary for germination controls to provide seedlings with the best possible chance of survival, germination responses would have to be highly plastic—able to change constantly in response to quite small differences in

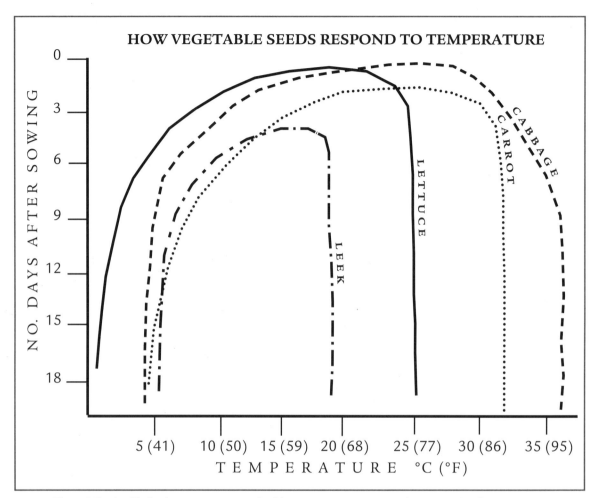

HOW VEGETABLE SEEDS RESPOND TO TEMPERATURE

Chart 6. Seeds of leeks, lettuces, carrots and cabbages were sown at a continuous range of temperatures between 0° and 40°C (32° and 100°F). Large differences occurred in the temperature ranges over which seeds germinated, and smaller differences occurred in the time taken for seedlings to emerge. Leek seed germinated (that is, the radicles emerged) over a narrow range from 6° to 18°C (43° to 64°F); the first seedlings appears after four days. Lettuce seed germinated from 2° to 26°C (36° to 79°F); the first seedlings appeared within one day. Carrot seed germinated from 5° to 32°C (41° to 90°F); the first seedlings appeared within two days. Cabbage seed germinated from 4° to 37°C (40° to 99°F); the first seedlings appeared within one day.

conditions in different parts of the range of a species. If it is necessary only for the controls to enable survival of sufficient seedlings to replace their parents, different populations of a species extending over considerable geographical ranges could all be endowed with similar responses, provided they enabled the minimum number of replacements to survive.

There need be no consistency from year to year. Occasional favourable years may be sufficient. In some situations, particularly with trees, the good years may be few and far between. Trees on the edge of their range, especially those growing in the taxing conditions posed by mountains, may fail to produce any seedlings for years on end. Then, one year, the coincidence of a good crop of seeds with ample summer rain, followed by an unusually mild winter, provides conditions unlikely to be repeated for decades that enable just a few seedlings to make a break for it and become sufficiently established to survive the return of harsher, more normal conditions during the following years.

When we try to link the conditions in which seeds produce seedlings with the conditions in which they survive naturally, it sometimes happens that attempts to draw conclusions based on average conditions produce red herrings. We would have more chance of reaching the correct conclusion by attempting the much more difficult task of spotting the occasional exceptional conditions responsible for fleeting opportunities.

The Dormancy Story

Seeds are produced by plants as a means of survival; they are used by gardeners as a means of propagation. Plant and gardener both achieve success when seedlings appear, but they measure success by different criteria.

Plants' needs are served wherever and whenever enough seedlings survive to replace their parents—hundreds, hundreds of thousands, or millions of seeds may be produced. Seedlings may emerge and perish for years or decades, but success is embodied in the single individual that grows and flowers and itself produces seed. A gardener's needs are served when the highest possible proportion of seeds germinate in the shortest possible time. We may have to be content with less, but that is what we aim for.

When seeds are sown but no seedlings appear, we conclude that the seeds are dead or dormant. We describe seeds as "dormant" when they "fail" to germinate in conditions which we deem favourable for germination. We talk about "breaking" dormancy when we expose seeds to low temperatures or apply other treatments which result in the appearance of seedlings. These words are well established in gardening lore, but they are based on unjustified assumptions and convey misleading impressions.

The word *dormant*, with its connotations of sleep, fails to express the fact that seeds lying in the soil constantly and actively sense what goes on around them and respond to their situation in positive and often subtle ways. "Breaking" dormancy suggests an action that is violent and irreversible, whereas the processes which change the responses of seeds to subsequent events are subtle, varied and often easily reversible. "Favourable conditions" is an entirely garden-centric concept. Seeds of one kind or another are able to produce seedlings under natural conditions at almost any temperature from 0° to 40°C, or 32° to 105°F (not excluding 0°C or 32°F), in almost every combination of day/night temperatures, with or without light. The inference that seeds which do not germinate have "failed" springs from a fundamental misunderstanding of their natural function and ignores the strategic significance of this event in the life cycles of plants.

Under natural conditions, seeds are presented continuously with options to germinate or remain as they are. Failure would be an appropriate description only when the option chosen exposes seedlings unnecessarily to danger. Germination becomes the unequivocally desirable option to adopt only under the extraordinary and unnatural conditions of cultivation.

Describing a seed as dormant creates a mind-set which hinders rather than helps an understanding of how seeds work. Apart from that, does it tell us anything about the seeds at all? When living seeds do not produce seedlings when we think they should, we label them "dormant" and conclude that the reason they do not produce seedlings is because they are dormant! That is the circular argument by which gardeners, horticulturists and plant physiologists define dormancy. It tells us precisely nothing about dormancy or the ways germination is controlled, and we are entitled to question whether there is such a phenomenon as dormancy or such a thing as a dormant seed, or whether the idea is a misbegotten and unhelpful concoction.

The concept of dormancy immediately creates two kinds of seeds: those that do not germinate (the dormant ones) and those that do germinate (the non-dormant ones). Another look at chart 2 on p. 43 reveals that just under 40 percent of *Primula japonica* seeds produced seedlings spontaneously without chilling, and that just over 60 percent produced no seedlings unless exposed to low temperatures for several weeks. The latter would be labeled "dormant" and, contrariwise, the rest "not dormant." We are immediately propelled into making the assumption that the batch contains at least two different sets of seeds, each responding in a different way to the environment. That big assumption is constructed on an extremely fragile foundation. Only a concept as deeply entrenched as dormancy has become could get away unchallenged with such a leap into the dark.

We can explore the possibility that this batch of seeds really does consist of two sets with different responses to their environment. If we do so, the first questions to ask are these: What underlies such differences? Could they be based on different genotypes?

Individual seeds do differ genetically, and the possibility that sibling primulas possess distinctively different genotypes which confer different responses is not hard to accept—when just two sets are involved. However, similar reasoning

applied, for example, to the behaviour of seeds of *Galeopsis dubia*, described in chart 4 on pp. 46–47, requires acceptance of the idea that the germination responses of seeds of this species are controlled by such a complexity of genes that almost every combination of light and temperature creates different proportions of dormant and non-dormant seeds. It is quite normal to find quantitatively different responses to different conditions of this kind whenever seeds are tested in a variety of situations. Even the long established, orthodox, regular, thoroughly converted to cultivation seeds of common vegetables like those shown in chart 6 on p. 50 can produce different responses.

The central questions are these: Do we accept that seeds which germinate under particular conditions are different from those that do not—as would be the case if the phenomenon of dormancy existed? Or could all the seeds of a particular species share similar genetic constitutions, and variations in the proportions which germinate would then arise from phenotypic responses, reflecting the way the genotype responds to different conditions?

If the latter were true, any seed may or may not produce a seedling in response to a particular situation. Its chances of doing so depend on the probability that a seedling will be produced by a seed with a particular genotype in response to a particular set of environmental conditions. For example, when 60 percent of the seeds of a particular species germinate in darkness, there is a 60 percent chance of any seed producing a seedling. In other words, three out of five will germinate, but any three out of five may produce seedlings. It is not necessary to draw the conclusion that they are genetically different from those that do not produce seedlings.

The significance of the distinction is that if dormant seeds are genetically different from non-dormant seeds, germination responses should be highly subject to genetic selection. If they are not genetically different, germination responses would not be highly sensitive to selection. The tacit assumption is often made that the responses

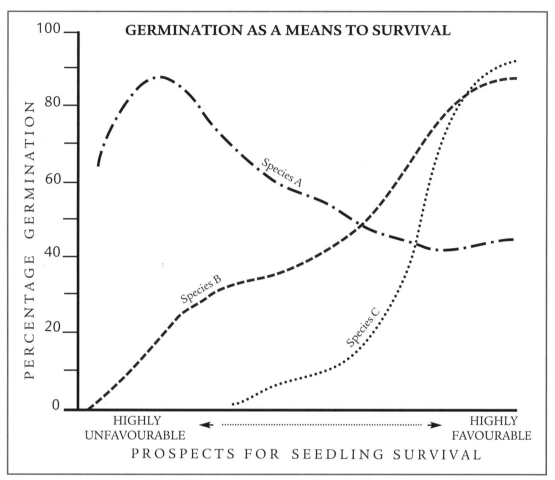

GERMINATION AS A MEANS TO SURVIVAL

Species A

Species B

Species C

PERCENTAGE GERMINATION

100

80

60

40

20

0

HIGHLY
UNFAVOURABLE

HIGHLY
FAVOURABLE

PROSPECTS FOR SEEDLING SURVIVAL

Chart 7. As shown here, species A represents a species whose seeds germinate more freely under unfavourable conditions for seedling survival than under those that are favourable. Species B represents one in which the seeds respond to conditions that favour seedling survival by producing high proportions of seedlings, but it also germinates to a considerable extent under moderately unfavourable conditions. Species C germinates only in conditions that are moderately or highly favourable for seedling survival. The implication is that the germination responses of species A are poorly adapted to maintain a natural population of the species in this particular area. Those of species C are very well adapted; and those of species B, although less specifically tailored for survival under these particular conditions, would provide good prospects for successful establishment of seedlings.

of seeds are sensitive to selection, particularly after wild plants have been adopted as cultivated plants. It is an assumption embodied in the belief that conscious and unconscious selective pressures in the course of cultivation convert wild plants into more amenable cultivated plants. This reasoning is used to explain why seeds of widely cultivated garden plants—the lettuces, pansies, tomatoes and delphiniums of our gardens—produce seedlings so readily when we sow them, whereas seeds of many wild plants, or less established garden plants, are more inclined to produce seedlings reluctantly—if at all—without special treatments.

The behaviour of the seeds of long-established, widely grown vegetables, such as lettuces and leeks, provides no support for the belief that they have undergone selection during the thousands of years they have been cultivated. Like many other long-cultivated plants, both still produce seedlings under the same conditions as their wild ancestors would have done, and they are subject to the same, sometimes quite stringent, restrictions on germination.

Widely cultivated plants, especially those grown from seed, originate predominantly from a few geographical regions—notable amongst which are Mediterranea and Central America. These are places where the natural germination responses of the native plants are already amenable to cultivation. Species that grow in them naturally—especially annual species—possess restrictions on germination, after-ripening responses and particular temperature responses which would not create problems for those attempting to raise seedlings from them but are likely to facilitate rather than complicate the gardener's job. The evidence suggests that our staple cultivated plants already possessed the desirable qualities needed for ease of cultivation when they were first adopted. This was probably one of the reasons they were originally successfully adopted as cultivated plants, and there is no need to propose subsequent changes.

CHAPTER 4

Setting up and Going on: Equipment and Facilities

Gardeners who are short of plants are often short of cash, time and space. This chapter describes how to make good use of all three. Cash is saved by producing your own plants—provided money is not spent on unnecessary facilities. Time can be saved by avoiding needless operations. Is pot washing essential? Is there an alternative to pricking out seedlings? Can plants be grown in ways that avoid or reduce the daily round of watering and feeding? Space is saved by matching container size to plant size and future expectations of growth—by grading (culling) plants to reduce waste, and by rigorously relating numbers grown to numbers needed. The methods used should be simple, flexible, and economical, avoiding dependence on special skills and judgments based on experience; establishing routines when sowing seeds, taking cuttings, making divisions, and caring for plants; standardising sizes and shapes of containers, methods of watering and feeding; and adopting techniques that are effective over a wide range of conditions.

Propagation is a craft in which success depends less on spending money on expensive equipment and more on simple things such as ensuring the containers in which seeds are sown do not fall over and spill their contents, that growing media do not dry out when the sun shines unexpectedly, and that seedlings and young plants do not serve as slug fodder.

One of the simplest ways to improve success rates is to avoid waste. Decide how many plants are needed, and grow only those that can actually be used, however tempting it may be to prick out every last seedling or sow every seed in the packet. Get the grading habit. Weak cuttings and puny seedlings are seldom worth growing; they waste containers, growing media, time and space. Commercial success is built on rejecting these second-grade plants, but soft-hearted amateurs acquire the habit with great difficulty. Good gardeners seldom grudge time and trouble spent on their plants, and the idea of ditching those that are struggling to survive is alien to most of us—but we would do better to follow the commercial model. Weak seedlings, very occasionally, turn out to be the ones with the exciting genetic combinations needed to produce new colours or forms. More often they are the incompetents with mismatches in their makeup that doom them to struggle and perform inadequately, or they have been crippled by infection with disease from which they will never fully recover. Dump them, and spend the time saved making sure their more promising brethren are well looked after.

Facilities

A widespread misconception exists amongst gardeners that glasshouses, frames and other more or less expensive structures are essential aids to plant propagation. This not only disregards the ability of plants to survive and propagate themselves naturally out of doors, but it also places them at the mercy of our regular tender loving care. If for any reason our care is less than regular, tender or loving they suffer, even die of neglect, often a much more potent killer than the weather. For your own and your plants' sake, remember that in many situations—especially for those who garden in milder climates—natural is likely to be the least demanding and can be the most successful option.

Nursery beds

Seeds can be sown, cuttings inserted and divisions brought on in nursery beds in a sheltered corner of the garden. Young plants and rooted cuttings lined out in the bed relieve us of the daily chores of watering and other duties plants in containers depend on for survival. Almost all the materials used can be well chosen salvage, and costs and trouble are more than offset once the bed is in use.

Raised beds approximately 15 cm (6 in.) deep, filled with well-prepared soil, are constructed in a sheltered corner of the garden. A bed need not be large—a 2 or 3 metre (5 to 10 ft.) long bed holds amazing numbers of seedlings and young plants. Do not make them more than 1.5 metre (5 feet) wide.

Paths are dug out, piling the earth on the beds. Well-textured soils and good drainage are essential. The first is achieved by mixing sand, grit, garden compost and other ameliorants to garden soil, and the latter by digging out the paths and partially refilling them with hardcore, scalpings, or gravel so that the beds themselves are raised above the surface of the path. Shelter from cold winds leads to better growth and extends the range of plants that can be grown. A trellis with ivy growing up it occupies virtually no space and provides a decorative as well as effective way to isolate a small space within the garden. Readily available water is a necessity, from a hose connected to a standpipe with a tap. Fertile soil is also a must. Top dress the beds before planting or sowing with a general, balanced fertiliser, depending on the nature of the soil—free-draining, hungry sands require more fertiliser than fertile loams. Freedom from weeds ensures good plant growth, and this is achieved preferably by mulching between the rows of plants, rather than repeated hand-weeding.

Tunnel cloches

A long cloche formed from polythene (polyethylene) protects seedlings of tender plants in cold situations and provides closed, humid conditions for cuttings of semi-mature shoots during summer and shelter for hardwood cuttings in winter.

Set up the cloche in an open, sunlit site, using light-diffusing milky-white or bubble polythene (polyethylene sheeting) containing a UV inhibitor, supported on a framework made from wide mesh stock wire. Mark out a bed with string a few centimetres wider than the cloche will be, and excavate a shallow trench approximately 15 cm (6 in.) deep all round the marked-out area, leaving a raised area in the centre. Cover the centre with a 4 cm (1.5 in.) deep mulch of organic matter and sand (2:1), before lightly mixing it with the upper layers of the underlying soil with a hand fork. It should not form a distinctly separate layer.

Make a tunnel with stock wire netting by inserting the cut ends into the ground on either side of the raised bed. Drape the polythene sheet over it, with one edge in the shallow trench along one side, held down by earth shoveled over it. Fold the other edge along the top of the cloche until seeds have been sown or cuttings inserted, when it, too, is drawn down, laid along the trench, and held in place with lengths of timber, to facilitate access.

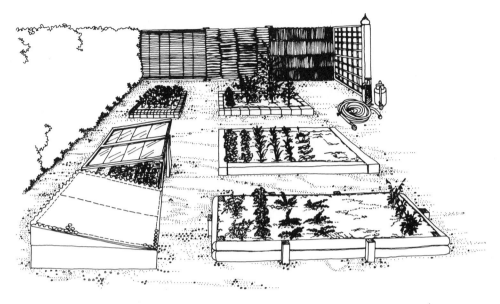

Figure 4. The time and skills needed to look after plants are greatly reduced when seeds are sown or plants are planted in nursery beds, a generally neglected but extremely valuable part of the equipment of a propagator. Raise the beds above the general ground level by digging out the paths and backfilling with hardcore (rubble) or quarry waste surfaced with gravel, using the excavated soil to top up the beds. Construct the sides of the beds from bricks, timber baulks (beams), blocks or whatever is available. Provide shelter by fencing, hedging or another means, and ensure ample water is available in the form of a standpipe—not just a water butt (rainwater barrel). The watering can may be adequate for damping down the frames, but a hose pipe fitted with a lance with a rose (hose, watering wand, and nozzle) is an essential part of the setup.

Frames

Frames are widely used to raise seedlings, nurture cuttings and protect young plants from frost. They are essential adjuncts to a glasshouse and should always be sited in sunlit situations. They can be set up independently outside or inside a glasshouse or poly tunnel.

Frames glazed with glass are heavy and fragile, possess poor insulating qualities, and become insufferably hot when the sun comes out, unless heavily shaded. Bubble polythene can be used in place of glass. It is lightweight and resilient, and it provides improved insulation and its own shade in the form of diffused light. Soil heating cables provide an economical, easily regulated source of supplementary warmth within a frame—whether within a glasshouse or outdoors.

Frames are cheap, flexible and productive. They are equally easily neglected through lack of attention, leading to serious problems. Growing media dry up, cuttings wilt and expire, and slugs, aphids or mice run rampant. All too often, more pressing concerns come before the simple need to open a frame once a day to check what is happening inside.

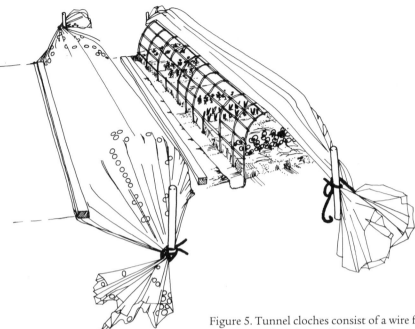

Figure 5. Tunnel cloches consist of a wire framework supporting a length of milky white or bubble polythene sheeting. Heavy gauge wire hoops, often used for support, are prone to collapse unless well secured. Stock wire with an 11 cm (4.5 in.) mesh provides a more satisfactory, flexible, but self-supporting framework. If necessary, "windows" can be made by removing some wires in order to improve access.

Poly tunnels

Poly tunnels, sometimes called hoop houses, provide most of the facilities of glasshouses at a fraction of the cost—especially in mild and warm temperate regions and in Mediterranea. In locations where frosts are light or unusual, extremely simple structures are sufficient to protect seedlings and cuttings from heavy rain or hail, and they provide shade from excessive sunlight. Their limitations include poor insulation, resulting in temperatures at night falling more or less to outside ambient temperatures; inadequate ventilation, resulting in high temperatures when the sun comes out; and limited life of their flexible polythene covers. UV-stabilising materials can be used to prolong the life of the covers, and protecting the sheet from direct contact with metal parts of the supporting structure prevents excessive wear and tear.

Despite their limitations, plastic tunnels provide excellent conditions in which to raise seedlings in nursery beds, grow young plants in containers, set up propagating frames for summer cuttings, and protect hardwood cuttings in winter. Many plants—notably trees—find the warm, humid conditions provided by plastic tunnels during spring and summer extremely congenial.

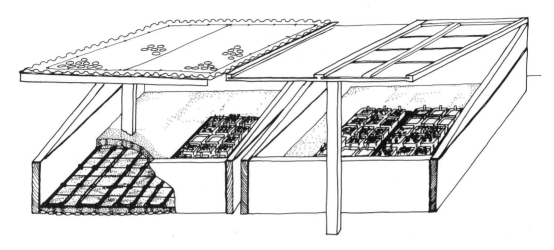

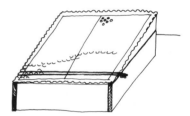

Figure 6. Frames are traditionally glazed with glass, originally using small panels, separated by glazing bars. Larger sheets of glass have become commercially popular because they transmit more light to the interior of the frame. More often than not, shading has to be used to reduce stress when cuttings are housed in a frame, and milky polythene or bubble polythene is a more suitable material to use, as well as being lighter to handle and less fragile. The most satisfactory way to hold down a framelight glazed with polythene is to string a length of twine across the frame toward the bottom—one end secured by a staple and the other looped round a nail.

Glasshouses

Glasshouses should be the boiler-rooms of gardens, especially in cool and cold temperate regions where winters are cold, days are short and light levels are low. Their high cost is justifiable only when they are used effectively—otherwise, poly tunnels are a more economically defensible alternative.

The most usual reasons for failing to use glasshouses effectively are the lack of supplementary heating and lighting; both are essential in a house used for propagation, and a source of electricity must be at hand to provide for them. In addition, backup facilities, including cold frames, nursery beds and standing out grounds (pot yards), are also necessary for using a glasshouse effectively.

A propagating house neither need be nor should be large. In the course of a year, thousands of plants—sufficient for the needs of almost any noncommercial gardener, even a small nursery—can be produced from a structure measuring no more than 2 by 3 metres (6.5 by 10 ft.). Reduced initial and running costs make the smallest glasshouse that will provide sufficient capacity the rational choice.

Electricity supply

Electrical services to a glasshouse must be professionally installed, with waterproof sockets and integral circuit breakers to avoid the dangers

Figure 8. Glasshouses are expensive structures with enormous productive capacity, provided they are supplied with electricity and backed up by ancillary structures, including frames, and room in which to stand out plants in containers. A plan of this unit appears in chart 8.

Figure 7. Soil heating cables installed in a bed of sand or grit in the bottom of a frame can be used to make it frost-proof, greatly increasing its versatility. A layer of insulation must be installed below the heating cables. Extra coverings, using reed mats or bubble polythene, may be laid on top as extra protection during cold weather.

of electrocution. Do-it-yourself electrical installations can damage your health to the point of death. They can also seriously damage your pocket—the installer may be liable should a visitor or a future owner of the property be injured due to poor workmanship.

Heating

The costs of heating a glasshouse vary with location, exposure, condition of the structure and ambient temperatures, but costs are significant

anywhere. Operating costs can be reduced by double-glazing the structure—an expensive option with glass and uncomfortably costly with polycarbonate—and lining with bubble polythene, which increases heat retention and reduces light levels and air movement. But be aware that low light levels and stagnant air during the winter lead to poor plant growth, inadequate performance, onset of pests and diseases, and other problems, especially during cloudy weather. Anything that further reduces light and ventilation in a propagating house should be avoided. Negotiate reduced rates for electricity, where available, as off-peak rates are likely to apply at night when consumption in

Chart 8 (opposite). Layout for a propagating unit comprising a glasshouse and necessary ancillary supporting facilities. Frames should provide at least three and preferably five times the space available on the benches of the glasshouse. Water and electrical supplies are essential for effective, economical management.

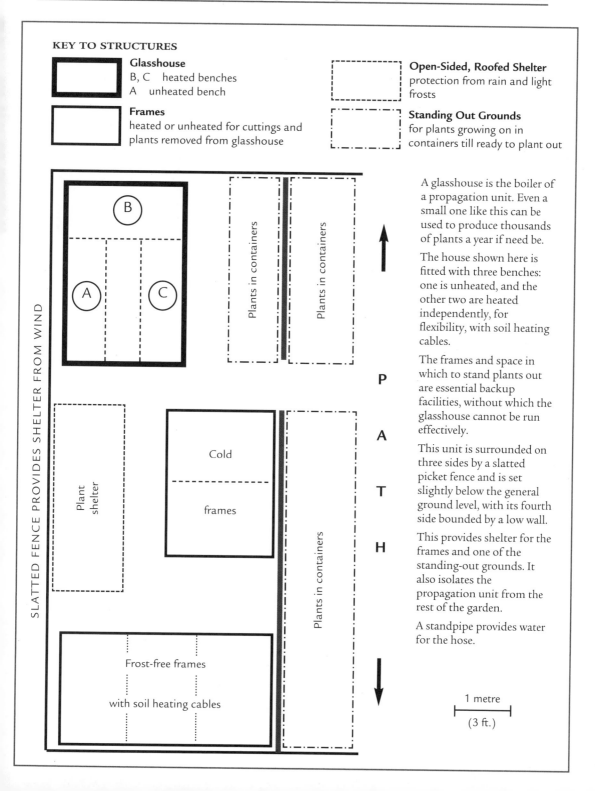

KEY TO STRUCTURES

Glasshouse
B, C   heated benches
A   unheated bench

Frames
heated or unheated for cuttings and
plants removed from glasshouse

Open-Sided, Roofed Shelter
protection from rain and light
frosts

Standing Out Grounds
for plants growing on in
containers till ready to plant out

B

A   C

Plants in containers

Plants in containers

SLATTED FENCE PROVIDES SHELTER FROM WIND

P
A
T
H

Plant
shelter

Cold

frames

Plants in containers

Frost-free frames

with soil heating cables

1 metre

(3 ft.)

A glasshouse is the boiler of
a propagation unit. Even a
small one like this can be
used to produce thousands
of plants a year if need be.

The house shown here is
fitted with three benches:
one is unheated, and the
other two are heated
independently, for
flexibility, with soil heating
cables.

The frames and space in
which to stand plants out
are essential backup
facilities, without which the
glasshouse cannot be run
effectively.

This unit is surrounded on
three sides by a slatted
picket fence and is set
slightly below the general
ground level, with its fourth
side bounded by a low wall.

This provides shelter for the
frames and one of the
standing-out grounds. It
also isolates the
propagation unit from the
rest of the garden.

A standpipe provides water
for the hose.

a glasshouse is likely to be highest. In addition, avoiding excessive temperatures can save expenses, as electricity consumption increases exponentially with temperature. Although plants are more likely to be damaged by than to benefit from high temperatures when light levels are low, needlessly low temperatures fail to promote plant growth and development and reduce the output and value of the facilities provided by a glasshouse.

Good management practices are important for cutting costs. Propagating houses are usually occupied by small plants, and even when the benches are fully occupied, nine tenths of the air space will be empty. Heating this air space may increase our comfort when we happen to be inside the house, but it is extravagant and wasteful. Costs are slashed by heating only spaces where plants are actually present. Soil heating cables installed on the benches beneath the plants are the most effective way to do this. On cold nights, a blanket of bubble polythene laid directly over the plants maintains a warm sandwich of air in the most economical fashion possible (see figure 9).

Glasshouse accessories

Following are advantages and disadvantages of a variety of accessories available for use in glasshouses.

Glazing

Glass is highly transparent and generates warmth by trapping infrared rays. It is also thermally stable compared to alternatives. However, glass is expensive and fragile, and it attracts dust and algae and requires regular cleaning.

Polycarbonate is highly transparent, resilient, lightweight and easily made up as double- or triple-glazed panels, greatly increasing insulation. However, it is expensive and liable to become scratched in exposed situations with permanent reduction in transparency.

Polyethylene is cheap and easily replaced. It diffuses light and maintains high humidities favourable for plant growth. On the other hand, its poor

Figure 9. Although it is freezing outside, soil heating cables and bubble polythene economically maintain temperatures of 10° to 15°C (50° to 60°F) around the plants.

insulation provides little protection against falling temperatures at night, and its short life makes regular replacement essential.

Ventilation

Automatic vents are essential in order to provide rapid responses to temperature changes without constant supervision. However, their operational range usually covers from approximately 10°C (50°F) upwards; at lower temperatures during the winter, they must be operated manually. Circulating fans are internal, low-volume fans that are a highly effective, economical way to disperse pockets of stagnant air. They are essential in a propagating house. Such fans have no serious disadvantages, and temporary failures are not significant.

Heating

Soil heating cables provide supplementary heating economically where it is most needed, in direct proximity to plants on heated benches or elsewhere. However, they are unsuitable for space heating, and their low inputs are insufficient to counter rapid falls in temperature unless the installation ensures a reservoir of warmth, which is best done by bedding them in sand or grit not less than 10 cm (4 in.) deep.

Fan heaters offer easily controllable space heating and are capable of rapid reaction to falling temperatures. They are a useful backup to soil heating cables. However, they are expensive to run and provide no reserves of warmth in the event of failure. Sheet heaters offer similar advantages and disadvantages to soil heating cables, but they are more expensive and less flexible. Tubular heaters are moderately economical, resilient sources of low-level background space heating. Unfortunately, their low response capacity can fail to provide protection when temperatures fall rapidly.

Insulation

Bubble polythene is lightweight, flexible, light diffusing and resilient to mechanical stresses; it provides excellent protection for small seedlings and leafy cuttings. The low-cost materials used for packing need frequent replacement; horticultural specifications incorporating UV inhibitors are essential for an economical length of life.

Horticultural fleece is lightweight, low cost, and versatile with good light transmission and diffusion properties and moderate usefulness as insulation. Fleece has no serious disadvantages.

Lighting

Lamps transform rates of growth and prospects of survival of seedlings or cuttings during short, dark days in high latitudes. Expensive to buy and run, they are economical only when carefully managed in situations where they make a real difference. Lamps tend to desiccate young seedlings and cuttings, so they are best used to supplement natural light for approximately four hours per day, either side of midday, rather than to extend daylight hours.

Watering

Capillary matting is highly effective and labour saving, but only when carefully and robustly installed to ensure that its base remains dead level to avoid dry or waterlogged patches. Unfortunately, capillary matting supports growth of algae and liverworts, and penetration by roots from bases of containers can cause problems that can be reduced by using a micro-perforated polythene sheet as an underlay.

Humidifier pumps, misting or fogging devices boost atmospheric humidity and are useful with cuttings and when growing ferns, some orchids and bromeliads, and streptocarpus. However, they are not fail-safe. Any breakdown quickly exposes plants dependent on high atmospheric humidities to disaster.

Micro sprinkler heads are suitable for small-scale automatic watering in a glasshouse; when used with a timer, they can partially replace hand-watering. Their circular spray patterns lead to uneven watering with rectilinear layouts, however, and they are unresponsive to day-to-day changes in the weather.

Water pumps convert stored water in tanks, such as rainwater, to standard household pressure for use with mist propagation or automatic irrigation. They are expensive to buy, though economical to run. No other serious disadvantages or restrictions are apparent.

Propagation

Plastic propagators based on seed trays with transparent lids (figure 10) make effective, versatile units for small-scale use. Electrically heated versions provide little space at a high cost. "Thermostats" used in such versions are usually voltage regulators that raise temperatures rather than control them at set levels. Propagators are not fail-safe.

Mist units provide excellent conditions for cuttings and many seeds, enabling difficult subjects to be propagated. However, the high costs are justified only when the scale of production and value of output are appropriate. These units are not fail-safe and failures quickly lead to disasters.

Warm bench and polythene, a closed frame with a polythene cover, provides a simple, flexible and economical system for cuttings. Such a system is often similarly effective to mist propaga-

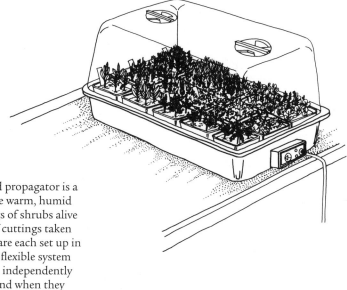

Figure 10. A self-contained, heated propagator is a convenient means of providing the warm, humid conditions needed to keep cuttings of shrubs alive and functioning. Small batches of cuttings taken from a variety of different shrubs are each set up in small plastic pots. This provides a flexible system in which each batch can be moved independently into less protected conditions as and when they have developed roots.

tion and the preferred option in most situations, and it has no serious disadvantages.

Controls

Time clocks (timers) are indispensable for operating heaters, lamps, fans and other electrical equipment economically. They should provide for minimum intervals of 15 minutes between switching with fail-safe battery backup. No serious disadvantages are apparent.

Thermostats are essential with any electrical heating system. Electronic thermostats are accurate (to 1°C, or 2°F) and easily and precisely installed, but they are relatively expensive. Make-and-break thermostats (accurate to 3°C, or 5°F) provide less precision, but they are inexpensive and adequate for most purposes concerned with propagation.

Containers

The containers in which plants are grown are central to the economy of a propagator's balance sheet. Temptations to convert plastic cups and salvaged food containers into flower pots or seed trays should be resisted and, nine times out of ten, rejected. Like their owners, some of these salvaged containers will be tall and thin, others short and fat, and many more something in between. Some will hold a pint, others more. Although there is no evidence that the shape of a gardener affects his or her ability to garden in any way, that is not so for the containers in which plants are grown. Different volumes of growing media in containers of different shapes dry out at different rates. Seedlings or rooted cuttings in a motley collection of salvaged receptacles are impossible to care for properly. Well-designed containers for plants cost pence (pennies) to buy, and failure to use them costs the lives of plants worth 50 or 100 times any-

Figure 11. A propagating frame used to raise plants from seeds and cuttings, set up on a bench provided with soil heating cables inside a glasshouse. The structure consists of a framework made from stock netting, draped with bubble polythene. Overhead lamps, controlled through a time clock, provide supplementary light when needed.

Figure 12. A mist propagation unit in a nursery growing Australian plants in California. In mild locations, simple, economical structures like this are sufficient to produce plants from seeds and cuttings.

thing saved by resorting to yoghourt pots. Standardising containers by using a limited and coordinated range of appropriate sizes and shapes is the key to making economical use of space in glasshouses, frames, and other areas of propagation.

Saving space on sizes

All too often, round rather than square containers and seed trays are the automatic and thoughtless choice when seeds are sown, irrespective of the numbers of seedlings needed. Using square rather than circular pots increases the capacity of a bench by up to a third. Replacing seed trays (flats) with pots increases glasshouse capacity by two or threefold—or even more!

It is worth reflecting that a standard seed tray has a volume of about 850 cm^2, or about 230 in.^{2} for the standard 1020 (10 by 20 in.) tray in North America. It holds about 4 litres of potting mix, or about 1.5 gallons of potting mix in North America, and accommodates 500 to 2000 seedlings until it is time to prick them out. It can accommo-date about 30 to 35 dahlia seedlings, 70 antirrhinums (snapdragons), or 100 lobelias. When those sorts of numbers are needed, a seed tray is an appropriate container; otherwise it is a waste of space.

Sow seeds in 7 to 9 cm (2.5 to 3.5 in.) square pots, following the methods described on p. 79, unless very large numbers of seedlings are required. Fifteen 7 cm square pots fit into a seed tray —in North America, eighteen 3.5 in. pots fit into a 1020 seed tray—which then provides a convenient holder for the pots. Each pot holds enough seeds to produce 50 to 100 seedlings, depending on their size. Similarly, prick seedlings out into square pots rather than seed trays. Square 9 cm (3.5 in.) pots each hold five hosta seedlings, or nine heather or six lavender cuttings, until they grow large enough to pot up individually. When larger numbers are needed, they can be accommodated in several containers.

CONTAINER ECONOMICS

Filled from a 10 litre (2.5 gal.) bag of potting mix

Number held on 0.5 m² of bench

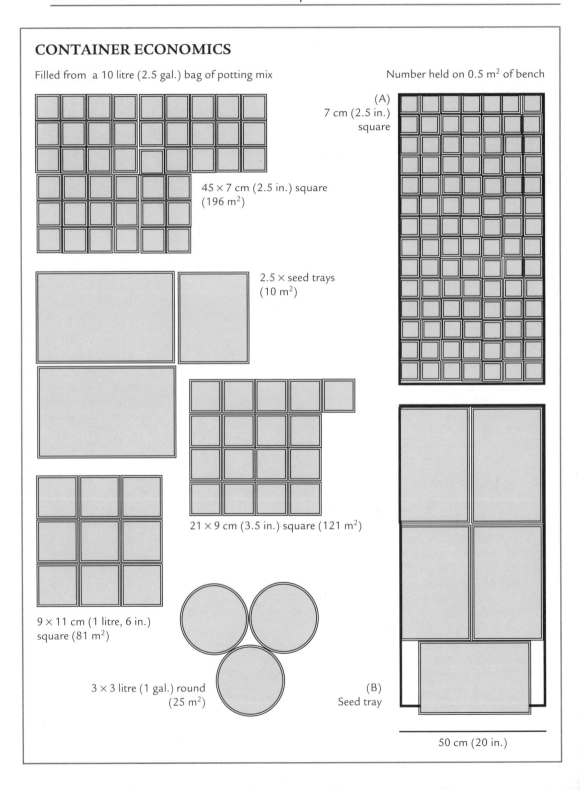

45 × 7 cm (2.5 in.) square
(196 m²)

2.5 × seed trays
(10 m²)

21 × 9 cm (3.5 in.) square (121 m²)

9 × 11 cm (1 litre, 6 in.)
square (81 m²)

3 × 3 litre (1 gal.) round
(25 m²)

(A)
7 cm (2.5 in.)
square

(B)
Seed tray

50 cm (20 in.)

Figure 13. Seedling annuals growing in 7 cm (2.5 in.) square pots. Each pot can hold up to 100 seedlings till they are ready to prick out. Substituting small pots for seed trays greatly reduces the space needed to raise seedlings.

Disposable, single use containers

A number of products, usually made of compressed peat, wood fibre or paper, are marketed as throw-away products in which to grow plants. They are better, so we are told, because plants need not be removed from them when they are planted in the garden, avoiding disturbance to the roots. That argument is less than convincing. Plants do not suffer when removed from their pots when

Chart 9 (opposite). The most economical, least painful way to save costs and space is to choose containers carefully. This illustration shows how many containers can be filled from a 10 litre (2.5 gal.) bag of potting mix. Seed trays and large pots run away with media and are used only when no alternatives are available. Even the choice of 9 cm (3.5 in.) in place of 7 cm (2.5 in.) pots more than halves the number filled—yet very often the plant will not benefit from the larger pot—bearing in mind that plants being propagated move on quickly from size to size as they grow. Judicious choices have equally great effects on the occupation of space in a glasshouse, as shown on the right.

this is done at the right time when the roots have developed sufficiently to hold themselves and the potting mix around them together. Turning a plant out may seem a little fraught the first time it is done, with fears in mind of smashed plants and roots bereft of growing medium. A little practice reveals it as a simple action that causes no ill effects at all.

Although useable only once, throw-away containers cost as much as multiple-use containers and are much more costly in the long run. Despite claims that roots penetrate them easily, the sides of the containers can act as barriers, preventing ready access to the soil when planting out—especially when the weather or soil is dry.

The choice of throw-away containers lies among those of peat, wood fibre or paper. Compressed blocks of similar materials eliminate the possibility of barrier effects, but their cost still compares unfavourably with multi-use alternatives. Blocks are most satisfactory in conjunction with capillary matting or similar automatic watering systems. When watering by hand, it is difficult to judge timing and amounts to apply, leading to overwatering in winter and underwatering during periods of hot weather or when pots are standing on a heated bench. Blocks on the margins of a batch are especially vulnerable to desiccation. Even with careful watering, they almost invariably suffer from drying out to a greater or lesser extent.

Multi-use containers are more economical than throw-away containers when appropriately chosen, and plants are almost always easier to manage when grown in them. Clay/terra-cotta pots are brittle, heavy, expensive, cumbersome to handle, harder to manage than plastic when growing most plants, and awkward to store. They are for diehards so wedded to tradition they cannot move forward, however logical it is to do so.

Black polythene bags are the cheapest of all containers; they are easily stored and can be used repeatedly. They are the ideal choice for plants that are to be given away. The soft, floppy bags are fiddly to open and awkward to handle, and it takes longer to install plants in them than in more rigid containers. At least 100 small plants can be

SIZES, CAPACITIES AND USES OF CONTAINERS

7 cm (2.5 in.)
square pot

Sowing seeds of annuals when up to 100 seedlings are needed
Sowing fern spores. Pricking out fernlets—5 per pot.
Cuttings—9 heathers, 1 delphinium, 1 protea, 6 lavenders, 4 forsythias, 3 conifers.
Divisions—single crowns of all but the more vigorous perennials.

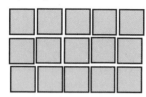

Standard seed
tray (flat)
Can be used as
a seed tray or
as a pot carrier

As a Seed Tray
Sowing seeds of annuals for large numbers, 500 to 1500 seedlings.
Pricking out seedlings of annuals, e.g., 35 dahlias, 60 antirrhinums, 80 lobelias.
Cuttings—60 lavenders, 40 hebes, 30 conifers, 24 dryandras.
Lily scales—30 to 60 depending on size.
Leaf cuttings of succulents—up to 60.

As a Pot Carrier
A seed tray holds fifteen 7 cm (eighteen 3.5 in.) pots securely. These accommodate enough seeds to raise up to 100 seedlings of each of 15 different kinds of plant until they grow big enough to be pricked out.
Or it can be used with a propagator top to hold cuttings set directly in cutting mix contained in the seed tray. It is more easily managed and flexible when each batch is set up separately in its own 7 cm (2.5 in.) pot, using the tray as a carrier.

9 cm (3.5 in.)
square pot

Sowing single, large, recalcitrant seeds of trees, e.g., oaks, nuts, palms and banksias.
Sowing seeds of perennials, bulbs, cactuses, small seeded shrubs and trees, when up to 100 seedlings are needed.

Pricking out seedlings—5 hostas, 9 freesias, 5 cactus, 4 medium sized shrubs, 1 or 3 trees until they grow large enough to pot up individually. Also fern sporelings—12 to 16.
Cuttings—16 heathers, 9 lavenders, 5 hebes, 5 callistemons, 4 choisyas.
Divisions—crowns of grasses and small perennials; single crowns of vigorous perennials.

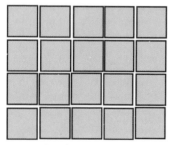

Carrier for 20 ×
9 cm pots

Constructed from moulded polystyrene in which each pot is securely held in a depression in the base of the carrier. Greatly facilitates handling, and prevents losses from accidental spills. A carrier of some kind should always be used when growing plants or sowing seeds in small pots.
Provides an easily manageable unit in which to set up batches of cuttings under mist or on a warm bench under polythene. Each plant in a batch of cuttings can occupy a single pot when only small numbers are needed.

One litre (6 in.)
square pot

Sowing moderately large-seeded perennials, shrubs and trees
Pricking out seedlings, e.g., 9 to 12 hostas, 25 tulips, 16 lavenders until ready to pot up
Cuttings of perennials, shrubs, trees—9 to 12 geraniums, 16 lamiums, 9 hydrangeas.
Stem and leaf cuttings of succulents.
Scales of lilies.

Growing on seedling bulbs—15 to 20; or perennials, shrubs, or trees singly.
Plants grown in containers require almost daily attention to watering, feeding and setting up. Time and effort can be reduced by planting out in a nursery bed rather than potting up, and plants are likely to grow better.

Two or three litre
(1 gal.) round pots

Pot washing

The ancient ceremony of pot washing raises its hoary head when containers are to be reused. This is an unnecessary and time-wasting activity, especially as practiced by amateur gardeners, who use containers to house an ever-changing variety of different plants. Very few pests or diseases are passed down through dirty pots—and whenever this is a serious risk it is more economical to use new containers for susceptible plants than spend time washing old ones. When the urge to wash becomes pressing, remember that time spent washing is time lost propagating. A few plants may be lost when unwashed containers are reused, but net gains accrue in the number of plants produced.

potted up in rigid containers in the time taken to put 70 into bags, and when time is limited (when isn't it?), that makes the difference between completing a job and never getting round to finishing it at all.

Polystyrene is widely used for the disposable seed trays and containers in which garden centres sell bedding and other low-cost plants. They are not intended for reuse, but with careful handling each can be used several times—but at the risk of collapses that result in the loss of plants within them. The risk offsets the advantage of their low initial cost.

Chart 10 (opposite). This illustration shows how different-sized pots are used to accommodate seedlings, cuttings and divisions. The numbers are intended only as a guide, but in principle, when propagating, put seedlings in small rather than large containers, crowd cuttings together for mutual support, and start divisions in the smallest container capable of holding them comfortably.

Hard plastic is used for a range of containers; it is intended to resemble clay in colour and shape. These pots are more practical than clay pots, but their circular profiles are equally wasteful of space. Moderate costs and relatively short lives reduce their appeal economically. Polypropylene, semi-rigid containers of all shapes and sizes are pleasant to handle, easy to work with, store well and last indefinitely. They are by far the best choice on practical and economical grounds.

Plants in cells and plugs

Garden centres sell small plants in individual cells, more or less the size of conventional pots or much smaller, when they are referred to as plugs. They are popular commercially because they make eco-

Container economics

Clay pots have been used for so long that gardeners have been converted to plastic only reluctantly and slowly. Once upon a time, all pots were round because they were thrown on a potter's wheel and that was the only shape possible. Plastic pots can be any shape—and pots square in section rather than circular have now become familiar items.

A little time spent setting out square or circular pots on a glasshouse bench shows that a circular container with a diameter of 10 cm (4 in.) contains the same amount of potting mix as a square one of equal depth, with sides of 8.5 cm (3.5 in.). As a result, 200 round pots can be replaced by about 276 square containers holding the same quantity of potting mix. Changing the shape of the container increases the capacity of a glasshouse by one third—a far more economical solution to shortage of space than buying a bigger glasshouse!

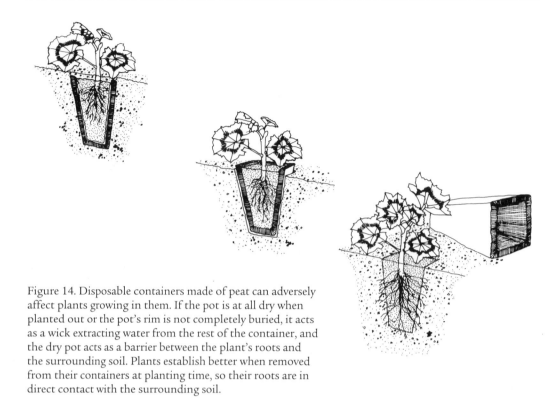

Figure 14. Disposable containers made of peat can adversely affect plants growing in them. If the pot is at all dry when planted out or the pot's rim is not completely buried, it acts as a wick extracting water from the rest of the container, and the dry pot acts as a barrier between the plant's roots and the surrounding soil. Plants establish better when removed from their containers at planting time, so their roots are in direct contact with the surrounding soil.

nomical use of potting mixes, and the subdivision into cells enables a few plants to be removed for sale without damaging those left behind—much! This appears to be a sensible idea that anyone could adopt. It is and it could be, but is not as simple as it looks.

Commercial growers manage these cells using specialised techniques that are not readily applied in informal situations. Watering is precisely regulated—usually using capillary matting to ensure every cell receives what it needs. Because each cell is separated from its neighbours, water cannot move between them to compensate for uneven watering. Precise sowing techniques are used to place a single seed in each cell. Premium quality seed is essential to ensure the presence of a plant in almost every cell. Routine feeding via the water

supply is used to encourage maximum growth and development. At home, where close supervision of the weather, the plants and the system as a whole is likely to be intermittent at best, the results can be disappointing.

Composts or Potting Soils?

Compost is a term widely applied in the UK to refer to the substrates in which plants are grown. It is also applied to the products of the compost heap, whether garden waste, municipal garbage or commercial products such as fermented bark or wood chips. *Potting soil* is also used to describe the substrates in which plants are grown; it is a word

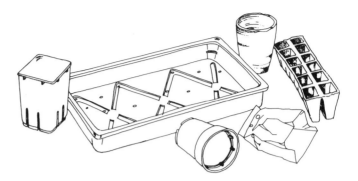

Figure 15. Containers are available in a wide range of shapes and sizes, made from many different materials. When propagating plants, it pays to work with a small number of carefully selected sizes of a particular type of pot or container. Square pots use space more economically than round ones, reusable pots are much more economical than disposable ones, and large capacity containers like seed trays should be used only when correspondingly large numbers of plants are needed.

which applies aptly to some but is less well suited to describe many of the substrates used for cuttings, which may contain few materials with close affinities to soil at all. The substrates in which plants are grown, seeds germinated or cuttings struck are referred to throughout this book as *potting, seed*, or *cutting mixes* or as *growth media*. Potting or cutting mixes are older names for these materials and have the advantage of accurately describing them while avoiding sometimes misleading connotations with other materials.

Loam, preferably as turf that had been stacked and left to decay for a year, was formerly the basis of almost all potting mixes. As commercial demands increased, particularly in hot, seasonally dry areas unfavourable for the development of loam, supplies failed to keep up with demand and peat became a widely used alternative. Alternatives to peat have been sought for some years, amidst often heated controversy about whether it should be used at all. The pros and cons of extracting and using peat are complex—as they are for several other materials used for potting mixes. They have been thoroughly aired; positions have been taken and nothing is to be gained by serving up the arguments yet again here. That said, peat finds its place as one amongst many alternatives in this chapter and elsewhere in this book as and when appropriate. It is up to individuals to form their own views on this subject and act accordingly.

Materials used for potting mixes can be broadly categorised as *organic* or *mineral*. That is more than just a convenient way to split the field—it is a fundamental division whenever and wherever potting mixes are composed. The bulk of all the organic materials used consists of cellulose, lignins and other more or less unstable carbohydrates, which are progressively broken down by oxidation and bacterial and fungal organisms into water and carbon dioxide. In time, what started as a potful of potting mix dwindles to a pot half full. Minerals provide a stable base, but apart from clays, generally lack the ion-exchange, water-holding and buffering properties provided by organic materials.

Organic materials, long represented almost exclusively by peat and to a small extent by leaf mould, are now increasingly numerous byproducts of commerce or the human genius for creating waste. Several materials, notably domestic rubbish generated by urban living, are produced in such quantities that getting rid of them has become an embarrassment. Converting them into materials acceptable for horticultural use would do us all a good turn.

Mineral components are derived from minerals of various kinds. To the extent that supplies are finite, these are nonsustainable materials. However, available reserves of some are sufficiently large to make that academic. Extraction, processing and transportation often involve considerable environmental costs.

Most potting mixes are made up of materials intended to produce an end product with the qualities of suitable texture, favourable pH, and freedom from pests and diseases. These are not always successfully achieved, even with commercial products.

A growing medium must be capable of supplying air (oxygen) and water (containing nutrients) to the plant's roots. Air-filled porosity (AFP), a measure of the air held in spaces between the solid components, is generally used as a means of assessing aeration. Optimum levels lie between 10 and 20 percent. Higher levels reduce water-holding capacity and make extra demands on watering; lower ones lead to waterlogging. Water content depends on the presence of porous materials able to absorb and hold water like a sponge.

Moderately acid pH levels between 5.5 and 6.5 are preferred. These are suitable for ericaceous plants and other calcifuges and tolerated by most calcicoles. Moderate to high ion exchange capacity reduces losses of nutrients from leaching and provides high buffering capacity to minimise changes in pH as nutrient concentrations change.

Some organic materials are potential sources of pest and disease trouble and should be treated before use to kill insects, eggs and larvae; weed seeds; and most pathogenic bacteria and fungi. This is accomplished either by pasteurisation

(heating while moist to 60°C, or 140°F, or just above, for 30 minutes) or by sterilisation (at 80°C, or 175°F, for 30 minutes). The latter destroys all the above and much else besides, including beneficial soil microorganisms. It may be beneficial to replace the lost microorganisms deliberately either with commercial microbial innoculants or by the addition of small quantities of unsterilised garden loam as an innoculum.

Mineral constituents

Clays

Clays such as calcined montmorillonite clays, with similar properties to Fuller's earth, are water absorbent and physically stable and are used to increase water and nutrient holding capacity. They are added to organic materials for the sake of their buffering capacity. This reduces losses of nutrients from leaching and shifts in pH as nutrients are absorbed.

Grits

These increase air-filled porosity and provide ballast for greater stability in exposed situations. They consist of sharp-edged fragments of hard stones between 3 and 8 mm in size. Millstone, granite or crushed flint with acid or neutral pH's are preferable to softer basic rocks, unless increases in pH are needed for lime-loving plants.

Lignite

A rarely used material, lignite is added at up to 30 percent of total volume. Air-filled porosity and water holding capacity are too low for solo use. Lignite is notable for its long-term stability, ease of management (it rewets readily), high bulk density (about three times the weight of bark) and free-flowing characteristics. It possesses a high cation exchange capacity, a pH between 4.5 and 5.0, and it is high in humic acids.

Perlite

This lightweight mineral is used as a substitute for sand or grit. Its modest, but significant, base exchange properties reduce losses by leaching of potassium and other basic ions. It is extremely dusty and should always be moistened before use.

Pumice/scoria

This highly porous, lightweight mineral is of mainly local significance. It is a promising component of potting mixes and provides a suitable substrate for cuttings under mist.

Rock wool

Cut into blocks as a growing medium, rock wool is used in hydroponic systems. Its aeration is excellent, but a constant supply of water is necessary to keep it moist. Rock wool is now being increasingly used commercially as a medium in which to set up cuttings in warm beds or under mist.

Sand

The longtime standby is used to increase air-filled porosity of loam and peat mixes but is generally inferior to grits for this purpose. Coarse, river-washed sands are best. Sand adds considerably to the weight of a growing medium—an advantage in windy situations where extra stability is needed, but a disadvantage when moving container-grown plants.

Vermiculite

This quarried mineral consists of lightweight plates of mica holding water between them, like the filling in a multi-layered sandwich. Vermiculite contains low levels of available potassium and magnesium. Coarse grades are most effective as additions to potting and cutting mixes. Fine grades are often recommended when sowing seeds, but they compact easily and become capped with mosses and liverworts, and intermediate grades are more satisfactory. Vermiculite marketed for insulation and other purposes is likely to be extremely alkaline and detrimental to plant growth.

Mineral/organic constituents

Fibre clay

Consisting of 50/50 cellulose fibre and mineral fillers, including clay, fibre clay is produced from recycled newspapers. It is generally recommended as a soil ameliorant, and it has been used in combination with chicken litter and garden waste. High levels of residual heavy metals derived from printers' inks can cause serious problems unless they are removed before use.

Loams

These are the substrates most similar to natural soils, but they are highly variable. Those containing excessive clay or high proportions of sand are unsuitable as base material for growth media in containers. Plants in loam-based mixes establish readily when planted in gardens. Loams contain reserves of nutrients, humus and trace elements held by physical forces that reduce losses from leaching. High buffering capacities reduce changes in pH as nutrients are taken up or leached out. High ion exchange capacities enable high levels of nutrients to be added without damage to plants. Plants can be grown in loam-based mixes for several years without the serious deterioration in structure suffered by predominantly organic materials. Loam can be readily rewetted after drying out, with few of the management problems posed by peat. Loam-based growth media stored in plastic bags deteriorate rapidly and become unusable within a short time. It is unusual to find the contents of a bag still in fit condition to use after the experience.

Organic constituents

Animal manure (composted)

Manure is used as a soil conditioner, but samples with suitably open textures can be used in potting mixes up to at least 25 percent of total bulk when combined with coir, wood chips, and other materials.

Bark (composted)

Almost invariably obtained from coniferous trees, bark is sometimes used with nitrogen-rich supplements, such as poultry manure. Bark is widely used as mulches or soil conditioners and in some parts of the world as a major component of growth media. It has moderate cation exchange capacity. Recommended rates of 20 to 40 percent in potting mixes provide acceptable alternatives to peat and are said to suppress certain pathogens—notably fusarium, and possibly botrytis and pythium. It is increasingly used, notably in North America, as an orchid growing medium, particularly fir and redwood bark.

Bark (milled or shredded)

Milled or shredded bark provides more open products than peat with higher air-filled porosities, requiring more watering but beneficial when plants are overwintered or held in containers for long periods. More finely milled products can be used directly as peat replacements. It provides little or no nutrients; pH levels can be very low, down to 4.0 or more usually around 5.0. Weed and disease levels are also low. Bark handles and retains its structure well and is sustainable and can be produced to consistent standards. It suppresses the activity of some pathogens, including fusarium, botrytis and pythium. A surface layer on containers suppresses the growth of mosses and liverworts.

Coir

The fibre found between the outer case and the coconut is a waste product of the coconut industry. The material has a history in horticulture dating back more than a century and a half. Numerous attempts to popularise its use have repeatedly failed due to the difficulty of producing a consistent product.

Compost (domestic rubbish)

This material is now available from some local authorities and is an acceptable product in terms of appearance and physical properties. The presence of printing inks, which contain heavy metals, make the inclusion of printed paper hazardous. Such residues can be extremely harmful, and once mixed with the soil are virtually ineradicable. Processes have been developed that can remove 99.5 percent of printing inks—perhaps opening the way for more extended use.

Compost (garden)

Produced domestically or on a large scale by local authorities or suppliers, it is an excellent and highly effective soil conditioner far superior to peat, with considerable promise as a component of potting mixes. Compost must be pasteurised to destroy weed seeds and pathogens. It is reported to be an effective substrate for cuttings. Compost contains high levels of nutrients and is credited with inhibitory effects on some pathogens.

Compost (worm)

This homemade product enables domestic waste to be turned into compost, usually based on the activities of *Eisenia foetida*. Of limited use as a potting mix, the finished product can be combined—up to 50 percent—with peat, coir or other organic constituents.

Leaf mould

Traditionally, leaf mould has been used as a component of growth media, a use that could be renewed wherever suitable supplies of leaves are available, both on a domestic scale or sourced from local authorities. Leaves take up to two years to decompose to a usable condition.

Peat (moss and sedge)

Consistency, ease of handling and the broad spectrum of plants that respond well to it have established peat's position as the favourite commercial product for potting mixes. Peat's physical structure provides very different conditions to those of garden soils, leading to establishment problems when plants are moved into the garden. Moss peat, derived from sphagnum, is more durable and has a better texture than peat derived from sedges. Generally free from weed seeds, pests and diseases and other contaminants, peat does not require pasteurisation before use. Microbial in-noculants containing a range of beneficial soil microorganisms can be used to compensate for peat's inherent sterility. It also has a high water-holding capacity combined with free drainage capacity. It is pleasant and clean to handle with no objectionable odours and visually attractive, though its appearance of rich fertility is mislead-ing. It contains virtually no nutrients naturally but has a moderate nutrient-holding capacity when these are added from artificial sources. Its naturally low pH is suitable for a wide range of plants and readily adjustable, usually by additions of calcium. Peat is lightweight and easy to lift and transport, but this can lead to instability in pot-ted plants. Its resistance to rewetting once it has become dry is peat's major physical shortcoming. This can be partially alleviated by the addition of wetting agents.

Sewage sludge

Produced in a number of forms, sludge is mainly used as a soil conditioner. Its physical properties are similar in many ways to peat, and the material has promise as a component of potting mixes.

Sphagnum moss

Usually dried and milled before use, it provides excellent aeration and high water-holding capac-ity and is credited with inhibiting effects on damping-off pathogens, though whether it ac-complishes this physically or chemically is open to question. It is a highly unsustainable material for which only small-scale, selective local exploita-tion would be acceptable.

Wood fibre

This is similar in most respects to milled or chipped bark.

Choosing potting mixes

Anyone who propagates plants has to make deci-sions about the composition of mixes used, and with so many materials available it can be difficult to see the wood for the trees. In the first place, the

---

> ## Significance of mineral versus organic materials
>
> The seedlings of many plants, especially those from woodland and forest communi-ties and impoverished situations such as the South African fynbos or Western Aus-tralian kwongan, display strong preferences either for organic or mineral soils, and the nature of the substrate strongly affects prospects of success or failure. Gardeners have paid little attention to these prefer-ences, perhaps because widely grown gar-den plants have been selected more or less inadvertently from those that are naturally amenable to a broad range of conditions.
>
> However, once we adventure beyond the standard fare of gardens—for example, when attempting to grow collections of native species, introducing ourselves or oth-ers to unusual, seldom cultivated plants—these preferences may hold the secrets of success or failure. When seedlings of a pio-neer tree species repeatedly damp-off on a peat-based mix, or those of a woodland per-ennial accustomed to germinating on a bed of leaf mould grow sickly on a mineral base, we should ask ourselves whether we have mismatched plant with substrate.

choice will depend on availability. Different mate-rials are used in different places simply because they are readily available in one place but not in another. For example, bark, pumice, lignite and even peat are all more or less local products. Coir almost invariably has to be transported long dis-tances to the places where it is used.

Preferences also play a major role, especially with long-established materials such as loam and peat; and the reverse of preferences, aversions based on convictions that have nothing to do with propagation itself, also influence use. Many people now avoid using peat. Others recognise the environmental costs of transporting coir or perlite and prefer to use more locally available alternatives.

The purpose for which the media is used, and the ways plants respond to it, also play a part in selection. For example, some growers avoid using peat-based mixes because they believe the mixes lead to establishment difficulties when planting out in the garden. Others, particularly growers of alpines, stick loyally to loam-based compounds because they find them easy to manage, and they believe their plants prefer them.

Sources of potting mixes

Some of the materials listed above are readily available—a few can be home produced, and oth-

---

Homemade loam-based potting mix

The classic formula for a loam-based potting mix suitable for homemade production is described here. This formula was developed at the John Innes Institute in England during the 1930s. Two variations exist: one contains double the quantities of base fertiliser, and the second contains three times the quantity.

- Locate a source of good-quality fibrous loam—preferably the top 25 cm (10 in.) of turf and soil from a well-established meadow or orchard. Avoid excessively clayey or sandy loams.
- Construct a stack of the material not more than 1.5 metres (5 ft.) wide and cover it. Black polythene with holes punched through it with a fork suffices. Much better is a sheet of the permeable plastic membrane on which nurseries stand out container-grown plants.
- Leave the heap for a year to mature into usable condition.
- Pasteurise the loam by heating it evenly to approximately 60°C (140°F) for 30 minutes. Small quantities can be done in an oven, but larger quantities need special arrangements.
- Mix pasteurised loam : [moss peat, coir, bark] : [sharp sand, grit]* at a ratio of 7:3:2, respectively.
- Add base fertiliser** and ground chalk (ground dolomite limestone) at the rate of 3.25 kg (7 lb.) and 0.75 kg (1.5 lb.), respectively, per cubic metre (cubic yard) and pro rata for smaller quantities.
- Allow the mixture to "mellow" for a fortnight and use within two or three months thereafter.
- Store the mix under cover beneath a sheet of permeable membrane, but do not enclose it in polythene bags.

A growth medium suitable for heathers, rhododendrons and other lime-hating plants is prepared in exactly the same way, but without the chalk (lime).

*Items within brackets should be read as alternatives.
**The simplest source of base fertiliser is a packet from a garden centre. However, those dedicated to self-help or sticklers for tradition can prepare it by mixing equal quantities of superphosphate, hoof and horn if available (or some other source of slowly released nitrogen), and sulphate of potash. Alternatively, mix with a controlled release fertiliser (see p. 106) according to the manufacturer's recommendations.

ers can be purchased as raw ingredients from which to compose our own mixtures, and these can provide economical sources of perfectly adequate growing media. Our choice of sources lies between proprietary manufactured products, modified manufactured products, or homemade growth media.

Proprietary manufactured potting mixes are comparatively costly and highly variable in quality. Many provide all that is needed for general—or even special—purposes. When available as consistent products, they can be adopted for standard, routine use. Many others are inconsistent from one batch to another, and a surprisingly high proportion of proprietary potting media fail to achieve even adequate results. Not surprisingly, many gardeners like to make their own additions to proprietary products to improve them—or tailor them to their own methods of management or the preferences of the plants they grow.

Modified manufactured products are produced by additions of grit, perlite, sand and other minerals intended to increase air-filled porosity—and sometimes to provide ballast for lightweight, organic materials. These additions reduce the proportions of nutrients available. This should be compensated for either by adding nutrient supplements to restore nutrient levels or by starting to apply feeds earlier.

Homemade growth media are a worthwhile option, especially when loam-based mixes are preferred. These are seldom obtainable in good condition unless bought from specialist suppliers. A certain amount of ingenuity is required to follow the recipe described in the facing box, but homemade is a viable option well worth considering.

Notation used for compost mixes

Recommendations for the composition of growth media in this book recognise that preferences, availability and other factors make it impracticable to quote generally applicable formulae throughout the world of temperate gardening. The notation used is based on the concept that with few exceptions, potting mixes consist of mixtures of organic and mineral components, and organic materials can substitute for one another, as can minerals.

Throughout this book, instead of specifying particular components—for example, peat coir, bark, leaf mould, and so on as organics, or grit, perlite, sand, pumice, and so on as minerals—mixtures are shown thus: *organic : mineral, 1:1*. Or they may be shown thus: *[peat, coir, bark] : [grit, sand, perlite], 3:2*. The organic or mineral components bracketed together are alternatives to be selected according to need, preferences and availability.

CHAPTER 5

Basic Techniques with Seeds and Cuttings

Seeds

Traditionally, seeds have been sown in containers by partially filling a seed tray or pot with potting or seed mix and then leveling and slightly compressing the surface before scattering the seeds over it. The seeds are covered with a layer of seed or potting mix, preferably delivered though a sieve. Watering is sometimes accompanied by a recommendation to water from below by partially immersing the container, rather than watering overhead from a watering can through a rose. However, this traditional method has some disadvantages and problems:

- Slight overcompression of the surface on which the seeds are sown can reduce germination.
- The depth at which the seeds are eventually buried is difficult to assess accurately.
- The initial watering, especially when using sifted potting mixes to cover the seeds, can lift the surface and the seeds with it.
- Subsequent watering from sowing to pricking out is not fail-safe. Small errors of judgment lead to waterlogging or drying out. Seeds may then fail to germinate and seedlings become more vulnerable to damping-off organisms.

The new standard method for sowing seeds, described below, is simple and almost ubiquitously applicable. It ensures excellent aeration in the immediate vicinity of the seeds and avoidance of any hint of waterlogging likely to encourage damping-off diseases. In addition, it must provide optimum conditions for growth and development of the roots—a consistently available supply of oxygen, water and nutrients, from the time seedlings appear until they are pricked out.

The secret of its success lies in the preparation of a two-layered substrate; in one layer seeds germinate and in the other roots develop. A base, or lower layer, consists of open, moisture retentive, fertile potting mix, occupying about two-thirds of the depth of the container, in which roots develop. A topping, or upper layer, occupies the upper third of the container, in which seeds are sown and germinate.

Minerals are more likely than organic materials to provide the well-aerated, moisture-retaining conditions needed in the topping. They are stable, retain their integrity for a long time, are easy to manage, are inert, hold water yet drain freely and are easily penetrated by emerging plumules and radicles. Grits and coarse sands possess most of these qualities but dry out too rapidly to be entirely satisfactory on their own. Materials which combine grittiness with the ability to absorb water better meet the specification needed for the topping—the accompanying box provides more information about suitable materials.

The way in which seeds are sown depends on their size and conformation:

- Tiny seeds, such as lobelias, begonias, campanulas, rodgersias, leptospermums and callistemons, are scattered over the surface. They are then watered, using a can with a fine rose, when they sink into the upper layers of the topping and lodge on irregularities just below the surface.
- Medium-sized seeds, such as pansies, aquilegias, primulas, and geraniums, are scattered over the surface and then "ploughed" in with the tip of a pointed stick, lightly stirring the surface and burying the seeds beneath it.
- Large or irregularly shaped seeds, such as hostas, clematis, sweet peas, acanthus, osteospermums, and banksias, are sown on a shallow bed of topping overlying the base, and then covered with more topping to bury them about 1.5 cm (0.75 in.) below the surface.

Seed trays should be used only when very large numbers of seedlings are needed. Fifty to one hundred fifty seedlings can be contained in 7 cm, 9 cm,

Figure 16. Annuals sown in 7 cm (2.5 in.) containers in a perlite topping over potting mix. The containers are securely held in a pot holder. Seedlings of some of the plants are ready to be pricked out, and others have not yet emerged. Each can be treated individually according to its needs.

Recommended materials for use as toppings

- Calcined clay minerals are marketed occasionally for horticultural use and widely used to soak up oil spills from garage floors.
- Horticultural perlite, medium or standard grades, are preferable; the fine grades marketed for sowing seeds are usually too fine. Vermiculite should be used only for seeds expected to germinate within one or two months. A 1:1 mixture of either material with grit produce excellent general-purpose toppings.
- Crushed brick, sometimes marketed as a covering for tennis courts, is likely to need sieving to remove dust.
- Crushed tufa, 4 to 7 mm (0.25 in.) in size, may need sieving to remove dust and larger fragments. It should not be used with calcifuge species.
- Milled, dried sphagnum moss provides excellent aeration and high water-holding capacity and is the best material to use for species that need organic substrates. The antibacterial and antifungal properties of sphagnum discourage pathogens, and it has been used successfully with difficult seeds, especially those prone to damping-off.

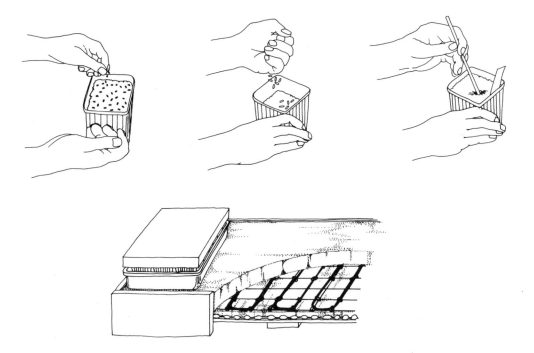

Figure 17. Most seeds are sown in small (7 or 9 cm) (2.5 to 3.5 in.) pots. Partially fill the pots with potting mix (base), before adding free-draining, water-absorbing material as a topping 2.5 cm (1 in.) deep. Sprinkle small seeds over the surface and water in. Distribute medium-sized seeds over the surface then plough backward and forward with a dibber to bury the seeds. Large or unevenly shaped seeds are sown on a layer of topping over the base and then covered with more topping. Pack the pots securely in a pot holder; stand them on a bench, heated if necessary, and water thoroughly. Cover with an expanded polystyrene tile until seedlings begin to appear.

or 1 litre (2.5, 3.5, or 6 in.) pots until they are ready to prick out, and pots provide the depth needed by the roots of almost all seedlings. Small containers like these are easily knocked over, with a risk of seeds being lost. This is prevented by placing them in pot holders (flats), which are widely used commercially. A standard seed tray holding 7 cm (2.5 or 3.5 in.) pots makes a serviceable, low-cost holder.

Watering

Thoroughly drench the containers immediately after sowing, using a fine rose to settle rather than disturb the surface of the topping. More than enough water is preferable to not enough; excess water drains into the base materials and eventually through the drainage holes or slits in the bottom of the container. Thereafter, watering is done as and when needed to prevent the topping from drying out. Excellent drainage in the upper layer in which the seeds lie avoids problems from any tendency to overwater; good aeration around the base of young seedlings reduces their vulnerability to damping-off diseases.

Do not use water from sources likely to be contaminated with pythium, phytophthora or other damping-off pathogens. Rainwater stored in tanks is a frequent source of these organisms, and tap water is usually a safer alternative.

After the initial soaking, cover the containers to maintain humidity and prevent rapid desiccation. Nothing serves better than lightweight sheets of expanded polystyrene cut to the size required. The polystyrene has good insulation properties and is translucent, allowing light to reach the seeds. It does not attract condensation; hence, no drips drop onto the seeds below.

Germination is heralded by the appearance of radicles. The covers should be removed—at least during the day—at the first visible signs of emerging roots. Any delay will lead to etiolation as the developing hypocotyls and plumules extend upwards to reach the light.

"Bog" watering method

This variation produces good results with some wetland species and alpines. After sowing the seeds, stand the containers in water in a shallow tray to about one-third of their depth. Water, raised by capillary attraction, maintains the zone in which the seeds are sown in a constantly semi-saturated state.

Some seeds do better with a layer of chopped, dried sphagnum moss over the topping. Remove the moss as soon as radicles appear; take the containers out of the water and place them on a bench. A topping of sphagnum moss gives good results in conjunction with a mist propagating unit with many seeds. Despite the repeated leaching effects of the mist, the excellent aeration within the moss avoids any semblance of waterlogging and provides conditions leading to the germination of seeds of a number of plants reluctant to germinate in more conventional conditions.

Weathering

Seeds of a great many perennials, bulbs, shrubs and trees require a period of weathering before they will germinate. This takes the form of more or less prolonged periods of exposure to warm (approximately 10° to 20°C, or 50° to 70°F) or cold (approximately 0° to 5°C, or 32° to 40°F) conditions—often in sequence—leading subsequently to the production of seedlings. A year, or even two years, may pass before seedlings appear, and seedlings of some species of paeonias, daphnes, hollies and roses, amongst others, may appear over periods of up to five years. Seeds not only remain at risk from pathogens, predators, accidents or other adversities throughout this time, but unless special precautions are used, they become lost to view and their progress and existence are otherwise almost impossible to check. Protect seeds from these risks and hold them readily available for periodic checks by containing them in polythene bags or boxes while they are weathering, as described in box on p. 83.

Natural temperature cycles should be used when weathering seeds whenever possible. The seeds of species that respond to weathering seldom need after-ripening, and the best time to start the process is immediately after harvest. However, that is not always possible. Seeds obtained from outside sources may not be available at an appropriate time. In warm temperate parts of the world or Mediterranea, winter temperatures may not fall low enough for long enough to satisfy the needs of seeds from colder places.

Warm weathering can be provided by placing bags containing seeds on top of a bed of sand in a heated propagator set to provide temperatures in the range 10° to 20°C (50° to 70°F). Cold weathering can be provided using a domestic refrigerator with temperatures between approximately 0° and 5°C (32° to 40°F). Weathering treatments should be maintained from one to three months.

Smoking

Fire is a major feature affecting plant growth in many parts of the world. The vegetation of the Mediterranean maquis, Californian chaparral, South African fynbos and Western Australian kwongan includes many species whose seeds germinate in spaces cleared of existing vegetation and open to colonisation after fires. The seeds of these plants respond to volatile substances in smoke.

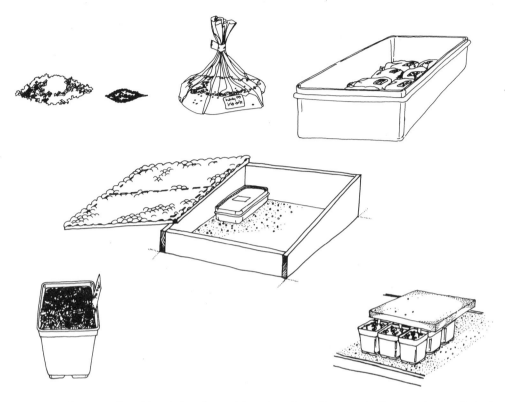

Figure 18. Seeds are weathered by mixing them with moist grit, perlite, vermiculite, or other media before packing the mixture into polythene bags. A number of bags are then packed into a single vermin-proof box—such as a transparent plastic box with a tight-fitting lid. Seeds weather most effectively when exposed to natural seasonal and diurnal changes in temperature; this is most easily done by placing the plastic box in a shaded frame. Examine the bags from time to time, and sow the seeds at the first signs of germination, using the contents of the bag as a topping.

Although the nature of these reactions remains obscure, their effects can be replicated in several ways.

Smoke produced by smouldering wood chips, sawdust or dry twigs of shrubs, preferably those that grow naturally in fire-adapted communities, can be used to treat seeds after they have been sown in much the same way food is smoked. A commercial "smoker" serves the purpose. Alternatively, a rough and ready but effective smoker can be constructed from a metal barrel.

Smoke pads—discs of absorbent paper impregnated with smoke—are commercially available, though sometimes difficult to find. These are saturated with water before placing the seeds on them to imbibe for 24 hours before being sown.

Charate is obtained by using a blowlamp, or blowtorch, to incinerate the twiggy stems of shrubs up to about 1 cm, or 0.5 in., diameter—preferably those that grow naturally in fire-adapted communities—until they become charred. They are then ground into a powder and

Weathering treatments for seeds

- Mix the seeds with a convenient quantity of moist grit, coarse sand, perlite or vermiculite to ensure they are fully imbibed with water.
- Put the mixture into a polythene bag or transparent plastic box with close-fitting lid. Seal bags by tying the tops in a knot, and label them.
- Pack the bags or boxes into a large polythene bucket with a lid to protect the contents from rats, mice, squirrels and other predators.
- Place them out of doors or somewhere where the seeds will experience the temperature fluctuations that accompany night and day and the changing seasons. Seeds sown, for example, in the autumn will first encounter diminishing temperatures, followed by variable periods of cold weather, dipping down to frosts in winter, succeeded by rising temperatures in the spring, when many of them will germinate.
- Examine the bags from time to time—at least once a month, especially in autumn and spring —looking for signs of germination.
- As soon as radicles start to emerge, use the contents of the bags or boxes to form a topping above a base layer of potting mix (as described for the standard method of sowing seeds).
- Depending on the species and the facilities available, place the containers on a bench in a glasshouse, in a cold frame or in the open. Thereafter, treat the seedlings like any others.

Seeds of different kinds of plants germinate at widely different times—some soon after the start of the weathering treatment, others months or even years later. Each bag must be examined individually and treated as a separate item, guided by the behaviour of the seeds within it. From time to time, check the viability of the seeds themselves by squeezing a few between your finger and thumb. Provided they retain their integrity and do not disintegrate into an amorphous smear, they are still alive and capable of germinating—sooner or later!

sprinkled over the surface of containers in which seeds are sown.

Other sources for smoke solutions can be produced by soaking substances heavily impregnated with smoke—such as a kipper or other smoked fish, or twigs, shoots and leaves from a bonfire— in water. Seeds are either soaked in the solution before being sown or watered with the smoke-infused water immediately after sowing. Successive applications during the course of several days enhances the effects of watering.

Seeds that have been "smoked" by fire under natural conditions germinate after the first moderate to copious rains. They do not usually respond to light showers and may fail to produce seedlings while temperatures remain high. In gardens, smoked seed should be thoroughly soaked after sowing and, if possible, not exposed to temperatures above 20°C (70°F) or so. Sometimes smoke treatments are effective only in combination with other environmental triggers, such as chipping the seed surface, thermal shocks (such as boiling water) or fluctuations in temperature between day and night.

Chemical treatments

A number of chemicals affect seed germination. Salts used as nutrients can inhibit germination at moderate concentrations. This is one reason for

Reduction of impermeable seed coats

Some species, particularly those in the pea family, develop impermeable seed coats that prevent water reaching the inside of the seeds. They produce seedlings only after damage to the seed coat enables water to pass through it to reach the embryos. This can be achieved in a number of ways when the seeds are sown.

Chipping

A knife can be used to slice off a section of seed coat, provided the seed is large enough to pin down with the finger of one hand. The cut should not be made close to the hilum—the part originally attached to the placenta and recognisable by the presence of a "scar." Seeds should not be sown immediately after chipping, but left exposed to the air for 24 hours. The tissues within them are extremely dry and the seeds need time to take up a little moisture from the atmosphere in preparation for imbibition. If sown immediately and watered heavily, damaged membranes and other imperfections can lead to the loss of solutes through cell walls as the seeds imbibe, providing focal points for invasion by pathogens.

Abrading

A more random, but usually effective, form of damage is inflicted on smaller seeds by rubbing them between two sheets of sand paper. Like chipped seeds, these should be left in the open for 24 hours before being sown.

Hot water

This method is widely used as a substitute for chipping. Boiling water is poured over the seeds and they are left to soak for 24 hours before being sown. Seeds that fail to take up water and swell are given a repeat treatment the following day. Alternatively, hot water at approximately 60°C (140°F) is poured over the seeds in a bowl, and they are left to soak in warm water for 24 hours, standing on a radiator, a warming plate or the edge of a cooker.

the traditional use of low concentrations of nutrients in seed mixes—the other is economy.

Gibberellins stimulate germination of many seeds, including those of gentians, primulas, meconopsis, pulsatillas and anemones, at least under some conditions, and have raised hopes for the use of this chemical. However, gibberellic acid (GA_3), the only member of this group of chemicals that is readily available, has seldom been used successfully to procure the germination of seeds that could not have produced seedlings without it. Simpler, more straightforward approaches using temperature fluctuations, exposures to low temperatures or light, or periods of after-ripening have usually been as effective as treatment with gibberellic acid and much easier to apply. Seeds of a few species in which germination problems do cause more intractable difficulties—notably a number of plants in the buttercup family—have been persuaded to produce seedlings after treatment with gibberellic acid, suggesting the possibility of limited practical applications.

Problems associated with the use of gibberellins include the high cost of gibberellic acid

Fire

The seed coats of some seeds fracture when exposed to the heat of a fire—either as they lie on the surface or immediately below the ground. Similar affects can be replicated in a rather arbitrary way by sowing seeds in clay containers and setting fire to straw, loosely laid on top. More practically, seed can be exposed to similar effects after they have been sown in nursery beds by setting fire to dried twigs, brushwood, or loose pine needles piled on top of the bed.

Sulphuric acid

Some seeds—mostly those of trees and shrubs and including species of ilex, crataegus and roses—have heavily thickened seed coats that cannot readily be chipped or damaged in other ways. These can be destroyed by soaking in concentrated sulphuric acid, *provided facilities are available to do this safely and the operator is fully aware of safety procedures necessary to avoid accidents.*

Remove the seeds from the fleshy tissues of the surrounding fruits, and leave them to air dry before pouring the concentrated acid over them. (Reactions between concentrated sulphuric acid and water create intense heat that can be dangerous to the operator and lethal for the seeds. Seeds must be absolutely dry before coming into contact with the acid. Acid treatments should never be applied to moist or imbibed seeds, not only because of the risk of overheating, but because this enables the acid to penetrate the interior of the seeds.)

Stir and leave seeds to soak. Only trial and error will establish the period needed for a particular kind or batch of seeds, but those with really thick seed coats need hours, rather than minutes, to break down the coats. As the seed coats disintegrate, the white or ivory coloured tissues inside them are revealed, marking the time to discontinue treatment.

Tip the mixture of seeds and acid into a large volume of cold water containing a little washing soda, stirring before and while pouring to ensure that the acid is rapidly diluted. Do not add the water to the seeds and sulphuric acid, as this increases the chances of a heated reaction.

Decant the dilute acid and rinse twice or more in the same mixture of water and washing soda to neutralise acidity and wash away most of the oxidised seed coats. Spread the seeds out to dry in preparation for sowing, and sow in the usual way.

and the unavailability of other gibberellins, including GA_4 and GA_7, which are generally much more effective. In addition, it will be difficult to avoid distorted growth, seen as extreme elongation of the hypocotyls, following treatment.

Other organic chemicals

The hormone weed-killer 2,4-D, coumarin and abscissic acid all adversely affect seed germination. Others, including thio-urea, kinetin and ethylene, increase the numbers of seedlings produced in darkness by some species that otherwise germi-

nate only in response to light. Sharing space in the propagator with a ripe banana might improve the germination of some seeds, but the practical applications of these responses appear minimal.

Making use of chitted seeds

Chitting is the word used to describe a technique in which seeds are germinated up to the point when radicles become just visible before being sown. Weathering in moist grit in polythene bags becomes a form of chitting when radicles are actually to be seen emerging by the time the mixture of seeds and grit is removed from the bags and used as a topping or to fill drills in a nursery bed. The technique is also used in a rather different fashion to improve chances of success when sowing the seeds of perennials, bulbs and some shrubs and trees in nursery beds.

Seeds of many species of these plants produce seedlings less predictably and more slowly than annual and biennial species. When sown in nursery beds without special precautions, seeds of delphiniums, primulas, aquilegias, eryngiums, bluebells, narcissus, irises and many other plants that are otherwise readily raised in nursery beds take so long to germinate that weed seedlings are already overwhelmingly present before they do so. Alternatively, germination may be so delayed that the seeds are irretrievably lost before seedlings show at all. These problems can be avoided by germinating the seed under controlled conditions and sowing it only when radicles are already emerging and the cotyledons on the point of breaking out. A technique for doing this is described in the facing box.

Pricking out (spotting off) versus space sowing

Two radically different approaches are used when growing plants from seed: seeds are sown relatively thickly, and soon after the seedlings emerge they are transplanted (pricked out) individually into seed trays or pots, to give each one space to develop; or seeds are sown individually or in very small groups (space-sown), either at separate stations in seed trays or pots, or in separate containers using cells or small pots.

Advantages and disadvantages of pricking out

Sowing is uncomplicated, quick and easy—equally so with large, medium, small or awkwardly shaped seeds. Pricking out makes economical use of space while seeds germinate and during the early stages of seedling development. It provides the flexibility necessary for seeds which germinate erratically

or over long periods, and it minimises space wasted on those which fail to germinate. This method makes it possible to grade seedlings, retaining only the best or those with particular qualities. This is a particular advantage with seeds which produce some malformed seedlings (such as old seed) or those whose seedlings carry pigments indicative of foliage or flower colours, or, like stocks, display characteristics which identify those which will produce double flowers.

On the other hand, pricking out introduces an additional time-consuming operation to the propagation process. It may damage and set back seedlings, something that is avoided by practice and by moving seedlings while they're still very small. The best time to prick out most seedlings is when the seed leaves (cotyledons) have expanded fully and before the true leaves start to grow. With practice, even the tiniest seedlings can be safely moved at this stage.

Advantages and disadvantages of spaced sowing

Spaced sowing avoids the possibility of setbacks when transplanting seedlings. However, this advantage is more perceived than real, as there should be no setbacks when seedlings are pricked out while they're still very small. It eliminates the need for a separate operation, which can be a considerable advantage when time is short and opportunities to prick out seedlings are limited.

However, spaced sowing makes uneconomical use of space while seeds are germinating and during the early stages of seedling development. It works well only with high-quality seeds capable of producing very high proportions of seedlings soon after sowing. Premium quality seed must be used if seeds are to be sown in individual stations. This is expensive and not readily available in the small quantities needed by most amateur gardeners. Sowing seeds individually by hand or in very small groups is time consuming, fiddly and frustrating—easier with large seeds but tedious and difficult with very small ones.

Groups of seedlings still need to be thinned out, an operation which takes time and which can

Chitting seeds to enhance prospects of germination in nursery beds

The following is applicable to seeds of perennials, bulbs and some shrubs and trees.

- Sow seeds on moist paper towels contained in transparent plastic boxes with close-fitting lids.
- Place the boxes somewhere light and warm at between 15° and 20°C (60° and 70°F) by day, dropping to 10°C (50°F) at night, keeping in mind that fluctuating temperatures are likely to produce better results than constant conditions.
- As soon as the first radicles can be seen breaking through the seed coats, carefully remove the seeds from the moist paper and mix gently but thoroughly with an appropriate amount of pre-prepared wallpaper paste, made a little thicker than it would be for use with wallpaper. The mixture of seeds and paste should resemble frog-spawn, with the seeds slightly more sparsely distributed than the frog's eggs would be.
- Note that at this stage, the seeds of most hardy plants will not be harmed by exposure to low temperatures in a refrigerator for up to a fortnight at least. This arrests further development of the emerging seedlings and provides an effective means of synchronising species with different germination rates. It is more practical to sow several batches together side by side in a nursery bed at the same time than repeat the operation separately for each one.
- Put the mixture of seeds and paste in a pastry cook's forcing bag fitted with a fairly fine nozzle: a plastic bag with a hole cut in one corner suffices but is much more difficult to use in a controlled way.
- Squeeze out a line of seed/paste mix along a shallow drill in a nursery bed with the seeds distributed along it—spaced according to the size and vigour of the plants being sown, from approximately 0.5 to 1.5 cm (0.25 to 0.75 in.) apart.
- Refill the drills to cover the seeds lightly.

damage the remaining seedlings. Sometimes, small groups of seedlings can be left unthinned; they will grow up together as though a single plant—for example, lobelias thin themselves out by natural competition.

Pot and container sizes

When clay pots were the norm, their sizes were measured according to the number obtained from a standard quantity of clay known as a cast—for example, 60's, 32's, 16's and 2's; the smaller the number, the larger the pot. Today's gardeners find this arcane system too confusing to cope with and now size pots by their diameters—so 60's became 3 in., 32's became 6 in., 16's became 10 in. and 2's

became 18 in. Containers now are always referred to by their size, but there is little or no agreement whether this should be by linear measurement—diameter (round pots) or width of sides (square pots)—or by volume—litres or gallons—or by assigning numbers to pots within different size ranges.

In this book, containers up to and including 1 litre are sized according to the width of their sides—for example 7 or 9 cm—relating only to containers that are square in section. Small, round pots waste space and should be avoided. Sizes above 1 litre are sized relating to containers that are usually circular in section. Confusion indeed—but confusion that can be rationalised. It is economical, and an aid to good manage-

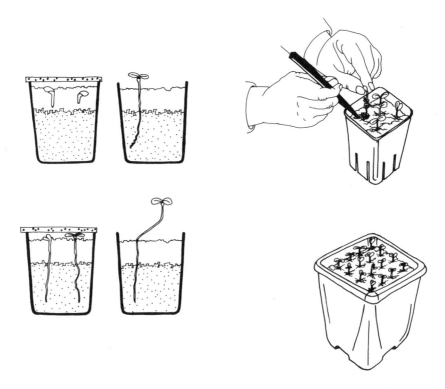

Figure 19. As soon as the very first signs of emerging radicles become visible, remove the polystyrene tiles used to cover seeds after sowing. Do not leave them in place any longer or the seedlings will become drawn up or etiolated in a search for light. The time to prick seedlings out is when the seed leaves have fully expanded. Knock them out of their containers and carefully separate the seedlings from the growing media, holding each one gently by one seed leaf. Prick them out close together into a suitable container. Unless very large numbers are needed, they occupy space more economically—and grow better—when moved into appropriately sized pots rather than seed trays.

ment, to standardise containers so far as possible. This principle is recognised in the following chapters by restricting container sizes to 7 cm, 9 cm or 1 litre square and 2, 3, 5 or 7.5 litre round pots.

To add to the confusion, in North America, container sizes are different still. Pot sizes range widely, from 2 to 8 inches, to 1, 2, 3, and 5 gallons or more. Conventions matching North American container sizes (approximately) to European counterparts are suggested throughout the book.

Matching container size with vigour

Putting a small plant into a large pot is like putting a small boy into his dad's suit in the hope that the child will grow into it. He is just uncomfortable. When seedlings or cuttings are *potted up* (the first occasion on which a seedling or rooted cutting is put into a container on its own) or *potted on* (the transfer from one container to a larger one as the plant develops), the size of the container should be matched to the size and vigour of the plant. When potting on, it is traditional to spec-

Tips for pricking out seedlings

Prick out seedlings with a dibber—a pencil-shaped stick—or a pencil serves perfectly well. Holding the dibber in one hand, pick up the seedling by the tip of one seed leaf (not by the stem), between the forefinger and thumb of the other hand. Set out planting stations individually with a dibber, rather than use a template. As each hole is made in sequence, it firms up the growth medium around the roots of the preceding seedling. The art of even spacing is not hard to learn, and it's a source of innocent pride once acquired.

Tiny seedlings are fragile and vulnerable to desiccation. Prick out in a shaded situation and water immediately afterwards. Apply light, refreshing sprays for a day or two until the seedlings reestablish.

Some seedlings cling together tenaciously and have to be gently separated to avoid damage. Risks are greatest with plants, including some grasses, in which the fragile connection between the cotyledon and the seed (caryopsis) is easily torn apart.

Prick out into seed trays or pots. The former are traditional; for most purposes, the latter are better. Pots are deeper, accommodate roots more easily and dry out less rapidly. They are also more flexible. A few seedlings can be grown together in a small pot, or in several small or one larger one, to hold greater numbers. Square 9 cm (3.5 in.) pots with five to nine seedlings to a pot make a good, flexible system, and the extra depth of the pot compared to a tray is very useful for plants with long roots.

Seed trays hold large numbers of seedlings and should be used only when large numbers are needed. When using seed trays, prick out on a grid, laid out by eye, placing 50 to 90 seedlings in a tray, apart from relatively large, fast-growing seedlings like dahlias, for which about 30 is enough. By aligning the grid accurately, gaps caused by losses from slugs and other threats are immediately obvious, and remedial action can be taken before serious damage is done.

ify a move into pots "one size larger" than those in which they currently reside. This did not make a great deal of sense in the days of clay pots; it makes none at all now—though the mantra is still to be read or repeatedly heard.

The extent of the move depends on conditions and prospects for growth. Plants should be treated generously when they are growing vigorously and favourable conditions for rapid growth lie ahead. When plants are not growing strongly, when growth is about to slow down due to the approach of winter or other adverse conditions, do not pot them on. A feed is the most they need to keep them going.

The sizes of pots used at different stages of the development of seedlings, cuttings or divisions can most readily be matched to vigour by using two series of container sizes: Small to medium-sized conifers, shrubs, and perennials, for example, can be contained in 7 cm, 1 litre, 3 litre, or 5 litre (2.5 in., 6 in., 8 in. or 1 gal.) pots. Vigorous perennials, medium-sized to large conifers, shrubs and trees can be contained in 9 cm, 2 litre, 4 litre, or 7.5 litre (3.5 in., 8 in., 1 gal. or 2 gal.) pots. Whenever possible, avoid using the larger pot sizes (2 litres, or 8 in., and above) by lining plants out in a nursery bed to grow on.

Potting up seedlings

Pricked out seedlings are potted up individually as and when they grow large enough. This is done when the plants can be easily handled—not delayed until space in the seed trays or pots is fully occupied, when the roots will have matted together.

Tip the seedlings out of their pots en masse, supporting the entire contents of the pot in the palm of one hand. Do not pry them out one by one. Similarly, remove them bodily from seed trays. Tap each side of the tray in succession sharply against the potting bench, and then eject the contents with a short, vigorous forward-throwing movement. Hang on to the container itself! Remove the plants individually using fingers or a dibber, and set them out ready to be potted up.

Pot up the plants individually, and as soon as they are all in place, move them into a sheltered, lightly shaded situation—such as in a frame or on a glasshouse bench—and water thoroughly. Protect the plants from the effects of excessive sunshine for the first few days.

Signs of health in seedlings

Seedlings should not appear stressed or suffering after being pricked out or potted up. After a day or two to recover, the result should be an almost immediate spurt of growth and an appearance of well-being—any hanging back is a sign that something is not right. Well-being takes many forms.

A rapid increase in size

Seedlings that fail to grow rapidly may be too cold or too hot (occasionally). They may be suffering from a growth medium that lacks airspace and fails to drain after watering. They may be too dry, particularly if they were not thoroughly watered in after being moved.

Retention of cotyledons (seed leaves)

Prolonged retention of the cotyledons in a green, healthy condition is a reassuring sign that the plants are well provided for. Early withering of the cotyledons is a sign that all is not well, usually an indication of a nutrient deficiency or poor root growth due to waterlogging or cold.

Overall appearance of foliage

A drab look is a pale look and an indication that something is wrong. Healthy seedlings develop a lustre on the leaves that varies from something akin to an "eggshell" glow to the bright "shellac" varnish seen in some strains of begonias.

Foliage colour

Healthy seedlings produce leaves that carry colours other than green, but pale yellow-green foliage is a sign of nutrient deficiencies due either to poor root development resulting from water-logged or acid mixes or a lack of nitrogen or potassium. Crimson and purple tints combined with hard growth indicate inadequate watering or cold conditions. Similar tints developing after initial healthy growth suggest a shortage of phosphate.

Sleep movements

Cotyledons and leaves change their posture, or stance, in regular and well-defined ways from night to day. At night, leaflets may close together, as in clovers. Cotyledons or leaves may assume a more vertical pose, as in tomatoes. These movements are most pronounced when seedlings are growing well.

Guttation

The nocturnal extrusion of droplets of water through pores around the margins of leaves is a sign that the roots are healthy and working effectively. It is most apparent in the morning in seedlings growing in glasshouses, where high humidities build up during the night.

Cuttings

Cuttings are bits of plant removed from their parent. Cuttings of shoots are usually removed by making the cut just under a node. This is because the nodes of dicots almost invariably contain buds and are the sites of meristematic tissues required for the initiation of roots. Griselinias provide a rare example of a partial exception to this rule. Although buds are frequently present in the axils of their leaves, they are almost equally likely to be distributed seemingly at random anywhere along the internodes.

Prospects for a cutting are bleak unless it can replace missing roots or shoots. The propagator's job is to keep it alive long enough to do so. The essential life-support systems that keep cuttings alive and functioning are water, oxygen, light and temperature.

Water must be freely and consistently available in the growth medium around the base of the shoots, whence it is taken up to supply the leaves, and as water vapour in the atmosphere around the leaves in order to reduce the rate of transpiration. Oxygen enables tissues to respire, and it must be available in the atmosphere around the leaves. No action is needed to ensure this—even a closed container (such as a sealed polythene bag) contains sufficient oxygen to support leaf respiration. Oxygen must also be available in close proximity to the base of the cutting, where missing tissues will be produced. Air should be able to diffuse freely through the cutting mix and is essential to avoid waterlogging. Light is needed by cuttings with leaves, to provide the energy through photosynthesis, on which plant metabolism depends. High light levels drive photosynthesis most effectively but lead to overheating in unventilated conditions and to drastic reductions in humidity in ventilated ones. Finding ways to combine high light levels with high atmospheric humidity is the key to success with cuttings. Shading reduces overheating and desiccation; it also reduces light levels and delays results. There are times when shading can be deliberately used to reduce demands on time and management—even though cuttings take longer to produce roots. Temperature affects dependent chemical and enzyme reactions which control rates of growth and the speed with which missing tissues are replaced. The optimum range, economically and effectively, usually lies between 12° and 25°C (54° and 75°F). Maintaining high humidities becomes increasingly difficult as temperatures rise, and temperatures above approxi-

mately 30°C (85°F) induce stress and reduce success, except with tropical plants. Lower temperatures slow growth and results take longer—which is not necessarily a bad thing. Very low temperatures cause injury from chilling or freezing with tender plants.

Making cuttings

The ideal tool to use to make cuttings is a matter of some dispute and ultimately individual preference. The choice lies among knives with fixed or disposable blades, secateurs (pruners), and fingers.

A small penknife or kitchen knife provides the obvious solution when faced with the prospect of making a cutting. However, in unskilled hands, knives are not easily maintained in a continuously sharp state and are all too capable of inflicting serious cuts (to the gardener, not just the plant). They also have the disadvantage of being the number one, ace carrier of virus diseases from one plant to another (see note on viruses on pp. 114–115).

Knives with disposable blades, such as craft knives of various sorts, avoid the need to learn the skills of keeping a blade sharp and provide a practical alternative. They are available with small blades that are easily used to make precisely guided cuts and reduce the chances of accidental slips. They can be replaced or sterilised as necessary to avoid possibilities of virus transmission.

Secateurs are widely available in a variety of shapes, sizes and fitness for the task. Cheap ones made with steel unable to maintain an edge soon become useless. Those that have been abused and strained so the blades no longer meet in a precise scissor fashion tear rather than cut plant tissues. A pair of well-maintained, sharp, high-quality secateurs are useful for many kinds of cuttings— particularly during the initial stages concerned with cutting suitable shoots from plants growing in the garden.

Thumbnails are the preferred tool for many gardeners when nipping off the softer tissues of cuttings, especially the leaves in the final stages of preparing a cutting. The delicacy of touch provided by fingers, combined with a suitably horny nail, makes the hand a highly effective precision instrument for this task.

Basic treatment of cuttings

The first decision to make when taking cuttings is whether to use individual containers for each batch of cuttings or set out cuttings of different plants side by side in a communal bed of cutting mix. The latter is less fiddly and is satisfying to set up, and freshly made cuttings neatly set out in rows looks efficient. However, community living has serious disadvantages.

Some species produce roots in a few weeks, others do so after many weeks, and some take months. Rooted cuttings should be removed as and when they are ready. One species will be ready at one time, but another may not be ready till weeks later. The slower, unrooted cuttings suffer disturbance in the process. In addition, space is wasted as one row of rooted cuttings is moved on while others are still occupied by unrooted cuttings.

Problems with hygiene occur as pathogens introduced to one part of the cutting bed travel freely to other parts. Second- and third-generation cuttings are stuck into positions previously occupied by other cuttings, increasing the potential for passing on pathogenic organisms. Unless the cutting mix is frequently renewed, mosses and liverworts become established.

These problems are avoided by setting up each batch of cuttings in its own container. This enables each batch to be handled independently in its own time, without interference from other batches of cuttings, and provided with fresh cutting mix, which is disposed of once the cuttings have produced roots.

Single sticking techniques

Pelargoniums, fuchsias, verbenas and many other plants grown in containers or used for bedding are produced commercially by sticking them individually into blocks of compressed peat, wood pulp and other organic materials. This simple labour-saving method is ideally suited to the rapid production of plants that form roots easily and

Figure 20. A propagating house in spring is filled with cuttings and seedlings. Pricked out seedlings of annuals appear on the left. A propagator filled with tip cuttings is in the centre (note the condensation), overwintered cuttings of perennials are at the back, and small pots sown with seeds in a tray and covered with a block of expanded polystyrene are partially visible on the right. The bench at the back is heated with soil heating cables.

consistently. A similar technique is used for cuttings of shrubs that produce inconsistent results using other methods or which transplant badly, including garryas, fremontodendrons, ceanothus, proteas, berberis and viburnums. These are stuck individually into small blocks of rock wool under a mist propagation unit.

Growth media for cuttings

Cutting mixes serve a specific purpose that is different from the potting mixes in which plants are grown. Successful mixes need to be sufficiently dense and stable to hold the cuttings in place, and sufficiently open to allow air (oxygen) to reach the parts of the cuttings where active growth takes place. They must be capable of absorbing water and making it consistently available to the tissues of the cuttings. Finally, they must be unfriendly to mosses and liverworts, most easily achieved by using materials that contain no nutrients, which are not essential during the time cuttings are replacing missing tissues. Although not essential, nutrients can assist root formation, but their pres-

Figure 21. Preparations for taking cuttings of fuchsias, pelargoniums and ericas, using a 1:1 cutting mix of grit and perlite and hormone rooting powder for the ericas and fuchsias, but not the pelargoniums.

ence encourages vigorous development of mosses and liverworts. On balance it is better to do without them.

Grit provides a good foundation for a cutting mix. It is widely available; obtainable with acidic or basic reactions, enabling it to be matched to the needs of different plants; open structured with excellent aeration; stable, providing firm support; and easy to manage, in that it accepts water readily and the excess drains away freely. However, grit holds water only on its surfaces, and with little in reserve, it dries out rapidly. Calcined clays, perlite, pumice and other minerals which are both gritty and absorbent avoid this problem.

Facilities used to produce plants from cuttings

Plants can be successfully grown from cuttings using equipment which ranges from the ultra-simple to the complex, from extreme economy to considerable expense, from a grit-lined trench dug in a sheltered corner of the garden or a flower pot enclosed by a polythene bag to a mist propagation unit. Only a minority of the plants propagated from cuttings depend for success on sophisticated equipment.

Container covered with a polythene bag

A flower pot enclosed in a polythene bag makes a simple, effective container for cuttings of leafy shoots. It is filled with cutting mix and drenched with water before sticking the cuttings in it. This simple, unventilated system overheats severely if exposed to the sun, even for a short time, and must be placed out of direct sunlight in a light, preferably warm place.

A 1 litre (6 in.) square container makes a convenient unit, and a firm support for the polythene is provided by a short length of stock fencing, with a 10 cm (4 in.) mesh cut to fit the container. It is easier to put the whole lot into a large poly bag and close the top with an elastic band than to attempt to fit a smaller bag over the container. A canopy of bubble polythene provides a simple means of protecting the bags of cuttings from direct sunlight.

Plastic propagator

Seed trays with transparent plastic tops are the most economical custom-made equipment for cuttings. They combine simplicity and flexibility with low cost, provided electrically heated versions are avoided.

Set up separate batches of cuttings in individual containers, using either quarter trays or 7 cm (2.5 in.) square pots. After setting up the cuttings,

---

Standard cutting mix

A suitable combination for use with a wide range of plants consists of a 1:1 mix of grit and perlite. Grit provides the weight necessary for stability; perlite holds a reserve of water. Both materials are sterile or easily sterilised. This is the standard cutting mix recommended throughout this book, unless an alternative is specified.

place the propagator on a heated bench; in a frame; under the bench in a glasshouse; out of doors in a shaded, sheltered situation; or on a window sill, depending on the needs of the cuttings and accommodation available.

These simple but effective units give excellent results, provided they are never exposed to direct sunlight and the cuttings are packed close together, disregarding old taboos about not letting the leaves of cuttings mingle or touch the sides of the propagator. A certain intimacy between the leaves of neighbouring cuttings provides mutual support and maintains a humid atmosphere, and leaves touching the sides of the container come to no harm. Do not remove the top to wipe off condensation, as condensation signifies that the atmosphere within is saturated with water vapour. Removing the top disturbs the cuttings and is unnecessary until the reduction or absence of condensation shows that the atmosphere is becoming dry; then thoroughly drench the cuttings with water and replace the top.

Plastic propagators with heating elements in the base are widely available. They are extremely costly in relation to the amount of heated propagating space they provide. Supplementary warmth is provided much more economically by standing the propagator on a bench fitted with soil heating cables.

Outdoor sun frames and tunnel cloches

These can be used to propagate all kinds of summer cuttings and protect overwintering hardwood cuttings of evergreen and deciduous trees and shrubs. Cuttings of semi-mature shoots during the summer are treated as follows:

- Cut suitable shoots off the parent plants. Put them straight into plastic bags to protect them from desiccation, and keep them in cool, shaded conditions until they're ready to make into cuttings.
- When using frames, set up each batch of cuttings in a separate container. In tunnel cloches, set up the cuttings in rows in a prepared bed

beneath the cloche.
- If possible, organise the collection of cuttings so that enough are available to fill substantial proportions of the available space in frames or tunnel cloches. High humidities are much easier to maintain in well-filled than partially filled frames. Ideally, a frame or a tunnel should be filled in one operation rather than with periodic additions of newly made cuttings.
- Water each batch of cuttings lightly as it goes in, and when all are in place, drench the cutting mix and the interior of the frame or cloche thoroughly to settle the cuttings in the cutting mix.
- Close the frame lights, or draw down the sides of the tunnel cloche. Do this even during short absences while setting up the cuttings to maintain a sealed atmosphere saturated with water vapour whenever possible.
- Leave everything undisturbed, disregarding condensation, until its reduction or absence indicates a drying atmosphere; then drench thoroughly.
- Provide extra shading in hot weather to prevent overheating beneath the plastic covers, using milky white polythene, shade cloth, or even newspaper.

The need for supervision and daily refreshing sprays of water when using frames to propagate plants from cuttings can be reduced to a minimum by laying thin-gauge plastic sheeting inside the frame, directly over the cuttings. This prevents water loss, and when applied in combination with extra shading will maintain a saturated atmosphere for long enough to leave a frame unattended during absences of at least a fortnight.

The cuttings are transferred in their containers to a weaning frame as soon as roots are produced, where ventilation can gradually be increased. Water the rooted cuttings heavily with a liquid feed (water-soluble fertilizer) at two or three times the standard recommended concentration as soon as they produce roots and/or the shoots start to grow.

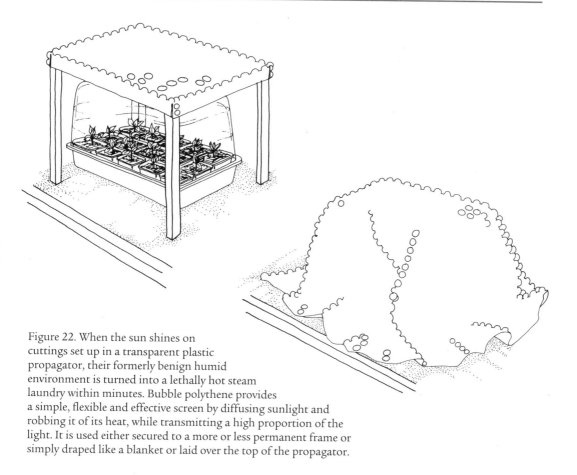

Figure 22. When the sun shines on
cuttings set up in a transparent plastic
propagator, their formerly benign humid
environment is turned into a lethally hot steam
laundry within minutes. Bubble polythene provides
a simple, flexible and effective screen by diffusing sunlight and
robbing it of its heat, while transmitting a high proportion of the
light. It is used either secured to a more or less permanent frame or
simply draped like a blanket or laid over the top of the propagator.

Heated frames in glasshouse or plastic tunnel

Frames set up inside other structures, especially in
cool and cold temperate regions of the world,
extend the range of plants that can be propagated
successfully, prolong the seasons when cuttings
can be taken, increase output by reducing the time
taken for roots to be formed, and provide extra
protection for tender plants during the winter.
Tropical and subtropical plants in particular are
likely to be dependent on warmth for successful
regeneration, and soil heating cables provide an
economical, flexible and effective way to provide it.

A warm bench combined with polythene provides a highly effective system for producing
plants from tip and semi-mature cuttings:

- Set up the cuttings on a bench within a glasshouse or plastic tunnel above soil heating
  cables controlled by a thermostat to maintain
  temperatures between 20° and 25°C (70° and
  75°F).
- When all the cuttings are in place, drench them
  thoroughly with water.
- Lay a sheet of thin, transparent plastic (80 to
  100 gauge) directly over them. Hold down the
  edges with battens to enclose the cuttings in

necessary by laying milky polythene (perhaps from an old fertiliser bag) or shade cloth over the bubble polythene.

- Check periodically for dry spots, especially when using soil heating cables.
- When more water is necessary, remove the overlying plastic sheet and drench the cuttings with a fine spray, before covering the cuttings once again with a sheet of plastic. It is easier to use a fresh sheet (or a dry, recycled one) than to attempt to replace the old, soggy one.

Mist propagation

The methods described so far have depended on maintaining saturated atmospheres by enclosing the airspace around cuttings and shading them to avoid excessive heat buildup. Shading reduces photosynthesis and the performance of the cuttings by limiting the energy available to them for renewed growth and development. Mist propagation avoids this by providing a fine mist in the air around the cuttings, enabling them to survive on an open bench at comparatively high light levels. This leads to more rapid root formation and sometimes greater success with plants that are reluctant to form roots when shaded and enclosed.

Figure 23. A veritable battery of propagators within a heavily shaded structure in Victoria, Australia, is used to propagate Australian native, drought-resistant shrubs.

The mist is produced by a pump which produces periodic bursts and is controlled either through a time clock set to switch on at predetermined intervals or through an electronic leaf located amongst the cuttings. When setting a time clock, it is difficult to judge how often and for how long a pump should operate, and insufficient or excessive watering almost always results. An electronic leaf disconnects the pump through a solenoid valve whenever a film of water covers its surface; as the water evaporates, the connection is restored, switching on the pump to rehumidify the air and the cuttings.

an almost airtight and watertight space. The plastic sheet lies on the cuttings in direct contact with their foliage. The air inside and around the cuttings quickly becomes saturated and drops of mist form on the sheet.

- Routine treatment of cuttings with a fungicide incorporated in the initial drench is usually recommended. However, it is seldom necessary and is done to reassure the propagator rather than for the sake of the cuttings.
- Protect the cuttings from direct sunlight with a canopy of bubble polythene, and in hot, sunny weather, reinforce the shading effect if

Mist propagation units provide an automatic system that adjusts to changes in weather, temperature and humidity. They operate with minimal need for supervision. Their use avoids the need for heavy shading—the leaves are kept cool by the evaporation of water from their surfaces.

Cuttings from plants from arid regions

Totally enclosed systems saturated with water vapour are unsuitable for cuttings of plants adapted to dry or exposed situations. More ventilation and less heavily saturated conditions are provided for plants with leaves that are needlelike or narrow with rolled margins, silver or grey, densely hairy or woolly, fleshy or succulent, or sclerophyllous (the hard drought-adapted foliage produced by banksias, proteas, dryandras and many other trees and shrubs from arid regions). *Eucalyptus* spp. are the prime example of plants with sclerophyllous leaves, but cuttings made from their shoots are so unlikely to produce roots they are virtually never used to propagate these plants.

These units are particularly useful with soft cuttings that are vulnerable to overheating from sunlight and lend themselves, in conjunction with soil heating cables, to the provision of warm conditions for the roots and cool tops, which is believed to encourage rapid root formation.

The great disadvantage of mist units is that they are not fail-safe.

- Failures rapidly lead to desiccation and are potentially disastrous.
- Overactivity can be difficult to detect and contributes insidiously to poor performance through waterlogging and excessive leaching of nutrients.
- Dry spots are created when jets become blocked, or a blocked jet close to the electronic leaf leads to repeated operation of the pump, causing saturation in other parts of the bed.
- The circular pattern of water distribution leads to overlapping and edge effects, causing uneven saturation. This can be used to advantage by inserting cuttings requiring less water in dry

areas and those with a preference for more in places where jets overlap.

- The leaves of cuttings subjected to mist for long periods lose nutrients through leaching, but adding nutrients to compensate for leaching leads to excessive development of mosses and liverworts.
- Roots produced under mist may be brittle, and special care is needed when potting them up for the first time.

The secrets of success with mist propagation lie in the following:

- Regular—weekly—maintenance of the pump, electronic leaf and spray nozzles.
- A supply of clean, particle-free, soft water, because hard water leads to problems with calcium deposits. Rainwater avoids such difficulties, but small specks of solid matter can block the nozzle of a jet.
- An easily cleaned, removable filter fitted between the pump and the jets to allow removal of solid particles before they cause problems.
- Use of high-pressure pumps, which produce the finest mist and are less likely to suffer from blocked nozzles; these are more likely to lead to leaks, however. To make leaks easy to detect, the pipe work from tank to pump to jets should all be visible and not discreetly concealed.
- Jets that are fed from pipes angled at 45 degrees over the bed from a supply running along the back; they should not emerge vertically from the centre of the bed.
- A circuit breaker to safeguard operator(s) in case of an electrical fault.

Cuttings under mist are weaned as and when they produce roots, before being moved and grown on. A similar installation with less frequent operation of the jets is sometimes recommended as a weaning unit, but this extravagance is seldom justified. It can be avoided, using minimal ingenuity, by moving containers holding recently rooted cuttings to the drier parts of the bed or along the margins. Cuttings finally removed from the mist unit should be lodged for a few days semi-enclosed in a frame covered with bubble polythene or some similar light diffusing, moisture retaining material.

Hormone rooting compounds

A group of hormones known as *auxins* play their part in the phenomenon of totipotency, supposedly as activators of the various developmental pathways leading to the formation of roots, shoots, flowers, leaves, and other plant parts. The precise ways in which auxins operate are obscure, but empirical observations suggest roots are formed in situations where levels of auxins are high. It follows that cuttings of shoots are more likely to produce roots if the concentration of auxins toward their cut ends, where roots are most likely to be formed naturally, can be supplemented—hence, the practice of dipping shoots in powder or liquid preparations containing auxin analogues in an attempt to reinforce natural processes. Conversely, shoots arise where auxin levels are low, and this explains why auxins are not applied to root cuttings.

Several chemicals are widely available for use as hormone rooting agents; these are known by acronyms standing for complex, chemical names. *NoA* and *NAA*, the two most generally available compounds used to make hormone rooting powders, can both cause excessive callus development and distorted or brittle roots when used to excess. *IBA* is generally more effective over a wider range of plants and is less likely to produce distorted roots, but it is less readily obtainable. Note that these hormones, especially IBA, are unstable when exposed to light in warm conditions. They should be stored in the dark in a refrigerator and replaced annually.

The most frequent misuse of these compounds arises from over-enthusiastic applications following the mistaken belief that if a little is good, more must be better. Cuttings taken from a high proportion of the trees and shrubs grown in gardens produce roots spontaneously, given the right conditions, with or without these chemical treatments. For a minority of species, the use of growth hormones is more or less essential for success, or at least greatly increases success rates, reducing the time required to form roots as well as increasing the number produced.

Liquid preparations are widely used for commercial plant production; powders are used for smaller scale amateur operations. Liquids make it possible to vary rates of use over a wide range to suit the needs of particular plants. This is particularly important when taking hardwood cuttings of trees and shrubs, including the large-flowered rhododendron hybrids, which are unresponsive to low concentrations.

Growing on cuttings

It is easy to produce a fine batch of rooted cuttings and then lose many, even all, of them later due to misguided treatment. Cuttings taken during the summer inevitably become self-sufficient and ready to grow on when winter is more or less imminent. In cool or cold temperate regions, especially, winter is a testing time for recently rooted cuttings. Those who garden in Mediterranea or in warm temperate regions can use the winter more effectively as a growing on period.

Cuttings suffer stress when they are potted up prematurely, before the roots have developed sufficiently to sustain the plant. Before starting to pot up a batch, check that all the cuttings have well-developed roots using oversized containers. The smallest container, usually 7 or 9 cm (2.5 or 3.5 in.), that holds the roots and provides space for a little growth is the right one.

If cuttings are potted up close to the onset of winter, stress ensues. In cool and cold temperate regions, mid-autumn provides the deadline for potting up cuttings. If they are not ready by then, they overwinter better crowded but undisturbed in their original containers and should be potted up when they resume growth the following spring. It is more economical and convenient to find space to overwinter one container filled with a dozen rooted cuttings than a dozen containers each holding a single plant.

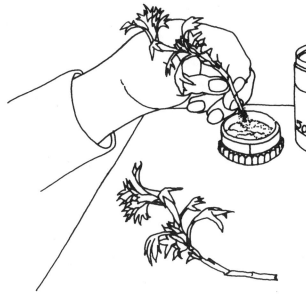

Figure 24. Proprietary rooting hormones consist of a variety of auxins similar to those known to be naturally involved in root formation in plants, mixed with talc. Dip the base of the cuttings into a thin layer of the hormone/talc mixture in the upturned lid of the container, to avoid contaminating the bulk of the powder. Dip only the extreme ends into the hormone and tap the cuttings against the rim of the lid to shake off any excess before setting them out.

If cuttings are potted up and simultaneously exposed to more rigorous conditions, they suffer. For this reason, whenever possible, cuttings should by returned to the conditions in which they were growing before they were potted up, for a short time while they establish.

Finally, if cuttings are potted into dry growth potting mix, they may not survive. A thorough soaking with water after potting up cuttings is essential to ensure no dry pockets remain—particularly when using peat-based mixtures.

Watering and feeding

Watering is crucial in determining success and failure when growing plants—and never more so than when looking after young plants. It should be given priority over every other operation. Capillary matting, overhead sprays and other automatic or semi-automatic watering systems are valuable aids on commercial nurseries, particularly when large batches of plants with similar requirements are being grown. As the diversity of plants increases and batches of the same kind become smaller, there is no substitute for the hand behind the can or the rose on a hose (hose and spray nozzle). A hose fitted with a short lance, or watering wand, and a rose produces more even flows, is less physically demanding and much quicker than using a watering can. It becomes essential when anything more than small numbers of plants are being grown.

Uneven growth in a batch of plants is almost always the result of poor watering skills or technique and is a sign of trouble. Problems are avoided by watering systematically, always going round the edges of each batch of plants before moving into the middle; forming a clear, preconceived idea of how much water to apply to each batch, before starting to water it; and avoiding the two cardinal sins of watering: giving a little bit for now with the promise of a return when time is less pressing, and going round picking out what obviously needs watering and leaving the rest for another day.

In winter, when plants are making little growth, overwatering quickly leads to problems—especially with recently potted cuttings and recently germinated seedlings. Most rooted cuttings tolerate remarkably dry conditions while more or less at rest during the winter, with no ill effects and with improved chances of survival and freedom from pests and diseases.

In cold regions with dark, short days during winter, overwintering cuttings should be watered only when absolutely necessary and whenever possible only in the morning on sunny days to give the foliage time to dry before sunset. Cuttings become much less sensitive to overwatering when they resume growth in the spring, and water should be freely applied to match demand.

When actively growing plants wilt, they suffer more than a short-lived, temporary setback—and recurrent wilting over several days seriously restricts the development of young plants. A dry plant reacts by cutting back—*hardening* in gardening terms—in order to adjust to reduced water availability. Recovery may appear to be complete, but the message will have been received, the impetus of growth reduced, and the plant may never make up what has been lost. This is not always undesirable, however. In hot, dry climates or situations, there may be advantages in encouraging plants not to grow at maximum pace continuously, and a certain level of hardening makes them easier to manage and less vulnerable to heat and drought.

Automatic watering systems

Many gardeners simply cannot arrange to be around as and when watering needs to be done. An automatic watering system of some kind

Figure 25. Watering is a crucially important skill and should always be done systematically. Decide how much water is needed before starting. Standardise the sizes of containers whenever possible and group together plants at the same stage of development. Whether using a can or a hose, use a rose, holding it close to the plants being watered and inverted to prevent the holes being blocked by grit and other materials. Always start watering around the edges, making sure they have been thoroughly covered before moving into the centre.

becomes essential if plants are to be grown at all. Automatic watering systems based on spray heads or sprinklers are difficult to set up in ways which ensure an even distribution of water. The balance between applying too much or too little is hard to achieve, they are not fail-safe, and even short breakdowns can have serious consequences.

In most situations, capillary beds provide a better answer to the problem. Pots are stood on matting or sand saturated with water from a reservoir, taking it up through the holes in their bases. The bed must be absolutely level and remain so when loaded with plants. Small deviations lead to dry areas where water fails to reach and wet ones where it floods. Unlike conventional watering, water and the nutrients it contains move upward towards the surface of containers—not downward. This can lead to excessive development of mosses and liverworts on the surface of the sand or matting of the bed and deposits of nutrient salts on the surface of potting mix in the containers.

CHAPTER 6

Plant Disorders Including Nutrition, Pests and Diseases, and Chimaeras

This should be a short chapter. Seedlings and young plants grown from cuttings are resistant to pests and diseases as long as they are stress-free. Problems arise from the sins and omissions of the gardener. When plants fail to thrive, succumb to diseases and pests or otherwise disappoint, the first place the gardener should look to find the cause is in the mirror.

Are the plants being watered and fed appropriately, and being grown in favourable conditions, where they might be expected to perform well? The main sources of trouble are summarised in the facing box.

Nutrition: Fertilisers and Feeds

Healthy plant growth depends on adequate nutrition. Seedlings and cuttings need feeding throughout the time they are making growth. Potting mixes in which seedlings and young plants are grown have nutrients added to them when they are mixed. As the plants develop, these are absorbed and must be replaced.

As a rule of thumb, start feeding when leaves reach the edges of containers or begin to overlap neighbouring seedlings in seed trays. Never as-sume, just because they are marketed by commercial organisations, that potting mixes are adequately endowed with nutrients; many branded potting mixes emerge from the bag woefully short of these necessities. Remember that adding grit, sand, or perlite even to well-endowed proprietary mixes to improve texture, drainage or density reduces nutrient levels. Early feeding is necessary to compensate.

Cutting mixes contain no nutrients. Their presence can cause problems, and they are not usually considered necessary, though they do enhance root formation and development in some situations. Drench with a nutrient solution as soon as cuttings develop roots, at two or three times the standard recommended rate. Repeat using standard rate applications at intervals till the cuttings are potted up individually or cease growth for the winter.

Plant nutrients

The chemical nutrients required by plants are summarised and divided into four groups in the box on p. 104. For practical purposes, group one is by far the most important when propagating plants from seeds and cuttings. Seedlings grown in proprietary potting mixes need supplementary feeding as they develop. It is usually sufficient to restrict these supplements to mixtures of the three

Main sources of problems experienced when propagating plants

- **Poor nutrition:** Starved plants are stunted and pest and disease prone. Overfed plants are easy meals for pests and vulnerable to diseases.
- **Careless watering:** Results in dry spots, especially around the edges of batches of plants, or overwatering, most likely in winter when plants are growing slowly.
- **Low light and short days:** Most severe during winter in high latitudes, this is deeply inimical to the health of young seedlings. It is alleviated by supplementary light or by delaying sowing.
- **Low temperatures:** Often associated with low light. Increased temperatures are effective only if light levels are also increased.
- **High temperatures and low light:** Lead to weak growth susceptible to pests and diseases.
- **High temperatures and high light:** When such conditions arise from exposure to the sun, scorch, wilting or, in enclosed conditions, Turkish bath effects are caused.
- **Airless, waterlogged growth media:** Caused by the use of unsuitable materials and/or overwatering, especially in winter when plants are growing slowly.
- **Lack of ventilation:** During the winter, the vents of frames and glasshouses should be opened whenever possible. Low-volume internal fans should be used to circulate air in glasshouses.
- **Hot, dry conditions:** Such conditions favour red spider infestations. Maintain ample watering and damp down walls, floors and benches thoroughly with a hose once daily—at least during the summer.
- **Cover for pests and diseases:** Remove old pots, boxes, anything not in use, and weeds from the vicinity of frames and within glasshouses, where mice or slugs, insect pests or fungal spores might lurk.
- **Chronic infestations:** Includes the entrenched presence of whiteflies, red spiders, mealy bugs and scale insects. Once established, these infestations require drastic remedies—including the removal of all plants for a period, followed by fumigation and treatment of woodwork with pesticides.
- **Contaminated water:** Rainwater butts harbour pythium, phytophthora and other disease organisms. They should be emptied, cleaned and disinfected regularly and the water renewed. Otherwise, be wary of using rainwater for young seedlings and cuttings.

group one chemical elements—nitrogen, phosphorous and potassium.

Cuttings need feeding as soon as they develop roots in order to sustain growth until they are potted up. Most cuttings contain sufficient reserves of groups two, three and four chemicals to keep them going through this phase. Once again, feeding can usually be confined to the three group one chemicals. A complete nutrient, one that supplies all the chemicals in groups one through four, becomes a necessity only when homemade mixtures of materials are used and must be incorporated during preparation.

The simplest way to feed plants is to buy proprietary liquid or soluble fertilisers and follow the directions on the label. Then all that is necessary is to decide what N:P:K formulation most closely matches the need.

<hr>

Mineral nutrients required by plants for healthy growth

The minerals listed here can be provided as salts applied in solution to the roots or as foliar sprays. Those who garden organically use sources derived mainly from plant and animal remains. Whatever the source, it is important to remember that all the chemicals listed here are essential for healthy and sustained plant growth.

Group One
Nitrogen (N) is a component of all amino acids, the building blocks of proteins, nucleic acids and other essential organic compounds.
Phosphorus (P) is a component of DNA, the material of which chromosomes are made; it also plays a critical role in the energy transfers that drive metabolism.
Potassium (K) balances the ionic composition of sap during the transportation and metabolism of other nutrients.
   A code, N:P:K, defines the percentages of the three group one chemicals—for example, *20:5:11* refers to 20 percent nitrogen, 5 percent phosphorus and 11 percent potassium.

Group Two
Magnesium is the central atom of every molecule of chlorophyll.
Sulphur is a component of several amino acids, necessary for the production of proteins.
Calcium is a component of cell walls; it is also involved in spindle formation during cell division.

Group Three
Iron is involved, as a catalyst, in the production of chlorophyll.

Group Four
Manganese, zinc, copper, boron, and *molybdenum* are required in minute quantities as catalysts and other facilitators of metabolic reactions.

<hr>

To encourage seedling growth in spring or the initial development of cuttings, a formula containing adequate amounts of potassium and phosphorus and a little extra nitrogen to sustain growth—for example, 25:15:15—would be right. Cuttings or seedlings in the autumn in need of hardening before the onset of winter would do better with higher ratios of potassium to nitrogen, such as 15:15:30.

High concentrations of mineral salts inhibit the growth of many plants. When applying supplementary nutrients to ageratums, azaleas, begonias, cactuses, cinerarias, impatiens, magnolias, polyanthus, streptocarpus, verbenas and viburnums, amongst others, the formulae used should be chosen from those with relatively low N:P:K levels, such as 15:15:15.

Proteas, banksias and other proteaceous plants, as well as Cape heaths and a number of other shrubs from the South African fynbos and West Australian kwongan, display extreme sensitivity to the presence of soluble phosphate. They should be provided with a formula such as 15:0:20, containing no phosphorus.

Homemade nutrient solutions

Proprietary feeds are unlikely to figure as costly items in plant production budgets, and the financial rewards of making your own are small. However, doing so adds flexibility when responding to the needs of different plants, contributes an extra dimension to the interest of growing plants, provides greater understanding of the responses of plants to nutrients, and leads to better, or more precise control, of growth and development.

Several of the compounds needed are widely available from garden centres; those that are not can be obtained from companies marketing horticultural sundries. The problem of weighing out small quantities of chemicals accurately can be avoided by using spoons to measure them out, based on the assumption that a slightly mounded dessert spoon (about 2 tsp. in North America) holds about 20 grams (0.75 ounce) and a tablespoon holds about 28 grams (1 ounce). (Note that different salts vary in density, and these approximations should be taken, appropriately enough, with a pinch of salt; they are accurate enough for practical purposes.)

Nutrient solutions for use when propagating plants

Recipes for three nutrient solutions are prescribed here. The first, composed simply of three chemicals, provides the essential trio of N, P and K and contains a supplementary feed for seedlings and a quick boost for recently rooted cuttings. The second recipe contains a full range of the nutrients needed to support plant growth and can be used to sustain growth and development of plants in containers, either as a foliar feed or in a nutrient solution when watering. The third recipe is for use with phosphate-shy species. In addition to proteas and Cape heaths, a number of widely grown temperate shrubs also suffer when grown in containers from a buildup of phosphates following repeated applications of nutrients. This solution should be substituted for the full nutrient solution for use on well-established shrubs in containers.

The measure used in the following is a slightly mounded dessert spoon (2 tsp., or about 20 grams), unless otherwise stated, in 20 litres (5 gal.) of rainwater. Dilute before use as follows: ×20 as a foliar feed; ×10 applied to pots containing young seedlings and salt-sensitive plants; ×5 applied to pots containing cuttings and growing plants.

Supplementary nutrient
Potassium nitrate: 1 (2 tsp.)
Urea: 1 (2 tsp.)
Potassium phosphate: 0.5 (1 tsp.)

General purpose complete nutrient
Potassium nitrate: 1 (2 tsp.)
Urea: 0.5 (1 tsp.)
Potassium phosphate: 0.5 (1 tsp.)
Calcium nitrate: 0.5 (1 tsp.)
Magnesium sulphate: 0.25 (0.5 tsp.)
Chelated iron: 0.25 (0.5 tsp.)

Phosphate-free nutrient
Potassium nitrate: 1.5 (3 tsp.)
Ammonium nitrate: 0.5 (1 tsp.)
Calcium nitrate: 0.5 (1 tsp.)
Magnesium sulphate: 0.25 (0.5 tsp.)
Fritted trace elements: 0.25 (0.5 tsp.)

Controlled release fertilisers

These fertilisers consist of soluble fertilisers enclosed in resin pellets. Nutrients are released through pores in the resin coating at varying rates, depending on the thickness of the coating, the size of the pores and soil temperatures. Different grades provide "lives" of three, six, twelve or more months before the nutrients in the pellets become exhausted. Nutrient release is not significantly affected by water saturation, pH values, microbial activity or the exchange capacity of the growth medium, but high soil temperatures or freezing adversely affect performance and rough handling when mixing growing media can damage the pellets. Plants grown on capillary watering systems or in loam-based mixes require reduced rates.

Controlled release fertilisers even out the supply of nutrients and avoid the high levels found in freshly made mixes based on orthodox nutrients, reducing damage to salt-sensitive plants. They minimise losses of nutrients by leaching and eliminate or reduce supplementary feeding as plants develop. On the other hand, they are expensive sources of nutrients compared to orthodox fertilisers.

Controlled release fertilisers suit those who grow large numbers of plants with similar requirements but are of limited value when growing small batches of plants with a variety of different needs, and they are generally unsuitable for use with plants that make most of their growth at low temperatures—such as bulbs from Mediterranea. Those who grow plants on a small scale will almost always find old-fashioned methods of feeding cheaper, more flexible and more practical.

Pests

Arsenic, cyanide, copper and nicotine, formerly prominent in the gardener's arsenal against pests and diseases, have been replaced by complex organic chemicals. The chemicals have changed, but the approach has not. Poisons continue to be used to treat the symptoms, while many gardeners pay little attention to underlying causes. Inevitably, the same troubles recur and when they do may be more virulent and difficult to control than on their first appearance—especially when using pesticides. All too often, these destroy beneficial predators even more effectively than their targets—the aphids and red spiders.

A sea change is taking place in our awareness of the world in which plants, insects, fungi and other organisms live and interact. Biological forms of pest and disease control are increasingly used when success depends on maintaining balanced environments in which predators and other agents can survive and work effectively. The extent and significance of symbiotic relationships between plants, fungi and bacteria, and the part they play in maintaining healthy plant growth, is becoming recognised. As a result, integrated biological approaches designed to support plants by sparing them unnecessary stress are gaining acceptance in place of sporadic offensives with poisonous chemicals.

Mankind has displayed its genius for claiming credit once again for inventing what Nature has been doing forever. Biological control may be a new concept to us, but it is nothing other than the balance through which predators and prey, diseases and hosts exist under natural conditions.

Simple and effective means of pest control and detection are provided by timely use of finger and thumb to squash incipient aphid colonies, caterpillars and vine weevils; torchlight excursions hunting for slugs, snails and caterpillars; search-and-destroy operations for leather jackets (crane flies), vine weevils and slugs and minor undesirables such as millipedes, woodlice (pill bugs) and ants, while repotting plants; and yellow sticky traps hung up above plants on benches in glasshouses to provide early warning of the arrival of aphids, whiteflies, and other insect pests. In very many situations, these are all that is necessary to keep plants free from pests and diseases in a propagation unit.

Soft and hard growth

Soft and *hard* are terms used by gardeners to describe the state of growth or condition of plants. Plants grown soft under opulent conditions are fulsome, with sappy, swollen stems and broad, dark green often glossy foliage, and they tend to develop foliage at the expense of flowers. Soft growth is encouraged by warmth and humidity, shelter from exposure, high nitrogen availability and ample water. Plants grown hard under an austere regime are wiry, with comparatively woody, slender stems and narrow, firm foliage with often light or mid-green leaves, and they tend to flower early. Hard growth results from low to moderate temperatures and humidity, ample ventilation, exposure to sunlight and wind, restrained watering regimes and high ratios of potassium to nitrogen.

A clear idea of the condition being aimed for when raising seedlings or growing on rooted cuttings is central to growing plants successfully. In spring and early summer, advantage can be taken of favourable conditions by growing plants slightly soft. As the time approaches to plant seedlings and cuttings out into the garden, they should be hardened to prepare them for the more austere conditions and the traumas of the move. In autumn, with hard times ahead, seedlings and cuttings grown hard have better prospects of surviving the winter, and during periods of adversity, including the winter in cold and cool temperate regions and summer in Mediterranea, young plants grown hard are less vulnerable and more likely to thrive than those grown soft.

Aphids

Winged aphids flying into glasshouses and cold frames in early spring are the forerunners of pioneering colonies. They can be controlled in several ways. Squashing colonies between finger and thumb as soon as they are noticed stirs up those that are not killed directly, many of which fail to reestablish themselves. Sprays of soapy water, repeated as necessary, can be beneficial. Biological control with parasitic insects—either the wasp *Aphidias matricariae* or a midge called *Aphidoletes aphidimyza*—should be released when temperatures reach 18°C (64°F) and before aphid colonies become well established. The parasites cannot be used effectively in the presence of insecticides of any sort. Ladybirds (ladybugs) and their larvae are effective aphid predators but are not widely available commercially—apart from North America, where they are easy to find at many garden centres. It may also be possible to introduce them from other parts of the garden.

Whiteflies

Whiteflies lay tiny eggs on the undersides of immature leaves, which hatch into small larvae. Established infestations are extremely difficult to eradicate, especially on fuchsias, daturas and other plants that the flies find particularly attractive. Control measures should start at the first sign of an incursion.

Biological control is possible with *Encarsia formosa*, a parasitic wasp. These lay eggs within the whitefly larvae (or scale) which turn black as the parasites develop within them. Although unlikely to eliminate whitefly completely, the wasps considerably reduce its numbers—provided night temperatures do not drop below 10°C (50°F) and daytime temperatures can be maintained at or above 18°C (64°F).

Whiteflies are controllable only in glasshouses, conservatories or other enclosed spaces, and the first signs of success should be detectable after a fortnight, with increasing proportions of dead, black whitefly larvae thereafter. The parasite persists, while whiteflies are present, only so long as favourable temperatures can be maintained. A fungal biological control, *Verticillium lecani*, also shows promise.

Sciarid flies or fungus midges (gnats)

These insects lay eggs immediately below the surface of the potting mix, with a particular preference for organic materials, especially peat. Their grublike larvae live on organic detritus, including plant roots. Established infestations are hard to control, but more or less effective methods include top dressing surfaces with a 0.5 cm (0.25 in.) deep layer of horticultural grit.

Use of the nematodes *Heterorhabditis* spp. and *Steinernema feltiae*, in the same way as for vine weevils (explained next), can offer some control. The nematodes should be applied when the surface is moist and in shaded, not brightly sunlit, conditions.

An alternative biological control is provided by a predatory mite, *Hypoaspis miles*, which feeds on a number of soil-dwelling pests, including other mites, enchytraeid worms and eelworms (roundworms).

Vine weevils

Vine weevils are seldom a problem with seedlings and cuttings but can cause serious losses amongst container-grown plants, later. Strong plant preferences include the roots of primulas, rhododendrons, skimmias, heucheras, begonias, vines and cyclamen.

Every vine weevil is female and capable of producing up to 1500 eggs before death intervenes. These develop without male participation of any kind. Eggs are laid in the soil and hatch into small, white C-shaped larvae that feed on roots. Adults cut semicircular "bites" out of the margins of leaves of mature plants that are unsightly rather than harmful and provide a warning of the presence of the insect.

Control measures include nocturnal search-and-destroy missions, which are seldom success-

ful because the weevils are expert at evading capture by dropping to the ground. Larvae can be destroyed by searching for them in spring in containers in which plants have overwintered.

Chlorpyrifos incorporated in potting mix as controlled release granules provides long-lasting, effective control and is present in many proprietary potting mixes. The chemical is stable and insoluble and does not migrate into untreated growth media when plants are potted on into larger containers. It has an active life of about two years. This broad-spectrum insecticide is also effective against sciarid flies, leather jackets, cutworms and root aphids, but it is extremely dangerous to fish and other aquatic life. Although an organic chemical, it has no organic credentials in the eyes of those dedicated to organic forms of gardening.

Biological control using nematodes, *Heterorhabditis* spp., is highly effective against larvae in containers and moderately so against those in nursery beds in the open ground at soil temperatures above 12°C (54°F), provided it is applied when the surface is moist. The nematodes are not usually persistent, and repeated applications may be necessary. Similarly, predatory nematodes occur naturally in some soils—but seldom in containers—and rarely in sufficient numbers to act as an effective control. Ground beetles eat vine weevil larvae and should always be encouraged, not destroyed.

Caterpillars

Caterpillars damage seedlings, especially in the autumn, and cuttings of tender perennials overwintering in glasshouses. Chewed leaves and deposits of frass, or excrement, reveal their presence. Caterpillars are nocturnal and hide under containers, amongst dead leaves or in the crowns of plants during the day. The most effective control measures include hand-picking and destruction at night—the damage is usually being done by only a few individuals.

Biological control with *Bacillus thuringiensis* is seldom justified on seedlings or cuttings unless plants are being propagated on a large scale and numerous caterpillars are present. The bacterium is sprayed on the leaves and eaten by the caterpillars, resulting in their death within a few hours. It is most effective on young larvae and unlikely to control leaf miners and stem borers or caterpillars that live in rolled-up leaves. Different strains of *B. thuringiensis* are used to control Colorado beetle, elm leaf beetle, sciarid and biting flies as well as caterpillars.

Mites

Red spider mites seriously affect young seedlings or cuttings only when growing conditions are poor. Overwintering cuttings, seedlings or stock plants are more at risk, especially in the warm, dry conditions found in many conservatories. Individual mites appear as minute, inactive dots, flushed with rusty, reddish tones and are hard to spot. Their presence become obvious when their webs visibly enshroud the surface of the plants on which they feed.

Humid conditions greatly reduce risks of infestations, but once established, the mites are hard to control. A predatory mite, *Phytoseiulus persimilis*, can provide effective control, but only when it is introduced at an early stage and only when temperatures exceed 10°C (50°F) for the greater part of each day.

Predator populations build up to effective levels quite slowly, and their effects may not become apparent for several weeks. Meanwhile, newly emerging foliage will be free of red spider. *Phytoseiulus* does not overwinter successfully in cool and cold temperate regions. Red spiders need to be reduced to the lowest possible levels before the onset of winter, and attempts to control them should be maintained late into the season. The mites congregate in inaccessible crevices and joints in woodwork during the autumn, where they overwinter, to emerge the following spring.

Red velvet mites are frequently mistaken for the red spider variety. They are readily visible, free moving, and clothed in sumptuous scarlet vestments. Far from damaging plants, these are predators, eating, amongst other undesirables, red spiders. They should be left alone.

Woodlice

Woodlice—also known as pill bugs, slaters, bibble bugs, sow bugs, cud worms, tiggy hogs, shoe laces, sink lice and coffin cutters—are viewed with suspicion by gardeners, no doubt because they are highly noticeable, hence, the abundance of colloquial names. They are capable of destroying small seedlings but prefer to dine on decaying plant material, and their attacks only occasionally cause damage to healthy green tissues.

Nematodes

Stem eelworms invade young seedlings or rooted cuttings in containers only when unsterilised materials are used or plants are grown in pots which have previously contained eelworm infested plants. Loams should always be pasteurised before being combined with other materials, and containers in which plants suspected of harbouring eelworms have been grown should be destroyed.

Propagation provides opportunities to eliminate eelworms from some infested plants by using root cuttings to propagate plants suffering from stem eelworm—such as phloxes—or by using tip cuttings from soft, rapidly grown plants—such as penstemons—to produce eelworm-free stocks.

Snails and slugs

In the robust conditions of an established garden, these creatures play vital roles in recycling nutrients from dead and dying plants, and outside the vegetable garden, despite the protests of hosta, delphinium and veratrum growers, they do little harm. In a propagating house, one can do irreparable damage to a tray of recently pricked out seedlings in the course of a single night. Few seedlings are capable of producing new buds after having their leaves nipped off—though a tiny minority, including linarias and linums, can develop buds on their hypocotyls from which replacement plants develop.

Damage is reduced or avoided by vigilance to detect the first signs of the presence of a snail or slug and catch the perpetrator before serious losses are suffered. The creatures can also be controlled by hand-picking on warm, humid nights or trapping them in saucers of beer.

Seedlings should be sown at times that encourage rapid growth to reduce the time they are at their most vulnerable, providing extra warmth and supplementary light. Hiding places for slugs and snails close to small seedlings should be eliminated and the area beneath containers in which seeds are sown should be treated to make them unattractive resting places for these creatures. Sharp grits are of little value by themselves; when sprayed with an aluminum salt or other liquid forms of deterrent they can be effective.

Avoid the use of slug pellets that are hazardous to other wildlife. Short-term benefits are outweighed by losses of ground beetles, frogs and toads, hedgehogs, carpet snakes, glow worms, birds and other natural predators.

Biological control is possible by encouraging the presence of natural predators and also the commercially available nematode *Phasmarhabditis hermaphrodita*, which is sprayed over the surface of benches and beds. This attacks all species of slugs, but few snails. It is most effective during warm, humid conditions in the evening, provided minimum temperatures do not fall below 5°C (40°F) and soil surfaces remain moist. Once *in situ*, the nematodes seem able to survive freezing temperatures and regain activity as temperatures rise. Activity drops off again as temperatures rise above approximately 20°C (70°F). One application remains effective for about six weeks.

Mammals

Rats, mice, gophers and voles eat seeds of many plants including cyclamen, scillas and grasses while still on the plant, and the first two pests can seriously reduce the prospects of successful weathering unless seeds are kept out of their reach. They eat bulbs and corms and graze the shoots of plants during the winter, with a particular fondness for clematis, dianthus and campanulas.

Plants in cold frames are at risk, especially when—as in the winter—they need little attention and can be left for long periods without being checked. Plants on benches in glasshouses are more regularly looked over, and damage should be spotted before it becomes serious. Traps provide a moderately effective answer, and cats are even more effective, but they can do more damage than mice unless they can be excluded from direct contact with plants. In some parts of the world, bulbs, fleshy rhizomes and tubers are regarded as essential items of diet by baboons, mole rats, squirrels and porcupines.

Phytoecdysones in ferns

With millions of years of ploy and counter ploy behind them in the struggle between plants and animals, ferns have developed chemical defenses against insects that even those Doctor Strangeloves in white coats who spend their lives devising ways of combating pests would acknowledge as cruelly inventive. Ferns produce small quantities of phytoecdysones—hormones resembling those that trigger "moulting" in insects. *Ecdysis* is the name given by scientists to the process by which animals shed their skins in the course of growth; most people would call it sloughing or stripping. As a result, insects feeding on them find themselves in a state of perpetual striptease, effectively preventing their growth and development. These hormones appear to be promising biological control agents for insects of all kinds but are not yet commercially available.

Diseases

Mildews, rusts, black spot of roses and many other fungal diseases that plague gardens are of little or no significance when plants are being propagated—apart from the obvious desirability of avoiding infected plant material when making cuttings. A small number of pathogens are more likely to cause problems.

Botrytis

Grey mould attacks dead plant material and other lifeless organic substrates as a rule, but it also invades living plant tissues that have been damaged or stressed. Its presence is almost always an indication of inattention to hygiene, neglect and/or poor growing conditions.

Sprays of Captan (banned in some countries) and other fungicides can be used, probably without much effect. By far the best protection stems from preventing or avoiding the conditions in which it flourishes in the following ways:

- By removing sources of infection, such as dead and dying leaves, especially amongst overwintering cuttings.
- By ensuring ample ventilation, particularly during overcast, muggy weather in the winter.
- By circulating air within a glasshouse, with a small (such as 15 watt) fan permanently switched on throughout the winter and spacing plants to enable air to circulate between them.
- By watering only on sunny days and early, so foliage dries out before nightfall.
- By providing supplementary illumination to reduce stress during short, dark days in high latitudes.

Pythium and *Rhizoctonia*

Several fungal organisms are responsible for disorders generally referred to under the heading "damping-off." They are prime causes of losses amongst young seedlings immediately after germination. Damping-off is encouraged by inappropriate growth media, poor growing conditions, crowded seedlings and lack of hygiene. Inappropriate growth media include those with low air-filled porosity that provide inadequate aeration or fail to drain freely. The system of sowing seeds described earlier (p. 79) avoids trouble from that source and greatly reduces risks from damping-off.

Damping-off can be greatly reduced by using free-draining, sterilised materials, organic or mineral, depending on the preferences of the plant; clean water; open patterns of seedling emergence; good growing conditions in the form of adequate warmth, high light levels, and plenty of ventilation; and timely pricking out.

Reducing losses from damping-off

Some species display strong preferences either for organic or for inorganic substrates. For example, seedlings of *Pseudotsuga menziesii* (Douglas fir) are likely to damp-off when sown on organic substrates but not on mineral, whereas the opposite applies to seedlings of *Tsuga heterophylla* (Western hemlock). Our understanding of such effects is based on empirical observations. No lists are available describing the preferences of different species, but it is likely they are much more widespread and significant than we realise.

Generally speaking, mineral substrates are favoured by pioneer species of trees and shrubs—especially those adapted to fire-dominated environments, including conifer forests and seasonally dry locations in California, South Africa and Australia. Organic substrates are favoured by climax species of evergreen broad-leaved and mixed forests and cool and cold temperate meadows and other situations in which seedlings grow up amongst established plants. When seedlings consistently damp-off in good growing conditions and despite efforts to prevent them doing so, it is worth considering changing from an organic to an inorganic substrate (or vice versa), at least for the topping used when sowing seeds and possibly for the base layer, too.

Persistent problems may be due to the presence of a source of infection in the water supply. Domestic water supplies are usually the safest source of water for small seedlings and for cuttings until they have produced roots. Rainwater stored in a tank is a likely source of infection unless the tank is emptied, dried out and cleaned regularly—or the water disinfected occasionally, using similar materials and methods to those used for swimming pools, followed by a period of several days for the oxidants used to disperse.

Like all living organisms, fungal spores and hyphae have natural enemies, and the growth and spread of damping-off fungi is restricted by certain bacteria. Open-structured, porous materials—including those derived from composted bark, garden waste and other organic residues—provide the well-aerated condition in which these bacteria thrive. They act like filter beds to form a bacterial matrix which destroys developing fungal hyphae. Sphagnum moss and immature sphagnum peat are said to have similar affects.

Seedlings growing at low light intensities and low temperatures suffer stress and fall easy prey to infection. Their reduced growth and transpiration rates, aggravated by low rates of evaporation from the surface, create conditions in which overwatering quickly leads to waterlogging—further increasing stress, while providing ideal conditions for the spread of the fungus.

In areas where winter days are short and light levels low, avoid early sowing whenever possible. A delay until mid- or even late spring minimises all these problems. Seedlings emerging during longer, lighter days are more likely to survive and grow so much faster they almost catch up with earlier sowings. When early sowing cannot be avoided, supplementary warmth and light are essential to support vigorous growth.

Alternative controls

Copper sulphate combined with ammonium carbonate provides an old and tried treatment for the control of damping-off diseases. The copper is intended to damp down the fungus, the ammonium to boost the seedlings—worth a try when seedlings are dying in spite of best efforts in other directions.

A biological control agent, the fungus *Trichoderma viride*, was originally developed as treatment for silver leaf in plums and has been used effectively to prevent the loss of seedlings from damping-off. It is available as pellets for inclusion in potting mixes and is also said to inhibit the growth of phytophthora.

Symbiotic associations between plants, bacteria and fungi

Mycorrhizal and bacterial associations with plants, once thought of as an unusual relationship applying to orchids, heathers, beech trees, alders, plants in the pea family and a few others, are now recognised as the norm. At least 85 percent of plants are now believed to form symbiotic associations with fungi, and almost all have relationships of some kind with bacteria. These associations improve uptake of nutrients—particularly nitrogen, which is obtained by fixing atmospheric nitrogen, and phosphorus—by making insoluble phosphates available. They also provide protection against pathogens and toxic soil substances and increase drought tolerance by greatly extending the effective root system.

Anyone who sows seeds of less usual plants—beyond the wide range available in colourful packets—encounters situations where seedlings emerge but then turn into ne'r-do-wells, hovering for a while between life and death. Some pull through; others decline and die, or spend so long hovering they become prey to slugs or snails. Their failure to thrive may be due to the absence of the fungal or bacterial partners on which the seedlings depend for healthy growth and development.

Four types of fungal associates are now recognised: *endomycorrhiza*, *ectomycorrhiza*, *ericoid mycorrhiza*, and *orchidaceous mycorrhiza*. The great majority, if not all, endomycorrhiza (arbuscular mycorrhiza) are members of a single family of fungi and have been identified in association with no less than 80 percent of the world's plants—including most tropical tree species, a wide range of temperate herbaceous plants and even some of the most ancient forms of plant life including liverworts and equisetums. They live inside cells in the roots of plants and do not produce toadstools, or fruiting bodies.

Ectomycorrhiza occur in association with many temperate woodland trees, including oaks, beeches, birches, pines, firs, spruces, willows and chestnuts. Dozens of different fungal species have been identified growing in association with a single tree species. They enclose the roots with sheaths of fungal hyphae and make contact by invading spaces between the cells, but they do not enter the cells themselves. In effect, they replace root hairs, and the roots become swollen and branch more freely than those not associated with fungi. Their conspicuous fruiting bodies include toadstools such as fly agarics, chanterelles, truffles, ceps and boletus. Endomycorrhizal and ectomycorrhizal associations may exist simultaneously in a single plant.

Ericoid mycorrhiza are specialists found in ericas and the Australian heaths known as epacrids. Their hyphae penetrate each cell independently, forming what look like spherical balls of wool under the microscope. They also occur in liverworts and are believed to act as intermediaries in the transfer of nutrients between liverworts and some flowering plants.

Rhizoctonia spp. are associated with orchids. They form associations within the cells of the seed, stimulating germination and supporting the plant nutritionally during early growth and later development.

Mycorrhizal associations are seldom crucially important when propagating plants—with the probable exception of orchids. However, plants of many kinds benefit from the opportunity to form these associations at an early stage in their development, and some widely used horticultural practices prevent this happening, including the routine use of fungicides, which can inhibit or completely prevent development of symbiotic relationships. Sterilisation at high temperatures can also prevent these associations. Pasteurisation at 60°C (140°F) is sufficient to reduce harmful organisms while leaving a proportion of beneficial organisms alive. Strict attention to hygiene during early seedling growth delays any symbiotic associations until the plant is eventually found a place in the garden—possibly with adverse effects on its prospects of establishing successfully (see the associated box).

Hygiene and cutting health—use of an innoculum

Hygiene in the potting shed is not an unmitigated virtue and can be overdone. Seedlings, like ourselves, need their peck of dirt from which they can form the alliances that provide them with the nutrients they require for healthy growth. Purists may throw up their hands in horror, but mixing an innoculum in the form of a small quantity of previously used growth media with the fresh when sowing or pricking out seedlings can contribute to the health of the plants. At the least, when seedlings stop growing, fail to thrive and begin to die, bear in mind that all they may be lacking is a little fungal or bacterial pick-me-up. Preparations containing mixtures of fungi thought to be appropriate to a wide range of plants are now available commercially but are probably no more effective than a handful of garden soil.

Bacterial disorders

Bacterial infections seldom cause serious problems when propagating plants—with the notable exception of black leg in pelargoniums and bacteria carried on the skin of the operator when growing orchids from seed asymbiotically (see p. 267).

Like fungi, bacteria also form symbiotic associations with plants, amongst them rhizobial bacteria found in nodules on the roots of legumes. Unlike the fungal symbionts described earlier, these are essential to the growth and development of their hosts, which are unable to assimilate nitrogen in their absence. Bacteria in the genus *Franklinia* are less familiar because they are less obvious, but they are more widely distributed amongst plants as widely different from one another as alders, ceanothus and coriarias.

Seeds and cuttings of shoots contain no friendly bacterial symbionts, and plants grown from them in sterile media cannot form the symbiotic relationships necessary for their healthy development, unless provided with a source. As with fungi, an innoculum consisting of a small quantity of unsterilised loam provides a source of bacteria and usually ensures that symbiotic relationships are established. Experimental studies consistently identify exclusive tie-ups between particular species of plant and particular strains of rhizobium, leading to fears that it might be difficult to provide an innoculum containing the right strain for a particular species—especially exotic species. In practice, this seldom causes problems, and a small amount of unsterilised

loam from almost any fertile loam richly endowed with organic matter—ideally from a long-established meadow—seems to do the trick.

Viruses

Seeds often, but not always, provide a means of raising virus-free plants. Cuttings, on the contrary, provide a notoriously effective way of spreading viruses. Knives are a frequent source of trouble. Viruses are picked up from an infected plant and then transferred to a healthy one and so on down the chain. Fingers, too, spread viruses, picking them up from cut surfaces and passing them on when we handle leaves of the next in line. Several widespread and potent viruses, such as tobacco mosaic, make themselves at home in

Plant disorders causing variegated effects in leaves

Chronic genetic instability caused by apparently random activation and inactivation of the genes responsible for producing particular pigments results in disorganised distributions of white, cream or coloured rays or blotches distributed haphazardly over the surface of the leaf. This tendency towards instability is sometimes genetically inherited, and seedlings—for example, *Lunaria annua*, *Barbarea vulgaris* and *Acer pseudoplatanus*—from parents with this type of variegation are also likely to be variegated.

Viral infections can also cause variegations. The leaves of plants infected with mosaic and vein-clearing viruses frequently display variegated patterns, giving rise to a widespread misconception that many, if not most, variegated plants in gardens owe their condition to the presence of viruses. That is a fallacy; most plants are so weakened by viral infections that they fail to survive. A minority, including *Lonicera japonica* 'Aureoreticulata' and cultivars of *Abutilon pictum* tolerate infections, though they grow less vigorously than their healthy counterparts. The variegated form is maintained in plants propagated from cuttings, but seedlings are unlikely to be variegated.

Air pockets develop spontaneously under the epidermis of the leaves of some plants as they unfold, producing the decorative silvery effects seen in forms of *Lamium maculatum* and *Pilea cadierei* (the aluminum plant) and the patterns on the foliage of *Silybum marianum* and species of *Pulmonaria*. The tendency to produce air pockets is inherited by seedlings, though their patterns and extent may differ from their parents. Cuttings of lamiums and divisions of pulmonarias retain their parents' patterns indefinitely.

Chimaeras cause the great majority of the variegations found in cultivated plants. A chimaera, in this sense, is an organism composed of two genetically distinct parts. Grafted and budded plants are examples of chimaeras composed of two distinctively different forms or varieties of the same, numerous different kinds of plants. By the end of an afternoon spent propagating this and that, both this and that—and a good many other things—may have been exposed to potentially disabling diseases.

The first precaution to take is the obvious one of avoiding diseased material as a source of cuttings, or, if there is a suspicion that viruses might be present, practicing forms of "barrier propagation" to avoid spreading the infection—for example, using disposable blades to make the cuttings and disposing of them afterwards. Lack of symptoms does not necessarily mean absence of viruses. Practical and effective routine precautions can be taken to reduce the chances of transferring disease. Blades can be sterilised between batches of cuttings using simple routines. A cigarette lighter or a small spirit lamp with a wick can be used to flame them—or, less conveniently, matches. Alcohol can be used to sterilise the blade after use; ideally, two blades are used, keeping one in alcohol (surgical spirit or gin) while the other is in use, and playing box and cox (taking turns). Viruses are not keen on gin, and used neat, it provides a readily available source of spirit.

Mosses and liverworts

Mosses and liverworts can grow luxuriantly on the surfaces of growth media, especially when germination is delayed. Their presence seriously reduces the chances of seedlings emerging successfully. Proprietary moss killers are not safe with young seedlings or cuttings, but measures that can be

---

or a closely related, species. Variegated leaves are chimaeras composed of tissues differing only in their ability to produce chlorophyll or some other plant pigment.

The more or less clearly defined zones of green, cream or white, sometimes crimson, on the leaves of chimaeras are due to the presence of tissues which are unable to produce chlorophyll or some other plant pigments, notably yellow flavones and sometimes crimson anthocyanins. These variegations are initiated when a single cell within the part of the apical meristem destined to form leaves suffers a genetic malfunction, which interrupts the processes leading to the formation of a pigment. Zonal patterns result because different parts of the meristem ultimately give rise to particular parts of the leaf.

Dicot leaves mostly develop from three layers in such a way that the loss of the ability to form chlorophyll by cells in the middle layer leads to the production of leaves with white margins round a green centre—a very common form of variegation. A similar loss of function by a cell in the inner layer produces leaves with white or cream centres, surrounded by a green border.

Monocot leaves are derived from two layers. The different form of their leaves and the ways they develop leads to the development of longitudinal stripes of different colours running the entire lengths of the leaves.

Conifer leaf tissues are less consistently linked to particular parts of the meristem. Entire shoots tend to develop needles lacking in chlorophyll—giving rise to stippling or patches of cream or white randomly distributed amongst the green.

Fern fronds lack structures linked to leaf areas and are not subject to chimaeras. A very few—notably *Athyrium niponicum* var. *pictum*—display patterned variations in foliage colour, but these are due to another form of genetic instability.

used safely include avoiding unnecessary use of fertilisers—for example, as the topping when sowing seeds or in the cutting mix when propagating plants from cuttings. The presence of nutrients stimulates the growth of mosses and liverworts and is better avoided.

Potassium permanganate solutions can be used to prevent the development of, or kill, mosses and liverworts once established. A very small bottle of crystals is sufficient for most purposes for many years. Dissolve a few crystals in rainwater—just sufficient to colour the water pale rose. Drench the surface of the bench or growth medium with the solution with a watering can fitted with a fine rose. Avoid watering for two days after the application. Mosses and liverworts usually shrivel and die within about 10 days. Early use of the solution will prevent establishment, and repeat treatments every two months throughout the summer will keep surfaces free from these invaders.

Chimaeras and Other Causes of Variegated Leaves

Tropical perennials and shrubs, including marantas, begonias, and crotons, often display colourfully marked foliage, as do some temperate plants, among them clovers, red-leaved dock, and *Geranium maculatum*. Variegations of this kind have no bearing on the difficulties or otherwise of propagating the plants; nor apart from the possibility of selecting for particularly vivid forms are any special precautions needed to maintain them. They are natural manifestations, displayed by normal, healthy leaves; but other forms of variegation—including those most widely grown by gardeners—are caused by a variety of plant disorders, as indicated in the box on pp. 114–115.

Cells having lost the ability to produce chlorophyll do not necessarily lose it forever. The genetic malfunction is quite frequently spontaneously reversed, resulting in the loss of variegation and reversion to plain green leaves. Cuttings or divisions produced from shoots with variegated foliage "inherit" the malfunctioning cells from their parents and reproduce similar patterns. However, shoots and leaves formed from root cuttings are derived from cells which contain the plant's basic genetic information—programmed to produce green leaves. They will produce variegated leaves only in the unlikely event that the genetic malfunction occurs independently in their cells. Similarly, seedlings do not inherit the condition, and variegations derived from chimaeras usually produce plain green offspring.

A few chimaeral variegations are inherited, not by genes carried in the nuclei, but by non-nuclear (cytoplasmic) material in plastids present in maternal tissues within the seed. When—as is the case with *Astrantia major* 'Sunningdale'—these tissues lack normal plastids, every seedling comes up with cream-coloured leaves containing a little flavone but no chlorophyll at all. They have no prospects of survival.

PART TWO

Ways to Propagate Plants of Different Kinds

Each chapter in Part Two deals with a particular group of plants, starting with bryophytes and pteridophytes, mosses and ferns, and from thence through gymnosperms to the flowering plants, grouped according to their growth forms— for example, annuals, perennials, shrubs, and trees.

The chapters are organised in two sections: The first section describes methods of propagation applicable to plants in the group in general, starting with propagation from seeds, then from cuttings, and then by division. The second section summarises methods of propagating different genera within the group. These summaries are presented in an extremely abbreviated form, and what follows here is a guide to the interpretation of the information contained in them. A typical entry appears as follows:

Hippophae—Dioecious. Succulent Fruit. **S.** fresh. **C.** semi-mature, mature, root. **D.** suckers.

This notation consists of the generic name followed by features of the plant of relevance when collecting seeds, and shorthand notation for propagation from seed (**S.**), propagation from cuttings (**C.**), and propagation from divisions (**D.**).

Features of relevance when collecting seeds include the following (note that very often only some or even a minority of species in the genus possess the feature listed):

Ballistic—some species produce seeds that are distributed ballistically when mature.

Dioecious—in some species, male and female flowers are produced on separate plants.

Liane—refers to genera in which some species are vines or climbers.

Parasite—some species are parasitic on other plants.

Recalcitrant—the seeds of some species are intolerant of desiccation and cannot be stored at subzero temperatures.

Serotinous—some species may retain mature seeds in persistent capsules, cones, or other containers until the tree or branch bearing them dies, for example, after fire.

Succulent Fruit—some species produce seeds surrounded by fleshy tissues which must be removed before storing or sowing seed.

Propagation from seed

S. fresh, spring; smoke, chip; viability variable. Commas are read as "or"; thus, sow fresh or in the spring. Seed with a recommendation to be sown fresh may need weathering before it will germinate.

Observations following semicolons describe possible treatments to improve germination rates, such as using smoke or chipping seed; treatments to improve seedling survival, such as an innoculum for species dependent on symbiotic relationships with bacteria and fungi; or a comment on viability ("variable" provides a warning of the possibility of high proportions of infertile seeds) or the likelihood of hybridisation with neighbouring species.

Propagation from cuttings

C. tip, semi-mature, mature, root, leaf. This indicates propagation from tip, semi-mature, mature, root, or leaf cuttings. Seasons of the year are not usually indicated because the times when cuttings are taken are defined by the condition of the shoots. Sometimes additional information is provided following a semicolon: "Sections," "Gouging," and other applicable terms refer to propagation of bulbs.

Propagation by division

D. layers, suckers. This indicates propagation from layers or suckers. When no method is entered, the plant is propagated from simple division of crowns. Seasons when perennials and grasses should be divided are indicated.

Definitions of Fruits

Fruits are frequently referred to in the summaries and elsewhere. The following provides a guide to the botanical names of fruits occurring in the text. Botanically speaking, many "seeds" are fruits, but when treated by gardeners as seeds, they are referred to as such throughout the book—unless the context demands a more precise approach.

Dry fruits

When the seeds ripen, they are released with no attached plant parts. Apart from separating them from associated bits and pieces of broken stems, leaves, and other materials, they require no other cleaning.

Fruits containing seeds

Capsules, such as poppies, heathers, rhododendrons, and paulownias, are many-seeded and split open to release seeds when ripe. Follicles, such as delphiniums and hakeas, are many-seeded and split open down one side to release ripe seeds. Pods (legumes), particularly members of the pea family, include beans, acacias, and brooms. These are few-seeded and split open down both sides to release seeds, often ballistically.

Seedlike fruits

Single-seeded fruits are enclosed within a horny or hard case or shell formed from the tissues of the carpel. Nuts include hazelnuts (enclosed by dry tissues) and walnuts (within a fleshy outer case). Almost all are recalcitrant and cannot be stored at subzero temperatures. In nutlets, such as geraniums and members of the mint family, each flower can produce up to four seeds. Achenes include potentillas, buttercups, lettuces and other members of the daisy family. Mericarps include the seeds of umbelliferous plants. Caryopses are the seeds of grasses.

Succulent fruits

Ripe seeds are surrounded by or closely attached to fleshy, sometimes leathery tissues which have to be removed before sowing or storing the seeds. Following is a list of succulent fruits: berries are produced by currants, fuchsias, and actinidias; drupes are produced by plums, dates, and olives and are single seeded, with stones surrounded by fleshy tissues; dry drupes are produced by pistacia and pterostyrax; drupelets are produced by raspberries; receptacles are produced by strawberries (the seeds on the surface are achenes), apples and many other members of the rose family in which the fleshy parts of the fruit are not derived from tissues which formed part of the ovule; and arils are produced by podocarps, yews, and euonymus, in which each seed is partially or completely enclosed by more or less fleshy tissues.

The Provinces of Mediterranea

The term *Mediterranea* is used as an inclusive name for locations in different parts of the world with a Mediterranean climate. It consists of the following regions.

The Mediterranean Basin

This is an area with an enormously rich flora, due to the diversity of locations often isolated one from another by seas and mountains. Species from this region display considerable frost hardiness—a quality which has enabled several of them to spread far afield as cornfield weeds. Many species extend north into southern Europe or east into Asia where cold winters are normal.

California and southern Oregon

This region covers a long, narrow strip between the Pacific Ocean and the mountains and deserts a short distance inland. The flora is less diverse than in the Mediterranean Basin, and the region has contributed correspondingly fewer plants to gardens. Nevertheless, many species are able to survive and play a valuable part in gardens with considerably more severe climates.

Western Australia

This comparatively small, relatively low-lying area in the southwestern corner of Australia is isolated by ocean or arid bush from other parts of the country. The winter climate is mild and few species are frost tolerant. Annuals grow on well-drained soils and are susceptible to waterlogged or poorly aerated soils. The climates of maritime South Australia and northern Tasmania are also markedly Mediterranean.

South Africa

Truly Mediterranean conditions are confined to a small area north and east of the Cape of Good Hope, but they extend in a modified form north into Namaqualand. Many species are intolerant of poorly drained, badly aerated soil but capable of surviving several degrees of frost.

Chile

This smallest region occupies an area in the centre of the country around Santiago from the coastal ranges beside the Pacific Ocean to the foothills of the Andes. A comparatively small number of annuals and shrubs from this part of the world are widely used in gardens. None tolerate more than occasional exposure to light frosts.

CHAPTER 7

Mosses and Ferns

There is much to be said for starting at the beginning, especially when it is a beginning almost ignored by most gardeners: algae, lichens, mosses, liverworts, clubmosses, horsetails and ferns—a roll call encompassing hundreds of millions of years of plant development and tens of thousands of different plants of which only a very few mosses and clubmosses and a minority of ferns are likely to make intended appearances in our gardens. Algae are nearly always unwelcome; lichens are regarded with lukewarm interest for their textures, strange forms and colours, and apparent harmlessness; mosses are sometimes welcomed, more often regarded with suspicion or hostility; liverworts are practically never welcomed; clubmosses are loved by a few; horsetails are detested by almost everyone; and ferns are valued and treasured by some, almost disregarded by most.

Each group includes plants that could be used much more in gardens than they are at present. But before we can explore their almost untapped possibilities, we need to find out more about them. How do they reproduce naturally? How can we propagate them? Where do they grow naturally? How can we use them in gardens? Are they tolerant of frost, drought and other garden hazards? What are the secrets to growing them successfully?

Sex and water are the twin springs on which these plants depend. Nothing new there—the same could be said for almost all plants, indeed for almost all living organisms. But the sexual arrangements of the plants featured in this chapter differ fundamentally from those of the flowering plants—in ways that vitally effect their reproductive processes and the ways they are propagated. Water plays the familiar roles of sustaining tissues, transporting nutrients and metabolites from one part of the plant to another and participation in chemical reactions. It also plays a part in matchmaking between male and female cells fundamentally different from the familiar story of pollen and ovules in the flowering plants.

Mosses, ferns and the rest do not produce seeds, but spores. The same difference, one might think, but not so! Spores are mobile and, like seeds, enable the plants to move around, but they are not the end product of any sexual process. A spore is a fragment, a single cell of the plant that produces it, with exactly the same genetic constitution; spores provide for mobility but they do not provide for sex. That comes later.

When spores settle in the right conditions—basically in moist situations—they germinate, but unlike seedlings, the spores of clubmosses, horsetails and ferns grow into plants quite unlike their parents. They are flattened or cylindrical, green or greenish, slightly succulent, leafless, and small. They are unremarkable, easily overlooked, short-lived, and referred to as *prothalli*, the plural of *prothallus*. As a prothallus matures, it develops sexual organs, which produce either small, mobile male cells (equivalent to pollen) or larger, immobile female cells (equivalent to ovules). Then water plays its vital part. The only way male cells can reach and fertilise the females is by moving through a film of water. After fertilisation, the ovules develop into small plants, equivalent to seedlings. They grow into the spore-bearing plants that we recognise as ferns, horsetails, clubmosses, and the like.

In the course of a complete life cycle from spore to spore, the plant exists in two distinctively different forms—a phenomenon known as alternation of generations. (The term *alternation of generations* is misleading, since a complete life cycle, comprising the two different forms of the plant, represents a single generation. It would reflect the situation more accurately to refer to *alternation of half-generations*.) The sexual form—represented by the prothallus, which develops from a spore—produces the male and female cells (or gametes) and provides for sex. The asexual form—represented by the ferns, liverworts and horsetails we all know and which grow from fertilised ovules—produce spores and provide for mobility.

Lichens

The propagation of lichens is a non-event in the gardening world. These complex, still mysterious plants formed from alliances between algae and fungi—usually with an algal core surrounded by fungal filaments—can be encouraged to grow on rocks, timber, and other surfaces, and many are extremely decorative. They are seldom, if ever, deliberately cultivated. The fungal partners produce spores in ascocarps—sometimes rarely as in the so-called reindeer mosses, and sometimes abundantly and regularly, as in the closely related goblet lichens (*Cladonia* spp.), in which the cup-shaped goblets are the ascocarps. The fungus depends on finding an algal partner before it can reproduce, but the processes involved are largely obscure and certainly not within the scope of gardening.

Some of the more loosely constructed lichens can be propagated vegetatively by detaching fragments and relocating them on suitable substrates—rocks, wood, or tiles. The lichen flora of the British Isles alone is more or less equivalent in numbers of species to that of the native flowering plants—worldwide the group offers vast opportunities for imaginative exploration.

Mosses

Another 1000 or more mosses and liverworts are found in the British flora—few with widely used vernacular names—a situation that is repeated with emphasis elsewhere, notably in the coniferous rainforests of the Pacific Northwest in the United States, the fjordlands of New Zealand and Chile, and the temperate rainforests of Ussuriland in the Russian Far East. Mosses and to a lesser extent liverworts introduce textures, shapes and effects not provided by other plants grown in gardens, but the opportunities they offer have scarcely begun to be explored—with the partial exception of gardens in Japan.

Mosses have neither vascular systems nor roots, and they anchor themselves with short rhizoids that cling to almost anything grippable without penetrating the surface. Both the sexual and asexual half-generations are represented by the plants familiar to us as mosses—there are no structures similar to the prothalli of the other groups. Male and female organs, often minute, are produced amongst the filaments of moss, sometimes close together on the same plant or, in the case of dioecious species, on separate plants. Male cells are attracted to females by chemicals akin to pheromones and depend on films of water to reach and fertilise the ovules. Capsules, developing from the fertilised ovules and filled with spores, are the sole visible manifestation of these plants' sexual existence.

Figure 26. Mosses and lichens growing wild in Chile under conditions where other plants cannot thrive create effects other plants cannot achieve. A lesson for gardeners?

Propagation from spores

The spores of some mosses are produced regularly in capsules held clear above the clumps of filaments and are easily obtained as they mature. Many other mosses produce spores only occasionally and erratically, and harvesting them may be a problem. Mosses can be raised from spores, either systematically using methods similar to those described below for growing ferns from spores, or informally, taking potluck by providing lodging places for wild spores.

For several hundred million years, mosses have been progressively squeezed out of all the better niches by a succession of "improved" plants—ferns and clubmosses, cycads and conifers, and eventually flowering plants. By and large, mosses survived by finding ways to live in situations other kinds of plants did not covet. As a result, mosses can grow in gardens where other plants cannot, achieving effects other plants cannot provide. If the moss you want to grow—and you do not need to know its name, just observe where you find it—grows on clay tiles on a roof, give it tiles. If it grows on bricks, give it bricks. If you find one growing on leaf mould in woods in dry places and another in permanently wet situations, provide leaf mould

and periods of drought for one and leaf mould and constant moisture for the other. If stones are its preference, provide it with stones—limestone for some, and granite for others—basic or acidic according to their natural tastes. Bogs should be provided for mosses that grow in bogs and bark for those that prefer bark.

The feature common to all is the need for consistent moisture for a period while the spores germinate and develop into established plants, almost invariably aided by shade to alleviate the desiccating effects of sunlight. Any surface to be clothed in mosses should be kept as constantly moist as is practicable; lightly or moderately shaded, depending on the time of year and the strength of the sun; and fertilised by additions of nutrients—for example, organic materials such as yoghourt or animal manures are often favoured, but watering with dilute nutrient solutions derived from salts is just as effective. Mosses are most likely to establish themselves successfully when surfaces are made ready to receive them between late summer and mid-autumn—with the prospects of a sustained period of moist conditions ahead—to encourage the germination of spores and the establishment of young plants.

Shaded situations beneath trees are notoriously "difficult" sites in gardens where, apart from ferns, relatively few recognised garden plants flourish. Mosses colonise these places spontaneously, provided the ground is first cleared by killing competing plants using sprays of glyphosate or paraquat. Subsequently, repeated applications of these herbicides are used to prevent other plants taking over, without harming the mosses.

The preferences of different species crucially affect prospects of success when trying to establish particular kinds. For example, lightly shaded situations drying out in summer are attractive to polytrichums, racomitriums and homalotheciums. Partially sunlit sites that remain moist attract calliergonellas and aulacomniums. Heavily shaded situations, moist in winter and dry in summer, provide homes for brachytheciums amongst others.

Propagation from cuttings

Mosses can be propagated from detached fragments, much as flowering plants can be propagated from cuttings. Unlike roots, their rhizoids do not penetrate substrates, and they need to be provided with a substrate capable of supporting them and holding together when moved. Choose one based on observations of the situations in which the plants grow naturally—for example, grit, peat, leaf mould, or composted or ground bark.

- Fill a seed tray or propagator to within 1.5 cm (0.5 in.) of the rim with the substrate.
- Cover with a single layer of fine, open mesh cotton or nylon net or stocking.
- Cover with a triple layer of absorbent paper—such as paper towel—and pour boiling water over it.
- Repeat three times to kill wild spores of mosses, liverworts, ferns, and other undesirables.
- Place a transparent plastic top over the tray while the cuttings are prepared.
- Cuttings are made from drought-tolerant mosses by rubbing clumps lightly between the palms of the hands. For non–drought-tolerant mosses, cut off the green filaments just above the soil level with scissors, or chop handfuls coarsely with a knife.
- Remove the lid of the propagator, peel off the paper towel, and sprinkle the fragments of moss over the exposed nylon net.
- Water thoroughly with clean rainwater or tap water containing half-strength nutrient feed (water-soluble fertiliser).
- Replace the tray lid.
- Place the seed tray or propagator in a cool, shaded situation—such as a north-facing cold frame or beneath the bench of an unheated greenhouse.
- Maintain constantly shaded humid conditions, watering whenever necessary, until growth resumes.

Cuttings taken in early autumn remain in their propagators throughout the winter with minimum care. Supplementary warmth is not usually necessary, but just enough to prevent the substrate from freezing is beneficial in places with very cold winters.

Propagation by division

Mosses are most easily propagated by pulling clumps apart and placing them on the surface of prepared weed-free ground. They must then be kept constantly moist until they reestablish themselves, which may take several months with some species. Divisions should consist of clumps not less than 4 to 6 cm (1.5 to 2.5 in.) in diameter. Autumn is the best season, and, except in perennially moist situations, dividing in spring, with the prospect of hot, dry weather ahead during summer should be avoided. Polytrichums, the mosses most widely used in Japanese gardens, respond particularly well to division.

Liverworts

Liverworts lack appeal to those familiar only with those that grow in the form of flat, lobed plates of green tissue—although a few of the more vigorous of these create interesting effects in more or less permanently wet situations. Familiarity with those species that more closely resemble mosses in the way they grow would revise unfavourable opinions of these plants. They are natural providers of deep, heavily textured, ground-covering carpets with obvious potential in gardens in mild and warm temperate regions.

Liverworts, like mosses, lack vascular systems and roots. They anchor themselves with rhizoids. We know the sexual "generation" as the plants familiar to us as liverworts. These produce male and female organs in conspicuous cup-shaped depressions on the surface, from which male cells swim in a film of water to fertilise the ovules. The asexual "generation" grows out of the fertilised ovules and develops into conspicuous spore-bearing organs resembling tiny umbrellas.

Some mosses worth a place in the garden

Plants are not usually described in this book, but most gardeners are so unfamiliar with mosses that a few species or genera are briefly described here as introductions to these plants.

Ceratodon spp. are tolerant of the most attenuated, least fertile, most subject to drought pollution and frost situations in many parts of the world. A useful rather than decorative ground cover most of the year, its reddish-brown, mahogany or russet-crimson seed capsules transform the mundane into carpets of colour in spring.

Climacium dendroides is widely distributed on damp ground in woodlands amongst grasses and even in low-lying, dampish places amongst sand dunes. Clusters of stems resemble miniature tree ferns. It scarcely ever produces spores in Britain.

Dicranella spp. are found in open woodlands and in sunlit pioneering situations on acidic soils in Eurasia and North America. These elegant, long-needled, clump-forming mosses always attract attention and are easily propagated by division of established clumps.

Dicranum spp. are perennially bright green, spiky tufts that spread slowly into flattened pillows. They are characterful, unmissable contributors to any situation in which mosses can play their part, equally at home on rocks, decaying tree stumps and the ground, as long as it is acid. The tips of the branches break off to form tiny "shuttlecocks" that produce rhizoids spontaneously, making them naturally predisposed to produce plants from cuttings.

Homalothecium spp. are easily grown, drought-tolerant species, common on hard ground, bases of trees and rocks where they form thick mats of golden or yellow-tinged, silky-textured foliage.

Hypnum spp. form dense mats of branching whipcord stems covered with scaly leaves on acidic rocks, stones, ground and tree stumps.

Class Psilotopsida

Species of *Psilotum* and *Tmesipteris* are the simplest vascular plants extant—conferring a botanical interest unmatched by any obvious garden qualities, and their claims for attention by gardeners are vanishingly elusive. They lack roots but possess a subterranean rhizome and a stem—both structurally very similar. Spirally arranged scale-like appendages on the stems function as leaves in species of *Psilotum*; similar but more leaflike organs serve for species of *Tmesipteris*, and in close encounters they resemble open-textured "leafy" mosses.

Horsetails

Once one of the dominant forms of plant life, horsetails are now reduced to fewer than 25 species distributed throughout the world, with the exception of Australasia and Antarctica, all in the genus *Equisetum*.

The sexual "generation," extremely rarely encountered, consists of inconspicuous branching or lobed prothalli. These are dioecious, and fertilisation is possible only when males and females grow close together—a proximity achieved by releasing the spores in small groups that drift away, clinging together, and germinate to produce clusters of prothalli. The asexual "generation" is represented by the familiar plants with well-developed vascular tissues and whorls of soft linear leaves on jointed

Mnium spp., *sens. lat.*, are dioecious, mat-forming, woodland mosses with fresh green fronds found on rotting wood and humus-rich substrates.

Plagiothecium spp. are robust carpeting mosses with flattened shoots formed by scalelike leaves closely pressed along the stems. They are broadly tolerant and at home, once established, in shaded and relatively open situations on acid soils. They make excellent ground cover beneath ferns.

Polytrichum spp. are dioecious, exceptionally dark green mosses. They spread steadily, once established, and are extremely persistent, drought-tolerant and easily grown in gardens in a broad range of different conditions. They are amongst the few mosses with conspicuous sexual organs in which male spores are produced amongst congested rosettes of tan-coloured or orange leaves.

Sphagnum spp. grow naturally in bogs as congested masses of foliage, often with distinctive crimson tones. They are easily propagated from coarsely cut sections in constantly saturated conditions.

Racomitrium spp. are mat-forming, drought-tolerant and amenable to a wide range of conditions in gardens. Ultra "mossy" mosses, some are adapted to permanently moist, waterside situations and others grow on the exposure and testing conditions of mountain tops.

Rhytidiadelphus spp. are often associated with grasses and a pest to those who cherish their lawns; some are spiky, and others have whipcord shoots formed from flattened, adpressed scales. They establish easily and spread moderately rapidly, and they are capable of quickly forming moss swards in shaded situations on poorly aerated soils where grass fails to form an acceptable lawn, simply by spraying out the grass with paraquat and concentrating on the moss. Several species develop attractive crimson shades in drought or spontaneously in the absence of stress.

Thuidium spp. are exceptionally feathery mosses; abundant on damp ground, rotting wood and wet rocks, they seldom produce fruiting capsules.

stems, growing from vigorous, deep-set subterranean rhizomes. Spores are produced in conelike structures at the tops of fertile shoots.

Many horsetails are handsome plants with distinctive forms capable of providing strikingly attractive effects in gardens; amongst them are *Equisetum palustre,* with distinctive, pale cones, or *E. myriochaetum,* a tender species with bright green, jointed stems, 5 metres (15 ft.) tall, in closely packed array, and resembling a most desirable, exotic looking bamboo. The vigorous subterranean rhizomes have conferred such rampageously tenacious reputations on their plants that most gardeners would not dream of planting them in their gardens.

Rashly optimistic gardeners with a spirit of adventure able to persuade themselves they have suitable situations for these plants can propagate them by division—digging down and cutting off sections of rhizome from plants growing in established colonies. A few species, including *Equisetum arvense* and *E. telmateia,* can be propagated from tubers formed in the autumn by enlargement of internodal sections of the rhizomes.

Clubmosses

Some 700 selaginellas and between 400 and 500 lycopodiums account for the vast majority of clubmosses. Most are tender subtropical or tropical plants and play extremely minor roles in cool or cold temperate regions, apart from providing lush, green settings for other plants in conserva-

Figure 27. Cones of the asexual "generation" of a horsetail (*Equisetum* sp.) composed of sporangia contained in sori massed at the tips of the shoots. Spores released in groups from the sporangia settle on the ground, where a minute proportion develop into subterranean, dioecious prothalli.

Figure 28. Clubmoss (*Lycopodium* sp.) growing amongst shrubs in New Zealand.

tories, where their presence helps maintain high atmospheric humidities.

However, *Lycopodium anotinum* from the mixed rainforests of Ussuriland, the very similar *L. clavatum* as well as *Selaginella helvetica* and the bog-loving *S. selaginoides* are sufficiently hardy to grow in gardens in colder parts of the world. The plants have considerable undeveloped potential in gardens in warm, moist situations where their resemblance to mosses on steroids make them excellent providers of luxuriant ground-carpeting greenery.

The seldom seen sexual "generation" comprises small, often subterranean prothalli usually growing in symbiotic relationships with fungi. Ovules may remain subterranean for some years after fertilisation before developing above ground. The asexual "generation"—the plants that gardeners grow—possess developed vascular systems capable during the Carboniferous Era of forming the trees that dominated the forests of the coal measures. Spores are produced in sporangia, sited

in axils of the leaves in selaginellas, and in cones at the tips of branches of lycopodiums.

Propagation from spores

Small, usually subterranean, unisexual prothalli, which may remain underground for a year or two before producing embryos, grow from the spores. Not surprisingly, few if any gardeners attempt to propagate clubmosses in this way. For those who want to make the attempt, the rich, cinnamon-red spores of *Selaginella helvetica* are easily collected and reasonably amenable; nevertheless, division provides a much faster and easier route to the same result.

Figure 29. *Lycopodium* sp. growing in Ussuriland, showing the cones produced by the asexual "generation" in which the spores are formed. After settling, the spores develop into prothalli, often below the surface, which form symbiotic relationships with fungi.

Propagation from cuttings

Lycopodiums produce dense, leafy growths resembling giant, ferny mosses. Cuttings of most of the widely cultivated species made from 3 to 5 cm (1 to 2 in.) sections, stuck into sandy cutting mix, and placed in a humid, shaded situation preferably with mist, produce roots within seven to ten days. Others can take longer to produce roots and some are reluctant to do so at all. Alternatively, mature fronds are cut into small sections 1 to 2 cm (0.25 to 1 in.) long and scattered over the surface before sifting just sufficient grit over them to hold them down. They are pricked out when roots form.

Selaginellas have a more open, rangy form of growth—sometimes markedly so. They are propagated from cuttings like lycopodiums, usually with much higher success rates.

Propagation by division

Divisions of lycopodiums and selaginellas are produced by cutting off ready-rooted sections. The former tend to produce roots sparsely and results are often disappointing, in striking contrast to the ease with which their cousins the selaginellas can be propagated in this way. Lycopodiums are encouraged to produce rooted sections more freely by layering them on sphagnum moss. Roots can be encouraged in two ways.

In the first method,

- Fill a pan or pot with sphagnum moss to the rim, pressing down well.
- Place alongside a lycopodium plant in a container of similar height.
- Draw down shoots and peg them to the surface of the moss with wire hoops.
- Water thoroughly.
- When roots form, cut off the shoots and pot up individually.

In the second method,

- Pack a handful of sphagnum moss tightly around the base of the plant, making sure it fills spaces between shoots.
- Pack more moss round and hold it in place with a belt of polypropylene twine.
- Water thoroughly.
- Two or three months later, loosen the belt.
- Gently remove the moss; cut off shoots with roots and pot them up individually.

Even when they have already developed roots, lycopodiums take some time to establish and need warmth, high humidity and careful watering while they do so.

Ferns

Ferns are more likely to be seen in gardens than the previous subjects of this chapter, but a well-stocked garden centre is unlikely to offer more than half a dozen species and forms, and even specialist sources offer only a tiny proportion of the variety available. The potential choice is so enormous that a collection consisting of none other than those in the four genera—*Asplenium, Polystichum, Dryopteris* and *Athyrium*—could draw on a pool of more than 1000 species. Many are tender, but a more than ample sufficiency is capable of growing in temperate gardens, supplemented by numerous—sometimes it seems endless—hybrids and forms. The greatest single impediment to their more extended use in gardens lies in the long and often forbiddingly complex Latin names with which they are burdened.

The fern's life cycle—including the vulnerable stage as a prothallus and the relatively inefficient provision for gene exchange—appears to confer fewer prospects for survival than corresponding arrangements developed by higher plants. But in one respect, ferns seem to have the edge. Higher plants reproduce from seeds produced by sexual processes involving exchange and recombination of genes. Each generation relies, therefore, on new, untested genotypes. Fern spores share the genetic constitution of their parents, and each spore possesses a genotype which has already proved itself. Sexual processes and genetic recombinations follow only after the prothallus has found itself a niche.

The sexual "generation" is represented by a small, often more or less heart-shaped prothallus, which produces male and female cells in small cup-shaped depressions on its lower surface. The asexual "generation" develops from fertilised ovules to form the large, conspicuous plants we know as ferns. Spores are produced in sporangia, spore-bearing structures located in pits known as sori on the surface of the fronds, covered with a lid called the indusium.

Many garden ferns are specially selected forms, often originally found growing in the wild. Some produce crested fronds and others are pleated, some divide repeatedly and others are arranged as fans or cock's combs.

The spores of ferns are produced by processes which make relatively ineffective arrangements for ensuring gene exchange during fertilisation. Consequently, while only a minority exactly reproduce their parents' characteristics, many will do so to some extent, with results that make it worth propagating selected forms from spores.

Fern spores

Some hybrids and cultivated forms produce few or no spores, but most ferns produce almost unimaginable numbers. Spore-bearing structures may be found in ranks of more or less circular sori on the undersides of the fronds. Green or olive green when immature, the indusia turn brown as they dry out and split open or peel back to expose the sporangia and release the spores. Genera producing spores in this way include *Dryopteris*, *Athyrium*, *Cyathea*, *Polystichum* and *Nephrolepis*. Cultivated forms of the last produce fertile spores so rarely they play no significant part in its propagation. Structures may also be found in parallel longitudinal fissures running at a slight angle to the midribs on the undersides of the fronds, characteristic of *Asplenium scolopendrium*, and in pockets along the margins of the fronds, formed by the rolled over margin of the fronds—as in *Adiantum* spp. Structures may also be found on modified fertile fronds. Unlike the sterile leaflike fronds, these develop into branched or columnar "twiggy" structures covered with dense masses of greenish, dark brown or mahogany sori—examples are *Blechnum*, *Matteuccia*, *Onoclea* and *Osmunda*. (The fertile fronds of some species of *Osmunda*, such as *O. cinnamomea*, combine normal leafy fronds with densely clustered masses of sori.)

Most spores mature and are dispersed in late summer and autumn, but some, including species of *Onoclea* and *Matteuccia*, overwinter *in situ* and mature the following spring.

Collecting fern spores

Spores are ready to collect as the sporangia mature—usually turning brown and slightly ragged in the process.

- Cut off the fronds, preferably early in the morning on cloudy, even humid days, when spores are less likely to blow around and contaminate other collections.
- Bring them into a dry, well-ventilated, but not draughty room.

- Lay each frond on a sheet of smooth, white, lightweight card stock or heavy paper, holding the stalk in place with a strip of masking tape.
- Place a second sheet of card over the frond to make it lie flat, guard against disturbance by sudden draughts and prevent contamination with extraneous fern, moss or liverwort spores.
- Spores are released from sporangia within the sori, dropping onto the lower sheet of card, where they form a shadowy imprint of the frond.
- Lift off the dried fronds and collect the spores by gently folding the card or paper to form a crease down its centre.
- Hold the folded card upright and tap it sharply several times to congregate the spores along the crease.
- Pour the spores into small, securely sealed envelopes, glass tubes or other appropriate containers.

If spores fail to appear within about a week, the fronds have been cut too early or too late, after all the spores have been shed. There is no point in keeping them longer. (Note that *Osmunda regalis* spores are produced on branched fertile fronds and released while still green—marked by a slight increase in the granularity of the sori as they mature. By the time the fertile fronds go brown, the spores have been lost.)

Spores are tiny, dustlike, and individually barely visible. The samples collected are likely to include the scaly coverings of the indusia. These are relatively large and easily discernible. Samples should be checked using a magnifying glass to make sure they do not consist exclusively of indusia, which tend to be light brown, rusty coloured and comparatively large. Spores are likely to be dark brown or black, or distinctly colourful. *Osmunda* spores are sage green or cinnamon, polypodiums are yellow, some tree ferns are ochre yellow, *Blechnum discolor* are donkey brown, and *Polystichum munitum* are a rich, chestnut brown.

Storing spores

Spores that are not sown soon after collection should be stored in an airtight box over silica gel. Most fern spores, including those of tree ferns, remain viable for several months at least and many for a year or two if kept dry at room temperature. They can be stored for much longer periods when treated in the same way as orthodox seeds—see pp. 34–35.

The spores of a few ferns, notably species of *Osmunda*, are recalcitrant. They lose their viability within a week or two and should always be sown as soon as possible after collection.

Propagation by sowing spores

It is not difficult—just different—to raise ferns from spores. The system described here is simple, effective and undemanding.

Spores which ripen during late summer and into autumn are most conveniently sown soon after collection, because the prothallial stages leading to the appearance of small ferns will then be completed during the winter, provided they are kept at 10° to 20°C (50° to 70°F). Fernlets will be large enough to prick out by spring, and young plants grow on during the summer. They are then ready to plant in the garden the following autumn or can be overwintered in a frame or cold glasshouse until spring.

Success depends on three essentials:

- Consistently moist, cool, shaded conditions must be maintained after sowing throughout the development of the prothalli, until tiny fern plants have appeared and become independently established.
- Competition from mosses and liverworts must be prevented. These play the part of weeds and can swamp prothalli and young fern plants.
- Recognise the unhurried nature of ferns. The processes that lead from spores to young plants take months to complete—a year or more for some species. Techniques and equipment must work effectively over longer periods

than those usually involved when growing flowering plants from seed.

The growing medium

The objective is to provide a water absorbing, consistently moist but not waterlogged substrate through which oxygen diffuses freely. Dense organic materials, such as fine peat, sand or composted bark, settle over time and may become so compact that the fine, threadlike rhizoids of some species of *Polystichum* and *Dryopteris* cannot penetrate them. Ferns with more vigorous rhizoids, including species of *Adiantum* and *Athyrium,* are less likely to suffer.

Mineral substrates applied as a 1.5 cm (0.75 in.) deep layer—provided, like calcined clay or perlite, they absorb water—are excellent physical conditions for many species. Acid substrates are preferred by most ferns and essential for some, including *Blechnum spicant, Cryptogramma crispa, Oreopteris limbosperma, Dryopteris cristata* and *Thelypteris palustris*. Base-rich (alkaline) substrates are preferred by a minority—amongst them *Phyllitis scolopendrium, Gymnocarpium robertianum* and some spleenworts, notably *Asplenium viride*. These benefit from additions of ground limestone or tufa to mineral substrates.

Containers

Sow spores in 7 cm (2.5 in.) square pots, placed in transparent or translucent plastic boxes with self-sealing lids—such as a cake box or food storage box—with 2 cm (1 in.) of boiled, cooled water in the bottom of the box. New pots reduce risks of contamination with spores of mosses and liverworts. Fill the pots with substrate, lightly pressed down to form a level surface. Replace the lids of the plastic boxes to ensure a constantly saturated atmosphere. They should not be opened again until the prothalli are well developed.

Hygiene

Kill weed spores on the substrate surface before sowing fern spores by scalding the surface with boiling water.

- Fold paper towels into pads just large enough to fit within the rims of the pots and lay them over the surface of the substrate.
- Pour boiling water from a kettle onto the pads of paper, and allow it drain.
- Repeat the scalding water treatment at least three and preferably five times.
- Place the scalded pots in the containers, without removing the paper pads, and replace the lids till ready to sow the spores.
- Write out labels before sowing and immerse them in boiling water or a dilute solution of kitchen bleach to kill any weed spores.

Sowing spores

Sow spores in the following way:

- Remove a pot from the plastic box, replacing the lid.
- Peel off the pad of paper towel just before sowing the spores, and throw it away.
- Put the appropriate label in place.
- Scatter a pinch of spores over the surface of the substrate as evenly as possible and moderately thickly. The tip of a table knife is an ideal tool for this purpose and can be wiped clean after each batch of spores. Avoid sowing too thickly, which is the usual tendency. Spores are so tiny they reveal little of their distribution, and mere mortals can be expected to do no more than their best in this direction. The relatively large indusia are more easily seen and may provide a guide.
- Put the pot back into the container; take out another and repeat.
- When all have been done, replace the lid of the box, making sure it is securely sealed round the edges.

Location

Aim to maintain a consistently humid atmosphere from the time spores are sown until young ferns start to develop—without needing to open the containers to replenish the water. This is easiest to achieve in cool, shaded conditions. Spores develop into prothalli more rapidly when warm

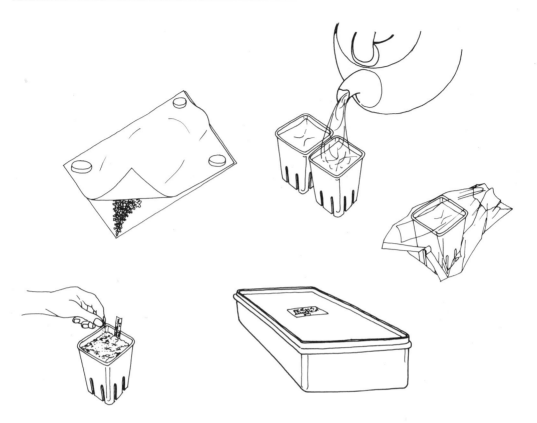

Figure 30. Fern fronds are dried between two layers of paper to collect the spores. Before sowing them, fill small pots with an organic-rich potting mix and cover the surface with pads of folded paper towel. Sterilise the surface by pouring boiling water over it; allow to drain and repeat several times. Hold the "sterile" pots in polythene bags until ready to sow spores. Remove the pots one by one. Peel off the paper towel and sprinkle spores lightly over the exposed surface. Place the pots in a transparent plastic box with a 2 cm (1 in.) layer of boiled, cooled water in the bottom, as each is sown. When all pots are sown and in place, close the lid and put the box in a warm, shaded place for the spores to germinate.

than when cool, but the atmosphere in the containers dries out more rapidly at higher temperatures. Management is simplified and stress to the plants reduced at temperatures of about 15° to 20°C (50° to 70°F) for hardy ferns. Diffuse light is sufficient for the needs of the prothalli, and exposure to direct sunlight for even a short time creates intolerable conditions in the closed containers.

Locations likely to be most successful include beneath the bench in a glasshouse or in a moderate to heavily shaded frame within it; in a corner of a well-lit shed or a little-used room in a house; in a heavily shaded cold frame in mild locations; or in a sheltered, shaded corner out of doors. In cool and cold temperate regions, supplementary warmth up to about 15°C (50°F) is necessary to enable prothalli to grow and produce fernlets dur-

Figure 31. Pots sown with fern spores, in a transparent plastic box (the lid has been temporarily removed). Prothalli growing from the spores cover the substrate in some of the pots. Condensation forming on the inside of the container maintains a saturated atmosphere and should not be wiped off.

Figure 32. Pots contained in a propagator or transparent boxes on a shaded window sill in a warm room provide a domestic-scale version for raising spores of ferns. Sown in the autumn, they will produce small fern plants in time to be pricked out in the spring.

ing the winter. In mild temperate regions and Mediterranea, supplementary heat is usually unnecessary.

Growing on

Throughout the time spores are developing until immature plants become visible, the atmosphere around the prothalli must remain humid, but the surface should not be sodden wet. Condensation in the containers in which the ferns are growing is a reassuring sign of a saturated atmosphere and should never be wiped off. Add more water only if condensation diminishes or disappears, by spraying boiled water over the surface, using a small hand-held sprayer. Provided the containers are well sealed, shaded and cool, it should not be necessary to add more water.

The first sign of success is the appearance of a green film over the surface of the pot. Gradually this assumes a textured appearance, as individual prothalli become visible. When these grow large enough, they produce sexual organs on their undersides; male organs most likely around the periphery and females towards the centre. Male

cells, or antheridia, migrate to and fertilise the ovules in a film of water. The stage is then set for the appearance of the first fronds of the young plants. Minute fronds develop from the fertilised ovules amongst the prothalli and grow into tiny, individual plants. At this stage, partially open the lids of the containers to accustom the fernlets to a more buoyant atmosphere. Spray with water when necessary and after a week or ten days, set them out uncovered in a shaded place in a glasshouse or frame to grow on. When the fernlets have grown large enough to handle, prick them out into seed trays to provide space for each one to develop.

Ferns develop at different rates, depending on the conditions and the species. Some, including *Cyathea australis*, *Pteris cretica*, *Dryopteris* and most *Polystichum* spp., develop rapidly and can grow large enough to prick out within six months. Others, including *Adiantum cuneatum*, *Cyathea medullaris*, *Cyrtomium falcatum* and *C. fortunei*, *Dicksonia antarctica*, *Doodia aspera*, and *Polystichum setosum*, grow more slowly, and it may be twelve months or more after sowing before they are ready.

Figure 33. Fern spores are sown in seed trays and enclosed in polythene bags on racks in a shaded house in a commercial nursery.

is a clumsy, gigantic object in relation to these tiny plants.

- Disentangle clusters of fernlets and prick them out individually—despite frequently repeated advice to prick out in small clumps. It is particularly important to separate ferns whose attractions lie in the individual character of their crowns in order to ensure they produce strong, well-developed crowns.
- As each container is filled with pricked-out fernlets, enclose it in a translucent polythene bag and drench the fernlets and the interior of the bag with a fine spray of water before closing the ends of the bags.
- Place the bags in a shaded cold frame (glazed with bubble polythene or shade cloth to diffuse sunlight) or similar situation.
- Open the ends of the bags after ten days to a fortnight, but otherwise do not disturb them.
- After a further ten days, remove the bags completely. From now on, water the plants when necessary from a can fitted with a fine rose.
- Grow the plants in the cool, shaded conditions within the frame, with the lights permanently raised, and provide ventilation till they are large enough to pot up individually.

Potting up

By now, the fernlets are large enough and independent enough to be grown like any other plant. Pot them up individually into 7 cm (2.5 in.) square containers when neighbouring fronds overlap in the seed trays or pots in which they were pricked out.

Pricking out

Even very small plants can be pricked out successfully, but delay the operation until the more forward fernlets have two or three tiny fronds. Young plants develop unevenly, and this gives time for the laggards to get going.

Work in cool, shaded conditions when pricking out fernlets. They have grown accustomed to life in almost water-saturated environments and are vulnerable to desiccation.

- Use a pencil or dibber with a sharp point—not the teaspoon sometimes recommended, as this

Propagation from cuttings

Ferns offer little to those in search of cuttings, although some with long, creeping rhizomes invite propagation in this way. Even those which produce the compact clusters of "shuttlecocks" typical of athyriums, dryopteris species, and others can be raised from cuttings. However, being ferns, these are cuttings of a somewhat special kind, made not from the organs that serve as stems or roots but from the bases of old fronds.

Old fronds wither and die, and having done so they lose contact with the plants that bore them. Many break clean off close to the stem. Others leave behind a short peg of tissue, the remains of the bases of the fallen fronds. In some tree ferns, these are highly conspicuous; in others, like the hart's tongue ferns and its many forms, they lie unnoticed amongst the debris at the base of the plant.

Frond pegs can be used to make cuttings (see figure 34).

- Remove the pegs by twisting each one down and slightly to one side until it breaks off at the junction with the main stem.
- Set them out, as though pricking out seedlings or setting out lily scales, in seed trays or pots (depending on how many there are) filled with cutting mix, burying each peg to about half its depth.
- Alternatively, pack them into plastic boxes after mixing them with moist vermiculite. This provides more secure and controllable conditions for an operation which may take several months to complete and makes it easier to inspect the contents to see what stage of development has been reached.
- Put seed trays or pots in a shaded situation in a glasshouse or cold frame, or, particularly in places with mild climates, a shaded cold frame.
- Plastic boxes are treated similarly or placed in a warm (15° to 25°C, or 60° to 75°F), well-lit room.
- Green protuberances appear near the bases of the pegs and gradually develop into offsets from which fronds emerge.
- Prick out the pegs in plastic boxes when the first signs of development become visible.
- Pot up the small plants individually in 7 cm (2.5 in.) square pots when they grow large enough to be self-supporting.

Propagation from frond pegs has long been the preferred way to propagate several attractive forms of the hart's tongue fern—such as *Asplenium scolopendrium* 'Crispum Bolton's Nobile', which is sterile and can be propagated by division only very

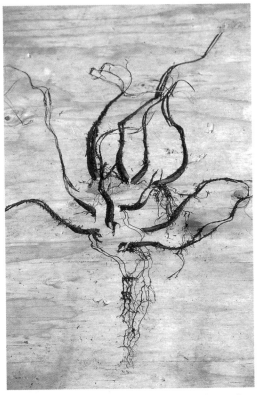

Figure 34. Frond pegs removed from the base of an old plant of *Asplenium scolopendrium* 'Crispum Bolton's Nobile'. The bases of the pegs (and "roots") are in the centre—the trailing extensions round the perimeter are the remains of the fronds' vascular tissues.

slowly. It remains a lengthy process, redeemed by the fact that numerous leaf bases can be obtained from a well-grown plant without doing it any damage at all. The method can be used to propagate other genera such as *Dryopteris*, which produce offsets more quickly, and—most spectacularly—with marattias, including the king fern, *Marattia salicina*, whose large frond bases, formed like the hooves of horses, can be removed, potted up individually and used as cuttings to produce new plants. Nevertheless, the small offsets which are to be found ready-made around the bases of the fronds are usually a more practical source of new plants.

Tree ferns

Many ferns possess "trunks" of various kinds; some never grow tall, but some of the tree ferns can compete with trees. The trunks of cyatheas, dicksonias, alsophilas and other tree ferns are not what they seem. In botanical terms, each is a caudex, constructed from the roots to form a semi-woody mass supporting the crown of fronds. Their remarkable powers of regeneration are seen in an extreme form in tree ferns.

Giant cuttings are produced in the following way: Cut off the top of the tree fern, with 1 or 2 metres (3 to 6 ft.) of caudex, surmounted by the crown. Remove all the fronds, apart from those contained within the bud. Insert the lower half into the ground, ensuring it is firmly held in place. Keep the caudex shaded and constantly moist until it produces new rhizoids.

This method of regeneration is widely used in the marketing of these ferns, using trees obtained from the bush. It scarcely constitutes a means of propagation, and since each plant provides only a single cutting, it is not a means of increase.

Propagation by division

Ferns can be divided, very broadly, into two groups, depending on whether they produce dense clusters of "shuttlecocks" from a clearly defined central stem or caudex, or rhizomes just below the ground or on the surface from which fronds arise at intervals singly or in small clusters.

Ferns with well-defined central rootstocks, including species of *Dryopteris*, crowned by shuttlecocks, produce buds at the base of the caudex and over the years develop into congested masses. These can be propagated by digging up a well-developed plant and dividing it by wrenching or cutting off individual crowns. Provided they are potted up and carefully looked after in a shaded situation, many of the detached crowns will eventually reestablish themselves to produce new plants. However, the crowns seldom separate readily, and more often than not the operation becomes a destructive process, risking the ruin of a good plant while gaining little.

Ferns with rhizomes lend themselves to division. It is only necessary to cut them into sections, each containing a length of rhizome and a few fronds, to produce a number of ready-made plants. These can be potted up and given a little care and attention while they reestablish themselves, or they can be planted straight out into the ground.

With some species, divisions provide even more tempting opportunities. Onocleas, polypodiums, some blechnums, phegopteris and cystopteris grow from subterranean rhizomes just below the surface. Apart from the active apical buds at the tips of the rhizomes, these possess nonactive (dormant) buds along their lengths that can be used as a source of new plants.

- Lift plants when they begin to grow in the spring.
- Cut off the active apical buds plus a short length of rhizome, and pot them up individually in small containers.
- Lay the remainder of the rhizomes flat on the surface in a partially filled seed tray, and cover with about 1.5 cm (0.75 in.) of a 1:1 mixture of [peat, bark, coir] : [grit, perlite].
- Water thoroughly, before placing a plastic propagator top over the seed tray or putting it into a polythene bag.
- Move the trays into a shaded cold frame, under the bench in a glasshouse or in another shaded situation.
- After a month, remove the propagator top or plastic bag, watering as necessary to keep the substrate moist.
- New shoots will emerge during the summer—many with juvenile fronds.
- Overwinter the seed trays, protecting them only from severe frost, if necessary, and in the following spring, separate the plants as they resume growth and pot them up individually.

Davallias can be propagated by a variation of this method. Lift the rhizomes in spring, strip off their old rhizoids and lay the rhizomes on a bed of organic : mineral, 1:1, mix, before covering with a layer of sphagnum moss about 2.5 cm (1 in.) deep. The small plants that develop from dormant eyes are potted up individually when they have formed roots.

Propagation from offsets

Some ferns—notably the New Zealand hen and chickens fern, *Asplenium bulbiferum*, and the bladder fern, *Cystopteris bulbifera*—produce small plants, bulbils or buds on their fronds which give rise naturally to new plants.

Figure 35. *Asplenium bulbiferum* showing small plants developing spontaneously on a frond, each of which is capable of growing into an independent plant.

Polystichum setiferum acutilobum and *P. proliferum* produce numerous small plants along the midribs of the fronds during late summer. Others, including *Asplenium monanthes* and species of *Woodwardia* are more reluctant, part-time mothers. They produce bulbils or small plants but do so less prolifically or readily.

Cut the fronds bearing bulbils or small, viviparous plants in the autumn. Peg them down on a bed of organic substrate with large fencing staples. Overwinter them in a cold frame or under the bench in a cold greenhouse, bringing them into warmer conditions, if space is available, in late winter. Small plants develop during the spring. Pot up individually into 7 cm (2.5 in.) containers when they are large enough to handle and growing more or less independently.

Propagation Summary for Ferns

S. = propagated from spores; the season is not specified because it can usually be chosen to meet the needs of the propagator
C. = propagated from cuttings
D. = propagated by divisions
+/− = more or less

Adiantum—**S.** marginal sori. **D.** spring; rhizomes, e.g., *A. pedatum*, also clump formers but less prolifically; not *A. diaphanum* (spores only).

Alsophila—tree fern. **S. C.** trunks.

Asplenium—**S.** sori oval or linear along the veins. Some forms, e.g., *A. trichomanes* 'Cristatum', reproduce +/− true. **C.** frond bases. **D.** viviparous plantlets, e.g., *A. bulbiferum* and *A. monanthes*; offset crowns, e.g., *A. oblongifolium* and barren forms, e.g., *A. trichomanes* 'Incisum'; Plantlets at tips of fronds, e.g., *A. flabellifolium*.

Athyrium—**S.** some forms, e.g., *A. filix-femina* 'Victoriae' and 'Frizelliae', reproduce +/− true. **D.** from offset crowns, often slow; short rhizomes, e.g., *A. niponicum* 'Pictum'.

Azolla—Aquatic. **D.** spring. In cold areas, overwinter a reserve stock in a bucket of water in a frost-free situation.

Blechnum—**S.** fertile fronds. **D.** short rhizomes, e.g., *B. penna-marina*, *B. fraseri* and *B. tabulare*; crowns on stolons, e.g., *B. discolor*.

Camptosorus—**D.** plantlets at tips of fronds.

Cheilanthes—**S.** marginal sori. **D.** short rhizomes.

Cryptogramma—**S.** fertile fronds; marginal sori. **D.** offsets.

Cyathea—tree fern. **S. C.** caudexes.

Cyrtomium—**S. D.** offsets.

Cystopteris—**S. D.** rhizomes, offsets, e.g., *C. bulbifera*.

Davallia—**S. D.** rhizomes.

Dennstaedtia—**S. D.** rhizomes.

Dicksonia—tree fern. **S.** spring. **C.** caudexes; not *D. fibrosa*. **D.** offsets, e.g., *D. squarrosa*.

Doodia—**S. D.** offset crowns, rhizomes, stolons.

Dryopteris—**S.** many forms reproduce +/− true, e.g., *D. filix-mas* 'The King'. **C.** frond bases. **D.** offsets, very slow.

Gleichenia—**S. D.** offsets on rhizomes.

Gymnocarpium—**S.** some forms, e.g., *G. dryopteris* 'Plumosum', reproduce +/− true. **D.** rhizomes.

Histiopteris—**S.**

Hymenophyllum—filmy fern. **S.** marginal sori. **D.** grow on under mist.

Lastreopsis—**S. D.** short rhizomes, offset crowns, e.g., *L. hispida*.

Leptopteris—**S.**

Marattia—**S. C.** frond bases. **D.** offset crowns at base.

Matteuccia—fertile fronds. **S.** spring. **D.** crowns on creeping rhizomes.

Nephrolepis—**D.** offset crowns, but mainly from stolons, freely produced by established plants.

Onoclea—fertile fronds. **S.** spring. **C.** rhizomes. **D.** rhizomes.

Oreopteris—**S.**

Osmunda—fertile fronds. **S.** fresh, very short-lived; forms reproduce +/− true. **D.** offset crowns, slow.

Pellaea—fertile fronds. **S.** marginal sori. **D.** tufted, creeping rhizome.

Phegopteris—**S. D.** rhizomes.

Phymatosorus—**S. D.** rhizomes, e.g., *P. diversifolius*.

Platycerium—fertile fronds (the antlers). **S.**, e.g., *P. superbum*. **D.** offsets from roots, all except *P. superbum*.

Polypodium—**S. D.** rhizomes.

Polystichum—**S.** except sterile forms, e.g., *P. aculeatum* 'Bevis'. **D.** offset plantlets, bulbils, e.g., *P. proliferum* and *P. setiferum acutilobum*.

Pteris—**S.** marginal sori; forms, e.g., *P. cretica*. 'Cristata' reproduce +/− true.

Rumohra—**S. D.** rhizomes.

Scolopendrium (Asplenium)—**S.** linear sori, some forms, e.g., 'Cristatum', reproduce +/− true, but not sterile forms, e.g., 'Crispum Bolton's Nobile'. **C.** leaf bases. **D.** offsets; slow.

Thelypteris—**S. D.** rhizomes.

Todea—**S. D.** offset crowns; slow.

Trichomanes—filmy fern. **S. D.** rhizomes grow on under mist.

Woodsia—**S. D.** short rhizomes.

Woodwardia—fertile fronds. **S. D.** plantlets at tips of fronds, rhizomes.

CHAPTER 8

Cycads, Conifers and Other Gymnosperms

The mosses, ferns and related plants introduced in the last chapter have never totally adapted to life on land. Each retains a memory—a backward nod towards a distant waterborne past—of the processes leading to the fertilisation of its ovules during sexual reproduction. Cycads, conifers and their allies, known collectively as gymnosperms, have escaped this dependency in a way that almost poetically represents a new life exposed to the challenges of terra firma. They have harnessed the winds as the agents that bring together male and female cells through the invention of pollen, and they have seized the opportunities of an earthbound existence by producing seeds.

The alternation of sexual and asexual lifestyles, so dominant and critical in ferns, both to the plant and to the gardener fades into insignificance in the gymnosperms. The sexual reproduction of ferns is unfamiliar territory to most gardeners. Sexual reproduction in the gymnosperms shares so many similarities with those of flowering plants that gardeners seldom think about such differences as do exist.

Cycads

Cycads dominated the vegetation toward the end of the Triassic period some 200 million years ago, when they were a significant presence in Gondwana. Mass extinction events and changes in climate progressively reduced their numbers and importance until today, when barely ten genera remain, including *Cycas*, *Dioon*, *Encephalartos*, *Lepidozamia*, *Macrozamia*, *Stangeria*, and *Zamia*, totalling only about 100 species. Their uncompromising, primitive forms create huge impact, an evocation of the past and a touch of the tropics—only too appropriate since, unless grown in conservatories, they are restricted to gardens in the warmer parts of the temperate world.

Propagation from seed

Cycad seeds are large—fingertip or thumbtip size—and enclosed by double-layered seed coats, similar to plums, in which the outer layer is fleshy and the inner one woody. They are produced in pairs between the scales of large and sometimes enormous cones. Seeds may not be produced in cultivation, or they may germinate badly because the plants are dioecious, and males and females must be grown in close proximity for ovules to be fertilised. Although most use the wind to transport pollen to the micropyles of the ovules, a few, particularly species of encephalartos, depend for pollination on small beetles which are unlikely to be present in gardens. Seeds continue to develop parthenocarpically if the ovules are not fertilised, and such seeds contain no embryos. Cycad seeds deteriorate rapidly after they mature and should be sown within a month of collection.

Some of these problems can be countered by artificial insemination:

- Cut off a male cone when the pollen is mature—if necessary, a male cone, or pollen from it, can be obtained from a plant growing elsewhere.
- Hold the cone over a sheet of heavy gauge white paper.
- Stroke it to dislodge ripe pollen onto the sheet of paper.
- Mix the pollen with distilled water containing a drop of detergent.
- Using an eyedropper, inject the suspended pollen between the scales of a receptive female cone.

Sowing seed

Lay the seeds on the surface of a bed of a free-draining substrate—[bark, peat, coir] : [coarse sand, grit, calcined clay], 1:1, and lightly cover with a thin layer of the organic component. Water thoroughly, but thenceforth apply water sparingly, taking care to avoid any hint of waterlogging. Maintain temperatures of approximately 25°C (75°F) by day, falling towards 15°C (60°F) at night. Pot up individually as soon as radicles are well developed into 9 cm (3.5 in.) square containers. Grow on at 20° to 30°C (70° to 85°F) under light shade.

Cycads grow slowly and take years to develop trunks. Nevertheless, even small plants are decorative and interesting and capable of making an impression out of proportion to their size.

Propagation from cuttings

Some cycads, among them the widely grown *Cycas revoluta*, continue to produce a succession of off-sets from truncated stems after the crowns have been cut off. The offsets can be removed and used as cuttings.

- Allow each to develop until it has several whorls of fronds.
- Cut offsets at the junction with the stem, and strip off the fronds.
- Pot up individually in a free-draining growth medium [bark, coir] : [grit, calcined clay, perlite], 1:3.
- Place pots on a glasshouse bench at a temperature of approximately 25°C (75°F).
- Shade lightly with increased shading in bright, sunlit conditions.
- Water extremely sparingly until roots appear; the plants are resilient and enduring, and more likely to be killed by kindness—especially overwatering—than by neglect.

Propagation by division

All cycads produce offsets (pups) or suckers around the base of their stems to a greater or lesser degree. These are removed after they have developed roots of their own but are otherwise treated as cuttings.

The Ginkgo

Ginkgo biloba is the last remaining living link between cycads and conifers. It resembles neither, but 120 million-year-old fossils show it has remained true to itself throughout this time—a remarkable example of a plant that can truly be said to have been unspoilt by progress. Being not only unique but almost unimaginably venerably ancient, it is always deferentially referred to with the definite article.

The ginkgo is dioecious. Female trees produce fruit only when their ovules are fertilised by pollen from neighbouring males. The round, orange fruits are drupes, as are plums, the size of small greengages, containing stones surrounded by fleshy tissues. The fruits add greatly to the tree's beauty after the leaves have fallen, and the kernels inside their stones are not only edible but enjoyable. However, some people dislike the unusual odour of the fruit, which is far less obnoxious in fact than its reputation suggests, and the mess created by fallen fruit can also lead to problems—especially when the trees are grown in public places.

Plants bought from garden centres are most likely to be male trees grafted onto seedling stocks. These have a reputation, based on slender foundations, for growing in a more regular, pyramidal shape than the females—a contributory factor to the preference for using them in gardens and especially for roadside planting.

Propagation from seed

The processes leading to embryo development are exclusive to the ginkgo. Pollen, produced by the male flowers in short catkins, is carried by wind to flowers on female trees, where it is caught on sticky surfaces at the entrances to the flowers. As the surface dries, the pollen is drawn closer to the site of the ovules, but no fertilisation occurs at this stage. Nonetheless, the tissues respond to the presence of pollen by growing rapidly to the size of a small cherry. As they do so, ovules develop within the fruits, and spermatozoids are formed within the pollen grains. Later, usually after the fruit has fallen from the tree, the spermatozoids move into the ovules and fertilise them—marking the start of embryo development. The embryos complete their development during the winter, leading to germination as temperatures rise the following spring.

Ginkgo fruits can be collected soon after they fall in the autumn, but the fleshy tissues should not be removed and on no account should the stones become dry.

- Mix the fruits with about five times their volume of coir, bark or coarse sand.
- Pack the mixture into plastic bags—with ample air space—and put them in a sheltered, shaded place where the processes leading to fertilisation can take place naturally.
- In late winter, after the embryos have developed, remove the mixture and pick out the

stones (seeds), separating them from any traces of fleshy tissues.
- Sow individually in 9 cm (3.5 in.) square containers.
- Place on a bench at temperatures between 20° and 25°C (70° to 75°F), or sow them in drills in a nursery bed.

The ginkgo produces two kinds of shoots: dwarf shoots with congested leaves emerging from barely separated nodes, and long shoots capable of growing a metre (3 ft.) in a year, on which the leaves are widely separated. The production of dwarf shoots is a response to austere conditions. Fertile soils, ample water, warmth and shelter are essential for rapid development of seedlings—and seedlings respond generously to glasshouse space during the summer.

Welwitschia

Principal contenders for the title of "World's Weirdest Plant," welwitschias start life with two leaves and end life with two leaves—even though they live for 1000 years. As the leaves become progressively more and more torn and tattered, they resemble bundles of tumbled, writhing ribbons emerging from the rim of a battered, partially hollow, woody stump. Few gardeners attempt to grow *Welwitschia mirabilis*, though plants have been raised from seed in botanic gardens.

Cultivated seedlings begin to produce cones when about 20 years old. At that stage, they bear little resemblance to the gnarled, woody Methusalahs made familiar by photographs of mature plants growing in the deserts of Namibia.

Those inclined to have a go at growing welwitschias need to remember a few points:

- They are dioecious, so one flower spike on a single plant does not found a colony.
- The male plants produce pollen in cones perched on branched stalks, like little chocolate-brown, clubbed antennae. This has to be transferred to cones on the female plants.

- Seedlings rapidly develop immensely long taproots and strongly resent disturbance—ample room is needed to allow these to develop.
- Sow seeds individually in deep containers in spring or summer in free-draining, gritty mix with an organic : mineral ratio of 1:3 or 1:4.
- As soon as seedlings grow large enough, add a topping of coarse grit or fine gravel, about 2 cm (1 in.) deep.
- Seedlings are extremely susceptible to fungal infections. Use fungicide routinely each time the plants are watered for the first six months.
- Xerophytic they may be, and tolerant of drought up to a point, but welwitschias depend on tapping into sources of water deep below the surface. The substrate should never be allowed to become completely dry, and watering from below to maintain a collar of dry grit around the neck of the plant is recommended.

Gardeners who hope to see their own home-raised seedlings achieve ultimate venerability are likely to be disappointed. One day, the heirs of their heirs might be so lucky.

Conifers

Pines, spruces and larches so dominate the boreal forests of Eurasia that they can create the impression that conifers are essentially plants of the colder parts of the world. That is an entirely false impression. Relatively few different genera and species grow in these northern forests compared to the numbers in the more temperate forests of British Columbia and the Pacific Northwest and the almost bewildering diversity through California and into Mexico. In the southern hemisphere, too, podocarps and relatives of yews growing in relatively mild, warm or cool temperate conditions introduce gardeners to novel views of conifers—not least because these plants produce no cones. Increasing emphasis on the search for novelty combined with the increased significance of gardening in warmer parts of the world, where

frost is not such a limiting factor, has raised interest in previously seldom-used species, particularly those from the southern hemisphere. Pines, larches, cypresses and cedars are being joined in gardens by plants with less familiar names.

From South America—alerces (*Fitzroya cupressoides*), Prince Albert's yew (*Saxegothaea conspicua*), mañios (*Podocarpus* spp.) and araucarias (*Araucaria* spp.).

From New Zealand—rimu (*Dacrydium cupressinum*), totara (*Podocarpus* spp.), kawaka (*Libocedrus plumosa*) and kahikatea (*Dacrycarpus dacrydioides*).

From Australia—Bunya pines (*Araucaria bidwillii*), Oyster Bay pines (*Callitris rhomboidea* and *C. oblonga*), King Billy pines (*Athrotaxis selaginoides*) and Huon pines (*Lagarostrobos franklinii*)—not one of which is a pine or even a close relative.

From South Africa—*Widdringtonia* spp. and yellow woods (*Afrocarpus falcatus* and *Podocarpus* spp.).

Propagation from seed

Seeds provide a practical, effective way to raise conifers, but seedlings can grow frustratingly slowly during the first two or three years, even when provided with good conditions. Species mostly come true from seed, with few tendencies to hybridise, but named varieties and forms are likely to reproduce variably and are seldom worth raising in this way.

Harvesting seed

The most difficult part of growing conifers from seed is likely to be the getting of it—unless it is obtained by purchase or otherwise from an outside source, when that becomes someone else's problem. Only mature trees produce seeds, and only those that are naturally low-growing, bushy, prostrate or precocious produce them within easy reach. The seeds of mature pines, firs, coast redwoods, and podocarps, among others, are borne high above the ground, inaccessibly placed towards the ends of the shoots. Few conifers produce fruits or seeds that can be gathered from the

Figure 36. The serotinous cones of *Pinus aculeata* do not open to shed their seed when mature but remain closely pressed to the branches until fire or the death of the branches releases the seeds inside them. As time passes, they become progressively more embedded in the bark.

ground after they have fallen, like acorns or beech nuts.

Trees can be felled or branches cut off and cones, arils or drupes gathered when they have been brought down to ground level. Large quantities of seed for forestry plantations are often obtained in this way, but it is seldom an option from trees grown in gardens. Windblown trees or branches provide opportunities for seed gathering. Most conifers produce orthodox seeds amenable to long-term storage. Occasional collections

from this source can be preserved for use over many years.

Many species of young trees become productive long before they reach their full size—for example, *Abies koreana*, *Larix* spp., *Thuja* spp. and *Chamaecyparis* spp.—and trees may provide accessible sources of seed while still quite small. Provided they are fertile, seeds produced by young trees are as good as those produced later in life. Seeds should not be collected from stunted or misshapen trees just because their condition makes the seeds accessible. They are quite likely to inherit the poor constitutions of their parents. Some of the other problems which beset those in search of conifer seeds are described in the facing box.

Cleaning seeds in cones

Cones of most species spontaneously open in warm, dry conditions after collection—a tendency that can be encouraged by the judicious use of artificial heat. Most open to release their seeds when set out in shallow layers in paper-lined seed trays in a warm room. A radiator can be used to speed up the process. Less amenable cones, amongst those of the fire-adapted pines and others, including *Pinus torreyana* and *P. monophylla*, *Cupressus macrocarpa*, *Callitris* spp. and *Actinostrobus arenarius*, should be dried in an oven set at 60°C (140°F) for six to eight hours. Larch (*Larix* spp.) cones often open reluctantly or partially. They may release their seeds only after being broken up by hand. A blow lamp played briefly over the surface, to simulate the effects of a bush fire, usually does the trick when all else fails.

Seeds drop out of the cones once the scales gape. Small batches are shaken in wide mesh (0.5 to 1 cm, or 0.25 to 0.5 in.) sieves to separate the seeds from the empty cones. It may be easier to lift off the cones of species with large seeds, including *Agathis* spp., *Araucaria* spp., *Pinus pinea* and *P. monophylla*. Except for those with large seeds, most conifers produce winged seeds designed to be transported by wind. The wings should be rubbed off before the seeds are sown or in preparation for storage.

Causes of infertility or unavailability encountered when collecting conifer seeds

Timing

Seeds of most conifers mature within six months or so of fertilisation. Some, including araucarias, piceas, junipers and sequoiadendrons, take two or even three years.

Irregular cropping

Most conifers produce fruit and seeds more or less regularly, though quantities and quality vary from year to year. Some, like the rimu, *Dacrydium cupressinum*, are notably irregular, and several years may separate one good harvest from another. Seed obtained during good years can be stored to provide a source of seedlings during the lean times.

Variable quality

Cones, with some exceptions, begin to shed seeds as and when they mature, and they usually continue to do so for some weeks—months, even. Seeds shed first are more likely to contain well-developed, fertile embryos than those shed later; delayed harvesting may result in inferior samples.

Variable viability

Fertility can vary greatly from year to year, and some, notably most *Abies*, *Chamaecyparis*, *Sequoia* and *Sequoiadendron*, tend to produce only small proportions of viable seeds in any year. The viability of a sample can be tested by cutting some of the seeds in half with a knife and examining them. Well-filled interiors with firm, white or ivory contents are likely to be viable. Those that are partially filled, which show signs of shriveling, or in which the contents are streaked or stained overall with brown, are most unlikely to produce seedlings.

Premature harvesting

Maturity is usually easily recognised. Green cones turn brown as they dry and their scales gape, particularly towards the base. Drupes, arils and other fleshy fruits change colour—pink, black, red, crimson or purple—and their fleshy tissues become soft and often sweet. Immature cones or unripe fruits are seldom worth gathering and certainly not worth storing. When the only alternative to harvesting green is not to harvest at all, it may be worth making a collection, extracting the seeds, taking care not to damage them by overheating, and sowing them at once. Otherwise, they should always be left until fully mature.

Losses from predators

Birds and squirrels play important roles in the consumption and distribution of conifer seeds, and some animals are capable of devouring an astonishingly high proportion of ripening seeds. Even very large crops can be stripped with remarkable speed. After collection, seeds must not be accessible to rodents.

Serotinous seeds

The cones of some species remain closed for years after they mature until they are exposed to heat from forest fires or the tree or branch bearing them dies. These include some junipers, such as *Juniperus oxycedrus*, and several fire-adapted pines, including *Pinus attenuata*, *P. radiata* and *P. contorta*. Seeds can be obtained only by manually removing the cones, when they usually open as they dry, or if not, after exposing them to heat.

Cleaning seeds in fleshy fruits

Numerous "conifers" do not bear cones at all, but produce fleshy fruits, as yews do, instead. If obtaining a collection of cones can be a problem, fruits can be a nightmare for anyone hoping for more than a very small share of the crop. Each bears only a single seed, they are available only for a short period due to competition from birds, and they deteriorate rapidly unless the fleshy tissues are removed soon after collection.

Small quantities are cleaned by hand, cutting open drupes to remove the stones and extracting seeds from the fleshy tissues of arils. Moderate quantities are cleaned by soaking the fruits in water for ten days, a fortnight, or more if necessary, and then rubbing the resultant soggy mixture of pulp and stones/seeds through a sieve to leave the seeds behind on the mesh. The seeds of a few, including *Taxus* spp., are small and hard enough to withstand mechanical maceration in a blender, provided the blades are padded. Large quantities are mixed with damp sand, packed into polythene bags and left in a shaded place out of doors—and inaccessible to rodents—to weather for a month or two while the fleshy tissues disintegrate. Seeds and pulp are then separated by rubbing the latter through a sieve. The remains of the pulp need not be removed before sowing seeds in nursery beds.

Cleaned, dried seeds are packed in paper or cotton bags and stored short-term in a refrigerator or cool cellar. With a few possible exceptions, including species of agathis and araucaria, the seeds of conifers have orthodox responses to storage. They survive long periods in a dry state at subzero temperatures.

Weathering seed

Seeds of most conifers from cool and cold temperate regions mature during autumn or early winter. A minority will germinate immediately when sown at 10° to 20°C (50° to 70°F). They are stored in dry, cool conditions until the time comes to sow them.

The majority need to be weathered before they will germinate. Exposure to low temperatures over

Figure 37. Cones of *Picea spinulosa* photographed in early summer. The open two-year-old cones shed their seeds during the previous autumn and early winter and are now empty. The closed cones will not mature and will not be ready for seed collection until the autumn—several months hence.

periods of a month or two are sufficient to satisfy this need for most of them. Seeds are weathered in the way described on p. 83. Frost-tolerant species can be placed out of doors, where they will experience temperatures down to freezing point and below. Frost-sensitive species from milder areas are placed in a shed or some other structure where temperatures do not fall far below freezing point. In mild or warm temperate regions and Mediterranea, or in other situations where natu-

Figure 38. *Afrocarpus falcatus*, like other podocarps, produces plumlike fruits known as drupes, each containing a single seed in soft, sweet pulp. Remove the pulp before sowing the seeds.

ral weathering is impracticable, a refrigerator can be used to provide low temperatures.

Sowing seed

Small batches, especially of rare or tender species, are best sown in containers, under cover. When supplementary heat can be provided, temperatures not exceeding 20°C (70°F) speed up germination and the development of young seedlings. Seeds are sown as described on pp. 78–80. Those that have been weathered are sown by spreading the mixture of seeds and grit as a topping over a potting mix base. Bear in mind that many conifers have strong preferences either for mineral or organic substrates—see p. 148.

Conifer seedlings need room to develop, and containers must provide sufficient depth for them to produce straight, uncongested roots.

- Sow thinly in 1 or 2 litre (6 to 8 in.) containers rather than 7 or 9 cm (2.5 or 3.5 in.) pots, and never in seed trays.
- Aim for about 20 seedlings in a 1 litre (6 in.) and 30 to 40 in a 2 litre (8 in.) container.
- Seedlings develop slowly. Provided they are not sown too thickly, they scarcely benefit from being pricked out and potted up individually

before they are into their second season of growth.

- Pot them up individually into deep containers with grooved sides to encourage uncongested root development.
- Line them out in nursery beds rather than in pots or into larger containers.

Nursery beds out of doors provide an effective means of raising hardy conifers from seed in cool and cold temperate regions and almost all conifers in warmer regions. They reduce demands on care and attention, avoid problems arising from congested or distorted roots, and provide favourable conditions for establishing symbiotic relationships with fungi.

A raised seedbed, prepared as described on p. 56, provides ideal conditions, top-dressed a month before sowing with a balanced NPK granular fertiliser and the magic ingredient—a few handfuls of soil and partially decayed needles from beneath an established conifer to provide the fungal symbionts needed for healthy growth and development.

Well-managed seedbeds have big, big capacities when seed is broadcast over the entire surface. A square metre, or square yard, can hold up to 500 pine seedlings, 700 spruces, or as many as 1000 thuyas or tsugas. Smaller numbers are sown in shallow drills drawn out 10 to 15 cm (4 to 6 in.) apart. Seeds stored dry in paper packets are trickled thinly along the length of the drills. Weathered seeds still mixed with grit or sand are tipped straight into the drills. Different kinds can be accommodated side by side, each marked and labeled, and perhaps occupying no more than a 30 cm (12 in.) long drill—sufficient for up to 60 young seedlings.

Growing on

Seedlings are thinned out manually soon after they germinate, leaving approximately 1 to 2 cm (0.5 to 1 in.) between each seedling and discarding weak or deformed plants. Lift and line out seedlings during their second year; slow-growing species, including *Thuja plicata* and *Tsuga hetero-*

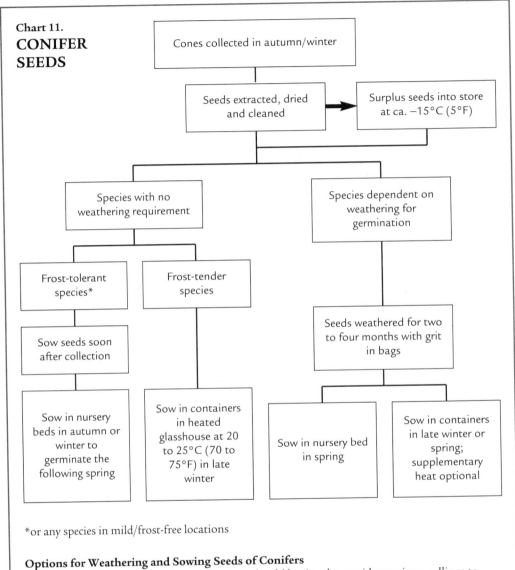

Chart 11.
CONIFER SEEDS

Cones collected in autumn/winter

Seeds extracted, dried and cleaned → Surplus seeds into store at ca. −15°C (5°F)

Species with no weathering requirement

Species dependent on weathering for germination

Frost-tolerant species*

Frost-tender species

Sow seeds soon after collection

Seeds weathered for two to four months with grit in bags

Sow in nursery beds in autumn or winter to germinate the following spring

Sow in containers in heated glasshouse at 20 to 25°C (70 to 75°F) in late winter

Sow in nursery bed in spring

Sow in containers in late winter or spring; supplementary heat optional

*or any species in mild/frost-free locations

Options for Weathering and Sowing Seeds of Conifers

In cool and cold temperate regions, operations should be timed to avoid exposing seedlings to frost. In mild and warm temperate regions and in Mediterranea, the seeds of many species will need to be artificially weathered in refrigerators before they will produce seedlings.

Management of nursery beds

Success with nursery beds depends on good management.

Avoid competition from weeds; seedlings are easily overwhelmed by weeds, especially in wet seasons. There are two aids to weed-free beds: First, top the seedbed with a layer of grit (about 1 cm, or 0.5 in., deep) immediately after sowing. Second, pass a blow lamp quickly and systematically over the surface of the bed to destroy the first flush of weed seedlings, just before conifer seedlings begin to emerge—usually ten days to a fortnight after sowing.

Avoid exposure to frost and sun. Seedlings, even those of hardy species, are more vulnerable to frost, sun scorch and exposure to drying winds than their parents. Almost all seedling conifers benefit from protection—and for more tender species it is essential. Flexible, economical and effective protection is provided by pinning 50 percent occlusion windbreak netting to a framework of light lathes. This is placed over the beds from the time the seeds are sown till past midsummer of their first year.

Predators, such as mice, rats and squirrels, eat the seeds, especially the large seeds of some pines, araucarias and agathis. Small areas of seedbed are particularly vulnerable and should be protected with small mesh wire netting. Moles, attracted to seedbeds by worms, burrow beneath and bury young seedlings, sometimes causing significant damage. Other destructive presences include pheasants, pigeons and, occasionally, finches. A good cat is the best deterrent for all these pests.

phylla, benefit from an extra undisturbed year. Protect the roots from desiccation while transplanting, especially particularly sensitive species, including *Pinus radiata* and some *Picea* spp. The best time to lift and transplant seedlings is when their roots are growing most actively during late summer to mid-autumn in their second year—with one proviso: Ample water must be available to ensure successful reestablishment. If this is in doubt, delay the move till the following late winter or early spring.

Propagation from cuttings

Cuttings are used to propagate selected forms unlikely to breed true from seed. They provide a practical, usually effective and economical way to propagate many cone-bearing conifers, including *Abies*,* *Actinostrobus*, *Calocedrus*, *Chamaecyparis*, *Cryptomeria*, *Cupressus*,* *Juniperus*, *Libocedrus*, *Metasequoia*, *Picea*,* *Sequoia*, *Taxodium*, *Thuja*, *Thujopsis* and *Tsuga*.

Cuttings of a number of other cone-bearing conifers are reluctant to produce roots and seldom provide the means to propagate selected forms of species. Amongst them are *Agathis*, *Araucaria*, *Callitris*, *Cedrus*, *Dacrycarpus*, *Fitzroya*, *Larix*, *Pinus* and *Pseudotsuga*.

Most fruit-bearing conifers in the family Taxaceae can be propagated from cuttings, including *Athrotaxis*, *Cephalotaxus*, *Dacrydium*, *Taxus*, *Phyllocladus*,* *Podocarpus* and *Prumnopitys*.*

Choosing material for cuttings

Shape and size are important attributes when growing conifers in gardens. Shoots to be used as cuttings should be chosen selectively and careful attention given to the ways the plants are grown. Important criteria are juvenile versus mature

*Success rates from cuttings of species in these genera are often low, and some take up to 18 months to develop roots.

Mineral versus organic substrates

Conifers can be broadly divided into two groups: pioneers and settlers. *Pioneers* are species that colonise areas stripped of most vegetation by fire, hurricane, volcanic eruptions, landslides and other events. Their seeds germinate on exposed bare mineral soils, often low in humus. Their seedlings grow up without the support and shelter of established trees. Pioneers occur amongst species of *Agathis*; *Libocedrus*; *Cupressus*; *Dacrycarpus*; *Juniperus*; some species of *Pinus* including *P. radiata*, *P. ponderosa* and *P. contorta*; *Pseudotsuga*; and *Sequoiadendron*. They germinate and grow naturally on mineral soils. On humus-rich substrates, their seedlings are vulnerable to the pathogens that cause death by damping-off. Peat, leaf mould, bark and other organic materials should be avoided as major constituents of seedbeds when propagating them in gardens.

Settlers are species that grow from seeds blown by the wind or carried by birds into established forests. Seeds germinate and seedlings develop in a humus-rich environment composed of remnants of decayed leaves, twigs, and other organic matter. They grow up in the shade and shelter of other trees. Settlers occur amongst species of *Abies*, *Chamaecyparis*, *Dacrydium*, *Picea*, some species of *Pinus*, *Podocarpus*, *Prumnopitys*, *Sequoia*, *Taxus*, *Thuja* and *Tsuga*. They germinate naturally on humus-rich soils. Additions of peat, leaf mould, bark or organic materials encourage healthy growth and development on mineral soils.

shoots, leading shoots, position of cuttings on the plant, trueness to type, and management of the plant material.

Juvenile shoots. Retinospora plant forms (*Thuja occidentalis* 'Rheingold' is a good example) often produce a mixture of juvenile and mature foliage. Shoots with juvenile foliage should be used as cuttings to maintain the juvenile leaf form and reduce rate of growth.

Leading shoots. The strict hierarchical growth form of spruces, pines, firs, araucarias and many other conifers depends on the apical dominance of the leading shoot. Cuttings made from side shoots may fail to gain the dominance needed to form a shapely plant. Special techniques can be used to increase the supply of apical shoots available for use as cuttings. (See the boxed section entitled "Production of shapely, symmetrical conifers from cuttings" later in the chapter.)

Position on the plant. Cuttings from shoots towards the top of a conifer, notably thujas, chamaecyparis, libocedrus, and other cypresses

(true or false), tend to produce taller, faster growing, more upright offspring. Those from around the base give rise to rounder profiled, slower growing trees. The effect is clearly seen in *Chamaecyparis lawsoniana* 'Fletcheri' and 'Elwoodii'. The former should be somewhat dumpy and is better propagated from shoots towards the base; the latter is ideally more upright and columnar and should be propagated from shoots towards the top. The effect is often maintained for many years before being lost.

Trueness to type. Choose cuttings from shoots likely to maintain the form and rate of growth of the plant being propagated—especially with dwarf forms. Narrow, upright shoots should be chosen when propagating columnar forms, and lax ones selected for those that are intended to weep. In particular, avoid selecting the more vigorous shoots from miniature forms—for example, *Juniperus communis* 'Compressa'. This is tempting, because they grow more rapidly; they also change the fundamental qualities and appearance of the plant, and many strains of this juniper in particular now grow very much faster than the snail pace of the original Noah's Ark junipers.

Management. Unlike deciduous trees and shrubs, the shape of a conifer, once lost, cannot easily be restored by judicious pruning. The loss of lower branches or foliage from drought, infertility or overcrowding causes more or less permanent damage.

Effects of size and maturity

Conifer cuttings can be made from snippets of shoots barely 2 to 3 cm (1 in.) long or from branchlets 20 or even 30 cm (8 or 12 in.) long. Naturally slow-growing forms produce smaller cuttings than more robust kinds, but much of this variation springs from the individual preferences of equally successful propagators.

Small cuttings occupy less space, and more can be accommodated in a frame or propagator. They also need to make more growth before they are large enough to plant out. The difference in the time taken to produce a garden-worthy plant can be as much as a year.

Large cuttings take up more space, are more likely to dry out, and can be clumsy to handle. They make good use of growth made while still attached to the parent plant and produce garden-ready plants more quickly.

Provided they can be conveniently accommodated and looked after properly, the size of the cuttings is less likely to contribute to success or failure than the condition of the shoots from which they were made.

What makes a good cutting?

Cuttings can be made from shoots at any stage of development. The more immature the tissues, the more care they need to keep them alive, and conifer cuttings are almost always made from mature or almost mature shoots taken towards the end of their growing season. A shoot can be cut at a number of different positions to produce a cutting—giving rise to different names, depending on the precise location of the cuts.

- *Nodal cuttings* are sections of stem usually cut at a node and sometimes at the point where the current season's growth started.
- *Basal cuttings* are formed by cutting side shoots off at their junction with the main stem.
- *Heel cuttings* are made by pulling shoots off at the point where they join the main stem, detaching each one with a sliver of the more mature tissues of the main stem attached to its base.

In general, heel cuttings are considered more likely to produce roots than basal cuttings. Basal are looked upon with more favour than nodal cuttings. These preferences can be academic—shoots are often too large to be used in their entirety, and then nodal cuttings are effectively the only option. Success usually depends more on the nature of the plant than the precise form of the cutting, but it is worth trying to obtain heel or basal cuttings when plants known to be disinclined to produce roots are being propagated.

Prospects of success with cuttings that produce roots slowly or reluctantly can be improved by wounding and/or applying root hormones. Wounding is the removal of a thin sliver of bark along one or both sides of the stem at the base of the cuttings.

Caring for cuttings

The sturdy awl-shaped, needle-shaped or scalelike leaves possessed by conifers enable them to remain alive and comparatively unstressed while they develop roots, with rather less care than cuttings made from the more vulnerable leafy shoots of broad-leaved shrubs and trees. Many conifers, especially cypresses and their relatives, are late starters. They do not begin to produce new shoots until towards mid-summer and then grow on strongly through late summer and into autumn. Their shoots are not ready to use as cuttings till well into the autumn. This provides two options: to take cuttings in the autumn or leave them on the plant till the end of the winter.

Figure 39. Three cuttings from a semi-prostrate juniper, showing the shoot from which they were removed. The cuttings vary in size from small to large. All have been pulled off with a heel. All three are equally likely to produce roots, but the size advantage of the larger ones will be maintained and they will develop into plants large enough to plant out one or two years before the smallest.

Timing

Cuttings taken in autumn need care and protection throughout the winter. The level of care and the equipment needed depends on the severity of cold and the nature of the winter in the place where the garden is situated. Roots are seldom produced before temperatures start to rise in the spring—especially in cool and cold temperate regions.

Late winter cuttings require care and attention for only a few weeks. They usually produce roots a little later than autumn cuttings and are ready to pot up a few weeks later. The situation of the garden, facilities available and other demands on time are more likely to define the season chosen and methods used than the needs of the plants.

In warm or mild temperate regions or Mediterranea, where no more than light frosts occur and winter rainfall is plentiful, minimal special equipment is needed. Cuttings taken in autumn can be set out in rows in a free-draining mix—organic : mineral, 1:1—as a topping beneath a tunnel cloche, or even in a nursery bed in a sheltered place out of doors. Apart from ensuring they do not dry out, the cuttings can be left more or less to themselves.

Dwarf conifers

A high proportion of conifers in gardens are selections of forms with restricted growth, widely considered more suitable for use in confined spaces, and often referred to as "dwarf conifers." (Note that the term *dwarf* is misleading. Most plants so-called are slow growing rather than innately small. Given time, these Peter Pans may eventually grow as large as their adult counterparts.)

Slow or restricted growth has a number of causes. Small species—low-growing or small conifers—grow naturally in alpine or exposed situations and remain so when brought into cultivation. Many of these produce cones and can be propagated from seed. Environmentally induced dwarfism can be caused by unfavourable conditions—for example, krummholtz trees are stunted individuals of normally large conifer species that are found growing close to the timber line in cold, exposed situations. These do not remain small in the kinder conditions provided by gardens, and seeds collected from their cones will not produce conifers of restricted growth in gardens. Genetic dwarfs, seedlings that are produced with genotypes that give rise to dwarf forms—such as selections of *Pinus mugo*, *Abies koreana* and *Picea mariana*—will reproduce more or less true from seed. Mutations such as bud sports (witch's brooms) occur from time to time on normal trees, producing congested masses of shoots with extremely short internodes—for example, *Picea mariana* 'Nana'. They are unlikely to produce cones or to come true from seed if they do. Juvenile forms (retinosporas) of thujas, chamaecyparis and junipers have softer, more divided foliage than their mature counterparts. Sometimes they fail to grow up, but they retain the juvenile form, usually accompanied by slower growth rates—for example, *Thuja occidentalis* 'Rheingold'. Cuttings of juvenile shoots maintain juvenility more or less indefinitely.

In cool temperate regions or in places where winters are mild but dry, autumn cuttings need the protection of a cold frame or tunnel cloche to protect them from frost or desiccation from wind.

In cold temperate regions where hard frosts are the norm, autumn cuttings need the protection of a frame, poly tunnel or glasshouse, and they benefit from supplementary warmth to protect them from extremes of winter cold. Soil heating cables, thermostatically controlled to provide minimum temperatures between 3° and 10°C (37° and 50°F) radically and economically improve performance—especially of less hardy species such as podocarps. Note, however, that supplementary heating always brings with it a danger of desiccation. Whenever soil heating cables are used, careful checks should regularly be made to ensure the growing medium remains moist around the base of the cuttings, and water must be provided to prevent it drying out.

Cuttings taken in late winter are set up on a warm bench under polythene or under mist in a poly tunnel or glasshouse. Soil heating cables are used when necessary to maintain temperatures of 15° to 20°C (60° to 70°F) in the growth medium around the base of the cuttings. As soon as roots are formed, the cuttings are weaned and potted up in 7 cm (2.5 in.) containers. They can then either be lined out directly in a nursery bed or potted on into 1 litre (6 in.) containers, from which they can be planted in the garden.

Conifers should be grown in the ground whenever possible and not in containers. They grow better and are less vulnerable to neglectful watering, feeding and overcrowding.

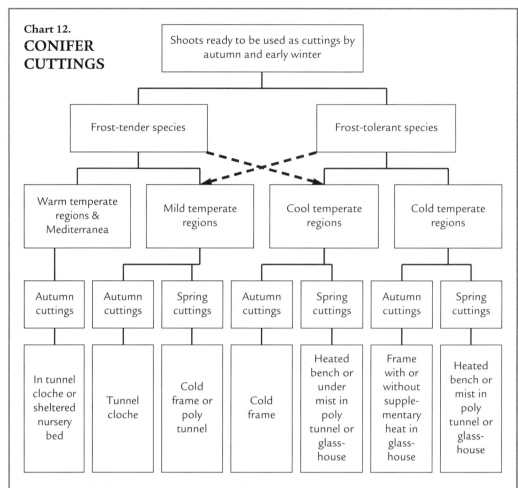

Chart 12.
CONIFER CUTTINGS

Shoots ready to be used as cuttings by autumn and early winter

Frost-tender species | Frost-tolerant species

Warm temperate regions & Mediterranea | Mild temperate regions | Cool temperate regions | Cold temperate regions

Autumn cuttings | Autumn cuttings | Spring cuttings | Autumn cuttings | Spring cuttings | Autumn cuttings | Spring cuttings

In tunnel cloche or sheltered nursery bed | Tunnel cloche | Cold frame or poly tunnel | Cold frame | Heated bench or under mist in poly tunnel or glass-house | Frame with or without supple-mentary heat in glass-house | Heated bench or mist in poly tunnel or glass-house

Options Available When Propagating Conifers from Cuttings
Cuttings of most conifers are made from mature shoots, ready in the autumn; cuttings can be taken either then or in late winter / early spring. The optimum time and the facilities needed vary depending on the frost tolerance of the species and the location of the garden. The chart illustrates optimum seasons and the facilities required for gardens located in different climatic regions. Cuttings of tender species, such as podocarps, must be protected from exposure to frost in cold locations.

Production of shapely, symmetrical conifers from cuttings

Seedling conifers grow naturally into forms inherited from their parents. Provided they are not neglected, few special precautions are needed to ensure they eventually grow into an attractive shape. However, this is not necessarily so when conifers are raised from cuttings, especially when growing upright, symmetrical forms dependent on the development of regularly spaced tiers of branches around a strong central stem.

The shoot most likely to give rise to well-shaped plants of this kind is the leading shoot at the top of the tree—inevitably, the supply of these is extremely limited. Shoots at the ends of side branches can also be used to make cuttings, but trees produced from them struggle to establish a single dominant bud, may never do so, and fail to produce a symmetrical tree with a strong, upright central stem.

The technique described here was originally developed to produce symmetrical Norfolk pines, *Araucaria heterophylla*, grown as pot plants. It can be applied to many other conifers, notably blue spruces, *Picea pungens* cvs. Using this method, 20 or 30 leaders can be obtained from a single seedling.

- Seeds are collected from selected plants with good conformation and foliage qualities.
- Seedlings raised from them are lined out, well spaced in a fertile situation out of doors and rogued to remove poorly shaped or otherwise less desirable plants.
- When five or six tiers of side branches have been produced, the leading shoot of each marked plant is taken as a cutting in the autumn.
- A cluster of potential replacement leaders develops from the top tier of branches during the following summer—one of which would eventually become dominant.
- All are removed as cuttings the following autumn, and the tops of the trees are cut off just above the next tier down, which in turn produces a cluster of replacement leaders.
- These provide another batch of cuttings, and the trees are reduced to the next tier down, and so on.
- When the lowest tier has been used, the trees are thrown away and replaced.

The technique can also be used when propagating inherited forms of *Abies, Agathis, Calocedrus, Cunninghamia, Dacrydium, Phyllocladus, Picea, Pinus, Podocarpus, Sciadopitys, Taxodium* and *Torreya*. The advantages of using leading shoots as cuttings is less marked with cypresses (true or false), red cedars, junipers and yews. Cuttings taken from almost any part of the plant are likely to develop leading shoots quickly and form attractive-looking plants.

Propagation by division

Some confers layer themselves spontaneously—notably Western red cedars, *Thuja plicata*. The lower branches of these trees dip to the ground, pulled down by their weight as they develop. Even substantial branches, once in contact with the ground, develop roots. In time, a single tree becomes the centre of a little grove formed by its offspring, arranged around it in concentric circles as successive layers grow up and produce branches that themselves reach down and form roots. This capacity for regeneration can be applied in gardens by layering young, pliable shoots rather than more mature branches, with all forms of *Athrotaxis*, *Chamaecyparis*, *Cephalotaxis*, *Thuja*, and *Thujopsis*, amongst others.

Propagation Summary for Conifers

S. = propagated from seed
C. = propagated from cuttings
D. = propagated by divisions

Abies—Cones, erect. **S.** weather—nursery bed, spring at 10° to 15°C (50° to 60°F). **C.** leading shoots; low success rate.

Actinostrobus—Cones. **S.** late winter, early spring. **C.** autumn, spring.

Agathis—Cones. Recalcitrant. **S.** fresh; takes 12 months to mature in cones. **C.** autumn, early winter, spring.

Araucaria—Cones. Dioecious. Recalcitrant. **S.** fresh; takes 12 months to mature in cones. **C.** autumn, early winter, spring.

Athrotaxis—Cones. **S.** late winter, early spring. **C.** autumn, early winter, spring. **D.** layers.

Austrotaxus—Succulent Fruit. **S.** fresh, spring.

Callitris—Cones. **S.** serotinous; weather—nursery bed, spring. **C.** autumn, early winter, spring.

Calocedrus—Cones. **S.** weather—nursery bed, spring. **C.** autumn, early winter, spring.

Cedrus—Cones. **S.** weather—nursery bed, spring; coloured foliage forms reproduce to some extent. **C.**

autumn, early winter, spring; preferably from water shoots.

Cephalotaxus—Dioecious. Succulent Fruit. **S.** weather—nursery bed, spring. **C.** autumn, early winter. **D.** layers.

Chamaecyparis—Cones. **S.** weather—nursery bed; coloured foliage forms reproduce to some extent. **C.** autumn, early winter, spring. **D.** layers.

Cryptomeria—Cones. **S.** weather—nursery bed. **C.** autumn, early winter, spring.

Cunninghamia—Cones. **S.** late winter, early spring. **C.** autumn, early winter, early spring; preferably water shoots.

Cupressocyparis—Cones. Hybridise. **C.** late winter, early spring.

Cupressus—Cones. **S.** Some species take 18 months to mature in cones. Weather—nursery bed, late winter, early spring. **C.** late winter, early spring.

Dacrycarpus—Succulent Fruit. **S.** weather—nursery bed, late spring. **C.** autumn, early spring.

Dacrydium—Dioecious. Succulent Fruit. **S.** weather—nursery bed, spring. **C.** autumn, early winter, spring.

Fitzroya—Dioecious. Cones. **S.** late winter, early spring. **C.** autumn, spring.

Glyptostrobus—Cones. **S.** spring.

Juniperus—Dioecious. Cones, e.g., *J. oxycedrus*/Succulent Fruit, e.g., *J. communis*. **S.** weather; germinates erratically, usually not before second year. **C.** late summer, autumn; success rates higher from species with needles than from those with scales.

Larix—Cones. **S.** weather—nursery bed.

Libocedrus—Cones. **S.** fresh, late winter, early spring. **C.** autumn, early winter, spring.

Metasequoia—Cones. **S.** weather—nursery bed, spring. **C.** autumn, early winter.

Microbiota—Cones. **C.** autumn, early winter, spring.

Microcachrys—Succulent Fruit. **S.** spring.

Microstrobos—Succulent Fruit. **S.** spring.

Phyllocladus—Dioecious. Succulent Fruit. **S.** fresh, late winter, early spring. **C.** autumn, early winter, early spring.

Picea—Cones, pendant. **S.** weather—nursery bed.

Pinus—Cones. **S.** serotinous; weather—nursery bed.

Podocarpus—Dioecious. Succulent Fruit. **S.** weather—nursery bed, spring. **C.** autumn, early winter, spring.

Prumnopitys—Succulent Fruit. **S.** fresh, late winter, early spring.

Pseudolarix—Cones. **S.** weather—nursery bed.

Pseudotaxus—Succulent Fruit. **S.** weather—nursery bed.

Pseudotsuga—Cones, pendant. **S.** weather—nursery bed.

Saxegothaea—Succulent Fruit. **S.** spring. **C.** autumn, early winter.

Sciadopitys—Cones. **S.** weather—nursery bed. **C.** autumn, early winter, early spring.

Sequoia—Cones. **S.** weather—nursery bed, spring.

Sequoiadendron—Cones. **S.** weather—nursery bed, spring. **C.** autumn.

Taiwania—Cones. **S.** spring.

Taxodium—Cones. **S.** weather—nursery bed, spring. **C.** autumn, early winter.

Taxus—Dioecious. Succulent Fruit. **S.** weather—nursery bed. **C.** autumn, early winter.

Thuja—Cones. **S.** weather—nursery bed. **C.** autumn, spring. **D.** layers.

Thujopsis—Cones. **S.** weather—nursery bed. **C.** autumn, early winter, spring. **D.** layers.

Torreya—Dioecious. Succulent Fruit. **S.** spring. **C.** autumn, early winter, early spring. **D.** layers.

Tsuga—Cones, pendant. **S.** weather—nursery bed.

Widdringtonia—Dioecious. Cones. **S.** late winter, early spring.

CHAPTER 9

Annuals, Biennials and Plants for Patios

After an orderly start, this chapter takes on something of the character of that ever-present source of help when all else fails—a ragbag. Annuals and biennials appear to be reasonably clearly defined groups—but patio plants need some explanation!

Annuals and biennials invite gardeners to experiment, to try out new ideas, to be a bit daring with colours and effects, to garden with a light touch, and to brighten up the places where we sit and relax and can enjoy the fruits of our labours. The results will be around for only a short time. Successes can be enjoyed while they last; mistakes and disasters are not long with us, and they provide a spur to try something different next time.

The plants we have come to know as patio plants are used in similar ways. They add to and make their own contribution to the bright and cheerful displays of annuals and biennials, and since many of them are used only for a season and then discarded, they are not unlike annuals in the ways we view them and the way we need to replace them repeatedly. It makes gardening sense to bring the field together in a single chapter and simplifies the business of surveying the options.

We are on first-name terms with most of these plants. They are pansies, marguerites, geraniums, snapdragons, and foxgloves—not formal Latin binomials—and this is the only chapter in which vernacular names play more than minor roles.

However, this homely approach brings its own problems. Vernacular names are not used consistently in different places, let alone in different languages, and they have to be used in tandem with their Latin equivalents to avoid confusion.

Annuals

Annuals are plants that grow for a few months, flower, produce seeds and then die. They reproduce only from seed and can be propagated only from seed. They include the familiar friends of our earliest gardening experiences. They are the vegetables and bedding plants whose pictures appear on brightly coloured packets of seeds labeled with comfortably familiar names. Others are less familiar. They are seldom if ever obtainable from colourful packets, and one of the great pleasures of growing plants for ourselves is the opportunity it provides to look beyond the familiar and discover some of these lesser known plants for ourselves.

In practice, a gardener's view of annuals and biennials is not as straightforward as it might be. A significant proportion of the "annuals" of gardens in cool and cold temperate parts of the world are perennials in warmer places, where they can survive winters out of doors. Petunias, lobelias and other perennials widely grown as annuals will be found in this chapter in the section on patio plants.

Origins of annual plants

The annuals which we cultivate are not drawn at random from the thousands of annual species which grow as wild plants throughout the world. They come predominantly from a few localities with well-defined climates. The great majority grow naturally either in Mediterranea in parts of the world where summers are hot and arid and winters cool, moist and free from severe frosts—around the Mediterranean Basin, in the southwestern corner of South Africa, the southwestern corner of Western Australia, coastal areas of California, and a belt across Chile centred on Santiago. They may come from subtropical or tropical climates in frost-free situations where seasons of abundant rain alternate with drought—notably in Mexico and Central America, and to a lesser extent from tropical parts of South America, Asia and Africa. These are all places where prolonged hot, dry seasons restrict competition from perennials and shrubs and preserve spaces where annuals can grow when their seeds germinate after rain.

Gardeners use the places where annuals grow naturally as guidelines when growing them in gardens—defined by their tolerance of frost. Because annuals are grown from seed, it is entirely practical to arrange the dates and places when they are sown and how they are treated subsequently, either to take advantage of their ability to withstand frost or to avoid exposing them to freezing temperatures.

Hence, orthodoxy divides annuals into two groups: hardy annuals—those able to survive freezing temperatures—and half hardy annuals—those killed by freezing temperatures. But this is a misleading and unsatisfactory classification from a gardener's point of view. "Hardy annuals" makes no distinction between plants tolerant of prolonged periods of sharp freezing weather and those able to survive only occasional moderate frosts. "Half hardy annuals" are killed by light frosts and are not hardy by any standards.

The traditional classification has been modified in this book to recognise three categories: *hardy*, or capable of surviving temperatures down to about −10°C (15°F); *half hardy* (retained for old-time's sake), likely to survive to about −5°C (25°F) under favourable conditions (see below); and *tender*, unlikely to survive freezing temperatures. Annuals listed in these categories are provided in the summary at the end of this chapter. The lists should be used in conjunction with the information that follows about growing hardy, half hardy or tender annuals in different locations.

This classification is used as a guide only. The susceptibility of plants to freezing temperatures are complicated by many other environmental factors, including these:

- *Rainfall*: Plants tolerate lower temperatures in areas with low winter rainfall than in wet locations.
- *Soil conditions*: Well-drained soils favour survival; waterlogged conditions reduce ability to survive frosts.
- *Exposure*: Situations sheltered from cold winds favour survival; close, airless locations increase risks of frost damage and pathogenic infections.
- *Light intensity*: Relatively high winter light levels and moderate day lengths increase tolerance to frosts. Low light levels combined with short days—experienced in high latitudes—greatly reduce winter survival rates.
- *Duration and frequency of frosts*: Occasional or intermittent frosts are less damaging than prolonged periods of subzero temperatures.

A garden's location and the conditions it experiences strongly affect the ways annuals can be used. This applies particularly to the large group of annuals capable of surviving light frosts—defined here and in the summary later as half hardy. In Mediterranea and in mild temperate regions, many of these can be sown in the autumn and grown through the winter to flower in the spring, as they would under natural conditions. In cool temperate regions, only hardy and a few half hardy annuals will survive winters out of doors, though many more half hardy plants will get by

with the protection of a cold frame. In cold temperate regions, few if any half hardy annuals overwinter successfully, even in cold frames. They need
to be raised under cover and planted out in frost-
free conditions. In any situation, survival rates are
improved by growing the plants in sunlit, open,
sheltered conditions, on well-drained soils.

Seed collection and storage

Under natural conditions, all annuals set seed
freely and reliably—they would not survive otherwise—and the great majority of those we grow in
gardens do so, too. The seeds of many annuals are
straightforward to collect, easy to handle, simple
to store and undemanding to germinate. They
represent the specification for the perfect seed,
and there is a widely held belief that this is the
result of unconscious selection for these qualities
during the period—often a very lengthy period—
they have been in cultivation. Evidence suggests
this presumption is mistaken. The qualities possessed by their seeds are the inheritance of the
natural adaptations which once enabled their
ancestors to survive in the wild.

They are straightforward to collect because
cycles of growth, including seed production, are
well defined. Seeds are produced predictably and
usually abundantly at particular seasons.

They are easy to handle because, in nature, the
best place to grow is likely to be the spot where
their parents were able to survive. Medium-sized
seeds with moderate storage reserves that fall
straight to the ground are more likely to achieve
this than more mobile, widely dispersed small or
winged seeds. Very large seeds are too easily
located by predators. The result is that many species produce moderate-sized seeds that are easily
handled during harvest, storage and sowing.

They are simple to store because seeds are shed
under natural conditions at the start of lengthy
periods of hot, dry weather. They must be able to
withstand intense desiccation and remain viable
till rains come—an adaptation that makes them
tolerant of desiccation and likely to survive well
in store.

They germinate without making special
demands because the optimum natural strategy
is to germinate without delay once conditions are
favourable. The germination of many species is
largely dependent on the presence of water—sow
them and water them, and they germinate. Under
natural conditions, rains create a starting-gate
effect, in which chances of survival are highest for
those seedlings which emerge first—placing a premium on rapid emergence of seedlings. Because
conditions are predictable from year to year, very
high proportions—often 100 percent—of seeds
germinate as soon as conditions are right. The
consequence is that high proportions of seed germinate more or less synchronously a few days
after being sown.

Total dependence on the presence or absence
of water would be a dangerous strategy; a late
shower just after seed had been shed, or a summer
thunderstorm, could lead to the emergence of
seedlings faced with the heat and drought of summer and with no hope of survival. Species originating from Mediterranea have two safeguards
designed to prevent this, both of interest to gardeners: A high proportion of the species produce
seeds with strongly developed after-ripening
responses. Many are unable to produce seedlings
at high soil temperatures. However, because
plants from Mediterranea are adapted to winter
growing seasons, their seeds germinate rapidly
even at low temperatures—sometimes only just
above freezing point—making them ideally suited
to early sowing in gardens in high latitudes.

Collecting seeds

Gardeners should take advantage of the amenable nature of annuals and collect and store their
own seeds of these plants whenever they can. A
one-off collection of Californian poppies, Swan
River daisies or scarlet flaxes can be dried, cleaned,
put into a plastic box over a layer of silica gel and
stored in a freezer to provide a source of plants for
many years to come.

A great many annuals not in the mainstream
of commercial production are hard to find and
available only intermittently. These almost invari-

ably are "unimproved" wild species and come true from seed. A rare or unusual annual need be obtained only once to provide seeds which can be stored almost indefinitely for future use or distribution to others who appreciate it.

However, worthwhile collections are limited by two considerations: F1 hybrids are the result of deliberately crossing two inbred lines to produce hybrids with extremely uniform qualities. The offspring of these hybrids inherit a random mix of the attributes of the original inbred lines. Individuals vary unpredictably and, apart from being uneven, may display distinctly unattractive qualities; flowers may be small with poor conformation, and it may be months before seedlings start to produce flowers. Avoid F1 hybrids as a rule when making collections of seeds.

Second, colour forms limit collections. The more popular annuals are available as selectively bred strains in which all the plants produce flowers of the same colour—and they often possess other qualities in common, too, such as a dwarf stance or particular shape of flower. Unless these are F1 hybrids, they will produce seed that generally comes true for colour and stance—provided the seeds are obtained from plants growing together away from other plants of the same kind. When these plants are grown alongside others of their kind, cross-pollination can lead to mixtures of colours or other qualities. There is no reason not to collect seed of these colour forms, provided the risk of some mixing is recognised and either guarded against by isolation or roguing, or regarded as acceptable.

Different ways to sow and grow annuals

Annuals can be grown in a variety of ways, depending on what they are wanted for, their ability to survive frosts, and the location of the garden.

Sowing straight into the garden

Annuals can be sown straight into the garden, more or less as they grow naturally. They can either be broadcast over the ground and then lightly raked in, or sown in shallow, spaced drills (weeding, thinning, and other tasks are simplified by sowing in drills).

The seedlings should be thinned out and gaps filled with some of the thinnings. This is best done in two stages: the first as soon as the seedlings can be distinguished from weeds, leaving about 2 cm (1 in.) between each seedling; the second after they become well established to remove weak and surplus plants. Distances between seedlings depend on the size to which the plants will grow. The more space each plant has, the larger it will grow, the more flowers it will produce and the longer it will remain in flower—though the appearance of the first flowers may be a little delayed. The various operations involved are essentially the same as those used to raise seedlings of biennials from seeds sown in drills, as illustrated on p. 163 (although annuals used to produce displays in borders are likely to be disposed in less formal arrangements than the parallel straight lines in the illustration).

Spring sowings produce plants in flower from mid-summer onwards in cool and cold temperate regions for all hardy and half hardy annuals, and in Mediterranea for most tender annuals, provided ample water is available to maintain growth through the summer. Autumn sowings produce plants in flower in spring and early summer. In Mediterranea and in mild and warm temperate regions, all hardy and most half hardy annuals can be sown then. In cool temperate regions in favoured situations, hardy annuals and a few of the more frost-tolerant half hardy annuals can be sown. In locations subject to frosts and heavy rainfall, the second thinning should be delayed till the worst winter weather is over.

Sowing in containers and planting out (bedding plants)

Annuals can also be grown in glasshouses or in poly tunnels to protect them from frost to a greater or lesser extent. They can be sown in autumn or late winter to late spring.

Autumn sowings in a glasshouse or poly tunnel protect seedlings from sharp frosts during the

Figure 40. Marigolds on the left, carnations on the right, sown into a vermiculite topping in 7 cm (2.5 in.) pots. Despite their different sizes, both sets of seedlings are the same state of development and ready to be pricked out.

winter. In cool temperate regions, all hardy and many half hardy annuals can be sown, depending on the protection available. In cold temperate regions, all hardy annuals can be sown. The range can be increased to include almost all half hardy annuals if sufficient artificial heat is provided to prevent temperatures falling more than a degree or two below freezing. Seeds should be sown in the standard way, as described on pp. 78–80. Then they are pricked out into trays or individual containers and overwintered in a cold frame or in a light, well-ventilated (fan-assisted) glasshouse to flower in spring or early summer. Excellent ventilation and free air movement are as important as protection from frost. Frames and glasshouses should be closed down only in freezing weather.

Late winter to late spring sowings occur in a glasshouse or poly tunnel—preferably with supplementary heat. In cool and cold temperate regions, all half hardy annuals can be sown and, provided supplementary heat is available, tender annuals as well. In mild temperate regions and Mediterranea, all tender annuals, either for the garden or for use in containers and window boxes, can be sown. Seeds are sown using standard procedures and pricked out, usually into trays, but then into individual containers when specimen plants are needed. Plants are moved into frames once they have established themselves and are hardened off before being planted in the garden. Tender annuals must be grown in frost-free conditions at all times and never planted in the garden till all danger of frost is past.

In cool and cold temperate regions, tender annuals should be sown late rather than early, except when there is an overriding need to produce plants in flower early and the considerable costs of doing so are acceptable. Tender annuals respond to temperatures of about 25° to 30°C (75° to 85°F), and they depend on minima of 20°C (70°F) to thrive. Supplementary heat at these levels is expensive and demanding when outside temperatures frequently fall below freezing point, but without it, the plants die or grow very slowly. Plants sown in late spring when ambient temperatures and light intensities are higher and days longer cost a fraction of the time and cash to produce and are susceptible to fewer problems than those sown in late winter. They very often catch up with earlier sowings.

Sowing and growing in containers as flowering plants

The seeds of half hardy annuals from Mediterranea germinate in the autumn; the plants grow steadily throughout the winter and flower in spring. They can be used for late winter/early spring displays in conservatories, by sowing them in early autumn, pricking out individually into 7 cm (2.5 in.) square containers and growing on in a well-ventilated, frost-free glasshouse or conservatory—preferably one capable of maintaining minimum temperatures of 5°C (40°F). They are then potted on individually into 9 cm or 1 litre (3.5 or 6 in.) pots, or communally into larger containers, troughs, hanging baskets or urns, and grown on with minimum temperatures of about 10°C (50°F) to flower from late winter through spring. Supplementary light improves growth rates and reduces risks of trouble from pests and diseases during short, dark days in mid-winter in high latitudes, but it should not be used after buds become visible.

Biennials

Biennials are broadly recognised as plants which germinate one year and flower the next, usually during spring and early summer; then they die.* Many biennials grow amongst trees or shrubs in competitive situations, and the strategy of building up a large, well-endowed plant in the first year capable of producing flowers early the following year is a response to this situation. Like annuals, they are entirely dependent on seed for survival.

The growth cycle of a biennial consists of a period of growth followed by a period of rest (winter), during which exposure to low temperatures leads to flower formation—provided the plants are large enough to support a flower. (If not, the plant will grow for a second season before flowering in the third.) The need for a period of rest and exposure to low temperatures before the plant can flower is the essential difference between a biennial and an annual. However, more and more strains of biennials, including hollyhocks, sweet Williams and others, are now being produced which are capable of behaving like annuals, without the need for low temperatures or a rest period.

Seed collection and storage

The comments about the seeds of annual plants apply to those produced by biennials. Most are equally easy to collect and equally suitable for long-term storage, and some are extremely prolific.

F1 hybrids are few, but numerous colour and flower forms exist—all of which reproduce satisfactorily true from seed, provided they are isolated from others of their kind. This applies even to the variegated form of honesty (*Lunaria annua varie-*

gata), one of the few plants with variegated foliage that can be propagated from seed—though, confusingly, the variegation does not appear until the plant starts to produce flowering stems.

Seeds provide a highly satisfactory means of maintaining stocks of unusual forms—of foxgloves, for example. A single plant of the once scarce *Digitalis purpurea* 'Suttons Apricot' grown in isolation within a small group of the same form produces hundreds of thousands of easily gathered seeds capable of being stored for decades. Other forms of *D. purpurea* come true from seed when grown in isolation, including the strange looking 'Campaniflora' and the white, split-petaled form known as 'Anne Reditsky', as well as var. *gloxinaefolia* 'The Shirley' and the dwarf 'Foxy'. There could be no simpler, more effective way to conserve plants like these than by their seeds.

Sowing seed

Under natural conditions, the following is true of biennials:

- They flower in spring or early summer.
- Seeds mature from mid-summer onwards.
- Seeds lying in favourable positions, essentially somewhere moist and warm, germinate.
- Seedlings grow for two or three months into well established, moderately large plants.
- Falling temperatures and the onset of winter prevent further growth.
- Buds within plants that have grown large enough respond to low temperatures by producing flower initials, but these are not formed in late-emerging seedlings or undersized plants.
- Growth is resumed as temperatures rise early the following spring, leading straight to flowering.
- Plants with no flower buds will continue to grow for another year.

In the garden, we cannot do better than follow nature's guidelines. Sow seeds in shallow drills in a nursery bed in early to mid-summer. Thin out the seedlings, filling gaps with surplus seedlings

---

*This definition is not entirely explicit; nit-pickers might point out that in the northern hemisphere, Mediterranean annuals, under natural conditions, flower during the calendar year after their seeds germinate. In the southern hemisphere, biennials complete their growth within a single calendar year.

in two stages: first to 2 to 5 cm (1 to 2 in.) apart, and then to 5 to 15 cm (2 to 6 in.), depending on the size of the plant. Wallflowers need little space, while foxgloves and mulleins benefit from more room. Only plants that have attained a reasonable size by autumn will produce flowers. Lift the plants in mid-autumn, so their roots can reestablish before soil temperatures fall, and plant them out in the garden.

Biennials for conservatories and patios

Canterbury bells, the chimney bellflower, the incense plant (*Humea elegans*), 'Excelsior' foxgloves and a number of others, when grown in containers, make decorative, extremely impressive plants. These can be grown in nursery beds, lifted in the autumn and containerised. Alternatively, they can be raised like annuals in poly tunnels or glasshouses.

- Sow the seed during late spring or early summer.
- Prick out seedlings individually into 7 cm (2.5 in.) pots.
- Pot on to produce plants in 3 or 5 litre (1 gal.) containers.
- Stand outside during the remainder of the summer, feeding and watering as needed; many will benefit from light shading. They will not do well in a glasshouse.
- Leave them outside till mid- to late winter to experience a period of cold.
- Bring them into a cool glasshouse or conservatory with minimum temperatures of about 10°C (50°F) and grow on to flower.

Seeds and seedlings of most annuals and biennials pose few problems for gardeners. Inevitably, some are less obliging and put greater demands on skills and the good judgment that lead to successful management.

The chimney bellflower, *Campanula pyramidalis*, is one of these. It is not difficult to grow; it germinates easily enough, but it provides examples of a number of problems that to a greater or lesser degree will be encountered when growing many other biennials and annuals.

It has tiny seeds. The standard advice is to mix them with a small quantity of dry silver sand to make it easier to ensure even distribution. This is not necessary when using the standard sowing technique described on pp. 78–80. It is enough to tip the seeds into the palm of one hand before distributing them carefully in small pinches over the surface of the topping; then water with a fine rose to settle the seeds in.

Susceptibility to damping-off, a common problem, is usually avoided by sowing on a mineral rather than organic topping; using a clean, disease-free water supply; sowing late in the season in warm, well-lit conditions in a well-ventilated glasshouse; and avoiding sowing in cool/cold, damp, poorly lit conditions early in the season.

Because of its extended germination period, seedlings emerge over a period of several weeks. Prick out the early seedlings when they are ready and lose those that emerge later. It may be necessary to sow extra seeds to compensate for the loss of slow emergers.

Rapidly developing roots necessitate that seedlings should be pricked out as soon as they can be handled—even though they will still be extremely small. Its fragile foliage means that leaves are soft and easily damaged, or even pulled off. Handle firmly, but very gently. Avoid pulling at the leaves to remove small plants from the seed mix—again, any delay in pricking out adds to the problem.

It is vulnerable to slugs and snails; reduce the vulnerable period to a minimum by providing warm, well-lit conditions to encourage rapid growth. Use prophylactic protective measures before troubles occur.

Patio Plants

During the last 25 years, plants with attractive foliage and/or brightly coloured flowers grown in containers or small beds close to the house have become enormously popular. Until recently, the variety available was quite limited—typified by

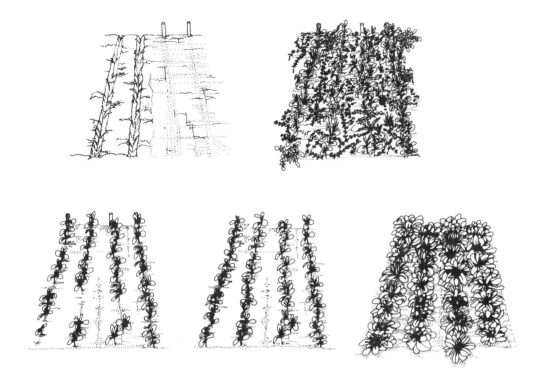

Figure 41. The most satisfactory way to grow biennials is from seed sown in drills in a bed out of doors. Sow the seeds in moist soil, and draw the soil back over the drills. When seedlings are clearly visible, remove weeds and thin out the plants to about 2 cm (1 in.)—it may be necessary to stretch twine along the line of the drills to make it easier to find the seedlings. Use some of the seedlings removed to fill any spaces. About a month later, remove any remaining weeds and thin out the plants according to their final size—5 cm (2 in.) is enough for wallflowers, and 15 to 20 cm (6 to 8 in.) for vigorous plants such as foxgloves, sweet Williams and Canterbury bells. Similar methods are used when growing annuals and perennials from seed out of doors.

pelargoniums, heliotropes, marguerites, petunias and a few others. Now the choice increases, year by year, as more and more plants are introduced.

This is one of those situations where propagation plays a particularly fulfilling and satisfying role—especially for gardeners in cool and cold temperate regions. Most patio plants are perennials. They can be grown from year to year but are tender and will not survive winters unprotected in places where even moderate frosts are experienced.

Added to that, young plants flower more freely and for longer and provide brighter and more attractive displays than their elders. In consequence, stocks of patio plants need to be renewed annually, and even quite small displays use large numbers of plants. These become costly to replace when purchased year after year—especially as generosity in the use of plants plays a vital part in the quality of the display. They cost very little to produce at home, however.

"Patio plants" do not make up a natural group; nobody ever heard the term till garden centres invented it to draw attention to plants they hoped to sell as more or less instant providers of summer colour. The extent of the category depends on the gardener's choosing and ingenuity, and a remarkable variety of plants already fulfill this role—revealed by a glance down the list in the summary at the end of this chapter.

A substantial number are naturally perennial—regarded as annuals and raised from seed in frost-prone parts of the world, because they have generally been grown as such. They can equally be grown from cuttings when need or opportunity arises. Many others are, and have traditionally been, grown from cuttings, including pelargoniums (now increasingly grown from seed), marguerites, verbenas, violas and scaevolas, and coleus. They tend to be amongst the easiest and most gratifying of all plants to grow in this way. Cuttings produce roots and renew growth extremely rapidly. Simple techniques make minimal demands with maximal rewards—and cuttings taken in early spring start to produce flowers often within a few weeks.

Figure 42. Cuttings of *Euryops pectinatus* (golden daisy bush) provide a means of overwintering a tender plant in cold locations and taken in the autumn will produce well-grown plants ready to flower the following spring.

Seed collection and storage

The relatively high individual value of patio plants means many of those sold are highly bred F1 hybrids—indeed, the advent of F1 hybrids opened the way to the propagation of pelargoniums from seed rather than from cuttings. Seedlings from seeds collected from F1 hybrid pelargoniums usually start to flower late in the season, display poor flower quality and variable colours, and grow up into less shapely, less compact plants than their parents. However, cuttings taken from the same F1 hybrids will come into flower early and reproduce the qualities of their parents precisely.

Sowing seed

Under commercial conditions, seedlings of patio plants are often grown in cells. This technique makes it possible to sow a single seed in each cell and avoids the need to thin or prick out seedlings. The attractions to hard-pressed gardeners are obvious, but unfortunately success depends on the use of specialised equipment, premium seed and forms of cultural care that are not easily provided on smaller, more domestic levels. Most gardeners would obtain better results by following standard methods of sowing and growing seedlings described previously (pp. 78–80). As with annuals, the key to growing these plants economically and successfully lies in taking their natural origins into account.

Plants from Mediterranea (origins are listed in the summary at the end of the chapter), including osteospermums, tracheliums and nemesias, are tolerant of temperatures down to 5°C (40°F) and will survive light frosts. Seed can be sown in late winter, and seedlings do not need constantly maintained high temperatures—although in high latitudes, early sowings benefit from supplementary light.

Plants from tropical regions, including busy Lizzies (impatiens), petunias and begonias, are dependent on temperatures between approxi-

Figure 43. Seedling pelargoniums sown in the autumn, and cuttings of marguerites and other tender plants, overwinter on a bench above soil heating cables in a glasshouse. The plants are grown cool and dry, in frost-free conditions, ensured by covering them with bubble polythene during periods of subzero temperatures.

mately 20° to 30°C (70° to 85°F) for successful development, and the plants start to show signs of stress when temperatures fall below 15°C (60°F).

In cool and cold temperate regions, it is more economical, and results are more likely to be successful, when seeds are sown later rather than earlier. Even late spring is not too late. Although the plants will start to flower a little later than those available from garden centres, they will maintain displays through the late summer well into autumn when earlier sowings are likely to be flagging.

Sowing pelargonium seed

Seedlings need to make considerable growth before they start to flower, and the usual recommendation is to sow seeds during mid-winter. Low temperatures reduce germination rates, and low light levels hazard the survival and slow the growth of seedlings. Unless conditions are exceptionally good (with supplementary lighting and ample heating), seedlings seldom produce flowers till late summer or early autumn. Plants perform

better and are easier to care for when seed is sown in early autumn. The high temperatures needed to germinate seeds and raise seedlings successfully are provided more economically. Seedlings develop in favourable ambient temperatures and relatively high light intensities, and when potted up individually they grow into small, well-established plants before winter.

Plants are overwintered in cool (about 10°C, or 50°F), frost-free conditions. They grow slowly but are much more resilient to suboptimal conditions than newly emerged seedlings. In late winter, they are potted on into 1 litre (6 in.) pots and grown on in a glasshouse or frost-free tunnel before being hardened off in frames. The first flowers are produced in early summer.

Propagation from cuttings

Most patio plants are evergreen perennials or shrubs capable of growing more or less continuously as long as they are warm and watered. Cycles of growth and rest are imposed either by cold winters or the hot, dry summers of Mediterranea. They are easiest to manage when grown in ways that take account of these natural cycles.

So long as the plants are growing, they produce a supply of cuttings over many months. Young shoots are soft and tender initially, becoming steadily firmer and eventually almost woody with age. Cuttings can be taken from them at any stage in their development. In warm temperate regions, cuttings are available at any time of the year to replace old plants, which become woody, unproductive and untidy with age. In cool and cold temperate regions and Mediterranea, where seasonal cycles of growth are imposed by cold or drought, cuttings are taken at particular times to produce plants ready to flower during favourable seasons and to ensure the survival of the plants in places with cold winters.

Cuttings in late winter/early spring

Cuttings taken at this time are used to produce plants for summer displays in gardens in mild, cool and cold temperate regions. They are ob-

Figure 44. Fuchsia cuttings taken in spring from shoots on a plant bought from a garden centre. Placed in a propagator or closed frame at 20° to 25°C (70° to 75°F) and lightly shaded—because these shoots are very vulnerable to desiccation—they will produce roots rapidly and be ready to pot on in a few weeks in time to develop into well-grown flowering plants by mid-summer.

tained from overwintered stock plants or shoots produced by cuttings taken in the autumn.

Plants sold by garden centres early in the season provide an excellent source for cuttings.

- Short shoots just firming at the base are removed, usually with three or four nodes.
- Lower leaves and flowers or flower buds are pinched off before inserting the cuttings in a 1:1 cutting mix of [coir, bark, peat] : [grit, calcined clay, perlite].
- A potting mix rather than the plain materials is used for the organic component of the mix to ensure newly formed roots have direct access to nutrients.
- Cuttings are placed in a closed frame, with supplementary warmth if necessary, to maintain temperatures of about 15° to 25°C (60° to 75°F) at the base of the cuttings. Cuttings made from immature shoots are vulnerable to excessive sunlight; on hot, bright days they need extra shading.

- Rooted cuttings are potted up individually into small containers and lightly shaded for a few days.
- Plants are grown on in warm, well-lit conditions before being transferred to the protection of a frame until all danger of frosts is passed.

Cuttings in autumn

These cuttings are used in cool and cold temperate regions to overwinter plants at risk from frost —and in Mediterranea to produce well-developed young plants to flower during spring and early summer. They are usually obtained from plants growing in gardens.

- Young, healthy shoots becoming firm throughout their length are cut off and placed in polythene bags until they are prepared.
- Lower leaves and flowers are removed and the cuttings set up in a standard 1:1 cutting mix of perlite : grit.
- Cuttings are placed in a closed frame or propagator shaded from direct sunlight and then thoroughly drenched with water.
- These cuttings are firmer than those taken in spring, and within a few days more ventilation should gradually be introduced, keeping conditions as light and airy as possible short of allowing the cuttings to wilt. They may wilt temporarily, but adjust the ventilation and exposure so they recover and remain firmly upright. No supplementary warmth is needed at this time of year.
- Drench rooted cuttings with double-strength feed; remove them from the shelter of the cutting frame, and stand out in a light, well-ventilated but frost-free glasshouse or poly tunnel.
- Leave the cuttings, packed together, in their containers. Feed them once more—a month after the first feed—at double normal strength.
- Keep them, making little or no growth, through the winter in cool, frost-free, well-ventilated, dry conditions, watering just enough to prevent the substrate from drying out.
- In late winter (mid-winter in Mediterranea),

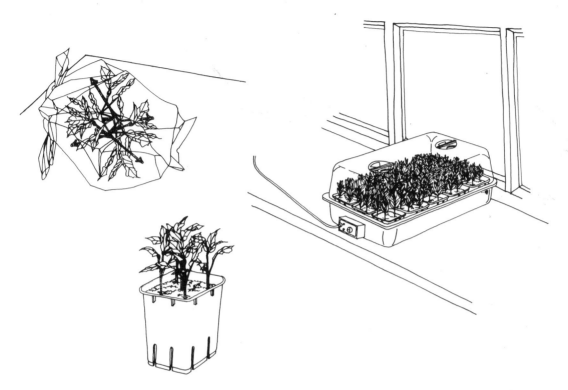

Figure 45. Many of the tender perennials and shrubs grown in containers to provide colour during the summer are propagated from cuttings of the first shoots produced during early spring. These soft tips are vulnerable to desiccation and are protected in a polythene bag from the time they are cut off till they are made into cuttings. They are stuck communally into cutting mix in small pots, held in a closed frame or propagator and, in order to encourage rapid development of roots, it is well worthwhile to use supplementary heating to maintain temperatures of about 20° to 25°C (70° to 75°F).

temperatures are increased to 10° to 15°C (50° to 60°F).

- As soon as they show signs of renewed growth, the rooted cuttings are separated and potted up individually into 1 litre (6 in.) pots.
- Young plants are grown on in warm, well-lit conditions with ample ventilation.
- Once well established and overlapping the edges of their containers, they should be moved to a frost-free frame till it is safe to plant them out.

Examples and exceptions

Begonia 'Gloire de Lorraine', the plant with single, pale rose-pink flowers, was one of the great standbys for winter colour in hanging baskets and containers in conservatories. Seldom seen nowadays because it cannot be rapidly mass-produced, the plant generously repays those who propagate it.

- Cut back stock plants hard in mid-autumn.
- Trim off the lower shoots and foliage to improve air circulation.

Chart 13. PATIO PLANTS FROM CUTTINGS

AUTUMN CUTTINGS

Autumn

Make cuttings from firm semi-mature or mature shoots. Remove all flowers and lower leaves before inserting in cutting mix.

Place in closed frame with light shade; reduce enclosure and increase ventilation after a few days as much as possible without harming the cuttings.

Winter

Drench with ×2 standard feed as soon as roots are formed. Repeat after one month.

Overwinter at 5° to 10°C (40° to 50°F), keeping the rooted cuttings as dry as possible with maximum ventilation short of causing losses from frost.

Drench with ×2 standard feed as soon as growth resumes. Pot up individually into 9 cm or 1 litre (3.5 or 6 in.) pots a week or ten days later.

Spring

Transfer to cold frame until all danger of frost is past. Then plant out in the garden.

Options for Raising Patio Plants from Cuttings

Cuttings made either in autumn or late winter into spring provide an effective way to produce large numbers of plants for summer display. Autumn cuttings are an economical means of overwintering tender plants in cold regions and produce early flowering plants the following spring. Spring cuttings provide a rapid means of increasing overwintered stock plants or plants bought in late winter from garden centres. Shoots from rooted autumn cuttings can often be used, too.

LATE WINTER/SPRING CUTTINGS

Make cuttings from tip or semi-mature shoots. Remove lower leaves and flower buds.

Place in closed frame with bottom heat ca. 15° to 25°C (60° to 75°F). Shade lightly, and increase shading in hot weather, especially in bright sunlight.

Pot up cuttings individually in 7 cm (2.5 in.) pots soon after roots appear. Set out with light shading on glasshouse bench at 10° to 15°C (50° to 60°F).

Pot on into 1 litre (6 in.) pots; or use plants to fill hanging baskets or troughs.

Protect from frost till all danger is past. Harden off outside for a week or ten days before planting in the garden.

Summer

Figure 46. A great many tender perennials, herbs and some shrubs grown as patio plants for summer display are propagated from cuttings in the autumn. Here, penstemon, hebe, sage and artemisia cuttings are shown ready to stick into cutting mix in 1 litre (6 in.) pots—9 to 12 cuttings per pot. Set up in a cutting frame over a heated bench if necessary to maintain minimum temperatures of about 15°C (60°F) while roots are being formed. The cuttings are given no more protection than is needed to prevent wilting, and a stock wire frame covered with bubble polythene is ideal. The ends are closed only for the first few days until the cuttings are capable of standing in a less than saturated atmosphere.

- Remove short shoots as basal cuttings during the winter, and set up cuttings individually in 7 cm (2.5 in.) pots in [coir, bark, peat] : [grit, perlite], 3:1. Alternatively, remove medium-sized leaves with about 2 cm (1 in.) of the petiole and stick them into 7 cm (2.5 in.) pots containing the same mix.
- Maintain at 20° to 25°C (70° to 75°F) with light shade until roots have been produced and young plants have developed.

- Pot on into 1 litre (6 in.) pots or hanging baskets, and grow them on through the summer, feeding as necessary, lightly shaded and as cool as possible.

Buds begin to form in early winter, and the plants will flower continuously provided temperatures do not fall below 15°C (60°F) for long periods. Established plants can be kept going for several years, increasing in size and flower power.

Figure 47. Recently rooted cuttings of a hardy fuchsia taken in the autumn. The basal buds developed by the plant on the left would enable it to survive if the shoot were killed by frost during the winter. The cutting at right has failed to form basal buds, probably because of competition from the flower. If the shoot were killed by frost, there would be nothing to replace it.

Viola cvs. tend to be short-lived unless frequently rejuvenated from cuttings. Cuttings taken in summer from flowering shoots may produce roots but usually fail to survive the following winter. The problem lies in the fact that these plants flower on annual shoots, destined to be replaced in the autumn by new shoots which will carry the following year's flowers. The trick lies in replacing the destined-to-die flowering shoots by a new set with better prospects.

- Prepare stock plants in late summer by cutting off all the flowering shoots.
- Basal shoots emerge rapidly from ground level, and when these are about 3 to 5 cm (1.25 to 2 in.) long, they are cut off and used as cuttings.
- Set the cuttings up in small pots filled with a 1:1 cutting mix of potting mix : [grit, perlite, calcined clay]. About 9 cuttings will fit in a 7 cm (2.5 in.) pot, 12 to 16 in a 9 cm (3.5 in.) pot, or 16 to 20 in a 1 litre (6 in.) pot.
- Place the cuttings in a cold frame, drench thoroughly with water to produce a humid atmosphere, and close the lights.
- Shade lightly for the first week in sunny weather.
- When the cuttings have produced roots—usually after three to five weeks—raise the lights slightly and gradually increase ventilation.
- During the winter, close the lights only during periods of subzero temperatures; otherwise, ventilate freely.
- Leave the cuttings in the frame in their containers until growth resumes in spring.
- Pot up the rooted cuttings individually.

Summary of the Natural Origins of Annuals, Biennials and Patio Plants

Med. Basin = the areas surrounding the Mediterranean Sea
Med. Calif. = parts of California with a Mediterranean climate
Med. S. Afr. = southwestern corner of Cape Province
Med. W. Aus. = southwestern Western Australia
Med. Chile = central belt of Chile
S. = propagated from seed
C. = propagated from cuttings
D. = propagated by divisions

Figure 48. Propagate violas from basal shoots produced in the autumn, following the removal of the flowering shoots in late summer. Cuttings about 3 to 5 cm (1 to 2 in.) long are set up communally in appropriately sized pots in the cutting mix. Overwinter the cuttings in a cold frame, providing maximum ventilation, as soon as roots are formed—short of incurring damage from frost.

Hardy annuals

Adonis aestivalis—Pheasant's eye. Med. Basin.

Ammi majus—False bishop's weed. Eurasia.

Anagallis arvensis—Scarlet pimpernel. Eurasia.

Argemone grandiflora—Prickly poppy. Med. Calif. and SW. USA.

Atriplex hortensis—Orache. Eurasia.

Brassica oleracea—Ornamental cabbage and kale. These plants are grown for foliage, not flowers, and are treated as annuals. Med. Basin, W. Europe.

Calendula officinalis—Pot marigold. Med. Basin.

Centaurea cyanus—Cornflower. Med. Basin.

Chrysanthemum segetum—Corn marigold. Med. Basin.

Clarkia grandiflora—Godetia. Med. Calif.

Claytonia perfoliata (*Montia perfoliata*)—Spring beauty, winter purslane. Eurasia.

Consolida regalis—Larkspur. Med. Basin.

Delphinium ajacis—Larkspur. Med. Basin.

Eschscholzia californica—California Poppy. Med. Calif.

Gypsophila elegans—Baby's breath. Asia Minor.

Iberis umbellata—Globe candytuft. Med. Basin.

Limnanthes douglasii—Poached egg plant, meadowfoam. Med. Calif.

Linum grandiflorum—Scarlet flax. Med. Basin.

Nigella damascena—Love in the mist, devil in a bush. Med. Basin.

Omphalodes linifolia—Annual navel wort. Med. Basin.

Papaver rhoeas—Poppy. Eurasia.

Papaver somniferum—Opium poppy. Med. Basin.

Phacelia tanacetifolia—Californian bluebell. Med. Calif.

Reseda odorata—Mignonette. Med. Basin.

Rudbeckia bicolor—Coneflower. North America.

Salvia horminum—Clary (sage). Med. Basin.

Scabiosa atropurpurea—Pincushion. Med. Basin.

Silene pendula—Hanging catchfly. Med. Basin.

Tripleurospermum perforata (*Matricaria inodora*)—False mayweed. Med. Basin.

Xeranthemum inapterum—Everlastings. Med. Basin, SE. Europe.

Hardy annual grasses

Agrostis spp.—e.g., *A. nebulosa,* cloud grass. Med. Basin, S. Europe.

Hordeum jubatum—Wild barley. Eurasia.

Lamarckia aurea—Golden shower. Eurasia.

Half hardy annuals

Agrostemma githago—Corncockle. Med. Basin.

Ammobium alatum—Winged everlasting. Med. W. Aus.

Anagallis linifolia—Blue pimpernel. Med. Basin.

Anchusa capensis—Cape forget-me-not. Med. S. Afr.

Antirrhinum majus—Snapdragon. Med. Basin.

Arctotheca calendula—Cape weed. Med. S. Afr.

Arctotis fastuosa—Marigold. Med. S. Afr.

Arctotis grandis—Cape marigold. Med. S. Afr.

Arctotis hirsuta—African daisy. Med. S. Afr.

Baeria gracilis (*Lasthenia californica*)—Goldfields. Med. Calif.

Bassia scoparia f. *trichophylla* (*Kochia scoparia*)—Summer cypress. Eurasia.

Borago officinalis—Borage. Med. Basin.

Brachyscome iberidifolia—Swan River daisy. Med. W. Aus.

Brunonia australis—Cornflower. Med. W. Aus.

Calandrinia grandiflora—Guanaco's foot. Med. Chile.

Calandrinia umbellata—Rock purslane. Med. Chile.

Callirhoe involucrata—Buffalo rose or purple poppy-mallow. S. USA.

Callistephus chinensis—China aster. China and Far East.

Carum carvi—Caraway. Eurasia.

Centaurea moschata—Sweet sultan. Med. Basin.

Cephalipterum drummondii—Pompom head. Med. W. Aus.

Cerinthe major—Honeywort. Med. Basin.

Chrysanthemum carinatum—Annual chrysanthemum. Med. Basin.

Citrullus colocynthis—Bitter apple. Med. Basin.

Clarkia amoena—Farewell to spring. Med. Calif.

Clarkia pulchella—Pinkfairies. Med. Calif.

Clarkia unguiculata—Elegant clarkia. Med. Calif.

Cnicus benedictus—Blessed thistle. Med. Basin.

Collinsia bicolor—Collinsia. Med. Calif.

Convolvulus tricolor—Dwarf morning glory. Med. Basin.

Coreopsis spp.—Tickweed. Med. Calif.

Cotula spp.—Goose eyes. Med. S. Afr.

Cynoglossum amabile—Hounds tongue. China and Far East.

Dianthus chinensis—Indian pink. China and Far East.

Didiscus caeruleus—Blue lace. Med. W. Aus.

Dimorphotheca aurantiaca (*Castalis tragus*)—Namaqualand daisy, Cape marigold. Med. S. Afr.

Dimorphotheca pluvialis—Rain daisy. Med. S. Afr.

Dimorphotheca sinuata—African daisy, jackal flower. Med. S. Afr.

Ecballium elaterium—Squirting squash. Med. Basin.

Eucharidium breweri—Pink ribbons. Med. Calif.

Euphorbia marginata—Snow on the mountain. North America.

Felicia bergeriana—Kingfisher daisy. Med. S. Afr.

Felicia heterophylla—Felicia. Med. S. Afr.

Gilia spp.—Gilia. Med. Calif.

Gorteria diffusa—Beetle daisy. Med. S. Afr.

Helenium tenuifolium—Annual helenium. Med. Calif.

Helichrysum orientale—Imortelles. Med. Basin.

Heliophila coronopifolia—Blue flax. Med. S. Afr.

Helipterum humboldtianum (*Rhodanthe humboldtiana*)—Everlastings. Med. W. Aus.

Helipterum manglesii (*Rhodanthe manglesii*)—Everlastings. Med. W. Aus.

Helipterum roseum—Everlastings. Med. W. Aus.

Hesperis tristis—Night scented stock. Med. Basin.

Ionopsidium acaule—Violet cress. Med. Basin.

Kallstroemia grandiflora—Arizona poppy. SW. USA.

Lavatera trimestris—Mallow. Med. Basin.

Layia platyglossa (*L. elegans*)—Tidy tips. Med. Calif.

Legousia speculum-veneris—Venus' looking-glass. Med. Basin.

Leptosiphon parviflorus—Coast baby-star. Med. Calif.

Limonium sinuatum (*Statice sinuata*)—Statice, wavyleaf sea lavender. Med. Basin.

Linaria maroccana—Moroccan toadflax. Med. Basin.

Lobelia lutea—Gold lobelia. Med. S. Africa.

Lobularia maritima—Sweet alyssum. Med. Basin.

Lupinus hartwegii—Annual lupin. Central America.

Lupinus subcarnosus—Texas bluebonnets. Texas.

Madia elegans—Showy madia. Med. Calif.

Malcolmia maritima—Virginia stock. Med. Basin.

Malope trifida—Malope. Med. Basin.

Malva mauritiana—Moroccan mallow. Med. Basin.

Matthiola annua—Ten week stock. Med. Basin.

Matthiola incana—Brompton stock. Med. Basin.

Matthiola sinuata—East Lothian stock. Med. Basin.

Mentzelia lindleyi—Blazing stars. Med. Calif.

Mentzelia laevicaulis—Blazing stars. Med. Calif.

Moluccella laevis—Bells of Ireland. Med. Basin.

Nemesia strumosa—Cape jewels, pouch nemesia. Med. S. Afr.

Nemophila menziesii—Baby blue eyes. Med. Calif.

Nierembergia caerulea—Blue bells. Argentina.

Nigella hispanica—Fennel flower, Spanish fennel. Med. Basin.

Nolana grandiflora—Little bells. Med. Chile.

Orlaya grandiflora—Orlaya. Med. Basin.

Oxalis valdiviensis—Yellow oxalis. Chile.

Phlox Drummondii—Annual phlox. SE. USA.

Podolepis canescens—Bright podolepis. Med. W. Aus.

Proboscidea louisianica (*Martynia louisiana*)—Unicorn plant. SE. USA.

Rhodanthe chlorocephala—Everlastings. Med. W. Aus.

Ricotia lunaria—Eastern honesty. Med. Basin.

Salpiglossis sinuata—Salpiglossis. Med. Chile.

Saponaria calabrica—Calabrian soapwort. Med. Basin.

Satureja hortensis—Summer savory. Med. Basin.

Scandix pecten-veneris—Shepherd's needle. Eurasia.

Schizanthus pinnatus—Poorman's orchid, butterfly plant. Med. Chile.

Sedum caeruleum—Blue stonecrop. Med. Basin.

Senecio elegans—Wild cineraria. Med. S. Afr.

Silene coeli-rosa—Rose of heaven, viscaria. Med. Basin.

Stylomecon heterophylla—Wind poppy. Med. Calif.

Trifolium incarnatum—Crimson clover. Med. Basin.

Ursinia anethoides—Ursinia. Med. S. Afr.

Ursinia speciosa—Ursinia. Med. S. Afr.

Vaccaria hispanica—Cow basil. Med. Basin.

Venidium fastuosum—Namaqualand daisy. Med. S. Afr.

Xanthophthalmum coronarium (*Chrysanthemum coronarium*)—Crown daisy. Med. Basin.

Zaluzianskya villosa—Drumsticks. Med. S. Afr.

Half hardy annual grasses

Briza maxima—Quaking grass. Med. Basin.

Eragrostis spp.—Love grass. Subtropics.

Lagurus ovatus—Hare's tail. Med. Basin.

Pennisetum ruppelianum—Fountain grass. East Africa.

Phalaris canariensis—Canary grass. Med. Basin.

Polypogon monspeliensis—Annual beard grass. Med. Basin.

Triticum durum—Durum wheat. Med. Basin.

Half hardy climber

Lathyrus odoratus—Sweet pea. Med. Basin.

Tender annuals

Ageratum houstonianum—Ageratum. Central America.

Amaranthus caudatus—Love lies bleeding. Trop. S. America.

Amaranthus tricolor (*A. gangeticus*)—Joseph's coat. Trop. S. America.

Amaranthus hypochondriacus—Prince's feather, Prince of Wales feather. Trop. S. America.

Angelonia salicarifolia—Angelonia. Trop. S. America.

Anoda hastata—Anoda. Central America.

Browallia grandiflora—Blue bells. Trop. S. America.

Cannabis sativa—Hemp. Trop. Asia and Africa.

Celosia cristata—Cock's combs. Trop. Asia and Africa.

Cleome spinosa—Spider flower. Trop. S. America.

Cosmea bipinnata—Cosmos. Central America.

Cucurbita pepo—Ornamental gourd. Trop. S. America.

Cuphea lanceolata—Firefly. Central America.

Datura fastuosa—Thorn apple. Trop. Asia and Africa.

Dorotheanthus bellidiformis—Livingstone Daisy. Med. S. Afr.

Emilia sagittata—Tassel flower. Trop. Asia and Africa.

Exacum affine—Persian violet. Trop. Asia and Africa.

Gomphrena globosa—Globe amaranth. Trop. S. America.

Helianthus annuus—Sunflower. Central America.
Hibiscus trionum—Flower of an hour. Trop. Asia and Africa.
Hunnemannia fumariifolia—Mexican tulip poppy. Central America.
Leonotis heterophyllus—Pink lion's tail. Trop. S. America.
Limonium suworowii—Lizard's tails, Statice. Central Asia.
Loasa spp.—Loasa. Med. Chile.
Ocimum basilicum—Basil. Trop. Asia and Africa.
Perilla frutescens—Beef steak plant. Trop. Asia and Africa.
Portulaca grandiflora—Purslane. Trop. S. America.
Salvia farinacea—Blue salvia. SC. USA.
Salvia splendens—Salvia. Central America.
Sanvitalia procumbens—Creeping zinnia. Mexico.
Tagetes erecta—African marigold. Central America.
Tagetes patula—French marigold. Central America.
Tagetes tenuifolia—Tagetes. Central America.
Tinantia erecta—Widow's tears. Trop. America.
Tithonia speciosa (**T. rotundifolia**)—Mexican sunflower. Central America.
Vinca rosea (**Catharanthus roseus**)—Rosy periwinkle. Madagascar.
Wahlenbergia pendula—Annual harebell. Canary Isles.
Xerochrysum bracteatum (**Helichrysum bracteatum**)—Straw flower. *Helichrysum* Med. W. Aus.
Zinnia elegans—Zinnia. Central America.

Tender annual grasses

Coix lacryma-jobi—Job's tears. Trop Asia and Africa.
Panicum miliaceum—Millet. Trop Asia and Africa.
Sorghum vulgare—Broom corn. Trop Asia and Africa.
Zea mays—Maize. Central America.

Tender annual climbers

Cucurbita spp.—Gourds. Trop. Asia and Africa.
Ipomoea tricolor—Morning glory. Central America.
Lagenaria vulgaris—Bottle gourd. Trop. Asia and Africa.
Luffa cylindrica—Luffa gourd. Trop. Africa.
Passiflora gracilis—Annual passion flower. Trop. S. America.
Thunbergia alata—Black-eyed Susan. Trop Asia and Africa.

Tropaeolum majus—Nasturtium. Trop. S. America.

Biennials and short-lived perennials

Alcea rosea—Hollyhock. Med. Basin.
Althaea rosea—Hollyhock. China and Far East.
Angelica sylvestris—Wild Angelica. **S.** fresh; weathered. Eurasia.
Aquilegia vulgaris—Columbine. **S.** fresh; weathered. Eurasia.
Calomeria amaranthoides (**Humea elegans**)—Incense plant. **S.** early/mid-summer. Overwinter plants, nearly dry in very cool glasshouse. New South Wales.
Campanula medium—Canterbury bell. Med. Basin.
Campanula pyramidalis—Chimney bellflower. S. Europe.
Campanula thyrsoides—Yellow bellflower. Eurasia.
Cheiranthus allionii—Siberian wallflower. Eurasia.
Corydalis sempervirens—Rock harlequin. Canada.
Cynara cardunculus—Cardoon. **S.** spring; **C.** spring from basal side shoots. S. Europe.
Dianthus barbatus—Sweet William. **C.** late summer, selected forms. S. Europe.
Digitalis purpurea—Foxglove. Selected forms, e.g., 'Alba', 'Excelsior', 'Suttons Apricot', 'Campanulata', 'Monstrosa', reproduce true from seed in isolation. Eurasia.
Dipsacus fullonum—Teasel. Eurasia.
Echium plantagineum—Purple viper's bugloss, salvation Sally. Med. Basin.
Eryngium giganteum—Miss Wilmot's ghost. **S.** fresh; weathered. Caucasus.
Erysimum cheiri (**Cheiranthus cheiri**)—Wallflower. Med. Basin.
Eustoma exaltatum (**E. russeliana**)—Prairie gentian. **S.** late winter, mid-summer; overwintered in light, airy frost-free glasshouse. SE. USA.
Ferula spp.—Fennel. Med. Basin.
Gaillardia pulchella—Gloriosa daisy. N. America.
Hyoscyamus niger—Henbane. Eurasia.
Lunaria annua—Honesty. Eurasia.
Lychnis coronaria—Crown campion. Eurasia.
Myosotis sylvatica—Forget-me-not. Eurasia.
Oenothera biennis—Evening primrose. N. America.
Onopordum arabicum—Scotch thistle. Med. Basin.
Papaver nudicaule—Iceland poppy. **S.** late winter, mid-summer. Boreal regions.
Penstemon barbatus—**S.** fresh, spring. **C.** late summer, autumn. USA.

Primula malacoides—**S.** summer. China.

Primula polyanthus—**S.** late spring, early summer. **D.** summer

Ptilostemon afer—Ivory thistle. **S.** mid-summer. S. Europe.

Salvia sclarea **var.** *turkestanica*—Hot housemaid. Central Asia.

Silybum marianum—Our lady's thistle. Med. Basin.

Smyrnium olusatrum—Alexanders. **S.** fresh, weathered. Med. Basin.

Tragopogon porrifolius—Salsify. Med. Basin.

Verbascum spp.—Mullein. Med. Basin.

Viola ×wittrockiana—Pansy. Eurasia.

Patio plants and decorative perennials

Acnistus—Blue datura. **S.** late winter. Australia.

Alonsoa warscewiczii—Mask flower. **S.** spring. Trop. S. America.

Althaea officinalis—Marsh mallow. **S.** late spring, early summer. Eurasia.

Anthemis cupaniana—Anthemis. **C.** spring, autumn. Med. Basin.

Antirrhinum majus—Snapdragon. **S.** late winter, early spring, early autumn. **C.** mid-autumn. Med. Basin.

Argyranthemum cvs.—Marguerite. **C.** spring; tips of shoots, autumn; flowering shoots produce roots as readily as non-flowering shoots—overwintered as rooted cuttings. Canary Islands.

Bacopa cvs.—**C.** spring, autumn.

Begonia—Begonia. **S.** late winter. *B. semperflorens* and tuberous—**C.** spring; basal. Trop. S. America.

Bellis perennis—Daisy. **S.** early summer. **D.** summer. Eurasia.

Bidens ferulifolia—Bidens **C.** late winter, spring, autumn. Central America.

Calceolaria—Slipper flower. **S.** mid-summer. Subtrop. S. America.

Campanula isophylla—**C.** late winter, autumn. Med. Basin.

Commelina coelestis—Sleeping beauty: **S.** late winter, spring. Central America.

Convolvulus sabatius—**C.** spring, autumn. Med. Basin.

Coreopsis tinctoria—Tickseed. **S.** spring, summer. North America.

Dahlia ×hybrida—Dahlia. **S.** spring. **C.** late winter, early spring. **D.** late winter, tubers. Central America.

Diascia—**S.** spring. **C.** spring to early winter. South Africa.

Dichondra sp.—Silver falls. **C.** or **D.** spring. Trop. America.

Euryops pectinatus—**C.** late winter, autumn. Med. S. Afr.

Gazania cvs.—**S.** late winter. **C.** spring, late summer, autumn. Med. S. Afr.

Glechoma hederacea—Ground ivy. **C.** spring to autumn. Eurasia.

Helichrysum cvs.—**S.** late winter, early autumn. **C.** autumn. Australia.

Helichrysum petiolare—**C.** late winter, autumn. S. Africa.

Heliotropium cvs.—Cherry pie. **C.** late winter, spring. Trop. S. America.

Impatiens sultani—Busy Lizzie. **S.** late winter, spring. **C.** autumn, spring. Zanzibar.

Lobelia erinus—Lobelia. **S.** spring. **C.** autumn, late winter. Med. S. Afr.

Lobelia valida—Lobelia. **C.** autumn, late winter. Med. W. Aus.

Lotus berthelotii—**C.** late summer, early autumn.

Mimosa pudica—Sensitive plant. **S.** late winter; chip. Palaeotropics.

Mimulus cvs.—Monkey flower, musk. **S.** spring. **C.** spring, summer; basal; **D.** spring to autumn.

Mirabilis jalapa—Wonder of Peru. **S.** spring. **C.** spring; basal. Overwinter like dahlia tubers. Trop. S. America.

Nemesia fruticans—**S.** late winter, spring; smoke. **C.** spring, autumn. Med. S. Africa.

Nicandra physaloides—Shoo-fly plant. **S.** late winter, spring. Trop. S. America.

Nicotiana cvs.—Tobacco. **S.** spring. Trop. S. America.

Osteospermum barberae—Veld daisy. **S.** spring, autumn. **C.** late winter, spring, autumn. Med. S. Africa.

Pelargonium cvs.—Geranium. **S.** autumn, late winter. **C.** autumn, spring. Eastern Cape, South Africa.

Petunia hybrids—**S.** late winter, spring. **C.** late winter, early autumn; Surfinia petunias are grown exclusively from cuttings. Trop. S. America.

Plectranthus spp.—**C.** spring, summer. **D.** summer. Subtrop. and Trop. Africa.

Ricinus communis—Castor oil plant, castor bean. **S.** late winter, early spring. Trop. Africa.

Rudbeckia hirta—Black-eyed Susan. **S.** early spring, late summer. **D.** late summer. North America.

Scaevola aemula—**C.** late winter, autumn. Australia.

Senecio cineraria—Silverdust. **S.** late winter, spring. **C.** late summer, autumn. Med. Basin.

Senecio cruentus—Cineraria. **S.** early to mid-summer. **C.** late winter. Canary Islands.

Solenostemon—Coleus. **S.** late winter, early spring. **C.** spring, single bud; autumn, early winter, semi-mature shoots. Trop Asia and Africa.

Sutera cvs.—**C.** spring, autumn. South Africa.

Trachelium caeruleum—Violet veil. **S.** spring, autumn. Med. Basin.

Venidium cvs.—**S.** spring, autumn. **C.** spring, autumn. Med. S. Africa.

Verbena cvs.—**S.** spring; quality variable, germination erratic. **C.** late winter to late autumn. S. America.

Viola cvs.—**S.** spring. **C.** autumn; cut plants back hard one month previously. Eurasia.

Climbing patio plants

Basella rubra (*B. alba*)—Malabar spinach. **S.** late winter. Trop. Asia.

Cobaea scandens—Cup and saucer plant. **S.** late winter. Central America.

Eccremocarpus scaber—Chilean glory flower. **S.** late winter, spring. Chile.

Ipomoea alba (*Calonyction aculeatum*)—Moonflower. **S.** late winter. Tropics.

Ipomoea lobata (*Mina lobata*)—Star ipomoea. **S.** late winter, spring. Central America.

Maurandya barclaiana—Maurandia. **S.** late winter. Mexico, Central America.

Rhodochiton atrosanguineus—Purple bell vine. **S.** late winter. Mexico, Central America.

CHAPTER 10

Perennial Herbaceous and Evergreen Herbs Including Carnivorous Plants

Gardeners automatically link the words *perennial* and *herbaceous* and hence link perennials to the herbaceous border—a combination that conjures up the image of a vegetarian lodger to those who are not phytocentrically inclined. But let us stay within the limits of the garden. *Perennial*, when applied to plants, means several things.

Herbaceous perennials, such as delphiniums, grow actively during spring and summer. In autumn they die back to ground level, and they survive the winter as congregations of resting buds, known as crowns, at or just below ground level. Like violas, but a little bit more so, these are perennial plants with annual shoots. Herbaceous perennials are divided into two group in this book: broad-leaved dicotyledons in this chapter, and narrow-leaved monocotyledons in the one which follows.

Evergreen perennials with persistent foliage and stems, such as pulmonarias, are not herbaceous. Many grow naturally in deciduous woodlands. They avoid competition with the dense overhead canopy of the trees during the summer, and they survive by making a living during winter and spring when trees are leafless.

Grey or silver-leaved perennials, often with some degree of shrubbiness—such as osteospermums and artemisias—grow mainly where summers are hot and arid. They make little growth in their native lands during the hot, dry summers but grow actively at other seasons whenever conditions are favourable. Favourable periods may be short and fleeting, confined to brief spells in spring and autumn, sandwiched between bitterly cold winters and oven-dry summers.

These differences are highly significant to the propagator. The seasonal cycles of growth of herbaceous, evergreen and eversilver perennials differ in major ways, posing different opportunities and problems when sowing seeds, taking cuttings or making divisions. The annual stems of herbaceous perennials are programmed to die at the end of every season. If they are to be successfully used as cuttings, precautions may be necessary to persuade them to forget their annual destiny and give rise to perennial plants. The shoots of the woodland evergreens are destined to live from one year to the next. However, their roots undergo cycles of comprehensive decline and replacement. These become significant when the plants are divided. Eversilvers are likely to be tenacious, persistent plants, more likely to be killed by kindness than neglect and are readily propagated from cuttings at almost any time of the year.

Seed Collection and Storage

Most perennials produce seeds in capsules or other dry fruits, which open, or dehisce, as they mature to release small seeds naturally tolerant of desiccation. Almost all can be stored at subzero temperatures for many years.

A minority of perennials, including actaeas, strawberries, mandragoras and phytolaccas, produce fleshy fruits. These are attractive to birds and likely to disappear rapidly soon after they ripen. Safeguards may be necessary to prevent this. Once gathered, the seeds inside them can be removed and stored in orthodox fashion.

The seeds of some perennials, as noted later in the summary and typified by geraniums and acanthus, are distributed ballistically as they become dry after maturing. These need to be picked over almost every day as they mature and collected just before they ripen or the seed will be lost. Once gathered, the seeds must be kept sufficiently enclosed to prevent them being hurled far and wide as they dry out—stored in paper bags, for example, rather than being laid out in an open tray.

Sowing Seed

The first hardy perennials to produce seeds, including species of adonis, eranthis, hellebores and hepaticas, come on stream about mid-summer, with increasing numbers as summer gives way to autumn, until the seeds of leucanthemellas, cimicifugas and a few other late flowerers that mature during early winter are produced. This time frame ensures that seeds of most perennials hit the ground at a time when the onset of winter is more or less imminent. They have a choice before them: they can either germinate at once, taking a chance on survival as seedlings during the winter in order to be well established, and favourably placed, the following spring; or they can wait till spring, overwintering in comparative security within the seed but vulnerable from established neighbours, when seedlings emerge into the competitive hurly-burly of the following spring.

Cold winters pose severe threats to seedlings with minimum storage reserves, whereas mild winter weather offers opportunities for seedlings to grow slowly but steadily into well-established plants by spring, advantageously placed to resist competition from more mature plants. However, although mild winters pose less dangers from frost, humid conditions increase risks of infection from pathogens and sharpen the appetites of slugs, snails and other pests.

There is no "best" solution to the conundrum whether to germinate in autumn or spring. In some years, favourable winter weather provides autumn seedlings with a flying start. In other years, catastrophic winter losses make waiting till spring the more successful strategy.

It is not unusual for seeds produced by a single plant to germinate at different seasons or in different years. Some may produce autumn seedlings, while others respond to low-temperature weathering and germinate in spring. Third, fourth, fifth or more flushes of seedlings may appear in successive autumns or springs during the following years. A proportion of the seed may become part of the soil seed bank, lying inert in the ground for years before producing seedlings—this is seen sometimes dramatically, when foxgloves germinate by the thousands in cleared woodlands many years after their parents have disappeared from the scene. When propagating perennials from seed, we can either attempt to familiarise ourselves with every trick possessed by each and every plant and try to reproduce every subtle twist and turn, or we can devise blanket strategies to enable us to produce seedlings of most of the plants most of the time.

As soon as we gather seeds, we are faced with the choice of sowing them at once or storing them for a while and sowing them later, perhaps in the spring. We do not have to make an irrevocable choice between one or the other; we can divide the seeds into two batches, sowing one immediately and the other in early spring. In the absence of inside information, that is exactly what should be done. It will not necessarily produce the best results, but it seldom fails entirely.

Seeds chosen for immediate sowing should be sown within a fortnight, if possible. Sow in the standard way and place the containers either in a cold frame with the lights propped open for ventilation or, preferably, on the bench of an unheated glasshouse. These aids provide shelter from extreme weather but are not essential. The seeds are watered when necessary and in cold locations protected from hard frost. Some seeds germinate within a short time and are left in their containers during the winter and the seedlings are potted up in early spring. Others start to germinate during the winter, probably reaching a peak in early spring.

Seeds chosen for delayed sowing are sown in late winter/early spring, and the containers are placed, preferably, on a bench in a glasshouse at temperatures between 12° and 20°C (54° and 70°F). Alternatively, they can be given no artificial heat, when they will respond to increasing temperatures during spring days. As and when seedlings grow large enough to handle, they are pricked out into suitable containers.

The division of the seeds into two batches maximises chances of obtaining seedlings, even when nothing is known about the ways they germinate. It identifies species which germinate only when sown fresh and weathered during the winter, and which are capable of germinating without special treatment. It reveals those that need special treatments of one kind or another. Once experience has been gained of the behaviour and requirements of different species, it becomes possible to vary the seasons when seeds are sown deliberately, to meet the needs of the seeds in ways that are convenient and economical for the propagator.

Advantages and disadvantages of sowing at different seasons

In late summer, many meadow perennials and some woodland species germinate naturally. Seedlings gain a head start the following spring. Seedlings should remain in their containers all winter in cold locations, but in Mediterranea and warm temperate regions they should be pricked out as soon as they are large enough to handle. Young plants benefit from protection in a frame or glasshouse but need no or minimal artificial heat. The long period of slow growth during the winter leaves seedlings vulnerable to slugs, mice and other pests—this may lead to heavy losses of susceptible plants such as campanulas, delphiniums and adenophoras. Early sowing exposes seed to warm weathering, before the onset of winter—an essential for some perennials, including hellebores.

In early autumn to early winter, seeds dependent on low temperature weathering during the winter should be sown by early winter if possible and exposed to natural winter weather—in a cold frame, for example. Most will then germinate during late winter into early spring. Seedling emergence and development can be speeded up by moving them into a warm glasshouse (10° to 15°C, or 50° to 60°F) after eight to ten weeks' exposure to cold. In places where winters are mild, a refrigerator can be used to substitute for natural weathering.

Late winter is an excellent time to sow seeds of species capable of germinating without weathering. They should be placed in a cold frame with the lights closed except on warm and sunny days, or on a bench over soil heating cables in a glasshouse at temperatures from 12° to 20°C (54° to 70°F). Many perennials will produce flowers during their first year when sown early with supplementary warmth. Seedlings can be pricked out as soon as they are big enough to handle, or if there are other things to be done, they can be held in their containers until it is convenient to prick them out. Tender species and those vulnerable to slugs, mice, and other pests may suffer severely in frames and are safer in a glasshouse.

Spring is the best time to sow tender species, but seedlings of many hardy species also thrive in the warmth and high light levels at this time of year. However, seedlings produced in spring need maximum attention and care at a busy season.

Chart 14. PERENNIALS FROM SEED

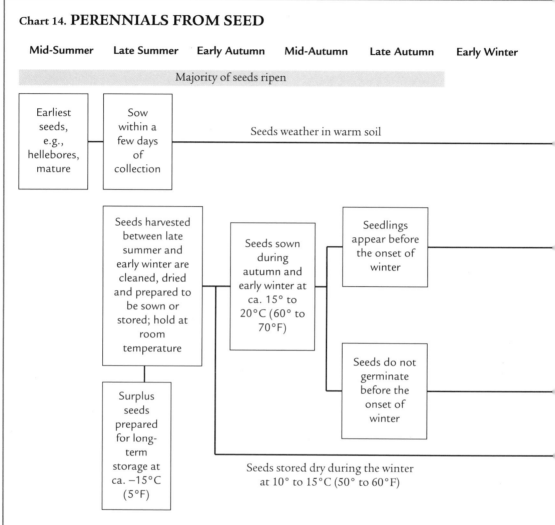

Options for Raising Perennial Plants from Seeds
- Seeds produced up to mid-summer: Sow as soon as possible to allow time for weathering in warm soils before the onset of winter cold.
- Seeds produced after mid-summer: Those capable of immediate germination can be sown either in autumn—when the seedlings are over-wintered in their containers before being pricked out in the spring—or sown when winter is over.
- Those in need of low-temperature weathering are sown as soon as possible.
- Those with unknown requirements are sown in two batches: one in the autumn, the other in the spring. Once their requirements are known, seeds are sown in later years at the most appropriate season.
- The great majority of perennials produce seeds suitable for orthodox long-term storage. Surplus seeds, dried and stored at ca. −15°C (5°F), remain viable for many years. These include seeds of primulas, meconopsis, delphiniums and other genera generally believed to be short-lived.

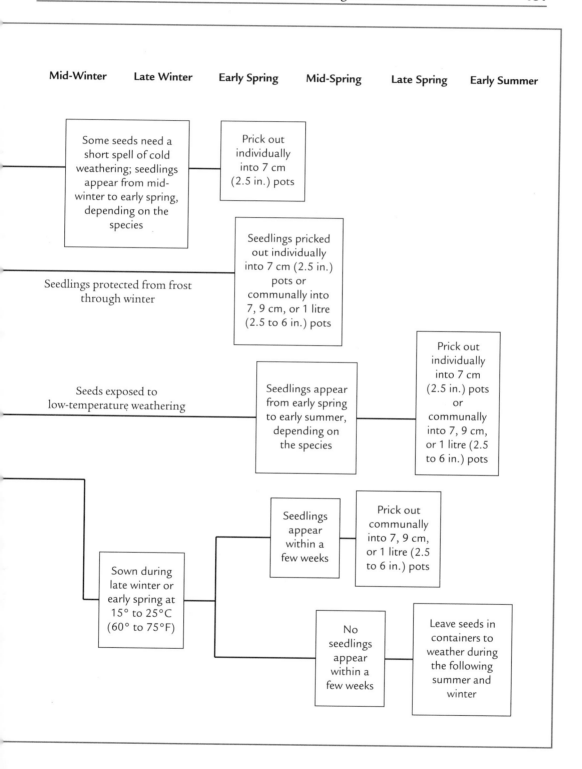

| Mid-Winter | Late Winter | Early Spring | Mid-Spring | Late Spring | Early Summer |

Some seeds need a short spell of cold weathering; seedlings appear from mid-winter to early spring, depending on the species

Prick out individually into 7 cm (2.5 in.) pots

Seedlings protected from frost through winter

Seedlings pricked out individually into 7 cm (2.5 in.) pots or communally into 7, 9 cm, or 1 litre (2.5 to 6 in.) pots

Seeds exposed to low-temperature weathering

Seedlings appear from early spring to early summer, depending on the species

Prick out individually into 7 cm (2.5 in.) pots or communally into 7, 9 cm, or 1 litre (2.5 to 6 in.) pots

Seedlings appear within a few weeks

Prick out communally into 7, 9 cm, or 1 litre (2.5 to 6 in.) pots

Sown during late winter or early spring at 15° to 25°C (60° to 75°F)

No seedlings appear within a few weeks

Leave seeds in containers to weather during the following summer and winter

In late spring/early summer, perennials can be sown (like biennials) out of doors in nursery beds, provided water is available to ensure they do not suffer from drought during the summer. This is a labour-saving way to produce plants ready to be planted out the following autumn or spring.

Pricking out and growing on

Perennials can be managed at a more relaxed pace than annuals. Seedlings emerging before the onset of winter, especially where winters are cold and light levels low, should not be disturbed till late winter or early spring, when growing conditions begin to improve. Seedlings from seeds sown in late winter in the warmth and shelter of a glasshouse can, if necessary, be moved into a cold frame and left to grow on slowly until more urgent sowings and other spring tasks are completed, when they can be potted on. They develop less rapidly than when pricked out early and grown on in a glasshouse in warmer conditions, but they do not suffer otherwise.

Seedlings grow large with tangled roots when left in their containers. The easiest, least damaging way to disentangle them is to immerse them in a bowl of lukewarm water before gently easing the growth medium away from their roots. Large plants are potted up individually in 7 or 9 cm (2.5 or 3.5 in.) containers, and small ones are pricked out to share similar containers.

It is neither necessary, economical nor beneficial to use seed trays (flats) when growing perennials unless large numbers are being grown of each. It is more convenient and flexible to prick out the seedlings into pots. A 9 cm (3.5 in.) container holds four large seedlings or nine small ones. A 1 litre (6 in.) container holds nine, twelve, or sixteen seedlings, depending on size, and seedlings are pricked out in units of four, nine, twelve or sixteen, using as many pots as are necessary, rather than juggling with partially filled seed trays capable of holding fifty or sixty seedlings.

Young plants are potted individually into 7 or 9 cm (2.5 or 3.5 in.) containers, before moving them into a frame or standing them out of doors

Figure 49. A batch of perennials sown soon after the seeds were gathered was photographed in mid-winter. Some seedlings have appeared, and others remain ungerminated. Hitherto, supplementary heat has prevented temperatures falling below 10°C (50°F) to encourage growth of emerged seedlings. From this point on, the heat will be turned off, and temperatures will be allowed to fall below freezing point, so seeds that have not yet germinated will be weathered.

until they fill the pots. At that stage, most are ready to plant straight into the garden. Those that are to be grown on can either be potted up in 2 litre (8 in.) pots or lined out in a nursery bed. Most will do better in the bed, where they will need much less care and attention.

Sowing perennials in the open

Perennial plants include numerous strong, enduring kinds capable of producing seedlings when sown during spring in a well-prepared seedbed in the open. Only species that do not require low temperature weathering should be grown in this way. However, similar methods can be used for those dependent on preliminary low temperatures by sowing seeds in autumn and protecting them from the worst of the winter weather under a polythene tunnel cloche.

Sow seeds in drills during late spring and early summer in cool and cold temperate regions or in

Points to bear in mind when sowing perennials

Square 7 or 9 cm (2.5 or 3.5 in.) pots make ideal containers for the seeds of most perennials using the standard technique described on pp. 78–80, although 9 cm (3.5 in.) pots are preferable when sowing seeds capable of germinating only after weathering, when several months or sometimes a year or more may pass before seedlings appear. Grit or calcined clays provide denser, more stable toppings than lighter or unstable materials such as perlite or vermiculite, which are more easily disturbed or blown or washed away. Containers should be held firmly in pot carriers or trays to guard against being knocked over, especially when seeds are being weathered in cold frames accessible to cats or other animals.

autumn in Mediterranea. The soil should be moist when the seeds are sown (if necessary, water thoroughly three or four days previously), and it should not be necessary to water again before seedlings emerge—nor is it desirable, since watering can lead to soil capping, making it harder for seedlings to break through the surface.

Thin out young plants in two stages: first when they are still very small to about 3 cm (1 in.) between each seedling, filling gaps with plants removed from more crowded parts of the row. Then thin to 10 to 20 cm (4 to 8 in.), depending on the vigour of the plants. Plants should not be moved until early autumn, when they are planted out in the garden if large enough, or lined out in a nursery bed to grow on for another year. It may be several years before seedling veratrums and cimicifugas grow large enough to be moved into the garden.

Examples and special cases when propagating perennials from seed

Anthriscus sylvestris 'Ravenswing' produces high proportions of crimson-leaved seedlings from parents grown in isolation. Seedlings should be rogued (selected) when still very small, keeping only those with intense colour. Other crimson-leaved perennials that can be treated similarly include *Foeniculum vulgare* 'Purpureum', *Angelica sylvestris* 'Vicar's Mead', sweet William *Dianthus barbatus* 'Sooty', and coloured-leaf forms of *Heuchera* such as 'Palace Purple' and 'Chocolate Ruffles'. There will be variations from parental forms.

Cyclamen seeds are collected as the capsules gape and sown immediately, when seedlings are produced in about a month at ambient temperatures of approximately 15° to 20°C (60° to 70°F). Irrespective of the time when they flower, the seeds of almost all species of cyclamen mature in the autumn. Pour near-boiling water over dried seeds and soak for 24 hours before sowing, but results are still likely to be disappointing. Small corms are formed immediately after germination from which leaves emerge. Pot individually into 7 cm (2.5 in.) pots with the corms just on the surface. Seedling roots are weak and do better when denied space to spread. Pot on when three or four leaves have developed, barely covering the corms, and grow on in cool conditions in a frame or cool glasshouse. Hardy species including *C. hederifolium, C. coum, C. purpurascens, C. repandum, C. cilicium, C. mirabile* and *C. pseudibericum* need protection only from severe frosts. Tender species including *C. creticum, balearicum, cyprium, graecum* and *persicum* should be grown on in cool but frost-free conditions.

Dicentra spectabilis, including 'Alba', seeds should preferably be collected while the capsules are still partially green, in late summer/early autumn. Sow immediately in small pots placed in an unheated glasshouse. Seedlings emerge irregularly, starting in mid-winter, and are potted up individually in 7 cm (2.5 in.) containers from early spring, and then moved to a cold frame about six weeks later, where they need protection from mice. The first seedlings are ready to line out in early summer.

Hepatica spp. and cvs. seed are collected as soon as they can be detached from the seed head by gentle rubbing; they should be sown at once. If that is impractical, they remain in good condition for several weeks when "sown" on damp paper towel in a transparent plastic box. Sow seeds on the surface of a generous topping of an open, free-draining organic and mineral mixture, such as [bark, coir, leaf mould] : [grit, calcined clay], 1:1, in 1 litre (6 in.) square containers, and plough in lightly to cover the seeds barely. After weathering in a cold frame, seedlings begin to emerge the following winter and until spring. Let them develop undisturbed until the beginning of their third growing season. Then knock them out of their containers. Carefully separate and pot up individually in 9 cm (3.5 in.) pots. Note that young plants are highly vulnerable to mice and slugs.

Meconopsis spp. and cvs. are frequently interfertile and cross-pollinate freely in gardens to produce infertile hybrids. Seeds are vulnerable to poor storage conditions, and mould infections are the most common cause of poor germination, but the seeds are orthodox and store well at subzero temperatures when thoroughly dry. Most species are not dependent on weathering for germination, and seeds should be stored and sown in early spring, avoiding peat-based mixes. A free-draining but water-retentive seed mix, such as perlite : leaf mould : light loam, at 1:1:1, is an acceptable alternative. The containers are best placed on a bench in an unheated, well-ventilated glasshouse, and damping-off is a major problem. Overwatering should be avoided, and light shading to reduce fluctuations in humidity is helpful.

Nymphaea, especially *N. ×pygmaea*, multiplies extremely slowly from divisions known as eyes. Seeds are produced in capsules surrounded by mucilage. The contents are spread more or less evenly over the surface of a loam-based mix and lightly covered with grit, before standing the containers in a tray deep enough for the seeds to be immersed—about 2 cm (1 in.) deep in water, at 15° to 20°C (60° to 70°F). When they first emerge,

seedlings produce tiny, translucent, exceedingly fragile submerged leaves. Leave undisturbed till two or three true floating leaves have been produced; then prick out into shallow containers, about 3 to 5 cm (1 to 2 in.) apart. They should be grown initially about 2 cm (1 in.) deep in water, gradually raising the water level as the plants develop. When growth resumes the following spring, pot them up individually into small containers and grow on through the summer.

Paeonia spp. and cvs. produce viable black seeds and infertile scarlet seed, which should be discarded. Mice are a major problem, eating both seeds and seedlings, and the seeds should be protected from them by mixing with moist vermiculite before putting the mixture into small plastic boxes with close-fitting lids, in which they can be weathered until germination starts. Even seed sown immediately after collection seldom germinates until the second winter or early spring, and seedlings may not appear for several years. Radicals emerge first and may be followed within a week or two by plumules; often the latter do not appear until the following year.

Primulas—primroses and polyanthus—produce seedlings successfully only in cool conditions, preferably below 15°C (60°F). They are best sown fresh or from packets in early to mid-summer, when ambient temperatures can be well above those they prefer; in as cool a condition as possible, placing the containers under a bench in a glasshouse or in a shaded cold frame. Sow the seedlings into a topping of grit : calcined clay, 1:1. The porous clay helps to maintain cool conditions by evaporation. Seedlings also need cool, moist conditions and do not thrive in bright sunlight and hot, dry conditions—a frame glazed with bubble polythene to diffuse sunlight with extra shading in sunny weather is the easiest way to keep them happy.

Salvia seeds produced by some species develop hard, impermeable seed coats and should be chipped before sowing to ensure that water reaches the embryo. Many species respond to fluctuating temperatures and produce few or no seedlings when temperatures remain constant night and day. Salvia seeds are frequently coated with a mucilaginous gum. This swells in contact with water to form a translucent jellylike covering that is easily mistaken for some kind of fungus. There is no agreement on its function, but it is possible it serves to anchor the seed against the downward thrust of the developing radicle immediately after germination, especially in loose, sandy soils. Seedlings of species from semi-arid areas may develop with spectacular rapidity; within 24 hours, radicles can penetrate several centimetres deep, often thrusting seeds up into the air above them. Sow salvia seeds thinly in deep containers and cover with a mineral topping at least 1 cm (0.5 in.) deep.

Veratrum spp. seeds need weathering and respond best to a sequence of warm temperatures followed by cold. Freshly gathered seed sown in late summer usually produces radicles during the following spring and summer, followed by leaves soon after or during the following spring. Stored seed may not germinate for several years. Flowers are unlikely to be produced till seedlings are five years old, but the foliage can be enjoyed after the third year. Under natural conditions, flowers are not produced annually, and in any year more than half the plants may not produce flowers. Fertile soils and generous feeding in gardens encourage regular flowering.

Propagation from Cuttings

Propagating perennials from cuttings is usually short, sweet and productive. Basal shoots of herbaceous perennials are likely to possess preformed root initials. Shoots of eversilver species mostly produce resilient, easily cared for and amenable cuttings which produce roots with few complications and with no need for expensive or special equipment such as mist propagation units. Cuttings of rhizomes and stolons are even easier. Roots or leaves can be used to propagate some species, and their possibilities can be investigated by those who enjoy a bit of mystery or uncertainty in their gardening.

Shoot cuttings

Basal cuttings are made from shoots emerging in spring from the crowns of herbaceous perennials. They are cut off as soon as they are large enough to handle and have developed a little firmness toward the base, and they often produce roots so rapidly their growth is hardly checked. When cut off just below ground level, some will already have young roots.

The process can be advanced by digging up plants in late winter and either potting them up or laying them in boxes with their roots lightly covered by soil, garden compost, peat, or bark. Stored dahlia tubers or chrysanthemums grown in pots can be treated similarly. If moved into a cool glasshouse with minimum temperatures of about 10°C (50°F), early crops of cuttings are produced from which plants capable of flowering the same year can be produced. Plants treated in this way should not be lifted from the garden too early. Herbaceous perennials are quiescent for a period after dying down in autumn, and vigorously renewed growth occurs only after they have experienced a period of cold weather. Those lifted too early may fail to produce the strong basal shoots needed to make cuttings.

- Cuttings are stuck into a mix of equal parts (1:1) organic and mineral components, such as [bark, coir, peat] : [grit, vermiculite, perlite] in square plastic containers.
- Large shoots, such as dahlias, delphiniums and euphorbias, are set individually in 7 cm (2.5 in.) containers. Smaller cuttings, such as chrysanthemums, diascias and codonopsis, are set communally in 9 cm or 1 litre (3.5 or 6 in.) containers.
- The containers are placed in a closed frame or propagator at 10° to 15°C (50° to 60°F) at the base of the cuttings. This supplementary heat is not essential, but it speeds up the development of roots and reduces risks of losses from damping-off organisms.
- Remove the cuttings from the closed case as soon as they form roots; feed with liquid fertiliser at standard strength.

- Rooted cuttings in communal containers are potted up singly.
- Transfer them to a cold frame to grow on after about a fortnight.
- Plant out in the garden early in the summer.

Semi-mature shoots

Semi-mature shoots from eversilver species with a more or less permanent superstructure of shoots containing more or less woody tissues lend themselves to propagation by cuttings, because they are adapted to cope with dry conditions and are less demanding than plants with softer, green leaves, which depend on highly humid conditions to remain alive and functioning. Nevertheless, attempts to propagate plants such as helichrysums, artemisias and dianthus often fail, because their tolerance of dry conditions is forgotten and they are exposed to the one element to which they are most vulnerable—excessive water.

Take cuttings in autumn or during late winter/early spring using the methods described for patio plants in chapter 9. Enclose them to the least possible degree consistent with keeping them alive and functioning. Ensure they have ample ventilation; moderate atmospheric humidities; and well-aerated, free-draining, moist but never soggy substrates—for example, a 1:1 mix of grit and perlite.

Semi-mature shoots from herbaceous species with annually recurring flowering shoots are most readily propagated from basal cuttings, as described above, or from divisions, as described below. Alternatively, cuttings can be made from the flowering stems of these plants. The method is used only for a limited number of plants including *Digitalis*, *Kirengeshoma*, *Cosmos*, *Hesperis* and *Verbascum*, for which simpler methods are unproductive.

Cosmos is an extreme example. Every plant in cultivation is believed to descend from a single plant brought to the Royal Botanic Gardens, Kew, in the 1970s. It is thought to be extinct in the wild and is self-sterile. No seed is set, and cuttings provide the only means of reproduction, apart from tissue cultures. Cuttings made from flowering shoots of these plants often produce roots and

shoots successfully and then fail to survive the winter. The problem stems from the herbaceous paradox embodied in the production of annual shoots on perennial plants. These shoots are destined to die after they have flowered and produced seeds: cuttings made from them will survive only if they are able to produce more persistent buds around the base of the cuttings before the onset of winter—or in the case of the cosmos, small tubers. They will do so, provided they are kept alive and growing long enough to form buds or tubers and stock them sufficiently with storage reserves. Once these have developed, although the shoots themselves die during the winter, replacement shoots are available to take their place.

- Cut off flower stems in their entirety just before flowers appear.
- Cut each into sections consisting of a short piece of stem (internode) topped by a leaf with a bud in its axil.
- Stick these single-bud cuttings into cutting mix with the bud immediately below the surface and the leaf sticking out above.
- Reduce large leaves by cutting them in half.
- Set up the cuttings in warm, light conditions—such as in a closed frame on a glasshouse bench or under mist—to promote rapid root development and renewed shoot growth.
- Roots are produced from the bases of the cut stems or develop from the buds in the axils of the leaves, after which the buds themselves grow out to form shoots.
- Pot up young plants as soon as they have sufficient roots and place them in conditions which encourage sustained growth and delay the onset of winter dormancy.
- A frost-free glasshouse is helpful, with a small amount of artificial heat (approximately 10° to 15°C, or 50° to 60°F, minimum) maintained into early winter, combined with supplementary lighting to keep the plants growing actively late into the autumn and early winter. This gives the plants time to develop the basal buds necessary to ensure survival, followed by renewed growth the following spring.

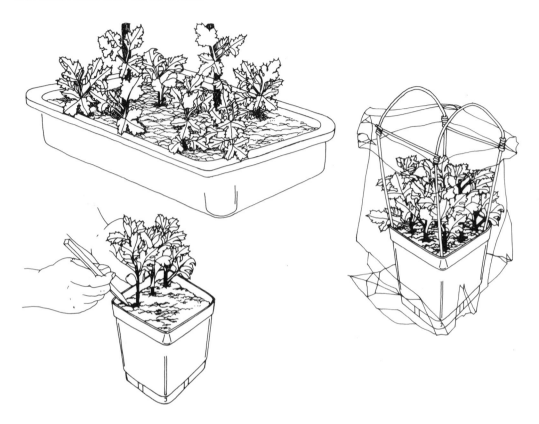

Figure 50. Chrysanthemums are propagated from cuttings of basal shoots. Cut the plants back to the ground when the flowers fade; pot up or stand in boxes and cover with potting mix. Shoots growing from the rootstock are removed when 5 to 9 cm (2 to 3.5 in.) long. Small numbers can be stuck into cutting mix in 1 litre (6 in.) pots, each enclosed in a polythene bag, supported on a stock wire frame (as shown) to make micropropagators.

Root cuttings

Roots are the complements of shoots. They are the cryptic, barely known and almost completely ignored aspect of the Janus head of plants, of which the flowers, foliage and shoots are the more familiar face. Although much less widely used than shoots, roots can also be made into cuttings. The roots of dicots contain cells capable of division, which, in the normal course of events, produce more roots, but thanks to the totipotency possessed by all the meristematic cells in a plant,

they can when occasion demands adapt their normal growth processes in order to produce shoots. Occasion demands when for any reason roots become detached from their tops and prospects of any sort of future depends on producing the leaves needed to sustain them. Dig up an acanthus, transplant it elsewhere, and in a short time new shoots spring up from roots left behind in the spot where it originally grew. Cells within the abandoned roots have divided, differentiated and formed replacements for what has been lost.

Figure 51. Many geraniums are readily propagated from cuttings. Some, like these *Geranium renardii*, may bear little resemblance to conventional cuttings. Shoots are cut off close to the rootstock and trimmed of almost all leaves, reducing them to the small stubs seen in the centre of the picture, and now ready to insert in a 1:1 cutting mix of grit : perlite.

The simplest way to make use of root cuttings is to let the plants do the work for you. Transplant oriental poppies, acanthus, or verbascums by lifting them during late winter and replanting them elsewhere. While doing so, take care not to lift them with all their roots, but slice through the latter some 15 cm (6 in.) below the ground. The truncated roots develop into a number of independent plants during the summer, which are dug up, separated and planted out the following autumn/winter.

Plants are propagated from root cuttings in a more formal fashion, as follows:

- Dig up parent plants in late winter and remove some of the strongest roots.
- Replant the parents. As a rule, remove no more than half the roots; but in case of extreme need, most plants manage to reestablish themselves and eventually make good the losses they have suffered, even when treated much more brutally.
- Cut the roots into convenient lengths—about 2 to 5 cm (1 to 2 in.).
- Fill a container deep enough to hold the cuttings, with a 1:1 cutting mix of [bark, coir] : [grit, perlite, calcined clay].
- Insert the cuttings vertically into holes made with a dibber, with the top of each just below the surface.

Roots, like all parts of a plant, possess polarity—that is, they have tops and bottoms. Root cuttings should be placed with their tops (the part that was closest to the crown of the parent) just below the surface, not inadvertently upended. The most economical way to do this is to lay out the cuttings methodically as they are made, in orderly rows on a tray on the potting bench with their tops pointing away from you. Standard advice to make a slanting cut at the base and a horizontal one across the tops wastes time and material.

- Put the pots containing the root cuttings either in a cold frame or on a bench in a glasshouse with supplementary heating from soil heating cables set to prevent temperatures falling below 5°C (40°F).

Gardeners follow this lead by cutting roots into sections and providing them with the wherewithal to continue to function, in the expectation they will not only continue to produce roots but also form shoots necessary to make up complete, functional plants. The anchor roots produced by many perennials during late summer are the key and provide the material, well provisioned with stored starches, from which cuttings can be made between mid-winter and early spring, just before growth starts. This is a season when the roots are naturally poised to release their storage reserves and the tissues are ready to grow actively as soon as the soil begins to warm up.

Figure 52. Many of the most attractive verbascum cultivars are sterile or do not breed true from seed. They are propagated during mid- to late winter from root cuttings made from the thicker roots. These are cut either into sections about 2 cm (1 in.) long and inserted vertically into cutting mix in pots with their tops just below the surface, or they are cut into discs up to 0.5 cm (0.25 in.) thick and inserted on edge with their upper rims barely protruding above the cutting mix. Water thoroughly after insertion and cover with bubble polythene laid on top of the pots till shoots begin to grow. Place either in a cold frame or on a bench with a minimum temperature of approximately 10°C (50°F).

- Shoots are produced from the cut surfaces at the tops of the cuttings, which grow through the thin covering of cutting mix.
- Delay potting up the young plants until it is quite certain they have developed enough new, young roots to support them—some plants, such as romneyas, are inclined to produce shoots enthusiastically unsupported by new roots.
- Feed at monthly intervals with a liquid nutrient.

Because they are out of sight and do not wilt or display signs of stress in other ways, looking after root cuttings is more hit-and-miss than caring for cuttings of shoots, and results are likely to be more erratic. Some years will produce excellent results, others will be no more than satisfactory or even disappointing. Sometimes cuttings placed on heated benches produce better results, and sometimes those in cold frames do better.

Root cuttings and plants with leaf variegations

Border phloxes are frequently propagated from root cuttings, despite the fact that basal cuttings provide a more predictable means of increase. The reason is stem eelworm—an extremely serious pest that infests phloxes and quickly reduces suscepti-ble varieties to shadows of their former selves. Stem eelworms invade plants from the soil and multiply rapidly in the tissues of the shoots. How-ever, they are steadfastly upwardly mobile, never descending into the roots. As a result, pest-free phlox plants can be raised from stocks riddled with eelworm by propagating them from root cuttings.

However, that is not the end of the story. A few border phloxes, including *Phlox paniculata* 'Norah Leigh', 'Pink Posie', 'Becky Towe' and 'Harlequin', are grown for their strikingly variegated foliage. When these become infested by eelworms, they, too, can be propagated from root cuttings—but not reproduced! Every plant will have plain green leaves, without a vestige of the variegation that is the only reason for growing these cultivars. This underlines the fact that variegated plants cannot be propagated from root cuttings (see p. 116) because the cells in the roots from which new shoots develop the original genetic constitution of the green-leaved plant, rather than the modi-fied constitution within the shoots and leaves which renders some cells incapable of forming chlorophyll.

Cuttings of rhizomes and stolons

Rhizomes are stems that have taken to life under-ground or grow horizontally on the surface—the "roots" of ground elder and the old stems of bergenias are familiar examples. Stolons are stems with greatly elongated internodes—typified by strawberry runners. Rhizomes can be wide-rang-ing, questing, attenuated and thin in cross-sec-tion, forming extended colonies of shoots—as in solidagos—or they can be short and stubby, ad-vancing steadily in stages measured in centime-tres a year—as in epimediums. They may resemble roots but can always be distinguished by the pres-ence of nodes and leaves. The leaves on under-ground rhizomes are nonfunctional; reduced to brown, scalelike organs; and not immediately recognisable for what they are.

Whatever their shape or size, rhizomes possess the hallmarks of all stems, the most important of which from the propagator's point of view is the presence of buds in the axils of each leaf, even the vestigial leaves of rhizomes. The consequence is that a new plant can be produced from every one of these buds. The rhizome carrying them is cut into sections, which are potted individually in 7 cm (2.5 in.) containers using a standard potting mix. Newly potted rhizome cuttings can be placed in a cold frame until they produce shoots and new roots. The time of year is seldom crucial, but spring and early summer provide the warmth nec-essary for rapid development with a long enough growing season ahead to build up a well-devel-oped plant.

Examples and special cases of perennials propagated from cuttings

Crambe maritima and *C. cordifolia* can be propa-gated from a combination of basal and root cut-tings in early spring. Lift the plants during the winter, cut off the roots and tie them in bundles of a dozen or so, and store them in sand in a cel-lar or cool shed. Adventitious buds develop at the top of the roots and are removed as basal cuttings when 3 to 5 cm (1 to 2 in.) long. The roots are planted and produce more shoots and eventually new plants.

Dahlia cvs. can be propagated from basal cut-tings produced in spring by their tubers. Set out the tubers in shallow trays in late winter and barely cover with soil : coarse sand, 1:1, before moving them into a frost-proof shed or under the bench in a glasshouse at around 10° to 15°C (50° to 60°F). After shoots emerge from the tops of the tubers, cut them off immediately below a node when 6 to 9 cm (2.5 to 3.5 in.) long and stick them into a 1:1 cutting mix of [peat, bark compost] : [perlite, grit] individually in small pots or in trays. Place them in a closed frame on a bench with soil

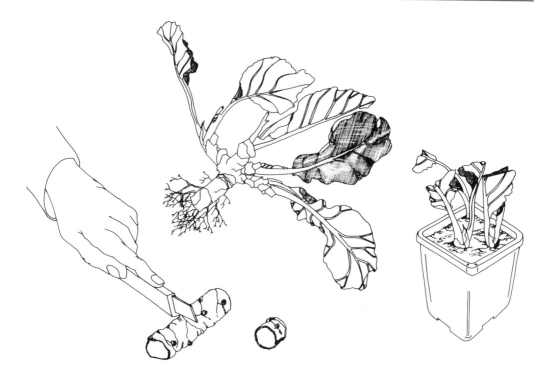

Figure 53. Now that bergenias have become popular, a general shortage of propagating material justifies cutting up the rhizomes to supplement the supply—even though such cuttings need a year longer than cuttings of shoots before they are large enough to plant out. Shoots are first cut off close to the rhizome; their leaves are reduced and they are stuck into cutting mix on a bench at about 15° to 20°C (60° to 70°F). They need very little protection from desiccation. Rhizomes are then cut into sections, 1 to 2 cm (0.5 to 1 in.) long, each containing at least one bud, and set out on edge, just below the surface of the cutting mix, either in a frame or on a heated bench.

heating cables providing supplementary heat of about 15° to 20°C (60° to 70°F). When roots develop, move the cuttings from the frame and grow them on with ample light and ventilation. Pot them up into 1 litre (6 in.) containers, before moving them into the protection of a cold frame until all danger of spring frosts is over. Then plant them out in the garden.

Delphinium cvs. can be propagated from cuttings of basal shoots just like dahlias. Alternatively, they are grown from "eye" cuttings in late summer. Cut back the flowering stems almost to ground level as soon as the flowers are over, and about a fortnight later, dig up the plants. The eyes are tiny dormant buds clustered around the base of the stems just above the crown. Detach each eye—pulled off or cut—as close to the root stock as possible, and pot up individually in small containers, with their tips immediately below the surface. Move them into a shaded frame and water only when clearly necessary. Shoots develop within a few weeks, and the small plants are over-

Figure 54. The writhing white "roots" of *Epilobium hirsutum* are underground stems, or rhizomes, identified by the upright pegs, which are vestigial leaves. A bud lies in the angle formed by each leaf with the rhizome, and, like dragon's teeth, provided it comes with a bud, every section is capable of developing into a plant.

wintered in a cold frame, with protection if necessary from slugs, potted on in late winter and brought into a cool glasshouse to grow on.

Geranium spp. and cvs., such as *G. pratense, G. himalayense, G. phaeum, G. psilostemon* and *G. endressi*, are dug up soon after the flowers fade in mid- to late summer, divided into single or small groups of crowns and potted up or lined out in nursery beds. *G. macrorhizum* and *G. ×cantabrigense*, amongst others, can be propagated from divisions, but better plants are obtained from cuttings taken in mid-summer. Very vigorous shoots of the former should be avoided, choosing those of lesser or moderate vigour. Species which produce a ring of shoots round a central rootstock, including *G. renardii* and *G. cinereum*, can be propagated only from cuttings. The shoots of some of these, such as *G. cinereum*, are so small it may be necessary to remove cuttings with part of the rootstock

attached in order to anchor them in the cutting mix. Elderly plants, particularly *G. cinereum* 'Ballerina', develop longer shoots that are more easily used as cuttings. *G. wallichianum* 'Buxton's Variety' is one of a number with sprawling annual shoots from a central, indivisible rootstock. Cuttings made from their shoots may produce roots, but they die back to nothing during the winter. These can be propagated only from seed.

Hesperis matronalis 'Alba Plena' and other double forms do not set seed and can be propagated only vegetatively. They seldom divide satisfactorily, and propagation from basal shoots in spring yields only small numbers of plants—the yield can be increased by earthing up the base of the plants with garden compost or composted bark during the winter. A more productive alternative is from single-bud cuttings made as the flowers fade. The old flowering stems are cut off and sliced into sections, each consisting of a leaf and the bud where it joins the stem, with 3 or 4 cm (1 to 1.5 in.) of stem below the leaf to provide a peg. This is stuck into a 1:1 cutting mix of [peat, bark] : [grit, perlite] in containers, with several cuttings sharing each container, and placed in a semi-enclosed, lightly shaded frame in a glasshouse, where they are kept sufficiently moist to prevent the leaves wilting until roots form, followed by shoots. Large leaves can be reduced by half. Sometimes axillary buds develop spontaneously in the inflorescences to form small, viviparous plants. These are detached and treated just like single-bud cuttings.

Romneya coulteri can be propagated from seed but seldom produces viable seeds in cool or cold temperate regions and, apart from erratic germination partially countered by smoke, very heavy losses often occur after pricking out. Root cuttings taken in mid-winter provide an alternative. These are most easily obtained by laying paving stones down alongside the plant. Lift the stones during late winter to expose the roots lying directly beneath them. Cut the roots into sections and set them out horizontally in shallow trays, covered with a layer of grit. The plants resent disturbance and often do not produce roots till long after the shoots have developed. Great care is necessary to ensure the roots are well developed before any attempt is made to pot up the plants individually.

Verbascum 'Helen Johnson' and other sterile cultivars must be propagated from root cuttings taken in November. Sections 2 to 3 cm (1 in.) long can be used, but many more plants can be obtained by using a razor blade to slice the roots into thinner sections—down to a minimum of about 0.5 cm (0.25 in.) thick. These discs of tissue are inserted in a 1:1 mixture of [coir, bark] : [grit, perlite, calcined clay], with the edge of the disc barely breaking the surface.

Propagation by Division

No gardener, however unobservant, can fail to notice the leaves, flowers and stems of herbaceous perennials coming and going with the seasons. Few gardeners, however keen, observe the equally significant annual cycles of growth, decline and renewal of the roots.

- Starting in late summer, strong, downward-tending roots emerge from the bases of subterranean buds or crowns. These anchor roots quickly penetrate the soil to provide a secure hold for the winter.
- During the autumn, storage reserves, mainly in the form of starch, are packed into the anchor roots to such an extent that their value to the plant as storage organs may well be even more vital than their anchoring effects.
- The following spring sees the mobilisation of these storage reserves to supply energy to the actively growing young shoots. At the same time, a network of feeding roots produced from the anchor roots ramifies through the upper layers of the soil, gathering water and nutrients.
- In early summer, when the need to sustain rapid growth becomes less vital, much of the root system wastes away, to be renewed when the cycle of growth starts again.

We are repeatedly advised to divide perennials during the winter "after the foliage has died down" or in the spring, when young shoots break through the soil and "renewed root growth helps the plants to reestablish rapidly." These directions may be hallowed by repetition, but they owe more to the management of traditional herbaceous borders than to the life cycles of plants. Their effect is to mutilate plants at times of the year when they are least able to repair damage and/or to deprive them of much of the storage reserves they depend on for vigorous growth.

Division of perennials in late summer

Bearded irises and polyanthus have long been divided during the summer, as soon as the flowers are over. Irises display their preferences particularly conspicuously by producing thrusting new anchor roots no one can fail to see. So, taking the hint, we have become quite accustomed to digging up irises in early July, dividing and replanting them in new soil after cutting back the old leaves. In dry seasons, we may encourage them with a sprinkling of water—but their new roots grow out so strongly and rapidly this is seldom necessary. Bearded irises and polyanthus are not exceptional plants. Their renewed growth and activity, marked by the production of vigorous roots soon after mid-summer, is simply the start of processes common to many other perennials.

The best time to lift and divide most perennials is in late summer extending into early autumn. Strong, young anchor roots may already be present, but they are seldom as conspicuous or immediately self-reliant as those of irises, and other plants need a little more help to reestablish.

- Cut off flowering stems and crop the foliage to reduce transpiration.
- Divide the clumps into single or small groups of two or three crowns.
- Set the crowns out in rows in a nursery bed, well watered and preferably protected by a shaded cloche for a couple of weeks. Alternatively, pot them individually into 7 or 9 cm (2.5

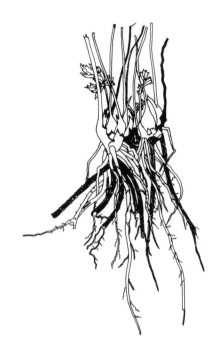

Figure 55. Crown from a plant of *Geranium psilostemon* removed in late summer, soon after flowering. The old flowering stem has been cut off. Two new buds have been produced, and new anchor roots can be seen thrusting down into the soil. This is the time to divide such plants. When replanting straight into the garden, the whole unit portrayed here is planted as it is shown. If potting up and growing on, the two new crowns are cut off and potted up individually—doubling productivity. By the following spring, they will have grown into fair-sized plants ready to plant out and produce flowers in the garden.

or 3.5 in.) containers, depending on their vigour.
• Place them in a cold frame and shade lightly.

These divisions establish rapidly, renewing roots and shoots at the start of the annual cycle of root growth, and they quickly produce the leaves necessary to stock the new roots with starch. By the end of the growing season they will have developed into fully competent small plants that can safely be held in their containers or in the nursery bed until places in the garden are ready for them.

Division of perennials in the spring

References to spring as the season of renewal are so trite they tend to set our teeth on edge, but even if it is not the best season to divide perennials, it is an inescapable truth that it is the season when gardening enthusiasm is renewed. This is no time to dampen enthusiasm by glibly reminding some-

one psyched up to replant a border with verve and imagination that he or she has missed the boat by going off on holiday the previous summer instead of staying at home to propagate daisies.

Apart from coinciding with the motivation to do something (no mean advantage in gardening), spring, leading into early summer, is not a bad time to divide most perennials. It can be a pleasant season to work out of doors, and the soil is likely to be in a receptive state for planting. It is not too difficult to picture how plants that are already developing new shoots will develop. Plants vulnerable to bad weather do not have to face the worst conditions of winter while in a delicate condition. Because the plants are growing actively, they recover quickly from injuries inflicted, and the networks of feeding roots they produce naturally at this time soon establish a roothold.

Plants divided at this season will need particular care to avoid unnecessary damage when digging up and dividing clumps. Refrain from greed and divide plants into clusters of crowns rather than ones or two. Cut back the tops or reduce the number of shoots a little to lighten the demands on the roots. Water when needed, and provide shelter from drying winds.

Division of perennials during the winter

The seasonal cycles of root growth described earlier provide the key to propagating perennials most economically and effectively; they also explain why the winter is a less than perfect time to attempt this. By the winter they will long previously have produced the anchor roots in which their storage reserves are held, and this is a season when plants are quiescent and vulnerable to damage. Injured roots and damaged tissues heal slowly and remain exposed to attacks by fungal and bacterial diseases and the predatory activities of millipedes, slugs, wood lice and other small creatures. But by tradition this is the time to make these divisions, and many gardeners remain convinced it is the only time to do it, conceding perhaps that late autumn or early winter might be preferable to mid-winter.

The timing at least has the advantage of providing something to do in the garden for those who enjoy working in the mud, and it is unlikely anyone ever yet managed to destroy a Michaelmas daisy, a helenium or a yellow loosestrife simply by dividing it during the winter. However, many attractive perennials—the very ones which have been responsible for the enormous increase in interest in this group of plants over the last couple of decades—do suffer when treated in this brutal way. Serious losses occur, even amongst the most tolerant, during severe weather or in cold, late springs in cold and cool temperate regions, particularly when newly divided crowns are lifted out of the ground by hard frosts or blasted by cold winds before their roots have started to grow. An occasional inspection to replace and firm back into position any plants lifted in this way should be a routine.

Figure 56. Even crudely made divisions can be an effective way to increase plants. These divisions of *Artemisia* 'Silver Queen' were obtained by cutting the rootball of a potbound plant from a garden centre into slices with a knife. More than a dozen divisions were obtained from a single plant.

Examples and special cases of propagating perennials by division

Aster spp. and cvs., such as Michaelmas daisies and other late-flowering perennials including heleniums, helianthus and cimicifugas, are propagated from cuttings made in spring from basal shoots or single crown divisions. Alternatively, plants can be divided in late summer by sacrificing their flowers, and single crown divisions made at this time produce excellent plants by the following spring for planting in the garden, which will produce multiple flowering stems by autumn.

Helleborus spp. and cvs. are readily propagated from seed, provided it is sown immediately after collection around mid-summer and exposed to the natural sequence of weathering as summer gives way to autumn followed by winter. Seedlings are vulnerable to damping-off and likely to survive better in a cold frame—or in the open—than in the apparently more clement conditions of a glasshouse. Named cultivars do not come true from seed and must be propagated vegetatively by division, since cuttings are not an option. *H. atrorubens* is slightly rhizomatous and the small stem extensions leading to different crowns make it relatively easy to divide. 'Orientalis' hybrids are divisible during late summer and tolerant of division, but courage and ruthlessness are at a premium when separating some of the more tangled crowns. *H. foetidus* and *H. niger* grow readily from seed, but named forms are not so readily propagated by division. Single crown divisions can be obtained either in early spring as the leaves start to develop after flowering or in early autumn. Replanted or potted up directly, they tend to make new growth reluctantly and benefit from being bedded down in a mixture of coarse, well-aerated, water-absorbing materials such as coarse coir or sphagnum moss and kept shaded and moist for a couple of weeks after separation from their parents. This encourages the emergence and rapid growth of new roots and enables the divisions to establish more rapidly when potted up.

Lathraea clandestina grows parasitically mainly on the roots of alders or willows but has been observed in gardens growing on a wide range of species including kniphofias, cordylines, podocarps, rhododendrons, nyssas, and chamaecyparis. Seeds germinate readily and are initially self-sustaining. They will then start to decline and eventually die unless potted up in company with a host plant such as a young willow cutting or alder seedling. Immature plants remain subterranean for several years before starting to produce flowers. Alternatively, propagate louseworts by digging up part of an established group and moving it to the foot of an alder, willow, maple, birch, hazelnut or other host. This is best done in late spring or early summer, when rhizomes and roots are growing actively and seeds are present in the spent flower heads. The latter will continue to mature and be scattered ballistically when they are ripe, providing additional prospects of successful establishment. Lay clumps of the plant in shallow trenches from which the fine, yellow roots will grow down to make contact with their host's roots—sometimes well below the surface.

Sanguisorba spp. are divided during late summer/early autumn, even though they are flowering then. Like many wetland plants, dividing them can be a vigorous project. In the competitive environments of wetlands, plants survive only by establishing a roothold and then holding it against all comers. Attempts to dig up established sanguisorbas and many other wetland perennials encounter considerable resistance. Crowns emerge from around the top of the rootstock and others from adventitious buds on the roots from which rhizomes grow out to produce shoots well away from the centre of the plant. The easiest way to propagate this and some other entrenched perennials is from young, relatively recently established plants or to search for and dig up the peripheral crowns, avoiding if possible direct engagement with the rootstock citadel itself.

Carnivorous Plants

Three things to avoid whenever carnivorous plants are grown and propagated: tap water or hard water, as rainwater carefully stored under clean conditions is best; artificial fertilisers of any kind; and closely compacted, poorly aerated growth media.

Darlingtonia californica, the cobra lily, grows naturally in cold-water bogs in western Oregon and northern California. It thrives only in situations where rhizomes and roots remain cool. Seeds are sown as soon after collection as possible on living sphagnum moss in closed containers and germinate in the spring, after weathering. Cuttings are made early in the growing season from sections of rhizome. Divisions are made from side shoots separated from their parents when about a quarter of their eventual size.

Dionaea muscipula, the Venus fly trap, is confined naturally to small areas of bogs, close to the Atlantic in the Carolinas. The black seeds, resembling tiny beads, cluster in open capsules before being dispersed during mid-summer. Sow seeds soon after collection on chopped sphagnum : sand, 1:1, in a closed frame or propagator. Prick out the seedlings individually in sphagnum moss in 7 cm (2.5 in.) pots, and immerse the containers to one third of their depth. Seedlings may take up to five years to grow into flowering plants. Make cuttings by detaching leaves and inserting them lightly in sphagnum moss. Small buds produced during the following three months develop into plants the following spring. Viviparous plantlets are occasionally produced and are removed and potted up in chopped sphagnum moss.

Drosera spp., sundews, are widely distributed across the world. Most grow in permanently waterlogged or seasonally wet situations. Seeds are produced from spring through autumn depending on the species. Sow seeds soon after they mature on the surface of a 1:1 mixture of chopped sphagnum : sand. Early sown seeds usually germinate within a few weeks. Autumn-ripening seed should also be sown at once and weathered. Seedlings are seldom produced by stored seed without weathering. Cuttings are made from rhizomes cut into short lengths and laid on the surface of a peat : sand mix. They are then lightly covered with sifted, chopped sphagnum moss and develop small buds that grow into new plants. Leaf cuttings made by removing young, mature leaves are placed on a bed of chopped sphagnum and lightly covered with a sprinkling of sphagnum. Plantlets develop on their margins and surface of the main veins in warm, shaded conditions. Divisions of species with numerous crowns are made in spring. Some deciduous species from cool temperate regions produce overwintering buds called hibernacula, composed of rounded clusters of tiny, tightly rolled leaves. These are picked off and potted up individually. Viviparous buds may also develop spontaneously at the bases of the leaves.

Heliamphora spp., sun pitchers, grow naturally in South America on a few inaccessible mountains, including Roraima, where levels of rainfall are amongst the highest in the world. Rhizomes are divided into sections, each with a few pitchers attached, and then laid on top of a layer of perlite,

half filling a small plastic pot before being covered with chopped sphagnum moss. The roots they produce are extremely fragile and need careful handling.

Pinguicula spp., butterworts, are widely distributed in bogs and around springs in permanently wet situations in many parts of the world. Unlike many carnivorous plants, they grow not only on acidic substrates but on basic rocks, including tufa, too. Seeds are sown as soon as possible after collection on a 1:1 mixture of peat : sand, in containers stood in trays of water, and weathered. Seedlings may not appear till the second spring. The surface should remain constantly saturated with water, and mosses and liverworts are a problem. Disturb the seedlings as seldom as possible and avoid transplanting while they are growing actively. Viviparous buds form spontaneously on the leaves and can be encouraged by removing the short, succulent, overwintering leaves just before growth recommences in spring, laying them flat over chopped moss in a closed frame or propagator. Buds, followed by plantlets, develop on the cut bases of the leaves.

Sarracenia spp., trumpet pitchers, all but one grow naturally in the southeastern corner of the United States. Only *S. purpurea* extends further north into Canada and is reliably hardy in cool and cold temperate regions. Sow seeds soon after collection on the surface of sand : chopped sphagnum, 1:1. They germinate either within about four weeks or in the spring, after weathering. Linear cotyledons are followed by tiny pitcher-form leaves, increasing progressively in size thereafter. All species hybridise freely in the wild where opportunities exist, and unless carefully isolated from each other, hybrids are almost the norm when grown in gardens. Rhizome cuttings are made by slicing rhizomes into 2 cm (1 in.) long sections, each preferably with a couple of roots still attached. These are potted up with the tops of the rhizomes just exposed. Alternatively, rhizomes growing from well-developed plants are exposed, leaving the roots undisturbed. The rhizomes are then partially cut through at intervals along their length. New buds appear at the sites of the cuts, and once these have produced roots, are separated and potted up as individual plants.

Propagation Summary for Broad-Leaved Perennial Herbs

S. = propagated from seed
C. = propagated from cuttings
D. = propagated by divisions

Some of these genera include annual or shrubby species. The following list should be read with reference only to perennial, non-woody species and cultivars. References to propagation techniques take no account of species usually grown as "alpines." (See the appropriate summary at the end of chapter 13.)

Abronia—**S.** autumn, spring; peel off outer covering of seeds before sowing. **C.** spring.

Acaena—**S.** spring, autumn; weathering may increase germination rates. **C.** mid- to late summer. **D.** summer, autumn.

Acanthus—**S.** ballistic. spring. **C.** late winter; roots. **D.** spring, early autumn.

Achillea—**S.** spring. **C.** spring; basal. **D.** late summer, autumn.

Achlys—**S.** fresh. **D.** late summer.

Aciphylla—Dioecious. **S.** fresh; germination often erratic, delay pricking out. **C.** spring; basal offsets.

Aconitum—**S.** fresh; seeds may not germinate till second spring. **D.** spring, early autumn.

Actaea—Succulent Fruit. **S.** fresh; may not germinate till second spring. **D.** spring.

Actinotus—**S.** fresh; smoke.

Adenophora—**S.** spring. **C.** spring; basal. **D.** late summer, early autumn.

Adonis—**S.** fresh; germination erratic. **D.** late winter, early spring.

Aegopodium—**D.** at any time.

Agastache—**S.** spring. **C.** late summer, autumn; for named forms.

Ajuga—**S.** spring. **C.** spring; basal. **D.** at any time.

Alcea—**S.** spring; chip.

Alchemilla—**S.** often apomictic. spring. **D.** late summer, early autumn.

Alonsoa—**S.** spring, autumn. **C.** autumn.

Amsonia—**S.** spring. **C.** summer.

Anaphalis—**S.** fresh; quality variable. **C.** spring; basal: summer. **D.** summer, early autumn; from natural layers.

Anchusa—**S.** spring. **C.** spring; basal: winter, spring; roots, e.g., *A. azureum*. **D.** late summer.

Anemone—**S.** spring, autumn. **C.** late winter; roots (japonica types). **D.** late summer, winter; offsets or corms.

Anemonella—**S.** spring.

Anemonopsis—**S.** fresh. **D.** early autumn.

Anisotome—**S.** fresh; **D.** late summer, early autumn from small plants. Long established plants have deeply penetrating taproots vulnerable to damage.

Anthriscus—**S.** fresh, winter; capable of germinating at temperatures just above freezing point. Forms with crimson foliage should be grown in segregated groups, and seedlings rogued to remove inferior plants.

Anthyllis—**S.** spring, autumn; chip plus innoculum.

Antirrhinum—**S.** spring; smoke with perennial species.

Aquilegia—**S.** fresh, spring; liable to hybridise, but *A. vulgaris* cvs., e.g., 'Norah Barlow', breed true with minimum isolation. **D.** late summer, early autumn; is possible but seldom productive.

Arctotis—**S.** spring, autumn; smoke. **C.** spring, late summer; perennial species should be renewed annually.

Armeria—**S.** spring. **C.** summer; rosettes. **D.** spring; from old plants.

Armoracia—**C.** winter; roots.

Arnebia—**S.** spring, autumn. **C.** autumn, winter; roots.

Arnica—**S.** spring. **D.** late summer, early autumn.

Artemisia—**S.** spring, autumn. **C.** summer, autumn. **D.** late summer; herbaceous species.

Aruncus—dioecious. **S.** fresh, spring. **D.** autumn from young plants.

Asarina (*Maurandya*)—**S.** late winter.

Asarum—**D.** early autumn.

Asclepias—**S.** fresh, spring; specialised pollination mechanisms often result in low seed production in gardens. **C.** late winter; roots.

Asperula—**S.** spring.

Aster—**S.** spring; quality variable. **C.** spring; basal. **D.** late summer, spring.

Astilbe—**S.** spring. **D.** late summer, winter.

Astragalus—**S.** spring; chip plus innoculum.

Astrantia—**S.** fresh. **D.** late summer, early autumn, for variegated and selected forms.

Ballota—**C.** summer, autumn.

Balsamorhiza—Hemi-parasitic. **S.** fresh; seedlings seldom thrive in gardens, likely to require a host plant. **C.** winter; roots.

Baptisia—**S.** spring; chip plus innoculum.

Barbarea—**S.** spring, autumn; including *B. vulgaris* 'Variegata'.

Begonia—**S.** late winter. **C.** summer; stems, leaves or single bud. **D.** winter, spring; offset corms or rhizomes.

Bellis—**S.** spring, autumn. **D.** summer; for selected forms.

Bergenia—**S.** fresh. **C.** late summer; shoots, rhizomes. **D.** winter.

Berkheya—**S.** fresh. **C.** summer; semi-shrubby species.

Bidens—**S.** late winter, spring. **C.** autumn.

Boltonia—**D.** late summer.

Brachyscome—**S.** late winter, spring. **C.** spring, autumn.

Brunnera—**D.** late summer.

Buphthalmum—**S.** spring. **D.** early autumn.

Bupleurum—**S.** fresh; quality variable. **C.** summer.

Cacalia (Adenostyles)—**S.** fresh, spring. **D.** late summer, spring.

Calandrinia—**S.** spring. **C.** summer.

Calceolaria—**S.** spring. **D.** summer, autumn.

Callitriche—Aquatic. **C.** spring, summer. **D.** summer.

Caltha—Aquatic. **S.** fresh. **D.** late winter, spring.

Calystegia—Liane. **C.** late summer, winter; roots.

Camissonia—**S.** spring.

Campanula—**S.** fresh, spring. **C.** spring; basal: summer. **D.** late summer, early autumn.

Cardamine—**S.** ballistic. fresh, spring. **C.** late spring; single bud, e.g., *C. pratensis*. **D.** summer; bulbils, e.g., *C. bulbifera*.

Carduncellus—**S.** spring, autumn. **C.** spring; basal offsets: late winter; roots.

Carlina—**S.** spring; variable quality.

Cassia—**S.** spring; chip or treat with boiling water. **C.** summer.

Castilleja—Parasitic. **S.** fresh; seedlings require a host plant, e.g., a grass seedling.

Catananche—**S.** spring, autumn. **C.** late winter; roots.

Celmisia—**S.** fresh, spring; viability variable, short-lived seed. **C.** summer, e.g., sub-shrubby species.

D. spring, late summer; layers, e.g., carpeting and sub-shrubby species.

Centaurea—**S.** spring. **C.** spring; basal. **D.** late summer, autumn, spring.

Centranthus—**S.** fresh. **C.** spring; basal: summer, autumn.

Cephalaria—**S.** fresh, spring.

Cerastium—**S.** spring. **C.** summer. **D.** winter, spring.

Ceratophyllum—Aquatic. **C.** spring, summer. **D.** winter; turions.

Chaerophyllum—**S.** fresh.

Chamaemelum—**S.** spring. **D.** summer.

Chelidonium—**S.** Ballistic. fresh.

Chelone—**S.** spring. **D.** late summer, early autumn.

Chrysanthemum—**S.** spring. **C.** spring; basal. **D.** spring.

Chrysocoma—**S.** spring.

Chrysogonum—**D.** spring, summer.

Cicerbita—**D.** late winter, spring with caution.

Cichorium—**S.** spring. **C.** roots. **D.** late autumn, early winter.

Cimicifuga—**S.** fresh. **D.** late summer; using young plants. Mature plants are not readily divided.

Cirsium—**S.** spring; quality variable.

Citrullus—Liane. Succulent Fruit. **S.** spring.

Clematis—**S.** fresh; quality variable. **C.** spring; basal: summer. **D.** late summer, autumn. Herbaceous species develop into large clumps and divide well.

Codonopsis—**S.** fresh. **C.** spring; basal. **D.** autumn from small tubers.

Colquhounia—**S.** spring.

Convolvulus—**S.** spring, autumn, e.g., *C. althaeoides*. **C.** late winter, spring, e.g., *C. sabatius*.

Coreopsis—**S.** spring.

Cornus—**D.** summer, early autumn, for *C. canadensis*.

Coronilla—**S.** spring, chip plus innoculum.

Cortusa—**S.** spring. **D.** summer; not very productive.

Corydalis—**S.** fresh, spring. **D.** summer; offsets: early autumn, e.g., *C. flexuosa*.

Cosmos—e.g., *C. atrosanguineus*; **S.** spring; but believed never to be available. **C.** summer; single bud, need time to form small tubers and accumulate storage reserves before winter.

Cotula—**S.** spring. **C.** spring, early autumn.

Crambe—**S.** spring. **C.** early spring; basal, roots.

Craspedia—**S.** spring; cultivated plants tend to be infertile.

Crepis—**S.** spring. **C.** late winter; roots. **D.** late summer, autumn.

Crucianella—**C. D.** summer.

Cyclamen—**S.** fresh; seeds of almost all species mature in autumn, irrespective of flowering time. **C.** spring, summer; sectioning corms.

Cycnium—Parasitic. **S.** fresh; seedlings need host plant.

Cynara—**S.** spring. **C.** spring from basal side shoots.

Cynoglossum—**S.** spring. **C.** late winter; roots.

Dahlia—**S.** spring. **C.** spring; basal. **D.** late winter, spring; tubers.

Darlingtonia—Carnivorous. **S.** spring on sphagnum moss. **C.** spring, summer from sections of rhizomes. **D.** offshoots when about a quarter of their eventual size.

Darmera—Semi-aquatic. **S.** fresh. **D.** winter; using peripheral rhizomes.

Delphinium—**S.** late winter, spring. **C.** spring; basal: late summer; eyes. **D.** late summer, early autumn.

Dentaria—**S.** spring; often infertile in cultivation. **D.** late summer, autumn.

Desmodium—**S.** spring; chip plus innoculum. **C.** summer.

Dianthus—**S.** spring, autumn. **C.** summer, autumn.

Diascia—**S.** spring. **C.** spring to early winter.

Dicentra—**S.** fresh. **C.** late summer; rhizomes. **D.** spring, summer; rhizomes—likely to lose their leaves following division: winter; offsets of bulbous species.

Dictamnus—**S.** Ballistic. fresh, plus innoculum. **D.** autumn; seldom productive and sometimes fatal.

Digitalis—**S.** spring, autumn; most forms of *D. purpurea* come true from seed if isolated. **C.** summer; single bud for infertile forms or hybrids.

Dimorphotheca—**S.** autumn, spring. **C.** summer, autumn, spring.

Dionaea—Carnivorous. **S.** fresh on sand/sphagnum moss mix. **C.** spring; leaf. **D.** summer; viviparous plantlets.

Dodecatheon—**S.** fresh, spring. **C.** winter; roots. **D.** autumn, winter; bulbils produced just below the surface around the crowns.

Doronicum—**S.** spring.

Drosera—Carnivorous. **S.** fresh; on sphagnum moss. **C.** spring; roots: summer; single bud with leaf or short sections of rhizome. **D.** summer.

Duchesnia—Succulent Fruit. **S.** spring. **D.** summer to early winter; stolons.

Echinacea—**S.** spring, autumn. **D.** late summer, early autumn.

Echinops—**S.** spring, autumn. **C.** early winter; roots. **D.** autumn.

Echinopsis—**S.** spring.

Elatostema—**D.** spring.

Eomecon—**S.** fresh, spring.

Epilobium—**S.** spring. **C.** spring; basal. **D.** late summer.

Epimedium—**S.** fresh; seed likely to hybridise, often sparingly produced. **D.** late summer, early autumn.

Eremophila—**S.** spring, autumn; seldom produce viable seeds in cultivation. chip or soak. **C.** spring.

Erianthis—**S.** fresh. **D.** spring; as flowers fade.

Erigeron—**S.** late winter, early spring. **C.** spring; basal. **D.** late summer.

Eriogonum—**S.** spring. **C.** summer.

Eriophyllum—**S.** spring; smoke. **D.** autumn.

Erodium—Dioecious. **S.** spring. **C.** spring; basal. **D.** spring, late summer.

Eryngium—**S.** fresh. **C.** late winter; roots. **D.** spring, late summer—often unproductive unless previously mounded up.

Erysimum—**S.** spring. **C.** spring to late autumn.

Erythrina—**S.** fresh, spring. **C.** basal shoots, e.g., *E. crista-galli*.

Eupatorium—**C.** spring; basal: summer; single bud. **D.** autumn.

Euphorbia—**S.** Ballistic. spring. **C.** spring; basal: summer. **D.** late winter, early spring.

Euryale—Aquatic. Succulent Fruit. **S.** late winter; store seeds in water. **D.** spring; offsets.

Farfugium—**D.** spring, late summer.

Filipendula—**S.** fresh. **D.** late summer, early autumn.

Fragaria—Dioecious. Succulent Fruit. **S.** spring. **D.** summer to winter; stolons.

Francoa—**S.** spring. **D.** spring, late summer.

Frasera—**S.** fresh. **D.** late summer, early autumn.

Gaillardia—**S.** late winter, spring. **C.** spring; basal: late winter; roots. **D.** spring.

Galax—**D.** late summer, early autumn.

Galega—**S.** spring; chip plus innoculum.

Galium—**D.** late summer.

Gaura—**S.** early spring.

Gentiana—**S.** variable viability; fresh, e.g., *G. asclepiadea*, *G. lutea*, *G. pneumonanthe*: spring, eg. *G. cruciata*. **C.** summer, e.g., *G. septemfida*. **D.** autumn, spring, e.g., *G. acaulis*.

Geranium—Ballistic. **S.** spring. **C.** summer, early autumn. **D.** spring, late summer, early autumn.

Gerbera—**S.** spring, autumn. **C.** spring; basal.

Geum—**S.** spring, autumn. **D.** spring.

Gillenia—**D.** late summer, early autumn.

Glaucidium—**S.** spring. **D.** mid-summer.

Glaucium—**S.** spring.

Glechoma—**C. D.** all year round; stolons with or without roots.

Gloxinia—See *Sinningia*.

Glycyrrhiza—**S.** spring; chip plus innoculum. **D.** spring; thongs (roots), each with at least one bud.

Gnaphalium—**S.** spring. **C.** spring.

Goodenia—**S.** spring, autumn. **C.** summer, autumn.

Gunnera—Dioecious. Succulent Fruit. **S.** fresh. **D.** spring; short stolons, e.g., *G. hamiltonii*.

Gypsophila—**S.** spring. **C.** spring; basal: summer; basal.

Hacquetia—**S.** fresh.

Halimodendron—**S.** spring; chip.

Harveya—Parasitic. **S.** spring; with host plant.

Hedysarum—**S.** spring; chip plus innoculum.

Helenium—**S.** spring. **C.** spring; basal. **D.** spring.

Heliamphora—Carnivorous **C. D.** summer; rhizomes.

Helianthus—**S.** spring. **D.** spring.

Helichrysum—**S.** spring; smoke.

Heliopsis—**D.** autumn.

Helleborus—**S.** fresh. **D.** late summer, autumn.

Hepatica—**S.** fresh. **D.** spring, late summer.

Heracleum—**S.** spring, autumn. **C.** late winter; roots.

Hesperis—**S.** fresh, spring; single forms only. **C.** spring; basal, aided by mounding: summer; single bud. **D.** summer; viviparous plantlets.

Heuchera—**S.** late winter, spring. **D.** spring, late summer.

Heucherella—**D.** spring, late summer.

Hibiscus—**S.** spring, herbaceous hybrids, e.g., *H. moscheutos*, tend to come true. **D.** spring; short rhizomes.

Hieracium—**S.** spring. **D.** spring to autumn.

Horminum—**S.** spring.

Hottonia—Aquatic. **D.** spring.

Houttuynia—Semi-aquatic, Apomictic. **S.** spring. **D.** spring, e.g., 'Chameleon' and 'Plena'.

Hovea—**S.** spring; chip, hot water.

Humulus—Liane. Dioecious. **C.** spring; basal.

Impatiens—Ballistic. **S.** late winter, spring. **C.** spring, summer; for doubles and selected forms.

Incarvillea—**S.** fresh, spring.

Inula—**S.** spring. **D.** late summer, autumn.

Ipomoea—Liane. **S.** late winter, spring; chip or soak. **D.** spring.

Iresine—**C.** late winter, spring.

Jasione—**S.** spring. **D.** spring, late summer.

Kirengeshoma—**C.** summer; single bud. **D.** spring.

Kitaibela—**C.** summer.

Knautia—**S.** fresh, spring.

Lactuca—**S.** spring.

Lamium—**S.** spring. **C.** early spring to late autumn. **D.** not recommended; cuttings are almost as easy and produce better plants.

Laserpitium—**S.** fresh. **D.** late summer.

Lathraea—Parasitic. Ballistic. **S.** fresh. **D.** spring as flowers fade.

Lathyrus—Liane. Ballistic. **S.** chip plus innoculum.

Laurentia—**S.** spring. **C. D.** summer.

Leonotis—**S.** spring. **C.** early summer; best from stock plants, cut back to produce suitable shoots early in the year.

Lespedeza—**S.** spring; chip plus innoculum. **D.** spring.

Leucanthemella—**D.** spring.

Leucanthemum—**S.** spring. **C.** spring; basal. **D.** late summer, autumn.

Levisticum—**S.** spring. **D.** spring, late summer.

Liatris—**S.** fresh, spring. **D.** spring; offsets.

Ligularia—**D.** late summer, autumn.

Ligusticum—**D.** late summer, autumn.

Limonium—**S.** spring. **C.** late winter; root. **D.** spring, late summer.

Linaria—**S.** spring; seedlings capable of regeneration from adventitious buds on the hypocotyls. **C.** spring; basal: summer. **D.** late summer.

Lindelofia—**S.** spring, autumn. **C.** late winter; roots. **D.** spring.

Linum—**S.** spring; seedlings capable of regeneration from adventitious buds on the hypocotyls. **C.** late summer.

Lobelia—**S.** spring; smoke. **C.** summer; many including *L. dortmanna*, single bud; e.g., *L. cardinalis*. **D.** spring, late summer.

Ludwigia—semi-aquatic. **S.** spring. **C.** summer. **D.** spring.

Lunaria—**S.** fresh, spring plus innoculum. **D.** late summer, e.g., *L. rediviva*.

Lupinus—Ballistic. **S.** spring; chip plus innoculum. **C.** spring; basal.

Lychnis—**S.** spring. **C.** spring; basal.

Lycopus—**S.** spring.

Lysimachia—**C.** spring; basal. **D.** spring, mid-summer to late autumn.

Lythrum—**C.** spring; basal. **D.** spring, early autumn.

Macleaya—**S.** fresh, spring. **C.** spring; basal. **D.** early autumn; suckers.

Malva—**S.** early winter, spring. **C.** spring; basal.

Malvastrum—**C.** summer.

Mandragora—Succulent Fruit. **S.** fresh, autumn.

Margyricarpus—Succulent Fruit. **S.** spring. **D.** spring.

Meconopsis—**S.** variable quality early, spring, autumn. **D.** spring, late summer; as flowers fade, e.g., 'Lingholm' hybrids.

Medicago—**S.** spring; chip plus innoculum.

Melianthus—**S.** spring. **C.** autumn.

Melissa—**S.** spring. **D.** autumn.

Mentha—**D.** spring to autumn.

Menyanthes—Aquatic. **D.** spring.

Mertensia—**S.** spring. **D.** late summer, autumn.

Meum—**S.** spring. **D.** late summer.

Michauxia—**S.** spring.

Mimulus—**S.** spring. **C.** spring, summer; basal. **D.** spring to autumn.

Mirabilis—**S.** spring. **C.** spring; basal.

Mitella—**D.** late summer, early autumn.

Monarda—**S.** spring, autumn. **C.** spring; basal. **D.** late summer, early autumn.

Morina—**S.** spring.

Musschia—**S.** spring.

Myosotidium—**S.** fresh, late winter; colour forms come true when grown in isolation. **D.** late winter, early spring.

Myriophyllum—Aquatic. **C.** spring. **D.** summer.

Myrrhis—**S.** fresh. **D.** late summer, early autumn.

Nelumbo—Aquatic. Recalcitrant. **S.** store in water; late winter, early spring; **D.** spring; all including the hardy *N. komarovii*, *N. lutea*.

Nemesia—**S.** late winter, spring; smoke. **C.** spring, autumn.

Nepeta—**S.** spring. **C.** spring, summer; basal.

Nierembergia—**S.** spring. **C. D.** autumn.

Nuphar—Aquatic. **D.** spring.

Nymphaea—Aquatic. Recalcitrant. **S.** store in water; spring; e.g., *N.* 'Pygmaea' cvs. **C.** spring; basal: summer; "eyes," minute buds produced on the roots. **D.** late winter, spring.

Nymphoides—Aquatic. Recalcitrant. **S.** store in water; spring. **D.** spring.

Oenanthe—Aquatic. **D.** spring or summer.

Oenothera—**S.** spring, autumn. **C.** summer.

Omphalodes—**S.** spring. **D.** late summer, early autumn.

Onosma—**S.** spring. **C.** late summer.

Origanum—**S.** spring. **C.** spring; basal: summer. **D.** late summer.

Osteospermum—**S.** spring, autumn. **C.** late winter, spring, autumn.

Othonna—**S.** spring, autumn; smoke. **C.** spring, autumn.

Ourisia—**S.** spring. **D.** late summer.

Oxalis—Ballistic. **S.** spring. **C.** summer, autumn. **D.** spring, autumn.

Pachysandra—Succulent Fruit. **S.** spring; seldom produce fruits in cultivation. **C.** spring to early winter. **D.** autumn, early winter.

Paeonia—**S.** fresh; black seeds are fertile, germinate erratically. **D.** late summer, early autumn—into single tubers each with at least one bud. "Blind" tubers sometimes produce shoots in the second year.

Panax—**S.** fresh; germinates erratically and seldom before second spring.

Papaver—**S.** spring. **C.** late winter; roots, e.g., *P. orientalis*. **D.** spring.

Parnassia—Semi-aquatic. **S.** spring. **D.** spring.

Patrinia—**S.** spring. **D.** spring.

Pedicularis—Parasitic. **S.** spring; seedlings require a host plant. **D.** spring, late summer with host plant.

Pelargonium—**S.** autumn, late winter. **C.** autumn, spring; roots.

Penstemon—**S.** fresh, spring. **C.** late summer, autumn.

Perezia—**S.** fresh. **C.** summer.

Persicaria—**C.** spring to late autumn. **C. D.** late summer, autumn, occasionally from bulbils, e.g., *P. viviparum*.

Petunia—**S.** late winter, spring. **C.** mid-autumn.

Phlomis—**S.** spring; chip. **D.** late summer.

Phlox—**S.** spring. **C.** spring; basal: summer: late winter; roots. **D.** late summer, spring—border phloxes make poor divisions.

Phuopsis—**C. D.** summer.

Phygelius—**S.** spring. **C.** spring; basal: autumn.

Physalis—Succulent Fruit. **S.** late winter. **D.** autumn, winter.

Physostegia—**C.** spring; basal. **D.** late summer, early autumn.

Phyteuma—**S.** spring. **D.** spring.

Phytolacca—Succulent Fruit. **S.** spring.

Pinguicula—Carnivorous. **S.** fresh. **C.** spring, summer; leaf. **D.** winter, spring; offsets.

Plantago—**S.** spring. **D.** late summer.

Platycodon—**S.** spring, autumn. **D.** late summer, spring; only when in active growth.

Plectranthus—**C.** spring, summer. **D.** summer.

Pleurophyllum—**S.** fresh, spring.

Podophyllum—Succulent Fruit. **S.** fresh. **D.** late summer, early autumn for species with rhizomatous roots, e.g., *P. peltatum*.

Polemonium—**S.** spring. **D.** late summer.

Potentilla—**S.** spring. **D.** spring, early autumn.

Poterium—Succulent Fruit, **D.** autumn.

Pratia—Succulent Fruit. **S.** spring. **D.** spring, summer.

Primula—Heterostyly, pin and thrumb-eyed flowers. **S.** fresh, late winter, spring. **C.** late winter; roots, e.g., *P. denticulata*. **D.** early to mid-summer, e.g., primroses, polyanthus: late summer, early autumn.

Prunella—**S.** fresh. **D.** spring to late autumn.

Pulmonaria—**D.** late summer, early autumn.

Pulsatilla—**S.** fresh. **C.** winter; root: spring; offsets.

Pyrethrum—**S.** spring; quality variable. **D.** late summer, early autumn.

Pyrola—**S.** fresh; immature embryos consisting of only a few cells. **D.** spring.

Ranunculus—includes Aquatics. **S.** fresh, germination often erratic; may be improved by harvesting seeds when still green. **C.** spring, summer, e.g., aquatics. **D.** spring, late summer, early autumn, early to mid-winter; *R. ficaria*.

Rehmannia—**S.** late winter, spring. **C.** late winter; root.

Rhazya—**S.** spring. **C.** summer.

Rheum—**S.** spring. **D.** winter.

Rhexia—**S.** spring. **D.** winter; tubers.

Rhodanthemum—**C.** summer.

Rodgersia—**S.** fresh, spring. **D.** late winter.

Romneya—**S.** fresh, smoke; germination erratic. **C.** mid-winter; root.

Rudbeckia—**S.** spring, autumn. **D.** late summer, early autumn; root.

Rumex—**S.** fresh, spring.

Salvia—**S.** spring; chip. **C.** spring; basal: summer, autumn. **D.** late summer, e.g., *S. nemorosa*.

Sambucus—Succulent Fruit. **D.** early autumn, winter, e.g., *S. ebulus*.

Sanguinaria—**D.** late summer, early autumn.

Sanguisorba—**S.** spring. **D.** late summer, autumn.

Sanicula—**S.** fresh.

Saponaria—**S.** spring. **C.** summer. **D.** spring to autumn.

Sarcodes—Parasitic. **S.** fresh; host needed.

Sarracenia—Carnivorous. **S.** fresh, on sphagnum moss. **D.** spring; rhizomes.

Saururus—Aquatic. **S.** spring. **D.** spring.

Saxifraga—**S.** fresh. **D.** summer, early autumn; stolons, e.g., *S. stolonifera*: division; *S. fortunei*: bulbils; *S. granulata*.

Scabiosa—**S.** fresh, spring. **C.** spring; basal: late winter; root. **D.** late summer, early autumn.

Scolymus—**S.** spring. **D.** early autumn.

Scrophularia—**S.** spring. **C.** spring; basal.

Scutellaria—**S.** spring. **D.** summer.

Semiaquilegia—**S.** fresh, spring.

Senecio—**S.** spring, summer. **C.** autumn, e.g., *S. cineraria*. **D.** mid-summer, early autumn, e.g., *S. pulcher*.

Serratula—**S.** spring.

Shortia—**S.** fresh; rarely available. **D.** late summer; stolons.

Sidalcea—**D.** late summer, early autumn.

Silene—Dioecious, e.g., *S. dioica*. **S.** spring. **C.** spring; basal.

Sinningia—**S.** late winter. **C.** summer; single bud. **D.** winter; corms, tuberous rhizomes.

Solanum—Succulent Fruit. **S.** spring. **C.** spring, summer, autumn.

Soleirolia—**D.** late spring, summer.

Solenostemon (Coleus)—**S.** late winter, early spring. **C.** spring; single bud: autumn, early winter.

Solidago—**S.** spring. **C.** spring; basal. **D.** late summer, early autumn, winter.

Solidaster—**D.** late summer, early autumn, winter.

Stachys—**S.** spring. **C.** late spring, summer.

Stackhousia—**S.** spring; smoke. **C.** summer.

Stokesia—**S.** spring; quality variable. **C.** late winter; root. **D.** late summer, early autumn.

Streptocarpus—Ballistic. **S.** late winter, spring. **C.** summer to late autumn; leaf. **D.** late spring; offsets.

Strobilanthes—Ballistic. **S.** spring. **C.** summer.

Stylidium—**S.** fresh.

Stylophorum—**S.** fresh, spring.

Succisa—**S.** fresh, spring.

Swertia—**S.** fresh.

Symphyandra—**S.** fresh, spring.

Symphytum—**S.** fresh, spring. **D.** spring, late summer.

Tanacetum—**S.** spring; quality variable. **C.** mid- to late summer.

Telekia—**S.** spring. **D.** late summer, early autumn.

Tellima—**S.** spring. **D.** late summer, early winter, spring.

Teucrium—**S.** spring. **C.** spring; basal: summer.

Thalictrum—**S.** fresh; germination erratic. **D.** late summer, early autumn, late winter.

Tiarella—**D.** spring, late summer, stolons.

Tolmiea—**S.** spring. **C.** summer, early autumn. **D.** late summer, spring; adventitious buds at tops of petioles.

Trachystemon—**S.** spring, autumn. **D.** late summer.

Trapa—Aquatic. Recalcitrant. **S.** spring, store in water. **D.** late winter, spring; tubers.

Trautvetteria—**S.** spring. **D.** early autumn.

Trifolium—**S.** spring, autumn. **D.** late summer.

Trollius—**S.** fresh. **D.** late summer, early autumn.

Tropaeolum—**S.** fresh, e.g., *T. polyphyllum* and *T. speciosum*. **C.** spring, summer; rhizomes and shoots, e.g., *T. tuberosum*: late winter, spring; root, e.g., *T. speciosum* and *T. polyphyllum*. **D.** late winter; tubers, e.g., *T. tuberosum*.

Tunica—**S.** spring.

Utricularia—Aquatic. **S.** spring. **D.** winter, turions.

Uvularia—**D.** late summer, early autumn.

Valeriana—**S.** fresh. **D.** spring, early autumn.

Valerianella—**D.** early autumn.

Vancouveria—**D.** spring, late summer, early autumn.

Veratrum—**S.** fresh. **D.** late summer, early autumn.

Verbascum—**S.** spring, autumn. **C.** summer; single bud: winter; roots.

Verbena—**S.** spring, e.g., *V. bonariensis*. **C.** late winter to late autumn.

Vernonia—**D.** spring, late summer.

Veronica—**S.** spring. **C.** spring, summer. **D.** late summer, early autumn.

Veronicastrum—**D.** late summer, early autumn.

Vicia—**S.** spring; chip plus innoculum.

Viola—Ballistic. **S.** late winter, spring, early autumn. **C.** late summer, autumn; prepare plants by cutting them back hard a month previously: spring; root, e.g., *V. pedata*. **D.** early to mid-summer, e.g., Parma cvs.: late winter, spring.

Wahlenbergia—**S.** fresh, spring; smoke. **D.** spring to late summer.

Waldsteinia—**D.** late summer to early winter.

Wulfenia—**S.** spring.

Wyethia—**S.** fresh, spring.

Xanthorhiza—**S.** fresh; **D.** late summer, early autumn.

CHAPTER 11

Herbaceous and Evergreen Monocots Including Grasses, Restios and Aquatics

Botanists divide the flowering plants into two great groups: Dicotyledons, familiarly known as dicots, embrace broad-leaved plants, generally with networks of veins in their leaves. Monocotyledons, or monocots, are narrow-leaved plants with more or less parallel veins running the lengths of their leaves.

From the gardener's point of view, monocots can be divided into several groups:

- *Grasses*, with their cousins the sedges and restios, are probably the epitome of the monocots for most of us and are included in this chapter.
- *Woody monocots*, the trees and shrubs of the group, include palms, bananas, bamboos, cabbage and grasstrees and are dealt with in chapter 17.
- *Petaloid monocots*, amongst them many outstandingly important garden plants, all produce flowers with what most of us would be content to call petals and yielding nothing in beauty, textural quality or brilliance in comparison with dicot flowers. They include day lilies, cannas, hostas, and some irises, all herbaceous perennials and covered in this chapter. Kangaroo paws, patersonias, arthropodiums, kniphofias, some watsonias, thysanotis and xeronemas with more or less evergreen foliage are also covered in this chapter.

- *Bulbs and corms*, such as daffodils, tulips, moraeas, lilies and gladioli are described in chapter 12.
- *Orchids* with flowers adapted to highly specialised forms of pollination are included in chapter 15.
- *Bromeliads*, including tillandsias, aechmeas and other plants of the pineapple family, are also included in chapter 15.

Monocots and dicots share habitats in inextricable medleys of associations, often growing together under exactly the same conditions. Both groups are propagated from seed and by division in broadly similar ways. The positioning and functions of meristems are quite different in the two groups, however. Monocots generally lack the capacity for secondary thickening of stems and continued or renewed growth once their tissues have matured, and their roots seldom contain meristematic cells of any kind They provide far fewer opportunities for propagation from cuttings.

Propagation from Seed

Most petaloid monocots produce seeds in dry fruits, such as capsules. On maturity, these gape open as they dry out, clearly revealing the seeds within them. Their contents can usually be tipped into a paper bag, and samples of seed, unmixed with other plant parts, obtained like this require minimum efforts to clean later.

Other petaloid monocots including convallarias, clintonias, dianellas and smilacinas produce fleshy berries. These soften and become brightly coloured as they ripen and are readily eaten by birds and animals. They should be collected just before they ripen fully or protected in some way. After collection, they are cleaned in the ways described for fleshy fruits in chapter 2.

"Seeds" of grasses, sedges and restios are technically fruits known as *caryopses*. Some are extremely easy to collect and clean; others pose great problems. Some grass seeds—including those produced by phalaris and miliums—separate naturally and easily from associated floral parts and are easily collected, and their well-defined, rounded caryopses are readily distinguishable from the irregular, amorphous remnants of bracts, awns and other parts of the flowers and are easy to clean.

Others pose greater problems. Seeds of fescues, stipas, bents and many other grasses are combined so intimately with other floral structures that they are almost impossible to separate from them. Cleaning becomes a matter of compromise between time and effort expended and rewards.

Restios create their own particular difficulties. They are dioecious, and male and female plants often differ considerably, complicating accurate identification. Their seeds may take months to mature, sometimes nearly a year after they have flowered.

The great majority of plants introduced in this chapter produce orthodox seeds. When dried and stored at low temperatures, they are capable of surviving for many years. A few produce recalcitrant seeds, including the fleshy coated seeds of several South African amaryllids, such as clivias and *Haemanthus* spp.; some aquatics, unable to survive out of water; and members of the arum family.

Seed sowing

Monocot and dicot plants with conspicuous flowers share life cycles, habitats and structural features to such an extent that their seeds have developed broadly similar germination strategies. Chart 14 in chapter 10, describing treatment of seeds of dicot herbaceous plants, applies to monocots, too.

Grasses and sedges

Many grasses and sedges grow naturally in communities—prairies, steppes or meadows—in which numerous species share similar life cycles. Flowers are abundantly produced during late spring and early summer, and seeds ripen by mid-summer. Competition from established grasses declines in the immediate post-flowering period, to be resumed as and when summer rainfall and high temperatures provide favourable conditions for renewed growth. This growth lull during mid- to late summer provides opportunities for seedlings to establish with some prospects of being able to grow large enough to survive the winter, and it marks the time when the seeds of many of these species germinate, a few weeks after maturing.

Seeds seldom need after-ripening. Seedlings are produced rapidly in response to high temperatures (15° to 25°C, or 60° to 75°F) and ample water. Lower temperatures inhibit germination in many species, and the seeds then wait till temperatures start to rise in the spring before producing seedlings. Weathering at low temperatures during the winter may enable seeds to respond to lower temperatures—10° to 15°C (50° to 60°F)—the following spring but is less likely to be an absolute must for monocot seed germination as it can be with dicot perennial seeds.

It is worth noting that many of the broad-leaved perennial species found growing naturally in association with grasses in dry meadows, steppes or prairies, including gypsophilas, dianthus, liatris and salvias, share similar germination responses with the grasses they live amongst. For gardeners, the choice lies between sowing seeds soon after they are gathered in order to grow on small plants before winter or storing seed in dry and cool conditions till late winter/early spring and then sowing it, preferably with supplementary heat to maintain a minimum of about 15°C (60°F). The first alternative can be used by gardeners anywhere, and it is the better option for gardeners in situations where winters are mild, and especially in those like Mediterranea, where summers are dry. The caryopses of grasses, mostly from warm temperate and subtropical regions, possess hard, impermeable seed coats. Chipping or even complete removal of their outer coverings may be necessary before they will produce seedlings.

Restios

Until recently, apart from *Elegia capensis* and a very few others, gardeners have paid little attention to the southern hemisphere reeds known as restios, and despite their often distinctive appearance, their value as garden plants has scarcely been explored. One reason has been the problems encountered when trying to propagate them. Seeds frequently fail to produce seedlings, and established plants respond grudgingly to being pulled to pieces and take many months to recover after division.

These plants grow naturally in the South African fynbos—a heathland community characteristic of infertile landscapes and subject to periodic fires. Plants from such places exist by developing strategies, enabling them to survive fires and by taking advantage of the opportunities they offer. The young shoots of established restios grow up from the centers of the clumps, where they are protected from the heat of the fire. Seeds germinate in response to exposure to volatile compounds contained in the smoke of a bush fire. Most restios respond extremely well to exposure to smoke. Almost every seed of some species germinates after exposure. In others, substantially greater numbers of seedlings are produced. A few respond to smoke treatment only in combination with other environmental triggers, such as brief exposure to very high temperatures, scarification of the seed coat, and exposure to light during germination. Restios with small caryopses, including species of *Chondropetalum*, *Elegia*, *Restio*, *Rhodo-*

coma, *Staberoha* and *Thamnochortus*, mostly respond well to smoke. Those with large caryopses—similar to small nuts—including *Cannomois*, *Hypodiscus* and *Willdenovia*, are likely to be less responsive.

Aquatics

Seeds of a few truly aquatic species—those that grow constantly in water—including nelumbos and euryale, need to be kept in water after collection. They are intolerant of desiccation and cannot be stored at subzero temperatures. They survive in water—contained, for example, in a screw-top glass jar—for months and some for a year or more, and provided they are kept at low temperatures (such as in a refrigerator at below 5°C, or 40°F) will not germinate. The seeds of most marginal aquatics, on the other hand, withstand drying and can be stored at subzero temperatures for long periods.

Seeds of aquatic species, stored under water, germinate when the temperature of the water rises to 10°C (50°F) or more. They are then potted individually into small containers and covered by 2 or 3 cm (1 in.) of water. Alternatively, seed is sown as described in chapter 10 for nymphaeas. The seedlings are pricked out when large enough to handle and grown on, gradually increasing the depth of water as they develop.

Seeds of marginal aquatic species frequently germinate on *terra firma* and display similar requirements to those of land-based perennials. Seeds of some species are provided with floats composed of corky tissues—particularly conspicuous in *Iris laevigata*. After dispersal, their seeds float on the surface of the water until stranded on mud at the water's edge, where they germinate. These seeds, and a number of dicot marginal aquatics with similar floats, including celery and gypsywort, avoid the possibility of germinating while still in the water by responding to diurnal fluctuations between day and night temperatures. Temperatures experienced by the seeds remain more or less constant as long as they are in water, but they experience considerable variations when lying on exposed mud. Seeds of these species pro-

duce seedlings only in response to diurnal variations in temperature, typically of about 7° to
10°C (15° to 20°F). A temperature controlled
apparatus, such as a bench in a glasshouse or an
electric propagator, needs to be used judiciously
when raising plants from seed. Supplementary
heating should be reduced or switched off at night
to provide the fluctuating temperatures on which
the seeds depend for germination—something of
the order of 20°C (70°F) by day falling to 10°C
(50°F) at night is likely to be about right.

Examples and special cases when raising monocot perennials from seed

Alstroemeria spp. and cvs. grow naturally in the
foothills of the Andes, in semi-Mediterranean climates with dry periods during mid- to late summer. Winters are relatively mild. Plants die down
after flowering as the soil dries out, and seeds are
shed into quite arid conditions. At this stage, they
will not germinate under any conditions. Imbibed
seeds respond to high temperatures during late
summer, leading to germination when temperatures fall below 10°C (50°F) in early winter. Seeds
are mixed with moist vermiculite, perlite or grit
and exposed to high temperatures (about 25°C,
or 75°F) for about six weeks; then they are kept at
temperatures of 10°C (50°F) or less, when radicals should appear within a fortnight. Germination rates can be further improved by chipping at
the time they are moved from high to low temperatures. A small area of seed coat and the underlying tissue should be removed at a place identified
by a brown spot on the seed coat.

Anigozanthos spp. and cvs., or Kangaroo paw,
seeds—*A. flavidus* in particular—germinate without
any special treatment. Most other species need
heat treatment at 60° to 70°C (140° to 160°F) for
90 minutes, using a water bath on a temperature-
controlled hot plate when available. Seeds failing
to germinate soon after being sown are exposed
to high-temperature weathering in dry conditions
during the following summer, and they are then
watered heavily in early autumn. Exposure to
smoke is often highly effective.

Asphodelus spp. and other liliaceous plants,
including anthericums, asphodels, cordylines, alliums, muscaris, sisyrinchiums and irises, may
respond to a form of chipping. Unlike many members of the pea family with hard seed coats which
also respond to chipping, these liliaceous seeds
imbibe water spontaneously, and chipping must
serve some other (presently unidentified) purpose.
It is effective only when done as close as possible
to the embryo, in the following way:

Cut a sample seed in half, usually lengthwise,
to establish the site and orientation of the embryo. Sow the remainder of the seeds on a pad of
moist paper towel for 24 hours to imbibe. This is
not essential, but imbibed seeds are easier to handle than dry ones and less likely to suffer damage.
Insert the point of a knife into the seed coat, 2 or
3 mm (1/8 in.) from where the embryo lies, and
twist to gouge out a small plug of tissue, without
damaging the embryo itself. Sow the seeds and
treat them thereafter in the normal way. Optimum temperatures after sowing vary between species. Fluctuating temperatures—for example 15°
to 20°C (60° to 70°F) by day, falling to 5° to 10°C
(40° to 50°F) at night—are likely to give better
results than constant temperatures.

Hosta spp. and cvs. seeds mature from late summer to early winter. They germinate readily and
rapidly at high temperatures (20° to 25°C, or 70°
to 75°F), slowly at 15°C (60°F) and very slowly
below 10°C (40°F). Results can be unpredictable,
apart from a few species. Centuries of cultivation
in Japan and China have led to all kinds of aber-
rant sexual tendencies amongst the hybrids and
even in some of the so-called species. These include apomixy and other forms of self-fertilisation which bypass the recombination of genes
during sexual reproduction, production of defec-
tive or sterile pollen, and formation of adventitious embryos in the nucellar tissues around the
embryo sacs, leading to the production of several
seedlings from each seed. Despite these uncertainties, growing hostas from seed can have rewarding results. Variegated forms will not produce
variegated offspring, but other foliage qualities
including tones of blue and yellow, leaf shape and

vigour can be selected for, as well as flower form and fragrance—two qualities that have been neglected in the search for ever more striking, complex or outrightly bizarre patterns of variegation.

Propagation from Cuttings

The distribution and function of meristematic tissues differs fundamentally between monocots and dicots, and this greatly reduces opportunities to propagate the former from cuttings.

Monocot stems lack the rings of subcutaneous meristematic tissues that enable shoots of dicots to continue to thicken and develop more or less indefinitely, and which give rise to roots and new shoots in cuttings. Monocot roots contain little or no meristematic tissue. They are continually replaced as they mature by new, or adventitious, roots from the base of the stems. With some exceptions, such as yuccas, monocot roots do not produce suckers and cannot be used as cuttings to propagate new plants. The stems of grasses, hostas, and bananas develop from meristematic tissues at the base of the plant, and all growth proceeds from the growing point enclosed and protected within layers of leaves at the base. Side shoots can be removed as divisions if they are producing roots, but it is not practical to use them as basal cuttings. Leaves produced on the stems of palms, bamboos, and other plants are very seldom associated with axillary buds at the point where they join the stem, and therefore the side shoots and single buds that are major sources of cuttings in dicots are seldom available from monocots.

Stem and rhizome cuttings

Monocots propagated from cuttings made from their stems include the following:

The creeping stems of tradescantias, commelinas, and other members of family Commelinaceae produce roots at their nodes and are propagated from cuttings. Rhizomatous grasses, amongst them *Agropyron repens* (an example that is uncom-

fortably familiar to many gardeners), like the rhizomes of dicots referred to in chapter 10, often provide ready sources of propagating material. *Arundo donax* and a few other clump-forming grasses produce side shoots, basal cuttings in effect, that can be removed without roots but produce them from pre-existing initials almost at once.

Saccharum officinarum and hybrids, or sugar cane, is propagated by cutting mature cane into sections 30 to 45 cm (12 to 18 in.) long. These are laid in a trench and lightly covered with soil, when they produce shoots and roots from the nodes.

Aquatic marginals include numerous monocots which can consistently be propagated from cuttings. Many of these are continuously radescent, producing roots from their nodes as they grow, to such an extent that when their shoots are removed it is a moot, but academic, point whether they should be referred to as cuttings or divisions. The stems of most aquatics lack woody tissues, and if stuck directly into the cutting media, the part below the surface is likely to rot. Cuttings should be laid on saturated surfaces and pinned down with a staple (about 2 to 3 cm, or 1 in., long), rather than inserted into the medium. Roots formed at the internodes grow out to establish new plants. Containers holding the cuttings should be partially immersed in water.

Propagation by Division

Petaloid monocots

Many petaloid monocots grow in woodlands and meadows amongst and alongside broad-leaved perennials and share similar cycles of root development. They are propagated by division at the same times and in the same ways as their dicot associates, described in chapter 10 and in chart 15.

The production of new roots during late summer into early autumn is particularly conspicuous in many perennial dicots, as anyone who digs up a day lily, hosta or *Iris unguiculata* at this time cannot help noticing. Plants are lifted, divided into

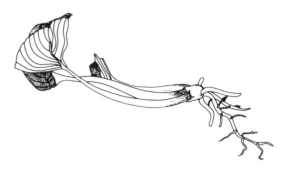

Figure 57. Strong anchor roots produced by hostas from mid-summer onwards mark the start of the annual renewal of the root system. Divisions made at this time establish well before winter, and plants can be divided up into single crowns for maximum productivity and potted individually or lined out in a nursery bed. Most leaves should be removed and those that remain reduced in size to lighten demands on the roots while these establish themselves.

their component crowns, and either planted straight back into the garden, lined out in a nursery bed or potted up while they reestablish and make some renewal growth. Potting up or lining out the divisions in a nursery bed make more work but may be more convenient than replanting straight back into the garden, because it is not necessary to find places for the plants immediately and they can be planted at any time up to or even beyond the following spring. In addition, increased chances of survival, even of very small subdivisions, make it possible to obtain the maximum number of plants.

Rhizomatous subtropical/tropical genera

Cannas, gingers, bananas, colocasias, alpinias and other broad-leaved tropical plants are increasingly widely used in temperate gardens in summer for their luxuriant foliage effects. In warm temperate regions and parts of Mediterranea, they can be left in the ground with minimal protection, but they must be lifted and overwintered in frost-free situations in colder places. They can be placed under the benches in a frost-free glasshouse or a shed; in shallow boxes with the roots and rhizomes lightly covered with peat, bark, or coir, kept barely moist throughout the winter; and propagated by division in the spring.

- The plants are started into growth in late winter, before being divided, when the young shoots provide a guide to the positions where cuts can be made.
- Boxes or pots containing the plants are placed on a bench over soil heating cables and then watered thoroughly before setting the thermostat to maintain temperatures around the roots of approximately 25°C (75°F).

- When shoots have grown large enough to be clearly visible, the rhizomes are divided so that each section includes at least one shoot.
- Pot up into 1 or 2 litre (6 or 8 in.) pots and grow on at 15° to 20°C (60° to 70°F), until their roots have developed sufficiently to fill their containers
- Pot on into 5 or even 10 litre (2 or 3 gal.) pots, depending on their size and vigour, and keep in a frost-free location while they continue to grow.
- Plant out or set the pots out in the garden when the last frosts are a memory.

Grasses, sedges and restios

These narrow-leaved, more or less surface-rooting, generally clump-forming monocots lend themselves to division by pulling the clumps apart. However, life for those who want to propagate them is more complex than that. Grasses and sedges respond well to this treatment but only when divisions are made when the roots are growing actively or just about to do so. In cold or cool temperate regions and in warmer areas with dry winters, divide in spring or early summer. In Mediterranea, where summers are dry, and in almost frost-free warm or mild temperate regions, divisions are made in early autumn.

Clumps are divided into small groups of crowns, rather than reduced to singles, doubles or triples. Most languish without company and are more likely to establish successfully in groups of at least six or seven crowns. "Weed" grasses which sow themselves into established clumps and gradually take over present a serious problem when growing grasses, not least because it can be difficult to distinguish the desirable greens from the weed. Dividing the plants provides an opportunity to remove these interlopers. Great care should be taken to note the characteristics of the species being divided and to exclude anything that seems strange.

Restios are intolerant of division and many take months to establish themselves and resume active growth afterwards. Their intolerance is due

Figure 58. Divisions obtained in mid-summer from a *Kniphofia* cultivar bought from a garden centre. The plant was knocked out of its container, the roots were washed and nine divisions into single or small clusters of crowns were made. When using divisions to produce the maximum number of plants, the young plants should be potted up and provided with some protection while they reestablish, rather than planting them straight out in the garden or a nursery bed.

to the fact that the new shoots arise from regenerative tissues in the centres of the clumps, and the peripheral, most accessible crowns are the oldest and least active. Young regenerating shoots can be reached only by completely dismantling the clumps and inflicting considerable damage to them in the process. Even more than with grasses and sedges, restios do not repay attempts to achieve maximum yields by separating them into small subdivisions.

Aquatics

Water plants growing in cool and cold temperate regions display very marked seasonal patterns of growth and development. Growth resumes as water warms up in the spring and dies down in autumn at the approach of winter. In Mediterranea, where ponds, streams and other sources of water are likely to dry up completely during the

Chart 15. MULTIPLYING PERENNIALS BY DIVISION

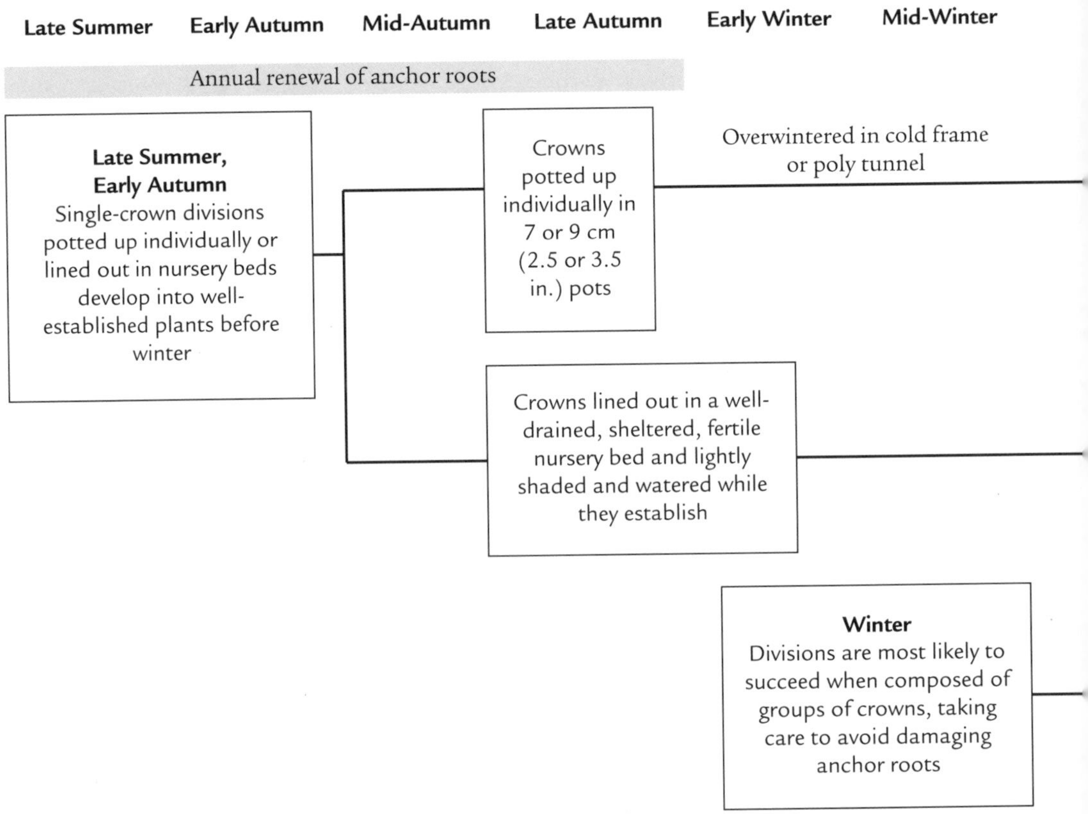

| Late Summer | Early Autumn | Mid-Autumn | Late Autumn | Early Winter | Mid-Winter |

Annual renewal of anchor roots

Late Summer, Early Autumn
Single-crown divisions potted up individually or lined out in nursery beds develop into well-established plants before winter

Crowns potted up individually in 7 or 9 cm (2.5 or 3.5 in.) pots

Overwintered in cold frame or poly tunnel

Crowns lined out in a well-drained, sheltered, fertile nursery bed and lightly shaded and watered while they establish

Winter
Divisions are most likely to succeed when composed of groups of crowns, taking care to avoid damaging anchor roots

Options for Making Divisions from Perennials
Cycles of root development are initiated in late summer with the production of anchor roots, from which networks of feeding roots emerge in the spring.

Divisions in the late summer are much more productive than those made at other seasons, because clumps can be subdivided into single crowns with very high survival rates.

Apart from extremely resilient plants, divisions made in winter and spring are most likely to be successful when composed of multiple crowns in order to reduce damage to existing and developing roots.

Grasses should be divided only when their feeding roots are growing actively: in spring in cool and cold temperate regions, and in autumn in Mediterranea and warm temperate regions.

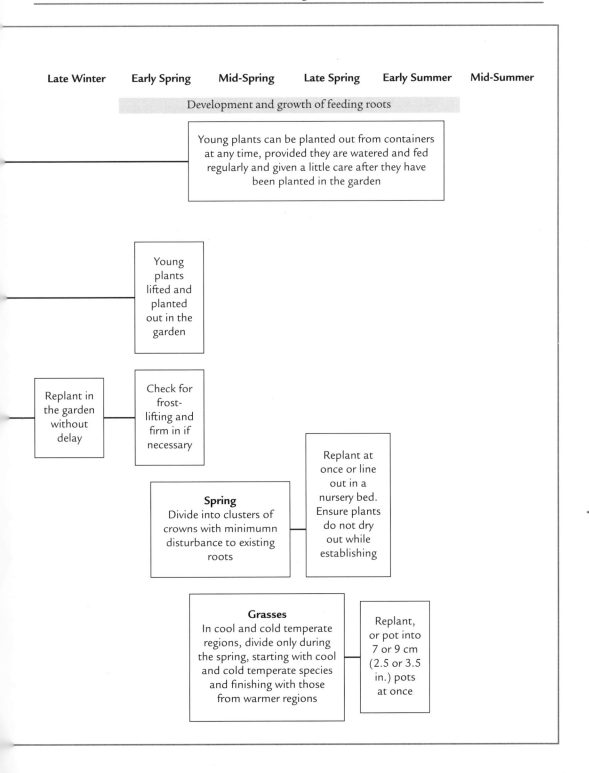

| Late Winter | Early Spring | Mid-Spring | Late Spring | Early Summer | Mid-Summer |

Development and growth of feeding roots

Young plants can be planted out from containers at any time, provided they are watered and fed regularly and given a little care after they have been planted in the garden

Young plants lifted and planted out in the garden

Replant in the garden without delay

Check for frost-lifting and firm in if necessary

Replant at once or line out in a nursery bed. Ensure plants do not dry out while establishing

Spring
Divide into clusters of crowns with minimumn disturbance to existing roots

Grasses
In cool and cold temperate regions, divide only during the spring, starting with cool and cold temperate species and finishing with those from warmer regions

Replant, or pot into 7 or 9 cm (2.5 or 3.5 in.) pots at once summer, renewal of active growth takes place in autumn.

Spring or autumn—depending on location—are the times when most aquatic and marginal plants should be divided, extending into summer for some of the true aquatics including eichhornia, hydrocharis, elodea, potamogeton, and stratiotes. These produce offsets, or young plants, viviparously so long as they are growing actively.

Because of the peculiar temperature inversion which causes water close to freezing point to be lighter than slightly warmer water, ice forms on the surface—not, as might be expected, at the bottom of ponds and lakes. As a consequence, the deeper layers of water in ponds and lakes are insulated by increasing amounts of ice as temperatures fall and seldom freeze. This enables many tender aquatics, including aponogetons, nelumbos, euryales and others, to survive cold winters by retreating to the bottom of the ponds. Most do so simply by adopting herbaceous forms of growth, dying down in winter to crowns buried in the mud, a metre (3 ft.) or so below the surface. Others, including hydrocharis and saggitarias, form detached resting buds known as turions. These sink and settle on the bottom, to resume growth as the water warms in the spring. They are propagated by collecting turions and growing them on, lightly lodged in growth media in containers covered with water.

Examples and special cases of monocot perennials propagated by division

Alstroemeria cvs. can be dug up from the garden and divided, but due to the depth to which their small, white, fragile rhizomes descend, this is easier said than done. Stock plants are grown in large pots (5 to 7.5 litres, or 2 to 5 gal.) in order to propagate these plants. Remove the plants from the pots in mid- to late autumn when new rhizomes have just been formed. These are small, blunt-ended, spindle-shaped objects between 1 and 4 cm (0.5 and 1.5 in.) long. They are translucent and white, with a consistency resembling the flesh of a lichee or cooked and skinned salsify root. Ease them out of the growth medium, snip them free from their attachments and pot them up separately in 7 cm (2.5 in.) square pots. They are overwintered in a frost-free situation but need no more supplementary heat than is necessary to achieve this. They are watered sparingly but should not dry out completely. When shoots appear, start watering more heavily and plant out in the garden or pot on into 1 litre (6 in.) pots when they are big enough.

Arum spp., such as *A. italicum pictum*, produce leaves from a bud at the apex of an annually replaced rhizome, which is the size of a strawberry. As the leaves develop, the old rhizomes shrivel to be replaced by others formed during the summer. Rounded, warty excrescences, about the size of small peas, form on the surface of the rhizomes, and these are left behind in the ground as the old rhizomes disintegrate. The plants are propagated by digging up the clumps as the foliage dies away in mid-summer. The rhizomes are separated from one another and replanted. The warty excrescences from the current year and past years (if any) are picked out and potted up individually in 7 cm (2.5 in.) containers. They spend the rest of the summer under cover in a frame, poly tunnel, or another covered area, watered sparingly but not allowed to dry out. Water more freely when leaves appear in autumn, and maintain growth throughout the winter; they are allowed to die down naturally in early summer. The young plants should be planted in the garden in the autumn when leaves reappear.

Astelia spp. and cvs. are divided in early spring when yields can be greatly increased by stimulating the production of offsets. During the previous summer, strip the leaves off some of the crowns to expose the growing points, located on the rootstock. After removing the leaves, scoop out the apical bud in the centre, taking care to avoid damage to the surrounding tissue. This stimulates the outgrowth of slender offsets from meristems in the axils of the leaves, which would otherwise have lain dormant. Remove the offsets as close to the rootstock as possible the following spring. Pot up

Figure 59. A one-year-old alstroemeria seedling grown in a container. Tuberous rhizomes develop deep below the surface, descending to 60 to 75 cm (24 to 30 in.) when able to do so. The rhizome is the cylindrical white object just below the centre of the photograph. It is difficult to dig up rhizomes of plants in the garden without doing them irreparable damage. Plants grown in containers can readily be propagated from the numerous small proto-rhizomes produced during late summer.

into small containers and grow on. Similar methods can be used to increase productivity of phormiums, hostas, day lilies and other monocots with similar forms of growth.

Xeronema callistemon can be raised from seed sown fresh at about 15°C (60°F). Germination may be erratic and prolonged, and the seedlings are highly susceptible to phytophthora unless planted in very free-draining, mainly mineral potting mixes. Older plants can be divided into single fans, provided each has some root, and preferably during the earlier part of the growing season. They are potted up individually into a very free-draining potting mix and grown on under a frugal watering regime—for example, a thorough soaking repeated at fortnightly intervals.

Zantedeschia spp. can be propagated by dividing their large, fleshy rhizomes. Much greater numbers can be produced by using the numerous, small, cylindrical rhizomes produced below the main body of rhizomes. Dig up the plants or knock them out of their containers toward the end of the summer. Remove most of the attached soil or growth medium from beneath the plants and pick out the little rhizomes found there—sometimes in considerable numbers. Pot up, either individually in 7 cm (2.5 in.) pots or, more economically, with five companionably sharing a 9 cm or 1 litre (6 in.) square container. Leaves are produced within a few weeks. The small plants are kept growing actively through the winter with minimum temperatures of about 10°C (50°F), when they will be ready to pot up or line out by the following spring. In places with cold winters, they need protection from frost in a glasshouse during the winter. In frost-free situations, they grow vigorously throughout the winter out of doors.

Propagation Summary for Perennial Monocot Genera

S. = propagated from seed
C. = propagated from cuttings
D. = propagated by divisions

Note that seasons shown for sowing seeds or making divisions are based on those applicable in cool or cold temperate regions. Gardeners in Mediterranea and also in mild or warm temperate regions can often propagate grasses, for example, in the autumn in place of—or as well as—spring.

Acorus—Aquatic. **D.** spring.

Agapanthus—**S.** late winter. **D.** spring.

Agrostis—Grass. **S.** summer, spring. **D.** early spring.

Alisma—Aquatic. **S.** fresh. **D.** spring.

Alocasia—**S.** spring. **C.** spring; rhizome. **D.** spring; offsets.

Alopecurus—Grass. **S.** spring. **D.** spring; variegated and coloured leaf forms.

Alpinia—**S.** fresh, spring. **D.** spring; from very short basal shoots.

Alstroemeria—Ballistic. **S.** fresh, late spring, summer. **D.** autumn; tuberous rhizomes from container-grown plants.

Ampelodesmos—Grass. **S.** fresh, spring. **D.** late spring.

Anigozanthos—**S.** spring; smoke, hot water or high temperature weathering. **D.** autumn, spring.

Aponogeton—Aquatic. **S.** fresh. **D.** spring; tuberous rhizomes.

Arisaema—Dioecious (rarely). Succulent Fruit. **S.** fresh, spring. **D.** late winter, spring; tubers usually, a few from offsets.

Arisarum—**D.** late summer, late winter; tubers and offsets.

Aristea—**S.** fresh, spring. **D.** mid- to late summer; resent root disturbance.

Arrhenatherum—Grass. **S.** spring. **D.** early spring.

Arthropodium—**S.** fresh, spring. **D.** spring.

Arum—Succulent Fruit. **S.** fresh. **D.** mid-summer; as foliage dies down; offsets or tubers.

Arundo—Grass. **D.** late spring.

Asparagus—Succulent Fruit. Dioecious. **S.** spring. **D.** late summer, spring.

Asphodeline—**S.** fresh, spring. **D.** early autumn.

Asphodelus—**S.** fresh, spring. **D.** early autumn.

Aspidistra—**D.** early spring; offsets.

Astelia—Succulent Fruit. Dioecious. **S.** fresh. **D.** late winter, early spring; yield can be increased by previously excising growing points.

Belamcanda—**S.** spring. **D.** late winter.

Biarum—**D.** late summer, early autumn.

Blandfordia—**S.** fresh, spring; five or more years to first flowers. **D.** summer; cut back hard immediately after flowers fade to encourage new shoots.

Bomarea—Liane. **S.** fresh. **D.** late summer to late autumn.

Bouteloua—Grass. **S.** fresh, spring.

Bromus—Grass. **S.** spring. **D.** early spring.

Bulbine—**S.** spring, autumn.

Bulbinella—**S.** fresh. **D.** autumn, spring.

Butomus—Aquatic. **D.** early spring; bulbils: mid-spring to early summer; rhizomes.

Calamagrostis—Grass. **S.** spring.

Calla—Aquatic. Succulent Fruit. **S.** fresh. **D.** early spring; rhizomes.

Calopsis—Restio. **S.** spring, autumn; smoke. **D.** mid-winter to early spring.

Canna—**S.** late winter; chip. **D.** late winter, spring; rhizomes.

Cannomois—Restio. Dioecious. **S.** spring, autumn; germination erratic. **D.** mid-winter to early spring.

Carex—Sedge. **S.** fresh. **D.** spring.

Cautleya—**S.** fresh. **D.** late summer, autumn.

Chasmanthium—Grass. **S.** fresh, spring. **D.** spring.

Chionochloa—Grass. **S.** fresh. **D.** late spring.

Chloris—Grass. **S.** late spring, early summer.

Chlorophytum—**D.** summer to early winter; viviparous offsets from inflorescences.

Chondropetalum—Restio. Dioecious. **S.** autumn, spring; smoke. **D.** spring.

Clintonia—Succulent Fruit. **S.** fresh. **D.** late summer; rhizomes.

Clivia—Succulent Fruit. **S.** fresh; sown on surface. **D.** autumn to spring; peripheral offsets; avoid unnecessary disturbance.

Collospermum—Succulent Fruit. **S.** fresh. **D.** spring.

Colocasia—**D.** late winter, spring; tubers

Commelina—**S.** spring. **C.** late winter, early spring. **D.** spring; tuberous rooted species, e.g,. *C. coelestis*.

Conostylis—**S.** autumn, spring; smoke.

Convallaria—Succulent Fruit. **D.** late winter.

Cortaderia—Dioecious. Grass. **S.** fresh. **D.** late winter to late spring; to propagate special forms, usually female plants.

Cynosurus—Grass. **S.** early spring.

Cyperus—Sedge. **D.** late winter, spring; short rhizomes or tubers.

Dactylis—Grass. **S.** spring. **D.** early spring.

Deschampsia—Grass. **S.** spring, autumn. **D.** mid- to late spring. Some have preference for light shade, e.g., *D.* 'Tatra Gold'.

Dianella—Succulent Fruit. **S.** fresh, spring; hot-water soak, light chip. **D.** spring.

Dierama—**S.** fresh, spring. **D.** late winter, spring.

Dietes—**S.** spring. **D.** autumn, spring; offsets.

Dioscorea—Liane. Dioecious. **S.** spring. **C.** spring; basal. **D.** late winter; tubers.

Diplarrhena—**S.** spring, autumn. **D.** late winter.

Disporum—Succulent Fruit. **S.** fresh. **D.** late winter, early spring.

Eichhornia—Aquatic. **D.** summer, autumn; overwinter stolons in frost-free conditions.

Elegia—Restio. Dioecious. **S.** autumn, spring; smoke. **D.** mid-winter to early spring.

Elodea—Aquatic. **C. D.** spring, summer.

Elymus—Grass. **S.** spring. **D.** spring, early summer; rhizomes.

Ensete—Succulent Fruit. **S.** late winter. **D.** late winter, spring; offsets.

Eragrostis—Grass. **S.** spring. **D.** spring.

Eremurus—**S.** fresh. **D.** winter.

Erianthus—Grass. **S.** fresh, spring. **D.** early spring.

Eriophorum—Sedge. **S.** spring. **D.** spring.

Festuca—Grass **S.** spring, autumn. **D.** spring, summer; viviparous plantlets in inflorescences of some alpine species.

Gahnia—Sedge. **S.** spring; germination slow and erratic.

Haemodorum—**D.** autumn, spring.

Hakonechloa—Grass. **D.** spring.

Hedychium—**S.** fresh, spring. **D.** late winter, autumn; rhizomes: summer; bulbils in leaf axils, e.g., *H. greenii*.

Helictotrichon—Grass. **S.** spring. **D.** spring.

Hemerocallis—**S.** spring. **D.** mid-summer to late winter; occasional viviparous plantlets.

Hierochloe—Grass. **S.** spring.

Holcus—Grass. **S.** spring. **D.** early spring.

Hosta—**S.** fresh, spring; blue and golden-leaved forms reproduce from seed to some extent, but not variegated forms. **D.** late summer, early autumn.

Hydrocharis—Aquatic. **D.** summer; runners: winter; turions.

Hypodiscus—Restio. Dioecious. **S.** autumn, spring; very erratic germination.

Hypoxis—**S.** spring, autumn. **D.** spring; offsets.

Hystrix—Grass. **S.** spring. **D.** late spring.

Imperata—Grass. **D.** late spring.

Iris—**S.** fresh, spring. **D.** mid-summer, bearded irises: late summer, early autumn, *I. sibirica*; Pacific Coast species and others similar: late autumn, winter, bulbous species.

Ischyrolepis—Restio. Dioecious. **S.** autumn, spring; smoke.

Isolepis—Sedge. **S.** spring. **D.** spring.

Juncus—Sedge. **S.** spring; **D.** spring; e.g., *J. effusus* 'Spiralis'.

Kniphofia—**S.** spring; likely to hybridise in gardens. **D.** late summer, early autumn.

Koeleria—Grass. **S.** spring.

Lagarosiphon—Aquatic. **C.** early spring to early autumn.

Lepidosperma—Sedge. **D.** autumn, spring.

Leymus—Grass. **D.** spring, early summer.

Libertia—**S.** fresh, spring; chipping may help. **D.** spring.

Liriope—**D.** late summer, spring.

Lolium—Grass. **S.** autumn, spring.

Lomandra—**S.** spring. **D.** autumn.

Luzula—Sedge. **S.** spring. **D.** spring.

Lysichiton—Succulent Fruit. **S.** fresh. **D.** late summer, autumn.

Machaerina—Sedge. **S.** spring. **D.** early spring to early summer; reduce foliage.

Macropidia—**S.** fresh; high temperature weathering.

Maianthemum—Succulent Fruit. **S.** fresh. **D.** late summer.

Melica—Grass. **S.** spring.

Milium—Grass. **S.** spring; *M. effusum* 'Aureum' comes true from seed. **D.** spring to early summer; rhizomes, preference for shade.

Miscanthus—Grass. **S.** spring. **D.** late spring to early summer.

Molinia—Grass. **S.** spring. **D.** early spring.

Monochoria—Aquatic. **D.** early spring.

Musa—Succulent Fruit. **S.** late winter. **D.** spring; suckers.

Narthecium—Aquatic. **S.** spring. **D.** spring.

Ophiopogon—**D.** spring to late summer.

Orontium—Aquatic. **S.** fresh. **D.** spring.

Orthrosanthus—**D.** spring, autumn.

Paris—Succulent Fruit. **S.** fresh. **D.** late summer, early autumn.

Patersonia—**S.** autumn, spring; viability variable. **D.** spring, autumn; short rhizomes.

Peltandra—Aquatic. Succulent Fruit. **D.** spring.

Pennisetum—Grass. **S.** spring. **D.** spring; overwinter stock plants in frost-free conditions.

Phaiophleps—**S.** spring.

Phleum—Grass. **S.** early spring.

Phormium—**S.** spring; may produce either upright, spiky or lax, arching forms. **D.** spring, autumn; increase yield by cutting back stock plants hard to rootstock to encourage the formation of numerous small offsets rather than a few large ones.

Pistia—Aquatic, **D.** spring to autumn; offsets.

Poa—Grass. **S.** spring. **D.** spring.

Polygonatum—Succulent Fruit. **D.** late summer to early winter.

Pontederia—Aquatic. **S.** fresh. **D.** late spring, early summer.

Potamogeton—Aquatic. **C.** early spring, summer; offsets.

Protasparagus—Succulent Fruit. **S.** spring. **D.** late winter.

Reineckea—Succulent Fruit. **D.** late summer, early autumn.

Restio—Restio. Dioecious. **S.** autumn, spring; smoke. **D.** spring.

Rhodocoma—Restio. Dioecious. **S.** spring, autumn; smoke.

Rhodohypoxis—**S.** spring. **D.** winter, early spring.

Roscoea—**S.** fresh, spring. **D.** late summer, early autumn.

Saccharum—Grass. **C.** spring to summer.

Sagittaria—Aquatic. **D.** spring, summer; offsets: winter; turions.

Sansevieria—**C.** spring, summer; leaf. **D.** offsets.

Schizostylis—**S.** spring. **D.** spring to autumn.

Scirpus—Sedge, Aquatic. **S.** spring. **D.** spring; rhizomes.

Setaria—Grass. **S.** late winter, spring.

Setcreasea—**D.** spring.

Sisyrinchium—**S.** fresh, spring. **D.** spring, late summer.

Smilacina—Succulent Fruit. **S.** fresh. **D.** late summer, early autumn; sections of rhizome each with a bud.

Smilax—Liane. Dioecious. Succulent Fruit. **S.** fresh. **D.** spring; rhizomes.

Sorghastrum—Grass. **S.** fresh, spring. **D.** mid-spring.

Sparganium—Sedge, Aquatic. Succulent Fruit. **S.** spring. **D.** spring.

Spartina—Sedge. Aquatic. **D.** spring.

Stipa—Grass. **S.** spring. **D.** spring.

Stratiotes—Aquatic. **D.** summer, autumn; offsets: winter; turions.

Strelitzia—**S.** fresh, spring; germination erratic. **D.** early spring; offsets.

Thamnocalamus—Restio. Dioecious. **S.** autumn, spring; smoke.

Thamnochortus—Restio. Dioecious. **S.** autumn, spring; smoke.

Thysanotus—**S.** fresh. **D.** spring; offsets.

Tradescantia—**C.** early spring to early autumn. **D.** Viviparous plantlets on peduncles of some species.

Tricyrtis—**S.** fresh, spring. **D.** late summer, early autumn.

Tulbaghia—**S.** fresh, spring. **D.** early spring, autumn.

Typha—Sedge, Aquatic. **S.** fresh, spring; erratic germination. **D.** spring.

Uncinia—Sedge. **D.** spring.

Vallisneria—Aquatic. Dioecious. Recalcitrant. **S.** store under water, spring. **D.** summer; stolons.

Wachendorfia—**S.** spring. **D.** late summer.

Willdenovia—Restio. Dioecious. **S.** autumn, spring; erratic germination. **D.** spring; recovery likely to be prolonged.

Witsenia—**S.** fresh, spring. **D.** autumn, spring.

Xeronema—**S.** fresh; germination erratic. **D.** spring.

Zantedeschia—Succulent Fruit. **S.** fresh. **D.** summer to autumn; offsets or rhizomes.

Zebrina—**C.** spring to autumn.

Zigadenus—**S.** fresh. **D.** autumn, early winter.

CHAPTER 12

Plants with Bulbs and Corms

Bulbs and corms are formed from quite minor modifications of standard plant parts. Tulip bulbs and crocus corms may not look like delphiniums or rose bushes, but they are propagated from seeds, cuttings or by division in much the same way, provided we recognise the underlying similarities between their leaves, shoots and stems.

Bulbs are subterranean buds. They consist of an extremely compressed stem, known descriptively as a basal plate, and variable numbers of short, fleshy leaves. Cut a daffodil bulb in half, look at it closely, and the basal plate and the leaves are clearly distinguishable. Snowdrop, tulip, hyacinth, nerine, onion and amaryllis bulbs are all minor variations on the same theme. Each is composed of modified stems and leaves all tightly wrapped in a package of dry, brown scales known as a tunic. Lily, nomocharis, and fritillaria bulbs lack the outer wrapping, or tunic, and their leaves, or scales, are easily separated one from another.

Bulbs are perennial, persisting for years. Daffodils, tulips and most other bulbs subdivide as they grow to form offsets that are readily propagated by removing and growing on. Urgineas, brunsvigias and a few others like them seldom subdivide but grow steadily larger year by year, increasing much more slowly.

Corms are rhizomes in disguise. They consist of short sections of swollen underground stems and vestigial, scalelike leaves. The latter are sometimes almost invisible but are closely associated with meristematic tissues on the surface of the corm. Cut a corm in half and examine it; there is no basal plate, no layers of leaves. The centre is composed of amorphous tissue—the rhizome—with tiny scales on the surface, enclosed in a fragile, papery covering. Gardeners may happily refer to the corms of crocuses, gladioli, ixias and freesias as bulbs, but botanist view them differently, and this is a situation where propagators should listen to the botanists. Things can be done to propagate bulbs that cannot be done with corms—and vice versa.

Many corms are annual. Each corm is replaced by one or more new corms as the flowers fade, and most disappear completely as they are replaced. Numerous tiny corms, called cormels, are also produced around the base of the corms themselves and can be used as propagules. A few corms are perennial. Those produced by crocosmias, babianas and others persist indefinitely, forming chains of superannuated corms beneath the currently active one. They are propagated by removing the redundant corms and resuscitating them.

The most significant difference between delphiniums or rose bushes and bulbs or corms is the latter's tolerance to desiccation and other adverse conditions. They provide a means by which plants can retreat underground to protect themselves from drought, heat, bitter winds and cold. They are akin to giant seeds that emerge only when better prospects are on the horizon—rising temperatures, more abundant rainfall, or in response to a significant event, such as fire. Like seeds, bulbs and corms can be left lying around, moved from one place to another or kept for long periods out of the ground without dying, all qualities gardeners have learned to use and abuse most effectively.

Daffodil bulbs unplanted one autumn are capable of surviving in nets in a potting shed until the next—and are still so forgiving they produce flowers the following spring. That does not mean such treatment is good for them—just that they can take it in an emergency. Lilies and other bulbs without tunics are less tolerant. Their cycles of growth provide no season when they do not suffer from being out of the ground. Even these can be dug up, left with the minimum of protection for several months, and then replanted—something that would be impossible with more vulnerable plants.

"The proper place for a bulb is underground" should be written up somewhere in every propagator's potting shed. This is easily forgotten, just because bulbs and corms are so amenable. But every day exposed to the air causes some loss of vitality and potential. Every extra day buried in the soil is another day when roots can explore, shoots can develop and preparations can be made for emergence and flowering later.

Propagation from Seed

Many gardeners do not take opportunities to grow bulbs from seed because they think it would be so long before they saw flowers, it would be a waste of time to set out on the journey. That is nonsense! Several lilies, as well as tigridias, lapeyrousias, galtonias, freesias and ixias sown early can produce flowers before the year ends. Seedlings of a great many other bulbs flower during their second or third season. Tulips and daffodils, and more specialist items including crinodendrons

and hippeastrums, are unlikely to flower until they are four, five, or even seven years old. But even these slow coaches produce seed so freely they can be used to raise more plants more quickly than is possible by any other means.

Seed collection and storage

Most bulbous plants produce seed prolifically, pollination problems are unusual, and they can be collected easily and stored without difficulty. Seeds are usually produced in conspicuous capsules, which go brown as they mature, dry up and split open to reveal the seeds. They are highly visible and leave no doubt about the time they are ready to collect.

There are exceptions. Crocus capsules develop at or just below ground level. They are easily missed and must be searched for, using such leaves as remain as a guide. Most amaryllids from South Africa produce more or less succulent seeds, intolerant of desiccation, and they cannot be dried and stored. A group of species from the Western Cape in South Africa, including a few kinds of lapeirousias, gladioli, pelargoniums, hesperanthas, babianas, and some of the paler flowered ixias, all produce nectar at the base of long spurs that are accessible only to proboscid flies—remarkable for the exceptional length of their tongues. Some fail to set seed in gardens in the absence of their natural pollinators and need to be hand-pollinated.

Germination and care of seedlings

Seeds of almost all bulbous plants can be sown using the standard technique in a free-draining base layer of [peat, bark, coir] : [coarse sand, grit, perlite], 1:1, with grit or perlite for the topping. Bluebells, ixias, galtonias and others with medium-sized, rounded seeds are scattered over the surface and ploughed in. The broad, flat-sided seeds of lilies, fritillaries, trilliums, and tulips are sprinkled over a shallow layer of topping and then covered to bury them about 1 cm (0.5 in.) below the surface.

Seeds of many species germinate spontaneously soon after being sown; others need to be weathered. The ways seeds germinate can be broadly grouped as follows.

Regale lily response

Seeds germinate spontaneously over a wide temperature range—optima 15° to 25°C (60° to 75°F). Sow seeds during late winter or early spring. In cool or cold temperate regions, supplementary heat speeds progress. Seedlings grow on rapidly to develop small bulbs by the end of the first season. Examples include many lilies, alliums and galtonias.

Bluebell response

Seeds are shed in mid-summer and germinate when temperatures fall in the autumn, after weathering at high soil temperatures during late summer. Sow seeds as soon as possible after collection, water thoroughly, and expose to the natural sequence of high temperatures—20° to 25°C (70° to 75°F), falling below 11°C (52°F) in autumn. Seedlings emerge during the winter and benefit from protection from frost in cold situations. Examples include *Hyacinthoides*, *Narcissus* and *Asphodelus*.

Freesia response

Seeds germinate spontaneously after a period of after-ripening when temperatures fall, during early autumn and winter. Store seeds dry after collection at about 20°C (70°F) for several weeks, and then sow at temperatures below 11°C (52°F). When seedlings appear, they are pricked out and grown on at higher temperatures—15° to 20°C (60° to 70°F)—to encourage rapid development. Examples include many bulbs from Mediterranea and especially South Africa.

Fritillary response

Seeds mature during the summer and are weathered by high soil temperatures during late summer/autumn followed by low temperatures during the winter. Seedlings appear during late winter or in early spring. Sow seeds as soon as possible

after collection, water thoroughly and expose to the natural cycle of summer, autumn and winter temperatures. When seedlings appear, they can be brought into a glasshouse at temperatures of 15° to 20°C (60° to 70°F) to encourage rapid growth and development. Examples include many Middle Eastern bulbs, including *Fritillaria* and *Tulipa*, and some lilies, including *Lilium chalcedonicum* and *L. pyrenaicum*.

Martagon response

Seeds shed during late summer and autumn respond to warm soil temperatures followed by low temperatures during the winter. In many places, soil temperatures do not remain high enough for long enough to satisfy the warm weathering requirement, and most seeds produce only a radicle when they germinate the following spring (this is known as hypogeal germination), into which the storage reserves are transferred from the seeds to form a minute bulb. They then respond to warm soils during the ensuing summer and low temperature weathering in the winter to complete the germination process the following spring. Sow seeds as soon as they mature and place the containers on a bench at 20° to 25°C (70° to 75°F) for three months. Then move them into a fully ventilated cold frame to experience natural winter cold. A high proportion should germinate during the following spring. Those that do germinate then spend the summer as minute bulbs, and seedlings appear the following spring. Examples include several lilies, amongst them almost all North American species and *Lilium auratum*, *L. japonicum*, *L. martagon*, *L. monodelphum*, *L. rubellum* and *L. szovitsianum*.

Trillium response

This is similar to the Martagon response, but not even hypogeal germination will occur unless the seeds are sown in time to experience high temperatures before the onset of winter. Seeds sown too late to experience high temperatures do not produce radicles until their second spring, and they produce no leaves till the third. Seeds should never dry out and if not sown immediately after

Chart 16. BULBS AND CORMS FROM SEED

| Early Summer | Mid-Summer | Late Summer | Early Autumn | Mid-Autumn | Late Autumn |

Freesia Response
Seeds mature

Seeds after-ripen in the summer. Sow at 10° to 15°C (50° to 60°F) any time after six weeks.

Bluebell Response
Seeds mature

Seeds sown as soon as possible

Seeds weather in warm soil during the summer and autumn

Fritillary Response
Seeds mature

Seeds sown as soon as possible

Seeds weather at high soil temperatures →

Trillium Response
Seeds mature

Seeds sown immediately after collection

Seeds weather at warm soil temperatures →

Regale Lily Response
Seeds mature

Seeds stored dry, overwinter at

Martagon Response
Seeds mature; sown immediately

Seeds weather

Amaryllid Response
Seeds mature

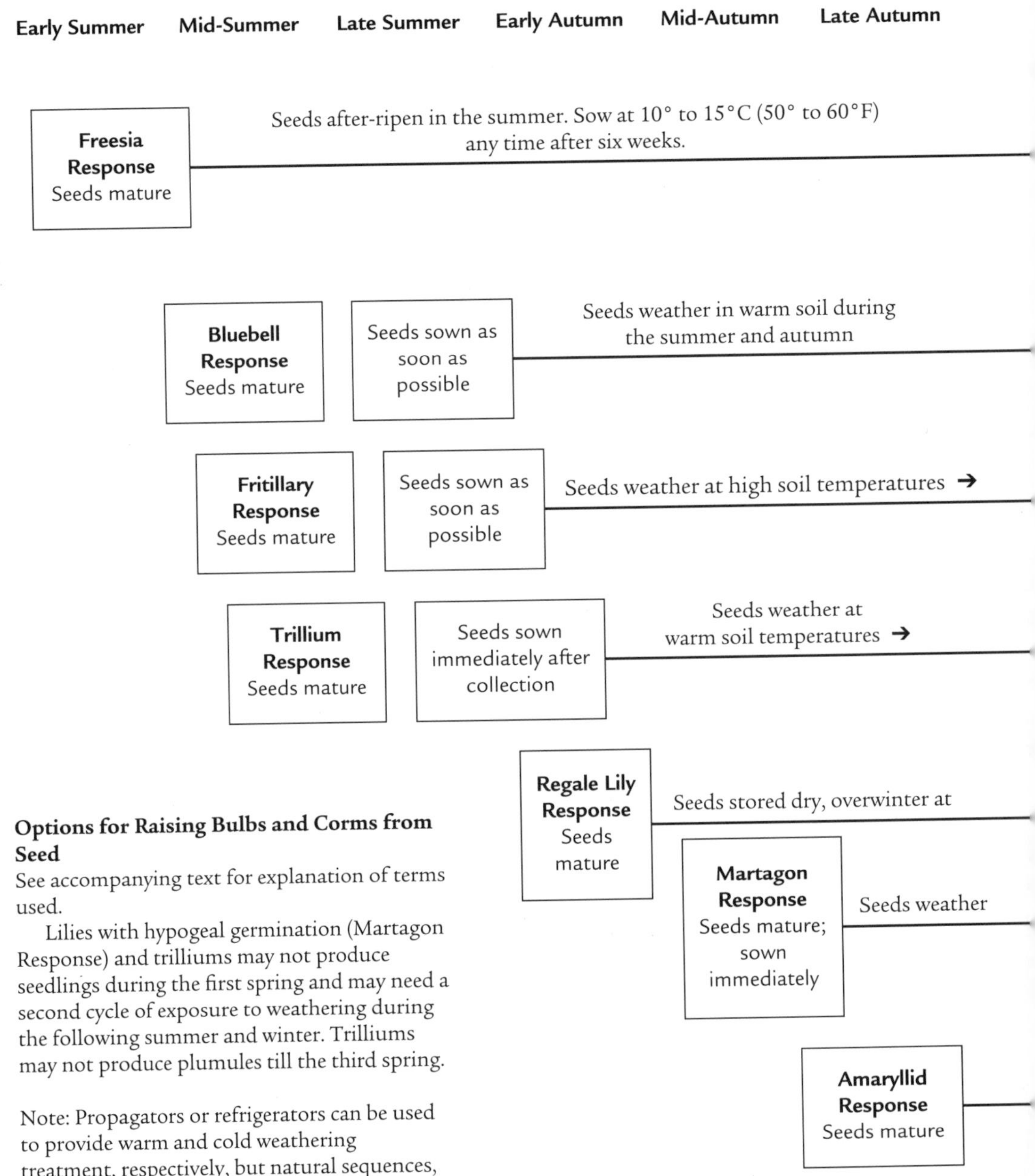

Options for Raising Bulbs and Corms from Seed

See accompanying text for explanation of terms used.

Lilies with hypogeal germination (Martagon Response) and trilliums may not produce seedlings during the first spring and may need a second cycle of exposure to weathering during the following summer and winter. Trilliums may not produce plumules till the third spring.

Note: Propagators or refrigerators can be used to provide warm and cold weathering treatment, respectively, but natural sequences, when available, may produce better results.

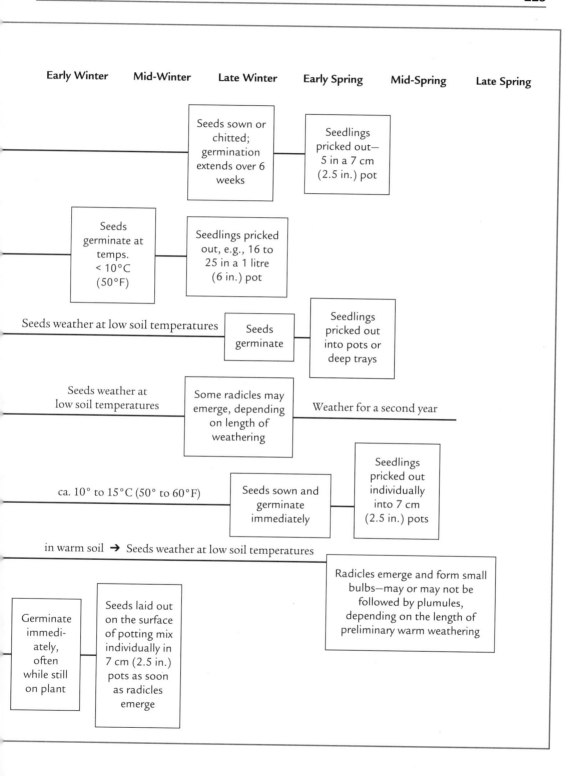

Early Winter | Mid-Winter | Late Winter | Early Spring | Mid-Spring | Late Spring

Seeds sown or chitted; germination extends over 6 weeks

Seedlings pricked out— 5 in a 7 cm (2.5 in.) pot

Seeds germinate at temps. < 10°C (50°F)

Seedlings pricked out, e.g., 16 to 25 in a 1 litre (6 in.) pot

Seeds weather at low soil temperatures

Seeds germinate

Seedlings pricked out into pots or deep trays

Seeds weather at low soil temperatures

Some radicles may emerge, depending on length of weathering

Weather for a second year

Seedlings pricked out individually into 7 cm (2.5 in.) pots

ca. 10° to 15°C (50° to 60°F)

Seeds sown and germinate immediately

in warm soil → Seeds weather at low soil temperatures

Radicles emerge and form small bulbs—may or may not be followed by plumules, depending on the length of preliminary warm weathering

Germinate immediately, often while still on plant

Seeds laid out on the surface of potting mix individually in 7 cm (2.5 in.) pots as soon as radicles emerge

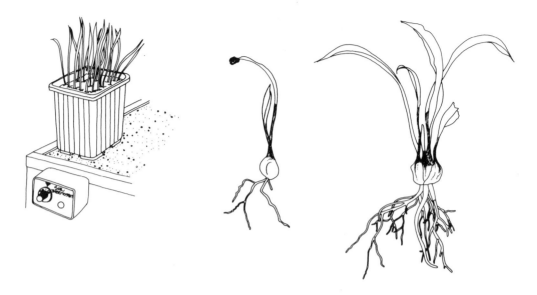

Figure 60. Seeds of *Lilium regale*, like many lilies, germinate readily soon after they are sown. When seeds of regale lilies are sown in late winter at 15° to 25°C (60° to 75°F) with supplementary heat, they rapidly produce seedlings, which are potted individually into 7 cm (2.5 in.) pots and grown on—first in a glasshouse and then in a cold frame—to form bulbs large enough to plant out by late summer or early autumn. Many will grow large enough to produce a single flower the following summer.

collection should be kept damp on moist paper towels in a polythene container. They are then sown and treated like Martagon lilies, or they can be held in the polythene box and exposed to the necessary sequence of high temperatures (20° to 25°C, or 70° to 75°F), low temperatures (0° to 5°C, or 32° to 40°F), and on into rising temperatures artificially using propagators or a refrigerator. The sequence may need to be repeated. Examples include species of *Trillium*.

Amaryllis response

Seeds mature just as the heat and drought of summer give way to cooler, moister conditions favourable for germination and seedling survival. They germinate at once, often beginning to do so while still on the plant. They are recalcitrant, and any attempt to store them is doomed to fail. Seeds are sparingly produced, and it is easy to miss the last vital days of maturation, only to find when attempts are made to collect them that they have been lost. Collect the seeds just before they mature and set them out on the surface of a well-drained, gritty growth medium. Water thoroughly—they must not dry out—and grow on at 20° to 25°C (70° to 75°F). Examples include species of *Boophane*, *Brunsvigia*, *Crinum* and *Haemanthus*.

Pricking out

Gardeners generally agree—a rare thing in itself—that seedlings of most plants grow better when separated one from another so they do not compete for water, nutrients and light. So they prick out seedlings soon after they germinate. Those who grow bulbs from seed are inclined to dissent, denying the benefits of pricking out the seedlings. Many prefer to leave them undisturbed for the

Figure 61. Seeds of *Lilium martagon* will produce seedlings
only after weathering. As soon as possible after collection, mix with
moist grit, perlite, and sand and pack the mixture into polythene bags. Weather
the seed initially at a minimum of about 15°C (60°F) for six to eight weeks and then at
low temperatures, down to 0°C (32°F), for two or three months, after which many of the seeds will
produce a short root on which a tiny bulb forms. A few may produce leaves, too, but most will not do so
till the following spring after further periods of weathering.

first and sometimes the second year after sowing. Then, when the infant bulbs and corms have grown large enough to be picked out (not pricked out), they are potted up individually or in small groups after they have died down. No grower of onions or leeks looking for prizes at the village flower show would suggest that the seedlings of these plants do not benefit from being pricked out, nor win any prizes if he or she failed to do so. Seedlings of other bulbs and corms share the amenable qualities of onions, respond well to pricking out and grow all the better for it,

provided it is done at the right time and in the right way.

Getting it right depends on being aware of the ways the seedlings of different bulbs and corms behave after they germinate. They can be conveniently divided into four groups based on their behavior.

Group one

Many plants in the iris family produce sword-shaped, leaflike cotyledons, followed by a succession of progressively larger leaves. They develop

Figure 62. Seedling *Allium giganteum* bulbs dividing precociously. When immature bulbs divide like this, they do so at the expense of the development of flowering-sized bulbs. The inclination to subdivide can be discouraged by ample feeding and by growing the bulbs in containers deep enough for them to develop at least 10 cm (4 in.) below the surface.

into fan-shaped plants with sizable corms by the end of the first year. Prick them out immediately after they germinate in order to encourage maximum development. Examples include freesias, anomathecas, sparaxis, babianas, ferrarias, and ixias.

Group two

Numerous lilies and onions produce a single, cylindrical cotyledon, the base of which swells to form a minute bulb from which roots emerge. Several more leaves are produced in rapid succession, leading to the development of fair-sized bulbs and sometimes, as with *Lilium formosanum* var. *pricei*, to the production of flowers within a few months. These should be pricked out as soon as they can be handled into deep containers (12 to 20 cm, or 5 to 8 in.) to provide the depth needed by species that form bulbs deep below the ground. Immediately after they germinate, the cotyledons of some bulbous plants push down deep below the surface. Bulbs or corms are formed at their

bases, close to the bottom of the containers in which they are grown. Prick seedlings out into deep containers a few days after they germinate. The cotyledons may even go though the drainage holes at the bottom of the pots and develop in the ground below, leading to losses if the containers are incautiously picked up and moved. Drainage holes in containers provide a means of escape that needs to be recognised and guarded against—especially for stoloniferous bulbs such as *Tulipa sylvestris* and *Lilium nepalense* and corms such as *Crocus nudiflorus*. Examples in group two include many lilies, alliums, and galtonias.

Group three

Species in many liliaceous genera (though no true lilies) and amaryllids produce similar cylindrical cotyledons, at the bottom of which roots emerge and a small bulb forms. However, they develop no true leaves during the first season's growth, and their bulbs may be no larger than a grain of rice when they die down. This provides little scope for improvement, but the slender cotyledons are not difficult to prick out and do produce slightly larger bulbs when this is done than they do when they are left crowded together. Examples include bluebells, hyacinths, tulips, colchicums, chionodoxas, and daffodils.

Group four

Species with delayed hypogeal germination are pricked out as and when the cotyledons first appear above the surface, whether during the first, second or third spring after sowing. Examples include some kinds of lilies and trilliums.

Growing on bulbous plants

Like all plants, bulbs are responsive to the changing seasons, and their growth cycles are strongly affected by environmental factors. The rate at which seedlings in groups one and two develop is strongly influenced by day length, temperature, water, light, and nutrition.

Day length

Many bulbs from cool and cold temperate regions, including most lilies and nomocharis, die down in late summer or autumn in response to decreasing day lengths after mid-summer. Bulbs from the Mediterranean Basin and the Middle East, including daffodils, tulips and crocuses, die down during early summer in response to increasing day lengths after the spring equinox. Day lengths have very powerful effects. Attempts to prolong growth by continuing to feed and water plants after they show signs of dying down leads to losses from fungal diseases.

Temperature

The times when leaves reappear above ground, or disappear, often depends on temperature. Bulbs from Mediterranea in general develop roots and initiate shoot growth in early autumn, as soil temperatures decrease. Conversely, in spring, increasing temperatures reinforce tendencies to die down, initiated by lengthening day lengths. But it is the overriding effects of day length that make it impossible to persuade tulips, crocuses, hyacinths, and other Mediterranean and Middle Eastern bulbs and corms to grow and produce flowers during the summer. Many bulbs from South Africa, including gladioli, freesias, ixias, sparaxis and other Cape bulbs, respond to temperature and drought and are relatively insensitive to day length. These can be grown as summer flowering bulbs in cool and cold temperate regions. Shading can be safely used to maintain cooler conditions and postpone the time seedlings of bulbs from Mediterranea die down, especially those from South Africa, and hence prolong their growing period.

Water

The presence or absence of water crucially affects the behaviour of bulbous plants, especially those from places where seasonal droughts are regular features. Seedlings of plants from dry regions—for example, tulips and moraeas—are extremely sensitive even to temporary water shortages. When grown from seed, it is critically important to maintain adequately available water right up to the time when they would die back naturally in response to long summer days; otherwise, they cease to grow and die back unnecessarily early. Plants from less arid places—for example, daffodils—are likely to be more tolerant of an occasional failure to keep them watered. When bulbs do start to die back naturally in response to day length or temperature, watering should always be discontinued; otherwise the bulbs are very likely to rot.

Light intensity

High light intensities encourage active, vigorous growth of seedling bulbs. Early sowings of species in groups one and two in places where winter light levels are low and days short benefit greatly during late winter and into early spring from supplementary illumination for four hours a day in total, distributed evenly on either side of midday.

Nutrition

Regular and at least adequate feeding is a key factor when growing bulbous plants from seeds. It promotes growth, leading to rapid formation of flowering sized bulbs and corms. Bulbs of tulips, alliums, scillas and others subdivide to produce offsets, rather than increase in size when deprived of nutrients. This can indefinitely postpone the development of flowering sized bulbs. Acute shortage of nutrients can lead to debilitation, death and the loss of small bulbs.

Examples and special cases when growing bulbous plants from seed

Lilies with regale response—epigeal germination

High proportions of seed germinate shortly after sowing. They grow on rapidly to produce small bulbs by the time they die down in the autumn, and when grown well some will produce a single flower during their second year; most will flower in their third. They respond rewardingly to good growing conditions, and maximum growth rates can be obtained.

- Sow early, moderately thickly, in late winter or early spring at about 20°C (70°F).
- Prick out early, as soon as seedlings can be handled—five seedlings per 7 cm (2.5 in.) square container.
- Provide supplementary light, especially where natural levels are low and days are short.
- Avoid extending the day length by switching lights on for three or four hours around mid-day.
- Pot on early, individually into 7 or 9 cm (2.5 or 3.5 in.) containers when three or four true leaves have developed.
- Grow on rapidly at temperatures of about 20°C (70°F) in a glasshouse, cold frame or outdoors depending on location.
- Plants should be well watered during the first part of the summer and fed regularly with a high potassium mineral feed until mid-summer.
- Plant out as the seedlings start to die down naturally after mid-summer, either into nursery beds for a year or straight into the garden.

Alternatively, seeds can be sown in drills in a nursery bed in early spring. This is an excellent way to grow large numbers of bulbs with little effort. Lift the bulbs in late summer, as the foliage starts to die down, and line out 7 cm (3 in.) apart. Plant out in the garden a year later. Eucomis, galtonias, ixias, sparaxis, watsonias, tigridias, gladioli and many other robust, hardy bulbs can also be raised in nursery beds in a similar way.

Lilies with martagon response—hypogeal germination

It can be difficult to observe the development of seeds sown in pots in the normal way. Seeds can be safeguarded and progress observed most easily by mixing the seeds with a quantity of moist vermiculite contained in a plastic box with a tight-fitting lid, so that the box is a third to a quarter full.

Weather for three months at 15° to 20°C (60° to 70°F) by placing the box in a heated propaga-

tor, followed by exposure to cold of less than 5°C (40°F) in a refrigerator for a similar period, before returning the box to the propagator. Radicles emerge from most of the seeds and develop small bulbils; variable numbers, depending on the success of the weathering treatments, also produce plumules.

Open the plastic box from time to time to observe progress. Seedlings with plumules are pricked out into containers, five grouped together in a 7 cm (2.5 in.) square pot. Grow on, with or without supplementary light or heat, until the plants are large enough to pot up individually. Seedlings that do not produce plumules during the first spring should be left in the box and exposed during the following months to the natural succession of the seasons. They will produce plumules the following spring.

Freesias from seed—express method

In gardens in Mediterranea and mild and warm temperate regions, freesias and other South African irids are sown in early autumn and grown on through the winter as nature intended. In cool or cold temperate regions where frosts make this impossible, they can be sown during the spring to develop through the summer. However, much larger plants capable of flowering by the autumn and producing a succession of flowers through the winter are obtained by sowing the seeds in mid-winter.

Freesia seeds germinate irregularly over periods of several weeks. Instead of being sown in the usual way, they are treated as follows:

- Scatter the seeds thickly over pads of damp kitchen towel (or capillary matting) in plastic boxes with close-fitting lids.
- Put the boxes in a room or propagator at approximately 10° to 15°C (50° to 60°F), but no higher, and not in the dark.
- Remove the seeds individually as radicles emerge.
- Set them out in 7 cm (2.5 in.) containers—five seeds to a pot, lightly buried in potting mix—and grow on at about 20°C (70°F) on a glass-

house bench or other well-lit situation. They benefit from supplementary illumination during short, dark days.

- When five or six leaves have developed, transfer the seedlings to 2 litre (8 in.) pots, moving them bodily as a group with as little disturbance as possible.
- As soon as danger from frost is over, move the containers into a well-ventilated cold frame.
- During the summer, they are kept as cool as possible—ideally in a north-facing frame, screened overhead with bubble polythene to avoid direct exposure to sunshine and adequately supplied with water. Aim to keep them growing steadily throughout the summer, feeding regularly with liquid feed or providing them with controlled release fertilisers when initially potted up.
- Transfer the plants to a glasshouse in the autumn and grow on with as much light and air as possible, short of allowing temperatures to fall below freezing point.
- Pick the flowers as they start to open to ensure a long succession through the winter months.

Geissorhiza spp.

Wine cups or sequins represent the less amenable face of South African bulbs. Most are frost tender, require stringently dry conditions in summer, and during their winter growing period must be consistently wet, even waterlogged. Short periods of water stress can lead to flower bud abortion, vegetative decline and dormancy. The corms are highly palatable to birds, rodents, guinea fowl, baboons, moles, and porcupines.

- Collect ripe seeds and store them dry in paper bags at room temperatures (20° to 25°C, or 70° to 75°F) for at least six to eight weeks, while they after-ripen.
- Sow the seeds fairly thinly in a calcined clay or grit topping, at approximately 15°C (60°F).
- Prick out—five to a 7 cm (2.5 in.) pot—as soon as they can be handled into a very free draining, gritty growth medium.

- Water frequently but judiciously while the seedlings establish.
- Once the seedlings are growing vigorously, the containers can be stood in shallow water up to a fifth of their depth. Feed regularly.
- At the end of the growing period, reduce watering drastically, and as soon as the foliage starts to die back, dry off completely, leaving the plants in their containers—protected from predators—till the time comes to resume growth.
- Soak the substrate to ensure it is thoroughly rewetted, and then transfer the entire contents of the pot with minimum disturbance to a 1 or 1.5 litre (6 to 8 in.) container, in which the plants will flower.

Babianas, lachenalias, gladioli, moraeas, watsonias, hesperanthas, romuleas, ixias, sparaxis and many other South African corms and bulbs respond to similar treatment.

Haemanthus spp.

Haemanthus seeds are produced in brightly coloured berries. Pick them as they mature, and remove the outer pulpy layer by washing them in a bowl of water.

- Sow the seeds immediately; if this cannot be done, they can be stored for a short time on pads of moist paper towel in a plastic container.
- Place the seeds on the surface of a free-draining, water-retentive substrate [bark, peat] : [grit, perlite], 1:1, and press seeds lightly onto the surface.
- Put the containers in a shaded, humid environment, watered sufficiently to prevent the seeds drying out.
- Some species produce a small bulb in the first year, and no leaves appear until the second.
- Pot on into larger containers at the start of the third year.
- Flowers are unlikely to be produced until the fourth or fifth year.

Nerines, crinums, amaryllis, brunsvigias, boophanes, clivias and scadoxus are treated in the same way.

Propagation from Cuttings

The possibility of propagating bulbs from cuttings might sound way-out optimistic. "Cuttings," as visualised in the mind's eye, look nothing like any part of a bulb or corm. However, once it is accepted that bulbs are composed of shoots and leaves, and corms are just a kind of rhizome, things sound a little less strange. After all, conventional cuttings are composed of shoots and leaves, and rhizomes provide the most obliging source of cuttings of any kind.

Any action that wounds a bulb or a corm—slicing with a knife, pulling leaf scales away from the basal plate, cutting corms into sections—stimulates the division of meristematic cells, and totipotency does the rest. Fresh tissues are produced to repair the damage, and new corms, bulbs or offsets develop to restore lost functions. The trick lies in knowing where, when and how the cuts should be made.

Cuttings from corms

Corms possess apical buds, from which most growth proceeds, and meristems in the angles between their vestigial scalelike leaves and the body of the corm. The simplest way to propagate them is to remove the apical bud. This has the same effect as pinching out the growing point of a plant, which stimulates the development of buds lower down the stem. The same thing occurs when the apical bud of a crocus or gladiolus corm is eaten by a mouse or excised by a gardener. Grasslike leaves develop from obscure buds on the surface of the corm and in their turn produce new corms. However, because most corms produce numerous offsets and cormels naturally, which provide even easier sources of increase, the method is seldom used.

Trilliums do not increase prolifically naturally, and the best way to propagate them vegetatively is to remove their apical buds.

- Dig up the rhizomes (no more than elongated corms) as the plants start to die down.

- Strip off the last remnants of foliage, and carefully excise the apical buds with the point of a knife.
- Leave in a dry, airy situation for six or seven days while the cut tissues dry out and begin to heal.
- Pot up in a free-draining growth medium, such as coir : perlite, 1:1, in a container amply large enough to hold the rhizome comfortably.
- Stand the container in a cold frame to protect the plants from excessive rainfall during the summer and frost during the winter.
- Feed shortly before growth resumes in spring with a standard liquid nutrient, and maintain healthy growth throughout the spring and early summer.
- As the leaves start to decline, knock the plants out of their pots, separate the offsets and line them out in a nursery bed.

Cuttings from bulbs

Bulbs, by comparison with corms, are likely to be reticent, reproducing steadily rather than rapidly from offsets, supplemented in a few extrovert kinds of lilies and alliums by the production of bulbils.

Sectioning and twin-scaling daffodils and other amaryllids

Building up stocks of new cultivars of lilies, daffodils, tulips, and especially amaryllids from offsets was a slow process until ways were found to speed up the rate of production. Gardeners who inadvertently slice in half a daffodil or other amaryllid bulb while digging a border are, in effect, propagating it. When done deliberately in the course of propagation, this is known as *sectioning*.

- Dig up a bulb(s) when the leaves have faded and are about to disappear.
- Slice it top to bottom into sections to make 4, 8, 16 or 32 divisions, depending on the size of the bulb.
- Set the sections aside for a few days while the cut edges dry.

- To discourage fungal infections, shake them in a polythene bag with a small quantity of flowers of sulphur (sulphur sublimed powder).
- Set them just below the surface in containers in a [peat, coir] : [grit, perlite], 1:1, mix and place them under the raised light of a cold frame.
- Water thoroughly and then as needed to keep them moist but not wet, closing the lights only during periods of freezing temperatures till leaves appear.
- Remove the lights and leave the plants to develop naturally during winter and spring.
- Knock the plants out of the containers as the foliage dies down, and line out the small bulbs in a nursery bed.

Figure 63. The bulbils produced on the stems of some lilies can be picked off, sown like peas and used to propagate them. Those that do not produce stem bulbils are propagated from the scales forming their bulbs.

Twin scaling is broadly similar to sectioning but more ambitious and more technically demanding. Each bulb is sliced into many more, much finer, divisions, producing dozens, even hundreds, of slices from a single bulb. Provided each section contains a fragment of the basal plate, with the meristematic tissues that occur there, it can give rise to grasslike leaves which produce tiny bulbs at their bases.

Twin scaling is a delicate operation, more suited to the laboratory when very large numbers of bulbs are needed.

- Slice bulbs into progressively finer sections, using a sharp knife—a craft knife with disposable blades is ideal. Each section consists of two or more thinly sliced scale leaves attached to a fragment of basal plate.
- Dust the twin scales with fungicide powder and then mix them with a quantity of moist vermiculite, perlite or grit and pack into a plastic box with a tight-fitting lid, partially filling it.
- Maintain temperatures of 15° to 20°C (60° to 70°F) for four to six weeks, and then transfer the boxes to normal ambient conditions—for example, a garden shed, beneath the bench in an unheated glasshouse, or a shaded cold frame—trying to avoid exposure to temperatures above 20°C (70°F).

- When the twin scales begin to develop microscopic shoots, distribute the contents of the box over the surface of a free-draining potting mix in a container and lightly cover with grit, perlite or vermiculite.
- Protect the young plants from the worst of the winter weather in a cold frame, poly tunnel or cold glasshouse and grow on till the leaves begin to die down naturally.

Numerous bulbs in the daffodil family can be propagated from sections or twin scales, including snowdrops, snowflakes, sternbergias, pancratiums, sprekelias, hippeastrums and amaryllis. Those that are tender need protection from frost. A warm glasshouse or a conservatory at about 20°C (70°F) during the winter greatly increases prospects of success.

Note that viruses are easily picked up from infected bulbs and transferred to others while making cuts. Craft knives of various sorts provide sharp, disposable blades that can be replaced between one bulb and the next or sterilised using a flame from a match or cigarette lighter or by dipping in alcohol—neat gin is also effective.

Lilies from scales

The scales of lily bulbs do not form a tightly wrapped mass like those of daffodils but are loosely attached to the basal plate and overlap like tiles. Not only is it easy to remove each one separately, but they often become separated when growing in the garden. It is quite usual to find detached scales in the ground, many of which will have a tiny bulbil, or perhaps two or even three, growing along the fracture line which marks their original point of attachment to the parent bulb.

This natural inclination to produce bulbils from detached scales is the basis of the technique known as *scaling*.

The best time of year to scale a lily bulb is in late summer or early autumn, when most lilies in the garden have finished flowering and are resuming natural root growth. However, scales can be removed at any time from lilies in almost any condition—not excluding the dried-up, semi-shriveled specimens left over on the shelves of garden centres in spring; long after they should have been planted.

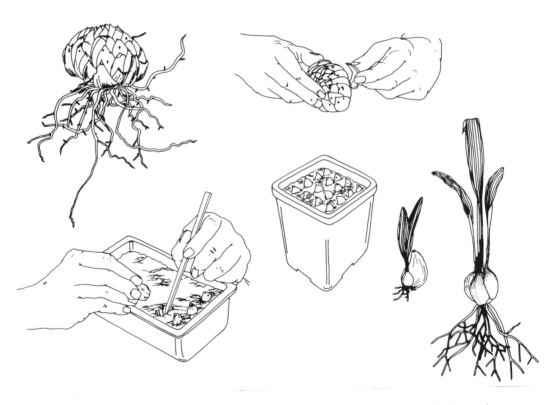

Figure 64. Lily scales, unlike those of narcissus or tulip bulbs, are independent of each other and easily removed individually. Scales removed from a bulb by gently pulling them sideways and slightly downward, are stuck into cutting mix with about a third of their length exposed. They are then placed in a frame or on an unheated or a heated bench in a glasshouse until bulbils form at the base of the scales, from which roots develop and leaves emerge into the air. They are knocked out of their containers during late summer to mid-autumn before being potted up individually in small pots.

Propagate a lily from scales using the following method:

- Discard rotten and hideously shriveled scales from the outermost layers of a bulb.
- Remove healthy scales one by one with a slight downward twist. Each should break off at the point of attachment to the basal plate. Meristematic cells along the broken edges divide to repair the damage done, at the same time, producing bulbils—usually one or two on each scale. Scales that break off halfway up lack this meristematic tissue and may fail to produce any bulbils.
- Stick the scales into a 1:1 mixture of horticultural grit : perlite in a seed tray, a half seed tray or another suitable sized container—perhaps a 1 litre (6 in.) pot—depending on the number obtained.
- Prepare a hole with a dibber and place the scales upright with their upper halves or thirds above the surface. It is not necessary to dust the scales with fungicide before insertion.
- Seed trays hold 40 to 60 scales depending on their size; a 1 litre (6 in.) square container holds 9 to 16.

- Place the containers on a bench in a cold or slightly heated glasshouse or conservatory or in a cold frame, and water thoroughly. They must not dry out—a particular hazard in a conservatory or when standing on a heated bench in a glasshouse.

Disregard advice to mix the seeds with moist vermiculite in a polythene bag placed in an airing cupboard. Scales set out in seed trays or other containers as described above occupy space economically, bulbils develop in accordance with the seasons, roots and shoots are orientated in the right direction, and they can grow and develop for some time without disturbance before needing to be potted on.

The time taken for bulbils to develop, new roots to form and leaves to emerge and grow depends largely on temperature—proceeding slowly in a cold frame, especially during the winter, and much faster on a moderately warmed bench in a glasshouse. Irrespective of the time when scales are removed, newly formed bulbils are potted individually into 7 cm (2.5 in.) square containers from mid-summer to early autumn, when foliage will be in natural decline, but renewed root growth

Figure 65. Young lily plants developing from scales. The remains of a scale still attached to the developing plant can be clearly seen at bottom right.

Figure 66. A batch of plants produced from scales obtained from three bulbs of *Lilium candidum*, shriveled and unwanted on the shelves of a garden centre, long after the due time to plant them had passed.

Chart 17. PROPAGATING LILIES FROM SCALES

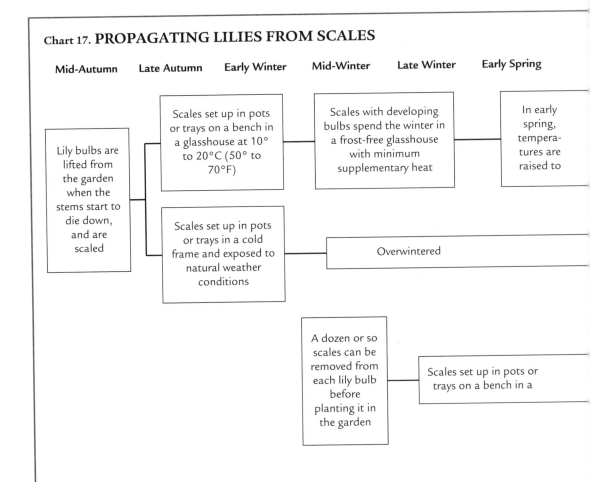

Mid-Autumn   Late Autumn   Early Winter   Mid-Winter   Late Winter   Early Spring

Lily bulbs are lifted from the garden when the stems start to die down, and are scaled

Scales set up in pots or trays on a bench in a glasshouse at 10° to 20°C (50° to 70°F)

Scales with developing bulbs spend the winter in a frost-free glasshouse with minimum supplementary heat

In early spring, temperatures are raised to

Scales set up in pots or trays in a cold frame and exposed to natural weather conditions

Overwintered

A dozen or so scales can be removed from each lily bulb before planting it in the garden

Scales set up in pots or trays on a bench in a

Options for Scaling Lily Bulbs

Lily bulbs can be successfully raised from scales taken at almost any time of year.

Irrespective of the time they are scaled, the resulting small bulbs are potted up individually between mid-summer and mid-autumn.

The best results are obtained from bulbs lifted as the stems die down during late summer until mid-autumn. This provides the developing bulbs with the maximum time to grow and enables them to be potted up early and become well established before the following winter. The scales can develop naturally in a cold frame, or supplementary heat can be used to speed their development.

Scales taken in mid- to late winter, or even in the spring, produce small bulbs successfully, but these are not ready to pot up till later—giving them less time to establish afterward. The differences are not crucial, but the earliest ones scaled will be the first to produce flowering-sized bulbs.

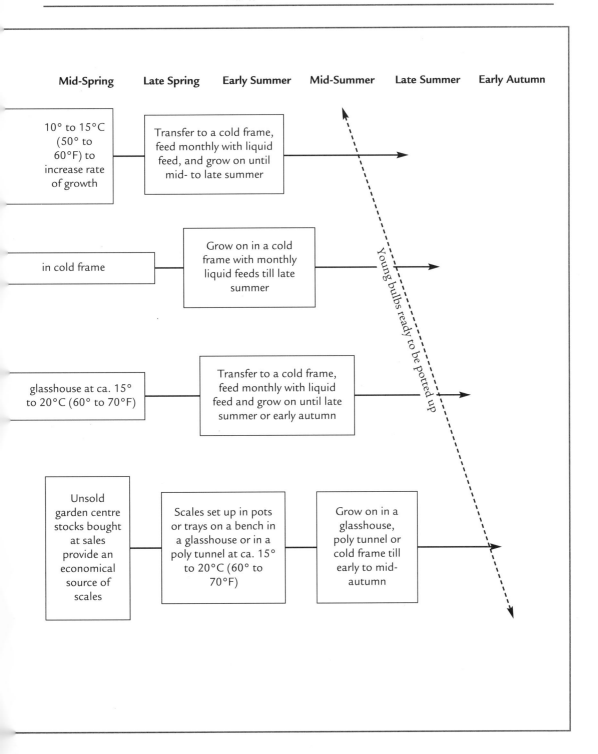

| Mid-Spring | Late Spring | Early Summer | Mid-Summer | Late Summer | Early Autumn |

10° to 15°C (50° to 60°F) to increase rate of growth

Transfer to a cold frame, feed monthly with liquid feed, and grow on until mid- to late summer

in cold frame

Grow on in a cold frame with monthly liquid feeds till late summer

glasshouse at ca. 15° to 20°C (60° to 70°F)

Transfer to a cold frame, feed monthly with liquid feed and grow on until late summer or early autumn

Unsold garden centre stocks bought at sales provide an economical source of scales

Scales set up in pots or trays on a bench in a glasshouse or in a poly tunnel at ca. 15° to 20°C (60° to 70°F)

Grow on in a glasshouse, poly tunnel or cold frame till early to mid-autumn

Young bulbs ready to be potted up

will enable them to establish themselves before cold weather brings growth to a halt. Their leaves are fragile at this time and often fall off during the operation, something that need cause no concern.

Some lilies, including several widely grown Asiatic hybrids, do not produce many, if any, leaves in the first year after they form bulbils. Although they appear to have failed to develop, they produce numerous bulbils below the surface and should be potted up in the normal way. Leaves appear during the following spring. Others, notably *Lilium martagon*, *L. hansonii* and their forms and hybrids, have a disconcerting habit of taking time off. Bulbs fail to produce leaves in the spring after being potted up, lying out of sight in their containers instead. Great care should be taken not to throw out containers without checking their contents. Healthy roots present in the container will confirm that the bulb is alive, even when no foliage can be seen, and new shoots will appear in due course.

Leaf cuttings of bulbs

Modified leaves in the form of scales have so monopolised this section that the fact that bulbous plants also produce regular, normal leaves could almost have slipped our memories. Lachenalias reproduce naturally from seeds or offsets, some generously and others rather frugally. They produce solid, semi-succulent, often spotted or mottled leaves, robust enough to resist wilting when detached from the parent plant, and at a time when these plants were more widely grown in conservatories, gardeners often propagated the less generous ones from bulbils produced by leaf cuttings.

- Remove fully mature leaves from the base of the plant.
- Cut them transversely into three or four sections. (Recommendations to dip the cut edges of the leaves into rooting hormone should be applied cautiously, if at all. Raised levels of these hormones inhibit bud and shoot development—or in this case, bulbils.)

- Set each section upright in a 1:1 mixture of perlite : coarse sand.
- Place them on a lightly shaded glasshouse bench at temperatures around 20°C (70°F).
- Water when necessary, without waterlogging the substrate.
- Bulbils are produced along the upper edges of the leaf sections.
- Allow the containers to dry out after bulbils have been produced, and pick the latter off the remains of the withered leaves. Set out individually, or five to a 7 cm (2.5 in.) container, at the start of the usual growing season, and grow on to produce larger, eventually flowering size bulbs.
- Leaf cuttings are used to propagate other South African bulbs, including species of scadoxus, haemanthus and ornithogalums (notably chincherinchees, *Ornithogalum thyrsoides*).

Gouging, scooping or cross-cutting hyacinths

Hyacinths produce offsets naturally around the base of the bulb. Left to themselves, few produce more than three or four each year and some scarcely any at all. Greater productivity can be encouraged by wounding the basal plate. This stimulates renewed meristematic activity, during which numerous new bulbs are produced. The bulbs are wounded either by gouging out the base or making deep transverse cuts across it. Both will increase the numbers of offsets produced, the first much more effectively than the second.

- Dig up the bulbs soon after the leaves have died down, and remove any loose, papery scales; wrench off any remaining roots to reveal a ring of tissue around the basal plate—often quite white and fresh looking.
- Remove and pot up any small offsets already present.
- Insert the point of a knife immediately above the ring of tissue revealed by removing the old roots. Run it at a slight angle around the circumference of the basal plate to pare away a

disc of tissue extending into the centre of the bulb.*

- Lay the bulbs out upside down in a light and airy situation for ten days or a fortnight while gums and other exudates from the cut surfaces dry out.
- Plant the bulbs individually, just below the surface, and place the containers in a cold frame.
- When the roots become well established, move the containers into a cool glasshouse.

The strong apical bud, typical of hyacinths, is usually destroyed by gouging out the basal plate. In its absence, numerous leaves emerge from around the base and from within the bulb. Bulbils about the size of hazelnuts form at the bases of these leaves. As the foliage shrivels, the plants are knocked out of the containers and the bulbs picked out. Store the bulbs, secure from predators, in paper bags and pot them up in late summer, early autumn—five to a 1 litre (6 in.) pot.

Propagation by Division

Offsets, bulbils or cormels provide bulbs and corms with an extremely effective means of increase, sometimes developed almost to the exclusion of other forms of reproduction. Bulbils and cormels in particular are a crucially important means of surviving predators, a strategy that is all the more remarkable because it involves the sacrifice of the parent plants. Bulbs filled with starch and other food reserves are tucked away out of sight below ground—but not really inaccessible

*Somebody once bizarrely suggested a sharpened teaspoon as the ideal implement for gouging out the basal plate of a hyacinth bulb. The advice has been repeated ever since by those who have never tried it. Gardeners with sharpened teaspoons in their kitchen drawers might like to give it a try, but any sharp-pointed, small knife can be used to remove a neat disc of tissue, shallow at the perimeter and a little deeper towards the centre.

Figure 67. A dense mass of shoots produced from bulbils developing from three gouged-out hyacinth bulbs planted in a 2 litre (1 gal.) pot. The treatment causes the disintegration of the bulb and the development of numerous bulbils in its place.

for all that—and provide a most useful source of food for many animals, birds and other creatures. Gophers go for them in North America; mole rats, porcupines and baboons dig them up and devour them in South Africa; pheasants enjoy tulips; and mice and squirrels eat crocus corms.

A minority of bulbs, including squills, boophanes and death camas, defend themselves by producing poisonous alkaloids. Others, including alliums and tulbagias, counter their attractions by being unpalatable to many animals. However, most bulbous plants appear resigned to act as uni-

Figure 68. Hyacinth bulbs produced by three flowering-sized bulbs after gouging out the basal plate. Those on the right are about the size of hazelnuts and capable of producing small but worthwhile flower spikes. The others will need to be grown on for another year or two to reach flowering size.

versal providers for anything with the sense to dig them up. Resignation in this case is an acceptance of the opportunities provided by predators, rather than a surrender to fate. Many bulbs and corms—particularly those from South Africa, where pressures from predators are particularly acute—can benefit from predation as an aid to survival and reproduction.

Cormels cluster round the bases of gladiolus corms. Dozens of minute replicas of the parent rhizomes are produced on the underside of a large arum lily. Old corms of babianas and crocosmias neither die nor fade away; each year another one is added to a string of predecessors going back ten years or more. While the parent corms live, few of these numerous offspring develop, but if the parent corm is dug up by a gardener, eaten by a predator or succumbs to fungal infection, some are left behind to replace their parent. Others are scattered around and find new resting places, where they can grow.

This enthusiasm for fragmentation could cause problems. All those cormels and bulbils could compete seriously with their parents for water and nutrients. Such self-defeating exuberance is reduced by devices which ensure either that some or most of the offspring remain dormant, as in gladioli cormlets and the back corms of babianas, or as in arums, the smaller ones emerge later than their larger and more mature brethren, giving the mature plants a head start.

Cormels may remain dormant for long periods under natural conditions, and those gathered from the base of gladiolus plants in gardens often grow erratically—some appearing the first year, others much later. Smoke treatments similar to those used to encourage seed germination can be an effective way to reawaken their interest in life.

Lilies from stem bulbils

Most lilies produce small bulbs and bulbils around the base of their stems to some extent. A few, particularly those that inherit the genes of *Lilium tigrinum*, *L. sulphureum* and *L. leucanthum*, produce numerous pea-sized bulbils in the axils of the leaves on the upper parts of the stems. These bulbils, just like the viviparous buds found on the inflorescences of some perennials, are ready-made plants waiting to be grown on, but if treated too casually, high hopes can lead to disappointment. When the bulbils first appear just after mid-summer, they are firmly attached to their parents but later become so tenuously linked that they drop at a touch. It is easy to postpone the moment of their collection, only to find they have all fallen and become lost before good intentions give way to action.

• Pick them off as soon as they can be easily detached.
• Sow them at once—nothing is gained by leaving them in the potting shed, where they will dry out or provide a mouse with a snack.
• Set them out, five in a 7 cm (2.5 in.) pot, about 1.5 cm (0.75 in.) below the surface.
• Place the containers on a bench in a glasshouse, if possible. The extra warmth enables them to grow roots, establish themselves and even produce a leaf or two before winter. Most do no more than produce roots.

- Those that produce leaves are encouraged to continue to grow as late into the autumn as possible to fatten their bulbs and give them a better foundation for a flying start the following spring.
- Overwinter them on a bench in a cold glasshouse if possible. This protects them from excessive rain during wet weather and the potentially lethal combination of frost and sodden growth media during cold. A place in a cold frame is second best, because mice enjoy the cover it provides to hunt out and eat the little bulbs.
- When shoots reappear early the following spring, transfer the contents of the small pots bodily into 2 or 3 litre (8 in. or 1 gal.) containers.
- Separate the bulbs, ready to plant in the garden, when the foliage starts to die down in late summer, early autumn.

Some lilies form stem bulbils if their flower buds are destroyed, and deliberate removal of flowers to stimulate bulbil formation is sometimes suggested as a means of propagation. However, most lilies produce few, if any, extra bulbils following the removal of their flowers, and little is gained from the sacrifice. It is better to use alternative methods of propagation, notably bulb scaling, which provide more effective means of increasing stocks without losing the pleasure of enjoying the plants in flower.

Some species of alliums, babianas and sparaxis also produce aerial bulbils or cormels—sometimes in place of flowers on inflorescences and sometimes in leaf axils. These should be treated like lily bulbils.

Dividing narcissus bulbs

Daffodils and other bulbs, including snowdrops, snowflakes, and the corms of ixias, some gladiolus, watsonias, and crocosmias, form congested clumps in which few flowers are produced. Failure to flower may be due either to virus infections—especially with daffodils—or starvation caused by congestion. Viral infection may not produce visible symptoms other than the absence of flowers. They are incurable in the absence of special facilities. Starvation due to congestion is extremely easy to remedy while producing large numbers of plants, and decisions about the possibility of viral infection is best left till this has been attempted.

- Lift the clumps as the leaves die down, or, with snowdrops, while the plants are still in flower or as they fade.
- Separate the bulbs or corms individually for maximum productivity or into groups of three to five for more effective floral displays.
- Replant in rows in a nursery bed or where they are intended to flower.
- Once relieved of competition from their neighbors, bulbs and corms regain flowering size within a year or two.

Those with no or very few flowers after two or three years should be regarded with suspicion. The most likely cause is infection with one or more virus diseases. Viral infections can be eliminated by prolonged high-temperature treatments, followed by tests to establish which bulbs are free of disease, but this is worthwhile only when the stock is unusually valuable. Bulbs which persistently fail to flower should almost always be dug up and destroyed.

Sandersonia aurantiaca can be propagated from seed. Germination is erratic, and small numbers of seedlings emerge in successive springs over periods of several years. Division is a slower but more certain process and is also applicable to *Gloriosa superba*. Both species produce flowers and shoots from V-shaped tubers. Each arm of the V has buds at the tip—one produces flowers and the other shoots. Divide the tubers just before growth starts in spring by cutting through the angle at the base of the V. Pot up each arm separately. Both usually flower during the first year. Divisions made from both arms produce new V-shaped tubers which can themselves be divided the following spring.

Propagation Summary for Bulbous Plants

(a) = genera that contain high proportions of species vulnerable to frost. In cold and cool temperate areas, these are sown or planted at seasons that do not expose seedlings or shoots to temperatures below approximately -3°C (30°F), usually in spring. In Mediterranea and other locations with mild winters, they are likely to do better when sown in the autumn.

S. = propagated from seed
C. = propagated from cuttings
D. = propagated by divisions

Note that the word *offset* is used to denote spontaneous divisions of the parent bulb or corm into subsidiary bulbs or corms—often of flowering size when removed. *Cormels* or *bulbils* denote numerous propagules, too small to flower and usually produced at the base of corms or in the shoots or inflorescences.

Acidanthera (a)—**S.** autumn, spring. **D.** offsets.
Albuca (a)—**S.** autumn, spring. **D.** offsets.
Allium—**S.** fresh, spring. **D.** offsets: summer; viviparous bulbils occur in inflorescences of some species.
Amaryllis—Succulent Seeds. Recalcitrant. **S.** fresh; sown on the surface. **C.** spring; section. **D.** offsets; left in place till they have developed roots of their own.
Androcymbium (a)—**S.** autumn, spring. **D.** offsets.
Anomatheca (a)—**S.** autumn, spring. **D.** offsets.
Anthericum—**S.** fresh. **D.** early to late winter.
Antholyza—**S.** spring. **D.** winter, early spring; offsets.
Arum—Succulent Fruit. Recalcitrant. **S.** fresh. **D.** late summer, autumn; bulbil-like rhizomes.
Babiana (a)—**S.** autumn, spring. **D.** summer; offsets, some species produce cormels in the leaf axils.
Bellevalia (a)—**S.** autumn, spring. **D.** offsets.
Boophane (a)—Succulent Seeds. Recalcitrant. **S.** fresh; on the surface. **C.** summer; section. **D.** bulbs seldom produce offsets spontaneously.
Brodiaea—**S.** autumn, spring. **D.** offsets.
Brunsvigia (a)—Succulent Seeds. Recalcitrant. **S.** fresh; on the surface. **C.** summer; section. **D.** Bulbs seldom produce offsets spontaneously.

Calochortus (a)—**S.** autumn, spring. **D.** offsets.
Camassia—**S.** fresh, spring. **D.** summer; gouge as hyacinths.
Cardiocrinum—**S.** fresh. **C.** autumn, winter; scale. **D.** autumn, early winter—small, bubils are produced after flowering as the bulbs decay, around the edge of the basal plate.
Chasmanthe—**S.** fresh, spring. **D.** offsets, stolons.
Chionodoxa—**S.** fresh. **D.** offsets.
Clintonia—Succulent Fruit. **S.** fresh. **D.** spring.
Colchicum—**S.** fresh. **D.** late summer; offsets.
Crinum (a)—Apomictic. Succulent Seeds. Recalcitrant. **S.** fresh; on surface of seed mix as soon as they ripen. **C.** summer; section. **D.** autumn, spring; offsets from leeklike shoots of evergreen, tender species, or rounded bulbs of deciduous more hardy species.
Crocosmia—**S.** fresh. **D.** autumn, late winter.
Crocus—**S.** fresh; produced in capsules just below ground level. **D.** autumn, winter; offsets.
Cyanella (a)—**S.** autumn, spring. **D.** offsets.
Cypella (a)—**S.** autumn, spring. **D.** offsets.
Cyrtanthus (a)—**S.** autumn, spring. **D.** offsets.
Dracunculus—**S.** fresh. **D.** late summer, autumn; tubers.
Erythronium—**S.** fresh. **D.** late summer, autumn; offsets, from species that grow naturally in E. North America; most species from W. North America seldom or never produce offsets.
Eucomis—**S.** fresh, spring. **C.** late summer; leaf; gouge as hyacinths. **D.** offsets.
Ferraria (a)—**S.** autumn, spring. **D.** offsets.
Freesia (a)—**S.** autumn, spring. **D.** offsets.
Fritillaria—**S.** fresh. **C.** summer; section, e.g., *F. imperialis*. **D.** offsets, bulbils, e.g., *F. uva-vulpis* and cvs. of *F. meleagris*. Never let bulbs or roots dry up.
Galanthus—**S.** fresh. **C.** mid-summer; section. **D.** late winter; offsets.
Galaxia (a)—**S.** autumn, spring. **D.** offsets; the corms are extremely small; disturb seldom and plant shallow.
Galtonia—**S.** spring. **C.** late summer; gouge as hyacinths. **D.** autumn, early winter.
Geissorhiza (a)—**S.** autumn, spring. **D.** summer; cormels.
Gladiolus (a)—**S.** spring. **D.** autumn, winter; offsets, cormels, viviparous offsets on inflorescence of some species.
Gloriosa (a)—**S.** spring. **D.** autumn; V-shaped tubers, each section with a bud.

Gynandriris—**S.** autumn. **D.** offsets.

Habranthus (a)—**S.** spring. **D.** autumn; offsets.

Haemanthus (a)—Succulent Seeds. Recalcitrant. **S.** fresh on the surface. **C.** late summer; leaf: summer; section. **D.** early spring; offsets.

Hermodactylus—**D.** autumn; thin, fleshy tubers.

Hesperantha (a)—**S.** autumn, spring. **D.** offsets.

Hippeastrum (a)—**S.** fresh. **C.** summer; section. **D.** late winter, spring; offsets, removed only when they separate easily from the parent bulb.

Homeria (a)—**S.** autumn, spring. **D.** offsets.

Homoglossum—**S.** autumn, spring. **D.** offsets.

Hyacinthoides—**S.** fresh. **D.** late autumn, early winter; offsets.

Hyacinthus—**C.** summer, early autumn; gouge basal plate. **D.** early autumn; offsets.

Hymenocallis (a)—**S.** fresh. **D.** spring; offsets.

Ipheion—**S.** fresh, spring. **D.** autumn, early winter.

Iris—**S.** fresh. **D.** autumn; offsets.

Ixia (a)—**S.** autumn, spring. **D.** offsets.

Ixiolirion—**S.** fresh. **D.** autumn, early winter; offsets.

Lachenalia (a)—**S.** autumn, spring. **C.** spring; leaf. **D.** summer, early autumn; offsets.

Lapeirousia (a)—**S.** autumn, spring. **D.** offsets.

Leucojum—**C.** summer; section. **D.** early winter.

Lilium—**S.** fresh, spring. **C.** late summer to spring; scales. **D.** late summer; offsets, bulbils.

Lycoris (a)—**S.** fresh. **C.** section. **D.** late winter, spring.

Massonia (a)—**S.** autumn, spring. **D.** offsets.

Merendera—**S.** fresh. **D.** early autumn; offsets.

Moraea (a)—**S.** autumn, spring. **D.** offsets.

Muscari—**S.** fresh, spring. **D.** late summer, autumn; offsets.

Narcissus—**S.** fresh. **C.** summer; section. **D.** late summer, early autumn; offsets.

Nectaroscordum—**S.** fresh. **D.** late summer, early autumn.

Nerine (a)—Apomictic. Succulent Seeds. Recalcitrant. **S.** fresh. **C.** summer; section. **D.** late summer to mid-autumn; offsets.

Nomocharis—**S.** fresh, spring. **C.** late summer, winter; scales. **D.** autumn; bubils, usually sparingly produced. Occasional plants produce them abundantly.

Notholirion—**S.** fresh. **C.** summer; gouge as hyacinths. **D.** autumn; bulbils produced around the edge of the basal plate of the old bulbs after flowering.

Nothoscordum—**S.** fresh. **D.** late summer; offsets.

Ornithogalum—**S.** fresh, spring. **C.** spring, summer; leaf; gouge as hyacinths. **D.** autumn; offsets, bulbils.

Pancratium (a)—**S.** fresh. **C.** summer; section. **D.** late summer, early autumn; offsets detached without roots; set out partially buried in sand till roots appear.

Paradisea—**S.** fresh. **D.** autumn; offsets.

Puschkinia—**S.** fresh. **D.** offsets.

Romulea (a)—**S.** autumn, spring. **D.** offsets.

Sandersonia (a)—**S.** late spring, early summer; germinate erratically. **D.** late winter; cut V-shaped tubers into two parts, each with a bud.

Scadoxus (a)—Succulent Seeds. **S.** fresh on the surface. **C.** early summer; leaf: summer; section. **D.** early spring; offsets, sparingly produced.

Scilla—**S.** fresh, spring, **D.** late summer, early autumn.

Sparaxis (a)—**S.** autumn, spring. **D.** offsets.

Stenomesson (a)—**S.** fresh. **D.** late winter; offsets, bulbils.

Sternbergia—**C.** summer; section. **D.** late summer, early autumn.

Tecophilia—**S.** fresh, spring. **D.** late summer, early autumn; offsets, cormels.

Tigridia (a)—**S.** late winter. **D.** autumn, early spring; cormels.

Trillium—**S.** fresh. **D.** late autumn; offsets can be encouraged by excision of apical buds.

Triteleia—**S.** fresh, spring. **D.** late summer; offsets.

Tritonia (a)—**S.** autumn, spring. **D.** offsets.

Tulipa—**S.** fresh. **D.** late summer, early autumn; offsets.

Vallota (a)—**S.** autumn, spring. **D.** offsets.

Veltheimia (a)—**S.** fresh, spring. **C.** summer; leaf: section. **D.** mid-summer; offsets.

Watsonia (a)—**S.** autumn, spring. **D.** offsets.

Zantedeschia—**S.** spring. **D.** late winter, spring.

Zephyranthes (a)—**S.** fresh. **D.** autumn, spring; offsets.

CHAPTER 13

Alpines

The cover of the bulletin of the Alpine Garden Society describes the society as "The International Society for alpine and rock plants, small hardy herbaceous plants, hardy and half-hardy bulbs, hardy ferns and small shrubs." That says it all! It establishes the society's view of the plants within its orbit, nodding piously towards those that are "hardy" but hinting even that criterion should not be taken too seriously. If a plant is covetable, the temptation to take it into the fold encounters minimal resistance from alpine enthusiasts.

We need look no further than cyclamen for proof. These plants have few pretensions to alpine lifestyles; many of the species are definitely not hardy, but that is no obstacle to their regular appearance at the society's shows. Most, but not all, of the plants introduced in this chapter do grow in conditions that are more or less alpine—and, incidentally, cyclamen are not included; they find their place in chapter 10. Bulbs and ferns, listed on the bulletin's cover, are also excluded: Each has a chapter to itself.

Plants become alpines only by adapting their lifestyles or physical forms to the conditions found in alpine situations, mitigating the effects of their severities and taking advantage of periods when conditions are more benign. Many lose the ability to survive in competition with less specialised plants in more favourable situations, and alpines are characteristically vulnerable to competition from neighbouring plants when grown in gardens—hence the need to grow them in special situations such as the rock garden or in alpine houses where they are protected from competition.

The extreme conditions in which alpines exist naturally strongly affect all their growth processes, including some of interest to those who propagate them. Alpine environments challenge plant survival in many different ways: short growing seasons, limited by low temperatures, result in late springs and early autumns; contrasting day/night temperatures often include subzero temperatures at night at any time of the year, and most significantly during the growing season; persistently low soil and water temperatures sometimes contrast strongly with high air and surface temperatures during summer; exposure to prolonged periods of subzero temperatures, day and night, are accentuated by lack of shelter and funneling effects of strong winds; extreme conditions of wet, drought, temperature, sunlight, and prolonged cloud are experienced, including the most severe effects of frost and drying winds, which may be alleviated by snow cover; and unstable surfaces are created by floods, frosts, rock falls, and landslips.

To survive in such situations, alpines have acquired characteristic adaptations, many with reproductive significance. Typical plant forms include tussocks, rosettes, cushions and mats.

Leaves may be rolled or have thickened cuticles, dense surface hairs and other forms of protection against the elements. These produce shoots with resilient constitutions relatively self-sustaining when removed to make cuttings.

Competition for pollinators (fewer insects overall, less diversity and reduced activity) leads to conspicuous flowers often associated in masses for greater effect and the absence of specialised pollination mechanisms. Flower forms are capable of providing stable platforms for insect visitors, despite high winds, and vivipary and self-pollination reduce dependence on pollinators. Short growing seasons lead to flower initiation in buds during autumn and winter, enabling them to open soon after growth resumes in spring.

Seeds are unlikely to have time to germinate and produce established seedlings in the autumn, and most postpone germination until the spring, when they may even germinate beneath a covering of snow to gain the best possible start. Unstable surfaces put a premium on pioneering species able to establish from seeds or reproduce vegetatively on mineral surfaces. Vegetative reproduction is often more significant than sexual reproduction.

Growth Media

Potting mixes used for alpines need to be more closely matched with their natural preferences than those used for most other plants, and alpine gardeners tend to preserve the traditional predisposition to devise and mix their own. The arcane arts of growing plants adapted to extreme circumstances is the justification for preferring their own recipes, but the need for such subtleties can be exaggerated. As a rule, a successful growth medium should drain freely, be well aerated, retain moisture without remaining waterlogged or becoming prematurely desiccated, and supply the nutrients needed to sustain the developing plants. These are the broadband qualities applicable to most plants—alpines are just less tolerant than most of failures to achieve perfection.

Potting mixes high in water-absorbent, free-draining minerals and relatively low in organic constituents are indicated. Grits, perlite, and calcined clays can be used as mineral constituents, using ground limestone to raise pH values when growing calcicole species and millstone grit or granite to depress levels for calcifuges. Under natural conditions, nutrient levels are usually low, dependent on the release of salts from rocks and the recycling of nutrients during the slow breakdown of organic debris, calling for low-nutrient status mixes. Nevertheless, alpines enjoy starvation no more than other plants, and they respond to frequent applications of very dilute nutrient feeds. In these circumstances, capacity and ability to retain nutrients characteristics of loams become particularly significant.

Mineral substrates, particularly porous minerals, combined 2:1 or even 3:1 with humus rich, fibrous loams rather than bark, peat or coir, are most likely to sustain healthy development. Low levels of controlled release fertilisers using formulations with high ratios of potassium and phosphorous and low nitrogen can be used. Well chosen and well used, these provide excellent sources of nutrients for alpines but have the disadvantage that any problems arising from the wrong choice of fertiliser are likely to be irretrievable.

Propagation from Seed

With few exceptions, plants grown as alpines produce orthodox seeds that can be stored dry for long periods. Collecting them is seldom a problem, provided they are present. Saxifrages, aubrietas, gentians, campanulas, lewisias, pulsatillas, cresses, and many others produce seeds in clearly visible capsules or heads in readily accessible situations. The capsules of some compact species with congested stems and foliage, including dionysias, may be partially hidden within the cushions of leaves and often rather sparingly endowed with seeds. Extracting mature capsules is fiddly, and a pair of forceps avoids frustrated efforts.

Others, including abrotanellas, produce capsules above the surface, from which seeds fall at the lightest touch to be lost amongst the congested leaves. A small hand-held vacuum cleaner has been suggested as a means of recovering them.

As with other plants, seeds are collected when fully mature—with significant exceptions, including buttercups and hepaticas. Seeds of both are more likely to produce seedlings when collected green, just before they mature but when they are easily detached by light pressure, than fully ripened seed. The bowl-shaped flowers of many alpines including saxifrages and the open bell-shaped flowers of campanulas are accessible to a broad variety of insect pollinators. Nevertheless, even under good conditions, many alpine species produce relatively few seeds and failures in unfavourable years are not unusual.

A few alpines protect their flowers from the elements in ways that make them inaccessible to casual pollinators. Amongst them are *Physoplexis* spp. and notably *Rheum nobile*, in which the flowers are protected within a shelter of overlapping bracts like tiles on a roof, or *Saussurea gossypiphora*, with flowers enclosed within an inflorescence resembling a ball of cotton wool. These depend on obscure and secret stirrings within hidden worlds that common or garden insects may fail to penetrate and in cultivation should be pollinated by hand. Other alpines—amongst them primulas and dionysias with pin- or thrum-eyed flowers on different plants—retain mechanisms designed to avoid cross-pollination, making it necessary to have plants of both forms in close proximity in order to obtain seed.

Sowing seed

Plants from high, cold situations on mountains exist in conditions where low temperatures and short growing seasons seldom provide time for seeds to germinate and produce seedlings sufficiently well established to survive the winter. Seeds seldom germinate in autumn but produce seedlings early the following spring, with the prospect of milder weather and a long growing season ahead in which to establish themselves. Significantly different strategies enable them to do this, each of which affects the ways seedlings can be produced in gardens.

When sowing seeds of alpines, it is worth bearing in mind that a sizable proportion, for example aubrietas, germinate rapidly and readily in moderately warm conditions (12° to 20°C, or 54° to 70°F) in a glasshouse, either with or without chipping. They do not depend on chilling treatments to do so. It should also be remembered that many plants grown as alpines are "honorary" alpines. They grow naturally in comparatively benign situations, like perennial plants in general, and consequently possess similar germination responses.

Unless reliable information is available about the conditions needed to produce seedlings, the seeds of alpine perennials are treated as illustrated in chart 14, using the information starting with "Seeds harvested between late summer and early winter . . ." as a guide. Many species of alpines do not require weathering but do respond to after-ripening. They should not be sown before the winter but stored dry in paper envelopes, preferably in a desiccator, at room temperature rather than at subzero temperatures, which would inhibit after-ripening processes. They are sown in late winter or early spring in the standard way, bearing in mind that seeds of alpines are more likely to germinate when temperatures fluctuate between day and night than when they remain constant.

Seeds known to germinate only after being weathered at low temperatures are treated by gardeners in cool and cold temperate regions as follows.

- Sow seeds as soon after they mature as possible and before the onset of the coldest period of winter weather.
- Most benefit from an all-mineral topping and a free-draining base—for example, standard potting mix : [grit, perlite], 1:1. (Species from markedly wet habitats require a topping of chopped, baked sphagnum moss.)
- Ensure the containers are stable by packing them in a seed tray or other pot holder.

Conditions under which seeds of alpines produce seedlings naturally and in cultivation

In nature
Seeds are able to germinate only after exposure to low temperatures during the winter or at temperatures above those likely to be encountered by seeds shed during the autumn and early winter. After-ripening changes during the winter enable these seeds to geminate at much lower temperatures, leading to early germination in spring. Seeds may also germinate only after hard or impermeable seed coats have been degraded, enabling them to imbibe water.

In cultivation
Treatment is needed to produce seedlings. Sow seeds when ripe and weather at temperatures close to 0°C (32°F) for at least six to eight weeks. Sow seeds either when they mature or after they have been stored. Use supplementary heat if necessary to provide diurnally fluctuating temperatures with a maximum of about 20°C (70°F). Reduce temperatures when seedlings appear. Chip and sow seed with added innoculum, at any time, at about 10° to 15°C (50° to 60°F).

- Place the containers on a bench in a cold glasshouse. It is not necessary, or desirable, to expose seeds to severe frosts. Cold frames provide equally effective quarters but suffer a greater likelihood of losses from mice, slugs, and other creatures.
- When seedlings appear, nothing is gained by exposing them further to frost or growing them slowly at low temperatures. Artificial heat is anathema to many growers of alpines, who insist it is not merely unnecessary, but

seriously harmful. They are right to warn against its use but wrong to condemn it utterly. Seedlings develop faster and vulnerability to pests and diseases is reduced by using soil heating cables under a glasshouse bench or in a frame to prevent temperatures falling below about 5° (40°) or even 10°C (50°F).
- Prick out the seedlings into small containers as soon as they can be handled; seed trays do not provide the depth of substrate needed by most alpines.
- Grow on in a light, airy, well-ventilated glasshouse.

In mild or warm temperate regions where natural conditions do not provide sufficiently prolonged or regular spells of cold to weather seeds effectively, mix the seeds with moist vermiculite or grit in polythene bags and store the bags in a refrigerator for two or three months. After removing the bags from the refrigerator, sow the seeds in the usual way by using the contents of the bags as the topping above a free-draining potting mix. Seeds of gentians, primulas, and other alpines may start to germinate during prolonged periods in the refrigerator. This is neither unusual nor a problem and reflects the natural behaviour of species whose seeds germinate while still covered with snow, in order to benefit from the longest possible growing season as the snows finally melt when spring arrives.

The critical environmental feature for most alpine seedlings is not temperature—provided this does not rise too high—but what might be described as the austerity of the atmosphere around the seedlings. High humidities, still air and enclosed conditions very quickly lead to losses, especially of species with congested leaves. They are countered by maximum use of ventilation, remembering that alpine seedlings are unlikely to be damaged by cold. Fans are invaluable to keep air moving within the glasshouse on still, humid days when there is little or no natural air movement.

Seedlings of many species—for example primulas and meconopsis—grow best in cool conditions in slightly humid rather than dry atmospheres but still require a buoyant atmosphere around them. This should be provided by light shading or a light diffuser, such as a bubble polythene screen, in sunny weather, not by restricting air movement.

Propagation from Cuttings

Few alpines are annuals. Survival in perpetually shifting, unstable environments puts a premium on retaining a hold once it has been obtained, and the alpine environment is one where possession once gained is held onto tenaciously. Vegetative reproduction from shoots, offsets, and rosettes becomes a major means of reproduction both in nature and in the garden.

Semi-mature shoots

A great many of the shrubs and evergreen perennials grown in gardens as alpines are readily propagated from cuttings made from their young growth from about mid-summer onwards in similar ways to those described on pp. 90–101 (basic techniques). Cuttings 2.5 to 5 cm (1 to 2 in.) long are inserted in cutting mix of grit : perlite, 1:1, and then placed in a closed frame. Shoots of alpines are vulnerable to desiccation, but the adaptations that enable alpines to survive harsh conditions not only make them more tolerant of more open, less consistently saturated atmospheres than softer cuttings but make them more vulnerable to excess humidity and overwatering. When managing frames to propagate alpines from cuttings, a little more air, a little less shading and careful attention to watering are the keys to success.

The lower leaves are usually removed when making a cutting, but this damages slender shoots with numerous, small or needlelike leaves—such as alpine phloxes, hebes, and saxifrages—and is tedious and extremely time-consuming. Idle gardeners who grow bored and irritated by this fiddly business stick in the cuttings, leaves and all. Their results are usually at least as good as those

of their more dedicated brethren who conscientiously remove the leaves.

Timing can matter. Cuttings of all species taken early in the season and provided with conditions leading to rapid root formation and development have time to grow larger than those started later. In other species, such as alpine phloxes and lithodoras, delays of only a week or two can greatly reduce success rates. Rooted cuttings are drenched with double-strength liquid fertiliser and weaned in more open, exposed conditions. They are potted up individually and after a few days moved into a cold frame with plenty of ventilation. In hot, sunny weather they benefit from a little protective shading at first.

Cuttings taken later which have barely developed root systems by early autumn are left in their containers until the following spring and potted up just before they resume growth. They are likely to take a year longer to produce flowers than similar cuttings taken only a few weeks earlier, in time to be potted up before the winter.

Rosettes and offsets, including wedge cuttings

The leaves of many alpines—saxifrages, chionohebes and raoulias—are designed to limit the damaging effects of drought and cold. Their tolerance to these conditions is often further increased by forms of growth, including rosettes, which reduce the surface area exposed to the desiccating effects of the wind and enable the plants to benefit from boundary layer effects, which slow the speed of air movement over the surface of the leaves.

Drought and cold tolerance enables cuttings of these plants to endure more rigorous, less protected conditions than conventional shoots. Rosette cuttings can be used to avoid the total loss of superannuated cushions in which rosettes have started to die—the common fate of many of the more difficult and desirable kinds. A few of the healthy rosettes are removed and used as replacements before the entire cushion dies.

- Remove each rosette and carefully strip the lowermost leaves off the stem to form a short peg—simple enough with large rosettes, but fiddly and intricate with the close-packed shoots of *Kabschia* saxifrages, raoulias and similar plants in which it is better not to attempt to strip off the leaves.

- Stick the peg, or the end of the cutting, into a container containing a 1:1 mix of grit : perlite with the body of the rosette resting on the surface.
- Place containers on a lightly shaded bench, for example by using a canopy of bubble polythene, not in an enclosed frame or propagator.
- Ventilate freely and water sparingly, just sufficiently to prevent the growth medium from becoming dry or the plants suffering from desiccation.
- When roots are produced, drench with a liquid fertiliser and then grow on in well-lit, airy conditions while the roots develop before potting up individually.
- Overwinter in a well-ventilated glasshouse or cold frame with the lights propped open. Few need protection from cold, but they do need protection from wet, which is held between their close-packed leaves, enabling fungal infections to gain a hold—by far the greatest threat to survival.

Rosette cuttings of many alpines do well under mist propagation units, contrary to what might be expected, provided they are set out on an open bench and not enclosed. Many cushion formers, including, inevitably, the more desirable ones—amongst them townsendias, dionysias, androsaces, and celmisias—are vulnerable to red spider mite in hot, dry conditions. They benefit from overhead shade in hot weather and periodic light sprays of water.

Single-bud cuttings

A number of tropical plants are propagated from leaf cuttings, but no plants from temperate regions, apart from some succulent plants and a few bulbs, are propagated in this way. Ramondas, haberleas and jankaeas are sometimes said to be propagated from leaf cuttings, but this is not accurate. These plants, like their cousins the African violets, are propagated from the meristematic tissues (buds) in the axils of their leaves (not the leaf tissues themselves). In other words, they are single-bud cuttings.

- Remove some of the older but still healthy leaves, holding them by the petioles and pulling them gently sideways, with a slight twist—much like scaling a lily bulb.
- Each petiole should break off at its point of attachment to the main stem, with its vestigial axillary bud at its base. Those that snap off part way up may form roots but are unlikely to produce plants.
- Stick the end of the petioles into standard cutting mix, at a slight angle and sufficiently firmly to support the leaves.
- Place the containers in a well-ventilated frame or propagator in a shaded but not enclosed situation.
- Water sufficiently to keep the substrate moist but not sodden.
- Roots grow from the base of the petioles. Then the axillary buds develop, quite slowly, first into minute and later into progressively larger rosettes.
- Pot up into the smallest container into which the small plants can be fitted, when roots and shoots are thoroughly established. This is better delayed than done too soon.

Bear in mind these plants live naturally on edges and crevices where they survive with minimal quantities of soil litter. They are very easily stressed when overpotted, by poor aeration and excess water, but they thrive on slender resources which most plants would find less than barely sufficient.

Propagation by Division

Many alpines live in those most characteristic of alpine habitats—screes. These provide highly unstable and disruptive conditions for plant life.

Repeated falls of rock, landslips and torrential floods force plants to produce new roots and shoots continuously and often to reestablish themselves from fragments of detached shoots in a process of natural division. Plants so well adapted to dividing themselves make the task particularly easy for those who wish to propagate them. Alpine inhabitants of screes form three main groups: ground-hugging carpeters, ground coverers, and compact, clump formers.

Ground-hugging carpeters produce roots spontaneously from their stems as they grow—such as thymes, campanulas, dryas, veronicas, and antennarias. These are amongst the easiest of all plants to propagate by removing ready-rooted shoots, potting them up and placing them in a shaded frame for a short time while they reestablish themselves.

Ground coverers, including celmisias, phloxes, primulas and androsaces, which produce shoots close to the ground level but do not hug the surface, produce roots readily and need little encouragement to do so. They are most easily encouraged by covering them with a layer of potting mix : grit, 1:1, and working it well down amongst the crowns—an operation known as blanketing. This can be done once several weeks before the plants are propagated or, much more effectively, several times over a period of months to build up a layer several centimetres deep, in which shoots have plenty of time and scope to form and develop roots. If done during the summer, the whole plant is lifted the following spring, and sections of shoots with roots are cut off and potted up individually.

Compact clump-forming plants respond to burial beneath fallen rocks by producing long, subterranean stems. These grow through the overlying layers of stone and rock to reach the surface. Eventually, they form colonies of what appear to be individual plants, the original plant from which they all developed dead and buried deep below the fallen rocks. A great many normally compact alpines can be propagated by making use of these abilities, by mounding, reverse mounding, or etiolation.

In mounding, grit or perlite with or without additions of peat, bark or some other organic material is piled over an established plant, either in the ground or in a container, to bury it eventually beneath an overlying layer 8 to 12 cm (3 to 5 in.) deep. When shoots produced from the buried crown grow through the mound to reach the surface, they are removed, complete with the roots they will have produced on the way, to make new plants.

Reverse mounding is similar, except that plants are prepared by planting them in deep holes in the ground. The holes are gradually filled with a 1:1 mixture of grit : bark to achieve the same results as mounding.

Plants are etiolated in containers by placing them in a frame with the lights covered with black polythene so the interior is almost dark. Etiolated shoots are produced, which may or may not form roots spontaneously. These are removed when they have grown several centimetres long, and those with roots are potted up. Those without roots are made into cuttings and usually root readily.

Examples and Special Cases when Propagating Alpine Plants

Gentiana spp., such as *G. acaulis* and *G. verna*, seeds are sown as soon as possible after collection and weather during the winter. Move onto a bench in a glasshouse in late winter or early spring, maintaining temperatures at about 20°C (70°F) by day, and 5° to 10°C (40° to 50°F) at night. *G. sino-ornata* and other autumn-flowering gentians are propagated from divisions; thonglike roots and shoots are dug up in the autumn, separated and potted up individually. Hybrids of *G. sino-ornata* and related species are easy and rewarding to grow from seed. They vary considerably, but almost all grow into attractive, desirable plants. Breeders of new varieties are interested only in seedlings that improve upon existing cultivars—as a result, they pay little attention to huge numbers of plants that most gardeners would be very content to see flowering in their gardens.

Lewisia spp. hybrids between species are freely produced but nearly always sterile and are propagated vegetatively. *Lewisia cotyledon* seed is sown fresh and weathered and germinates during the winter or early the following spring. *Lewisia tweedyi* produces numerous crowns and can be propagated by cuttings made from the rosettes or from seed. Seed is sown in mid-autumn and weathered till late winter; then it is moved into a frost-free glasshouse. Erratic germination in the first spring ranges from prolific to sparse and sometimes nothing till the second spring. *Lewisia rediviva* seeds are sown thinly in autumn and placed in an unheated glasshouse. Grow the seedlings on for the first year without pricking them out. Under natural conditions, the plants stop growing in the summer, but seedlings should be kept watered and will continue to grow. Pot up the seedlings individually in deep containers and grow on in a cool glasshouse throughout the winter. Many will flower in the spring. The plant can also be propagated from rosette cuttings and has such extraordinary powers of recovery from desiccation that herbarium specimens have been revived to grow again.

Propagation Summary for Alpines

S. = propagated from seed
C. = propagated from cuttings
D. = propagated by divisions

Generally speaking, those species whose seeds are sown in spring do not need weathering treatments and are likely to benefit from mildly warm (minimum 5° to 12°C, or 40° to 55°F, at night) temperatures. Seeds sown fresh are likely to respond to low temperature weathering and

should be exposed after sowing to natural low temperature cycles during the winter or, when that is not possible, to temperatures of about 0° to 5°C (32° to 40°F) in a refrigerator for least one and preferably several months.

Acaena—**S.** spring, autumn. **C.** summer. **D.** summer, autumn.
Acantholimon—**S.** spring. **D.** summer.
Acinos—**S.** spring. **C.** summer; basal. **D.** spring.
Adonis—**S.** fresh. **D.** mid- to late summer. Almost all cultivated forms of *A. amurensis* are sterile and propagated by division.
Aethionema—**S.** fresh, spring. **C.** mid-summer.
Alyssum—**S.** fresh, spring. **C.** late summer.
Anacyclus—**S.** spring. **C.** summer.
Androsace—**S.** fresh. **C.** summer; shoot or rosette. **D.** summer.
Anemone—**S.** fresh. **C.** winter, early spring; root.
Antennaria—Dioecious. **S.** fresh, spring; some species, e.g., *A. alpina*, appear to be exclusively female and apomictic. **D.** summer.
Arabis—**S.** spring. **C.** mid- to late summer.
Arenaria—**S.** fresh, spring. **C.** early summer.
Artemisia—**S.** spring. **C.** summer. **D.** spring, early summer.
Astragalus—**S.** spring; chip plus innoculum.
Aubrieta—**S.** spring. **C.** summer; basal shoots produced after the removal of flowering shoots.
Azorella—**S.** fresh, spring. **C.** late summer. **D.** blanket and divide following spring.
Bolax—**S.** fresh. **C.** late summer.
Caiophora—**S.** spring. **C.** winter; root.
Calceolaria—**S.** spring. **C.** late summer. **D.** spring to autumn.
Campanula—**S.** fresh, spring. **C.** spring, summer. **D.** spring, late summer.
Carduncellus—**S.** spring. **C.** winter; root.
Carlina—**S.** fresh, spring. **C.** winter, early spring; root.
Cassiope—**C.** late summer, autumn. **D.** summer; cut back, mound and layer.
Celmisia—Hybridise freely. **S.** fresh; viability often poor, short lived unless well stored. **C.** spring, summer—sub-shrubby species: summer; rosette formers. **D.** spring; self-made layers of sub-shrubby species or rooted rosettes.
Chaetanthera—**S.** fresh.
Chionohebe—**C.** summer.
Corydalis—**S.** fresh, spring. **D.** spring; offsets—tuberous species only, e.g., *C. cava*.

Cyananthus—S. spring. C. late summer; basal.

Daphne—Succulent Fruit. **S.** fresh. **C.** late summer, autumn. **D.** layers.

Dianthus—S. fresh, spring. **C.** summer; pull shoots from joints to make cuttings (known as pipes).

Dionysia—S. fresh; pin and thrum-eyed forms needed for pollination. Seeds sparsely borne in capsules hidden within cushions. **C.** spring; rosettes in pure sand or ground pumice.

Donatia—S. fresh; seeds hidden within cushions. **D.** summer; detach from margins of clumps.

Douglasia—C. summer.

Draba—S. spring. **C.** summer. **D.** spring, summer; rosettes.

Dryas—S. fresh. **C.** summer. **D.** summer; blanket.

Dudleya—S. spring. **C.** summer; rosettes.

Edraianthus—S. spring. **C.** spring; basal.

Epilobium—S. spring. **C.** summer.

Erinacea—S. spring; chip plus innoculum.

Erinus—S. spring.

Eritrichium—S. fresh.

Erodium—S. spring. **C.** spring; basal: late winter; root.

Gaultheria (formerly *Pernettya*)—Succulent Fruit. **S.** fresh. **C.** late summer, autumn. **D.** blanket and/or layer.

Genista—S. spring. **C.** spring, summer.

Gentiana—S. fresh, e.g., *G. verna*. **C.** spring; basal, e.g., *G. septemfida*. **D.** spring, e.g., *G. acaulis*: autumn; from thongs, e.g., *G. sino-ornata*.

Gentianella—S. fresh. **C.** spring, summer.

Globularia—S. spring. **C.** late summer. **D.** late summer; natural layers or blanket.

Gnaphalium—S. spring. **C.** spring.

Gypsophila—S. spring. **C.** summer.

Haastia—S. fresh. **C.** spring; avoid overwatering; may appear to die but usually recover if kept dry. **D.** rosettes on perimeters of clumps may produce roots spontaneously.

Haberlea—S. spring. **C.** summer; single bud.

Hebe—S. fresh, spring. **C.** summer, autumn.

Hectorella—S. fresh. **C.** summer.

Helianthemum—S. spring. **C.** mid-summer.

Helichrysum—S. fresh, spring. **C.** summer; water minimally—no more than enough to maintain life. **D.** spring, summer; blanket, e.g., *H. bellidioides*.

Hepatica—S. fresh. **D.** late summer.

Herniaria—S. spring. **D.** summer; natural layers or blanket.

Hutchinsia—S. fresh. **C.** summer. **D.** late summer.

Hypericum—S. spring. **C.** summer; basal. **D.** late summer; natural layers or blanket.

Iberis—S. spring. **C.** during summer.

Ionopsidium—S. spring. **D.** autumn, in mild localities.

Isotoma—S. spring; extremely small, and should be sown on the surface. **C.** summer. **D.** summer.

Jankaea—S. spring. **C.** summer; rosettes or single bud with leaf.

Jeffersonia—S. fresh.

Junellia—S. spring. **C.** summer. **D.** spring, summer, e.g., blanket/carpeting spp.

Ledum—S. spring. **C.** late summer. **D.** layers.

Leontopodium—S. fresh, early spring. **D.** spring.

Leptinella—S. fresh, spring. **D.** offsets on stolons or rhizomes.

Leucogenes—S. fresh; high proportion of infertile seeds are likely. **C.** late summer. **D.** best from large, mature clumps.

Lewisia—S. fresh, spring. **C.** early summer from individual rosettes.

Linaria—S. spring. **C.** spring; basal, winter; root. **D.** late summer.

Linnaea—C. late summer. **D.** mound, layers.

Linum—S. spring. **C.** late summer.

Lithodora—S. spring. **C.** late summer.

Lobelia—S. spring. **C.** late summer. **D.** spring.

Lupinus—S. spring; chip and bacterial innoculum.

Mazus—S. spring. **D.** summer.

Micromeria—S. spring. **C.** summer.

Mimulus—S. spring. **C.** basal; spring, late summer. **D.** spring to autumn.

Minuartia—S. fresh. **C.** spring to late summer.

Morisia—S. spring; produced from capsules buried below the surface. **C.** summer; rosettes: winter; from roots.

Myosotis—S. spring. **C.** summer; for reliable perennial species.

Nassauvia—S. spring.

Nertera—Succulent Fruit. **S.** fresh, spring. **C.** late summer. **D.** spring from spontaneously rooted pieces.

Notothlaspi—S. fresh; often sparingly produced in cultivation. Prick out early before extensive root system develops.

Nototriche—S. fresh.

Onosma—S. spring. **C.** late summer.

Origanum—S. spring. **C.** spring; basal.

Ourisia—S. fresh, spring. **D.** late summer, spring.

Oxalis—**S.** spring. **D.** spring to autumn; offsets.

Parahebe—**S.** fresh, spring. **C.** autumn, winter. **D.** autumn; layers.

Parochetus—**S.** spring. **C.** at any time. **D.** late summer.

Paronychia—**S.** spring. **D.** summer; mound and layer.

Penstemon—**S.** spring. **C.** mid-summer to late autumn.

Perezia—**S.** fresh. **C.** summer.

Petrocoptis—**S.** fresh, spring.

Phlox—**S.** spring. **C.** mid- to late summer. **D.** late summer or spring.

Phyllachne—**S.** fresh. **C.** summer.

Phyllodoce—**S.** fresh, spring; **C.** summer to autumn.

Physoplexis—**S.** fresh; seldom produced in gardens without hand-pollination.

Phyteuma—**S.** spring. **D.** spring.

Potentilla—**S.** fresh, spring. **C.** early summer; basal perennial species: mid- to late summer; shoots of shrubs. **D.** late summer, spring.

Pratia—Succulent Fruit. **S.** spring. **D.** spring.

Primula—**S.** fresh, spring. *P. petiolaris*, section collected green and sown at once. **D.** late summer.

Pterocephalus—**S.** fresh. **C.** mid-summer.

Ptilotrichum—**S.** spring.

Pulsatilla—**S.** fresh; may germinate immediately or after weathering. **C.** winter; root; very erratic.

Ramonda—**S.** spring. **C.** summer; single bud with leaf. **D.** late summer; ready rooted rosettes.

Ranunculus—**S.** fresh; germination may be improved by collecting and sowing seed while still green. **D.** late summer, winter.

Raoulia—**S.** fresh. **C. D.** spring to late autumn.

Rhodohypoxis—**S.** spring. **D.** autumn through winter; offsets.

Sagina—**S.** spring. **D.** summer.

Saponaria—**S.** fresh. **C.** summer; basal. **D.** late summer, spring.

Sarmienta—**C.** summer.

Saussurea—**S.** fresh.

Saxifraga—**S.** fresh. **C.** summer. **D.** spring.

Soldanella—**S.** fresh. **D.** summer.

Tanacetum—**S.** spring. **C.** late spring, summer. **D.** late summer or mound and layer.

Thlaspi—**S.** fresh. **C.** late spring, summer.

Thymus—**S.** spring. **C.** summer. **D.** summer to autumn, mound and layer.

Townsendia—**S.** fresh.

Umbilicus—**S.** spring. **C.** summer.

Vaccinium—Succulent Fruit. **S.** fresh. **C.** late summer. **D.** late summer, autumn; suckers.

Veronica—**S.** spring. **C.** summer; basal. **D.** spring to autumn, mound and layer.

Viola—Ballistic. Cleistogamous. **S.** fresh. **D.** spring, summer; runners, offsets.

Vitaliana—**D.** late summer; mounded.

Wahlenbergia—**S.** spring. **C.** spring. **D.** spring, late summer.

CHAPTER 14

Succulent Plants

When faced with the problems of living with drought, plants have five alternative strategies: they can produce seeds that lie on the ground until rain comes to sustain a new generation, retreat into bulbs, reduce water loss through their leaves, tap into subterranean sources of water through deep roots, or store water in their tissues during the good times as a reservoir to draw on when the world dries up. This chapter is about the plants that have adopted the fifth option, broadly known as succulents and typified by cactuses, aloes, pachypodiums, agaves and sedums.

Despite being widely distributed amongst many different plant families—both monocot and dicot—succulents share essential features associated with their lifestyle. They are a remarkably homogenous group of plants from a propagator's point of view. Recognising and responding to their distinctive features is an essential part of growing and propagating succulents successfully.

Water is stored in thin-walled cells within swollen, fleshy leaves, shoots or main stems. Low salt concentrations in the stored water and few spaces between the cells provide little protection from ice formation within their tissues; consequently, many are highly vulnerable to frost. Layers of wax and other impermeable substances covering leaves and stems prevent loss of water by evaporation. Fleshy leaves have few stomata and are often inset or protected in other ways to reduce rates of movement of water vapour and, incidentally, gases. This drastically reduces photosynthetic efficiency, a handicap that is partially relieved either by producing ephemeral, normally photosynthesising leaves during seasons when water is readily available. This response is adopted by some euphorbias, alluaudias and cyphostemmas. Or succulents may produce leaves that are photosynthetically effective with little protection from water loss while immature. As they mature, their function as water stores becomes preeminent and photosynthetic efficiency declines, a response found in sedums, stapeliads, and some mesembryanthemums.

Clearly defined growing and resting seasons are characteristic of succulents. When active, they are capable of making rapid growth and need to be well supplied with water. Contrariwise, when resting, especially when subzero temperatures may occur, they should be kept almost totally dry.

High day and low night temperatures are characteristic features of their habitats. Similarly, fluctuating temperatures greatly improve the germination of seeds and growth of seedlings of many species. Cuttings or divisions are more or less constantly available throughout the year. Timing is less critical than with other plants. Nevertheless, better results can be expected when plants are propagated while growing actively.

Networks of fine roots close to the surface, designed to mop up periodic and often highly erratic showers, are typical of many succulents. They respond better to periodic drenching, followed by a period to dry out, rather than constantly moist conditions, and apart from stapelias, most grow better restricted in their containers than when provided with room to spread.

Seeds of many succulents germinate naturally and seedlings develop in the shadow of other plants. Succulence is less about tolerating heat and sunlight and more about storing water, and a cactus with its network of fine roots close to the surface makes a complementary companion for a shrub with deep taproots. The former mops up surface water, while the latter draws from more consistent sources deep below ground and keeps the sun off its succulent friend. In cultivation, seedlings need protection from exposure to direct, bright sunlight.

Succulents are drought adapted. That may appear to be stating the obvious, but it is a fact often forgotten when succulents become sick or unthrifty. They are more likely to be cured by depriving them of water than by trying to revive them by watering. Similarly, cuttings or divisions produce better results in dry than wet conditions.

Propagation from Seed

Apart from the spiny nature of their producers—and sometimes of the fruits themselves—it is seldom difficult to collect seeds of succulents. Their fruits, like their flowers, are conspicuously displayed, and it is easy to judge when they are mature. Seeds of many cactuses range from small to tiny, apart from the large seeds of most opuntias. The plants are long-lived, and under natural conditions, an individual seed's chances of growing into a mature plant are almost infinitesimal, and the strategy adopted is one of minimal commitment of resources to forlorn hopes. Seeds of agaves, haworthias and some other liliaceous succulents are fitted with wings—some conspicuous,

others rather rudimentary—to aid dispersal by wind. Many cactuses and a few others, including lomatophyllums, carpobrotus and cyphostemmas, produce berries or other fleshy fruits as an incentive to birds to eat them and distribute the seeds. All, or almost all, store well under orthodox conditions.

Seed collection and storage

Collecting seed may present few problems; persuading plants to produce it in cultivation may not be so easy for a number of reasons.

Sterility problems

Many species are self-sterile and produce seed only when fertilised with pollen from a genetically distinct individual—not one of the same clone. Because these plants are so easily propagated vegetatively, clones are widespread in cultivation and it can be difficult to find a suitable partner.

Hybridisation

In the absence of a genetically distinct and compatible partner of the same species, another species often fills the gap, and any seeds produced are hybrids.

Specialised pollination requirements

The tubular, red flowers of some succulents—kalanchoes amongst them—are pollinated by nectar-eating birds and fail to produce seeds in their absence. Huernias depend on complex arrangements with particular species of flies that are seldom reproducible in cultivation. Other asclepiads, the producers of carrion flowers, are sinister looking and sinister in fact. Flies, while investigating the source of the smell of rotting meat produced by the red or dull crimson flowers, become trapped by their legs, held tight by structures on the anthers. They can escape only after their struggles detach one of the sacks—or pollinia—in which the pollen is stored. Then they fly off with it still hanging on to their legs and transfer it to the stigmas of the next flower they visit.

Seed dispersal mechanisms

Mesembryanthemums are readily pollinated by short-tongued flies and bees as well as beetles. They set seed freely, but seed is not released when it matures, as long as the capsules remain dry. Seeds are dispersed naturally by raindrops after the flanges of the capsules open in response to rainstorms. The capsules should be kept dry after collection—just as with other seeds—but will release their seeds only in humid atmospheres.

Predation

Seed capsules of aloes, in particular, harbour predatory insects which destroy the seeds. In some locations and in some years, these seriously reduce the production of viable seeds.

Sowing seed

The seeds of succulents germinate, and the young seedlings develop, under conditions very different to those we associate with the lifestyles of their parents. Water, nutrients, warmth and light shade are essential prerequisites for germination and rapid development, and seedlings are ill-equipped to cope with the stresses their parents are built to survive. In nature, suitably generous conditions may occur seasonally as interludes in the prevailing austerity and periodically only in exceptional years. Because, once established, plants are long-lived and the rate of replacement is low, plant populations are able to survive and replace themselves despite dire prospects for seedling survival in the great majority of years. Once they have made their break, the plants are designed to hold their ground through thick and thin.

Favourable conditions are easily provided by gardeners, and seeds are a practical and effective means of propagating many succulents.

- Sow early in the growing season—late winter or early spring—to ensure the longest possible period of growth.
- Sow on the surface, following the standard method for sowing seeds.
- Use [peat, loam, bark] : [grit, perlite], 1:1, as a base, and use minerals—for example, calcined clay, grit, or coarse sand—as a topping. Less stable minerals, such as perlite or vermiculite, are better avoided.
- Place in a propagator or closed frame at approximately 20° to 25°C (70° to 75°F) by day, reducing temperatures at night by at least 10°C (20°F) if possible.
- Shade lightly with bubble polythene and more heavily, perhaps by adding a layer of milky-white polythene, in hot, brightly sunlit conditions to protect young seedlings.
- Seedlings have little resistance to and are easily killed by drought and excessive sunlight at this stage.
- Damping-off and sciarid flies (*Sciara* spp.) are the main hazards. Routine additions of fungicide to water helps prevent the first, and an all-mineral topping reduces the likelihood of damping-off and discourages sciarid flies.
- Water generously as and when the surface starts to dry out, using a very fine spray and incorporating quarter-strength high potash, medium nitrogen, low phosphate fertiliser.
- As seedlings develop, reduce shading and increase ventilation, and prick them out when their cotyledons have been absorbed by the developing plants—usually when around two or three months old.
- Keep lightly shaded, and water sparingly till young plants reestablish after pricking out. Seeds of aloes, agaves and other plants with rosettes should be sown thinly and the young plants allowed to develop three or four leaves before they are pricked out.
- Maintain active growth for as long as possible before letting seedlings rest. Supplementary lighting, used with caution to avoid drying up the seedlings, can be helpful. Seedlings benefit from being held communally in the containers they were pricked out into, at least until the beginning of their second period of active growth and usually till the start of the third, provided they have space to develop.
- Pot up well-grown seedlings individually into containers just large enough to hold them.

Fresh seed usually germinates rapidly. Old seed, especially from species of opuntias, can be very slow. As a rule, succulents germinate within a few weeks, and cactuses take a little longer. Those that have not produced seedlings within four months at approximately 20°C (70°F) are unlikely to do so.

Some mammillarias and mesembryanthemums produce their first flowers during their second period of active growth; most other succulents and rebutias, notocactuses, gymnocalyciums and lobivias amongst cactuses, during their third or fourth period. Cyphostemmas, opuntias, cereus, ferocactuses and columnar aloes take longer, and a few, including species of *Doryanthes*, *Agave* and *Alluaudia*, are unlikely to produce flowers till they are 10 to 20 years old—sometimes considerably more.

Propagation from Cuttings

Regeneration from cuttings is a natural way of life for many of these plants, to such an extent they are designed to shed shoots as a regular means of reproduction. The jointed stems of opuntias, senecios and kalanchoes fall apart naturally or at a touch. They produce roots while lying on the ground and rapidly develop into new plants. The swollen leaves of mesembryanthemums, kalanchoes, sedums and crassulas are similarly tenuously attached to the stems and a regular source of renewed growth. Most succulents provide easy cuttings that can hardly fail to produce roots unless they are killed by misguided attempts to be kind to them.

The most effective and simplest way to propagate most succulents in gardens in mild, dry situations is to break off shoots or offsets and stick them lightly into the ground. This direct, extemporary method imitates nature and introduces fewer man-made hazards than potting them up.

Standard advice when taking cuttings of almost all succulents is to lay them out in a dry, warm place for a few days to dry out the cut ends to reduce risks of fungal infections. This is sound practice but has the disadvantage that time must be found to go back and complete the business by setting up the cuttings. Meanwhile, it can be inconvenient to have unattached prickly bodies lying around. The double shuffle can be avoided by using very well-drained substrates and high temperatures to encourage rapid regeneration, reinforced by setting up the cuttings dry and withholding water for several days.

Offsets

Many succulents produce offsets, miniature replicas of their parents, clustered round the base—amongst them agaves and other plants in which the central cluster of leaves dies after it has produced a flowering stem. These pups, as they are called, may form roots spontaneously and are detached as divisions, or those without roots are removed as cuttings. They are kept almost completely dry until roots start to emerge from the base of the detached offsets.

Offsets develop from meristems in the angles between the stems and the fleshy leaves of many succulents. Their origins within the tightly congested, densely ranked leaves are deeply buried amongst the leaf bases. Unless great care is taken to delve down deep, especially with haworthias, it is all too easy to end up with a handful of detached leaves, leaving behind the growing point on which future development depends.

Shoots

The jointed pads of an *Opuntia*; the tip of a *Cereus*; the tubercles from a *Mammillaria*; a section of stem from a *Mesembryanthemum*, preferably with a small length of old wood at the base; the top of an *Aeonium*, *Kalanchoe* or tree aloe—all these are cuttings in the world of succulents. Cut them off the parent plants and lightly insert or lay on a bed of dry sand, grit, perlite or calcined clay. Leave them unwatered for three or four days. Then water them thoroughly once, and keep them in a lightly shaded, well-ventilated, buoyant atmosphere at approximately 20° to 25°C (70° to 75°F). They should not need to be watered again until they produce roots.

A price is to be paid as well as a bonus gained when removing the top of a cereus or other columnar cactus, the upright, spiny cylinders of some euphorbias, or the top of a tree aloe. The amputation wrecks them as specimen plants, but the new shoots which develop on the cut surfaces of cactuses and euphorbias provide offsets for future use. Single-stemmed tree aloes—such as *Aloe ferox*—are less accommodating. The tops develop roots after removal, the truncated stems do not produce shoots, and nothing is gained by decapitating them.

Epiphyllum cvs. are propagated from large cuttings about 30 cm (12 in.) long. The fleshy tissue towards the base is pared back to expose some of the midrib, from which roots emerge. Cuttings are made from vigorous shoots in flowering condition. Their removal inevitably reduces the numbers of flowers produced, but they will themselves produce flowers the following year. Alternatively, cuttings can be made from older, damaged or woody shoots after they have produced flowers. These are more easily spared, but it is likely to be two or three years before they produce flowers.

The shoots of mesembryanthemums, as a group, have a reputation for providing the duffer's cuttings—almost impossible to fail with. Nevertheless, it is entirely possible to fail, as batch after batch damp-off without forming roots. The obvious remedy is to reduce watering to the minimum necessary to keep the shoots alive, and it also helps to take the cuttings with a small bit of the previous year's growth at the base.

Leaves

The fleshy, thickly cuticled, heavily waxed leaves of sedums, cotyledons, mesembryanthemums and other succulents can be used as cuttings. Remove them with a slight downward pull and a twist to ensure they break off at the point of contact with the stem—like lily scales. Scatter them over the surface of a mineral potting mix, and

shade them lightly to reduce stress, leaving them unwatered till they start to produce roots. New plants develop from meristems at the base of the leaf—not from the tissues of the leaves themselves. As small plants develop, remove the shading and water with a liquid mineral fertiliser to drench the potting mix thoroughly. Keep them moist, but not overwatered, while they grow and establish as new plants.

Kalanchoes, echeverias, aeoniums and other succulents with broader, more normal leaves are also propagated from leaf cuttings. Remove some of the younger, more vigorous but fully expanded leaves, complete with their petioles. These will come from the centre of the rosettes of aeoniums and similar plants. Detach the petioles at the point where they join the stem. Those that break off higher up may produce roots but are less likely to form the buds necessary to develop into a complete plant. Stick the bases of the petioles just below the surface of the cutting mix. Keep them almost dry till new plants have formed and started to produce roots. Shading helps to reduce stress until this happens.

Sansevierias and a few other succulents with long, narrow, fleshy leaves are propagated from leaf cuttings by slicing the leaves into 4 to 5 cm (1.5 to 2 in.) long sections and sticking them vertically into well-drained cutting mix. Small buds develop along the cut edges.

Propagation by Division

Divisions, like cuttings, are something that succulent plants do rather well on their own. Many succulents are propagated by division simply by allowing side shoots or rosettes to develop their own roots before removing them from their parents. As with cuttings, a few days of shade and light watering while they reestablish themselves helps to ensure success. Some reproduce in more curious ways—few more so than the viviparous plantlets of *Kalanchoe tubiflora* arranged along the margins of cup-shaped structures on the sides and tips of the tubular, fleshy leaves. Raindrops striking the rounded cups depress them, and on the rebound, the plantlets are flicked off their perches to land up to a metre (3 ft.) away. Gardeners do not need to go out in a rainstorm and catch these jet-propelled plantlets midair. Simply pick them off and scatter them over the surface of a well-drained substrate.

A problem with divisions—and with cuttings—arises from the presence of pests—mealy bugs in particular, and also red spider mites, greenhouse thrips, scale insects and sometimes eel worms, hidden amongst the basal leaves. These receive free transfers to a renewed and invigorated plant. When these pests are present, the entire plant should be immersed in insecticide before potting it up.

Propagation Summary for Succulent Plants

mesemb = genera within the reclassified genus *Mesembryanthemum*
S. = propagated from seed
C. = propagated from cuttings
D. = propagated by divisions
C. D. = parts, such as stems, that may or may not already possess roots when used as a propagation material

These plants need different growing regimes depending on whether they are grown in gardens in warm or mild temperate regions and Mediterranea where frosts are seldom severe, or in cool or cold temperate regions where moderate to severe frosts are experienced. The winter is often the growing season for succulent plants in mild areas, especially those from South Africa, and autumn through winter to early spring are busy seasons for the propagator. In colder areas, most succulents need protection from winter frosts, and spring through summer to autumn is the growing season and the time when they are most likely to be propagated. The seasons quoted below for

sowing seeds, taking cuttings and making divisions should be interpreted with this in mind, following the rule that seeds should usually be sown and divisions made early in the growing season, and that cuttings can usually be taken throughout the growing season.

References to *spring* should be read as the start of the growing season, *summer* and *autumn* as the growing season, and *winter* as a season of restricted growth or rest.

Aeonium—**S.** spring. **C.** spring to autumn; rosettes, leaves; use only the inner leaves.

Agave—**S.** fresh, spring; flowers may need hand pollinating to produce fruits in cultivation. **C.** spring; offsets or pups; tend to be most freely produced by potbound or senescent plants. **D.** summer, autumn; viviparous bulbils on inflorescences—e.g., *A. sisalana.*

Aichryson—**S.** spring. **C.** spring to autumn; rosettes or leaves.

Alluaudia—**S.** spring; seed leaves (cotyledons) lie in a horizontal plane; thereafter the small paddle-shaped leaves are vertically aligned to reduce their exposure to sunlight.

Aloe—**S.** fresh, spring; hybrids likely. **C.** spring, summer—e.g., *A. arborescens.* **C. D.** spring, summer; offsets and suckers with or without preformed roots.

Anacampseros—**S.** spring.

Argyroderma—**S.** spring, summer; do not prick out or disturb till at least a year old. **D.** summer.

Astrophytum—**S.** early spring; inclined to damp-off.

Beschorneria—**S.** spring; seedlings develop slowly. **C. D.** spring, summer; offsets.

Carpobrotus (mesemb)—Succulent Fruit. **S.** fresh, spring. **C. D.** any time; sections of stem with or without roots.

Cephalocereus—**S.** spring; slow growing. **C.** any time, preferably summer.

Cephalophyllum (mesemb)—**S.** fresh, spring; plants fail to flower unless kept very dry during resting season. **C.** spring, or immediately after flowering.

Cereus—**S.** spring. **C.** at any time.

Cheiridopsis (mesemb)—**S.** spring. **D.** spring, as flowers fade.

Chiastophyllum—**C.** summer; stems, leaves.

Conicosia (mesemb)—**S.** spring. **C.** spring, as flowers fade.

Conophytum—**S.** spring, summer; leave undisturbed till at least a year old. **D.** summer.

Cotyledon—**S.** spring; hybrids likely. **C.** summer; stems, leaves, rosettes.

Crassula—**C.** summer; stems, leaves. Dry off cuttings before insertion. **D.** viviparous plantlets—e.g., *C. multicava*.

Cyphostemma—Succulent Fruit. **S.** fresh, spring. Keep very dry through resting season.

Delosperma (mesemb)—**S.** spring. **C.** spring, as flowers fade.

Didierea—**S.** spring.

Disphyma (mesemb)—**S.** fresh, spring. **C. D.** any time.

Dorotheanthus (mesemb)—**S.** late winter, spring; reach flowering size within six to eight months. **C.** spring, as flowers fade.

Doryanthes—**S.** fresh, spring. **D.** summer, autumn; offsets produced following the development of flower stems, which may take more than a decade from seed.

Drosanthemum (mesemb)—**S.** spring; smoke. **C.** spring, immediately after flowering.

Dudleya—**S.** spring. **D.** spring, summer; offsets.

Echeveria—**S.** spring. **C.** at any time; shoots, rosettes, leaves.

Echinocactus—**S.** spring, early summer; rapid germination at ca. 20°C (70°F). **D.** at any time; offsets, usually very sparingly produced.

Echinocereus—**S.** spring, early summer. **D.** any time; offsets.

Echinopsis—**S.** spring, early summer. **C.** summer; offsets.

Epiphyllum—**S.** spring; develop very slowly. **C.** mid-spring, late summer.

Euphorbia—**C.** spring to autumn; stem.

Ferocactus—**S.** spring, early summer.

Gasteria—**S.** spring, summer. **C.** summer; leaf. **D.** some species form clusters of bulblets along fractured surfaces of broken leaves.

Gibbaeum (mesemb)—**S.** spring. **D.** spring, as flowers fade.

Glottiphyllum—**S.** spring; hybrids likely. **D.** summer.

Graptopetalum—**S.** spring. **C.** summer.

Greenovia—**S.** spring. **C.** spring to autumn; rosettes, leaves, using only the inner leaves.

Haworthia—**S.** fresh, spring; hybrids likely. **C. D.** spring or summer; offsets, preferably removed with roots, otherwise treated as cuttings; also leaf cuttings. **D.** viviparous buds on inflorescence.

Huernia—**S.** spring. **C.** spring to autumn; light shade is essential for the health of seedlings and young plants.

Jovibarba—**S.** fresh, spring. **D.** spring to autumn; offsets, division of rosettes into four to eight sections, e.g., *J. heuffelii*.

Kalanchoe—**S.** spring. **C.** summer to autumn; shoots preferably, leaves. **D.** spring to early autumn; viviparous plantlets at the tips of the leaves—e.g., *K. delagoensis*.

Kleinia—**C.** spring to autumn; shoots.

Lampranthus (mesemb)—**S.** spring; smoke. **C.** spring, as flowers fade.

Leipoldtia—**C.** spring, as flowers fade.

Lithops—**S.** spring, summer; leave undisturbed till at least a year old. **D.** summer.

Lomatophyllum—Succulent Fruit. **S.** fresh, spring. **C.** spring, summer. **C. D.** spring, summer; offsets, suckers; more or less ready-rooted.

Mammillaria—**S.** spring, early summer. **C.** summer; tubercles. **D.** spring to autumn; offsets.

Mesembryanthemum—**S.** spring; smoke. **C.** spring, as flowers fade.

Opuntia—Succulent Fruit. **S.** spring, early summer; rapid germination at ca. 20°C (70°F). **C.** at any time from paddle-shaped shoots, or even fruits.

Ophthalmophyllum—**S.** spring, summer; leave undisturbed till at least a year old. **D.** spring, summer.

Oreocereus—**S.** spring, early summer.

Othonna—**S.** spring; viability often low. **C.** spring, summer.

Pachypodium—**S.** spring. **C.** summer.

Pelargonium—**S.** spring. **C.** summer, autumn; austere water regimes are the key to success. The more succulent the species the greater the need to avoid excess water.

Portulacaria—**C.** spring, summer; using the stronger shoots off main stems.

Rebutia—**S.** fresh, spring.

Rhodiola—**C. D.** spring, summer.

Rosularia—**S.** spring. **C.** spring to autumn; rosettes. **D.** offsets.

Ruschia (mesemb)—**S.** spring; smoke. **C.** spring, as flowers fade.

Sansevieria—**S.** spring; rarely produced in cultivation. **C.** spring, summer; pups, side shoots when about half their mature size. Leaf cuttings produce buds along the cut upper edges; may be very slow before full-sized plants develop. Variegated forms produce all green offspring.

Sarcocaulon—**S.** spring. **C.** spring to autumn.

Sedum—**S.** spring. **C.** spring; basal—e.g., *S. spectabile*: summer; shoots, leaves. **D.** spring to autumn.

Sempervivella—**C. D.** spring to autumn; rosettes.

Sempervivum—**S.** spring. **C. D.** spring to autumn; offsets.

Senecio—**S.** spring; viability often poor. **C.** spring to autumn; shoots, by separating jointed stem into sections—e.g., *S. articulata*.

Stapelia—**S.** spring; fruits take a year to mature, but seed germinates very rapidly; grow on in shade. **C.** spring to autumn.

Stoeberia (mesemb)—**S.** spring. **C.** early summer, as flowers fade.

Tylecodon—**C.** spring, summer; shoots preferably, or leaves.

Zygocactus—**C.** spring; flattened shoots cut into sections at joints.

CHAPTER 15

Bromeliads and Orchids

Bromeliads and orchids are not closely related; in fact, they have little in common botanically. They share this chapter because many species in both families are epiphytes—they grow amongst the branches of trees, and they lodge in crevices in the bark, in the forks and even, seemingly in defiance of gravity, on the bare, exposed wood of dead branches. Some, mainly bromeliads, are lithophytes, perching on the even less hospitable surfaces of rocks and boulders, and a few tillandsias are available to make themselves at home on a telephone wire.

Epiphytes lodge, but they do not parasitise. The lifestyle provides its advantages. It lets plants escape the intense plant-to-plant competition found amongst terrestrial communities and lifts the plant from the shaded recesses of the forest floor to places where light intensities are higher. It brings with it disadvantages, such as exposure to wind; exposure to drought, since the plants are almost entirely dependent on rainfall; exposure to large fluctuations in temperature between day and night; exposure of roots to drought and wind, since they cannot penetrate the substrate; and reliance on exiguous nutrient levels from decaying plant and animal matter, bird droppings, and other organic material lodged in crevices. As a result, epiphytic plants are unusually tenacious, resilient and enduring. They are adapted to survive and thrive in conditions that would kill most other plants.

Impressions of exotic luxury, opulence, a fragile beauty even, conveyed by the word *orchid*, and leading on to thoughts of a life of pampered ease, could not be further from actuality. Bromeliads and orchids thrive on benign neglect. They tend to respond to misjudged attempts to pamper them by dying. As a rule, they prefer the following conditions:

- Temperature regimes which include large diurnal fluctuations
- Clearly defined periods of rest, during which they are kept almost dry, coinciding in high latitudes with the low light and short days of winter
- Potting mixes composed of fibrous, impeccably free-draining materials in small volumes, just sufficient to provide a roothold
- Watering regimes when growing actively that allow the substrates on which they grow almost to dry out between one application of water and the next—such as light, misty sprays of water to refresh the foliage
- Low levels of nutrient feeds applied at frequent intervals only during their growth phases
- Clay or wood rather than plastic containers

Both families include terrestrial species. These grow in the ground in a more or less normal fashion. Terrestrials and epiphytes require quite different treatment in gardens. The epiphytes are no more difficult to grow than the terrestrials. They could be said to be rather easier because of their enduring natures—but they are different and must be recognised for what they are and treated accordingly.

Bromeliads

Few of these members of the pineapple family are hardy, but many make excellent and rewarding conservatory plants—especially the epiphytic species. The leaves of aechmeas, neoregelias, and some vrieseas characteristically enclose cup-shaped hollows in the centre of the plant. This holds water, and a widely held belief decrees it should be regularly topped up. That is unlikely to cause much harm when the plants are growing actively, when the softer leaved kinds, which grow naturally in shaded, humid situations, benefit from the extra humidity it creates. However, this is not necessary and can be positively harmful when the plants are at rest—especially during cool periods when light levels are low—and when propagating the plants from divisions. If the practice cannot be resisted, it should be confined to active growth periods, and the cups should be refilled only when water has disappeared entirely—not constantly topped up.

Bromeliads do not cope well with frost. In general, a bromeliad is considered hardy when it is not harmed by temperatures down to about 5°C (40°F). Some puyas, fascicularias and dyckias tolerate light to moderate freezing temperatures. Species with rigid, stiff or spiny leaves—including some aechmeas, billbergias, neoregelias, and those mentioned in the previous paragraph—are the most hardy. Guzmanias, vrieseas and tillandsias with softer foliage are unlikely to thrive when temperatures fall below 10° to 15°C (50° to 60°F). Light intensities are of major significance; tillandsias, dyckias, puyas, and those aechmeas and billbergias with spiny, stiff leaves respond to high intensities. Softer leaved aechmeas and tillandsias

need some shade, and most vrieseas and guzmanias are positively shade loving.

Propagation from seed

Hybrids are frequently produced between genera as well as species. They are likely to produce fertile seeds but do not necessarily reproduce the characteristics of their parents. The striking patterns of stripes on the leaves of many bromeliads, including aechmeas, some vrieseas and notably *Cryptanthus zonatus*, are produced by bands of water-absorbing scales and are likely to be inherited by seedlings. Variegated leaf patterns, such as those of *Cryptanthus bromelioides* var. *tricolor*, are not inherited.

Seed collection and storage

Seeds are produce either in berries, as in aechmeas and billbergias, and the fleshy tissues must be removed before sowing, or in capsules, as in pitcairneas, dyckias and puyas. When carefully collected, the seeds should need little further cleaning in preparation for sowing or storage. Seeds of tillandsias, vrieseas, and guzmanias may be attached to a pappus, similar to a dandelion seed. These are not removed before sowing. Dried seeds are orthodox for storage at subzero temperatures.

Sowing seed

Bromeliad seed is sown and seedlings raised in ways that allow for the surface nature of their roots—and for tillandsias, known as air plants, in ways that take account of the complete absence of roots.

Bromeliads with roots

To propagate such bromeliads from seed,

- Sow seeds on the surface of a free-draining, absorbent mineral topping—scoria, pumice, calcined clay or perlite—overlying a free-draining but water-absorbent organic : mineral, 1:1, base.
- Water with a fine spray, taking care not to disturb the surface (especially when using perlite).

Figure 69. Neoregalias form pups on stolons and spread to form open clumps of rosettes. The leaves often form cups, which hold water. These should be filled only when plants are growing actively and not kept topped up but allowed to dry out before refilling.

The addition of a fungicide reduces risks of damping-off.

- Place in a closed propagator or frame, lightly shaded in sunny situations, at 20° to 25°C (70° to 75°F).
- Increase ventilation as soon as seedlings appear.
- Prick out the seedlings communally into small pots—five in a 7 cm (2.5 in.) pot, nine in a 9 cm (3.5 in.) pot—when they have developed two true leaves.
- Grow on with ample ventilation.
- Water sparingly—just sufficiently to prevent the substrate from drying out.
- Pot up individually into small, preferably clay, containers.

Rootless tillandsias

The pappus attached to the seed enables these seeds to float in the wind and acts as an anchor when they come to rest on the bark of a tree. These plants are uncompromisingly epiphytic. Sown on the surface of potting mixes, they will germinate but are then more than likely to damp-off. The silvery scales on their leaves absorb moisture from humid air.

Sow the seeds on surfaces to which they can become attached. Two sowing methods can be used:

- Scatter seeds over damp twigs with rough rather than smooth bark, in a propagator over moist bark to maintain a humid atmosphere. Then water periodically with a fine spray, including fungicide. Growth is slow. When large enough to handle—two or three months—transfer the seedlings individually to small plates of bark.
- Stretch fine material—cheesecloth, nylon gauze or a bit of a stocking—over a piece of bark. Spray with water to saturate the material. Scatter the seeds thinly over the surface, and then spray again lightly to flatten the parachutes against the material. Suspend the bark in a cool, lightly shaded, warm, humid situation. Repeat sprays when the surface dries out, but try to avoid doing so on humid days with little air movement.

Seedlings are more likely to rot when overwatered than die from lack of water. Germination may take several months—usually less. Transfer the seedlings onto pieces of bark when they are large enough to manipulate, using a small stick with a notch on the end, and grow on. They benefit from increasing amounts of light, drought and exposure as they grow bigger.

Propagation by Division

Billbergias are popular, easily managed plants, widely grown out of doors in frost-free places and in conservatories or as house plants in colder places. Their life cycles are characteristic of bromeliads in general. Each rosette of leaves is monocarpic: it grows for several years, produces a flower and then dies—not immediately, but after a period of decline. As flowers develop, offsets, or pups, appear in the axils of some of the lower leaves—neoregelias produce them on stolons several centimetres long. Under natural conditions, these grow for a few years, flower and die, producing more pups before they do so. This cycle of death and regeneration leads in time to the production of large clumps of rosettes.

In gardens, the plants are propagated from the pups. Leave the pups on the parent plant till they are about one-third to half the size of the mature rosette—tillandsias till they are even larger. Remove them with a downward twisting action, and pot up individually in the smallest container that will hold them. Water sparingly until new roots are produced; if water lodges in their cup-shaped centres, tip it out.

Even well-developed pups, especially those of aechmeas, may have no roots of their own. Treat them as cuttings. Remove the lower leaves, trim the base with a sharp knife and set up in pots in a well-drained organic : mineral, 1:2, mix. Pot up the original (dying) rosettes after removing the pups. These continue to produce a succession of pups, sometimes for several years.

Figure 70. Many bromeliads produce side shoots, or pups, only as the flowers fade and the original shoot starts to die back. Pups emerge from the base of the plant, and each one should be allowed to grow to at least half or two-thirds its final size before being removed. The old plants are kept after removing the pups and frequently produce several more "flushes" of side shoots during the following year or two. The pup on the left in the illustration is ready to remove by carefully cutting or twisting it off close to the point of attachment to the old shoot; the one on the right should be left in place until it has grown larger.

Pups removed from billbergias and some aechmeas produce flowers within about 18 months. Neoregelias, guzmanias and other aechmeas flower within about 30 months. Vrieseas and tillandsias flower in between two and ten years, depending on the species and how they are grown. Epiphytic species often respond to drought by producing flowers. A reluctant plant may be stirred into flowering mode by withholding water for a period, followed by a return to normal periodic soakings.

Tillandsias, such as *Tillandsia usneoides* and *T. argentea*, with no roots, are also propagated by division. Some produce offsets on creeping rhizomes, others in closely packed clusters. Allow the offsets to develop before removing them, like other bromeliads. Stick them onto suitable mounts using silicone glue. Hang the mounts in a lightly shaded situation and spray them sufficiently to moisten, but not drench, them, twice weekly. They absorb the water they need through the scales on the surface of their leaves.

Propagating Orchids

Few epiphytic orchids are hardy enough to be grown in cool or cold temperate regions, but a number are used in gardens in warmer parts of the world. They are becoming increasingly popular as conservatory plants, appreciated for their endurance of variations in humidity and temperature, low light levels and other conditions many other plants find intolerable. Terrestrial orchids are likely to be hardy enough to be grown in the coldest gardens, and in frost-free or near frost-free situations, literally hundreds of species could be used—if only reliable and effective ways could be found to propagate them. As a group, terrestrial orchids are one of gardening's great blank areas.

A few species of orchis, bletillas, and to a lesser extent bletias, pleiones and calanthes can be found in gardens. We are scarcely aware of the pleasures of growing cypripediums, serapias, ophrys and calypsos from Eurasia and North America; chloraeas and gavileas from Patagonia; eulophias, disas and satyriums from Southern Africa; and caladenias, diuris and thelymitras from Australasia. This is partly because terrestrial orchids are not particularly amenable to cultivation in gardens, mainly because methods of propagating them are too underdeveloped for them to be produced economically in sufficient numbers to try them out under different conditions in different situations.

Propagation from seed

Orchid seed to orchid flower is a time span measured in years, but not as many years as garden lore suggests. Think in terms of two to four years, rather than the six to seven often quoted. Of a dozen epiphytic species grown from seed on nutrient cultures at the Jodrell Laboratory at the Royal Botanic Gardens, Kew, two flowered in less than two years, eight in under three, and only two between three and four. Terrestrial species have been observed in the wild flowering profusely on newly created sites within three or four years. Once established, orchid plants are long lived. Seeds provide an entirely practical, economical and effective way to build up a collection.

Epiphytic orchids are raised from seed with little difficulty. What goes on happens on the surface, making it possible to observe the progress of seedlings and respond to their needs. Terrestrial orchids develop underground, lost to sight and understanding for several years before leaves appear. We know little about their needs, rates of development and responses to different conditions.

The belief that orchids form partnerships with fungi in the genus *Rhizoctonia* at an early stage is generally accepted, often with the assumptions that their seeds cannot germinate until they form such a partnership and that they must maintain symbiotic relationships with their fungal partners when they are mature. Neither assumption is fully confirmed by observations of the behaviour of epiphytic orchid seedlings raised under laboratory conditions on nutrient media.

Orchid seeds can be germinated and grown under sterile conditions. Seedlings provided with mineral nutrients and a source of carbohydrate such as sugar produce chlorophyll and develop without forming symbiotic relationships. Plants raised asymbiotically in this way grow into mature plants when potted up in standard orchid potting mix and produce flowers. There is no indication that the plants form symbiotic relationships after they are potted up, though the possibility cannot be excluded. Orchids may depend on their fungal partners for the competitive edge necessary for survival in plant communities growing naturally, but we should accept with caution the idea that such partnerships are invariably necessary when orchids are grown in gardens, whether as an aid to germination or in support of healthy growth and the production of flowers.

Seed collection and storage

Orchids are notable for the ingenious and complex partnerships they have formed with insects and other animals to ensure pollination of their flowers. Despite the often elaborate arrangements for cross-pollination, most orchids appear to be self-fertile, and seed can be produced by hand-pollinating the flowers on a single plant. The flowers of cultivated plants should always be hand-pollinated when seeds are wanted, to ensure their production and as a safeguard against hybridisation.

Orchid pollen is produced in specialised anthers known as pollinia. These do not open to release the pollen but are transported intact to receptive tissues on the styles of neighbouring flowers. The most effective substitute for the natural pollinator is a short length of stick—for example, a match stick—instead of the customary paint brush or rabbit's tail. This is inserted deep into the flower. As it is withdrawn, one or both pollinia become attached to its surface. The match stick is inserted into another flower, pressing one of the pollinia against the stigmatic surface of the style as it enters, where it remains when the stick is withdrawn.

Seeds are produced in capsules. Deciduous terrestrial species produce mature seed a few weeks after fertilisation. Epiphytic species may do so within five or six weeks, others take up to six months, and some take more than a year.

Capsules contain enormous numbers of minute seeds which are released when they mature, and within a few days, several hundred thousand seeds may escape into the air. The capsules open quite discreetly along the seams, splitting rather than gaping. Cut off the capsule as soon as the first signs of maturity are detected. Label it and put it individually into a glass tube. Cover the top with gauze to ensure good ventilation while the capsule continues to dry out. Place the tube in a desiccator to make sure the seeds dry completely. Orchid seeds tolerate desiccation over silica gel or similar desiccants and once dried are orthodox for storage. Many, perhaps most, can be stored for up to ten years in a refrigerator and considerably longer in a freezer.

Sowing seed

Orchid seeds are minute, barely dustlike in appearance. They contain virtually no storage reserves and no differentiated embryo. Upon release, the seeds drift through the air, and some land in situations where it is possible for them to grow. Such situations are few and far between, and the establishment, growth and successful maturation of a wild orchid seed is a rare event. After landing, the cells divide and develop into a roughly spherical corpus of undifferentiated tissue—supposedly with the assistance of a fungal symbiont. Chlorophyll is produced within the cells and an apical meristem forms. This gives rise to leaves and a recognisable seedling.

Epiphytic orchids are likely to give good results when attempts are made to grow them from seed. Terrestrial orchids with pseudobulbs on or just below the surface also mostly respond well. Terrestrial orchids with subterranean tubers are chancy at best and likely to be unsuccessful at worst.

Symbiotic methods have been largely neglected since methods for growing orchid seedlings on sterile nutrient cultures were developed during the 1920s. That is a shame, because their min-

Options for propagating orchids from seed

Symbiotic propagating methods
Seed/seedlings are given opportunities to establish symbiotic relationships with fungal partners.

- Using fungal symbionts already present in a mature plant—preferably of the same species or genus—thoroughly saturate the substrate around a well-established plant with water.
- Sprinkle seeds on the surface of the growth medium around the roots.
- Spray lightly with a fine mist of liquid nutrient at a quarter standard strength.
- Place at 20° to 25°C (70° to 75°F) in a shaded, humid situation.
- Spray regularly with water to ensure the surface of the growth medium and seeds remain moist, but do not drench.
- When protocorms are visible, perhaps after two to three months, start regular feeds with quarter-strength nutrient at monthly intervals.
- When leaves appear, prick out individually on a bed of chopped sphagnum moss : bark, 1:1.
- Continue to feed regularly.
- Pot up into small pots of orchid growth medium.

Using a semi-sterile method similar in many respects to that used to raise fern spores, wash a kitchen work top or formica-covered table with domestic sterilising solution to prepare a clean working surface.

- Sterilise new 9 cm (3.5 in.) plastic containers.
- Cover the sterilised containers with cling film (plastic wrap).
- Cut off the ends—about 1 to 2 cm (0.5 to 1 in.) long—of the roots of established orchid plants, preferably the same species or genus as those to be sown.
- Put them in a clean saucer, spray lightly with boiled water and cover with a sheet of glass.
- Mix sphagnum : bark : fairly coarse coir, 1:1:1, and pasteurise by pouring boiling water over it, repeating several times.
- Include a small innoculum of fibre from which an orchid has been growing, if possible.
- Wrap handfuls of the mixture in squares of clean, boiled cotton gauze or nylon stocking, to make packages sufficient to fill a 9 cm (3.5 in.) pot.
- Remove the cling film, put the gauze-wrapped packets into the pots, tamp down to form a level surface and spray with boiled water to saturate the gauze and its contents.
- Sprinkle orchid seeds over the surface.
- Add the tips of a few roots and spray lightly with quarter-strength nutrient feed. (The root tips increase prospects of success but are not invariably necessary.)
- Replace the cling film with new film.

- Put the pots in a polythene box with a transparent top (such as a cake box) and about 2 cm (1 in.) of boiled, cooled water in the base.
- When all the pots have been sown, close the lid of the box firmly.
- Put it somewhere well illuminated but not in direct sunlight, at about 25°C (75°F).
- Leave undisturbed until protocorms are formed and the first small leaves are developing.
- Partially raise the lid of the box and increase ventilation progressively as the seedlings grow.
- Feed with quarter-strength nutrient at monthly intervals.

Asymbiotic propagation methods

Seedlings are produced under sterile conditions with no opportunities for contact with fungal partners. Seedlings are grown under aseptic conditions on nutrient media containing sugars. Some bacterial as well as fungal spores grow freely on these media and compete with or destroy seedling orchids. Success depends on being able to provide the seedlings with completely sterile conditions during their initial development. Asymbiotic methods are likely to be successful only when the operator has some experience of working under sterile conditions and equipment and facilities are available to make this practicable.

A method for growing orchids asymbiotically is set out in chart 18. Details of nutrient solutions are provided in a separate box. A brief summary of the method is provided here.

- Prepare nutrient solutions containing a complete range of minerals and sugar.
- Combine with agar to form a jelly on which the seeds are sown.
- Pour small quantities of the jelly into suitable containers—glass tubes, jars or flasks—and sterilise.
- When the jelly has cooled and set, sow small quantities of seed on the surface.
- Close the tops of the containers to prevent contamination with spores of fungi, bacteria, ferns, mosses or liverworts.
- Put the containers in a warm, well-lit situation, where the orchid seeds can germinate and develop.
- When the seedlings are large enough to handle, prick them out onto fresh, sterile nutrient solution (described later in boxed text), and grow on till each one has several well-developed leaves.
- Pot up individually in a finely divided orchid potting mix, scrupulously removing all traces of the nutrient jelly while doing so.
- Grow on under normal conditions in a glasshouse or poly tunnel.

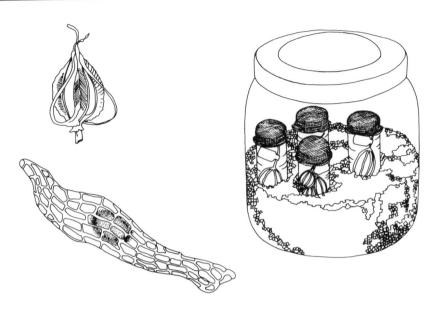

Figure 71. Orchid capsules split along their sides to release the dustlike seeds within them, and the first signs of splits are easily missed. Unless a careful watch is kept, most of the seeds can be lost before their escape is noticed. Seeds are minute, composed of a group of undifferentiate cells enclosed by a filamentous network within which they can float through the air for enormous distances. Cut off the capsules as soon as they begin to dehisce, and put them with labels attached straight into small specimen tubes, capped with a square of muslin. The tubes are enclosed over silica gel in a suitable airtight container while the capsules open and all the seed is released. Then the empty capsules are removed and the containers stored either in a refrigerator or a freezer cabinet.

imal special requirements offer opportunities for growers of orchid seedlings with few facilities, and there is no doubt they could be improved on with every prospect of being almost as useful and effective as the far more complex sterile techniques which require more elaborate facilities and skills.

Asymbiotic methods based on nutrient solutions also offer scope for simplification, particularly in the composition of the base nutrient solution. There is no reason to think that appropriate proprietary liquid feeds could not be used to replace the laboratory chemicals specified here. Orchid seedlings grow best with low levels of calcium and comparatively high levels of potassium and nitrogen. They also respond to a number of complex organic additives including oatmeal, banana pulp and yeast extract. The addition of these and others can considerably improve success rates—even with some of the unamenable terrestrial, tuberous species.

Propagation from cuttings

In common with monocots generally, orchids offer few opportunities for propagation from cuttings. A few epiphytic species, including angraecums and dendrobiums, produce elongated, shootlike pseudobulbs, which they retain almost indefinitely.

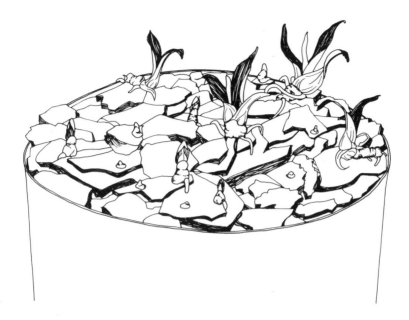

Figure 72. Orchids are now almost exclusively raised from seed by asymbiotic methods based on nutrient solutions containing sugar, for which sterile conditions are essential. Seedlings of many epiphytic but fewer terrestrial orchids, including some cypripediums and paphiopedalums, can be raised more naturally by sowing them on growing media containing an innoculum consisting of a small quantity of potting mix on which an established orchid has been grown. Minute seeds develop first into translucent green blobs of undifferentiated cells from which a tiny bud emerges, gradually giving rise to leaves; meanwhile, roots develop from the base of the mass of cells. Over a period of several months, small orchid plants develop and are potted up individually. The tiny seedlings need protection from the overwhelming presence of mosses and liverworts.

- Remove some of the redundant pseudobulbs.
- Cut the stems into sections, each with several joints.
- Either strap them to pads of osmunda fibre or bed down in sphagnum moss.
- Put them in a closed propagator or frame at 20° to 25°C (70° to 75°F).
- Spray lightly from time to time sufficiently to prevent the moss or fibre from drying out, but do not waterlog or maintain constantly water-saturated atmospheres until roots are produced.
- Pot up and grow on normally.

Propagation by division

The key to growing most orchids successfully lies in providing them with clearly defined periods of rest and growth. In cool and cold temperate regions, rest periods usually coincide with winter, when deciduous species lose their leaves. In Mediterranea and other locations with hot, dry summers and mild winters—especially with terrestrial species—they coincide with summer.

Different species vary in their tolerance to cold and their treatment while resting:

Chart 18. ORCHIDS FROM SEED (ASYMBIOTICALLY)

Successive stages in the preparation of nutrient media, the collection of seeds, sowing seed and growing on seedlings

Preparation of Sterile Nutrient/Sugar Solutions	Pollination and the Collection and Preparation of Seeds	Sowing Seeds and Growing on Seedlings
Nutrient solutions prepared—make concentrated stock solutions of each chemical individually	Hand-pollinate flowers and label by writing date and identification on tags	**Sow seeds on nutrient agar in jars. Hold the jars at an angle, and use a mounted needle to introduce the seeds**
Dissolve agar in boiling water; add sugar and nutrients to produce nutrient gels	Remove ripe capsules as soon as they start to gape; dry over silica gel to release seeds	**Prick seedlings out; use a mounted needle to space them on fresh nutrient agar in a jar**
Pour hot nutrient gel into jars. Sterilise at min. 80°, preferably 100°C (175°, 215°F)	Store* dried seeds in airtight tubes in a refrigerator or freezer	Remove seedlings from jars and pot them up individually in orchid mix in 7 cm (2.5 in.) pots
Tighten lids on jars and allow to cool, setting jars at an angle to form slopes	**Sterilise seeds, using a solution of kitchen bleach immediately before sowing**	Transfer the pots to a glasshouse and wean in a closed frame at 20° to 25°C (70° to 80°F)
		Grow on under appropriate conditions for the species till flowers are produced

*Seeds of most species of orchids can be stored for several years, at least, dry in a refrigerator. Seeds survive for much longer periods at sub-zero temperatures.

- Deciduous epiphytic species—for example, *Dendrobium nobile*, pleiones, catasetums and some calanthes—should rest in a dry house at about 10° to 15°C (50° to 60°F), minimum 5°C (40°F), until growth restarts. Provide just enough water to prevent pseudobulbs from shriveling.
- Evergreen epiphytic species—such as oncidiums, many dendrobiums, some calanthes, cymbidiums and odontoglossums—should rest with similar temperatures, preferably with a slightly higher minima, but kept less stringently dry.
- Deciduous terrestrial species—such as orchis, chloraea, ophrys, dactylorhiza, cypripedium and other species with tubers or tuberous roots—should be watered sparingly, just sufficiently to prevent the substrate drying out

---

Note to Chart 18 (opposite): Concentrated stock solutions of nutrient minerals can be made up and kept in a refrigerator—make enough to produce several batches of useable strength solutions.

Boxes with bold margins and bold type in the diagram refer to stages in the process accomplished under sterile conditions.**

It is essential to avoid contamination with fungal or bacterial spores during these operations. Some form of equipment that makes it possible to work under sterile conditions is needed when sowing and growing orchid seedlings on nutrient solutions containing sugar. Sources of contamination include spores in the air and on the surfaces of equipment—and, not the least, those on the hair and skin of the operator.

The most practical way to sterilise seeds is to fold them in facial tissue. Put the pads formed into a nylon sieve and pour diluted kitchen bleach solution over them. Rinse repeatedly in boiled cold water afterward.

**Detailed instructions for raising orchids from seed asymbiotically are provided in the booklet *Orchids from Seed* by P. A. Thompson, published by Her Majesty's Stationery Office (HM8540).

completely. Air temperatures can go down to freezing point but not below.

- Evergreen terrestrial species—such as bletias, bletillas, calypso, and paphiopedilums—should be provided just enough water to prevent shriveling and wasting of green tissues, with minimum temperatures down to about 5°C (40°F).

All resent closed, humid conditions. Fan-assisted air movement within the glasshouse and as much ventilation as possible consistent with maintaining minimum temperatures are the rule.

The plants start to grow spontaneously in the spring, and with few exceptions, including bletias and bletillas, this marks the time to divide them. Species with back bulbs are divided, either by splitting well-developed plants into several large sections, each containing a number of active growth centres and pseudobulbs, or by cutting off some of the redundant pseudobulbs individually. In both cases, meristematic tissues at the base of the pseudobulbs develop new roots and shoots. While they are doing so, they should be lightly and regularly sprayed with water, taking care not to saturate the substrate. Some, including odontoglossums, take time to reestablish. They should be shaded during periods of sunshine.

Terrestrial orchids with tubers or tuberous roots provide fewer opportunities for multiplication by division. The tubers are seldom perennial and usually replaced annually. A few produce offsets fairly freely or regularly, but many do little more than replace themselves. Remove plants from their containers or dig up established clumps when they are available, as growth starts in spring. Carefully disinter the tubers. Divide and repot or plant out individually. A few, amongst them *Dactylorhiza elata* and *D. foliosa*, increase steadily once established. Leave them to build up numbers and divide periodically at intervals of about five years.

A nutrient solution for growing orchids from seed asymbiotically

The Jodrell nutrient solution is a modified form of one developed at the Jodrell Laboratory at the Royal Botanic Gardens, Kew. It has the unique advantage of making it possible to vary the concentration of nitrogen, calcium, phosphorous and potassium independently, and it has been used successfully to raise seedlings of some 150 different orchid species. The project provided the foundation for the later development of the Orchid Propagation Unit at Kew.

Recipe for stock solutions (×10 concentration)
Urea: 6.3 grm/litre (1 heaped tsp./quart)*
Orthophosphoric acid: 3.0 grm/litre (0.5 tsp./quart)
Calcium acetate: 1.0 grm/litre (0.25 tsp./quart)
Magnesium sulphate: 3.7 grm/litre (0.5 tsp./quart)
Potassium acetate: 3.9 grm/litre (0.5 tsp./quart)
Chelated iron: 0.25 grm/litre (a pinch/quart)
Chelated trace elements: a few drops
Sugar (sucrose): 30 grm/litre (1 oz./quart)

*Note that measurements using teaspoons do not achieve the accuracy of a chemical balance, but they provide an acceptable means of making a serviceable nutrient solution for those unable to weigh chemicals precisely.

Making the nutrient solution
If working in grams, take 100 mls of each stock solution and make up to a litre in total. If working in teaspoons and quarts, take one cupful of each stock solution and make up to ten cupfuls.

Setting up
Take approximately half the nutrient solution and bring to a vigorous boil. Add 10 grm (1 tsp.) of agar flakes. Stir continuously while adding the agar and until it has dissolved completely. Remove from heat and add the remainder of the nutrient solution. While still hot, pour into screw-top jars to form a layer about 1.5 to 2 cm (0.75 to 1 in.) deep and replace the screw tops. Ease the tops off about half a turn, and sterilise the jars and their contents in an oven at about 250°C (480°F) for half an hour. Take the jars out of the oven, and while they are still hot tighten the screw tops. Stand the jars at an angle by raising one side about 3 cm (1 in.) on a length of wood so that the agar forms a sloping surface when it sets.

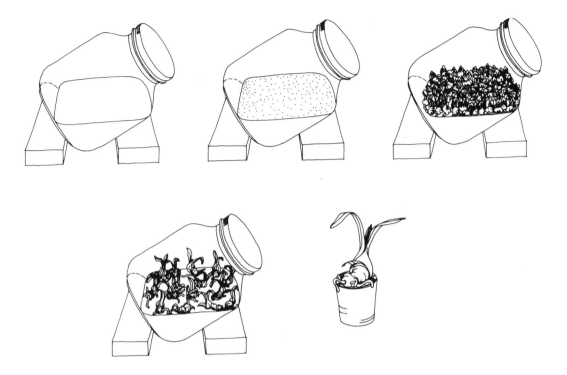

Figure 73. Orchid seedlings are raised on solutions of mineral salts and sugar, but this is possible only when strictly sterile conditions can be maintained until the seedlings grow large enough to pot up individually on orchid growth media. Provided facilities are available to do this successfully, seedlings can be sown, pricked out and grown on, on nutrient agar slopes in wide-mouthed jars. The jars should be kept in warm, well-lit conditions, out of direct sunlight. Bubble or milky polythene sheeting can be used to diffuse sunlight while still exposing the developing seedlings to comparatively high light intensities.

Propagation Summary for Bromeliads and Orchids

S. = propagated from seed
C. = propagated from cuttings
D. = propagated by divisions

Bromeliads

Abromeitiella—Terrestrial. **D.** pups after flowers die.

Aechmea—Epiphytic. Succulent Fruit. **S.** spring. **C.** unrooted pups. **D.** Rooted pups—sometimes produced on stolons.

Ananas—Terrestrial. Succulent Fruit. **C.** top of mature fruit with rosette of leaves. **D.** pups produced in leaf axils after fruits mature.

Billbergia—Epiphytic. Succulent Fruit. **S.** spring. **D.** pups from offsets at base of flowering shoots.

Cryptanthus—Terrestrial. **S.** spring. **D.** offsets; freely produced in leaf axils, even before flowering.

Dyckia—Terrestrial. **S.** fresh, spring. **D.** pups; after flowers fade.

Fascicularia—Terrestrial. **D.** offsets when about two-thirds their final size.

Guzmania—Epiphytic. **S.** spring. **D.** offsets in leaf axils; remove when about one-third full size.

Neoregelia—Epiphytic. **S.** spring. **D.** offsets; stolons emerge from leaf axils.

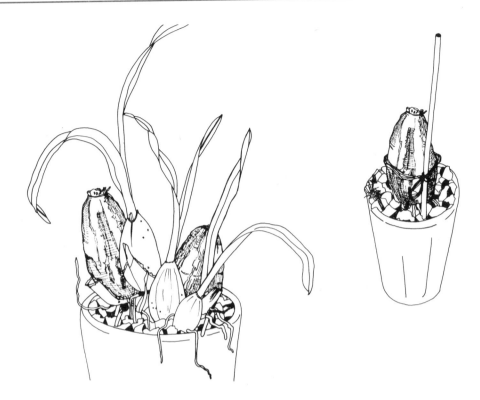

Figure 74. As orchid plants grow, they sometimes produce a series of shoots, as in dendrobiums, similar to a conventional stem but more often a bulblike object, topped by leaves—one arising from the base of another. Eventually the leaves drop off, and the pseudobulbs, now known as back bulbs, become redundant and somewhat desiccated. New plants are propagated by detaching the back bulbs and setting them on a bed of coarse orchid mix, supported in an upright position with their bases touching but not buried in the mix. When kept warm and barely watered no more than necessary to moisten the growing medium, new roots and then a shoot emerge from the base of the back bulb to form a new plant.

Nidularium—Epiphytic. **D.** pups in leaf axils, after flowers die.

Ochagavia—Epiphytic. **D.** pups; in leaf axils as flowers develop. Leave till half full size before removal.

Pitcairnia—Terrestrial/Lithophytic. **D.** evergreen clump-forming and grassy spp.—e.g., *P. andreana*; produce offsets freely with or without flowers; deciduous species—e.g., *P. pungens*—produce offsets from a bulbous base as flowers develop in spring.

Puya—Terrestrial. **S.** spring. **D.** pups produced after flowering.

Tillandsia—Epiphytic/Lithophytic/Terrestrial. Seeds with pappus. **S.** fresh; on muslin or nylon gauze. **D.** from offsets on creeping rhizomes or in clusters; *T. usneoides*, *T. argentea* and other rootless species stuck on to bark or twig substrates; viviparous buds on inflorescences.

Vriesea—Epiphytic. Seeds with pappus. **S.** fresh; on nylon or muslin gauze. **D.** from pups after flowering; except *V. splendens*, which forms single rosettes that cannot easily be divided successfully.

Orchids

Anacamptis—Terrestrial. Tuberous. **S.** self sows, but unamenable in cultivation. **D.** tubers—very slow to increase.

Angraecum—Epiphytic. Pseudobulbs. **S.** spring. **C.** species with jointed stems—e.g., *A. eichlerianum*. **D.** species with rhizomatous pseudobulbs—e.g., *A. gracilipes*.

Bletia—Terrestrial. Pseudobulbs. **D.** as flowers fade.

Bletilla—Terrestrial. Pseudobulbs. **D.** after flowering.

Caladenia—Terrestrial. Tuberous. **S.** spring: symbiotic. **D.** very slow to increase.

Calanthe—Terrestrial. Pseudobulbs. **S.** spring. **D.** late winter; evergreen species—even old, shriveled pseudobulbs will regenerate; late winter/spring; deciduous species—can be lifted and stored overwinter.

Calypso—Terrestrial. Tuberous. **D.** offsets.

Cephalanthera—Terrestrial, Tuberous. **D.** offsets.

Chloraea—Terrestrial, Tuberous. **D.** offsets.

Coelogyne—Epiphytic. Pseudobulbs. **S.** any time. **D.** pseudobulbs, singly or in groups.

Cymbidium—Epiphytic/terrestrial. Pseudobulbs, **S.** any time. **D.** small groups or individual back bulbs after flowering.

Cypripedium—Terrestrial. Bulbous. **S.** symbiotic. **D.** offsets; very slow.

Dactylorhiza—Terrestrial. Tuberous. **D.** from established plants after several years. Stocks of the most widely distributed species—e.g., *D. elata* and *D. foliosa*—widely severely affected by stem eelworm. Retain only the tubers when propagating.

Dendrobium—Epiphytic. Pseudobulbs. **S.** any time. **C.** sections of jointed pseudobulbs. **D.** nonflowering, back pseudobulbs; viviparous buds in inflorescences occasionally produced.

Disa—Terrestrial. Tuberous. **S.** any time. **D.** spring; offsets.

Diuris—Terrestrial. Tuberous. **D.** offsets.

Epidendrum—Epiphytic. Pseudobulbs. **S.** any time. **D.** groups of back bulbs; rooted shoots of species with stems produced after cutting back about 50 percent.

Epipactis—Terrestrial. Creeping Rhizome. **D.** after flowering.

Eulophia—Terrestrial. Tuberous a few with pseudobulbs. **D.** spring.

Gavilea—Terrestrial. Tuberous. **D.** spring; from established clumps.

Goodyera—Terrestrial/Epiphytic. Fleshy Rhizomes. **D.** very slow to increase.

Habenaria—Terrestrial. Tuberous occasionally with fleshy rhizomes. **D.** very slow to increase.

Liparis—Terrestrial/Epiphytic. Tuberous. Pseudobulbs. **D.** late winter; pseudobulbs: spring; tubers; very slow to increase.

Lycaste—Epiphytic/terrestrial. Pseudobulbs. **D.** individual back bulbs.

Odontoglossum—Epiphytic. Pseudobulbs **S.** any time. **D.** into small groups or individual back bulbs. Take some time to establish. Remove old back bulbs when new ones develop.

Oncidium—Epiphytic. Pseudobulbs. **S.** any time. **D.** individual back bulbs; a few produce buds viviparously in their inflorescences.

Ophrys—Terrestrial. Tuberous. **S.** self-sows but unamenable in cultivation. **D.** tubers, but seldom do better than a one for one replacement.

Orchis—Terrestrial. Tuberous. **S.** symbiotic. **D.** tubers from established clumps, in autumn as the plants die down.

Paphiopedilum—Terrestrial. Rhizomatous. **S.** any time. **D.** spring; from large plants to form comparatively large subdivisions.

Platanthera—Terrestrial. Tuberous. **D.** but annual replacements of old tubers seldom produce more than one for one.

Pleione—Terrestrial/Epiphytic. Pseudobulbs. **S.** any time; seedlings must have cool resting period when they have developed pseudobulbs. **D.** after flowering—usually replaced two for one.

Pogonia—Terrestrial. Tuberous. **D.** from small natural increase (if any).

Pterostylis—Terrestrial. Tuberous. **D.** offsets, spring.

Satyrium—Terrestrial. Tuberous. **S.** fresh.

Serapias—Terrestrial. Tuberous. **S.** self-sows, but unamenable in cultivation.

Spathoglottis—Terrestrial. Rhizomatous Pseudobulbs. **D.** spring.

Spiranthes—Terrestrial. Rhizomatous or more or less tuberous. **S.** self-sows, but unamenable in cultivation. **D.** spring.

Thelymitra—Terrestrial. Tuberous. **D.** usually only replaces previous tuber, but some species multiply steadily.

CHAPTER 16

Shrubs Including Lianes

Shrubs are long-lived, woody and persistent, with steadily expanding frameworks of branches on which they spread out their leaves and display their flowers. The persistent, woody structure of shrubs fundamentally affects their survival strategies under natural conditions and influences their propagation in important ways.

The odds against any individual seed growing up to replace its parents become ever more astronomical. Nevertheless, seeds play vital roles in finding places to grow. Production and distribution are often economically combined in a package by producing seeds in succulent, sweet, brightly coloured and sometimes aromatic fruits. These are eaten by birds, mammals, reptiles and other creatures, which distribute the seeds within them far and wide.

Shrubs use the woody persistence of their branches as a means of self-perpetuation denied to annuals, biennials and herbaceous perennials with annual shoots. When in contact with the ground, their branches produce roots, giving rise to new plants which do the same in their turn to form a series of linear descendants leap-frogging away from a founder to form a thicket. Gardeners imitated this expression of totipotency in the simplest possible way by making layers. They also use the ability of almost any shoot to form roots and give rise to a new plant, provided it remains alive and functioning to make cuttings; the ease and certainty with which so many of these plants can be propagated from cuttings has made this by far the most widely used way to propagate shrubs in gardens.

Propagation from Seed

Restrictive controls on germination, including hard seed coats and prolonged weathering, often spread the production of seedlings from a particular vintage of seeds over several years, sometimes extending to decades. Plants benefit because this provides time during which changes in the surrounding vegetation may produce new sites where seedlings can gain a roothold. Gardeners find such strategic delays irksome and have devised ways to speed up natural responses.

Seed collection and storage

Many shrubs produce seeds in readily visible, easy to observe, accessible, moderately productive capsules, pods, follicles and other dry fruits. These pose few problems for the seed collector. More care and attention are needed to collect others successfully. Ballistic seeds—spartiums, genistas, carmichaelias, hoveas and many members of the pea family and a few others including boxes, the pistol bush (*Duvernoia adhatodoides*) and cean-othus—discharge their seeds ballistically as soon as they ripen. Collections must be repeated at frequent intervals just before the seeds mature. Fleshy fruits of various kinds, including berries, drupes, and arils, are produced by many shrubs.

Small seeds, like those contained in the fruits of fuchsias, actinidias, akebias and passifloras, can safely and easily be separated from the pulpy tissues by maceration. Larger seeds produced singly or in small numbers by daphnes, coprosmas, cornus, cotoneasters, roses and viburnums, amongst others, are more likely to be damaged during maceration. Small quantities can be extracted manually; large quantities are extracted by mixing with grit and weathering.

Dustlike seeds, produced by a minority of shrubs including kunzeas, callistemons, rhododendrons, hydrangeas and carpentarias, easily become almost inextricably mixed with hairs, leaf fragments, undeveloped seeds and other matter. The capsules should never be broken up but shaken gently in a paper bag to extract the seed, avoiding plastic bags in which static electrical charges bind small seeds to the plastic. A few shakes are sufficient; seeds that do not detach readily are usually those that have failed to develop.

Serotinous seeds are produced by a number of shrubs including callistemons, calothamnus, leptospermums, melaleucas, banksias and hakeas from semi-arid or seasonally dry areas where fires are a significant feature of the environment. These are held in the fruits—sometimes for years—until the parent plant dies, often as a result of fire. The woody fruits may become partially embedded in the tissues of the stems and can be collected only by removing the sections of stem that bear them, after which the woody capsules usually open to release the seeds inside them as the stems start to dry. When this fails to happen or more rapid results are needed, the cut fruits and stems can be placed on a shelf over a radiator or in a low oven for a few hours.

Problem seeds produced by a few shrubs are difficult or laborious to collect in any quantity. *Agathosmas*—the South African buchus—produce successions of flowers over long periods. Seeds are well hidden, produced sparingly and mature over correspondingly long periods so numerous repeat visits are necessary to make a worthwhile collection. In addition, the capsules spring open to disperse the seeds ballistically as they mature, and seed collected from immature, green capsules seldom germinates.

Some Western Australian shrubs including chamelauciums, darwinias, actinodiums, calythrix and verticordias are similarly unrewarding. There is scarcely any fruit development as such, and the single seed produced by each flower lies surrounded by the wilted remnants of the floral parts. They are extremely fiddly to collect, infuriating to clean and usually germinate reluctantly, especially when planted in the soil. Under natural conditions, the seeds germinate among the plant debris on the surface, including the remains of the flowers, which surrounds them and act as their own personal, transportable seedbed.

Exceptions apart, most shrubby species produce seeds that are easy to handle and clean. The vast majority can be dried and stored at subzero temperatures under orthodox conditions.

Sowing and pricking out

Under natural conditions, seeds produced by shrubs produce seedlings and eventually mature plants relatively seldom, mainly because of the long lives enjoyed by the parents they replace, not because the seeds are reluctant to germinate. Gardeners can propagate shrubs from their seeds readily and regularly, provided they are aware of the conditions that lead to germination. Many seeds will grow into flowering plants within a few years—not much longer than from cuttings.

Seed germination and subsequent successful development very often depend on exposure to weathering treatments, which may involve sequences of warm, cool and cold weathering, and sometimes one or more phases need to be repeated; positive or negative reactions to the organic/mineral balance of the potting mixes on which they are sown and grown; and symbiotic

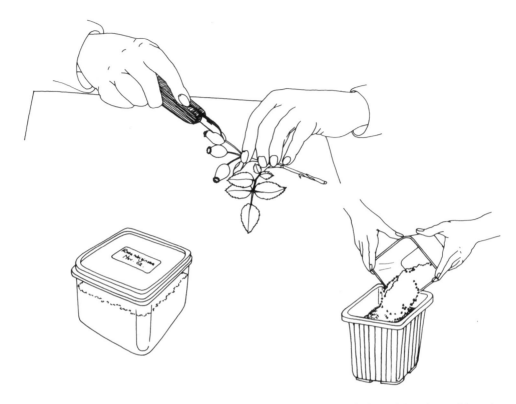

Figure 75. Rose seeds are removed from the hips by hand and weathered after mixing them with moist grit, perlite, or vermiculite. Few, if any, will germinate before the second spring and many not till the third. A transparent plastic box provides a suitably robust container in which to weather seeds for such long periods. It should be opened from time to time to check the seeds and ensure the mixture remains moist. When seedlings begin to emerge, tip the contents of the box out to form the topping above a base of potting mix in a container, or use it to fill a drill drawn out in a nursery bed.

relationships with bacteria and fungi. The inclusion in the potting mix of an innoculum of partially sterilised or unsterilised loam (or the addition of a commercial product containing mycorrhizal fungi) can transform the health of young plants in containers, their resistance to undesirable pathogens, and rates of development.

Shrubs from similar habitats often share similar germination responses, and the germination responses of shrubs from a variety of natural habitats are summarised in the box on pp. 280–281.

There are very many exceptions, notably amongst members of the pea family, with hard, impervious seed coats. These usually germinate when chipped or treated with boiling or hot water without any further treatment.

Small numbers of seedlings are produced by sowing shrub seed and treating the seedlings in similar ways to those described earlier in the book for perennial plants. They are pricked out or potted on individually, depending on their size, as soon as that is practicable, and they are grown on till large enough to line out in nursery beds or plant in the garden. Even hardy shrubs are likely to benefit from and repay the extra protection provided by glasshouses, poly tunnels or cold frames, which greatly increase the speed at which seedlings develop.

Sowing seeds in nursery beds

Large numbers are produced by raising seedlings in similar ways to those used for trees in nursery beds out of doors. (For further details, see pp. 331–332.) Seedlings raised in this way are directly exposed to the natural climatic events of the place where they are being grown, and obvious precautions need to be observed. Tender species are not sown without protection in areas with cold winters. Water must be available and effectively used in order to grow seedlings in drought-prone situations. Shading is necessary to protect seedlings, especially those from forest or woodland habitats, from excessive sunlight.

The effects of fire may have to be reproduced, either by treating the seeds with smoke before sowing them or by laying a loose layer of straw and/or fine brushwood over the beds after the seeds have been sown and setting it alight. Burns engendered in this way should be short and sharp, exposing the seeds to the smoke and heat of the fire for no more than five minutes. As soon as the fire is over, the beds should be watered thoroughly to wash aromatic combustion components down to the seeds and provide the moist seedbed conditions needed to encourage germination.

Soils with a low phosphate content are essential for successfully growing seedlings of many species from the South African fynbos or Western Australian kwongan. *Phytophthora*-free soils and water supplies are essential when growing a wide range of shrubby species, especially members of the protea family and many other southern hemisphere species.

Examples of shrubs grown from seed

Banksia and *Protea* spp. are sown in 1 litre (6 in.) containers in spring or early autumn (in Mediter-

ranea). Use coarse grit, perlite or calcined clay for the topping and [bark, peat, coir] : [grit, perlite], 1:3, for the base. Optimum temperatures are about 25°C (75°F) by day falling to 10° to 15°C (50° to 60°F) at night. Prick out seedlings as soon as they can be handled into 7 cm (2.5 in.) containers using the same mix as the base layer, with no added fertiliser of any kind. Nutrients contained in the seeds of these species are said to be sufficient to maintain the seedlings for a year. While this may not be strictly—or even approximately—true, it is worth taking the hint and being at the very least extremely sparing with the use of fertilisers for the first year and niggardly thereafter. Keep seedlings on the dry side in winter in cool and cold temperate regions, watering only when the surface layer of substrate has dried out, and ensure ample ventilation and air movement. Supplementary light for four hours around midday increases survival rates of seedlings in high latitudes. Grow under frost-free conditions for at least the first two years.

Carmichaelia spp. pods do not open as they mature, but the seeds fall through them to leave a hole. Soak seeds in hot water or chip them and leave them in a humid atmosphere for 24 hours before sowing. Sow in late winter or early spring at 20° to 25°C (70° to 75°F) by day falling to 10° to 15°C (50° to 60°F) by night. Prick the seedlings out individually into 7 cm (2.5 in.) containers as soon as possible after the radicles emerge; subsequent growth of the roots can be extremely rapid. Seedlings are leafy for the first year or so and become broomlike later.

Daphne spp. hybrids and cvs. seed production varies among species and the locations where they are grown. Some species, such as *D. odorata,* are dioecious. Individual plants of others may produce predominantly male or female flowers. Suitable pollinators may be absent; daphnes have a long, narrow calyx tube that is accessible only to small insects or those with long mouth parts, and yields of seed can be increased by hand-pollination. Low temperatures can lead to abortion shortly after fertilisation of the ovules of early flowering species; this can be prevented by hous-

A guide to the conditions under which seeds of shrubs from different natural habitats produce seedlings

Heathland communities on mountains or at high latitudes

Many evergreen, low-growing or prostrate shrubs produce succulent fruits. Seeds mature during late summer and early autumn just before the onset of winter when soil temperatures have started to fall. Examples include *Calluna, Cassinia, Cassiope, Coprosma, Daphne, Empetrum, Epacris, Gaultheria, Hakea, Hebe, Olearia, Philesia, Phyllodoce, Potentilla, Rhododendron, Richea* and *Vaccinium*. Seeds are likely to respond to weathering treatments involving exposure to low temperatures (about 1° to 5°C, or 35° to 40°F) for periods of one or three months. Some germinate spontaneously between 15° to 20°C (60° to 70°F) whether sown fresh or in the spring.

Shrubs of deciduous or mixed woodland

Evergreen or deciduous shrubs flower during spring or very early summer—the latter often displaying early bud break in spring. Fruits mature during the summer when the soil is moderately warm and more or less moist, but the overhead leaf canopy is at its most dense and conditions are unfavourable for the survival of seedlings. Examples include *Berberidopsis, Berberis, Chaenomeles, Cornus, Daphne, Exochorda, Forsythia, Fothergilla, Hedera, Holodiscus, Jasminum, Kalmia, Lapageria, Ligustrum, Lonicera, Parthenocissus, Philadelphus, Pieris, Ruscus, Skimmia, Symphoricarpos, Symplocos* and *Viburnum*. Seed success is highly likely to depend on weathering treatments. Many require warmth (of approximately 15° to 20°C, or 60° to 70°F) for several weeks, followed by low temperatures (of approximately 1°to 5°C, or 35° to 40°F) for six to eight weeks; they germinate naturally as temperatures start to rise in early spring. Without the preliminary warm weathering, seedlings may not appear till the second spring. Organic substrates are likely to provide more successful growing media than mineral ones.

Scrub in open situations in cool and cold temperate areas

Scrub grows on impoverished, free-draining soils or acid, waterlogged ground. A high proportion of these shrubs are deciduous. Flowers are produced during the summer, and seeds are shed while soil temperatures remain moderate to high. Examples include *Berberis, Buddleja, Cornus, Corylus, Cotinus, Cotoneaster, Cytisus, Discaria, Genista, Mulinum, Mutisia, Myrica, Perovskia, Pyracantha, Rhamnus, Rosa, Rubus, Salix, Syringa, Ulex, Viburnum*, and many genera in the pea family. Some germinate spontaneously when sown fresh or in spring at temperatures of from 15° to 25°C (60° to 75°F); others respond to cold weathering. Many, particularly those in the pea family, respond to chipping or hot

ing the plants in a glasshouse. Pollination failures due to self-sterility, pollen sterility or ploidy effects also reduce seed yields. Self-sterility is a major cause of failure in cultivation, because many species have a very narrow genetic base—sometimes every plant is a descendant of a single founder. Berries are collected as soon as they ripen; seeds may germinate better from berries harvested just before they ripen. The fleshy pericarp is removed, preferably by hand, wearing gloves as a protection against toxic compounds in cell sap. Sow seeds as soon as possible and weather. Many species need warm followed by cold weathering, after which seedlings emerge late water treatment. Some, including roses, combine hard seed coats with requirements for warm and cold weathering. Free-draining, mineral substrates reduce losses from damping-off. Root development occurs immediately after the radicles emerge and can be extremely vigorous, and seedlings may need to be pricked out within a few days of germination.

Mediterranean or other seasonally dry communities

Shrubs are almost invariably evergreen. They are tolerant of light frosts but likely to be killed by severe ones. Flowers are produced during winter or in spring, and seeds mature during early summer/summer at the start of or during the dry season. High soil temperatures inhibit germination. Fire is a major environmental factor in most areas, and the release of seeds and germination responses may depend on it. Examples include *Acacia, Arctostaphylos, Banksia, Boronia, Callistemon, Carpenteria, Ceanothus, Cistus, Erica, Garrya, Grevillea, Lavandula, Leucadendron, Paliurus, Phlomis, Pimelea, Psoralea, Rosmarinus, Salvia, Solanum, Spartium, Sutherlandia, Thymus, Verticordia, Vitex* and *Zauschneria*. Many species display after-ripening responses and fail to germinate or do so only at low temperatures (10° to 15°C, or 50° to 60°F) when sown fresh. Most germinate spontaneously at moderate temperatures (up to 25°C, or 75°F) after dry storage for a month or so. Seeds from serotinous fruits usually germinate spontaneously at moderate temperatures. Smoke treatment increases germination rates of many species—also chipping, particularly for species in the pea, mint and cistus families. Species from southern Africa and Western Australia are sensitive to phosphate, and levels used should be extremely low. They are also vulnerable to pathogens that cause damping-off, and seeds should be sown only on mineral substrates.

Shrubs of mild or warm temperate evergreen forests

Evergreen, with little tolerance to frosts, a high proportion is likely to produce succulent fruits. Flowers may be produced at almost any season with a correspondingly wide distribution in times when fruits mature. Plant-to-plant competition is much more significant that climatic hazards. Examples include *Alberta, Azara, Carissa, Clianthus, Coprosma, Dombeya, Dracophyllum, Freycinetia, Hebe, Macropiper, Mitraria, Olearia, Pandorea, Pittosporum, Pseudopanax, Solanum, Telopea, Thunbergia* and *Tibouchina*. Many species germinate spontaneously at temperatures from 15° to 30°C (60° to 85°F) when sown fresh or after storage. With some exceptions, including dracophyllums, organic, humus-rich substrates are likely to be more successful than mineral ones.

the following winter or in early spring. Seeds sown too late to experience preliminary warm weathering are unlikely to germinate until the second spring. Daphne seeds deteriorate rapidly in warm, moist situations, but they can be dried and stored at subzero temperatures in orthodox storage conditions. Nevertheless, stored seeds are likely to produce seedlings slowly and erratically, compared to seeds sown fresh.

Dracophyllum spp. cuttings are seldom successful, apart from *D. recurvum*, and other species are better raised from seed. Sow, using a mineral topping, and germinate at 15° to 20°C (60° to 70°F), fresh if possible. If not, prevent drying out by storing on moist paper towel in a plastic box in a refrigerator. Prick out and pot on into a free-draining potting mix—loam : [grit, calcined clay], 1:2. Seedlings grow slowly and are vulnerable to smothering by mosses and liverworts. Apart from developing slowly, seedlings tend to die erratically for no obvious reason, so that the numbers in a batch decline as time goes by.

Erica spp., or Cape heath, flowering shoots are removed after the flowers have faded; strip off as many leaves as possible without damaging the dead flower heads, before drying them in open trays or loosely packed in paper bags till the seeds are released. Avoid contaminating the seeds with broken bits of leaf and other plant parts. Sow from autumn to early winter in warm temperate regions and Mediterranea, and in spring elsewhere, on an acidic grit topping above a well-drained, predominantly mineral base—organic : mineral, 1:3—with an innoculum of partially sterilised loam to provide fungal symbionts. Seeds usually germinate freely, and success rates can be further improved by smoke treatment. Use new, previously unused containers when sowing, pricking out and growing on the seedlings. Water with clean rainwater, keeping the containers consistently moist, but not overwatered. Shade the containers after sowing, and maintain shading until the seedlings are well established, before gradually bringing them into full sunlight. Early growth is very slow, likely to be two to three months before the seedlings are big enough to prick out when 1 to 2 cm (0.5 to 1 in.) high. Avoid artificial fertilisers entirely or use them sparingly in extremely dilute form. Pot up individually into small containers. Nip out tips of plants to encourage bushy growth. Plant out when seedlings are about 6 to 9 cm (2.5 to 3.5 in.) high.

Grevillea spp. and cvs. capsules containing a few large seeds are often produced by only a few flowers in a cluster, depending on the species. The small, oval or purse-shaped capsules, with persistent styles, often open while still green, and repeated visits are needed to make collections successfully. *Grevillea* seed has a reputation for erratic germination at best. Seed coats, though thin, are tough, but they germinate without special treatment—if at all. Hit-and-miss results can be reduced by ensuring seeds are viable by removing seed coats from one or two, whose contents should be ivory white and firm, not yellowish; soaking seeds in warm water for 24 hours, stirring occasionally, discarding seeds that remain floating; and treating with smoke. Sow thinly in a grit or perlite topping over a mainly mineral potting mix—such as [peat, bark] : [perlite, calcined clay], 1:3. Water thoroughly after sowing, and then maintain moist, well-aerated conditions in the vicinity of the seeds, ensuring that they never dry out. High temperatures (20°C, or 70°F, or higher), especially at night, tend to inhibit germination.

Leptospermum spp. and cvs. seeds, sown in late winter/early spring, between 15° to 25°C (60° to 75°F), germinate freely. Some species respond positively to the bog method. Prick out as soon as the seedlings grow large enough to handle. Pinch out the tips when they are 3 to 4 cm (1.5 in.) tall to encourage bushy growth. Large numbers of seedlings can be raised in nursery beds. Cut off complete flowering shoots as the seed capsules mature, and lay them crisscross in two or three layers over a completely weed-free bed with a finely raked, level surface. Seeds fall from the capsules as they dry out onto the surface of the bed. The dying leaves also drop off and act as a light mulch, and the crisscross of stems provides shelter and a little shade for the developing seedlings.

Rhododendron spp. and cvs. seeds are effective in propagating deciduous species in situations where their inclination to hybridise is acceptable. It is a less rewarding way to propagate large-flowered hybrids and evergreen azaleas. Seeds mature in capsules while the latter are still green from late winter till spring. Capsules can be collected green and split open manually or left till they start to open naturally, and then put in a warm, dry room to dry thoroughly and release the seeds. Early collections, if sown immediately, enable seedlings to make maximum growth and development in their first year. Seeds store well under orthodox conditions. Sow on a topping of finely sieved [peat, bark] : [sand, grit] over a lime-free potting mix or on sphagnum moss under mist. Place in cool, shaded conditions with maximum temperatures held below 15°C (60°F) if possible. Seedlings are intolerant of high fertiliser levels; use attenuated, lime-free potting mixes and dilute liquid feeds. Prick out when seedlings have produced a third or fourth true leaf. Growth during the first year is very slow, and dilute potassium permanganate should be used to suppress the growth of mosses and liverworts.

Telopea spp. inflorescences consist of many flowers, amongst which a small minority produce the relatively large seed capsules that open when mature to release numerous straw-coloured, winged seeds. Sow fresh just below the surface at about 20° to 25°C (70° to 75°F). Unlike many proteaceous plants, fluctuating temperatures are not essential for germination. Soak seeds in fungicide before sowing to reduce losses from damping-off. Pot up individually as soon as seedlings can be handled in 9 cm (3.5 in.) containers. Spray seedlings regularly with fungicide to maintain protection against damping-off organisms. Avoid potting mixes containing artificial fertilisers for young seedlings, and feed older ones very sparingly. Telopeas are not thought to form symbiotic fungal associations, but like other proteas, they produce special scavenging roots, known as proteoid roots. These develop only in low-nutrient status growth media.

Viburnum spp. and cvs. produce flowers followed by clusters of single-seeded, rather dry drupes in autumn. Under natural conditions, seedlings seldom appear until the second spring, although radicals may be produced during the first spring. Collect and clean the fruits before sowing. Either sow in the standard way and expose to natural warm weathering, followed by cold weathering, or mix the seeds with moist vermiculite in a plastic box and place in a propagator at approximately 20°C (70°F) for six to eight weeks, followed by a similar period in a refrigerator. Alternatively, seed collected from green drupes may germinate without being weathered.

Seedlings may appear during the first spring. If not, stand the containers out of doors to experience natural cycles of weathering.

Viscum album, or mistletoe, is one of a small number of parasitic shrubs that grow epiphytically on trees and tap into the sap-conducting tissues of the trees themselves. The plants are dioecious, pollinated by flies, and the females produce berries only when male plants are growing nearby. The flat, greenish-grey seeds are enveloped in sticky gum (viscin) within the berries. Pick the berries. Those freshly harvested in late mid-winter, rather than the dried remnants of Christmas boughs, give the best results. Do not clean the berries, but squash those containing the seeds against the shaded underside of a vigorously growing young shoot to deposit the seed onto the bark. Apples, poplars, willows and hawthorns all make good hosts. The seeds first become green, and then in early summer radicles emerge, equipped with discs at their tips which press against the bark. No further growth occurs till the following year. Meanwhile, the bark of the tree grows around the disc and secures the seedling firmly in place. A small outgrowth from the disc penetrates the underlying bark during the winter to establish contact with the cambial layers of the host tree, followed by the emergence of cotyledons during the second spring and the development during the summer of two true leaves. Two short branches, each bearing two leaves, are produced during the third season, and thereafter further branches, each bearing two leaves, develop year by year.

Propagation from Cuttings

It is very difficult to define exactly why one shoot makes successful cuttings while another similar shoot is a poor prospect. Common sense, aided by experience, is the best guide to choosing shoots from which to make cuttings. If that is not much help to the beginner, it might be comforting to learn that cuttings of many plants produce roots so easily that success is much more likely than failure, almost irrespective of the precise condition of the shoots used.

Cuttings are made from shoots at almost any stage of development during their first year. Shoots more than a year old are much less likely to produce roots and are used only for a very few plants. Cuttings made from shoots at successive stages of development are customarily described as "tip cuttings" when made from shoots in the earliest stage of development and only traces of woody tissues are present. Semi-mature cuttings are made from shoots described as "firming towards the base," in which developing woody tissues can be felt throughout the lower half to two-thirds of their length. Mature or hardwood cuttings are made from shoots with fully developed woody tissues throughout their length. Apart from the shoot's maturity, other considerations must be taken into account when choosing shoots to use as cuttings.

Avoid misshapen or diseased shoots. This is an obvious and sensible rule to follow, although plants raised from hardwood cuttings from rose bushes stripped of their leaves by blackspot will be neither more nor less susceptible to the disease than those taken from plants sprayed weekly to suppress all signs of infection. Some willows are deliberately grown for their unusually thickened and distorted forms.

Use short-jointed, compact shoots in preference to elongated ones. However, there is little reason to suppose this is a rational preference, and some evidence shows that etiolated shoots are more likely to produce roots than compact ones grown at high light intensities. Avoid weak or spindly shoots and those with exceptional vigour. There is more than a suspicion that gardeners choose shoots that display a normal or average degree of vigour, not because experience has shown that they make better cuttings but because the middle way seems safer and produces nice, even-looking batches of cuttings. Nevertheless, it is easier to set up and care for batches of evenly formed shoots than mixtures of shapes and sizes.

Avoid flowering shoots. However, when other material is in short supply, these are not a forlorn hope and can be used. Any flowers and buds should be removed as the cuttings are made.

It is often taken for granted that for each and every shrub there is a season to take cuttings, and the key to success lies in knowing what that season is; occasionally, that is so. For example, the shoots of *Syringa vulgaris* cvs. produce roots only when taken at a precise stage of development that happens to coincide with the time the flowers are fully out. Shoots of *Cotinus coggygria* produce roots for a period of only a few days at a certain critical stage as the very soft, immature shoots begin to develop the first traces of woody tissues. Such precision is rare. More often, choosing which shoots to use depends on a combination of the plant's ability to produce shoots and the convenience, skills, and facilities available to the gardener.

The shoot's capacity to produce roots is only occasionally a critical limiting factor. Usually, a particular shrub can be propagated from cuttings with more or less equal chances of success from shoots at different stages of development. Only a few, such as lilacs and cotinus, demand close attention to timing. Immature shoots require much more TLC than more mature ones and put correspondingly greater demands on skill. Some types of cuttings make minimal demands on the gardener or equipment, while success with others depends on the availability of well-equipped and endowed propagation facilities.

Lavenders—*Lavandula* cvs.—for example, can be propagated from cuttings at any stage of development, and the method used depends largely on the gardener's circumstances, needs and opportunities.

- *Tip cuttings* are available in large numbers, from bought plants, if necessary. They produce the highest success rates in the minimum time. They produce roots in late spring/early summer with a long growing season ahead of them, during which they are easily trained into compact, bushy plants. But tip cuttings can be produced successfully only when a closed frame or propagator is available—preferably within a glasshouse or poly tunnel—and supplementary heat is desirable.

- *Semi-mature cuttings* give high success rates and produce roots in late summer, making little growth before winter, but they grow on well the following summer. They are likely available only in small numbers because almost every shoot on many kinds of lavenders produces flowers. They require at least a tunnel cloche and preferably the protection of a closed frame for success.

- *Mature cuttings* are available in quantity from early-flowering cultivars but may be hard to find on late-flowering kinds. They can be produced in the open, with the minimum of equipment and make very small demands on time. They produce variable results from one year to another and almost total failures in bad years and tend to produce less shapely, more straggly plants than other cuttings.

Lavenders have been traditionally raised from mature cuttings, and despite drawbacks it remains the best option for those with minimal facilities and little time. Success rates can be greatly improved by the use of tunnel cloches or poly tunnels. When a frame or glasshouse is available, and some attention can be paid to them, tip cuttings provide by far the best way to produce lavenders from cuttings. It is also worth remembering many lavender cultivars reproduce almost true from seed, and this option is well worth consideration. Similar considerations affect the times when cuttings can be taken and the methods chosen to propagate many other shrubs.

Tip cuttings

Gardeners in cool or cold temperate regions are familiar with the way shrubs burst into growth in spring; those who garden in Mediterranea observe a very similar reawakening as temperatures fall and autumn rains relieve the summer drought. These shoots are soft, extremely vulnerable to desiccation, and dependent on warmth and moisture

for survival. However, because they are growing so rapidly, their cells are dividing actively and they are capable of producing roots rapidly when used as cuttings.

- Make nodal or basal cuttings by cutting off 3 to 5 cm (1.25 to 2 in.) long tips of actively growing shoots, choosing those that are just beginning to firm up.
- Keep the cuttings in polythene bags until ready to prepare and insert them.
- Stick them into a 1:1 cutting mix of grit : perlite in small containers, and put them under mist or on a warm bench under polythene or in a propagator, at 20° to 25°C (70° to 75°F).
- Unless under mist, drench with a fine spray of water to settle them in, and enclose them to maintain a saturated atmosphere.
- Roots are produced extremely quickly—in as little as a fortnight for rapid responders such as abelias and fuchsias.
- When the first roots appear, drench with liquid feed (at two times the standard rate).
- Then wean by gradually increasing ventilation till the rooted cuttings are able to stand on their own without the protection of mist or polythene.
- Pot up individually and grow on in a warm, well-lit situation.

The immature shoots used as tip cuttings contain no storage reserves. They can support new growth only by using sunlight as a source of energy, but they cannot endure exposure to direct sunlight. A careful balance must be struck between excessive and inadequate sunlight. Use a light-diffusing material such as bubble polythene to provide high light intensities without exposure to direct sunlight and consequent overheating within the enclosed containers.

Tip cuttings are more delicate than those made from more mature shoots. Short periods of neglect or inattention lead to disasters. Consequently, they are usually used to propagate shrubs less easily propagated in other ways or to produce plants rapidly for summer display and other special purposes.

Chart 19. PROPAGATING SHRUBS FROM CUTTINGS

| Mid-Spring | Late Spring | Early Summer | Mid-Summer | Late Summer | Early–Mid-Autumn |

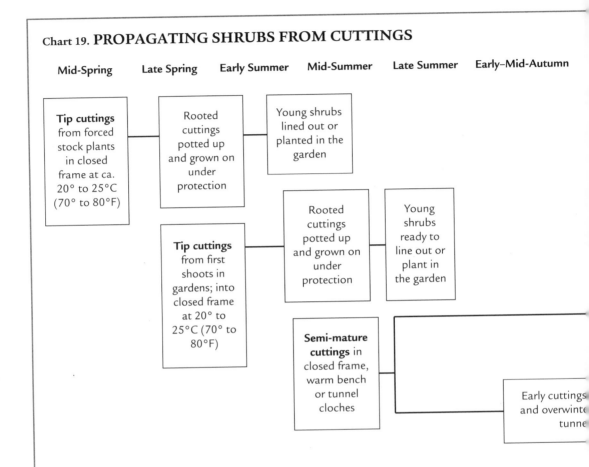

Options for Raising Shrubs from Cuttings

- **Tip cuttings** are made from immature shoots which have scarcely begun to develop woody elements. When a very early start is wanted, stock plants can be brought on in a glasshouse. Alternatively, shoots are taken from early growth in the garden.
- **Semi-mature cuttings** are made during the summer from shoots just past the first flush of growth. Those that are taken early and have produced roots by mid-autumn are potted up before the winter. Later cuttings will survive winter weather better in cold climates when left crowded in their containers till late winter or early spring.
- **Mature or hardwood cuttings** taken at the end of the growing season can either be made in autumn or left till spring. In places with mild winters, mature cuttings of evergreen shrubs should be made in autumn.

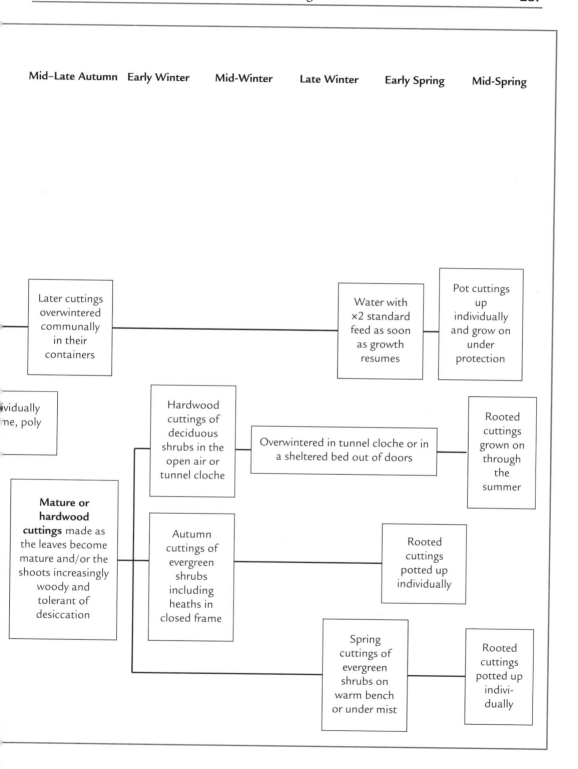

Mid–Late Autumn   Early Winter   Mid-Winter   Late Winter   Early Spring   Mid-Spring

Later cuttings overwintered communally in their containers

Water with ×2 standard feed as soon as growth resumes

Pot cuttings up individually and grow on under protection

ividually
ne, poly

Hardwood cuttings of deciduous shrubs in the open air or tunnel cloche

Overwintered in tunnel cloche or in a sheltered bed out of doors

Rooted cuttings grown on through the summer

Mature or hardwood cuttings made as the leaves become mature and/or the shoots increasingly woody and tolerant of desiccation

Autumn cuttings of evergreen shrubs including heaths in closed frame

Rooted cuttings potted up individually

Spring cuttings of evergreen shrubs on warm bench or under mist

Rooted cuttings potted up indivi-dually

Figure 76. Part of a large lavender plant showing three or four young shoots in spring. These are at the right stage to make into tip cuttings before they produce flowers. Narrow-leaved, silver-foliaged shrubs such as lavenders and rosemaries resent enclosure in humid atmospheres and should be exposed to more ventilation than softer cuttings of broad-leaved shrubs such as fuchsias.

Figure 77. Cuttings of shrubs set up in moderately large containers. The one in the foreground contains cuttings of two different hebes. Setting up different kinds of cuttings in the same container works only if both produce roots more or less at the same time. Otherwise, it is better to set out each kind in a separate container, where they can be treated according to their individual progress and needs.

Semi-mature cuttings

Mid-summer to early autumn is the bonanza season for taking cuttings of shrubs in cool and cold temperate regions of the world. Shoots are cut off when they have almost finished elongating but are still immature with a built-in capacity for renewed, regenerative growth. Use shoots 5 to 10 cm (2 to 4 in.) long, depending on the shrub involved. They can be nodal, basal or heel cuttings (it is seldom necessary to be too particular about which); convenience and the nature of the material usually governs the choice. Generally speaking, cuttings taken at this time produce good results with fewer demands on the propagator than tip cuttings, because their more fully developed leaves and stem tissues are less dependent on constant, skillful care; ambient temperatures are higher; and artificial warmth is not necessary in order to promote root formation. Simple equipment can be used to provide conditions that will keep cuttings alive and enable them to produce roots.

Only the gardener can decide how much care and attention can be spared to look after cuttings and the method most appropriate to his or her situation. Those whose activities are likely to be limited by time available and commitments that make it impossible to be at hand during most days, with periodic absences on holiday, may have to adapt their methods accordingly.

Tunnel cloches, propagators or frames can be adapted to require minimum input when time is short by setting up the cuttings in the usual way, thoroughly drenching cuttings and substrate with water, and then shading heavily so they receive only diffuse sunlight. In frames, an internal layer of polythene just above the cuttings and below the lights can be used to reinforce the effect. The space around the leaves of the cuttings remains saturated for three or four weeks, without further attention. Grown cool and shaded like this, the cuttings will eventually produce roots; they do so more slowly than when exposed to more light and warmth, but they need so little attention that their caretaker's absence for a fortnight or so passes unnoticed.

Equipment	Advantages	Disadvantages
Tunnel cloche	Ideal when large numbers of cuttings of species that readily produce roots are needed. Requires little attention.	Less suitable for numerous small batches of different subjects. Careful attention to siting and shading are crucial for successful operation.
Shaded sun frame	Low cost, high capacity, flexible in use. Can be heavily shaded to work well with very little attention but with relatively low output.	Most productive when only lightly shaded, but careful attention to watering is needed to keep cuttings alive and functioning actively.
Propagator	Economical and convenient for small numbers of cuttings. Flexible, easily sited and effective. The number of units readily matched to cuttings available.	Small capacity. Liable to overheat in sunshine unless carefully sited and shaded.
Warm bench under polythene	Economical alternative to mist unit. Usually as effective even with difficult subjects, and with fewer potential problems.	Not flexible. Most suitable for relatively large numbers of cuttings. To work well, a large section needs to be set up in one go.
Mist propagation unit	Potentially effective and flexible while making few demands on time. High outputs are possible due to the speed with which roots are produced.	High initial cost. Economical only for high-output situations. Not fail-safe; failures of control systems can lead to serious losses.

Table 2. Advantages and disadvantages of equipment available to propagate shrubs from semi-mature cuttings

When more time is available for regular attention, cuttings are set up with less shading and greater exposure to the light and warmth of sunshine. Roots are produced rapidly, but the cuttings need more care and attention. They dry out more rapidly and in hot, sunny weather may need overhead sprays of water several times a day. If a mist unit is not available, this must be done by hand. When a mist unit is available, it reduces time spent looking after the cuttings and can also be used to produce "instant" large plants from oversized cuttings 20 to 30 cm (8 to 10 in.) long

Figure 78. *Banksia* cuttings potted up individually into 7 cm (2.5 in.) pots, into a 1:1 mix of bark : perlite. These plants require excellent drainage and minimum levels of nutrients until well established.

or more. Shoots of pyracanthas, potentillas, ceanothus, philadelphus and many others can be left on the mother plant to grow on till early autumn instead of removing them when quite small in mid-summer. Cuttings taken in this way at the end of the summer produce roots during the winter and are potted up in late winter, early spring. They are ready to plant in the garden during the summer.

Insuring against losses of tender and short-lived shrubs

Most gardeners dice with death, deliberately growing plants they know to be on the borderline of hardiness for their conditions. These and others with no hope of survival during the winter are grown to enhance summer displays and can be safeguarded by propagating them from cuttings taken during the autumn.

Penstemons, marguerites, hebes, felicias, fuchsias, lantanas, tagetes and tibouchinas are a few of the more widely grown shrubs propagated in this way, but depending on the location of the garden and the opportunities and hazards of its situation, a huge number of tender and semi-tender plants may be involved. The tissues of the shoots used to make these cuttings verge on the mature, and at a season when the heat of summer is past and levels of sunshine are declining, the combination of more self-sufficient tissues and less stressful conditions means that the cuttings are more tolerant of desiccation than more tender shoots at earlier stages of development.

- Cut off conveniently sized shoots and remove the lower leaves and any flowers or flower buds.
- Stick them into cutting mix in 1 litre (6 in.) containers with 9 to 16 cuttings in each.
- Set them up on a bench in a glasshouse or in a poly tunnel and water them to saturate the cutting mix.
- Protect them in an enclosed atmosphere under a light-diffusing canopy.
- Spray lightly, if necessary, to prevent wilting.
- After a few days, start to provide a little more ventilation, applying sprays of water judiciously to keep the cuttings upright and turgid.
- Eventually, the cuttings should require no more protection than a sheet of bubble polythene set up as an overhead canopy and open at the sides.
- Speed is not of the essence. As long as ambient temperatures do not fall below about 10°C (50°F), supplementary heat is not necessary. In cold climates, soil heating cables are used to prevent temperatures falling below 5°C (40°F) during the winter. In warmer locations, these temperatures will be held without recourse to artificial heat.
- Roots are produced during late autumn and early winter, and the cuttings are left undisturbed in their containers during the coldest, darkest days of winter.
- Keep the rooted cuttings as dry as possible, short of wilting, and water only when absolutely necessary in the morning on sunlit days, so that the foliage dries out by nightfall.
- Pot up individually into 9 cm (3.5 in.) containers in late winter/early spring and grow on at about 15° to 20°C (60° to 70°F).
- Pot on into 1.5 to 2 litre (8 in.) pots, and a short time afterwards stand the plants out protected

Options available when propagating evergreen shrubs from mature cuttings

The fundamental choice lies between taking cuttings before or after winter. Cuttings of tender or borderline hardy shrubs should be taken before winter in cold locations in order to ensure their survival. Otherwise, the choice depends on what is most convenient and what facilities are available.

Cuttings taken in late autumn/early winter
Line out cuttings in a sheltered nursery bed. This method is likely to be successful only with the toughest shoots that are well protected against desiccation. It is recommended only in warm temperate regions and Mediterranea and for hardy evergreens in mild temperate regions. For most evergreen shrubs in mild temperate regions and in Mediterranea, and for hardy evergreens in cool and cold temperate regions, cuttings are lined out in a polythene tunnel cloche or set up in a cold frame. This is an economical and effective method. They can also be set up in a frame in a glasshouse. Soil heating cables are used to maintain frost-free conditions, at a minimum of about 5°C (40°F) if necessary, which is recommended for all evergreen shrubs in cool and cold temperate regions.

Cuttings taken in late winter/early spring
Set up under mist or on a warm bench in a glasshouse or poly tunnel, using soil heating cables to maintain minimum temperatures of 15° to 20°C (60° to 70°F) at the base of the cuttings. This is recommended for any evergreen shrub in mild or warm temperate regions and for those hardy enough to survive winters in cool and cold temperate regions.

from frost, if necessary, by cold frames until they are large enough and the weather is mild enough to plant them in the garden.

Mature cuttings

Hardwood cuttings provide one of the easiest means of propagation, even for those hard-pressed for time and unconfident of their skills. There are major differences in the treatment of deciduous and evergreen shrubs. Deciduous shrubs lose their leaves, enter a resting period, resume growth only when buds break in the spring, and are mostly extremely frost tolerant. Evergreen shrubs retain their leaves, remain photosynthetically active, can grow during the winter, and are at best moderately frost tolerant. These differences define the ways cuttings of mature shoots are used to propagate these plants.

Deciduous shrubs and vines
By the autumn, shoots have developed fully formed woody tissues, their cells are filled with starch and other storage compounds and their leaves fall. They may not look promising as material from which to make cuttings, but beneath their inactive exteriors, their meristematic tissues are ready to support renewed growth when spring comes and mobilise the hidden totipotency of their cells to create the roots they will need to survive.

Cuttings made from them are almost unaffected by desiccation and forgiving of treatment that would lead to the rapid collapse of more ten-

Figure 79. Shoots produced during the summer by argyranthemums and other tender or dubiously hardy plants are used to make cuttings in autumn as an insurance against losses during the winter.

Figure 80. *Argyranthemum* cuttings taken during the early autumn. These will produce roots before the onset of winter but in cold climates they should not be potted up individually till spring. They survive cold weather better crowded together in their containers and kept as dry as possible short of dehydration.

der tissues. The storage reserves packed away in their cells provide them with the self-sufficiency needed to survive and prosper with minimal demands on the gardener's time or attention.

The best shoots to use are vigorous, straight shoots produced during the current growing season, of the kind which appear spontaneously after shrubs have been cut back hard. These are produced in the normal course of cultivation by plants such as bush roses, black currants and buddlejas, which are pruned hard each spring to maintain their shape and flower power. They can be obtained from many other shrubs by anticipating the need and pruning them back in a similar way during the preceding winter; alternatively, shrubs will sometimes respond to a heavy dressing of fertiliser sprinkled round their roots during the previous spring. Young plants still making vigorous growth usually provide the best material.

Hardwood cuttings of deciduous trees and shrubs have, by long tradition, been taken throughout the winter. However, the best results are obtained when cuttings are made either immediately after leaf fall in late autumn/early winter or just before the buds resume growth in spring. These leafless shoots do not need enclosed atmospheres but are lined out in a sheltered nursery bed while they produce roots.

- Cut off strong, young shoots as close as possible to the junction with more mature wood.
- Remove and discard the tips of the shoots with less firmly developed woody tissues.
- Cut the remainder into sections of about 10 to 20 cm (4 to 8 in.) long, each with about four buds. A cluster of buds is often located at the base of the shoot, and their presence improves prospects of root formation.
- Wound the cuttings by removing a sliver of

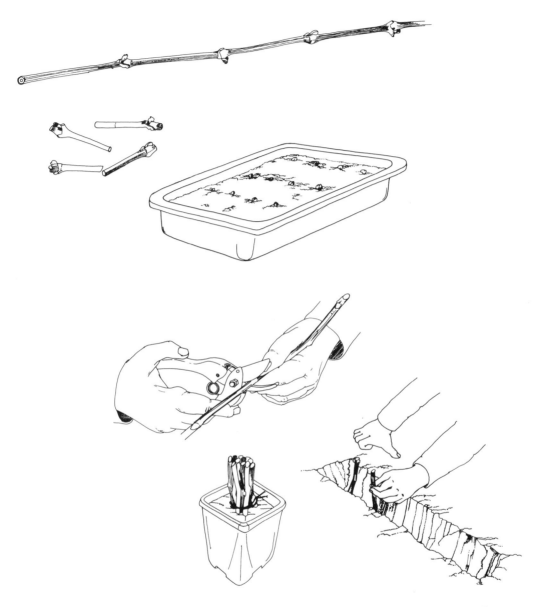

Figure 81. Vines are propagated from single-bud cuttings made by cutting rods into sections, each containing one bud. These are set out, secured by a short length of stem, almost on the surface of potting mix in a tray on a glasshouse bench, preferably at 15° to 20°C (60° to 70°F). Alternatively, vines and many deciduous shrubs are propagated from sections of stem, each with three or four buds, set out in a trench in a sheltered part of the garden. In cold situations or with less hardy plants, better results are obtained by bundling the cuttings and holding them in pots filled with cutting mix for a period of several weeks—if necessary, until spring—at 10° to 15°C (50° to 60°F) before setting them out in the garden or under a tunnel cloche.

bark from the lowest part of each section, avoiding damage to any buds.

- Cut V-shaped trenches about 10 to 15 cm (4 to 6 in.) deep, and pour a small amount of grit along the bottom.
- Set out the cuttings with their bases lodged in the grit and the uppermost bud of the cutting at or just above the surface.
- Backfill the trenches. The cuttings are left *in situ* throughout the following summer and lifted in the autumn.

This method has the twin advantages of needing no equipment and making minimal demands on care and attention. The disadvantage is that the cuttings are maximally exposed to the weather. Severe weather leads to failures, and exposure to wintry weather of any sort restricts its usefulness to plants hardy enough to survive it. Some protection improves results in cold locations, and when growing less cold-tolerant shrubs, use the following method:

- Either set up the cuttings in exactly the same way within a tunnel cloche, keeping the sides partially open in all but the coldest weather and removing the cover in late winter just before growth starts; or set up the cuttings in 2 or 3 litre (8 in. or 1 gal.) containers or in boxes filled with potting mix : grit, 1:1.
- Insert the cuttings 2 to 3 cm (1 in.) apart with their uppermost buds just above the surface.
- Put the containers in a cold frame, polythene tunnel or unheated glasshouse (for small numbers and less hardy shrubs).
- As soon as shoots start to grow in the spring, pot up individually into 9 cm (3.5 in.) containers.
- They benefit from being grown on with minimum temperatures of 10° to 15°C (50° to 60°F) in a glasshouse if one is available.
- Once they are established, harden off the rooted cuttings and line them out in a nursery bed.

Evergreen shrubs

Shrubs from mild or warm temperate regions and Mediterranea are more likely than not to be evergreen. Their leaves are robust as a protection

against storms and cold, and they remain perennially active, enabling them to respond to warmth and light. They are able to grow and form new organs, such as roots, at any time.

Mature shoots of callistemons, hakeas, grevilleas, dryandras and other evergreen shrubs from dry, arid parts of the world often appear discouragingly hard. Their leaves are narrow and needle-like, or sclerophyllous, with a tough, dry unrewarding feel to them. Their stems lack any signs of succulence. To those accustomed to the softer textures of the shoots of deciduous shrubs, they appear a less than obviously promising material for use as cuttings.

Appearances are deceptive. Most can be propagated from hardwood cuttings without difficulty. Their inherent toughness enables them to survive with less care than more vulnerable shoots. They may take longer to form roots than more obviously amenable shoots. They are more likely to benefit from wounding, and they are much more likely to be less frost tolerant. Decreased resistance to freezing temperatures is the penalty for remaining active throughout the winter.

Single-bud cuttings

A typical shrub cutting consists of a shoot composed of an apical bud and a number of leaves separated by short lengths of stem. It would be almost impossible to handle and set up cuttings of lianes* (climbers, creepers, and vines) if they consisted of three or four pairs of leaves and the attenuated lengths of stem between them. The problem is resolved by abandoning one of the golden rules of propagation—to make all cuts immediately beneath a node. Single-bud cuttings consist of one or a pair of buds attached to a short length of stem, cut off about 2 cm (1 in.) below the node.

*The term *liane* is used in this book to provide a neutral term for plants free from the various connotations raised by the alternatives in different parts of the English-speaking world.

Figure 82. Cuttings, from left to right, of *Elaeagnus ebbingei*, *Choisya ternata*, *Viburnum henryi*, *Hedera helix* and *Pyracantha* 'Orange Glow' all have been cut off immediately below a node and have had their lower leaves removed. The large-leaved *Elaeagnus* and *Viburnum* have had their remaining leaves reduced to facilitate handling. The ivy (*Hedera*) is a mature form, and the cutting, from the fork down, consists of second-year wood. It is unlikely to produce roots. Much longer shoots of *Pyracantha* than the one shown can be made into satisfactory cuttings when mist is available.

Cut the stem 2 or 3 cm (1 in.) below a node. Make a second cut immediately above the node. The result is a neat little cutting composed of a single leaf or pair of leaves, with a piece of stem conveniently providing a peg to stick into the potting mix. The cuttings are then treated like any other. Buds from semi-mature shoots of clematis are treated like other cuttings made from semi-mature shoots. Buds from mature shoots obtained from leafless vine rods in winter are treated like other cuttings made from mature shoots.

Apart from lianes, numerous shrubs can be propagated from single-bud cuttings, but conventional cuttings are easier to handle and produce bigger plants more rapidly—so single-bud cuttings are usually used only when conventional cuttings pose problems (as with mahonias). The clumsy cuttings produced conventionally from their large leaves and substantial shoots are avoided by making each cutting from a single node and then cutting off most of the leaf to reduce its area. Single-bud cuttings are also used

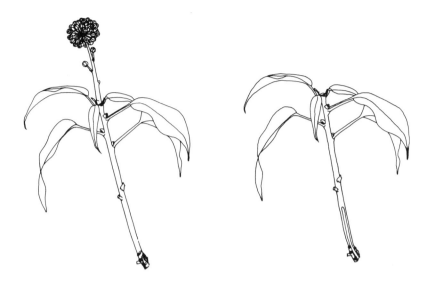

Figure 83. Cuttings made from mature forms of ivies remain mature and are used to produce shrubby versions of the more familiar climbers. They are made in the autumn when every shoot may end in a flower; shoots too weak to produce flowers are unlikely to make satisfactory cuttings. Cut off the shoots at the cluster of buds at their base, remove the flowers, strip off basal leaves, and if necessary reduce leaf areas of those remaining. Wound the base of the cutting by slicing off a sliver of bark and dip into hormone rooting powder. Set out individually in cutting mix in 7 cm (2.5 in.) pots in a cold frame.

when propagating material is limited and maximum numbers of plants are needed. For example, a single shoot of a rose, removed as a conventional hardwood cutting in autumn, provides perhaps four cuttings. The same shoot removed during the late summer would make a dozen or so single-bud cuttings.

Root cuttings

Any shrub that produces suckers is a potential candidate for root cuttings, as are many that do not sucker naturally. However, root cuttings are usually the resort of the propagator who has been unable to propagate a shrub by other means. The shoots of a few shrubs either fail entirely to produce roots or do so erratically and often unsuccessfully. The roots of some of these can be used

to make cuttings with greater prospects of success. Parts of the root closest to the stems are most likely to work satisfactorily, but differences are unlikely to be great and entire roots should normally be used.

- During the winter, dig around an established shrub to expose some of the roots.
- Cut off a few close to their origins, choosing medium-sized roots (for the plant) rather than the thickest or thinnest.
- Cut into sections 7 to 10 cm (3 to 4 in.) long.
- Dip the roots in fungicide.
- Partially fill deep containers with a 1:1 mixture of potting mix : grit.
- Lay out the sections of root horizontally or vertically, and cover with 2 to 3 cm (1 in.) of the mixture of potting mix and grit.

- Shoots almost always precede roots, and roots usually appear adventitiously from the base of the new shoot.
- Pot up the cuttings individually when roots are clearly visible ramifying through the potting mix and grit mixture.

Propagation from juvenile tissues

Plants, like animals, go through a juvenile stage when young prior to the development of flowers. It can be 10 or 20 years before tree seedlings produce their first flowers. Ivies grow for years as lianes; then, after reaching the summit of their ambitions, they change radically, producing short shoots and flowers. Cuttings made from them produce plants that maintain this mature form and grow into shrubs.

The shoots of seedlings of many trees native to New Zealand repeatedly branch and branch again, developing tangles of divaricating stems bearing undistinguished leaves. As they mature, they change to an adult form, and in the process develop trunks and often splendid, broad, glossy foliage. Cuttings taken from mature forms retain their trunks and fine foliage, avoiding the necessity to be patient until ugly duckling seedlings turn into swans.

The terms *juvenile* and *immature* tend to be used indiscriminately—a habit that confuses the different meanings of the two terms. *Juvenile* refers to the phase associated with seedlings typified by the inability to produce flowers or seeds. *Immature* refers to the still-developing or growing tissues of a plant at any stage during its life span. Immature shoots, like juvenile tissues, are generally more likely to produce roots when used as cuttings than mature shoots—but not always. Their soft tissues, vulnerable to desiccation and stress, demand more care and attention than the harder stems and foliage that come with maturity, and unless time and facilities are available to provide the care immature shoots need, mature shoots may be a safer bet for those in search of plants.

Figure 84. Single-bud cuttings of roses are made from actively growing shoots during the summer. Cut off any flowers and the immature ends of the shoots. Then divide the rest of the stems by cutting above and below the nodes to form cuttings comprising short lengths of stem, each with a single leaf.

Examples of shrubs propagated from cuttings

Calluna and *Erica* spp. and cvs. should be trimmed back by shearing off the tips of the shoots as the flowers fade. Numerous shoots are produced, which are used as cuttings as they mature in autumn. Set up a frame in a shaded, sheltered corner. Glaze the framelight with bubble polythene. Partially fill with lime-free potting mix, topped with a 5 cm (2 in.) deep layer of organic : mineral, 1:1, cutting mix. Cut off the ends of the new shoots to make short cuttings 2 to 4 cm (1 to 1.5 in.) long. Set the cuttings out systematically in lines in the frame 2 to 3 cm (1 in.) apart, and carefully label each batch. Do not attempt to remove the leaves on the lower parts of the stems before setting them up. Water thoroughly, drenching the bed of cutting mix. Close the frame. When cuttings are made in autumn and the frame is adequately shaded, no further watering is usually necessary till spring, but water if necessary to ensure the growth medium does not dry out. In very cold

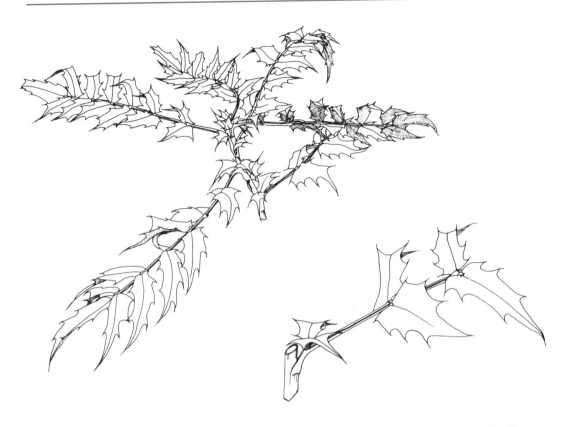

Figure 85. A mahonia shoot is formidably prickly, ungainly and almost impossible to contemplate for use as a cutting. These problems are resolved by making single-bud cuttings consisting of short sections of stem, each with a single leaf. Entire leaves would still be highly unwelcome occupants of the cutting frame and are cut back to the basal two pairs of leaflets to reduce them to a semblance of compliance. Each is set up individually in cutting mix in a 7 cm (2.5 in.) container.

areas, extra protection from frost may be needed. Otherwise, the cuttings are overwintered with just the protection provided by the shelter of the frame. Roots form during late winter. As they do so, the frame lights are progressively opened to provide more ventilation, and the rooted cuttings are fed with a proprietary liquid feed. Pot up the rooted cuttings individually in early summer into 7 cm (2.5 in.) pots, or, preferably, line out in a nursery bed. Conifer cuttings respond to similar treatment, as do cuttings of mature shoots of ever-

green shrubs. In both cases, attention must be paid to the frost tolerance of the species being propagated and arrangements made to protect tender subjects.

Camellia cvs. single-bud cuttings are made from mature shoots of the previous year's growth containing a stem and a single leaf. Wound by removing a sliver of bark, opposite the bud. Reduce leaf areas by cutting transversely across half-way along the midrib. Stick the cuttings into an organic : mineral, 1:1, cutting mix individually in 7 cm (2.5

in.) pots or communally with nine cuttings in a 1 litre (6 in.) pot. Push each down till the base of the leaf is just below the surface of the growth medium. Set up under mist or on a bench and cover with polythene at 20° to 25°C (70° to 75°F). Wean when roots form, and pot up individually if necessary. Grow on in a glasshouse or poly tunnel. Young plants are sensitive to excess fertiliser in potting mix and should be fed sparingly.

Semi-mature nodal cuttings of camellias are made in mid-summer, each with three or four buds, with the soft tips pinched out. Set up in a organic : grit, 2:1, cutting mix in a closed frame or under mist. The cuttings produce roots by early winter, but the shoots seldom grow before the following spring.

Clematis cvs. single-bud cuttings of semi-mature shoots provide a long-established means of propagating these plants. Results are variable and sometimes thoroughly unsatisfactory. Cultivars derived from *C. viticella* and *C. texensis* make very little growth before every bud develops into a flower. Cuttings made from these may produce roots but make no top growth. By far, the most satisfactory cuttings are made from the short shoots produced in early spring. Cut off the shoots before they start to elongate and treat them like tip cuttings. Stick them approximately 3 cm (1 in.) apart into grit : perlite, 1:1, cutting mix in containers. Set up under mist or preferably on a warm bench under polythene at about 20°C (70°F). Wean as soon as they start to develop roots and pot up individually into 9 cm (3.5 in.) containers. These early cuttings, especially from mother plants brought into a glasshouse in late winter, make considerable growth by autumn. Young clematis shoots are much appreciated by mice during late winter and care should be taken to protect them if necessary. Some species—such as *C. tangutica* and *C. orientalis*—produce flowers in their first year.

Rhododendron spp. and cvs. are not difficult to raise from seed, but they hybridise so promiscuously that vegetative propagation is essential to reproduce cultivars and many species true to type. For rhododendrons and deciduous azaleas,

Figure 86. Make heather cuttings from 2 to 4 cm (1 to 1.5 in.) long young shoots in late summer/early autumn. Do not strip off lower leaves. Set up in small pots in grit : perlite, 1:1, or set out in lines in a bed of similar cutting mix in a cold frame.

including Exbury, Mollis, Knaphill, Occidentalis and Rustica, bring stock plants in containers into a glasshouse or poly tunnel in late winter. Cut off young shoots when they are 6 to 10 cm (2.5 to 4 in.) long and set up individually in 7 cm (2.5 in.) pots filled with lime-free cutting mix : [grit, perlite], 1:1. Set up under mist or preferably on a warm bench under polythene. For evergreen azaleas, including Japanese, Diamant Group and many smaller-leaved species, take semi-mature cuttings in mid- to late summer and set them up communally, 9 to 16 cuttings in 1 litre (6 in.) containers under mist or on a warm bench under polythene.

Large-flowered hybrids and many species are propagated from cuttings of mature shoots. Success rates vary greatly between different cultivars and the condition of the shoots. They succeed best in locations where growing seasons are long enough to ensure the wood becomes fully mature before the cuttings are taken. Make nodal cuttings about 10 cm (4 in.) long from thin rather than thick shoots in early winter. Remove terminal buds and basal leaves and reduce the area of

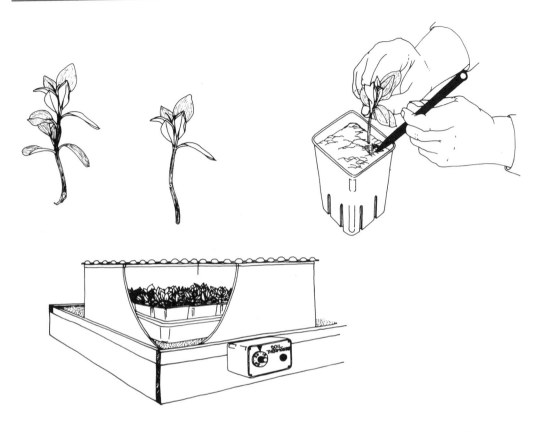

Figure 87. Cuttings of evergreen Japanese azaleas are made from fairly firm semi-mature cuttings, preferably with heels, from mid- to late summer. They produce roots most rapidly in a closed frame above soil heating cables and will do so equally successfully, but more slowly, in a sun frame out of doors. Set the cuttings in a perlite : acidic grit, 1:1, cutting mix with 5 sharing a 7 cm (2.5 in.) pot or 16 to 20 in a 1 litre (6 in.) pot. Overwinter communally and pot up individually as soon as growth is renewed in the spring.

remaining leaves by 50 percent. Wound by removing slivers of bark from both sides of the base of the stems. Dip the base of the cuttings in full-strength or extra-strength rooting hormone. Stick them into individual containers filled with organic : mineral, 1:1, cutting mix. Set up under mist or on a warm bench under polythene.

Vireya rhododendrons are propagated from semi-mature to mature cuttings of new wood from mid-autumn till early winter. Cut off young shoots when firm rather than soft, and remove lower leaves. Stick into organic : mineral, 1:1, cutting mix, with no added fertiliser, with 9 to 16 cuttings sharing a 1 litre (6 in.) container. Set up under mist or on a warm bench under polythene at 20° to 25°C (70° to 75°F). Pot up individually when roots have had time to make considerable development, either into orchid compost or chopped dry bracken : oak leaf mould : moss peat, 1:1:1, plus a pinch of growth medium from an established plant. Feed regularly with quarter-strength, low phosphate liquid feed. Rhododendrons grow leggy, lose their lower leaves and become irretrievably half-starved unless they receive persistent, unremitting attention to watering and feeding. Apart from vireyas, they should be lined out in a nursery bed as young as possible. They transplant so readily this poses no problems.

Skimmia spp. and cvs. tip or semi-firm cuttings are taken in summer and usually produce good results. Hardwood cuttings lined out in a shaded bed in early winter, and left undisturbed throughout the following summer, produce high success rates. Alternatively, insert hardwood cuttings in blocks of oasis during late autumn, early winter. Set them up on a bench with soil heating cables to prevent minimum temperatures falling below 5°C (40°F). Cuttings made from the current season's wood are most successful, but high proportions of two- or even three-year-old shoots usually produce roots. Rooted cuttings develop slowly out of doors; they do better for the first year in a glasshouse or poly tunnel. Line out in a nursery bed after the first year.

Viburnum spp. and cvs., *V. carlesii* group, stock plants are moved into a cool glasshouse in late winter. Cut off the ends of the shoots to make tip cuttings about 5 cm (2 in.) long as soon as they lose their initial softness. Stick individually into grit : perlite, 1:1, cutting mix in 7 cm (2.5 in.) pots. Set up under mist or on a warm bench under polythene at 20° to 25°C (70° to 75°F). Rooted cuttings develop slowly and are grown on in a glasshouse through the summer, but they are unlikely to exceed 15 cm (6 in.) in height by winter. For deciduous species, such as *V. farreri*, place tip cuttings (taken as above) under mist or on a warm bench under polythene in late spring. Alternatively, mature cuttings in a cold frame in late autumn will produce roots during winter. It is usually necessary to cut back stock plants hard the previous spring to obtain shoots suitable for use as cuttings. For evergreen species, such as *V. tinus* and *V. davidii*, set up mature cuttings in late autumn or early winter in a cold frame, as described earlier for heathers, or take similar shoots in late winter or early spring. Remove any visible flower buds. Set up under mist or on a warm bench under polythene. For lacecaps, such as *V. plicatum* and forms, place hardwood cuttings in a cold frame in late autumn, as described for heathers, or set up tip cuttings under mist in spring as described for *V. carlesii*.

Propagation by Division

Shrubs can be propagated from suckers or layers. By and large, gardeners regard suckers with suspicion, associating them with the problems they experience with budded and grafted plants of roses, lilacs, viburnums, plums and cherries, and view them as undesirable nuisances. Such suckers are indeed of no use to most gardeners.

Suckers from shrubs growing on their own roots are a different matter, however, and they should be assessed for the opportunities they offer. They are a ready-made source of plants, ideally suited to the needs of amateur gardeners. Dig them up, with some attached roots, and plant them elsewhere. Those that possess very few roots when lifted are potted up and looked after for a while, but even these represent a ready supply of well-grown plants.

Layering occurs naturally when a trailing branch comes in contact with the ground. Similar effects when reproduced in gardens are the basis of propagation from layers. In nurseries, layering is done systematically, in an organised, relatively complex way designed to obtain the greatest possible number of layers from each mother plant. On a smaller, more domestic scale, layering can be done quite casually to cater to the needs of anyone who wants a few shrubs from time to time by following one of the procedures described in the box on pp. 304–305.

Few gardeners attempt to propagate shrubs or trees from layers, perhaps because it appears to be a lengthy process, demanding exceptional patience. Nevertheless, it is a most useful form of propagation for several reasons: It provides a means of obtaining shrubs which are difficult to propagate by more familiar methods. Layers need virtually no further attention while forming roots. They are made initially from much larger shoots than cuttings and continue to grow while they are forming roots, quickly developing into plants much larger than anything obtainable from a cutting in the same time.

Tip layering

Propagation from tip layers is almost confined to *Rubus* spp. of one kind or another—apart from one or two ferns—all of which practice it highly effectively as their normal means of reproduction. The long, arching shoots of some species of *Rubus* are bent over during late summer, and their tips are pegged to the ground or into a pot filled with potting mix. A simple way to make sure that they stay securely lodged in their containers is to thread the end of the flexible shoot through the drainage hole in the bottom of a clay pot, before filling it with potting mix. Roots are produced at the tips of the shoots and at the same time buds develop into small plants. Cut the young plants free during the winter and set them out in the garden. Most will still be very small and their positions should be marked with short lengths of cane.

Lapageria rosea can be propagated from seeds or cuttings, but the simplest and usually most successful method is from layers.

- Peg sections of old stems, from which most of the leaves have been lost, down onto a layer of organic : mineral, 1:1, potting mix in a large box.
- Arrange the stems backward and forward across the box, and cover them with about 2 cm (1 in.) of the potting mix. At least half of any leaves present should emerge above the surface.
- Buds form in the axils of the buried nodes and develop roots.
- Lift and separate these when they have produced roots, and pot them up individually.
- Grow on the young plants in cool, shaded conditions.

Note that the young shoots are vulnerable to slugs and snails. Similar methods, adapted according to the flexibility or inflexibility of the shoots, can be used to propagate many other kinds of lianes.

Propagation Summary for Shrubs

S. = propagated from seed
C. = propagated from cuttings
D. = propagated by divisions

Note that seed sown "fresh" may germinate immediately or may respond to weathering. Seeds that do not produce seedlings within four to five weeks at temperatures above 10°C (50°F) should be exposed to natural weathering or analogous treatments, using supplementary heat or refrigeration.

Abelia—**C.** tip, semi-mature, mature.
Abeliophyllum—**C.** semi-mature.
Abutilon—**S.** spring; e.g., *A. vitifolium* and *A.* ×*suntense*. **C.** tip, mature; autumn, spring.
Acacia—**S.** spring; chip or treat with boiling water. **C.** tip to semi-mature; e.g., most Australian (*Racosperma*) species.
Acalypha—**C.** tip, mature.
Acanthopanax—Succulent Fruit. **S.** fresh; germination often erratic. **C.** mature, root.
Acer—**S.** autumn; viability variable. **C.** tip; produced from forced mother plants to ensure a long growing season. **D.** layers—e.g., *A. circinnatum*.
Acmena—Succulent Fruit. **S.** spring.
Acnistus—**S.** late winter, spring. **C.** semi-mature, mature.
Actinidia—Liane. Dioecious. Succulent Fruit. **S.** spring. **C.** semi-mature, mature. **D.** layers.
Actinotus—**S.** fresh, green; smoke; variable germination.
Adenandra—**S.** fresh; slow. **C.** mature.
Adenostoma—**S.** spring; smoke. **C.** semi-mature.
Agathosma—**S.** Semi-ballistic. spring; mature over a long period. **C.** tip, semi-mature; with mist; produce roots slowly; resent disturbance.

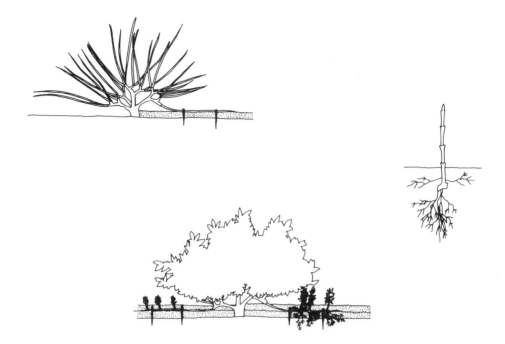

Figure 88. Numerous layers are produced from a single shrub, such as a dogwood, by cutting it back hard during the winter and feeding it well to encourage the production of long, straight shoots. These are drawn down the next winter and pinned to the ground with pegs. During the following summer, shoots grow from buds along the lengths of the shoots. As they grow, a 1:1 mixture of earth : grit is spread around them, burying all but their tips until a layer some 10 cm (4 in.) deep builds up. When the leaves drop, fork out the shoots, complete with the roots formed at their bases, and line them out to grow on for another year.

Akebia—Liane. Succulent Fruit. **S.** spring. **C.** semi-mature, mature. **D.** layers.

Alberta—**S.** spring; low viability usual; shade seedlings. **C.** semi-mature; mist; success rate usually low.

Aloysia—**C.** tip, semi-mature.

Alyogyne—**S.** spring. **C.** semi-mature.

Ampelopsis—Liane. Succulent Fruit. **C.** mature; with minimum of four or five buds.

Andromeda—**S.** fresh. **C.** semi-mature, mature. **D.** layers; produced naturally.

Anthemis—**S.** spring. **C.** semi-mature; spring, autumn; flowering shoots produce roots as readily as nonflowering shoots.

Aralia—Succulent Fruit. **S.** spring. **C.** root. **D.** layers.

Araujia—Liane. **S.** fresh, spring. **C.** semi-mature. **D.** layers.

Arctostaphylos—Succulent Fruit. **S.** fresh; weathered, smoke, soak in sulphuric acid for four-plus hours. **C.** tip, mature.

Argyranthemum—**C.** semi-mature; at almost any time—usually late winter, spring, autumn.

Aristolochia—Liane. **S.** spring. **C.** mature; preferably early spring.

Aronia—Succulent Fruit. **S.** fresh. **C.** semi-mature. **D.** suckers.

Artemisia—**S.** spring. **C.** semi-mature. **D.** spring.

Asteranthera—**C.** semi-mature to mature.

Atriplex -Dioecious. **S.** spring. **C.** semi-mature.

Some ways layers can be used to obtain small numbers of choice shrubs for gardens

Method one

For shrubs with more or less permanent structures—such as magnolias, proteas, hamamelis, and rhododendrons.

- In winter, cut back two or three major branch systems almost to the base.
- Apply about 100 grms/m² (3.5 oz./yd²) of low-phosphate garden fertiliser to the ground around the base of the shrub.
- Several strong, new shoots develop during the summer.
- Lightly fork the ground beneath the shrub in the autumn, and bend each shoot into a U shape, with the base of the U against the ground.
- Wound by removing a sliver of bark from the underside of the U to stimulate root formation.
- Insert bamboo canes.
- Tie each shoot to a cane, with the end held more or less upright, and the curve of the U firmly pressed to the ground.
- Lay a brick over the base of the U to hold it in place, while providing the cool, moist conditions needed to encourage the production of roots.
- Lift the bricks to examine the layers the following autumn, disturbing them as little as possible.
- Sever the connections with their parent plants by cutting the stems of those that have formed roots, and leave them *in situ*. Some may not form roots until the second season after being layered.
- Dig up the rooted layers in early spring and line out in a nursery bed.

Method two

This is a variation on method one, used to propagate shrubs that are not already growing in the garden.

Aucuba—Dioecious. Succulent Fruit. **S.** fresh. **C.** mature.

Aulax—Dioecious. **S.** spring. **C.** semi-mature.

Baccharis—**S.** spring; viability variable. **C.** semi-mature, mature.

Backhousia—**C.** semi-mature, mature.

Bacopa—**S.** spring; slow and erratic. **C.** semi-mature.

Baeckea—**C.** semi-mature.

Banksia—**S.** serotinous except *B. integrifolia*, spring, autumn. **C.** mature.

Barosma—**S.** fresh; smoke. **C.** mature.

Bauhinia—Liane. **S.** spring. **C.** semi-mature. **D.** layers, suckers when available.

Bauera—**C.** semi-mature, mature.

Beaufortia—**S.** spring. **C.** semi-mature, mature.

Berberidopsis—Liane. Succulent Fruit. **S.** spring. **C.** tip, semi-mature. **D.** layers.

Berberis—Succulent Fruit. **S.** fresh. Hybrids likely. **C.** semi-mature; while still quite soft with small piece of mature wood attached; mature.

Bignonia (*Macfadyena*)—Liane, e.g., *M. unguis-cati*. **S.** fresh. **C.** semi-mature.

Billardiera—Liane. Succulent Fruit. **S.** fresh; germination often erratic; colours of berries likely to be inherited by seedlings. **C.** semi-mature.

Boissiea—**S.** spring; chip, hot water treatment.

Boronia—**S.** fresh; species from eastern Australia. Spring; species from Western Australia. Smoke,

- Obtain a young plant in a container from a nursery or garden centre, choosing one with several vigorous, long stems.
- Plant it on its side in a well-prepared nursery bed.
- Lay the young shoots along the ground with their tips tied to bamboo canes to hold them upright.
- Cover the shoots, except for their tips, with 5 to 7 cm (2 to 3 in.) of cutting mix.
- Then treat as for method one.

Method three

For shrubs in which older shoots are pruned to encourage the growth of new wood—such as dogwoods, flowering currants, and forsythias.

- In the autumn, fork the ground lightly around the shrub, working in a generous amount of coarse grit.
- Pull down several young shoots, pinning them to the ground at intervals with several pegs cut from branches.
- Cover the entire shoot with about 1 cm (0.5 in.) of organic : mineral, 1:1, cutting mix.
- Side shoots growing from the buried stems emerge through the layer of growth medium during the summer.
- Add more cutting mix, leaving the tips of the shoots exposed, to build up a layer 7 to 10 cm (3 to 4 in.) deep.
- In the autumn, lift the buried stems with a fork.
- Cut them into sections, each bearing an upright shoot, with roots close to the base.
- Line out the rooted layers in a nursery bed, cutting them back to three or four buds from ground level.

chipping, boiling water or harvesting green may promote germination. **C.** semi-mature, mature.

Bougainvillea—Liane. **C.** semi-mature; over bottom heat, with mist. Mature; over bottom heat. **D.** layers.

Brachyglottis—**S.** fresh. **C.** semi-mature, mature; reduce leaf area of large-leaved species.

Brachyloma—Succulent Fruit. **S.** fresh; very uncertain, best chance with bog method, smoke. **C.** tip, semi-mature.

Browallia—**S.** late winter, early spring.

Brugmansia—**C.** mature.

Brunfelsia—**C.** semi-mature.

Brunia—**S.** spring; smoke. **C.** tip. semi-mature; mist.

Buddleja—**S.** spring. **C.** semi-mature, mature.

Bupleurum—**C.** semi-mature.

Burchellia—**S.** spring. **C.** semi-mature.

Buxus—**S.** Ballistic. fresh; erratic, slow germination. **C.** mature.

Caesalpinia—**S.** spring; chip, soak in warm water. **D.** layers.

Calamintha—**S.** spring. **C.** semi-mature. **D.** layers.

Calliandra—**S.** spring; chip. **C.** semi-mature.

Callicarpa—Succulent Fruit. **S.** fresh. **C.** tip, semi-mature.

Callistemon—**S.** Serotinous—not all, e.g., *C. acuminatus*. Late winter, early spring; smoke. **C.** semi-mature, mature; under mist.

Calluna—**S.** spring; smoke. **C.** semi-mature.

Calothamnus—**S.** serotinous, spring. **C.** semi-mature, mature.

Calycanthus—**S.** spring. **D.** layers, occasionally suckers.

Calycotome—**S.** spring; chip.

Calytrix—**S.** spring. **C.** semi-mature.

Camellia—**C.** tip, spring; semi-mature; all do best with bottom heat under mist, or on warm bench beneath polythene.

Campsis—Liane. **S.** spring. **C.** semi-mature, mature, root. **D.** layers.

Cantua—**C.** semi-mature.

Capparis—Succulent Fruit. **S.** spring. **C.** semi-mature, mature.

Caragana—**S.** autumn, early spring; chip. **C.** root. **D.** layers.

Carissa—Succulent Fruit. **S.** spring. **C.** mature. **D.** layers.

Carmichaelia—**S.** spring; chip and hot water soak. **C.** semi-mature, mature.

Carpenteria—**S.** spring; smoke. **C.** tip, mature; both in spring, usually low success rates. **D.** layers.

Carpodetus—**S.** spring. **C.** mature.

Caryopteris—**S.** spring. **C.** tip, semi-mature, mature.

Cassia—**S.** spring; chip, boiling water. **C.** semi-mature.

Cassinia—**C.** mature; heel, basal cuttings.

Cassiope—**S.** spring. **C.** semi-mature, mature. **D.** layers.

Ceanothus—**S.** Ballistic. Fresh, green; smoke, hot water soak plus weathering. **C.** semi-mature, mature.

Celastrus—Liane. Dioecious. Succulent Fruit. **S.** fresh. **C.** tip, mature, root. **D.** layers, suckers.

Celmisia—**S.** fresh; viability variable, hybrids likely. **C.** semi-mature, mature.

Centradenia—**C.** tip, semi-mature.

Ceratostigma—**C.** semi-mature. **D.** suckers.

Cestrum—Succulent Fruit. **C.** semi-mature in spring best, also produce roots readily at other seasons.

Chaenomeles—Succulent Fruit. **S.** fresh. **C.** mature, root. **D.** suckers.

Chamaedaphne—**S.** fresh. **C.** semi-mature. **D.** layers.

Chamelaucium—**S.** spring. **C.** semi-mature.

Chimonanthus—**S.** late winter; seldom set seeds in cultivation. **C.** semi-mature; usually low rates of success. **D.** layers, air layers.

Chionanthus—Succulent Fruit. **S.** fresh. **C.** tip. **D.** layers.

Choisya—**C.** semi-mature, mature.

Chordospartium—**S.** spring; chip and hot water soak. **C.** semi-mature, mature.

Chorizema—**S.** spring; chip, hot water. **C.** semi-mature.

Chuquiraga—**S.** spring; hot water.

Cissus—Liane. **C.** tip; early spring with small section of mature wood at base.

Cistus—**S.** spring; chip, hot water. **C.** semi-mature, mature.

Clematis—Liane. **S.** fresh; viability variable. **C.** tip; in early spring from dwarf shoots before the internodes start to elongate; semi-mature; internodal cuttings in mid- to late summer. **D.** layers.

Clerodendrum—Liane. **S.** fresh, spring. **C.** semi-mature, root. **D.** suckers.

Clethra—**S.** spring. **C.** tip, semi-mature. **D.** layers, suckers.

Clianthus—Hand-pollinate. **S.** spring; chip lightly, hot water, very vulnerable to damping-off; colour forms come more or less true from seed. **C.** semi-mature.

Clytostoma—**C.** mature. **D.** layers.

Cobaea—Liane. **S.** late winter, early spring. **C.** tip, semi-mature.

Coleonema—**S.** spring. **C.** semi-mature, mature.

Colletia—**S.** spring; seldom set in cultivation. **C.** semi-mature.

Colutea—**S.** spring; chip. **C.** mature.

Conospermum—**S.** Serotinous. spring; smoke, each flower produces a single seed; viability usually low, very vulnerable to damping-off. **C.** semi-mature, with soft tips removed; success rates usually low except for *C. triplinervium*.

Convolvulus—Liane. **C.** tip, semi-mature, mature.

Coprosma—Dioecious. Succulent Fruit. **S.** fresh; germination likely to be erratic; hybrids likely. **C.** semi-mature, mature. **D.** layers, prostrate species form natural layers.

Coriaria—Succulent Fruit. **S.** fresh, spring. **C.** semi-mature. **D.** suckers.

Cornus—Succulent Fruit. **S.** fresh. **C.** tip, e.g., *C. florida*, *C. kousa*; mature, e.g., *C. alba*, *C. stolonifera*. **D.** layers in stool bed, e.g., *C. alba*. **D.** air layers, e.g., *C. kousa*.

Corokia—Succulent Fruit. **S.** fresh; germination often erratic. **C.** mature.

Coronilla—**S.** spring; chip. **C.** tip, semi-mature.

Correa—**S.** spring; soak in water, innoculum; seed seldom produced by cultivated plants in cool climates unless hand-pollinated. **C.** tip, semi-mature soon after flowering.

Corylopsis—**S.** spring. **C.** semi-mature; low success rates likely. **D.** layers.

Corylus—Nut. Recalcitrant. **S.** fresh. **C.** mature; wrapped in damp moss till spring, then over bottom heat. **D.** layers from stool bed, suckers.

Cotinus—**S.** fresh. **C.** tip, semi-mature. **D.** layers, air layers.

Cotoneaster—Succulent Fruit. **S.** fresh; hybrids likely; some species in cultivation are apomictic. **C.** semi-mature, mature.

Crowea—**S.** fresh, spring; chip, hot water soak, innoculum. **C.** semi-mature.

Cuphea—**S.** spring. **C.** semi-mature.

Cyathodes—Succulent Fruit. **S.** autumn, spring sown on sphagnum; smoke. **C.** tip, semi-mature; from shoots produced on recently cut-back plants.

Cyclopia—**S.** spring; chip.

Cydonia—Succulent Fruit. **S.** fresh. **C.** mature; up to three-year-old wood at 15° to 20°C (60° to 70°F), after storage in damp moss. **D.** suckers.

Cytisus—**S.** spring; chip, hot water. **C.** semi-mature; basal.

Daboecia—**S.** spring. **C.** semi-mature, mature.

Dampiera—**S.** spring.

Daphne—Dioecious, e.g., *D. odora*. Succulent Fruit. **S.** fresh. **C.** semi-mature. **D.** layers.

Daphniphyllum—Succulent Fruit. **C.** semi-mature, mature.

Darwinia—**S.** fresh; viability variable. **C.** tip, mature.

Datura—**S.** spring. **C.** mature; spring or autumn.

Daviesia—**S.** spring; chip, hot water soak.

Decaisnea—Succulent Fruit. **S.** late winter, early spring; germination often erratic. **C.** semi-mature, mature.

Decumaria—Liane. **C.** semi-mature.

Dendromecon—**S.** fresh, spring; smoke, germination usually slow and erratic. **C.** mature, root.

Desfontainia—**C.** tip, mature; basal.

Deutzia—**S.** spring. **C.** tip, semi-mature.

Dichroa—Succulent Fruit. **C.** semi-mature.

Dictamnus—**S.** fresh; innoculum.

Diervilla—**S.** spring. **C.** semi-mature, mature. **D.** suckers.

Dillwynia—**S.** spring; sand, hot water, chip.

Dipelta—**C.** semi-mature, mature.

Diplolaena—**S.** spring; smoke. **C.** semi-mature, mature.

Disanthus—**S.** fresh; may not germinate till second or third spring. **C.** mature. **D.** layers.

Discaria—**S.** spring. **C.** semi-mature.

Dombeya—**S.** fresh, spring. **C.** semi-mature.

Dracophyllum—**S.** fresh, spring, in a mineral seed mix, e.g., calcined clay, grit (or bog method)—seedlings liable to sudden death syndrome at any stage of development. **C.** semi-mature. *D. recurvum* only.

Dryandra—**S.** autumn, spring; vulnerable to damping-off. **C.** mature; prostrate forms only, e.g., *D. nivea, D. obtusa, D. calophylla*. Upright forms are very unrewarding.

Ebenus—**S.** spring; chip, innoculum.

Eccremocarpus—Liane. **S.** late winter, early spring.

Edgeworthia—Succulent Fruit. **S.** fresh; seldom available. **C.** semi-mature.

Elaeagnus—Succulent Fruit. **S.** fresh. **C.** semi-mature, mature, root. **D.** layers, suckers.

Elsholtzia—**C.** semi-mature.

Embothrium—**S.** spring. **C.** semi-mature, root. **D.** suckers.

Empetrum—Dioecious. Succulent Fruit. **C.** semi-mature, mature.

Enkianthus—**S.** spring. **C.** semi-mature, mature. **D.** air layers.

Epacris—**S.** fresh; on sphagnum, smoke. Germination likely to be erratic. **C.** semi-mature; from vigorous shoots after cutting back.

Ephedra—Liane. Dioecious. Succulent Fruit. **S.** spring. **D.** suckers, layers.

Eremaea—**S.** spring; smoke. **C.** semi-mature, mature.

Erica—**S.** spring; fluctuating temperatures, smoke. **C.** semi-mature, mature. **D.** layers after mounding.

Eriocephalus—**S.** spring; smoke. **C.** tip to semi-mature.

Eriophyllum—**S.** autumn, spring; smoke. **C.** semi-mature.

Eriostemon—**S.** spring; smoke. **C.** semi-mature, mature.

Escallonia—**C.** semi-mature, mature.

Euonymus—Succulent Fruit. **S.** fresh. **C.** semi-mature. (evergreen species), mature (deciduous and evergreen species). **D.** layers.

Euryops—**S.** late winter, spring; smoke. **C.** semi-mature, mature; autumn, late winter, spring.

Exochorda—**S.** spring. **C.** tip; slow but usually eventually successful; semi-mature; seldom produce plants with satisfactory roots. **D.** layers, suckers.

Fabiana—**C.** tip, mature.

Fallopia—**S.** fresh. **C.** mature. **D.** layers.

Fatshedera—**C.** single bud. **D.** air layers.

Fatsia—Succulent Fruit. **S.** fresh. **C.** semi-mature, mature. **D.** air layers.

Felicia—**S.** spring, autumn; smoke. **C.** semi-mature; late winter, spring, autumn.

Fendlera—**S.** spring. **C.** tip. semi-mature.

Forsythia—**S.** spring. **C.** semi-mature, mature.

Fothergilla—**S.** fresh; usually germinates during second spring. **C.** semi-mature, root. **D.** suckers, layers.

Fouquieria—**S.** fresh.

Fuchsia—Succulent Fruit. **S.** late winter, early spring. **C.** tip, semi-mature. **D.** from prostrate species, e.g., *F. procumbens.*

Gardenia—Succulent Fruit. **S.** late winter; seedlings develop slowly. **C.** mature; early winter, shoots with three to four buds with minimum bottom heat of ca. 20°C (70°F).

Garrya—Dioecious. **S.** fresh. **C.** mature. **D.** layers.

Gaultheria—Succulent Fruit. **S.** fresh; on sphagnum moss. **C.** semi-mature; slow and erratic. **D.** natural layers, encouraged by blanketing, suckers.

Gelsemium—Liane. **C.** semi-mature.

Genista—Ballistic. **S.** late winter; chip. **C.** semi-mature, mature.

Grevillea—**S.** fresh; smoke, viability variable, performance erratic. **C.** mature; preferably nodal or basal.

Grindelia—**S.** spring. **C.** semi-mature.

Guichenotia—**S.** spring. **C.** mature.

Hakea—**S.** serotinous, spring. **C.** tip, semi-mature, mature.

Halimiocistus—**S.** spring; chip. **C.** semi-mature.

Halimium—**S.** spring; chip. **C.** semi-mature.

Haloragis—**S.** fresh, spring; coloured-leaf forms come true from seed. **C.** semi-mature; remove soft tips.

Haplopappus—**S.** autumn, spring; viability variable.

Hardenbergia—Liane. **S.** spring; chip, hot water. **C.** tip, semi-mature.

Hebe—**S.** fresh; seedlings of whipcord species have normal leaves while juvenile. **C.** mature.

Hedera—Succulent Fruit. Liane. **S.** fresh; germinates in second spring. **C.** semi-mature, mature; mature forms propagated from cuttings produce non-climbing plants. **D.** layers.

Heliotropium—**S.** late winter, spring. **C.** semi-mature; spring or autumn after flowers fade.

Hibbertia—**S.** spring; germination erratic. **C.** mature.

Hibiscus—**S.** spring. **C.** mature; up to three-year-old wood, wounding may improve results.

Hippocrepis—**S.** spring; chip.

Holodiscus—**S.** fresh; weathered. **C.** semi-mature; with heel, variable performance. **D.** layers.

Hovea—**S.** Ballistic. spring; chip, boiling water.

Hoya—Liane. **C.** tip, semi-mature. **D.** layers, especially *H. carnosa.*

Hunnemannia—**S.** spring.

Hydrangea—Including liane. **S.** late winter, spring. **C.** tip, e.g., *H. petiolaris*; mature. **D.** suckers, e.g., *H. quercifolia* and *H. arborescens*; layers.

Hylomecon—**S.** spring.

Hymenanthera—Succulent Fruit. **S.** spring. **C.** semi-mature. **D.** layers.

Hypericum—**S.** spring. **C.** semi-mature. **D.** suckers.

Hypocalymma—**S.** fresh, spring. **C.** semi-mature, mature.

Hypoestes—**S.** late winter, spring. **C.** semi-mature.

Hyssopus—**S.** spring. **C.** semi-mature.

Iberis—**S.** spring. **C.** mature.

Impatiens—**S.** late winter, spring, autumn. **C.** semi-mature.

Indigofera—**S.** spring; chip, innoculum. **C.** semi-mature; nodal.

Iochroma—Succulent Fruit. **C.** semi-mature.

Isopogon—**S.** spring. **C.** mature.

Itea—**S.** fresh. **C.** semi-mature, mature. **D.** divide clumps of stems.

Jamesia—**C.** semi-mature, mature.

Jasminum—Liane. **S.** spring. **C.** semi-mature, mature. **D.** layers, e.g., trailing species.

Jovellana—**S.** spring. **C.** tip, semi-mature. **D.** suckers.

Justicia—**C.** semi-mature.

Kalmia—**S.** fresh, spring. **C.** semi-mature; under mist; mature; wounded. **D.** layers.

Kalmiopsis—**S.** fresh. **C.** semi-mature, mature.

Kalopanax—Succulent Fruit. **S.** spring. **C.** root.

Kennedia—Liane. **S.** spring; chip, boiling water. **C.** semi-mature, mature.

Kerria—**C.** mature. **D.** suckers.

Kolkwitzia—**C.** tip, mature.

Kunzea—**S.** fresh, spring. **C.** mature.

Lambertia—Liane. **S.** fresh.

Lantana—**S.** spring; modern hybrids are almost all sterile. **C.** tip, mature.

Lapageria—Liane. **S.** fresh, germinates best when entire capsule is lightly buried; seedlings develop very slowly, may not start to twine till third year. White forms reproduce more or less true. **D.** layers.

Lardizabala—Liane. Succulent Fruit. **S.** spring. **C.** semi-mature. **D.** layers.

Lavandula—**S.** late winter, early spring—extended and irregular germination. Most forms reproduce more or less true. **C.** tip, mature.

Lavatera—**S.** spring. **C.** semi-mature, mature.

Ledum—**S.** spring. **C.** mature. **D.** layers.

Leiophyllum—**C.** semi-mature.

Leonotis—**S.** spring. **C.** tip, semi-mature.

Leptospermum—**S.** Serotinous except *L. laevigata*. Late winter, spring. **C.** tip, semi-mature, mature; wounded.

Leschenaultia—**S.** autumn, spring; smoke. **C.** semi-mature, mature.

Lespedeza—**S.** spring; chip, hot water soak. **C.** semi-mature.

Leucadendron—Dioecious. **S.** spring; smoke. **C.** mature.

Leucophyllum—**S.** spring.

Leucophyta—**C.** semi-mature.

Leucopogon—Succulent Fruit. **S.** fresh, viability variable.

Leucospermum—**S.** spring; smoke. **C.** mature.

Leucothoe—**S.** fresh; sphagnum. **C.** mature. **D.** rhizomes.

Leycesteria—Succulent Fruit. **S.** fresh, spring. **C.** semi-mature.

Ligustrum—Succulent Fruit. **S.** fresh; may not germinate till second spring. **C.** mature.

Lindera—Succulent Fruit. **C.** semi-mature.

Lithodora—**S.** spring. **C.** semi-mature.

Lithospermum—**S.** spring. **C.** semi-mature.

Lobostemon—**S.** spring. **C.** mature.

Lomatia—**S.** spring. **C.** semi-mature, mature.

Lonicera—Liane. Succulent Fruit. **S.** fresh. **C.** tip, semi-mature, mature.

Lophospermum—**S.** late winter, spring.

Lophostemon—**C.** mature.

Lotus—**S.** late winter, early spring; chip, hot water soak. **C.** semi-mature.

Macfadyena—Liane. **S.** fresh. **D.** layers, tubers.

Mackaya—**C.** semi-mature, mature.

Macropiper—Succulent Fruit. **S.** fresh; very vulnerable to phytophthora. **C.** tip, semi-mature.

Magnolia—**S.** fresh. **C.** tip; in spring from forced stock plants to provide a long growing season. **D.** layers, air layers.

Mahonia—Succulent Fruit. **S.** fresh; erratic germination from first autumn to second spring; hybrids likely. **C.** autumn, early winter; single bud. **D.** suckers, layers.

Mandevilla—Liane. **S.** fresh, spring. **C.** semi-mature, mature—from small side shoots.

Marrubium—**S.** spring.

Maurandya—Liane. **S.** late winter, spring. **C.** semi-mature.

Medicago—**S.** chip, innoculum. **C.** mature, e.g., *M. arborea*.

Melaleuca—**S.** Serotinous but not *M. leucadendron*; spring. **C.** tip, semi-mature, mature.

Melicytus—Dioecious. Succulent Fruit. **S.** fresh. **C.** semi-mature. mature.

Metrosideros—Liane, e.g., *M. fulgens* and *M. albiflora*. **S.** fresh, spring; prick out when two or three true leaves have developed. **C.** semi-mature to mature, e.g., *M. kermadecensis*.

Michelia—**S.** fresh. **C.** tip, mature.

Microloma—Liane. **S.** spring, autumn.

Micromeria—**S.** spring. **C.** semi-mature.

Mimetes—**S.** spring.

Mimulus—**S.** spring, autumn. **C.** semi-mature, e.g., *M. aurantiacus*.

Mitchella—Succulent Fruit. **D.** division of stems with roots.

Mitraria—Liane. Succulent Fruit. **C.** semi-mature. **D.** rooted sections of stem.

Monsonia—**S.** spring. **C.** semi-mature to mature.

Monstera—Liane. Succulent Fruit. **C.** sections of stem, each with two or three nodes, laid horizontally and partially buried.

Muehlenbeckia—Liane. Dioecious. **S.** fresh. **C.** semi-mature, mature. **D.** divisions of rooted stems, e.g., *M. axillaris* and *M. ephedroides*.

Mulinum—**S.** spring; chipped, hot water.

Mutisia—Liane. **S.** spring; viability variable, usually infertile in cultivation. **C.** semi-mature. **D.** suckers, e.g., *M. decurrens*.

Myrica—Dioecious. Succulent Fruits. **S.** fresh. **D.** suckers.

Myrsine—Dioecious. Succulent Fruits. **S.** fresh. **C.** semi-mature, mature; may be up to a year before roots are produced.

Nandina—Succulent Fruit. **S.** fresh. **C.** semi-mature, mature; single node or basal. **D.** suckers.

Neillia—**S.** spring. **C.** semi-mature.

Nerium—**C.** mature.

Notospartium—**S.** spring; chip or hot water. **C.** semi-mature, mature.

Nototriche—**S.** fresh.

Nuttallia—Dioecious. **C.** semi-mature.

Nylandtia—Succulent Fruit. **S.** spring; smoke.

Nymannia—**S.** fresh, spring.

Oldenburgia—**S.** fresh, spring. **C.** semi-mature.

Olearia—**S.** spring; viability variable. **C.** semi-mature, mature, root.

Osmanthus—Succulent Fruit. **S.** fresh; weathered, germination unlikely before second spring. **C.** semi-mature; short side shoots, e.g., *O. burkwoodii*, **C.** semi-mature, mature.

Osmaronia—**S.** fresh. **D.** suckers.

Oxylobium—**S.** spring; chipped, hot water.

Oxytropis—**S.** spring; chipped, hot water.

Ozothamnus—**S.** fresh. **C.** semi-mature.

Pachystegia—**S.** fresh, spring; vulnerable to damping-off, slugs and snails. **C.** semi-mature, mature.

Paeonia—**S.** fresh; epicotyl dormancy ensures first seedlings will not appear before second year, may be considerably later. **D.** air layers.

Paliurus—**S.** fresh. **C.** root.

Pandorea—Liane. **S.** fresh, spring; seldom produced by cultivated plants. **C.** semi-mature; cuttings of flowering shoots may remain shrubby. **D.** layers.

Parahebe—**S.** fresh, spring. **C.** semi-mature, mature. **D.** layers.

Parsonsia—Liane. **S.** spring. **D.** layers.

Parthenocissus—Liane. Succulent Fruit. **S.** fresh. **C.** semi-mature, mature—need at least four nodes to ensure the presence of an active bud, e.g., *P. tricuspidata*.

Passerina—**C.** mature.

Passiflora—Liane. Succulent Fruit. **S.** fresh, late winter, spring; germination often erratic, *P. incarnata* and *P. edulis* seeds sown early can produce flowering plants in the first season. **C.** semi-mature, mature. **D.** suckers.

Periploca—Liane. **S.** spring. **C.** semi-mature. **D.** layers.

Pernettya—Dioecious. Succulent Fruit. **S.** fresh. **C.** semi-mature. **D.** suckers.

Perovskia—**C.** semi-mature. **D.** suckers.

Persoonia—Succulent Fruit. **S.** fresh; chip, smoke; germination erratic, up to two or three years.

Petrea—Liane. **C.** semi-mature. **D.** layers.

Petrophile—**S.** Serotinous. Fresh; smoke. **C.** mature.

Phaenocoma—**C.** semi-mature; preferably tips of shoots.

Phellodendron—Dioecious. Succulent Fruit. **S.** fresh. **C.** mature; preferably with heels in autumn, stored in sphagnum, set in spring.

Philadelphus—**S.** spring; hybrids likely. **C.** semi-mature, mature. **D.** suckers.

Philesia—Succulent Fruit. **S.** fresh; rarely produces seed in cultivation. **C.** semi-mature; prolonged period needed to form roots. **D.** suckers.

Phylica—**S.** spring. **C.** semi-mature.

Phillyrea—Succulent Fruit. **S.** fresh. **C.** semi-mature.

Philodendron—Liane. Succulent Fruit. **C.** from continuously radescent sections of stem, each with two or three nodes.

Phlomis—**S.** spring; chip, hot water treatment. **C.** mature.

Photinia—Succulent Fruit. **S.** fresh. **C.** mature.

Phyllodoce—**S.** spring; with sphagnum. **C.** semi-mature. **D.** suckers.

Physocarpus—**S.** fresh, spring. **C.** semi-mature, mature.

Pieris—**S.** fresh. **C.** tip. semi-mature. **D.** air layers.

Pileostegia—Liane. **C.** semi-mature, mature. **D.** layers.

Pimelea—Succulent Fruit. **S.** fresh, spring; smoke. **C.** tip, semi-mature. **D.** layers, prostrate species.

Piptanthus—**S.** spring; chip. **C.** tip. **D.** air layers.

Pisonia—Succulent Fruit. **S.** late winter, early spring. **C.** semi-mature to mature.

Pistacia—Dioecious. Succulent Fruit (dry drupe) **S.** spring, autumn; soak for three or four days before sowing. **C.** mature.

Pittosporum—**S.** late winter, early spring; hot water treatment, hybrids likely. **C.** mature; wounded.

Plumbago—Liane. **C.** tip, mature, root, e.g., *P. indica*. **D.** layers.

Podalyria—**S.** spring; chip, innoculum—germinates erratically and seedlings grow slowly. **C.** semi-mature.

Polygala—**S.** fresh, spring.

Poncirus—Succulent Fruit. **S.** fresh.

Prostanthera—**S.** fresh. **C.** mature; may be slow.

Protea—**S.** spring, early autumn; smoke. **C.** semi-mature, mature.

Pseudopanax—Succulent Fruit. **S.** fresh. **C.** mature; best results likely from the slimmer, smaller shoots.

Pseudowintera—**S.** fresh. **C.** mature; wounded.

Psoralea—**S.** spring, autumn; chip, hot water treatment, smoke.

Pultenaea—**S.** spring; chip, hot water treatment. **C.** semi-mature to mature.

Punica—Succulent Fruit. **C.** mature. **D.** layers.

Pyracantha—Succulent Fruit. **S.** fresh. **C.** semi-mature, mature.

Rhamnus—Dioecious. Succulent Fruit. **S.** fresh. **C.** tip. semi-mature, mature.

Rhaphiolepis—Succulent Fruit. **S.** fresh. **C.** mature.

Rhodochiton—Liane. **S.** late winter, early spring; will flower during first year. **C.** semi-mature.

Rhododendron—S. Hybrids likely. Late winter, early spring. **C.** tip, e.g., Exbury, Knaphill, Mollis azaleas; semi-mature, e.g., many species, evergreen Japanese, Indian and vireyas; mature, wounded, e.g., large-flowered hybrids. **D.** layers, air layers.

Rhodothamnus—S. spring. **C.** mature. **D.** layers.

Rhus—Dioecious. Succulent Fruit (dry drupe). **S.** fresh. **C.** semi-mature, mature, root. **D.** suckers.

Ribes—Succulent Fruit. **S.** fresh, spring. **C.** semi-mature, mature. **D.** layers, e.g., *R. speciosa.*

Richea—S. fresh; allow seedlings to grow for 12 months before potting up individually. **C.** mature; strike rates are likely to be low.

Ricinus—S. late winter, early spring.

Rosa—Succulent Fruit. **S.** fresh; unlikely to produce seedlings before second spring, unless treated with sulphuric acid. **C.** semi-mature, mature, root, e.g., species in groups Cinnamomeae, Carolinae, and Gallica. **D.** suckers.

Rosmarinus—C. mature.

Rubus—Succulent Fruit. **S.** fresh. **C.** semi-mature, root. **D.** divisions, tip layers.

Russelia—C. mature.

Ruta—S. late winter, spring. **C.** mature.

Salix—Dioecious. **S.** hybrids likely; remains viable for only a few days. **C.** mature; including truncheons.

Salvia—S. fresh, spring. **C.** tip, semi-mature.

Sambucus—Succulent Fruit. **S.** fresh, spring. **C.** semi-mature, mature, with heels to avoid exposing pith; root; not variegated forms.

Santalum—Parasite. Succulent Fruit. **S.** fresh; nuts placed whole or cracked in plastic bag with moistened vermiculite at 15° to 25°C (60° to 75°F). Chitted seed removed and potted individually. Host plant required when potted on.

Santolina—C. semi-mature, mature.

Sarcocaulon—C. mature, root.

Sarcococca—Succulent Fruit. **S.** fresh. **C.** mature. **D.** division, suckers.

Sarmienta—C. semi-mature.

Satureja—S. spring. **C.** semi-mature, mature.

Schefflera—Succulent Fruit, **S.** fresh. **C.** mature.

Schizandra—Dioecious. Liane. Succulent Fruit. **S.** fresh. **C.** semi-mature, root. **D.** suckers, layers.

Schizophragma—Liane. **S.** fresh. **C.** semi-mature. **D.** layers.

Senecio—Liane, e.g., *S. macroglossus* and *S. scandens.* **S.** fresh, spring; viability variable. **C.** semi-mature, e.g., *S. tamoides*; mature.

Senna—S. spring, autumn; chip, hot water treatment.

Serruria—S. late winter, spring.

Shepherdia—Dioecious. Succulent Fruit. **S.** fresh.

Sideritis—S. spring. **C.** semi-mature.

Simmondsia—S. fresh.

Sinocalycanthus—S. fresh. **C.** mature.

Sinowilsonia—S. fresh. **D.** layers.

Skimmia—Dioecious. Succulent Fruit. **S.** fresh, spring; make very little growth during first year. **C.** semi-mature, mature.

Solandra—Liane. **C.** semi-mature; preferably with heels.

Solanum—Liane. Succulent Fruit. **S.** spring. **C.** tip. semi-mature.

Sollya—Liane. **S.** late winter, spring. **C.** mature.

Sorbaria—S. fresh. **C.** mature, root. **D.** suckers.

Spartium—S. late winter, spring; chip. **C.** semi-mature.

Sphaeralcea—C. semi-mature.

Spiraea—S. spring. **C.** semi-mature, mature. **D.** suckers.

Stachyurus—Succulent Fruit. **S.** fresh. **C.** tip.

Staphylea—S. fresh, spring. **C.** tip; from forced stock plants. **D.** suckers.

Stephanandra—S. fresh. **C.** semi-mature, root. **D.** suckers.

Stephanotis—Liane. **C.** semi-mature.

Stirlingia—S. spring; smoke.

Streptosolen—Liane. **C.** semi-mature.

Styrax—Recalcitrant. **S.** fresh. **C.** semi-mature; strike rates usually low.

Sutera—C. semi-mature.

Sutherlandia—S. autumn, spring. **C.** semi-mature.

Swainsona—S. spring; chip. **C.** tip, semi-mature.

Sycopsis—S. fresh. **C.** semi-mature, mature.

Symphoricarpos—Succulent Fruit. **S.** fresh. **C.** semi-mature, mature. **D.** suckers.

Symplocos—Succulent Fruit. **S.** fresh; seldom germinate before second spring. **C.** semi-mature.

Syringa—S. spring. **C.** tip, semi-mature; shoots used for cuttings should be taken when the flowers are in bloom. **D.** suckers.

Tagetes—S. late winter, early spring, autumn. **C.** semi-mature, e.g., *T. lemonii.*

Tecoma—Liane. **S.** spring. **C.** semi-mature. **D.** layers.

Tecomanthe—Liane. **S.** fresh. **C.** semi-mature.

Telopea—S. Serotinous, fresh; very susceptible to damping-off. **C.** semi-mature; from basal shoots produced below the inflorescences.

Templetonia—**S.** fresh; chip, boiling water. **C.** semi-mature, mature.

Tetrapanax—Succulent Fruit. **C.** semi-mature, mature, root.

Tetratheca—**S.** fresh, spring; hot water treatment. **C.** tip, semi-mature, mature.

Thermopsis—**S.** spring, autumn.

Thomasia—**S.** spring, autumn; viability variable. **C.** semi-mature, mature.

Thryptomene—**S.** fresh, spring; germination improved under mist.

Thunbergia—Liane. **S.** spring. **C.** semi-mature. **D.** layers.

Thymelaea—**S.** spring. **C.** semi-mature.

Thymus—**S.** spring. **C.** semi-mature. **D.** divisions most productive when blanketed.

Tibouchina—**S.** fresh, spring. **C.** semi-mature.

Trachelospermum—Liane. **C.** semi-mature; preferably with heels. **D.** layers.

Tripterygium—Liane. **S.** spring.

Tweedia—Liane. **C.** semi-mature.

Ulex—Ballistic. **S.** spring; chip, hot water treatment. **C.** mature.

Vaccinium—Succulent Fruit. **S.** fresh. **C.** tip, mature. **D.** suckers.

Verticordia—**S.** autumn, spring; smoke; viability variable.

Vestia—**C.** semi-mature.

Viburnum—Succulent Fruit. **S.** fresh; seedlings unlikely to appear till second spring. **C.** tip, e.g., *V. carlesii* group, *V. farreri*; semi-mature; mature, e.g., *V. tinus*. **D.** layers.

Vigna—Liane. **S.** spring; chip.

Vinca—**C.** tip, semi-mature. **D.** division.

Viscum—Parasite. Dioecious. Succulent Fruit. **S.** late winter; *in situ* on living branch.

Vitex—Succulent Fruit. **S.** spring, autumn. **C.** semi-mature.

Vitis—Liane. Succulent Fruit. **S.** fresh. **C.** mature; shoots with three or four buds stuck vertically, or single-bud cuttings laid horizontally.

Weigela—**C.** semi-mature, mature.

Westringia—**S.** spring. **C.** mature.

Wisteria—Liane. **S.** spring; chip, hot water treatment. **C.** semi-mature; under mist, root. **D.** layers.

Zanthoxylum—**S.** spring. **C.** root. **D.** suckers.

Zauschneria—**S.** spring. **C.** semi-mature. **D.** natural layers.

Zenobia—**S.** fresh, spring. **C.** tip, semi-mature.

CHAPTER 17

Woody Monocots Including Bamboos and Palms

The vital differences between the propagation of monocots and dicots lie in the meristems, those centres of cell division from which all new developments spring. Meristems are almost entirely absent from the stems, leaves and roots of grasses, hostas, bananas, and other herbaceous monocots. The cells within them can expand to complete the growth of existing tissues. They cannot divide to initiate new developments. The meristems from which offsets, side shoots, new leaves and flowers of monocots arise are centred around the rim of rootstock at or below ground level. As a result, these plants can seldom be propagated from cuttings—the few exceptions include the plantlets sometimes produced viviparously in the inflorescences of some grasses and hemerocallis.

Woody monocots—dasylirions, palms, dragon trees (*Dracaena draco*) and grasstrees (*Xanthorrhoeae*)—are treelike. Their meristems, like those of the herbaceous plants, are more or less confined to a ring of tissue from which new leaves and flowers develop. However, their meristems also give rise to new tissues beneath them, creating a growth zone which progressively raises them into the air. As they mature, these tissues become woody and form the trunks of the trees. The trunks of monocots can grow continuously upwards, reaching enormous heights in the case of palm trees, but their girths cannot expand—hence their slender, columnar appearance.

Palms and bamboos very rarely produce side shoots or produce axillary buds in the angles between the leaves and their stems. Exceptions include a few species of cordylines, pandanus, freycinetias, yuccas and a few palms which are more likely to possess meristematic tissues in their leaf angles, but less consistently than dicots. Consequently, cuttings are much less useful as a source of new plants from woody monocots than they are from dicot trees and shrubs. Divisions made from rarely produced basal offsets or side shoots also play minor roles when propagating woody monocots. Seeds become sometimes the only, and almost always the major, means of vegetative propagation, apart from tissue cultures under laboratory conditions.

Tree forms are comparatively rare amongst monocots. They occur predominantly in the three groups of plants covered in this chapter: bamboos, which are, in effect, woody grasses; shrubs and trees broadly related to lilies, such as dragon trees, grasstrees, yuccas and cordylines; and palms, which are alike only in that they are all more or less woody and all are monocots.

From the propagator's point of view, the problems the different groups pose and the opportunities they offer are so different it is impracticable to cover them together. Consequently, each has a section of the chapter to itself.

Bamboos

With few exceptions, bamboos are not born to suffer adversity patiently. They thrive in wet, warm, fertile situations to which they respond by rapid growth and development. Deprived of any of these three comforts, they struggle. In chilly locations, the use of a glasshouse or poly tunnel to supplement natural temperatures and provide the humid, cosy conditions they need is likely to be amply rewarded.

Propagation from seed

The belief that a species of bamboo flowers simultaneously all over the world, sets seeds, and then dies is too clear-cut and clean an end to survive scrutiny. It can happen more or less like that—when bamboos over considerable areas after years of looking magnificent are suddenly inflicted with the urge to reproduce. Scruffiness replaces magnificence, and untidy little grasslike inflorescences appear, reminding us that these plants are woody grasses. Seed may be set, and for a year or two the plants look progressively more miserable as their leaves wither and their stems die. The clump may duly expire or totter on for years, wispily regenerating from a few surviving shoots. The underlying cause of this behaviour is a puzzle, its extent a matter of dispute between those who believe it to be a major and clearly definable feature of the reproduction of these plants and those who claim its occurrence and intensity is less clear-cut and more limited than reports suggest. Nevertheless, the phenomenon certainly exists.

Attempts to explain the causes behind episodes of synchronised flowering have failed to establish links with such things as the age of the plants; the density of culms (shoots) in a group; the thickness of their stems; climatic factors such as cycles of warmth or cold, dry or wet seasons; and soil fertility. Some species produce abundant crops of seed. Others produce no more than a miserable few—far below anything commensurate with the apparent effort involved. Some are appar-

ently sterile, producing no seed at all, and species that fail to produce seed may die in the attempt; stocks of plants in gardens have been entirely lost as a result, to be replaced only by reintroductions from the wild.

Bamboos produce seeds similar to those of grasses or cereals. They germinate like any other seed, usually with no special requirements, and develop rapidly into young bamboo plants. Growth is limited during the first year to the development of a single culm. This may reach 30 to 40 cm (12 to 15 in.) before it stops growing—but sometimes reaches barely 10 cm (4 in.). In later years, additional shoots are produced from buds at the base of the culms. These grow progressively longer, building up the pattern of upright shoots typical of a clump of bamboo.

Bamboo seeds are orthodox for storage. Dried seeds remain viable at subzero temperatures for very long periods. Since seeds are produced sporadically and erratically, opportunities to put some away in store as and when they become available should always be taken.

Propagation from cuttings

The woody stems of bamboos cannot be used to make cuttings, but some of the vigorously rhizomatous species including phyllostachys, pleioblastus and sasas are propagated from sections of their underground rhizomes. Excavate around the peripheral shoots of a clump to expose the rhizomes. Remove stems with short sections of rhizome attached and replant as divisions. Lift several rhizomes in the longest lengths possible. Cut them into sections 15 to 30 cm (6 to 12 in.) long and line out in shallow trenches.

Propagation by division

Bamboos are not particularly amenable to disturbance, and their tough, rhizomatous stems can be remarkably resistant to division. Species which spread vigorously are comparatively easily propagated by sawing rhizomes into sections, each containing several nodes with or without a culm. Line

Figure 89. Bamboos produce new shoots from subterranean rhizomes. The more desirable garden species have short rhizomes which form compact clumps of shoots. They are propagated by digging up a clump and cutting the woody rhizomes between one shoot and another to form clusters of three or four shoots. Both the digging up and the cutting encounter great resistance from well entrenched, established plants. The easiest shoots to use are those on young plants which have been in place for only a few years.

out in rows, 20 to 30 cm (8 to 12 in.) deep. Cut the culms back after planting to reduce windrock. Clump-forming species, which are by far the more desirable in most gardens, require ruthless determination to get in and force a separation between the congested rhizomes. Divide into groups of three or four culms, preserving as much root as possible. Replant at once, taking care they do not dry out. If they have to be transported, keep them temporarily in plastic sacks until replanting. The transplants are likely to sulk afterwards, losing their leaves and apparently heading towards death, but they seldom take things to this extreme. New buds form at the base of the culms, and during the second year these emerge to replace those that have gone before. From then on, the plants build in strength year by year.

Liliaceous Plants Including Woody Agaves

Propagation from seed

Cordylines, yuccas, species of xanthorrhoea and other woody, liliaceous monocots produce seeds in dry capsules or succulent berries in accessible positions. Harvest presents few problems, and once cleaned, seeds tolerate drying and can be stored under orthodox conditions for many years.

Most genera do not depend on specialist pollinators and are likely to set seed when grown in gardens—with the notable exception of yuccas. These develop alliances with moths, amongst which *Yucca whipplei* is the extreme example. Large, creamy white flowers develop in spring on flowering stems up to 4 metres (12 ft.) high. In southern California and northern Baja California, where it grows naturally, hundreds of plants may come into flower synchronously. They die after flowering and depend for survival on the yucca moth, which gathers pollen from one flower with which it pollinates another, meanwhile laying eggs in the ovary. The caterpillars feed on some of the developing seeds before pupating in the fruit. In the absence of the yucca moth, the flowers of these plants must be hand-pollinated.

Sow seeds and raise seedlings using standard procedures described earlier for other plants. As a matter of prudence and with regard to the conditions in which these plants grow naturally, use free-draining potting mixes, for example 1:1 mixes of loam : [grit, calcined clay, perlite] and mineral toppings for yuccas, dasylirions, furcraeas and other species from arid areas. More fertile moisture-retentive substrates, such as 2:1 mixes of [peat, bark, coir] : [grit, perlite], and mineral toppings are more appropriate for cordylines, pandanus, freycinetias and other forest-dwelling species.

Figure 90. One-year-old seedling grasstrees, *Xanthorrhoea* sp. Seeds germinate readily, but seedlings take many years to develop stems and 20 years or so to flower.

Propagation from cuttings

Dasylirions, dragon trees, nolinas and beaucarnias, amongst others, produce side shoots, the first occasionally and invariably sparingly and the others more generously. These are used to make conventional cuttings.

- Remove the lower leaves.
- Set up individually in 7 or 9 cm (2.5 or 3.5 in.) containers filled with standard cutting mix.
- Place them on a warm bench at 20° to 25°C (70° to 75°F) under polythene.
- After a few days, provide a little ventilation, increasing it gradually. The more the cuttings are able to tolerate without wilting the better.

Stem cuttings are made from cordylines, freycinetias and screw pines (*Pandanus*).

- Cut mature shoots into sections, each containing at least one node where the meristematic tissues are located.

- Partially fill a deep tray or large pot with potting mix.
- Lay out the cuttings horizontally on the surface of the substrate and bury them about 3 cm (1 in.) deep with a layer of a 1:1 mixture of potting mix : [grit, perlite].
- Place on a warm bench at 20° to 25°C (70° to 75°F) and water thoroughly.
- Pot up the young plants individually after roots have developed and shoots have appeared.

More specialised cuttings are made in a very similar way from the swollen underground shoots bearing buds produced on the roots of those yuccas which sucker and cordylines. Yuccas start to produce these shoots, known as knees, while still immature. A plant bought from a garden centre will sometimes provide a dozen or so; they can be felt through the sides of the container as uneven protuberances.

- Excavate around an established plant or obtain a plant in a container in spring.
- Locate and cut off the knees, which are similar to semi-woody tubers with buds more or less clearly defined on the surfaces.
- Cut the knees into sections, each containing at least one bud.

- Partially fill a tray with a 1:1 mixture of grit : perlite.
- Lay out the sections of knees, and bury them beneath a layer of the mixture about 3 cm (1 in.) deep.
- Place them on a bench with supplementary heat, if necessary, to maintain minimum temperatures of 15° to 20°C (60° to 70°F).
- Feed at two times normal strength with a liquid nutrient as soon as shoots appear.
- When roots have developed, pot up the young plants individually in 9 cm (3.5 in.) containers.

Yucca filifera and *Y. guatemalensis* produce no suckers, and hence no knees. Cuttings are made from the aerial parts of well-developed plants in several ways.

- Dismember the plants, branch by branch.
- Stick each branch into the ground, like a truncheon, tying each to a bamboo cane to support it.
- When roots have been produced, remove individual branches and lay them horizontally in shallow trenches.
- Cover with a gritty potting mix.
- Numerous shoots are produced from meristematic tissues in the axils of the former leaves.
- Remove them when they are 7 to 10 cm (3 to 4 in.) long and treat like cuttings.

Alternatively, decapitate several shoots. When side shoots emerge below the cut ends of the stems, cut them off to provide cuttings.

Propagation by division

Beschornerias and some xanthorrhoeas are propagated by removing offsets from the base of the plant, preferably when they have grown large enough to have produced some roots. Others, including *Ruscus* spp. and *Danae racemosa*, form clumps of woody stems. These are dug up, divided into groups of three or four and replanted.

Furcraeas are a group of monocarpic plants which grow usually for between three and fifteen

Figure 91. A yucca plant removed from a container, showing the subterranean outgrowths, known as knees, amongst the roots.

Figure 92. Yucca knees are cut up to produce cuttings. As shown here, they do not have to be made from the tips of the shoots, provided each section contains at least one bud.

Figure 93. Shoots and roots growing from cuttings made from yucca knees. Once they reach this stage they are ready to pot up individually into 9 cm (3.5 in.) pots.

as they mature, or pick them up from the ground after they fall. Set them out individually in 9 cm (3.5 in.) pots in a well-drained, loam-based potting mix mixed with equal parts of coarse grit. Water very sparingly until roots are produced. Grow on at 15° to 25°C (60° to 75°F).

Palms

Knock a coconut off its perch at a fair or buy one—preferably one that is still heavy with the milk, or liquid endosperm, inside it. Plant it with the "eyes" uppermost, barely covered by potting mix, in a large container. Water thoroughly. Put it somewhere warm and continue to water sufficiently to stop the growth medium drying out. In six months or so, it will grow into a seedling palm tree. A great deal more time and space is needed before it produces coconuts.

Propagation from seed

Palms produce seeds—some regularly in profusion and others less abundantly. A few, amongst them raphias, save everything up during lifetimes lasting for decades before producing enormous inflorescences followed by huge crops of fruit. Then they die, exhausted by the stresses of procreation. Most palms furnish neither cuttings nor offsets. In the absence of alternatives, seeds are by far the most usual way to propagate these plants.

Apart from inaccessibility at the tops of tall, columnar trees, palms pose few problems for seed collectors, provided allowances are made for the lengthy periods their fruits take to mature. These are invariably measured in months and can exceed a year.

Palm fruits are drupes composed of a stone (the seed) surrounded by more or less succulent tissues. In some, those we know as dates, the tissues are soft, sweet and appetising. In others, they are dry or almost leathery and almost or quite inedible. Whatever their form, these surrounding tissues may contain inhibitors which reduce the

years, depending on the species and the conditions. They then develop soaring inflorescences and die. Some inflorescences produce normal flowers, followed by seed, which can be sown to raise new plants. Forms with variegated leaves, such as *Furcraea foetida* var. *mediopicta* and *F. selloa* var. *marginata* cannot be propagated in this way.

Many inflorescences produce numerous small, viviparous offsets in place of flowers. These offsets provide a simpler, more rapid form of propagation than seed and can be used to reproduce forms with variegated foliage. Pick off the offsets

Figure 94. Furcraeas produce large inflorescences after growing for a number of years. Many of these produce viviparous buds where there would normally be flowers. The buds provide an extremely easy way to propagate the plants.

Figure 95. Palm inflorescences often contain thousands of flowers. After pollination, these develop into masses of drupes. Most take months to mature; some take more than a year.

chances of germination and should be removed before seeds are sown. If the stones are not readily extracted by hand, soaking in water for several days, followed by brisk scrubbing, is usually the best way to clean them.

Seeds of most species lose viability rapidly after cleaning and should be sown with the least possible delay once this has been done. The embryos of the great majority of palms are extremely vulnerable while being dried and unless this is carried out with great care are destroyed in the process. Although probably technically orthodox for seed

storage if drying can be successfully achieved, in practical situations the seeds should be regarded as recalcitrant.

The stones of palms are thickened with hemicellulose and extremely hard. The white endosperm surrounding the embryos within the stones also hardens as the seeds mature. The result is that the embryos themselves are surrounded by obdurate tissues which resist the entry of water and delay the processes of germination until the hard tissues of the stones begin to break down due to microbial activity while in the ground.

Figure 96. The seed leaves (cotyledons) of palms resemble broad blades of grass. Seedlings are potted up when the first true, divided leaves appear, very soon after the stage reached by the seedlings in the photograph.

Seeds of palms take at least two to three months to produce seedlings, and some take much longer.

- Sow seeds individually in small pots or communally in trays in a free-draining organic : mineral, 1:1, seed mix.
- Cover with 2 to 4 cm (1 to 1.5 in.) of mix, depending on the size of the stone.
- Water thoroughly.
- Maintain minimum temperatures of 20°C (70°F) and preferably from 25° to 30°C (75° to 85°F).
- Seed leaves (cotyledons) of most palms resemble broad blades of grass; the first true leaf is divided and more palmlike, and its appearance marks the time to pot up seedlings individually.
- Storage reserves in the endosperm and the hemicellulose forming the stone itself continue to support growth for some time after germination, and the remnants of the stones are not removed when the seedlings are potted up.

Propagation by division

A few palms, including *Chamaerops*, *Chamaedorea* and *Rhapis*, produce clumps from offsets or suck-ers. They can be propagated by division, removing the offsets with a spade in spring and potting them up individually. Numbers obtainable are usually quite small, and the plants take some time to establish. They are set out in sheltered, shaded conditions and never allowed to dry out until new roots are developing freely.

Propagation Summary for Woody Monocots

S. = propagated from seed
C. = propagated from cuttings
D. = propagated by divisions

Bamboos

Almost all bamboos can be raised from seed sown in spring at 15° to 25°C (60° to 75°F), provided seed is available. Because seeds are produced extremely erratically and are generally unavailable, they are seldom included below as an option. However, seeds from a single event can be stored dry at subzero temperatures for many years, and there is no reason why intermittent crops of most species should not be harvested when an opportunity arises and remain available for years thereafter.

Arundinaria—**C.** spring, summer; rhizome. **D.** spring. Recent revisions, based on the availability of seeds, have reassigned nearly all the original species to *Pleioblastus* and other genera.

Bambusa—**D.** spring; apart from *B. glaucescens*, these are not frost hardy and are damaged or killed by only a few degrees of frost.

Chusquea—**D.** spring; recover and establish rapidly from small buds at the base of the culms.

Dendrocalamus—**S.** spring; seedlings are grasslike for the first year, before developing culms. **D.** spring. Subtropical to tropical and few are hardy, but *D. strictus*, one of the largest, is unexpectedly tolerant of light frosts.

Fargesia—Clump-forming. **D.** Spring; into small groups of culms retaining as much root as possible.

Phyllostachys—Some vigorously rhizomatous. **C.** spring, summer; rhizome. **D.** spring; single culms or small groups.

Pleioblastus—Vigorously rhizomatous. **C.** spring, summer; rhizomes. **D.** spring; single culms or small groups.

Pseudosasa—Clump-forming. **D.** spring; divide into small clumps, retain roots and avoid drying out.

Sasa—Vigorously rhizomatous. **C.** spring, summer; rhizomes. **D.** spring; small clusters.

Shibataea—Short rhizomes, open clump formers. **D.** spring; small clusters.

Thamnocalamus—Seldom invasive. **D.** spring.

Liliaceous, agaves and others

Agave—Flowers may need hand-pollinating in cultivation. **S.** may be produced only after many years' growth; fresh, spring. **C.** spring; offsets or pups; tend to be most freely produced by potbound plants. **D.** summer, autumn; pups; viviparous bulbils produced on inflorescences, e.g., *A. sisalana*.

Beaucarnea—**S.** spring. **C.** summer.

Cordyline—Succulent Fruit. **S.** spring; purple forms reproduce purple in the absence of green-leaved or variegated plants with some variation in depth of colour; variegated forms reproduce green. **C.** late winter, spring; sections of stems. Also subterranean toes, like Yucca knees.

Danae—Succulent Fruit. **S.** fresh. **D.** spring, autumn.

Dasylirion—**S.** spring. **C.** summer; very sparingly produced.

Dracaena—Succulent Fruit. **S.** autumn, spring. **C.** summer; sections of stems.

Draco—**S.** spring. **C.** summer.

Freycinetia—Succulent Fruit. Liane. **S.** fresh. **C.** summer; sections of stem. **D.** offsets; most likely to be available from young plants.

Furcraea—**S.** autumn, spring. **D.** late spring, summer; viviparous plantlets periodically produced on inflorescences.

Kingia—**S.** fresh, spring; very slow growing.

Nolina—**S.** spring. **C.** summer. **D.** autumn, spring; offsets.

Ruscus—Dioecious, Succulent Fruit. **S.** fresh, spring. **D.** winter, early spring.

Xanthorrhoea—**S.** fresh; germination may be prolonged and delayed; seedlings grow very slowly. **D.** spring, e.g., *X. minor* and *X. macronema*.

Yucca—Hand-pollination may be necessary in gardens. **S.** spring. **C.** summer; sections of stem, "knees" (rhizomes).

Palms

Archontophoenix—**S.** germinates within two to three months; seedlings develop rapidly.

Arecastrum—**S.** germinates within two months; seedlings grow rapidly.

Brahea—**S.** germinate within two or three months.

Butia—**S.** germinates in up to six months; initial growth of seedlings tends to be slow.

Caryota—**S.** germinates in three or four months. **D.** suckers; available in small numbers.

Chamaedorea—**S.** can germinate in a month but may need six. **D.** late winter, spring; e.g., *C. microspadix*.

Chamaerops—**S.** germinates freely within two or three months. **D.** early spring; offsets.

Hedyscepe—**S.** germinates within four months; tolerant of cool conditions.

Howea—**S.** germination erratic; may take from two months to a year.

Jubaea—**S.** fresh; germination up to six months.

Laccospadix—**S.** tolerant of low temperatures but germination very prolonged below about 15°C (60°F), and seedling development slow.

Linospadix—**S.** germinates usually in around 12 months. Seedlings need heavily shaded, warm, moist conditions.

Livistona—**S.** germination in less than a month, e.g., *L. chinensis*. Other species take several months.

Parajubaea—**S.** germination in two to three months. Tolerates cool conditions.

Phoenix—Dioecious, e.g., *P. dactylifera*. **S.** germinates within two or three months.

Rhapis—**S.** germinates within two or three months but seldom available. **D.** late winter; offsets establish slowly.

Rhopalostylis—**S.** fresh, germination may take 12 months; seedlings of *R. sapida* grow very slowly. *R. baueri* grows faster in gardens.

Sabal—**S.** germinates within two or three months; young plants develop rapidly.

Syagrus—**S.** fresh; germinates in two or three months. Stored seed more likely to take twelve months.

Trachycarpus—**S.** germinates freely within two months. Tolerates low temperatures.

Trithrinax—**S.** germinates in two or three months.

Washingtonia—**S.** germinates in about two months; seedlings grow rapidly.

CHAPTER 18

Trees

Procreation might seem one of the least of a tree's priorities. Short-lived trees live for decades, while many have life spans measured in centuries and some in millennia. A harvest missed, or hundreds of harvests missed, count almost for nothing. It is enough if, in the course of these immense life spans, sufficient seeds produce seedlings to replace their parents. Provided that average is achieved, the population survives, and even if it fails for some reason to reach that average—if, for example, only every other tree produces a mature offspring—a population of trees will still persist for generations, declining steadily in numbers perhaps for thousands of years. How remarkable, then, that trees put so much energy into the production and so much ingenuity into the distribution of seeds—all the more remarkable since seed and fruit production imposes significant strains on trees' resources. Many trees have "off" years, when they produce very few seeds, or more significantly "on" years separated by several off years because bumper harvests strain resources to such an extent that time is needed to rebuild reserves. Scarcely any of the energy and ingenuity devoted to seeds benefits the trees at all—almost infinitesimally little.

But plants, however incidentally useful they may be to man and beast, are not altruistic. Seeds play a critical role in their survival, and every viable seed of every year's harvest carries a promise of producing a seedling and eventually a mature tree. The fact that so few fulfill this destiny does not make the ways they germinate or the methods they employ to distribute their seeds any less interesting to those who have an interest in using the seeds to propagate the species for themselves. Successful propagation of trees from seeds, just as for any other plant, depends on understanding the life processes and life cycles of a tree and the roles seeds play to enable it to fulfill them.

Seeds, seedlings and young saplings are amongst the most vulnerable members of their communities for many years. Seriously disadvantaged in competition with their much larger neighbours, seedlings hang on under adverse conditions, making little growth but slowly increasing their grip on the ground as their roots develop and they build up reserves. They may scarcely grow from one year to the next, but, given the opportunity, the speed at which they develop in response to light, nutrients, water and warmth can surprise us.

In the favourable conditions of the nursery seedbed, or cloistered in a poly tunnel, tree seedlings can be amongst the most amenable and responsive of all plants—so amenable, in fact, that problems arise, not from the difficulties of inducing seeds to germinate and produce seedlings, but from the freedom with which they do so and the embarrassment of producing far more plants than can possibly be used. The secret of growing trees successfully is to grow no more than are needed and to provide those we do grow with the very best conditions.

Propagation from Seed

Trees from seed! The thought raises images of interminably long waits for anything to happen. Stories of liriodendrons (tulip trees) and *Magnolia campbellii* taking 20 or 30 years or more to produce a flower come to mind. Many trees do enjoy long juvenile periods, during which they neither flower nor fruit—as those who sow an apple pip discover—but not all. *Lagerstroemia* seedlings very often start to flower in their second year and can look the proverbial picture by their fifth. And trees offer more rewards than their flowers. Very many trees are scarcely grown for their flowers at all, but for the effects their presence creates, and young trees possess a grace that makes them amongst the most valued contributors to the attractions of a garden.

Seed collection and storage

Collecting seeds from anything as large and inaccessible as trees poses the obvious problem of how to reach them. Gunfire can be used to bring down clusters of fruits, or trees can be felled to obtain their seeds, but generally, more orthodox, less drastic means are available—and preferable. The fruits and seeds of many trees become readily accessible when they fall to the ground; low branches may provide enough for modest needs, and it may be possible to reach a supply by climbing.

Seed cleaning

Generally speaking, the seeds of trees are no more difficult to clean than those of other plants, and possibly rather easier as a rule. They are, perhaps, more likely to produce seeds that appear to be fertile but are not. Beeches may produce quantities of nuts between mast years, all of which are empty. Beetles may destroy the embryos and inner tissues of seeds, while leaving little trace of their activities. Seeds present in parthenocarpic fruits, or those produced following hybridisation, may contain no embryos. The presence of embryos and supporting tissues can usually be confirmed either by cutting open samples of a few seeds or by flotation—by throwing a sampling of seeds into a bucket of water. After stirring thoroughly, fully developed seeds sink to the bottom, leaving rubbish and dead and empty seeds floating on the surface. The method depends on viable seeds being sufficiently dense to sink in water—something that does not apply to all seeds, notably those with hard or heavily waxed seed coats impenetrable to water.

Storing seeds

The seeds of trees are more likely to be recalcitrant than those of other groups of plants. Large, permanently moist seeds, including nuts of all kinds and acorns, are not tolerant of desiccation; they cannot be dried and stored at subzero temperatures like orthodox seeds, making it impossible to store them for long periods. This becomes particularly significant with species which crop erratically or which seldom produce seed at all in cultivation.

These large, moist seeds must not be allowed to dry out at all. Immediately after collection, mix them with a substantial quantity (at least five times their bulk) of barely moist peat, bark, sand, perlite or other available material. Pack the mixture into heavy gauge polythene bags. They can be held in a refrigerator at temperatures as close to 0°C (32°F) as possible, but not falling below freezing point. Temperatures in the range of 1° to 3°C (34° to 37°F) are ideal. Higher temperatures speed up germination and reduce storage life but are not otherwise harmful. The maximum storage life of recalcitrant seeds under these conditions is about 18 months; for many, it is closer to 6 months. Alternatively, seed can be held in a cellar, outhouse or other cool, sheltered place. The seeds

Causes of problems when collecting seeds of trees

Dioecious species
Plants available may be exclusively male or female. This is particularly likely when vegetative propagation is an easy option—as with poplars.

Clones
Every neighbouring tree may be the offspring of a single, self-sterile clone. This frequently occurs in vegetatively propagated species, such as elms, which are readily available as suckers.

Absence of pollinators
Many subtropical and tropical trees are pollinated by bats, birds, mammals, and even reptiles while foraging for pollen or nectar. Even familiar insect pollinators, such as the appropriate bees, may not be present when trees are grown in gardens away from their native haunts.

Sterile hybrids
The flowers may be incapable of setting fertile seed, though not necessarily unable to produce parthenogenic fruits.

Fertile hybrids
Seeds are produced, often abundantly, but they produce bastard offspring.

Juvenility
Seedlings of many species remain juvenile for years, during which they produce no flowers. Even after they start to bear flowers, a further lengthy period may occur, as in mulberries and some acers, before the flowers become fully fertile and capable of producing seed.

will start to germinate within a few months, when they must be sown. If sown thickly and left unfertilised, tree seedlings make little growth and can remain in a seedbed for several years, during which batches are removed and lined out as they are needed during successive springs, when they will rapidly grow on into saplings.

Nuts and other large, moist seeds are easily recognised as recalcitrant and can be treated appropriately. Other seeds, not so obviously large and moist, might be described as "semi-recalcitrant." These include acers, fraxinus, liriodendrons, citrus and pterocaryas with large but less obviously fleshy seeds. These can be dried and stored at low temperatures, but unless they are

treated very gently, they are likely to be killed in the process. Dry the seeds in a desiccator (a biscuit tin, plastic cake box or other sealed container with silica gel crystals over the bottom), avoiding the use of heat, either artificial or from sunlight.

Maples (*Acer* spp.) produce seeds which deteriorate rapidly after collection unless carefully dried, when viability is well maintained at subzero temperatures. Even when dried successfully, the seed coats harden, making the seeds more difficult to germinate, a problem common to the seeds of many deciduous trees and one of several reasons why tree seeds should almost always be sown fresh unless there are good reasons for doing otherwise.

Predation
Insects may destroy seeds while maturing on the plant. Bruchids, weevils and other beetles can infest seeds, such as those of trees in the pea family. Caterpillars burrow into the almost mature seeds of plagianthus and hoherias and destroy them while in store or when lying on the ground.

Erratic flowering
Flowers and seeds may be produced prolifically only during "mast" years, characteristic of species of *Quercus*, *Fagus* and *Nothofagus*, amongst others, with intervals of several years between productive years. Seeds produced during off years are likely to be low in storage compounds (fats, oils and carbohydrates), unlikely to store well, and capable of producing only feeble seedlings.

Unfavourable weather
Frosts, prolonged cold spells, or sustained periods of mist or rain may inhibit pollen development, dispersal or fertilisation. Seed production of cultivated trees may not follow normal patterns and may be intermittent, with seeds produced only in exceptionally favourable years. For example, a number of chestnuts (*Aesculus* spp.) are grown in Britain, but only *A. hippocastanum* produces seed abundantly and regularly; *A. indica* is a little less regular or reliable. *Aesculus flava* produces seeds only in above average warm years, and *A. parviflora* produces only in unusually hot, dry ones.

Adaptations to fire
Serotinous seeds are retained on the tree in woody capsules after they mature. They are released only after fire or when the tree or the branch bearing them dies.

Seeds sown fresh usually produce seedlings during the first spring; seeds dried and stored till the following autumn seldom germinate till the second spring and often do so erratically over a period of several years. The extent of the problem varies with different species. Some, including *Acer capillipes*, *A. pensylvanicum*, *A. rufinerve*, *A. ginnala*, *A. tartaricum*, *A. japonicum*, *A. griseum*, *A. nikoense* and *A. campestre*, tend to develop hard seed coats naturally as they mature. This is accentuated by drying, and whenever possible they should be collected green, just before they mature, and sown at once. Others, including *A. pseudoplatanus*, *A. trautvetteri*, *A. platanoides*, *A. palmatum*, *A. opalus*, *A. crataegifolium*, *A. davidii*, *A. grosseri*, *A. hersii* and *A.*

macrophyllum, are less likely to develop hard seed coats. They can be left to mature on the tree—but they do develop hard seed coats when dried and stored. Seeds of *A. rubrum* and *A. sacharinum* mature in early summer and germinate freely when sown fresh. Attempts to remove the wings of acer seeds are likely to do more harm than good. Sow the seeds entire, as they come off the tree.

Despite exceptions and partial exceptions, the great majority of trees produce orthodox seeds. These are collected as and when they mature and can be stored dry at subzero temperatures between one collection and another even when the intervals between these are lengthy.

Sowing and germination

In cool or cold temperate regions, the existence of trees in places where frosts are a significant threat to survival depends on developing strategies that avoid exposing young seedlings to its effects. Responses to weathering are very widespread. Succulent fruits are used by many species as a means of distributing their seeds. Recalcitrant seeds are widely represented. Hard seed coats, either inherent as in members of the pea family or as a result of drying, commonly occur. Severally, or taken together, these responses provide good reasons for sowing seed freshly gathered rather than stored, whenever possible.

Weathering serves two purposes: It ensures that seedlings from seeds shed in the autumn and early winter do not emerge while still very small, only to face frosts and short, dark days; instead, they appear in more promising conditions in the spring. In combination with squirrel-, bird- or wind-aided transportation, it is a way of distancing seedlings in space and time from the overbearing presence of their parents.

Beneficial though it may be to the tree, weathering is something of a nuisance to a gardener who wants to obtain seedlings with as few delays or complications as possible. The most obviously natural way to cope is to sow seeds in an outdoor seedbed as they become available, in the expectation they will weather during the winter and seedlings will emerge in due course in the spring. This is the simplest and most labour-saving approach. It can work very well.

It also leads to problems and failures. Large seeds, such as nuts, are food resources, highly sought after by birds and animals. Without protection, few if any are likely to survive until spring. Soaking in paraffin serves as a temporary deterrent. Seedling emergence in spring is not a foregone conclusion; some will not appear till the second spring or even later. Effective management of a nursery seedbed is complicated and usually unsatisfactory when some species are represented by actively growing seedlings and others by seeds lying hidden in the ground.

Succulent fruits present problems. The succulent tissues often contain compounds that inhibit germination and must be removed before seedlings will emerge. Seeds sown in autumn are exposed to the adverse as well as the beneficial affects of weather during the winter. Rain can cause soil capping, impeding seedling emergence, or wash away parts of a seedbed. Frost can lift and loosen the soil around the seeds, creating unfavourable conditions for germination, especially for species with small seeds. Weed seedlings as well as mosses and liverworts may take over the bed during the winter, making it more difficult for tree seedlings to emerge and competing with them for light, water and nutrients. Moles, worms, field mice and other burrowing creatures can seriously disrupt seedbeds during the winter and move seeds from one part to another, leading to confusion by mixing plants in adjacent rows.

These problems are avoided by treating "weathering" and "germination" as separate phases. Weathering becomes a form of active storage during which the seeds are maintained in a fully imbibed condition and exposed to the successive periods of warmth, cold, and so on, that lead to germination. Throughout this phase, the seeds remain under the control of, and visible to, the gardener, protected from predators, adverse weather and other hazards. Germination involves sowing the seeds in similar conditions to those used for seeds from a packet or any other situation where seedlings are expected to appear within a short period.

Weathering treatments

Collect fruits as they mature. Clean the seeds either by placing dry, dehiscent fruits in a warm, airy room for a few days or by mechanically macerating or hand-picking succulent fruits to extract their seeds. Alternatively, mix larger quantities of succulent fruits with moist grit or sand. The fleshy tissues decay as the seeds are weathered.

Mix seeds with five to ten times their volume of grit, coarse sand, or vermiculite, and half fill polythene bags with the mixture. Expose to weathering by packing the bags in heavy-gauge plastic sacks or buckets with lids—the latter provide better protection from rodents. Place them in a sheltered place out of doors, where their contents will experience a more or less natural progression of temperatures through the seasons. For seeds collected during the autumn, these consist of several weeks of mild, progressively reducing, temperatures from about 15° to 5°C (60° to 40°F) (warm weathering) followed by several months of cold temperatures of about 10° to 0°C (45° to 32°F) and below (cold weathering), succeeded by rising temperatures in spring of 10° to 20°C (45° to 70°F), when seedlings emerge.* Inspect the contents of the bags from time to time, looking for signs of the emergence of radicals. These are almost invariably ivory or white and conspicuous. Their appearance marks the conclusion of the weathering phase and the time to start the sowing phase leading to the production of seedlings within a short time.

Different species respond to weathering in critically different ways (see chart 20). Many respond to low temperature weathering lasting from one to three months; they then produce seedlings as temperatures rise. A substantial minority, amongst them species of carpinus, cotoneasters and hamamelis, need warm weathering before the onset of cold. Their seeds fail to produce seedlings unless they experience both in the correct sequence, and when sown too late to experience the preliminary warm weathering, their seeds do not germinate during the first spring. Subsequently, their need for warm weathering is met during the following summer, and cold weathering during

*These values are approximations for guidance only. Temperatures in winter fall well below 0°C (32°F) in many places but are believed to have little or no effect on weathering responses. Temperatures do not have to be consistently low to induce the changes that lead to germination, and fluctuating conditions, during which temperatures fall to low levels for part of the time, are not only more natural, but probably more effective, too.

the winter leads to germination during the second spring. A few, amongst them liquidambars, some ilex and crataegus species, seldom germinate during the first spring, but do so during the second spring after experiencing cold weathering (first winter), followed by warm weathering (first summer), leading to a second period of cold weathering (second winter). A small minority, including some ilexes, roses, crataegus and tilias, seldom produce seedlings before the second spring, followed by more seedlings in the third and sometimes subsequent seasons.

Germination

The seeds of many trees found in places with cold winters germinate readily even without being weathered and can be sown in the standard way used for all seeds. Those that have received weathering treatments are sown in containers, as follows.

- Partially fill containers with potting mix to provide a base.
- Empty the mixture of seeds and grit from the bags in which they have been weathered onto the base to form a topping.
- Seeds germinate more rapidly, once they have been weathered, when warm rather than when cold. If supplementary heat can be provided, they benefit from temperatures between 15° and 20°C (60° and 70°F).
- Prick out the seedlings individually into separate containers, remembering to limit numbers strictly to those actually needed.
- Standard pots can be used, but tree seedlings do better in deeper containers with grooved channels down their sides; these are designed to ensure that their roots grow straight down rather than coil in a tangle within the pots.
- Large quantities are sown in nursery seedbeds by tipping the contents of the bags in which they were weathered into drills or distributing them evenly over the surface and covering lightly.

Chart 20. TREES AND SHRUBS FROM SEED

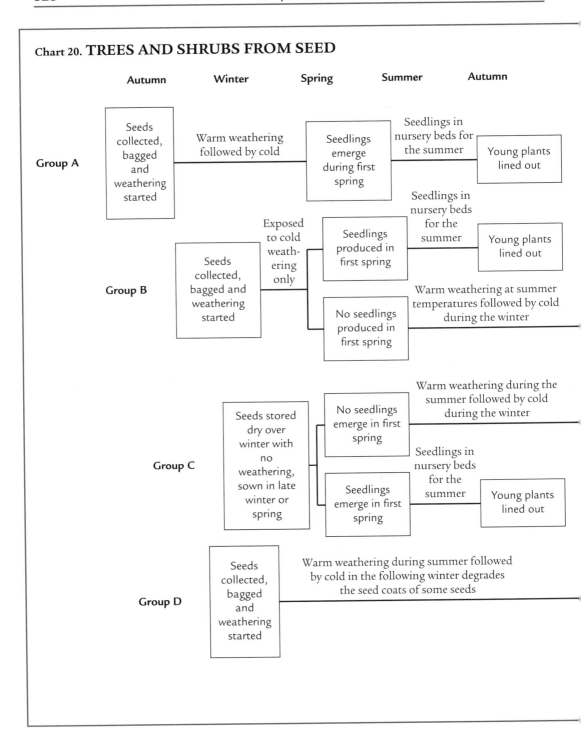

Winter	Spring	Summer	Autumn	Winter	Spring

How Sowing Times and Weathering Affect the Germination of the Seeds of Woody Plants

- **Group A:** Freshly collected seeds sown in autumn before soil temperatures fall receive warm weathering before cold weathering during the winter and are ready to produce seedlings the following spring.
- **Group B:** Seeds sown only a few weeks later, when soil temperatures have fallen, experience reduced warm weathering before winter. Many species will still respond to cold weathering and produce seedlings the first spring. Species that require a sequence of warm followed by cold weathering will not germinate till the second spring, following exposure to warm soils during the summer and cold during the winter.
- **Group C:** Seeds of species capable of immediate germination produce seedlings within a few weeks when stored dry and sown in the spring. Those dependent on warm and/or cold weathering will not germinate till the following spring.
- **Group D:** Some seeds, especially those with heavy seed coats such as roses and hollies, need repeated cycles of warm and/or cold weathering. Germination may not occur till the third spring after sowing, or even later.

Note: "Sowing" in these contexts dates from the start of weathering after seeds are mixed with grit, bagged and exposed to natural seasonal temperature cycles.

Seedlings emerge during second spring

Seedlings emerge during second spring

Some seedlings emerge in second spring

Repeated warm followed by cold weathering degrades the seed coats of more seeds

Most seedlings emerge during third spring

Weathering in practice: how to obtain the best results

- Start weathering treatments immediately after harvesting the seeds. This is not always practicable, but it does point to the value of collecting your own seed whenever possible.
- Use natural seasonal cycles, if available, to provide sequences of mild and cool conditions rather than resort to a propagator or the refrigerator. Use artificial aids only where winters are not cold enough to provide chilling treatments or when seeds obtained from elsewhere arrive too late to be weathered naturally.
- A propagator set to maintain minimum temperatures from 10° to 15°C (50° to 60°F) can be used to provide preliminary mild treatments for four to six weeks, to seeds mixed with grit, packed in polythene bags—followed by two to three months in a refrigerator.
- When obtaining seeds from elsewhere, try to arrange for them to be mixed with moist grit and stored in polythene bags at ambient temperatures from the time they are collected till they are dispatched. This satisfies their need (if any) for warm weathering, and they can then go straight into a refrigerator on arrival.
- Seeds in polythene bags may start to germinate at unexpected times—perhaps during the preliminary mild period or even while experiencing chilling treatments. Examine the bags periodically—emerging radicles are easy to spot, and if they appear, fast forward to the germination phase.

Seeds of some species, amongst them cotoneasters and sorbus, can be dried after the completion of weathering treatments. They can then be stored and handled just like any dry seed.

Trees from warm temperate regions and Mediterranea

Great numbers of trees, mostly evergreens, grow in places free from severe frosts during the winter in warm temperate regions and Mediterranea. They provide almost unlimited—still only partially explored—opportunities for gardeners in the milder parts of the world. Seeds of these trees are likely to germinate without weathering, although many benefit from a few weeks of after-ripening before being sown. They can be sown in the expectation that they will produce seedlings rapidly.

In gardens where winters are mild, sow seeds during late summer and autumn, when they will germinate before winter. Prick out the seedlings individually into separate containers and grow on steadily. They benefit from the protection of a poly tunnel. Line out the seedlings the following spring. Alternatively, sow in late winter or early spring, but only where summers are not too dry or water is available for irrigation.

In gardens with cold winters and short, dark days, store the seeds after collection and dry at room temperatures. Sow in late winter in a glasshouse or poly tunnel at minimum temperatures of about 10°C (50°F). Prick out individually into separate containers. Pot on into 3 litre (1 gal.) containers, and later into 5 or 7.5 litre (2 gal.) containers, and grow on through the summer, preferably under cover. Overwinter under cover in near frost-free conditions. Plant out in suitable, sheltered positions in the spring.

A great many trees from these parts of the world produce seeds with more or less hard seed coats. These may need chipping or treatment with hot water before they are able to imbibe water and germinate. They seldom possess other restrictions on germination, and once the barrier of the seed coat has been broken down, their seeds can usually be relied on to germinate without further delays—sometimes with startling rapidity and vigour.

Managing trees in nursery seedbeds

Trees raised in nursery beds suggest images of forestry enterprises with long beds filled with thousands of seedlings. But tree seeds can be raised on any scale. A hundred seedlings of ten, perhaps fifteen, different species can be raised in a nursery bed just 1 metre (3 ft.) square. One metre (3 ft.) wide beds separated by 0.5 metre (1.5 ft.) paths are accessible and easy to manage.

Sow in drills when raising small numbers, or broadcast over the surface for larger quantities. Use a board to press broadcast seed lightly into the surface. Cover the bed with coarse grit (alternatively, and always for species that grow better in organic substrates, use composted bark in place of grit) about 1 to 2 cm (0.5 to 1 in.) deep after sowing the seeds. This reduces water loss by evaporation, maintains even humidity around the seeds, discourages the emergence of weed seeds, facilitates the removal of weed seedlings blown in by the wind, eliminates water runoff due to capping of soil surface, and discourages the growth of mosses and liverworts.

When seedlings emerge and while seedlings are growing during the summer, water generously, feed regularly, and provide shade and shelter from excessive exposure to sunshine and wind. In the winter, especially in cold areas or locations exposed to spring frosts, protect the seedlings with a light, overhead canopy. Even seedlings of many seemingly bone-hardy species such as ashes and beeches are vulnerable to frost. A moderate frost soon after seedlings germinate can be a killer, and even a light one defoliates and checks growth severely.

Many trees are capable of growth rates far in excess of those possible in the semi-natural con-

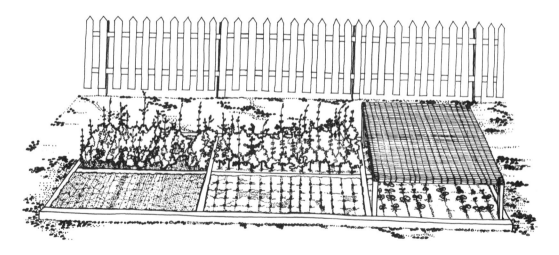

Figure 97. Tree seeds are sown in nursery beds, in drills, scattered, broadcast or, if large, set out individually. Sowing in drills simplifies weeding. Beds should not be more than 1.5 metres (5 ft.) wide with good access from firmly based paths on either side. When small batches are being raised, sowing, weeding and other operations are simplified by dividing the bed down the centre to enable all operations on a particular batch to be done from one side. Large seeds attractive to rodents and young seedlings vulnerable to frost or exposure may need protection in the form of appropriate covers.

ditions of a seedbed out of doors. By the end of their first year, trees in containers with ad lib watering and feeding in the shelter and warmth of a glasshouse or poly tunnel can grow to two or three times the size of those in a nursery bed. Birches, oaks, rowans and sweet chestnuts, amongst others, can grow to 2 metres (6 ft.) in a single season in a glasshouse, compared to at most half a metre (1.5 ft.) for well-managed seedlings out of doors. When maximum growth is required, perhaps to produce a few specimen trees, lift seedlings early from the nursery bed, pot them up, and grow on under cover.

Examples of trees grown from seed

Acacia spp., including *Racosperma* spp., seed viability can be extremely low, especially on isolated trees growing in "foreign" climates. Some species germinate more freely after a period of after-ripening of one to two months. All are likely to produce seeds with hard seed coats. Chipping is the simplest and most effective way to allow water to enter the seeds. Germination can then be startlingly rapid, sometimes within 24 hours of sowing. Equally, seeds of some species may take a month or six weeks to produce seedlings. Hot water treatments can also be used, either as an overnight soak in hot water or a short, sharp shock, repeated if necessary, by pouring boiling water over the seeds, or by prolonged soaking for two or three days after pouring boiling water over the seeds. Seeds that have still not germinated two months after hot water treatment may respond to chipping. Pot up seedlings individually when their radicles emerge.

Davidia involucrata nuts are collected as they fall. Pack into polythene bags with moist peat, bark, or coir and weather naturally. Each nut contains up to six embryos and can produce several seedlings. Seedlings seldom appear during the first spring, but radicles begin to emerge during the second winter and may continue to do so until late spring. Pot up the seedlings individually as soon as the cotyledons separate naturally from the endosperm. Protect young seedlings from frost in

a cold glasshouse or frame. As soon as all danger of frost is over, line out in a nursery bed. The roots tend to develop slowly and take up water and nutrients ineffectively, and seedlings grow better lined out in a nursery bed than in containers. Transplant seedlings into their final positions, with great care during their first winter. Wait 10 to 15 years for the first flowers and bracts to be produced.

Eucalyptus spp. cuttings and layers are seldom if ever successful, and seeds usually provide the only means of propagation. The capsules remain closed for long after the seeds mature, and most species can be collected at any time of the year. They release their seeds freely when dried. Capsules develop even when very few of the ovules have been fertilised, and gums tend to produce large amounts of duff seeds present as pale brown or reddish-brown chaff, readily distinguished from the dark brown or black viable seeds. Seed samples should be winnowed to remove most of the chaff, if possible. A great many species germinate freely at 15° to 25°C (60° to 75°F) and in most situations should be sown during late winter and early spring, under glass or in a poly tunnel in colder parts of the world with supplementary heating. Some species or provenances respond to cold weathering, and this should be tried if they do not germinate spontaneously. Examples include *E. delegatensis*, *E. glaucescens*, *E. kybanensis*, *E. niphophila*, *E. nitens*, *E. pauciflora*, *E. debeuzevillei* and *E. regnans*. Seedlings grow so rapidly, particularly their roots, that they very easily become potbound. They are pricked out individually into 9 cm (3.5 in.) containers as soon as they can be handled. Young plants are lined out in a nursery bed as soon as possible—usually within only six to eight weeks. They may still be no more than 10 cm (4 in.) high but even by then are likely to have developed formidable roots. Plants from seeds sown in late winter and lined out during the spring can be 1 to 2 metres (3 to 6 ft.) high by autumn with a well developed and well spaced out root system, ready to be set out in their permanent positions. None should be left behind in the nursery bed but dug up and dumped if not needed.

Left *in situ*, they grow embarrassingly large and too big to transplant successfully by the following year.

Fraxinus spp. seeds of most species need to be weathered. Mix them immediately after collection with moist grit or sand, without removing the wings. Excelsior group embryos are still immature when the fruits fall, and when dried the seed coats harden rapidly. Preliminary warm weathering is required, during which the seed coats become permeable and the embryos mature. This should be followed by cold weathering for about three months, after which the seeds germinate as temperatures rise. Without preliminary warm weathering, seedlings are unlikely to appear before the second spring. Manna ash group embryos are mature when the seeds fall. Their seeds do not develop hard coats, and germination follows a period of low temperature weathering. When available, seeds of both groups gathered green and sown at 10° to 20°C (50° to 70°F) produce seedlings without weathering.

Nuytsia floribunda, the Western Australian Christmas tree, is semi-parasitic, tapping into the roots of neighbouring shrubs. Semi-mature cuttings provide a possible, but usually not very productive, means of propagation. Seeds sown in autumn in Mediterranea or spring elsewhere germinate readily at 15° to 25°C (60° to 75°F). Prick out the seedlings individually into 7 cm (2.5 in.) pots. Pinch out the tips of the shoots while the plants are still very small. Seedlings will grow for a year or more without a host plant, and it is unnecessary to provide one while they are in containers. Line out young plants in nursery rows close to a potential host; nuytsias are not choosy in this respect, and many shrubs or perennials serve the purpose, provided they are not too vigorous. Mulch with coarse grit to reduce the rate of water loss, and keep the roots cool. At first, the trees grow as shrubs, resembling a coarse cytisus. A series of shoots emerge from a subterranean rootstock over several years. Eventually, one shoot develops vigorously as an upright stem and assumes a tree form. The trunk is made up of concentric rings of bark and wood—possibly as a pro-

tection from fire. Seedlings take 10 or 15 years to produce their first flowers.

Pittosporum spp. hybridise freely, unless isolated, when even selected forms usually reproduce more or less true to type. The capsules open while still green. Extract the shiny black seeds from the surrounding mucilage; then mix them with dry sand and rub vigorously to remove as much mucilage as possible. Sow fresh in the standard fashion at 15° to 25°C (60° to 75°F). Most species produce seedlings without further treatment. Some seeds contain inhibitors; soak these for 48 hours in warm water, changing the water twice. Others require cold weathering. Seeds germinate erratically, often over unpredictably long periods. Pot up seedlings individually as soon as they can be handled, taking care not to damage their fragile roots.

Quercus spp. cuttings of some evergreen oaks, notably *Q. ilex*, can be used for propagation, but cuttings are not an option with deciduous species and acorns provide by far the best means of raising oaks of all kinds. Acorns are most freely produced from cross-pollination amongst groups of trees. Isolated trees, dependent on self-pollination, produce small crops of poor quality acorns. Species hybridise freely when grown close together. Acorns deteriorate and lose viability rapidly when stored dry even for short periods. To keep them moist and alive temporarily—for example, in transit—wrap them in moss in a polythene bag. For the longer term, mix the acorns with five to ten times their volume of bark or grit and pack the mixture into heavy gauge polythene bags. Keep them overwinter in a frost-free, shaded situation or in a cool store at temperatures of about 5°C (40°F). Open the bags in late winter. Tip the contents of the bags into 7 cm (3 in.) deep drills, or distribute them over the surface of a nursery bed. Many will have produced short radicles while in the bags, but this has no effect on subsequent performance. Close the drills or press the distributed seeds into the surface with boards, and cover with a 3 cm (1 in.) deep layer of composted bark. Leave them to grow in the nursery bed during the summer; the seedlings will be a few centimetres high by autumn. Alternatively, pot up a few seeds or lift selected seedlings soon after they germinate, pot them up and grow on in a glasshouse or tunnel. Amply supplied with water, regularly fed and potted on when necessary, they will be a metre (3 ft.) or more high by the end of the season. Oaks appear to be the epitome of the truly hardy tree, but the centre of distribution of the genus is in subtropical and warm temperate regions. Northern species, such as *Q. robur*, *Q. mongolica*, *Q. coccinea* and *Q. velutina*, for all their appearance of being at home are a little out of their element. Memories of a warmer existence are not dead, and oaks respond to the warmer conditions provided by a glasshouse or poly tunnel by growing extremely rapidly. As an alternative sowing method, sow the acorns thickly and leave the seedlings crowded in their seedbed for several years. They make minimal growth but provide a supply of young plants to draw on to bridge gaps caused by failures to produce acorns between one good year and another.

Sorbus spp. and cvs. fruits, when available, are collected as they start to colour. Doing so before they are fully ripe avoids losses due to birds, and seedlings are more likely to be produced during the first spring. Seeds within the fruits are soft and likely to be damaged by mechanical maceration. Small quantities of seeds should be extracted manually and sown in containers and weathered in a cold frame or on a bench in an unheated glasshouse or poly tunnel. Larger quantities are simply crushed before weathering. Weather fruits plus seeds mixed with moist grit in polythene bags and sow in late winter in nursery beds. Germination rates vary erratically and unpredictably, from as low as 10 percent to more than 80 percent. Fruits left till they are fully ripe are treated similarly, but species and cultivars in the *S. aucuparia* group are unlikely to germinate till the second spring. Leave them in the polythene bags till emerging radicles are visible; then sow in a nursery bed. Seedlings of the *S. aucuparia* group (recognised by their pinnate leaves) respond extremely well to the extra warmth provided by a glasshouse or poly tunnel during the growing season. Protected plants may reach

1.5 metres (5 ft.) compared to barely 10 cm (4 in.) in the open. Species and cultivars in the *S. aria* group (white beams) are unlikely to respond to extra warmth.

Propagation from Cuttings

The shoots of a few trees, including gums, deciduous oaks, tupelos and beeches, obdurately refuse to produce roots when attempts are made to propagate them from cuttings. Others, including nothofagus, sorbus, many maples and pterocaryas, seldom do so more than sparingly at best. The majority of trees can be propagated from cuttings of one kind or another. As with shrubs, but even more often, the main problem lies in obtaining suitable material rather than persuading them to produce roots.

Tip cuttings

Few trees are regularly propagated from tip cuttings, but those that are, including magnolias, maples and some flowering cherries, are extremely significant. The cuttings need a long growing season to establish themselves before the onset of winter, and success depends on making an early start. In locations where mild winters are followed by long, warm summers, this can be achieved within the framework of natural growing seasons. In cool or cold temperate regions, the growing season has to be prolonged by bringing on stock plants in a glasshouse or poly tunnel.

In autumn, put young trees with several strong stems into 10 to 15 litre (3 to 5 gal.) pots. Alternatively, obtain similar plants from a nursery or garden centre.

- Cut each stem back to about half its length.
- Move the plants into a glasshouse or poly tunnel just after mid-winter, and maintain minimum night temperatures of about 10°C (50°F), with day temperatures from 15° to 20°C (60° to 70°F).

- When the shoots have produced three or four leaves and are still soft at the tips, barely firming towards the base, cut them at the point where the new growth starts.
- Hold them in polythene bags until ready to prepare them as cuttings.
- Remove the lower leaves, and dip the tips of the cuttings into rooting hormone.
- Set up under mist or on a warm bench under polythene, at 15° to 25°C (60° to 75°F).
- Wean the cuttings as soon as they produce roots, and pot individually into 7 cm (2.5 in.) containers for the smaller ones—such as maples and flowering cherries—and 9 cm (3.5 in.) for magnolias and other larger cuttings.
- Grow on in warm, 20° to 25°C (70° to 75°F), moist conditions.
- Pot the cuttings into 2 or 3 litre (1 gal.) containers, and grow them on through the summer in a poly tunnel with regular feeds to maintain growth.
- Overwinter in nearly frost-free conditions.

Other trees, including amelanchiers, davidias and hoherias, are sometimes propagated in a similar way. Many others could be, but less demanding methods are usually preferred.

Semi-mature cuttings

The most suitable shoots for use as cuttings are likely to be found on immature, actively growing trees. When these are not available, it may be necessary to cut back judiciously selected branches on established trees to stimulate the development of a flush of new shoots. Vigorous young shoots, known as water shoots or water sprouts, spring spontaneously from the trunks and main branches of some trees, and these can be used to make cuttings as and when they appear. Mist or a warm bench with polythene provide the best conditions in which to set up semi-mature cuttings, though when appropriate shoots are available, any of the methods and equipment used for semi-mature cuttings with shrubs and perennials can also be used.

Root cuttings

A few trees, amongst them ailanthus, catalpas, paulownias, quinces and rhus, are regularly propagated from root cuttings, mainly because easier ways are available for most others. However, almost by definition the roots of any tree capable of producing suckers can be used to make root cuttings.

Exposed lengths of root, preferably between 1.5 and 2.5 cm (0.5 to 1 in.) thick during the winter, are cut into sections some 6 to 12 cm (2.5 to 5 in.) long. Treat these in the same way as similar cuttings from shrubs.

Mature cuttings

The methods and equipment used for mature cuttings of evergreen shrubs, described in chapter 16, are equally successful with trees. They provide one of the main means of propagating a great many of the evergreen trees from Mediterranea and warm and mild temperate regions.

Cuttings made from the leafless shoots of many deciduous trees can also be treated in the same way as similar cuttings from deciduous shrubs. Cuttings of deciduous trees (and, indeed, of shrubs, too) do not need to be placed immediately in the open ground, and in cold locations, they benefit from protection during the worst of the winter before being lined out in a nursery bed in late winter.

Cut and divide the shoots into sections each containing three or four buds. Tie them in bundles and prevent them drying out by partially burying them in a bed of moist sand, grit or composted bark or moss in boxes or large pots in a sheltered place. An open shed where they are protected from exposure to very low temperatures is ideal.

The opportunity can be used to stimulate root formation, before setting them out in the open, using the following routine.

- Remove the shoots in early winter and tie into bundles of 10 to 20 cuttings.
- Dip the base of the bundles into a liquid for-

mulation of a rooting hormone, immersing them no more than 2 cm (1 in.) deep, for about a minute.

- Drain, and then partially bury the bundles in moist grit, sand or composted bark in large pots with the upper half of the cuttings exposed to the air.
- Stand the pots in a box over soil heating cables to raise temperatures around the base of the cuttings to about 20°C (70°F) for two to three weeks.
- Keep the exposed tops as cool as possible.
- During late winter, open up the bundles of cuttings and line them out in a sheltered place or protected by a tunnel cloche.

The method greatly increases the success rate with hardwood cuttings of plum and apple rootstocks as well as limes, many maples, quinces, ornamental cherries and crabs, alders, London plane, and a variety of shrubs. Wounding, even splitting, the base of the cutting can also be used to encourage root formation.

Extra large, mature cuttings (truncheons)

Willows, poplars, olives, mulberries and erythrinas can all be propagated from large cuttings, known as truncheons. These are not demure snippets of shoots a few centimetres long, but actual branches. Poplar and willow truncheons can be 3 or 4 metres (9 to 13 ft.) long, producing a cutting that one immediately has to look up to.

Make truncheons by cutting off large, leafless shoots during the winter. They need no special treatment but are simply stuck straight into the ground where they are intended to grow.

Alternatively, cut shoots into sections and make a number of smaller, more conventional hardwood cuttings, which will produce roots equally obligingly. Set them out in a nursery bed for the winter, and leave them *in situ* till the following winter. Dig them up and cut back hard to a bud close to ground level before planting out in a nursery bed or in the garden.

Examples of trees propagated from cuttings

Elaeocarpus spp. seeds germinate slowly and erratically—possibly due to their hard endocarps. Seedlings may not produce flowers for up to 20 years. Cuttings are the only way to propagate mature forms and cultivars. Propagate from tip to soft, semi-mature cuttings during the summer produced from young, vigorously growing shoots. It is usually necessary to cut back branches on mature trees to stimulate production of cutting material or to obtain cuttings from young, container-grown plants.

Hamamelis cvs. tip cuttings from forced plants produce roots relatively rapidly under mist or in a closed case with bottom heat, at about 20°C (70°F). Producing rooted cuttings is relatively easy; the main problem is persuading them to grow large enough to survive the following winter. Pot up the rooted cuttings individually in 9 cm (3.5 in.) pots as soon as they have formed roots. Keep them in a glasshouse or poly tunnel in pots through the summer, but do not pot on. They are sensitive to high salt concentrations in the growth medium; use fertilisers and apply liquid feeds at half strength. Overwinter the young plants in a frost-free glasshouse. Pot on into 3 litre (1 gal.) containers the following spring.

Magnolia cvs., yellow-flowered hybrids, are derived from the North American *M. acuminata* crossed with the closely related East Asian *M. liliiflora*. They can be propagated from semi-mature cuttings in mid- to late summer. Cut young shoots at the junction with the previous year's growth. Pinch off the soft tips of the shoots with any unexpanded leaves. Remove the lower leaves, and reduce the leaf area of those remaining by 50 percent. Skim off a sliver of bark from the base of the cutting, and dip the base into hormone rooting powder. Stick the cuttings individually into a 1:1 mix of grit : perlite in 7 cm (2.5 in.) containers and set them up under mist or on a warm bench under polythene at about 20°C (70°F). Overwinter without potting them on, and move them into 2 litre (8 in.) containers just before growth starts the following spring.

Metrosideros spp., *M. excelsa*, *M. robusta* and *M. umbellata*, are inclined to be erratic or downright disobliging from cuttings. The more shrublike *M. kermadecensis* is seldom a problem. The climbing species produce roots more readily, but when taken from mature plants they produce shrubby rather than climbing forms. Use water shoots produced adventitiously at the base of the plant to propagate *M. excelsa*, or make cuttings from two-year-old shoots on which the leaves have lost their covering of soft, silvery hairs, preferably using flowering shoots on which the flowers have just faded.

Pennantia corymbosa seeds give rise to plants that remain for a number of years in a juvenile, divaricating condition before developing into trees. The juvenile form has few attractions for gardeners, but mature trees have handsome, deep-green foliage and beautiful, creamy white, fragrant flowers. The juvenile phase can be avoided by taking cuttings of mature plants of either sex, according to need. Semi-mature to mature cuttings taken in autumn provide the least uncertain means of propagation. The initiation and development of roots is usually a prolonged process, and a year may pass before they become visible.

Propagation by Division and Layers

Trees, like shrubs, can be propagated from suckers and by bringing their branches into contact with the ground and layering them. The latter presents obvious problems when working with plants with long, clear stems and no branches within reach of the ground. Air layering, a technique that might be said to bring the ground to the branch, provides a feasible alternative.

Air layering

The principle is simple enough, but the practice less so. In principle and in brief,

- Select young, straight shoots. It may be necessary to encourage their development by cutting back one or two branches in advance.
- Wrap a bundle of moist, water-holding material—sphagnum moss is the preferred choice, but rock wool can also be used—around the shoots, including at least one node.
- Enclose the bundle in several layers of opaque polythene sheeting. Wrappings must be opaque because light inhibits root formation, and direct sunshine turns an unshaded interior into a lethal steam bath.
- Close the top and bottom ends tightly with tape.
- The development of roots may be encouraged by partially ring-barking the stem just below the site of the layer and/or wounding the stem on one or two sides by removing slivers of bark.
- Roots produced by the stem grow out into the moss or rock wool.
- Cut off the stem just below the layer once roots have developed.
- Remove the wrappings and pot up the rooted layer together with the sphagnum or rock wool.
- Grow on in a shaded, cool situation until the plant has established itself.

Air layering is used to propagate some kinds of house plants, which grow rapidly in warm, humid atmospheres. When an India rubber plant (*Ficus indica*) threatens to grow through the ceiling, an air layer produced from the top of the plant provides an easy means of starting it from ground level again.

Problems arise when similar methods are applied to hardy plants growing out of doors in every kind of weather, which take months rather than weeks to produce roots. It is difficult to devise a weatherproof package capable of keeping out rainwater, yet remaining moist long enough for the new roots to grow. Seals formed by taping the polythene sheet to the stems usually break down when exposed to heat and cold. Rainwater runs down the stems, causing waterlogging at any time and damage from freezing during cold weather.

These problems lead to high failure rates, and air layering is less useful and less frequently used than it might be. Nevertheless, it provides a means of propagating a number of trees and shrubs that cannot be readily propagated in other ways. Inevitably, these tend to be rare and choice, and the technique does offer a gleam of hope in circumstances where otherwise there would be none.

Examples of trees propagated by division

Ailanthus altissima—the tree of heaven—is dioecious, and some people find the smell of the male flowers offensive. Seeds may produce either male or female plants, and suckers are preferred because they provide a simple means of ensuring that all the plants propagated are females.

Cedrela sinensis 'Flamingo' plants are raised from suckers. These are produced extremely freely and are used to propagate the pink-leaved form grown in gardens.

Maytenus boaria can be raised from seed in situations where these are produced or from semi-mature cuttings where seeds are not available. Some trees produce suckers, an easy means of increase but one that should be used with caution, since it perpetuates the inclination to sucker—something many gardeners would prefer not to encourage.

Ulmus spp. seed viability varies greatly from species to species, place to place, and year to year. Those elms which produce few or no seeds, including the English elm, are propagated from suckers. They are simply dug up during the winter and lined out, very often *in situ*, to form a hedge. As a result, the elms in thousands of miles of hedges may constitute a single clone, all uniformly susceptible to the ravages of Dutch Elm disease—an extreme example of the dangers of abandoning genetic diversity.

Propagation Summary for Trees

S. = propagated from seed
C. = propagated from cuttings
D. = propagated by divisions

Acacia—**S.** spring; chip, hot water soak. **C.** semi-mature.

Acca—Succulent Fruit. **S.** spring; cultivars come moderately true from seed. **C.** tip, semi-mature.

Acer—Dioecious, e.g., *A. negundo*; some semi-recalcitrant. **S.** fresh. **C.** tip; from forced stock plants.

Aesculus—Nut. Recalcitrant. **S.** fresh. **C.** not *A. hippocastanum*; tip, root. **D.** layers, e.g., *A. parviflora*.

Agonis—**S.** spring.

Ailanthus—Dioecious. **S.** fresh, spring. **C.** root. **D.** suckers.

Albizia—**S.** fresh, spring; hot water soak. **C.** semi-mature; heel, can be very slow.

Alectryon—Succulent Fruit. **S.** takes a year to mature; fresh.

Allocasuarina—**S.** fresh, spring.

Alnus—**S.** fresh, spring; viability variable. **C.** mature. **D.** suckers.

Amelanchier—Succulent Fruit. **S.** fresh. **C.** tip. **D.** suckers, e.g., *A. canadensis*.

Amomyrtus—Succulent Fruit. **S.** fresh, spring. **C.** semi-mature, mature.

Amorpha—**S.** spring; chip. **C.** tip, mature.

Angophora—**S.** fresh, spring; unlike *Eucalyptus* spp. their seeds are released as the capsules mature.

Arbutus—Succulent Fruit. **S.** fresh. **C.** mature.

Aristotelia—Dioecious. Succulent Fruit. **S.** fresh.

Atherosperma—**S.** fresh. **C.** semi-mature.

Azara—Succulent Fruit. **S.** fresh. **C.** mature.

Banksia—Serotinous, except *B. integrifolia*. **S.** fresh; viability variable; weathering at ca. 5°C (40°F) may be beneficial.

Beilschmiedia—Succulent Fruit. **S.** fresh still in the fruit, scarcely buried in organic substrate.

Betula—**S.** fresh, spring on mineral substrate. **C.** semi-mature; *B. nana*; other species inclined to produce roots but no shoots. Initial growth very slow.

Bolusanthus—**S.** fresh, spring; chip.

Brabejum—Recalcitrant. **S.** fresh—best results with seed pressed lightly onto the surface of the seed mix.

Brachychiton—**S.** spring; chip, hot water.

Broussonetia—Dioecious. Succulent Fruit. **S.** fresh, spring. **C.** tip. semi-mature, mature; heel to protect the pith; root.

Carpinus—Semi-recalcitrant, **S.** fresh; dried seed seldom germinates before second spring. **C.** semi-mature to mature.

Carya—Nut. Recalcitrant. **S.** fresh.

Castanea—Nut. Recalcitrant **S.** fresh; protect from rodents and other pests.

Castanopsis—Nut. Recalcitrant. **S.** fresh; protect from rodents and other pests.

Casuarina—**S.** fresh, spring. **C.** semi-mature.

Catalpa—**S.** fresh, spring. **C.** semi-mature, mature, root.

Cedrela—**D.** suckers, e.g., *C. sinensis* 'Flamingo'.

Celtis—Succulent Fruit. **S.** spring. **C.** mature. **D.** layers.

Ceratonia—**S.** spring; chip, hot water soak. **C.** mature; slow and often unsuccessful. **D.** air layers.

Ceratopetalum—Nut. **S.** fresh, spring; best results from green seed sown fresh.

Cercidiphyllum—**S.** spring. **C.** tip from forced stock plants.

Cercis—**S.** spring; chip; seedlings of the white form have paler foliage and lack crimson tones on petioles and young stems. **C.** tip; from forced stock plants.

Cheiranthodendron—**S.** fresh, spring. **C.** mature—usually low success rates.

Chorisia—**S.** spring.

Chrysolepis—Recalcitrant. **S.** fresh.

Cinnamomum—Succulent Fruit. **S.** fresh. **C.** tip.

Citrus—Recalcitrant. Succulent Fruit. **S.** fresh.

Cladrastis—**S.** fresh; chipped and weathered. **C.** root; laid in moss.

Cola—Recalcitrant. **S.** spring; sow individually in small pots, avoid unnecessary disturbance. **C.** mature.

Cornus—Succulent Fruit. **S.** fresh, e.g., *C. capitata, C. mas, C. nuttallii.* **C.** tip, e.g., *C. kousa.* semi-mature/mature, e.g., *C. capitata.* **D.** air layers, e.g., *C. nuttallii.*

Corynocarpus—Recalcitrant. Succulent Fruit. **S.** fresh; partially buried; germination erratic. **C.** tip; for preference, semi-mature; often unsuccessful.

Cotoneaster—Succulent Fruit. Some species apomictic. **S.** fresh; including preliminary warm treatment, may not germinate till second spring. **C.** semi-mature, mature.

Crataegus—Succulent Fruit. **S.** fresh; seldom germinates before second spring.

Crinodendron—**S.** fresh, spring.

Cunonia—Succulent Fruit. **S.** spring. **C.** semi-mature.

Cussonia—Succulent Fruit. **S.** spring. **C.** mature.

Cydonia—Succulent Fruit. **S.** fresh. **C.** mature, roots. **D.** suckers.

Cyphomandra—Succulent Fruit. **S.** spring; seedlings produce fruit in two or three years.

Davidia—Recalcitrant. Succulent Fruit. **S.** fresh; seedlings seldom appear before second spring. **C.** tip. semi-mature, preferably basal at junction with mature wood. **D.** air layers.

Diospyros—Dioecious. Succulent Fruit sometimes produced parthenocarpically. **S.** fresh. **C.** semi-mature. **D.** air layers.

Dodonaea—Dioecious. **S.** fresh, spring; purple-leaved forms produce purple seedlings. **C.** semi-mature, mature.

Drimys—Dioecious. **C.** tip.

Dysoxylum—Recalcitrant. **S.** fresh; seedlings very susceptible to damping-off.

Ehretia—Succulent Fruit. **S.** fresh.

Ekebergia—Succulent Fruit. **S.** fresh.

Elaeocarpus—Succulent Fruit. **S.** fresh; germination slow and erratic, long juvenile period delays appearance of first flowers. **C.** semi-mature.

Embothrium—**S.** fresh, spring, on mineral substrate. **C.** semi-mature, root. **D.** suckers.

Entelea—**S.** fresh, spring.

Eriobotrya—Succulent Fruit. **S.** fresh.

Erythrina—**S.** fresh, spring. **C.** tip; basal shoots; mature; including truncheons.

Eucalyptus—Serotinous. **S.** fresh, spring; viability variable, often low.

Eucryphia—**S.** fresh, spring; viability often low. **C.** semi-mature, mature.

Exocarpos—Parasite. Succulent Fruit. **S.** fresh, provide host plant. **C.** semi-mature; success rates likely to be low.

Fagus—Recalcitrant. **S.** fresh; seedlings of purple forms include high proportions of purple seedlings; intensity may vary. Fastigiate forms produce ca. 40 percent of fastigiate seedlings.

Ficus—Dioecious. Succulent Fruit. **S.** fresh. **C.** semi-mature, mature. **D.** layers, suckers.

Franklinia—**S.** spring. **C.** semi-mature.

Fraxinus—Semi-recalcitrant. **S.** fresh; protect young seedlings from frost.

Fremontia—**S.** spring. **C.** semi-mature.

Fremontodendron—**S.** fresh; hot water soak plus weathering. **C.** tip, semi-mature in autumn as the flowers are almost over.

Genista—Ballistic. **S.** spring; chip. **C.** semi-mature, mature.

Gevuina—Recalcitrant. **S.** fresh. **C.** semi-mature.

Gleditsia—**S.** spring; chip or hot water soak.

Gordonia—**S.** fresh. **C.** semi-mature. **D.** layers.

Greyia—**S.** spring. **C.** semi-mature, mature.

Griselinia—Dioecious. **S.** fresh. **C.** mature; wounded.

Gymnocladus—**S.** spring; chip or hot water soak.

Hakea—Serotinous. **S.** fresh, spring. **C.** semi-mature, mature.

Halesia—**S.** fresh. **C.** tip, root.

Halleria—Succulent Fruit. **S.** fresh, spring.

Hamamelis—Ballistic. **S.** fresh; may not germinate till second spring; seed gathered green produces seedlings more rapidly. **C.** tip; from forced stock plants. **D.** layers, air layers.

Harpephyllum—Dioecious. Succulent Fruit. **S.** spring. **C.** mature; large basal shoots.

Hedycarya—Dioecious. Succulent Fruit. **S.** fresh. **C.** semi-mature.

Hippophae—Dioecious. Succulent Fruit. **S.** fresh. **C.** semi-mature, mature, root. **D.** suckers.

Hoheria—**S.** fresh. **C.** tip. semi-mature, mature.

Hymenosporum—**S.** spring. **C.** semi-mature.

Idesia—Dioecious. Succulent Fruit. **S.** spring. **C.** semi-mature, root.

Ilex—Dioecious. Succulent Fruit. **S.** fresh; seedlings emerge during second spring. Seedlings from yellow or white berried forms usually produce red berries. **C.** mature; evergreen species; wounding encourages root formation. semi-mature; deciduous species.

Jacaranda—**S.** spring; hot water soak; pot up early to avoid transplant shock. **C.** semi-mature.

Juglans—Nut. Recalcitrant. **S.** fresh; protect from squirrels.

Kigelia—**S.** spring; extract seeds manually from large, fibrous fruits.

Kiggelaria—Dioecious. **S.** fresh. **C.** mature.

Knightia—**S.** spring; on mineral substrate; seedlings vulnerable to phytophthora.

Koelreuteria—**S.** fresh, spring. **C.** root; success rates likely to be moderate at best.

Laburnum—**S.** spring. **C.** mature, late winter; rooted cuttings scarcely grow till following year.

Lagerstroemia—**S.** fresh, spring; seedlings flower from second or third year. **C.** mature.

Lagunaria—**S.** spring.

Laurelia—**S.** spring. **C.** mature.

Laurus—Succulent Fruit. **S.** spring. **C.** mature.

Ligustrum—Succulent Fruit. **S.** fresh; may not germinate till second spring. **C.** semi-mature, mature.

Liquidambar—**S.** fresh; may not germinate till second spring. **D.** air layers.

Liriodendron—Semi-recalcitrant. **S.** fresh; viability likely to be low; seedlings intolerant of disturbance.

Lithocarpus—Recalcitrant. **S.** fresh.

Lophomyrtus—Succulent Fruit. **S.** fresh; seedlings vulnerable to damping-off. **C.** semi-mature, mature.

Luma—Succulent Fruit. **S.** fresh. **C.** mature.

Maackia—**S.** fresh; chipped and weathered. **C.** root.

Maclura—Succulent Fruit. **S.** fresh. **C.** semi-mature, root.

Magnolia—**S.** fresh. **C.** tip from forced stock plants. semi-mature cut at junction with previous year's growth, wounded, e.g., *M. acuminata*. **D.** layers, air layers.

Malus—Succulent Fruit. **S.** fresh; a few species are apomictic.

Maytenus—Dioecious. **S.** fresh, spring. **C.** semi-mature; **D.** suckers.

Melia—Succulent Fruit. **S.** fresh, spring.

Melicope—Dioecious. Succulent Fruit. **S.** fresh, spring. **C.** semi-mature.

Meryta—Dioecious. Succulent Fruit. **S.** fresh. **C.** semi-mature; reduce leaf area.

Mespilus—Succulent Fruit. **S.** fresh; seedlings may not appear till second spring.

Metrosideros—**S.** fresh, spring; prick out when two or three true leaves have developed. **C.** semi-mature, mature; *M. excelsa, M. robusta, M. umbellata*; may be erratic or downright disobliging.

Mimosa—**S.** spring; chip.

Morus—Succulent Fruit. **S.** fresh. **C.** mature; including truncheons.

Myoporum—Succulent Fruit. **S.** fresh; warm water soak. **C.** tip. semi-mature.

Myrtus—Succulent Fruit. **S.** fresh. **C.** semi-mature, mature.

Nothofagus—Recalcitrant. **S.** fresh. **C.** tip, semi-mature, e.g., *N. dombeyi* and *N. procera*—success rates usually low.

Nuytsia—Parasite. **S.** fresh, spring; able to grow without a host plant until planted out. **C.** semi-mature.

Nyssa—Succulent Fruit. **S.** spring. **D.** layers, air layers.

Ochna—Succulent Fruit. **S.** fresh; germination usually poor, but self-sows in favourable situations. **C.** semi-mature.

Olea—Succulent Fruit. **S.** fresh; chipped. **C.** semi-mature, mature; including truncheons.

Olearia—**S.** spring; viability variable. **C.** semi-mature, mature; with heel.

Ostrya—**S.** fresh.

Parrotia—**S.** fresh. **C.** semi-mature; usually very low success rate. **D.** layers, air layers.

Parrotiopsis—**D.** layers, air layers.

Paulownia—**S.** spring. **C.** semi-mature, root; laid horizontally just below surface.

Pennantia—Dioecious. **S.** fresh; chipped. **C.** semi-mature, mature; erratic and usually very slow. Juvenile (divaricating) and mature forms both retained from cuttings.

Persea—Succulent Fruit. **S.** fresh; set each seed upright with pointed end just above the surface, in separate containers.

Peumus—Dioecious. Succulent Fruit. **C.** mature.

Photinia—Succulent Fruit. **S.** fresh. **C.** semi-mature, mature; basal.

Pittosporum—**S.** fresh, spring; warm water soak; germination tends to be erratic. **C.** semi-mature, mature; wounded.

Plagianthus—Dioecious. Succulent Fruit. **S.** fresh. **C.** semi-mature, mature; enable mature forms of selected sexes to be propagated.

Platanus—**S.** spring. **C.** semi-mature; with heel, mature. **D.** layers.

Plumeria—**C.** mature in late winter; just before flowers and leaves emerge.

Poinciana—**S.** spring; chipped, hot water treatment.

Pomaderris—**S.** spring; chipped, hot water treatment. **C.** semi-mature.

Populus—Dioecious. **S.** fresh; extremely short-lived. **C.** mature; including truncheons.

Prunus—Succulent Fruit. **S.** fresh. **C.** tip; from forced stock plants, e.g., *P. subhirtella, P. triloba, P. tenella*. semi-mature, e.g., Japanese cherries, mature; inc. *P. cerasifera* and forms of *P. laurocerasus*.

Ptelea—**S.** fresh; often infertile in cultivation.

Pterocarya—Semi-recalcitrant. **S.** fresh; seedlings very vulnerable to frost. **C.** root. **D.** suckers; most successful when removed as woody tissues develop at base and treated as cuttings.

Pterostyrax—Succulent Fruit. **S.** spring. **C.** semi-mature.

Pyrus—Succulent Fruits. **S.** fresh.

Quercus—Recalcitrant. **S.** fresh: hybrids likely.

Radermachera—**S.** spring. **C.** semi-mature. **D.** layers.

Rhododendron—**S.** spring; hybrids likely. **C.** mature; wounded; success rates with arborescent forms often low. **D.** layers, air layers.

Rhus—Succulent Fruit. **S.** fresh; hot water soak. **C.** mature. **D.** layers, suckers.

Richea—**S.** fresh; e.g., *R. pandanifolia*; allow seedlings to grow for 12 months before potting up individually.

Robinia—**S.** spring; chipped, hot water treatment. **C.** root. **D.** suckers.

Salix—**S.** fresh; very short lived; hybrids likely. **C.** mature; including truncheons. **D.** layers.

Sassafras—Dioecious. Succulent Fruit. **S.** fresh. **C.** root. **D.** suckers.

Schefflera—Succulent Fruit. **S.** fresh.

Schinus—Succulent Fruit. **S.** fresh. **C.** mature.

Sophora—**S.** late winter, spring; chipped, hot water treatment. **C.** semi-mature; wounded. **D.** layers.

Sorbus—Succulent Fruit. **S.** fresh; germination and viability variable; most seedlings likely to appear during the second spring. Species in the *S. aria* group are often apomictic; different forms come more or less true from seed and seldom hybridise.

Sparrmannia—**C.** tip.

Stenocarpus—**S.** spring. **D.** air layers.

Sterculia—**S.** spring. **D.** layers.

Stewartia—**S.** fresh. **C.** semi-mature.

Syzygium—Succulent Fruit. **S.** fresh, spring. **C.** semi-mature.

Tamarix—**S.** spring. **C.** semi-mature, mature, including truncheons.

Tasmannia—**S.** spring. **C.** semi-mature to mature.

Telopea—Serotinous. **S.** fresh, spring; yellow flowered forms, e.g., *T. truncata* f. *lutea*, seedlings usually produce about 25 percent yellow-flowered plants. **D.** layers, air layers.

Tetracentron—**S.** spring.

Tetradium (Euodia, Evodia)—**S.** fresh, spring. **C.** semi-mature, root.

Tilia—**S.** fresh; germination is usually erratic, spread over several years, starting, in the second spring. **C.** semi-mature; e.g., *T. cordata* and *T. europaea*. **D.** layers from stool beds.

Toona—**S.** spring. **C.** mature, root. **D.** suckers.

Tristaniopsis—**S.** spring. **C.** semi-mature.

Trochodendron—**S.** fresh.

Ugni—Succulent Fruit. **S.** fresh, spring.

Ulmus—**S.** fresh; fertility highly variable. **D.** suckers.

Umbellularia—Succulent Fruit. **S.** spring. **D.** layers.

Virgilia—**S.** fresh, spring; seedlings are very vulnerable to frost.

Vitex—Succulent Fruit. **S.** spring; germination may be protracted.

Weinmannia—**S.** fresh. **C.** semi-mature.

Xanthoceras—Recalcitrant. **S.** fresh. **C.** root.

Xylomelum—**S.** serotinous; fresh, spring; on mineral substrate.

Zelkova—Succulent Fruit. **S.** fresh.

Ziziphus—Succulent Fruit. **S.** fresh, spring. **C.** semi-mature, root.

Plant Index

Note that this index includes only generic names. Plants referred to in the text under specific or vernacular names must be searched for by genera.

Abelia, 302
Abeliophyllum, 302
Abies, 142, 143, 147, 148, 151, 153, 154
Abromeitiella, 273
Abronia, 198
Abutilon, 114, 302
Acacia, 281, 302, 332, 338
Acaena, 198, 249
Acalypha, 302
Acantholimon, 249
Acanthopanax, 302
Acanthus, 198
Acca, 338
Acer, 114, 302, 324–325, 338
Achillea, 198
Achlys, 198
Acidanthera, 240
Acinos, 249
Aciphylla, 198
Acmena, 302
Acnistus, 175, 302
Aconitum, 198
Acorus, 216
Actaea, 198
Actinidia, 302
Actinostrobus, 142, 147, 154
Actinotus, 198, 302
Adenandra, 302

Adenophora, 198
Adenostoma, 302
Adiantum, 128, 130, 132, 136
Adonis, 171, 198, 249
Aechmea, 273
Aegopodium, 198
Aeonium, 255, 257
Aesculus, 32, 338
Aethionema, 249
Afrocarpus, 141, Figure 38
Agapanthus, 216
Agastache, 198
Agathis, 142, 147, 148, 153, 154
Agathosma, 277, 302
Agave, 255, 257, 321
Ageratum, 44, 173
Agonis, 338
Agropyron, 209
Agrostemma, 20, 172
Agrostis, 172, 216
Aichryson, 257
Ailanthus, 338
Ajuga, 198
Akebia, 303
Alberta, 281, 303
Albizia, 338
Albuca, 240
Alcea, 174, 198
Alchemilla, 198

Alectryon, 338
Alisma, 216
Allium, 226, 240
Allocasuarina, 338
Alluaudia, 255, 257
Alnus, 338
Alocasia, 216
Aloe, 256, 257
Alonsoa, 175, 198
Alopecurus, 216
Aloysia, 303
Alpinia, 216
Alsophila, 136
Alstroemeria, 208, 214, 216, Figure 59
Althaea, 174, 175
Alyogyne, 303
Alyssum, 249
Amaranthus, 173
Amaryllis, 240
Amelanchier, 338
Ammi, 171
Ammobium, 172
Amomyrtus, 338
Amorpha, 338
Ampelodesmos, 216
Ampelopsis, 303
Amsonia, 198
Anacampseros, 257

General Index